THE COVER STORY

The cover of *In Search of God and the Ten Commandments* is reflective of where we stand today in regards to what has always been considered traditional American values and freedoms in the United States.

This photo was taken in Toledo, Ohio in September 2012 on a cloudy, cool Saturday morning. The landscaping around the Ten Commandments monolith had not been tended to in quite some time. There was garbage tossed about the entire area. The monolith, which was partially covered by a small bush, was presented to Lucas County in 1957. It had three bullet holes in its granite surface that had begun to erode.

The American flag, now faded and worn, that was placed beside the Ten Commandments monolith was dedicated on April 19, 1959 by the Catholic War Veterans "For God, Country, and Home." There was a bullet hole under the brass eagle that was perched at the very top of the tilted flagpole. The stained memorial base was caused by the neglected mast which had rusted over time.

The original photo used for the cover of this book was intentionally altered to look like it was old and water damaged – like a photo that you would find in a long-forgotten, neglected box in the back of a farm house attic that had a leaky roof at some point. Like that old, ignored box, we, who have held America up on a pedestal as a light to all nations, and who have honored our Founding Fathers who recognized this country's beginnings as a gift from God, have been silent and ignored for too long. We have neglected to protect our God-given way of life as our traditional values and freedoms have been trashed and eroded over the past several decades. We have allowed ourselves to believe that we needed to be tolerant of others and their beliefs, so we have sat idly by while our American heritage has been trampled upon, mocked, and nearly eradicated.

We are standing at a precipice at this moment in time. We can either be pushed off the cliff and let our country be run by those who wish to forever change the America that we once knew, or we can stand our ground and fight for our right to believe that this is a country based on Judeo-Christian principles.

As you peruse the following pages, you will encounter a national project that began with all of the hopes and promises of a better tomorrow. What you will discover is that through neglect, fear, and absence of resolve, a story that has been allowed to be rewritten by others who wish to do it harm. May this be the beginning of a new hope for this Ten Commandments Project from a bygone era, and with the new beginning, hopes for a stronger America that has returned to its God-given values and freedoms.

Photo by Sue A. Hoffman (September 2012)

Toledo, Ohio (June 1957)

When Lucas County's Ten Commandments monolith was dedicated on May 22, 1957, several judges, the mayor, and the county commissioner were present. On November 26, 2003, the American Civil Liberties Union (ACLU) of Ohio, on behalf of Charles Boss (a practicing attorney in Lucas County and a dues-paying, registered member of the ACLU), filed a lawsuit against the Board of Commissioners of Lucas County. The lawsuit stipulated that "the monument offended him (Charles Boss) and diminished his use and enjoyment of the courthouse and its grounds." US District Judge James Carr suspended the case until arguments were heard, and a decision was made, in the US Supreme Court ruling in the 2005 case regarding the Ten Commandments monolith on the state capitol grounds in Austin, Texas. Based on the High Court's five-to-four ruling allowing the monolith to stay in Texas, in April 2006, Carr ruled that the monolith may remain where it was originally placed at the Lucas County Courthouse. He stated, "I am persuaded that an objective observer could not conclude that the monument, despite the sectarian antecedents of its text, has the effect of endorsing religion in general or the specific tenets of any particular sectarian assembly."

A Few Kind Words

It is not only an honor, but gives me great pleasure to endorse Sue Hoffman's book, IN SEARCH OF GOD AND THE TEN COMMANDMENTS.

What a journey! Mrs. Hoffman has made this her life's historical venture. Her initial research, which began thirteen years ago, led her to the man behind the entire project, Judge E. J. Ruegemer. The Judge, then retired and elderly, welcomed her phone calls and cross-country visits, and gave what background and information he could to assist with her project. His oldest daughter, Nita, was invaluable in providing information that the Judge, because of his impaired hearing, was unable to convey. Nita would have been thrilled to see what Sue was able to accomplish with her help. Nita, sadly, died in 2011.

My pride in this endorsement is that I am the youngest child of Judge Ruegemer. I was in elementary school when Dad's project began. Our basement became an operational area and I did my share of washing and drying the glass that went into the frames of the original copies of the Ten Commandments.

Dad, too, is now gone, having died in 2005. But, because of IN SEARCH OF GOD AND THE TEN COMMANDMENTS, *his work will live on. Thank you Sue, (and Jeff, for your encouragement and driving stamina throughout the US) for your work, your vision, and your belief in what God, Himself, gave us!*

~ Anne Berg, daughter of Judge E. J. Ruegemer

A fascinating project and clearly a labor of love. Anyone who cares about the past and the future of our uniquely blessed nation should consider the history of Ten Commandments monuments as symbols of our religious and ethical heritage. Sue Hoffman's work may even play a role in our eventual reconnection to surge in faith and patriotism that seemed to sweep the nation sixty years ago.

~ Michael Medved, nationally syndicated talk radio host

The sole feature that reliably distinguishes cultures that flourish from those that fail is fealty to the Ten Commandments. Sue Hoffman offers a definitive directory of America's relationship with these permanent principles. Her compelling account belongs in every patriot's library and not only points the way, but inspires the reader to be a part of a better tomorrow.

~ Rabbi Daniel Lapin, American Alliance of Jews and Christians

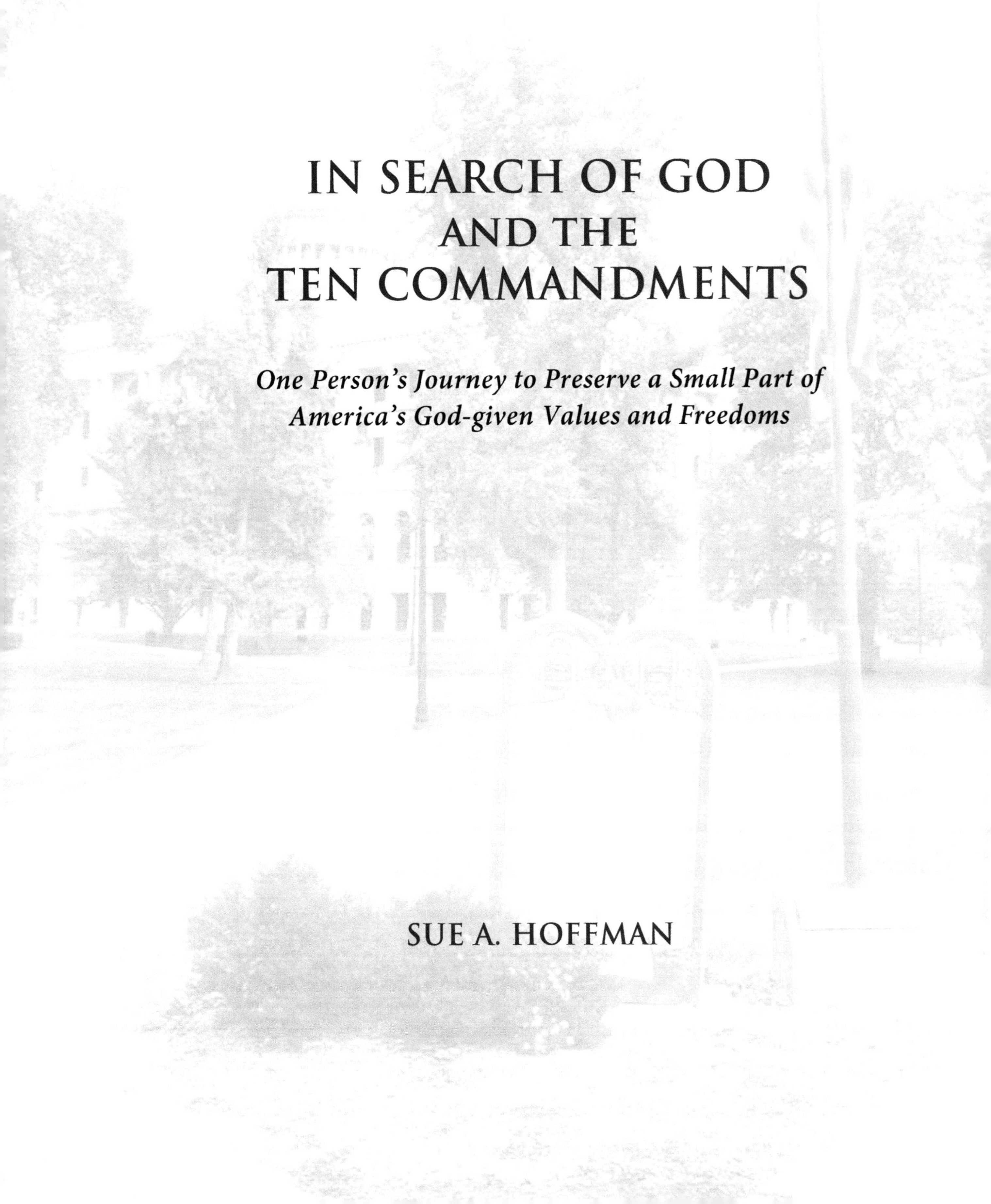

IN SEARCH OF GOD AND THE TEN COMMANDMENTS

One Person's Journey to Preserve a Small Part of America's God-given Values and Freedoms

SUE A. HOFFMAN

Printed by CreateSpace, an Amazon.com Company.

ISBN-13: 978-0615960296
ISBN-10: 0615960294

DEDICATION

JEFFREY A. HOFFMAN

Without my wonderful husband, this book would never have been possible. His willingness to take over most of the household chores, do the grocery shopping, run all of the errands, and handle everything that could be passed off to someone else, allowed the following pages to be created. Jeffrey has remained my main support and biggest cheerleader for the now-thirteen years that I have been working on this book. Most of all, he has kept me smiling. Follow this dialogue, if you will:

"Jeffrey, would you like to read some of this book while I am writing it?" I question in hopes that he will volunteer his great editing skills for the cause.

"That depends. What's it about?" he quips knowing full well exactly what the book is about.

"The Ten Commandments," I mutter with feigned disgust.

"No thanks. I think that I'll wait for the movie. Oh, wait! I think that I've already seen the movie!" Chuckle, chuckle, snort, snort . . .

If anyone would have asked him what it was like to have his wife "chained" to her desk and computer over the past few years, Jeffrey probably would have said something like, "Well, she sure didn't say that much. All I ever heard from her was, 'Blah, blah, book, blah, blah, Ten Commandments, blah, blah.' Other than that, she pretty much ignored me."

Jeffrey has allowed me to "do my thing" for so long (having been married since 1976), he deserves to be recognized for his loving contribution of being there for me all of the time, and in all ways. With a grateful heart, deepest admiration, and much love . . .

The story of these monoliths is the story of good intentions . . . on everyone's part. No matter how much of what DeMille did was (or was not) related to promotion, he thought his film would actually make a positive contribution to the world. The Eagles thought that bad kids could be turned around simply by exposure to the words of the laws. The ACLU was concerned about unnecessarily hurting the feelings of those who aren't in the majority.

All good intentions, and yet, each so simplistic that the goals couldn't possibly succeed without negative fallout or repercussions. But isn't that a lot like most of what happens in life? There is a famous saying from a Scottish poem by Robert Burns:

"The best laid schemes o' mice an' men gang aft a-gley."
(The best laid plans of mice and men often go astray.)

True, but that doesn't mean that we should stop making plans.

~ Scott E. Meyer ~

CONTENTS

IN SEARCH OF GOD
AND THE
TEN COMMANDMENTS

FOREWORD

I met Sue Hoffman when we were both young first-time mothers. Her daughter Lisa and my son William were infants, and we shared a parent education class at a local community college. The bond formed between women who are first-time mothers sharing their love, worries, and concerns is a strong one, formed at a time in a woman's life like no other, and our bond has survived over the twenty-nine years since. We, along with a core group of four or five others, still meet regularly for dinner. We share news of our kids. We help each other with their weddings. We work through our joys and sorrows together. We are friends, sisters in spirit, mentors to one another, trusted confidants, allies, and cherished travelers through our lives.

We have shared joyous occasions – new babies, personal successes, new jobs, moves to new homes, college graduations, and the advent of grandchildren. We have also shared lost jobs, a divorce, the death of a husband, painful losses of parents, various illnesses, car crashes, and financial challenges. We care deeply about each other and that care has grown incrementally over the years.

Despite all of these shared experiences, it would not be fair to assume that we share philosophies, religions, faiths, or political persuasions – not surprising in a group brought together more by the chance dates of the births of their firstborns. This, in the long run, has proven to be among the most valuable aspects of this group for me.

This brings me to the unusual aspect of my story. Sue and I are just about as radically different as two women can be in terms of religious beliefs and political persuasions. I do not share her faith, her religion, or her political views. My enthusiastic participation in the development of this book was not born of the same passion as hers. Mine was from another passion altogether – the passion to see a friend achieve a huge milestone that is important to her.

I followed Sue's early work on this project with interest, as I would follow any other friend's interesting projects, but then one day we had a conversation about one of the motivating factors for her. Sue shared with me that one of the big reasons she wanted to complete this book was that she was a bit concerned that by the time her grandchildren were old enough to really remember her well, she might be incapacitated and they would not have a memory of her as the capable person she is now. She said that if that turned out to be the case, that this book would serve as proof that their grandmother had, at one point, been capable of accomplishing a major, important project like this. Well, I was IN at that exact moment, ready to do anything that was needed to help her get this done.

So I started to incorporate side trips to photograph monoliths into my travels. I took a cab in Florida between an airline flight and a cruise to capture one. I stopped at many monoliths along the way to drop my daughter at college, enjoying her company on the way there (and including her in one early morning picture) and alone with my tears on my way home with an empty van and a full camera (taking a different route, of course, so I could capture more monoliths). I took mini-vacations in the middle of family gatherings in Minnesota during two different years, once traveling east in a big loop and the next year traveling north and west in a different loop. I extended a visit to the Fiestaware factory in West Virginia to visit some monoliths in the northeast. A work trip to Cincinnati doubled in length to accommodate an elaborate figure-eight route through Ohio and Indiana. I engaged my parents in the quest as I visited them in Nebraska (Sue included a very touching memorial to my father who passed away a few years ago.) Trips with my mom to Chicago and Kansas City yielded a few more photos. No trip to Glacier National Park would be complete without a few monoliths along the way. (My husband and I even found one on that trip that Sue was not aware of as we drove through a lovely little town in Montana.) And I ensnared friends and family in the search, sending my son and his wife to capture a southern California site, family friends to visit a few in the Midwest, and an ex-boyfriend to find one of the monoliths in Texas.

I saw monoliths that needed to be propped up, one or two with lights focused on them, one with a time capsule at its base, a few in front of Aeries, many in parks and cemeteries, and on courthouse lawns. Many were well-tended and out in the open, and others were damaged, neglected, or in remote areas. Some were parts of extensive displays of other monuments, but most stood sentinel alone. One was buried in such a way that the dedication information was not visible. Most were quite similar, but one or two were completely different from their counterparts, and those were always a treat to find. Finding something on the back of a monolith was an occasional fun surprise. Some made me feel sad (like the one nearly overgrown with bushes); some inspired anger (vandalism is never acceptable, despite one's beliefs about these monoliths); one made me laugh out loud as I drove around the park four times and finally saw the monolith right on the road, but under an Air Force plane which caught my eye on each passing – this apple didn't fall far from her pilot father's tree!; one made me cry (sited as it was right next to a cemetery plot for infants); and those I couldn't find made me feel very frustrated. The one next to the river in Cedar Rapids which was lying on the ground shortly after a devastating flood in the area reminded me of the occasional wrath of Mother Nature, and seeing it a year or two later upright in a new location reminded me of the perseverance of human nature. The very best part of each and every single find was my phone call to Sue to tell her where I was and what I was seeing, trying to have her share the experience with me.

It has been a great adventure. Life is a little less interesting without my side trips to seek out one more monolith, and a little less rich without the visits to small towns all across the land. I miss the phone calls to Sue with one more find, and the anticipation I felt as I approached each potential location and the thrill of the sighting.

Thank you to Sue for letting me be part of her magnificent work, and please know this, Sue: your life has enriched everyone you have known, your passion for this work has been a true inspiration to everyone around you, and your grandchildren have the extraordinary good fortune to have an extraordinary woman for a grandmother with, or without, this book.

Karen Madsen

PROLOGUE

My sister-in-law, Judy, and I were doing our thing – taking photos, measuring, writing notes – when the disc in the camera flashed "FULL." Not quite finished, in a rush trying to make it to the next town before sundown, already overwhelmed by the heat of the day, a full camera disc was just one more thing to slow us down. Trying to rifle through bags and boxes of things that have been in the car for three weeks was no easy task in the attempt to find one tiny disc in a camera case that hadn't been seen in days.

As I waited for Judy to flush out the car and come back to the corner of the courthouse where we were frantically trying to complete this site's photo episode, two people emerged out of the front doors of the building and started to descend to the street. A woman followed them with a camera, stopping them midflight to pose for photos. It was so obvious that they had just been married – the joy in their faces overflowed.

Judy and I both knew it was "a God thing." We stopped in our tracks to witness something very special. Almost feeling like intruders on their special day, we asked to take their photo. There were no other people around – there were no family or friends to witness what had just taken place. The bride was born and raised in this town. After moving away years before, she felt that she had to come back just for the weekend to get married. They currently live in a town not very far from where I live in Washington, and they were going to head right back after the ceremony. The groom's mother lives in Wisconsin where Judy lives. With God, there are no coincidences. If the disc in the camera had not been teeming with monolith photos, we would have been long gone and not been a part of this. We wouldn't have stopped to "smell the roses." Even as I write these words, I still smile about how truly happy they appeared.

Congratulations to
Cameron and Kimberly Crawford
of Bellingham, Washington

Just as we were all aglow and giddy, the Justice of the Peace, who also happened to be the district attorney, came down the steps to hand this couple their marriage license. Bringing us back to the reality of the moment, he asked what we were doing taking photos in front of the courthouse (which was not the first, nor the last, time that we were questioned regarding our intentions).

"I want to tell the story of these monoliths that were placed across the country." This is a story that I could tell in my sleep, but his next question came as a bit of a surprise, and I was not quite prepared to answer it. The district attorney then asked, "What is our town's story?"

Truth be told, a monolith that was originally placed and still remains sitting in front of a courthouse, has no story. At least it doesn't today – and that's a good thing. I explained that when a Ten Commandments monolith was dedicated, however many years ago, it was usually quite a big deal. It was something that the town wanted, probably dedicated with great pomp and circumstance, and it held an honored place in the town's history. If no one ever complained, or threatened a lawsuit, or tried to vandalize it, the monolith was just there biding its time. In most cases, people don't even know that it's there. If they have noticed it, they probably don't have an opinion regarding its existence one way or another.

He looked a little miffed, or perhaps disappointed, that I couldn't tell him anything more than that – that his town's monolith seemed almost boring. That's when I realized that this town was fortunate, and blessed, in so many ways – it still had a connection to its past values. This connection was so strong that someone who had moved away years before thought it was important enough to come back just for the weekend to get married – to be immersed in a part of the past in a way that made this wedding day more heartfelt and meaningful, even though it was just the newlyweds who experienced this special day.

That is when the full realization came to me that I cannot bring harm to any of these towns, or be responsible for "outing" any of the Ten Commandments monoliths to those who wish to do them harm. There are individuals and organizations that would come into a small town like this one, find someone who needs his or her "fifteen minutes of fame," and create havoc, division, and cost the town money just to line their own pockets – just because they can. It has happened time and time again, and I do not want to be the person who gives any of these organizations that opportunity.

Unfortunately, what this means is that there are photos contained in this book that have no town recognition. Building names, street signs, license plates, flags, monolith dedications, etc., have been blurred so that it is difficult to know where these protected monoliths are. It is with great sadness that I do this because these towns, and the people that reside in them, have been wonderful in this Ten Commandments adventure over the past thirteen years. I have many stories that I wish I could share with everyone regarding these protected monoliths, but it's not the time to do so. Every monolith that has been made known to me is represented within the following pages in one way or another. If a monolith is already known to those groups who wish to do it harm, or if it is on private property, then its location is part of the narrative. If it is a protected monolith, then I have not disclosed its location. The information, locations, and photos that have been collected over the years will be preserved for future generations to access so that this collection will not be lost.

It is a sad world in which we live that a few individuals and organizations cannot tolerate, or even attempt to pretend to appreciate, a national program that occurred over sixty years ago for its historical and cultural significance. And yet, I do not want to leave out any of the known monoliths, pictured within their current settings (or at least where they were at the time the photos were taken). Please accept my most sincere apology for altering a number of photos and documents that are contained within these pages. This was done out of the utmost respect and concern for each town's historical integrity and financial wellbeing.

CHAPTER 1

IN THE BEGINNING

It was Flag Day, Thursday, June 14, 2001, at 4 AM, and I was spending some "personal time" in the bathroom as I was beginning to get ready to finish one more week with my students at West Seattle High School before summer break. I was flipping through the June 9 issue of *World* magazine looking for something to catch my interest, when I came across an article with a photo of a HUGE Ten Commandments monolith. I had never seen anything like that before. The one-page article, *Road kill and stone tablets* by Gene Edward Veith, had me mesmerized. Before I was even finished reading through the story, I got that "slap" that nearly knocked me over.

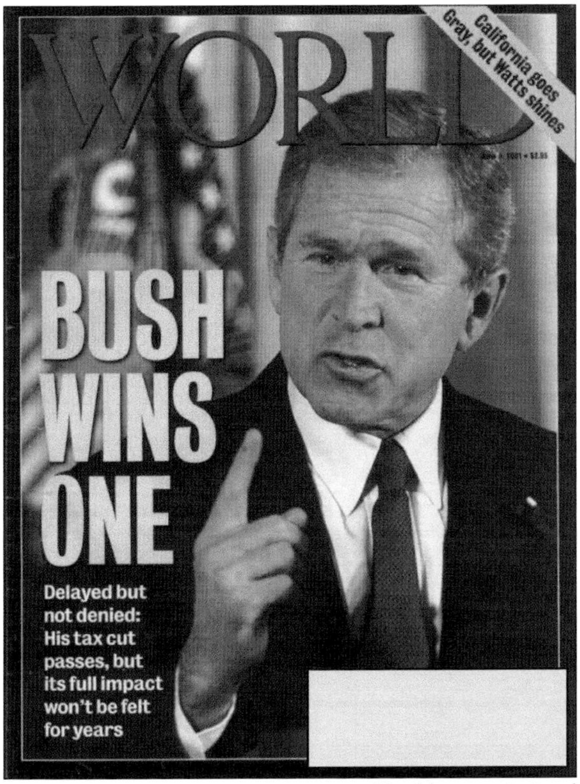

CULTURE BEAT

Road kill and stone tablets

If art should be offensive, why object to a Decalogue monument? ▸ by GENE EDWARD VEITH

A raccoon that had been run over by a car. A deer skull. Turkey feathers. A dead crow. Put them all together and you have a work of art.

Ben Jennings, an art major at the University of Wisconsin-Marathon County, created his masterpiece by cruising for road kill on Highway 29 in rural Wisconsin. He assembled his materials in a glass box and displayed the work in the college's exhibit room.

His purpose was to create what he called "dynamic art," a sculpture that would change without the help of the artist. The appearance of the carcasses would change every day as they rotted.

But then the *objet d'art* started to stink. Although, presumably, the sense of smell could be considered part of the work's sensory aesthetic, the stench got really, really bad. It became too much for the gallery-goers, however sophisticated they were when it came to contemporary art. The odor could not be contained within the exhibit space, and it wafted down the halls into the rest of the building. The aroma of the rotting road kill threatened to disrupt a big end-of-the-year awards ceremony.

Finally, the dean stepped in and told Mr. Jennings and the Art Department to just throw the thing away. "I was kind of flattered that I had to remove it," said the artist. "The reaction is the best part of it, even if it's negative."

Mr. Jennings may be only a college student in the hinterlands right now, but he may have a great career ahead of him in the arts establishment. Look at artistic superstar Damien Hurst who carves up not only dead animals but human cadavers. Having scorned the notion of "Beauty," artists are experimenting with creating works of calculated ugliness. Instead of trying to create an aesthetic response, they are trying to create other kinds of responses: shock, anger, disgust. Taking advantage of the widespread public ignorance about the arts ("who is to say what art really is?"), many artists are defining art in a circular way as "anything an artist does."

When the philistine masses object to works of art that offend them, the art establishment is pleased. The negative reaction validates the work's purpose.

Hispanic Catholics in New Mexico are currently objecting to a painting of the Virgin Mary wearing a sexy bikini. Two years ago, Mayor Giuliani and other New York taxpayers found fault with another Virgin Mary covered with elephant dung and clippings from porn magazines. Christians of all stripes are offended at a depiction of the Last Supper featuring Jesus as Mrs. Butterworth and the disciples as advertising cartoon characters. The squeamish and hygienic are bothered by the displays currently in vogue of artist's excrement and bodily fluids.

"Art is supposed to be offensive," the art establishment tells them. Works of art are supposed to stretch people's perceptions and make them uncomfortable. The offensiveness of art is proof that it is working.

Back in 1956, filmmaker Cecil B. DeMille teamed up with a Minnesota judge, E. J. Ruegemer, and his service club, the Fraternal Order of Eagles, to install granite reproductions of the Ten Commandments in parks and on the grounds of municipal buildings.

IT'S SUPPOSED TO BE OFFENSIVE: Elkhart's monument.

Mr. DeMille bought into the plan as a way of promoting his new movie *The Ten Commandments*. Judge Ruegemer, concerned by a juvenile offender who said that he didn't know what the Ten Commandments were, wanted to educate the public about the then uncontroversial notion that the Decalogue is the foundation for all subsequent legal systems. The Eagles chipped in some money and offered the sculptures to their local communities. Altogether, some 4,000 replicas—six feet tall, weighing 2,500 pounds—were installed across the country, with Hollywood's Moses, Charlton Heston, presiding at some of the unveilings.

Elkhart, Ind., had its Ten Commandments monument just outside the municipal building. Over the years, it became overgrown with shrubs, out of sight and out of mind. But recently, after some new landscaping, the monolith became visible again. A man named William A. Books rode by on his bicycle and became offended.

He sued. According to his affidavit, he was "extremely upset and bothered" to see the Ten Commandments, which, he said, symbolizes religions he does not practice. The Indiana Civil Liberties Union took up the case, demanding that the city remove the sculpture. City officials refused. They won the first round, but a federal appeals court ruled that the stone tablets are unconstitutional. The city of Elkhart—to its credit, unlike many cities that cave at the first threat of an ACLU anti-religion lawsuit—appealed to the U.S. Supreme Court, which last week declined to hear the case.

Maybe Elkhart should have argued that the Ten Commandments monument is a work of art and that, as the expression of God's Law, it is *supposed* to be offensive. ◼

WORLD | June 9, 2001 15

Road kill and stone tablets ~ If art should be offensive, why object to a Decalogue monument?
by Gene Edward Veith (*World* June 9, 2001)

The article was centered on a court case regarding the Ten Commandments monolith on public property in Elkhart, Indiana. The fact that these monumental stone tablets were anywhere amazed me in general, and that I had never heard of them, was even more astonishing. As I was reading, I *heard* the following words, "You will travel around the country, find these monoliths, and you will write *In Search of God and the Ten Commandments*." Talk about a fearful moment. I knew that I had just heard from God. I had never heard from Him before, and sitting where I was in the bathroom, was the last place that I would have imagined that it would have happened. I was scared, excited, and I do believe I even laughed and cried at the same time. All I knew was that I was going on a mission – a mission from God. Convincing the family would be crucial, but fortunately, whether they believed it was the voice of God or not, they were pretty much okay with it.

I immediately started writing letters. Some of my early letter-writing campaigns addressing politicians and media personnel produced some interesting responses. Unfortunately, none of them were overly helpful as to the locations of the monoliths, or knowing if they would be allowed to stay where they were placed. The letter from Charlton Heston, though, touched my heart.

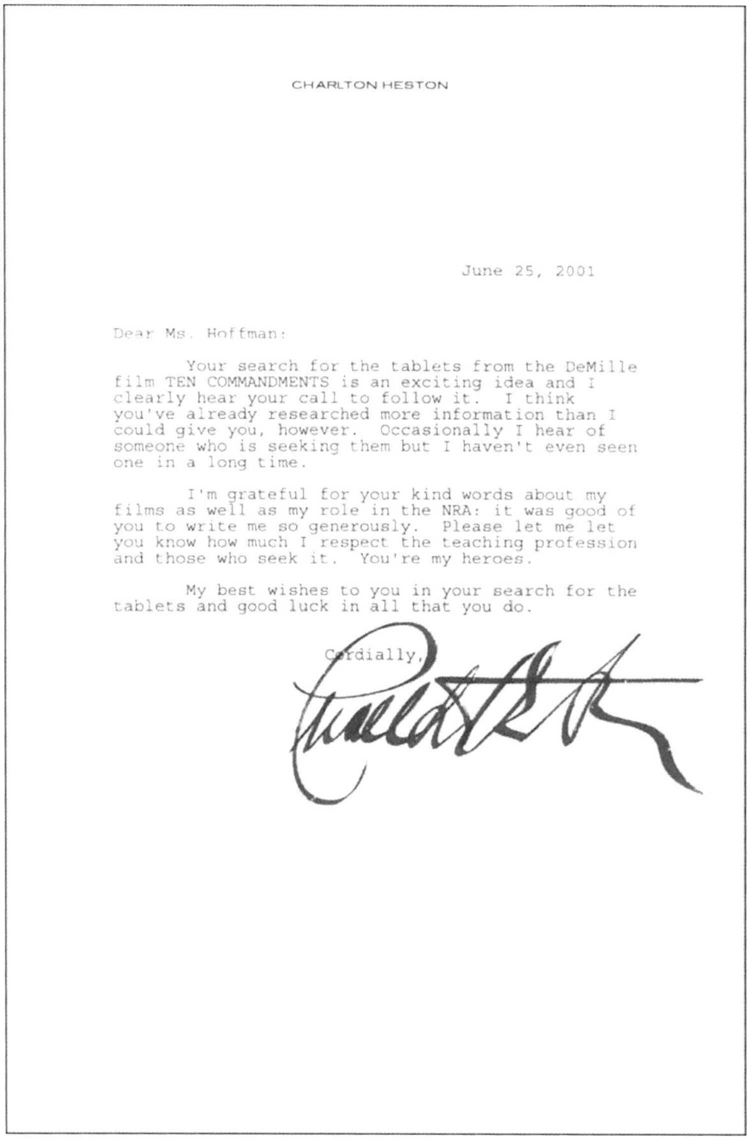

CHARLTON HESTON

June 25, 2001

Dear Ms. Hoffman:

Your search for the tablets from the DeMille film TEN COMMANDMENTS is an exciting idea and I clearly hear your call to follow it. I think you've already researched more information than I could give you, however. Occasionally I hear of someone who is seeking them but I haven't even seen one in a long time.

I'm grateful for your kind words about my films as well as my role in the NRA: it was good of you to write me so generously. Please let me let you know how much I respect the teaching profession and those who seek it. You're my heroes.

My best wishes to you in your search for the tablets and good luck in all that you do.

Cordially,

Letter from Charlton Heston written on June 25, 2001

At the time that I received Mr. Heston's letter (this one and another one shortly thereafter), there was no indication that in just shortly over a year he would announce his upcoming battle with Alzheimer's disease. I was truly saddened on April 5, 2008, to hear that Charlton Heston had died.

Another reply to one of my letters came in the form of a tongue lashing from Chief Justice Roy S. Moore (see pages 4 and 5). This was during the early stages of his own personal battle with his own Ten Commandments monument. It appeared to me that it would make more sense to consider the monoliths more of a cultural or historical icon as an argument against their removal. Moore did not like that approach and misunderstood my intentions as to why the monoliths had to be viewed in that way in order to fight for their existence.

I had to admire his convictions and his willingness to lose his job for his personal beliefs. I also appreciated the time that he took out of his hectic schedule to respond so thoroughly. On the other hand, his methods of keeping his own monument in place brought a lot of unwanted and negative attention to the Fraternal Order of Eagles' Ten Commandments monoliths. People had the monuments confused and used Moore's monument as an argument to have all of the Ten Commandments monoliths removed.

In 2003, a judicial panel barred Moore from his position for refusing to remove a Ten Commandments monument from the rotunda of the Alabama Judicial Building. He went on to serve as President of the Foundation for Moral Law in Montgomery and gave speeches all across the country regarding constitutional issues. In November 2012, the good people of Alabama voted overwhelmingly to reinstate Chief Justice Roy S. Moore, returning him once again to the Supreme Court of Alabama.

I was in constant conversation with anyone who would listen about the logistics, the possibilities, and the promises of things unknown regarding these Ten Commandments monoliths. I had a great family, a great job, and now a God-given mission, a journey, a quest so to speak. I thought I was going to write a book about monoliths and Americana, and then my search led me to the man who started it all, Judge E. J. Ruegemer in Alexandria, Minnesota, and the mission took a slight detour.

Just when you think that you know what you are doing, God steps in and shows you His way. Judge E. J. Ruegemer, who was ninety-nine years old when I first met him, made it very clear to me when I asked him what I should do with all of the information that I was given regarding the Ten Commandments monoliths. He very simply and humbly said, "They should know about the Ten Commandments." As I forged my way through the copious amounts of documentation regarding the Judge and all that he had done for teenagers and the people that he had come in contact with, I felt very honored that I was granted the privilege of being able to talk with him in person. There was so much more to the story than what I had ever imagined. Enormous and heart-felt thanks and gratitude go out to the Judge and his family for their continued support and generosity. The more I learned from them, the more I realized that I had to go back to our beginnings and what our forefathers had in mind for our nation.

It was less than two months after I had met Judge E. J. Ruegemer when the most unimaginable and horrific thing happened – September 11, 2001. Our nation as a whole truly needed God and all of His promises, and it looked like we were going to grow closer to Him. People were openly praying in public and caring about each other. There was hope mixed in with the pain and fear. Sadly, as time moved on from that horrendous day, it appears that we have moved even further away from God.

My original intent in gathering information regarding the Fraternal Order of Eagles' Ten Commandments Project was to personally try to find each monolith and get the individual story from each town where a monolith was placed. That was when the guesstimated published number stood at 4,000 monoliths. It did not take long for me to realize that there were probably fewer than

200 monoliths in place since the production of the first monolith in 1954. Little did I realize in 2001 that due to the many years since the project began that so much information had vanished.

SUPREME COURT OF ALABAMA
JUDICIAL BUILDING
300 DEXTER AVENUE
MONTGOMERY, ALABAMA 36104-3741
(334) 242-4609

ASSOCIATE JUSTICES
J. GORMAN HOUSTON JR
CHAMP LYONS JR
DOUGLAS INGE JOHNSTONE
THOMAS A. WOODALL

CHIEF JUSTICE
ROY S. MOORE

ASSOCIATE JUSTICES
HAROLD SEE
JEAN WILLIAMS BROWN
ROBERT BERNARD HARWOOD JR
LYN STUART

October 30, 2001

Sue A. Hoffman
3501 Auburn Way S. #14
Auburn, WA 98092

Dear Mrs. Hoffman:

Having received your letter of October 14, 2001, I read with great interest your sincere desire to stop the removal of granite displays of the Ten Commandments across our Nation. I appreciate your concern and commitment to those principles and values which have made America great and your support for my effort to restore the acknowledgment of God in our land.

Nevertheless, I perceive some misunderstanding in your logic. You must never relegate God's Word to an object of art, history, or a national relic of the past. We may be a Nation of many backgrounds and faiths, but not of many gods. A simple deception of modern teaching is its attempt to equate the one true God with Buddah, Allah, Taoism, Hinduism, etc. Our Nation was founded in law and fact on the God of the Holy Scriptures. While no government can make one think or believe in any particular manner, we must always acknowledge that which forms the basis of our law and our legal rights. Americans would be advised to read the Declaration of Independence and learn the meaning of "laws of nature and of nature's God."

I am not aware that the recent decision of the United States Supreme Court in refusing to opine as to the display of the Ten Commandments casts the obligation upon States to defend religious liberty. The First Amendment of the United States Constitution is applicable to all people and the United States Supreme Court must eventually address this issue. Howbeit, I am not willing to excuse anyone who will not defend his or her right to acknowledge God to focus on secular concerns as poverty, unemployment, transportation, and housing. The role of government was to secure the rights God gave us according to the Declaration of Independence. It is no wonder that we are loosing our rights when we have forgotten from whence those rights flow.

Letter from Chief Justice Roy S. Moore written on October 30, 2011 – Page One

October 30, 2001
Page Two

I agree that Judge E. J. Ruegemer is a man to be admired and one who will receive his heavenly reward for his devotion to God's Holy Laws. Please give him my regards should you have occasion. I, too, have children and will continue to work to promote an understanding of those principles which made us a great people. I am enclosing for your review a pamphlet which we recently published in our court system. Thank you for your concern and support.

Sincerely,

Roy S. Moore
Chief Justice

RSM/wha
enclosure

Letter from Chief Justice Roy S. Moore written on October 30, 2011 – Page Two

The biggest break came in August 2003 with a trip to Buffalo, New York when I attended the Fraternal Order of Eagles' International Convention. I presented a visual display with everything that I had gathered regarding sixty-three monoliths in hope that representatives from each state would take notice and offer more information. At the end of three days, the number of known monoliths increased to 112 thanks to the many individuals who were willing to share what they knew about the monoliths in their hometowns.

The Fraternal Order of Eagles' Grand Aerie made an effort to try to encourage Aeries, from the state level on down, to reply, or at least acknowledge, my inquiries regarding the monoliths. For the most part, everyone agreed that it would be a good idea to have the information in one location for the overall Ten Commandments Project. In 2004, letters went out regarding the collection of data, but there was very little response (fewer than five Aeries replied).

Even with so little information available, the number of known monoliths grew to 157 by the spring of 2005. It was very difficult to get information from the local Aeries. Just knowing that a monolith existed was not enough proof for me – I wanted photos, dedication information, and stories. People continued to contact me through those early years, but it seemed like the interest in the Ten Commandments monoliths declined after the US Supreme Court decision in 2005 regarding Van Orden v. Perry. A lot of individuals thought that would end all of the angst towards the monoliths. In reality, it was the calm before the storm.

Everyone deserves at least one shot at their "fifteen minutes of fame," and because of the Ten Commandments monoliths, I have been the fortunate recipient of several such moments. I received an invitation to attend the unveiling of the Grand Aerie's very own Ten Commandments

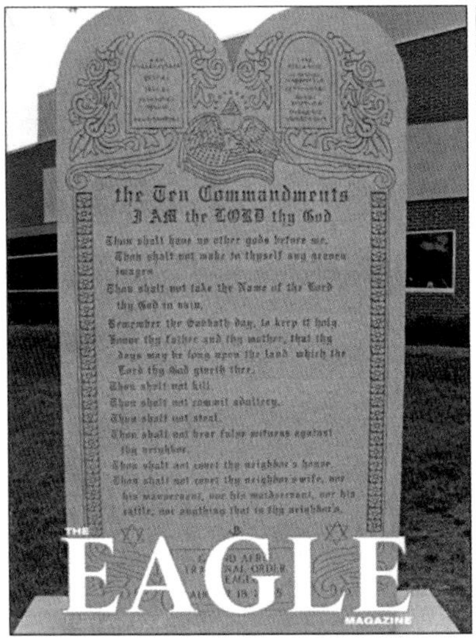

FOREVER CHANGED

The Eagle Magazine (February 2006)

Sue A. Hoffman speaking at the Fraternal Order of Eagles' Headquarters, Grove City, Ohio, for the dedication of the Ten Commandments monolith in August 2005

monolith in August 2005. I was honored that they had asked me to share a few words. I took this opportunity to step down from my search of the Ten Commandments monoliths. I was tired and frustrated from the lack of response from the local Eagle Aeries. I had also just medically retired from teaching because the multiple sclerosis that I had been living with since 1999 was beginning to take a physical and emotional toll.

My speech ended with a challenge to the Fraternal Order of Eagles to stand up for what they believed in so that history would not repeat itself as more and more monoliths were being removed from public land:

> My work is now done. At this time, there is no need for me to write a book regarding the Ten Commandments monoliths. Considering that I am not a member of the Eagles, and because my disability and early retirement together have affected my financial resources to the extent that I am no longer able to continue down the path that I began four years ago, I am now returning this project over to you. The Eagles need to embrace the complete ownership of this important legacy. I encourage you – no, I challenge you – to continue on now with what has become larger than any one of us, something that began over fifty years ago, that I know has now become a shining light in a world of darkness for all to see.

The Fraternal Order of Eagles honored me with The Ten Commandments Award in October 2005, "For your inspiration in strengthening the moral and the spiritual fabric of our organization." The Grand Auxiliary of the Fraternal Order of Eagles' gifted me with an Honorary Life-time Membership in Auburn, Washington Aerie 2298, "In recognition of your true American Spirit and for your dedication to research on the Fraternal Order of Eagles Ten Commandments Monoliths and for embracing the ideals and principles of our beloved Order." I felt duly blessed and truly appreciated by both organizations for all of the efforts in documenting the history of the Ten Commandments monoliths.

Eventually, though, I began to experience the guilt of having so much information regarding the monoliths at my disposal. This story belonged to the Fraternal Order of Eagles, and I knew that I had to give back to them what was rightfully theirs. During a chance meeting in February 2008 with

Anne Berg, the daughter of Judge E. J. Ruegemer, I knew that I had to finish what I had started. Unfortunately, there still was not enough information to satisfy my desire for the complete and final picture.

In order to make one last-ditch effort to collect information, I mailed 192 letters to Aeries with known, and suspected, monoliths. Each Aerie was sent everything that had been collected regarding their possible monolith. In some cases, there was no information other than "someone said a monolith was in that town somewhere."

Knowing from past experience how difficult it was for people to respond to the letters, I sent thirty-five additional packets to the State Aeries with the same information that was sent to the local Aeries requesting information. I hoped that the State Aerie people would remind the local Aerie people to get the information sent in a timely manner. Had the response been immediate, there would have been a lot of information to work with on my end. Unfortunately, this was the spring of 2008 with horrific floods and tornadoes throughout the Midwest, and those storms definitely, and understandably, affected some Aeries' greatly. They had much larger problems to ponder than gathering information regarding a fifty-year-old project.

Out of the 192 letters I sent to Aeries, only fifty Aeries responded with varying degrees of information. That meant that 142 Aeries did NOT respond. Out of those 142 Aeries, 123 Aeries actually had known monoliths.

I took all of the information that I had and produced a book entitled, *"I AM the LORD thy God" - An Overview of the Fraternal Order of Eagles' Ten Commandments Project 1946 - 2008.* I firmly believed that FINALLY, the Eagles would try to finish the work that I had started and at least get the blanks filled in. After all of the excitement of "finishing" what I thought was the book that I was supposed to write. I placed the printed pages in a canvas bag behind the couch to collect dust. Every now and then, I brought it out to show someone what I had accomplished. It was over 400 pages, so I told them just rifle through to take note of the photos and the kinds of things that were in there. No one ever read it - it was too long and they were just supposed to appreciate all of the work that went into its creation. Every now and then I would get a phone call requesting information regarding the Ten Commandments Project, and I would pull the book out to get some statistics or refresh my memory so that I could speak with conclusive authority on the topic at hand. I never looked through it again. Deep in my heart I knew that it wasn't finished, but I also knew that I lacked what it would take to put it all together in a way that was pleasing to God.

If I were to have actually completed this book in the first couple of years, or would have considered it done in 2008, it would have been a book about stone monuments. What was I thinking? God gave me the first clue - the title of the book, *In Search of God and the Ten Commandments -* and somehow I missed that for years. The second clue was meeting Judge E. J. Ruegemer - it wasn't just about granite monoliths. There was a specific man behind the story who brought context and the human condition into the forefront. He was not perfect, but his heart for young people when dealing with them in the courtroom was contagious. The third clue was my personal struggle with trying to put everything together, and not just once, but on three separate occasions. Getting this book not only done, but doing it the way that God intended, turned out to be a journey thirteen years in the making.

I had wasted so many years attempting to "fight the good fight," that I took my eyes off of God and tried to do it on my own. In Matthew 7:5-7 (ESV), it says, "You hypocrite, first take the log out of your own eye, and then you will see clearly to take the speck out of your brother's eye. Do not give dogs what is holy, and do not throw your pearls before pigs, lest they trample them underfoot and turn to attack you. Ask, and it will be given to you; seek, and you will find; knock, and it will be opened to you."

I was not spiritually ready to handle all of the adversaries and their lies. No matter how sure I was of my relationship with God, I had so much more to learn. Even though I was under a marvelous pastor for twenty years whose messages were Biblically sound, it took moving to another congregation, which had not only a pastor who sat at the feet of God, but members of the congregation who were prayer warriors. There were also fellow congregants who had a strong grasp on what was happening to America's freedom, and who understood the cultural decline that America was experiencing.

Karen Madsen

Judy Pankow

Diana Bunch

Deborah Arnett

God is truly marvelous in how He uses people and circumstances to make things come together for His glory. I had to not only be in a class to have my eyes opened, but I had to lead the class several times so that I got to experience the material four times before it got into my heart. *The Truth Project* by Focus on the Family raises the question in relationship to what is found in the Bible and what your daily walk is – Do you really believe that what you believe is really real? That is truly a profound question because if you do believe what is in the Bible, then how do you live your life in thoughts, words, and deeds? It affected me down to my very core. Add that to the Leadership class that I did not have the time to take, but discovered that it was EXACTLY what I needed to prepare me for the journey that I was about to undergo. It equipped me with not only looking more into who I was in God's eyes and being able to apply that to life's challenges, but it also offered me the privilege of knowing individuals who became the prayerful encouragers that I needed alongside me.

God has always provided individuals to help me in ways that I will never be able to repay. Throughout this book, you will be able to appreciate that almost half of the photos were taken by Karen Madsen over several years of traveling around the United States. For reasons beyond understanding, she has inspired me to never give up on this journey. Karen continues to reassure me that she is always there for me should I ever begin to falter or stumble.

My beloved sister-in-law, Judy Pankow, has been willing and able to "go on an adventure" at a moment's notice. She was with me when I first met with Judge E. J. Ruegemer in Minnesota in 2001, when I did the infamous "Southwest Tour" in 2012, and then continued on her own and took a few more photos here-and-there without me. Judy is more than just family – she is also a true friend.

Through my church, The Truth Project class, and the Leadership class, a new-found friend and sister in God, Diana Bunch, gifted me with her amazing editing skills as "midnight approached." To be able to step in at the last moment and offer to be "another set of eyes," has blessed my socks off.

A long-time friend and cohort, Deborah Arnett, has always encouraged my efforts and has listened to endless tales of the inane people and organizations that I have encountered. She was even brave enough to travel with me on a whirlwind monolith photo tour which could have easily ended any friendship, but ours endures.

The Grand Aerie of the Fraternal Order of Eagles has given me so much support by providing archived documentation of photos, articles, meeting minutes, records, etc. Their trust and encouragement in this project has been there from the early days of this journey. Although this story is much bigger than the Eagles, my wish is, although there are no "sacred cows" in these pages, that the Fraternal Order of Eagles will be honored for all of the excellent charitable work that they accomplish.

Grand Secretary Chuck Cunningham has lent his unending support for thirteen years. Office Assistant Marilyn Bozich, who has since retired, spent relentless hours researching and copying copious amounts of old documents, letters, and magazine articles. Bob Wahls, Past Grand Secretary, was the first person that I had contact with who had the faith in me to set the record straight.

There are so many people that I am privileged to have crossed paths with in this adventure. They have been extremely generous with their time and talents, and I will be forever grateful. Without the many hands that God has provided, this story could not have come together.

Chuck Cunningham

As you can witness, this story is bigger than any one person can handle, but if God gave His approval, as it says in Romans 8:31 (ESV), "What then shall we say to these things? If God is for us, who can be against us?" I was busy for years trying to put out the fires of misinformation regarding these Ten Commandments monoliths. In reality, I was just wasting time attempting to provide facts to people who were unwilling to accept them. They have been so wound up in the lies that they have believed for so many years, that they may still be unwilling to give up those dogmas even when the evidence is laid before them. Now I will be better prepared because of the work that God has done in me to handle, or ignore, their continued onslaught of fabrications and desire to destroy a symbol of America's history.

Marilyn Bozich

Seeking God's face was the answer to all of the issues regarding writing this book. I had what I needed to bring truth forward thirteen years ago, but it eluded me. In Exodus 34:29 (ESV), it says, "When Moses came down from Mount Sinai, with the two tablets of the testimony in his hand as he came down from the mountain, Moses did not know that the skin of his face shone because he had been talking with God." I had been searching God's face for two months, physically sequestered from family and friends, for the final journey of putting words on paper. As I entered the final few days, I felt my heart beginning to "glow." It wasn't until then that I found "the smoking gun." I cried out, "Why didn't I see this before?" And then I immediately knew, simply clarified, that I wasn't prepared for the truth in a way that I was able to explain it. God is so great, and as always, greatly to be praised.

Bob Wahls

The experience of *finally* doing the task at hand, in a way that was pleasing to God, I could feel His approval from the inside out. This journey was truly about searching for God and His truth. Then, and only then, could the injustice that has rained down on the Fraternal Order of Eagles' Ten Commandments monoliths be brought into the light of day.

May the following written words anger, frustrate, but ultimately, enlighten, and encourage you. Enjoy the journey, and may you be truly blessed in the process.

CHAPTER 2

THE MAN - JUDGE E. J. RUEGEMER

It was truly an awe-inspiring experience to meet the Honorable Judge E. J. Ruegemer in August 2001. Even at ninety-nine years of age, he was still a "judge" in every sense of the word.

To understand the Fraternal Order of Eagles' Ten Commandments Project is to understand who Judge E. J. Ruegemer was - a decent, loyal, and humble human being with an intense passion for what he did. His strong belief system, and the work that he was able to accomplish with misdirected young people, was extraordinary. The Stearns History Museum, which is located in the Judge's jurisdiction, has boxes of newspaper articles and documentation regarding the Judge.

So much has been written about the Judge in the past seventy years that the best way to give you a glimpse of the man behind the monoliths is to highlight some of his accomplishments.

Steve Erickson (friend), the Judge, and Nita Hofmann (daughter) in 2001

Stearns History Museum, Saint Cloud, Minnesota

JUDGE E. J. RUEGEMER

- Judge E. J. Ruegemer attended grade school in Richmond, Minnesota plus ninth grade (school only went through ninth grade).
- At age sixteen, he worked as Assistant to the Postmaster in Richmond, Minnesota for twenty dollars per month.
- He was advised by the Saint Cloud Business College to NOT finish high school, but instead, to attend the business college, which would be more useful.
- He enrolled in the business college at age seventeen.
- At age eighteen, he started working as a clerk at the Saint Cloud Reformatory for forty dollars per month plus room and board.
- While being a clerk at the reformatory, he decided to study law, but in order to take correspondence courses in law through the LaSalle Extension University in Chicago, he needed to finish the remaining three years of high school.
- He attended Tech High School and Cathedral High School at night.
- After finishing the university correspondence course, he found that he also needed to study law in a lawyer's office in order to take the Bar Exam.
- His day started at 5 AM when he stoked the furnace and studied until the family got up.
- He continued his job at the reformatory where he was promoted to Secretary to the Superintendent and also Secretary to the Board of Criminal Classification.
- At night, he went to the Atwood and Quinlivan Law Office to study law.
- He then was told that studying law in the evening did not meet the qualifications necessary to take the Bar Exam.
- While working part-time at the reformatory during the day, he also worked with Judge Roeser in the Judge's Chambers and the Courthouse Law Library.
- He was informed that this study would not qualify him for the Bar Exam because Roeser was not a practicing attorney.
- Harry Burn's Law Office agreed to let him study with them starting at 1 PM while he worked for the reformatory in the morning.
- In 1930, he passed both the oral and written exams – fifty-seven percent of those tested did not.
- He then took a course in public speaking at Saint Cloud Teachers' College, along with a course at Northwest College of Speech Arts.
- After passing the Bar Exam, he joined the law firm of Atwood and Quinlivan, and because of the Depression, most of his earnings came in the way of vegetables, sheep manure, and moonshine (which he passed on to his colleagues and friends). He accepted whatever means his clients could afford as payment for his legal services.

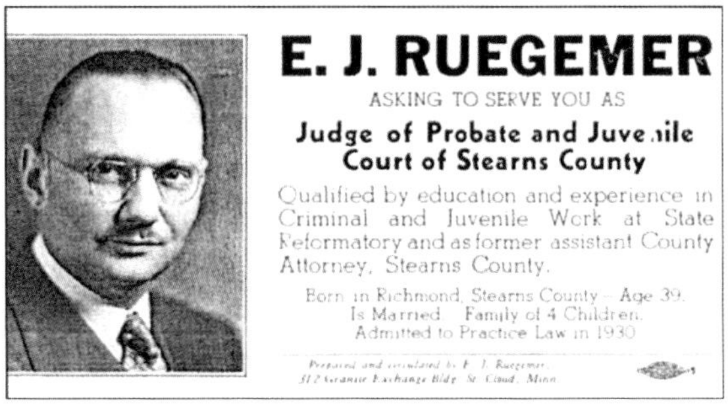

E. J. RUEGEMER
ASKING TO SERVE YOU AS
Judge of Probate and Juve.ile
Court of Stearns County
Qualified by education and experience in Criminal and Juvenile Work at State Reformatory and as former assistant County Attorney, Stearns County.
Born in Richmond, Stearns County – Age 39.
Is Married. Family of 4 Children.
Admitted to Practice Law in 1930

- Judge E. J. Ruegemer became the Assistant County Attorney to Harry Burns for three years.
- He was elected Judge of Probate and Juvenile Court of Stearns County in Saint Cloud, Minnesota in 1940.

- Judge E. J. Ruegemer became a member of the White House Commission of Youth under Congressman C. Estes Kefauver.
- He was appointed District Court Judge of the Seventh District in Saint Cloud, Minnesota in 1947 by Governor Luther Youngdahl.
- Re-elected in 1948, 1954, 1960, and 1966, he chose to retire in 1967 even though his term went to 1973.
- He was instrumental in initiating the first probation officer position in Juvenile Court.
- He started Big Brothers in Saint Cloud, Minnesota.
- The Judge held the following civil positions: President of the Minnesota Probate and Juvenile Judges Association, Secretary to the Superintendent of the Minnesota State Reformatory, Secretary of the Board of Criminal Classification, member of the Minnesota Youth Conservation Commission, Secretary of Saint Cloud City Charter Commission, Trustee of Saint Paul's Catholic Church, and appointed a member of the committee on Underprivileged Children for Kiwanis International.

Stearns County Courthouse
Saint Cloud, Minnesota

- He was awarded the Sertoma's Annual "Service to Mankind" Award, and was also awarded the title of Senior Counselor by the Minnesota Bar Association in recognition of more than fifty years of honorable service.
- The Judge held the following positions for the Fraternal Order of Eagles: President of the Saint Cloud, Minnesota Aerie, President of the Minnesota/North and South Dakota District, Chief Justice of the Eagles' Judiciary Committee, Chairman of the National Youth Guidance Commission (meetings were frequently attended by Father Flanagan, J. Edgar Hoover, and Hubert Humphrey), Grand Aerie Trustee, and co-author of the *Youth Guidance Handbook.*
- He was inducted into the Eagles' Hall of Fame in 1992.

Plaque in Stearns County Courthouse
Saint Cloud, Minnesota

Memorial engraving on the steps leading up to Stearns County Courthouse, Saint Cloud, Minnesota, in honor of Judge E. J. Ruegemer

In 1989, at eighty-seven years of age, Judge Ruegemer granted a sworn affidavit in the first Colorado case of Freedom from Religion Foundation (FFRF) v. State of Colorado as one of the few individuals who could provide first-hand knowledge of the Fraternal Order of Eagles' Ten Commandments Project. His testimony led to a successful conclusion – the monolith could remain in Denver.

Photo courtesy of the Ruegemer Family

Judge E. J. Ruegemer speaking at the dedication of a Ten Commandments monolith at the International Peace Garden, Dunseith, North Dakota in 1956

On April 13, 1992, upon his induction into the Eagles' Hall of Fame, Judge E. J. Ruegemer at ninety years of age stated, "I will say the same thing I said to the boy many years ago in my court. Man made thousands of laws. God made only ten. They should suffice. And if mankind would heed those ten, it would be a better world in which to live."

When Judge Roy Moore defied the court system and refused to remove the Ten Commandments monument in Alabama, Judge E. J. Ruegemer, at 100 years of age, said the following, "I can only say that the Ten Commandments are one of the oldest codes of conduct handed down to man, and I still say that they are a good code of conduct. I wish that all of the monoliths could remain; however, in areas where the courts have ruled that they must be removed, we have to obey the law. I would hope that in those areas they could do as was done in Grand Junction, Colorado. There, the Ten Commandments monoliths are allowed to stand on public grounds, but along with other monoliths which are inscribed with other historical documents such as the Bill of Rights, the Magna Carta, the Preamble to the Constitution, and the Mayflower Compact."

My husband and I had the privilege of attending the Judge's 100th Birthday Celebration in 2002. He was surrounded by family and friends. His niece, Renee Ruegemer Miller, penned the following:

A CENTENARY PRAYER

Thank you, O most Gracious God
For the gift of one hundred years
For the cup of life
For moments and milestones
Hours of hope, of hurt, of heartbreak
Days of daring and dreaming
And months of memories
For years of youth and of yearning
Decades of dedication and devotion
Periods of prayer and petition
For seasons of studies and startings
Autumns of achievement, of anxiety
Winters of wit and of wisdom
Spring times of strivings and success
And summers of sunshine and song
A lifetime
Of loving, living, laughter, learning
O, how full the cup, Gracious God
We look deeply inside
We, who call him father,
Grandfather, uncle, neighbor,
Judge, mentor, friend
And what we see is rich and golden
We raise that cup to You, Gracious God
And as You, too
Consider its contents
We know You are greatly pleased
With what You and he, together,
Have wrought
For from the fruits of one hundred vines
You have made a full-bodied wine
We offer
Here and now
A toast and a tribute
To this man of faith
So bountifully favored with blessings
His cup truly runneth over
And we thank you, Gracious God
That it is so.
AMEN.

The Ruegemer Family Home in Saint Cloud, Minnesota

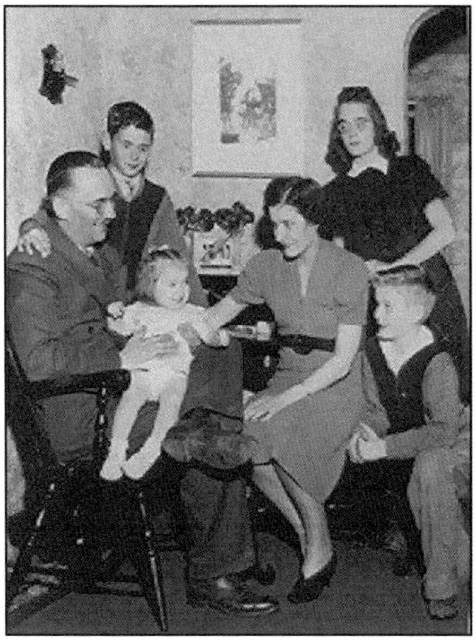
The Ruegemer Family
Sitting: Judge Ruegemer, Anne (in his lap), Mrs. Ruegemer, and Karl
Standing: James and Nita

Judge Ruegemer's home in Alexandria, Minnesota in 2001
(The house was sold, torn down, and replaced since the Judges' passing.)

A FEW PERSONAL FACTS ABOUT JUDGE E. J. RUEGEMER

- The Judge was born on July 29, 1902 in Richmond, Minnesota.
- He met Joan Steidl at the Saint Cloud Business College while he was also working at the Saint Cloud Reformatory.
- He married Joan in 1924.
- Wife, Joan, and new daughter, Nita, were present at his high school graduation.
- Together, they had five children, Nita (died in 2011), James (died in 1992), Karl, Dorothy (died in 1931), and Anne.
- His wife, Joan, died in 1943.
- In 1945, he married Agnes Steidl Gilloley (whose husband also died in 1943), bringing her son, Jack (died in 1981), into the marriage.
- The Judge moved from Saint Cloud, Minnesota to his home on Lake Carlos in Alexandria, Minnesota.
- His wife, Agnes, died in 1975.
- Gardening and making rock gardens were his hobbies, along with woodworking and making furniture.
- An avid reader even while his eyesight was failing, he continued to read with the help of a reading machine.
- In 2003, he moved to Bonnie's Senior Haven where he had wonderful care.
- At the time of the Judge's death on January 12, 2005, he was survived by three children, twelve grandchildren, five step-grandchildren, nineteen great-grand-children, and three great-great-grandchildren.
- The Judge always stood firm in his belief that all laws dealing with human relations stem from the oldest code of conduct – The Ten Commandments.

Regarding the
Ten Commandments Project,
Judge E. J. Ruegemer
commented:

This was never intended as religious instruction of any kind, but rather to show youngsters that there were such recognized codes of behavior to guide and help them.

Judge E. J. Ruegemer and his "Reader"
Alexandria, Minnesota in 2001

Photo courtesy of the Ruegemer Family
The Honorable Judge E. J. Ruegemer
July 29, 1902 ~ January 12, 2005

Judge E. J. Ruegemer's
favorite quote:

If we work upon marble, it will perish. If we work upon brass, time will efface it. If we rear temples, they will crumble to dust. But if we work upon men's immortal minds, if we imbue them with high principles, with the just fear of God and love of their fellowmen, we engrave on those tablets something which no time can efface and which will brighten to all eternity.

~ Daniel Webster ~

CHAPTER 3

THE ORGANIZATION - FRATERNAL ORDER OF EAGLES

What, or who, is the Fraternal Order of Eagles (FOE)? When I first heard of the Ten Commandments monoliths in 2001 while reading a magazine, in addition to being totally enthralled with the monoliths themselves, I was a little more than a tad "suspicious" of the organization that put them up. Other than seeing a building in my local town with FOE on it, I had no idea who the Eagles were or what they did. I envisioned them as some kind of secret society or infamous lodge organization. If that was the case, then my search for the monoliths would have ended before it began. I did not want to get involved with, or be connected to, any organization that was contrary to my belief system or my relationship with God. My search of the Ten Commandments monoliths began with a breakdown of the Fraternal Order of Eagles.

Their Story and Contributions

As in all things, I usually start at the top and work my way down (which has frustrated all of the organizations that I have ever been involved with). I wanted to know from "the powers that be" what kind of organization this was. They had every reason to be as cautious of me as I was wary of them. The timing was horrific – the Eagles were in the midst of lawsuits concerning the monoliths all over the country. People were misrepresenting themselves trying to obtain information from the Eagles to use it against them to remove the monoliths. My efforts to try to locate the monoliths might have been seen by them as a strategy to find them, and then attempt to take them down. There

"The Fraternal Order of Eagles, an international non-profit organization, unites fraternally in the spirit of liberty, truth, justice, and equality, to make human life more desirable by lessening its ills, and by promoting peace, prosperity, gladness, and hope."

appeared to be a level of trust that I had to earn in order to obtain information that was not publicly accessible.

The Eagles' Mission Statement gave me some hope in the initial search: "The Fraternal Order of Eagles, an international non-profit organization, unites fraternally in the spirit of liberty, truth, justice, and equality, to make human life more desirable by lessening its ills, and by promoting peace, prosperity, gladness, and hope." Phone calls to the International Headquarters of the Fraternal Order of Eagles in Milwaukee, Wisconsin (and then to Grove City, Ohio when they moved the Headquarters in 2002) were always pleasant, supportive, and educational. Internet research produced a goldmine of information that needed clarification regularly. Chuck Cunningham, FOE Grand Secretary, has been my constant source of information and help for thirteen years. His knowledge and love of historical matters has been a true inspiration and has guided me through the plethora of monolith information throughout this entire adventure.

The International Headquarters collects, oversees, and distributes charitable funds, organizes national events, coordinates and retains all records and statistical information, and is the source of all things Eagles. It also warehouses historical information and objects representing over 115 years of Eagledom history. The chain of command starts at the local level with the town or city Aerie (which literally means eagle nest or home), who reports to the district or region, who in turn reports to the state, who then answers to Headquarters.

As in any large organization that has small groups within it, not all groups adhere to the philosophy of the parent organization. A few of the small, local Aeries are known for "doing their own thing." There are also a "few bad apples" in the groups that turn out to be "rotten" individuals. Because Eagle members come from all walks of life, they bring into their membership parts of other organizations that they belong to. It is not unheard of that some Eagle members are also members of Masonic lodges, and have tried to influence their local Aeries with some of the Masonic traditions. These Aeries are few and far between, and any changes or additions to the bylaws passed by the Headquarters would be highly discouraged. Some ingrained traditions may be hard to oust (I equate that with trying to herd cats), but the Fraternal Order of Eagles has come a long way to become the modern, truly fraternal, organization that it is today.

Some towns view their local Eagle establishments as event rental halls, taverns, or bars. In some cases, this tends to be true, and it is these individual Aeries that will eventually become extinct, even though they have made attempts to do their minimal share to contribute to the whole of the organization. Some of the older, established Aeries are having problems getting into the technological era of the twenty-first century, and eventually, with younger members coming in, their ability to make use of social networking and correspondence will bring them up to speed. This all has to be taken with a grain of salt. The desire of the Headquarters is to be modern, advanced, and technologically astute. This would increase productivity and their ability to be more proactive in their capability to help people.

Some things just have to be experienced firsthand, so as an Honorary Life-Time Auxiliary member, I attended my local Eagle Auxiliary monthly meetings in Auburn, Washington for one year. The people were welcoming and wonderful. They truly cared about each individual. The meetings were filled with tradition and pomp and circumstance. From my background of being raised in a liturgical church, being a girl scout, and joining the US Army, there was comfort in all of the meeting rituals, none of which were contrary to my faith or religious beliefs. If you had never experienced any of the above organizations, the rituals may seem awkward at first, or at least old fashioned, but these rituals have historic significance which was explained at each meeting.

The other functions and events of the Auxiliary, besides the monthly meetings, were meant to be fun, community oriented, and beneficial to others – anything from potlucks, dances, bingo, barbeques, participating in Auburn parades and community events, as well as coordinated efforts with other charitable organizations, churches, and individuals. Overall, it was a great experience. One would only hope that other Aeries are as organized, caring, and fun as Auburn, Washington. This did give me an instrumental insight to the Eagle organization as a whole which was needed to be able to report with more accuracy the story of the Ten Commandment monoliths. If there were not so many other items on my plate, I would have continued to be part of that community. As in any fraternal organization, they rely on time commitments from their members to help them do what they do best – helping others. I felt that I could not, at that time, be as active as I would have liked.

The more I learned about the Eagles and what they contribute both financially, and with hands-on help to their communities and on a national level, the more I discovered an organization that shines above many others. As of October 2013, the Eagles had 538,927 members and approximately 1,500 local Aeries in the United States and Canada. Women's auxiliaries totaled more than 1,300, with 262,071 members – that is approximately 801,000 people strong. Although most of the Aeries are located within the United States, Aeries can also be found in other countries such as Canada, Europe, New Zealand, and Australia.

What is even more astonishing than the number of members in the FOE is the amount of money that is raised to help individuals and organizations worldwide. In 2013, local Aeries raised $7,550,042 for charitable contributions. These funds are collected by the Grand Aerie and redistributed in total as grants. In 2013, more than 1,000 grants were gifted to organizations and individuals for a total of $6,966,193. It is estimated that the Eagles annually donate approximately $100 million in money, goods, and services to charities, communities, and individuals. This is only an approximation because the Grand Aerie only distributes grants, but the rest of the monies donated at the local and state levels are given out through the individual Aeries to their local charities. With 801,000 members and $100 million a year donated to charitable organizations and people in need, one cannot help but take notice of the Eagles' success as a fraternal organization.

On February 6, 1898, the Fraternal Order of Eagles was founded by six theater owners while they were sitting on a pile of lumber in Moran's Shipyard in Seattle, Washington.

The Fraternal Order of Eagles has been around for over 115 years. They have done a lot of good to not only aid those people in their immediate communities, but they have also reached out to help build schools and training facilities internationally. Their vision of a charitable organization outweighs any issues that the individual Aeries may have, and those issues are getting fewer and farther between. Over the past thirteen years, I have personally witnessed local benefits for flood and fire victims, fundraisers to help pay for doctor and hospital bills, and I have been on the receiving end of the always welcoming smiles and generous, good nature of the people involved within this organization, from the top on down. With the permission of the Grand Aerie, along with information gathered from other resources over the past several years, the following is a portrait of the Eagles' extraordinary history and their continued charitable works.

On February 6, 1898, the Fraternal Order of Eagles was founded by six theater owners while they were sitting on a pile of lumber in Moran's Shipyard in Seattle, Washington. Competitors in the theater industry, they met to discuss a musicians' strike. After deciding what to do on that issue, they decided to bury the hatchet and form an organization dubbed "The Order of Good Things."

The first meetings were held on the stages of various local theaters, and after the business was settled, a keg of beer was rolled out and all enjoyed a few hours of social activities. A few weeks later as their numbers increased, they chose the bald eagle as their official emblem and changed their name to "The Fraternal Order of Eagles." The membership formed a Grand Aerie in April 1898, secured a charter, drew up a constitution and bylaws, and elected its first president, John Cort.

Most of the initial Eagle members were connected with the theater (actors, stagehands, playwrights, etc.), and as they went on tour, they carried the story of the new Order with them across the United States and Canada. This is why the Eagles grew so quickly nationwide. The Order was unique in its concept of brotherhood, and its early success has been attributed to its establishment of a sick and funeral benefit (no member of the Eagles was ever buried in a "Potter's Field"), along with provisions for an Aerie physician and other benefits unknown in other fraternal organizations up to that time.

As the Eagles grew, so did its responsibilities to its members. Its first constitution and bylaws were copied from those previously used by a defunct fraternal organization. It took a member like Frank Hering ("Father" of Mother's Day and long-time editor of the *National Eagle* publication) to revise the bylaws and make them unique from any other organization.

Hering, a member of South Bend, Indiana Aerie 435, who had been Notre Dame's first athletic director and a great football quarterback and baseball player, wrote the Order's funeral service. When he died in 1943, his stirring words were recited over his own body by Grand Worthy President Lester Loble. It was men like Hering who kept the Eagles from going under during the difficult days at the turn of the century, and built the solid foundation that it rests on today.

Over the years, the Eagles have fought and won many bitter battles for a Workmen's Compensation Act, Mothers and Old Age Pensions, Social Security laws, and "Jobs After Forty." They are still fighting to liberalize present social benefits along with combating vicious diseases plaguing mankind through their sponsorship of the Fraternal Order of Eagles Diabetes Research Center located at the University of Iowa, the Art Ehrmann Cancer Fund, Max Baer Heart Fund, Jimmy Durante Children's Fund, D. D. Dunlap Kidney Fund, Robert W. Hansen Diabetes Fund, as well as many other charities.

Many great social and political leaders have belonged to the Eagles. Noteworthy members include: former US presidents Theodore R. Roosevelt, Warren G. Harding, Franklin D. Roosevelt, Harry S. Truman, John F. Kennedy, Jimmy Carter, and Ronald Reagan; Bob Hope, comedian, performer; Charlton Heston, actor; Max Baer, boxer, heavyweight champion; Gordie Howe, Hockey Hall of Fame; William Allen Egan, former Governor, Alaska; NASCAR drivers Sam Hornish and Tony Stewart; musical performers Tony Orlando and Billy Ray Cyrus; every Eagle Brother; former US president wives Bess Truman and Eleanor Roosevelt; Virginia Graham, radio and TV personality; Susan Wagner, wife of former New York Mayor Robert Wagner; and every Eagle Sister.

The story of the Eagles is a story of fraternal crusading. There is something about the Fraternal Order of Eagles that is different, distinctive, and something not to be found in any other order. Since February 1898, the Eagles have not only welcomed the average man as a member, but fought for his right to a life of dignity and self-respect.

With a motto of "People Helping People," Eagle members are very actively involved in their local communities. Many of the activities focus on children and improving their quality of life. Eagles' Aeries and Auxiliaries conduct toy drives, send young victims of domestic violence to camp, hold baby showers for needy families, provide Christmas and Thanksgiving baskets, provide backpacks and school supplies, make quilts for nursing homes, and the list goes on.

During any kind of disaster such as floods, hurricanes, fires, or tornadoes, Eagle members will be onsite to provide supplies and lend a helping hand. For example, local Aeries and Auxiliaries raised thousands of dollars for victims of Hurricanes Katrina and Sandy, and helped distribute food, water, and other supplies.

Eagles donate millions of dollars each year to hospitals and research centers, churches, schools and universities, and other organizations, such as the Leukemia, Multiple Sclerosis, Lymphoma, and Muscular Dystrophy Societies, as well as Make-a-Wish Foundation, and many others. Funds are raised through any number of activities including bake sales, car shows, bingo, bus trips, auctions, dinners, dances, and golf outings.

Photo by Karen Madsen (September 2008)
Iowa City, Iowa

"People Helping People" is a value that the Fraternal Order of Eagles has held for more than a century. It is a statement that guides the charitable actions to help members and their families, as well as fellow Americans, affected by illness, injury, or catastrophe. It is this philosophy that has inspired their leadership to work towards a Fraternal Order of Eagles medical research facility dedicated to eliminating diseases that afflict so many.

FOE Headquarters sponsors several events each year including the International Convention, golf tournaments, bowling and horseshoe competitions, NASCAR, newsletter and photo contests, children's art contest, an oratory competition for young people ages ten-to-fifteen called God, Flag and Country, just to name a few.

Almost every local Aerie has individual groups based on their members' interests - bowlers, RVers, motorcycle riders, card players, golfers, horseshoe players, softball enthusiasts, dart throwers, etc. If there is an activity that some individuals want to do as a group and that group does not exist, then the opportunity is there to start one.

Something that the Fraternal Order of Eagles is very proud of is their "History of the Four Pens." Through the years, the FOE has encouraged federal programs and legislation that benefit many Americans - especially the young and old. The "Four Pens" are the actual instruments three US presidents and a governor used to sign the documents that made these federal programs a reality. These pens are displayed at the Eagles' International Headquarters.

Joseph M. Dixon, Governor of Montana, signing into law America's first Old Age Pension Act in 1923 said, "You Eagles have planted this seed. . . . If the Eagles of the United States never do anything else, they have more than justified their existence in their advocacy of this great humanitarian movement."

"The pen I am presenting the Order is a symbol of my approval of the Fraternity's vision and courage. May its possession inspire your members to dedicate their efforts and those of the Fraternity . . . to bring a greater degree of happiness to our people," Franklin D. Roosevelt, US President, was quoted as saying while signing into law the Social Security Act in 1935.

President Lyndon B. Johnson, while signing the federal "Jobs After Forty" Bill, which outlawed upper age limits in hiring, said, "The Eagles started this whole idea. That is why I invited the Eagles to be at this private bill signing, and the reason I am presenting this pen to the Fraternal Order of Eagles."

And again, President Johnson, in a message to the Eagles on the signing of the Medicare Amendment to the Social Security Act, "For your energetic and dedicated espousal of social justice, and for the generous support you have given to all measures designed to further economic opportunity and the compassionate treatment of the sick and disabled."

On a personal note, I believe that these Four Pens are symbols of a progressive movement in which the government gains more control over individuals' lives. This is where I do step back and separate myself from the Fraternal Order of Eagles. All of the good that they have done, and continue to do, in their charitable work for communities, organizations, and individuals, would have been enough. Their naïve belief that the government can do better for individuals than they can do for themselves, or fraternal organizations like the FOE, or churches, or family, has helped create this downward spiral of people becoming dependent on the government. Had the Eagles not encouraged this kind of dependent behavior, individuals may not be so reliant on government assistance today. Then again, if the Eagles had not initiated such government dependency, perhaps other organizations or individuals may have.

I have often contemplated the initial beginnings of the Fraternal Order of Eagles in the early 1900's, and the individuals who were involved in the theater and the arts coming out of the Pacific Northwest. The spread of progressive thinking across the United States runs parallel to the spread of the Fraternal Order of Eagles. These were all good people trying to do good things for the benefit of many. It was, and still is, a good thing to a certain extent. People from all walks of life were involved with the Eagles, and many were not only involved in theater, but they were also involved in the legal system and local governments. These individuals were activists at every level. It is not very difficult to make the connection that the Eagles were a major influence in the spread of the progressive movement and social justice. This is just a reflective observance that I have happened to ponder on and off over the past several years. In no way should this demean the great civic and social work that the Eagles have done, but yet one has to wonder about the possible correlation.

Their Initial Lackadaisical Efforts Regarding the Ten Commandments Monoliths

On March 10, 1958, F. C. Schroeder of the Schroeder & Schroeder Law Offices in Detroit Lakes, Minnesota penned a letter to Robert W. Hansen at the Fraternal Order of Eagles Grand Aerie concerning the actions of the Minnesota Branch of the American Civil Liberties Union (ACLU) to disrupt any further dedications of Ten Commandments monoliths. The letter stated:

> We are going to have to stay on top of this until the matter is settled – once we make our position clear, that is that the program is non-denominational and non-sectarian, we should be able to get the ACLU to withdraw all objections. The Minnesota State Aerie is in no position to handle this situation, though, of course, some of the members will be working thereon. In my opinion, the Grand Aerie must handle the matter – it is a national program, but more than that, we are going to need some national prestige behind us. . . . I write to alert you to the situation as I see it, and to suggest that the Grand Aerie should step into the picture in more ways than having the Judge carry the burden. Judge will go ahead – but he should have help. And there is not time to waste. . . .

Judge E. J. Ruegemer, working on the same problem in his letter to Rev. Ray Boehlke of the Ministerial Association of Minnesota on February 25, 1958, wrote: "I am afraid if we do not take immediate steps to counteract the actions of the ACLU and the American Jewish Congress [who wrote the brief for the ACLU], we may run into some difficulty."

The Grand Aerie of the Fraternal Order of Eagles did not "grab the bull by the horns and put a stake in its heart" at this point as they should have. Hindsight is twenty-twenty, but it should not have taken much brain power to realize, even back in 1958, that the ACLU was not an organization to roll over and take "No" for an answer. When you add other anti-religious organizations to the mix, you have a recipe for a disaster. In the case of the Ten Commandments monoliths, you have the program being explained with lies and twisted fabrications on a national level.

Case in point, the Freedom from Religion Foundation (FFRF) continually uses the following argument:

> The Eagles campaign started when a devout judge and Eagle member, E. J. Ruegemer – who wanted to promote religion and Minnesota granite – teamed up with film director Cecil B. DeMille, interested in promoting his 1956 epic, *The Ten Commandments.* In 2002, FFRF successfully removed one of the first such monuments placed on government property, in the City of Milwaukee. Yul Brenner had turned up for the dedication.

This is what happens when you allow someone else, in this case, the FFRF, to rewrite your story. Yes, the Judge was a devout Catholic, but that is beside the point – he was a JUDGE, a man of the law, and he had no reason to want to promote religion. Minnesota granite did, and does, just fine without special promotions. As stated in the Publicity Stunt's section of Chapter 6, Cecil B. DeMille had no need to promote *The Ten Commandments* film through the Fraternal Order of Eagles and their existing Ten Commandments Project for the Youth Guidance Commission. Timing made a win-win situation, and there is no known law regarding one organization benefitting with the help of another based on timing. Yul Brenner was present at the rededication in 1957 during Law Enforcement Week in Milwaukee, Wisconsin, and the Ten Commandments monolith had not been placed at that time.

Why are these two lawsuits (Everett and Frederick), cited at every court case, allowed to be continued to be used when they have false information contained within them?

In actual law suits filed in district courts, it has been propagated that Cecil B. DeMille actually financed Ten Commandments monoliths across the country. In the ACLU of Ohio's case against the Ten Commandments monolith given to Lucas County (see cover story), it states:

> Some of the cases addressing similar monuments the Eagles provided also mention that, on learning about the Eagles' program (which originally involved distribution of printed copies of the Decalogue), Cecil B. DeMille, producer of the film *The Ten Commandments*, offered to underwrite distribution of hundreds of monuments to local governments on behalf of the Eagles. *See, e.g., Card v. City of Everett*, 386 F. Supp. 2d 1171, 1174 (W.D. Wash. 2005); *Chambers v. City of Frederick*, 292 F. Supp. 2d 766, 769 (D. Md. 2003). DeMille did so under the belief that distributing the monuments might promote his "Hollywood blockbuster movie. . . . " *Card*, 386 F. Supp. 2d at 1176. The parties have not, however, submitted evidence showing DeMille paid for the Lucas County monument.

To this day, it has not been proven that he did so because he did not, and yet this false belief continues to be part of the scenario every time a case is brought before a judge. Why are these two lawsuits (Everett and Frederick), cited at every court case, allowed to be continued to be used when they have false information contained within them? The lawyers keep citing these lies as facts and no one disputes them openly. Just because the information is documented in court cases does not mean that it is correct, and yet here they stand.

There is a plaque next to the Ten Commandments monolith in Canal Park, Duluth, Minnesota attempting to explain why the monolith was placed there. Although it was a phenomenal exhibit of what a community can do to maintain its history, the plaque is factually incorrect. It is these kinds of errors that have been repeated so many times over the past sixty years, that people assume that they are true. The plaque states (with corrections in parentheses):

Duluth's Ten Commandments Monument

> In 1946, Judge E. J. Ruegemer of Saint Cloud, Minnesota, who was also a leader in the Fraternal Order of the (no "the") Eagles, sentenced a sixteen-year-old boy to memorize the Ten Commandments (the Judge did not "sentence" the boy at all, and referred him back to his mother). This led to local chapters of the Eagles financing the construction of over 4,000 tablet-shaped granite monuments (there are only 184 known monoliths as of 2013) to be dispersed (most were initiated locally) around the nation. Two Minnesota granite companies produced the massive monuments (there were several that were produced elsewhere). In 1957 (1954), the monuments were donated to public places (only after the public places told the Eagles where to place them) across the United States. This was coordinated with the release of the film *The Ten Commandments* (it began prior to the release of the movie and continued, as of this writing, through 2010) and movie stars (three) were used in some dedication ceremonies.
>
> This monument was given to Duluth and displayed in front of City Hall for almost forty-eight years. It was then removed from public property and put up for auction as a result of a threatened lawsuit by the American Civil Liberties Union (ACLU) of Minnesota. Concerned local citizens rallied but the winning bid came from Celebration Church in Lakeville, Minnesota. They returned the monument to a group of Duluthians who had it placed on private property in 2004.

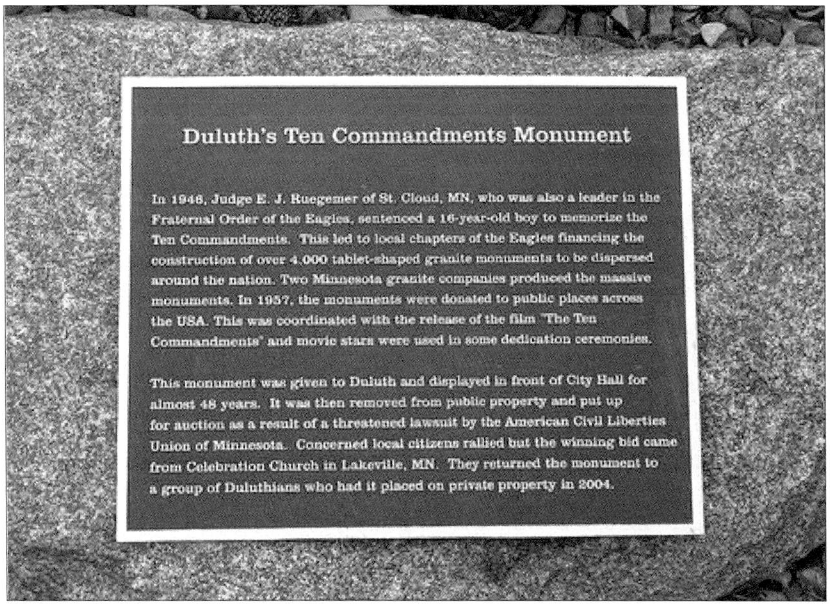

Explanation plaque placed next to Duluth, Minnesota's Ten Commandments monolith

This plaque is newly seen by hundreds of people every year – some of them from international communities. Even with the best of intentions, it continues to mislead people with inaccurate information.

How many errors can ONE paragraph have in the *New York Times*? In an article by Frank Rich in March 2005, the corrections are made in parentheses:

The God Racket, From DeMille to DeLay

Frank Rich/*New York Times*/March 27, 2005

> As DeMille readied his costly Paramount production for release a half-century ago, he seized on an ingenious publicity scheme (this may have been a win-win situation, but it was not publicity scheme for the sake of a publicity scheme). In partnership with the Fraternal Order of Eagles (there was no partnership – it was a suggestion to one man, again with a few win-win circumstances), a nationwide association of civic-minded clubs (Aeries) founded by theater owners, he sponsored (he did NOT sponsor or finance anything) the construction of several thousand Ten Commandments monuments (184 known monoliths as of 2013, most of which were dedicated long after the movie was released) throughout the country to hype his product (it is hard to hype a product with a few dozen monoliths). The Pharaoh himself – that would be Yul Brynner – participated in the gala unveiling of the Milwaukee slab (Brynner was NOT at the unveiling in 1955). Heston did the same in North Dakota. Bizarrely enough, all these years later, it is another of these DeMille-inspired granite monuments (hard to claim DeMille-inspired since DeMille passed away in 1959 and the monolith was not placed until 1961, which was FIVE years after the movie was released), on the grounds of the Texas Capitol in Austin, that is a focus of the Ten Commandments case that the United States Supreme Court heard this month.

I personally attempted to contact Frank Rich and point out the errors in his article to no avail. This was in the *New York Times* – how many individuals in 2005 were hanging on to every word written as if it was truth, especially in the heyday of the US Supreme Court decision in Austin, Texas?

The History Channel presented a two-part documentary regarding the history and application of the Ten Commandments. Toward the end of Part Two, Cecil B. DeMille was mentioned. According to Gary DeMar, "The History Channel gave the impression that the placement of the Ten Commandment monuments by DeMille was purely a publicity stunt to promote his movie." The DVD set of this documentary will have this lie living into eternity. Television, newspapers, magazines, radio – the lies live on and who is stepping up to denounce them?

The FOE Headquarters is definitely the place where the buck stops, but I lay a lot of blame on the individual Aeries when it comes to protecting their very own monoliths. Each Aerie that has dedicated a Ten Commandments monolith located on public property should have the distinct responsibility to know the history of that monolith, and take charge of keeping the record straight regarding the Ten Commandments Project. At the very least, they should have, in written form, communication with Headquarters as to the whereabouts and historical facts of their monolith. Even back in the mid-1950s and through the 1960s, annual pleas were made at the International Conventions for Aeries to let Headquarters know about the monoliths that they had placed. This was not only to publicize the successes of the Ten Commandments Project, but also to document the dedications for FOE records.

Each Aerie that has dedicated a Ten Commandments monolith located on public property should have the distinct responsibility to know the history of that monolith, and take charge of keeping the record straight regarding the Ten Commandments Project.

No matter how many hundreds of letters I wrote, or hundreds of emails that I sent, or phone calls that I made, Aerie after Aerie had no recollection of having a Ten Commandments monolith, or even if they had one at one time, where it was currently located. Some Aeries, after acknowledging that they had a monolith, lacked the courtesy to supply information regarding it. Even in an accidental sighting of a monolith as I drove down a main street in Ohio, where there was a monolith placed into the wall of the Aerie, the Aerie leaders and members did not know that the monolith was out front or how it got there. The people had to go outside and see for themselves what I was talking about. At another Aerie that I visited, I was surprised to learn that even though they had a monolith, they had only recently learned that it was a national program based on the Youth Guidance Commission – they thought that the Ten Commandments Project was only in their state.

When will the Fraternal Order of Eagles set the record straight once and for all? They need to step up and speak for themselves each and every time a case goes to court. Their briefs have to be accurate and very distinct in each of the above issues, each and every time. They cannot rely on the arguments that they relied on in the past. They need to forget all of the legalese and just be very forthright that these lies have been told and told so often that even the Eagles have let them slide as "truth." One Eagles' brief mentioned the 4,000 monoliths that were placed across the country, even after the attorney was told at the time, that there were approximately 175 known Ten Commandments monoliths. They need to use a number that is known, or at least believed to be accurate, at the time of the lawsuit, and have lawyers who know the history of the Youth Guidance Commission and the Ten Commandments Project. If not, this history will continue to be rewritten and retold with lies and half-truths.

When history is no longer based on truth, the Ten Commandments monoliths will be sacrificed, one at a time, to the changes being made in our American culture as it spirals downwards into the vat of political correctness and moral decline.

Francis Manion, an attorney with the American Center for Law and Justice (ACLJ) in Washington, DC stated, "These monuments have been around for decades. Now all of a sudden, they're unconstitutional. Or so we're asked to believe. But that's the nature of America's current legal culture – virulently anti-Christian." At least the ACLJ has been relentlessly fighting these cases.

When history is no longer based on truth, the Ten Commandments monoliths will be sacrificed, one at a time, to the changes being made in our American culture as it spirals downwards into the vat of political correctness and moral decline. At what point will there be no semblance of how great and strong we once were as a nation? As long as there are individuals and organizations intent on wiping out "every public trace of America's Christian heritage," there will be lies and lawsuits. Only the Fraternal Order of Eagles can officially set the record straight. To do so, they must take ownership and total control of the truth with fortitude and conviction. They are such a grand organization in so many ways, it would be a shame that this very important project that they took on so many years ago disappeared from our American heritage.

CHAPTER 4

THE PROGRAM - YOUTH GUIDANCE COMMISSION'S TEN COMMANDMENTS PROJECT

Flag Day, June 14, 2014, marked thirteen years since I began this God-given journey to record the history of the Fraternal Order of Eagles' Ten Commandments Project. I have been truly blessed to have had the honor to talk with Judge E. J. Ruegemer face-to-face, and to be there for his 100th birthday celebration. His daughters, Nita Hofmann (who has since passed away) and Anne Berg, have been generous with their time and in sharing their family-owned photos and documents. Grand Secretary Chuck Cunningham has opened up the historic Fraternal Order of Eagles' vaults of letters, receipts, telegrams, photos, magazine articles, and all things pertaining to this project. I am truly grateful for the generosity that he has shown to me throughout these past thirteen years. People from all over the country have provided newspaper articles, personal stories, photos, and well wishes to complete this research. I have been surrounded by people who love and care about me, and have prayerfully guided me through the travels, trials, and successes of the fact-gathering and creative process.

It has always been my heartfelt desire to use all of the resources available to me to get this narrative told honestly once and for all. The Ten Commandments Project history has been hijacked from the Fraternal Order of Eagles, twisted, misaligned, gutted, and retold so many times incorrectly that no one knows for sure exactly where truth and fiction cross lines. Even those individuals who have done serious research to gather the truth have not had their eyes totally opened to have been able to see ulterior motives of those who wish to do the Ten Commandments Project harm. It has also been my observation that younger researchers cannot discern the rationalization of those individuals who are facing their twilight years. Until you have walked in their shoes, either through growing old or being in declining health, the ability to see things that others cannot is clouded by youth or lack of experience of life in general.

Maybe it is because I have exposed myself to the depths of those who have spewed horrific injustices, as well as to those who have praised and placed this project on a heavenly altar, that I can step back and share the facts as they are available through written words and interviews. So much time has passed, and there are missing documents that would presumably fill in a few blanks. There are some things that even I am curious about regarding the responses to some of the letters that were written by the Judge and by others, but those letters are long gone or have not yet surfaced.

> *May this current retelling of the history, which is done to the best of my ability, be the one that lies to rest all rumors, lies, doubts, and uncertainties.*

May this current retelling of the history, which is done to the best of my ability, be the one that puts to rest all rumors, lies, doubts, and uncertainties. May this be the story of the Ten Commandments Project that continues from this point on unless some truth is unearthed after this moment in time.

The Judge's Court Room

During a Fraternal Order of Eagles convention in 1943 in Cincinnati, Ohio, a group of individuals developed a program to "help solve the problems of our youth – those under-privileged and unfortunate boys and girls, now in their teens, who are publicized in the press and sometimes ostracized from society as so-called juvenile delinquents." It was out of this Grand Aerie International Convention that the first Youth Guidance Commission was instituted. According to a report by Judge E. J. Ruegemer, "An earnest study was made as to the approach to the problem of juvenile delinquency and behavior, and the preparation of a program to be offered to all Eagles by which they could participate in the prevention of delinquency and preserving the youth of America from yielding to the temptations of modern-day living." It was out of this Commission that the first Youth Guidance Committee Handbook was published in 1946.

It was during this same year, while Judge E. J. Ruegemer was serving as a juvenile and probate court judge in Minnesota that a sixteen-year-old young man came before him charged with seriously injuring a man whom he struck while driving a stolen car. It was recommended that the boy be sentenced to the State Training School, but the Judge ordered a background check and discovered that the boy came from a broken home. This boy also had hearing difficulties, poor vision, and was sitting in the back of his classroom in school. The Judge decided to give him a suspended sentence with the warning that he should stay in close contact with the officer who brought the boy in, and to learn and keep the Ten Commandments.

The young man stated that he did not know anything about the Ten Commandments and asked where he could find them. The Judge took the boy into his back chambers and pointed to the large library of law books. The Judge told him that the Ten Commandments were contained in all of these books. Shocked and slightly confused, the boy asked the Judge how he was expected to find the Ten Commandments in those hundreds of books. The Judge explained that the books contained thousands of laws, but he needed to seek out only ten of them because all of the laws in the country dealing with human relations were based upon those ten. Those ten laws alone would be sufficient to guide him and to keep him out of trouble. The Judge then made arrangements with a pastor of the boy's mother's faith to teach the boy the Ten Commandments.

A few years after that court room incident, while chairman of the Minnesota Youth Guidance Committee, Judge E. J. Ruegemer initiated the Ten Commandments Project. He firmly believed that the Ten Commandments were the oldest code of conduct handed down to man, and he "always understood that the Ten Commandments were a guide to basic moral conduct."

Prints and Scrolls

The Fraternal Order of Eagles' Ten Commandments Project had very humble beginnings. From the individuals who brainstormed for months on end regarding how this project should develop, to the individuals who did the actual footwork and got the project off the ground – this project began with the best and proudest of intentions.

Starting in 1948, several conversations among prominent major religious groups, law enforcement entities, family professionals, and marketing specialists took place. After three years of discussions, the Eagles employed the artists of Brown and Bigelow to prepare a decorative twenty-by-twenty-six inch version of the Ten Commandments which would be suitable for framing. It contained not only what they thought to be a universally acceptable translation of the Ten Commandments, but it also displayed an American flag, an eagle, two tablets of the Ten Commandments, the All-seeing Eye of God super-imposed on a triangle, the Star of David, and the Greek letters of Chi Rho (representing the first two letters of Christ). There were hundreds made in the twenty-by-twenty-six inch size, but in 1954, the size was reduced to thirteen-by-eighteen inches to make it more cost efficient for Eagle members to purchase and for mailing.

Photo courtesy of *The Eagle Magazine* (March 1954)
The Ten Commandments haven't always been unwelcome in public places. President Harry S. Truman was happy to accept a framed copy at the White House on August 18, 1952 from Eagle Albert Schmitt of Saint Cloud, Minnesota Aerie 622.

Photo courtesy of *The Eagle Magazine* (February 1954)
Grand Aerie Youth Guidance Commission maps plans for nationwide program at the first meeting in Fargo, North Dakota

The State of Minnesota initiated the Ten Commandments Project in 1951 by distributing more than 7,000 smaller replicas of the framed Ten Commandments.

The Ten Commandments Project went national in December 1953. By March 1954, 10,000 prints were made available for national distribution. According to Eagles' Manny Meyers in July 1954:

> There is no single pattern for the distribution of the Ten Commandments. Both public

and private schools display the scrolls. There are clubs, civic headquarters, YMCA buildings, and fraternal homes other than Aerie homes, which exhibit the Eagle-sponsored Decalogues. They grace walls of offices and factories, too.

Often a Ten Commandments presentation by an Aerie is marked with a formal ceremony with public officials present. Skip around the country and you can see how extensively this Eagle idea has been adopted. At Cle Elum, Washington, the Aerie presented a scroll in the city hall during a regular council meeting. In Atlantic City, New Jersey, City Detective Mortimer Hayes received a copy in recognition of his long years of service to youth. At Bicknell, Indiana, Boy Scouts and Cub Scouts received scrolls. At Dubois, Pennsylvania, Mayor Pat Dillman hung a scroll on a council chamber wall after a formal ceremony. At Brookings, Oregon, the Young Peoples' Association of the Community Church gratefully accepted a scroll. In Marlboro, Massachusetts, Judge George E. Dewey was honored with a scroll in recognition of his role in curbing juvenile delinquency.

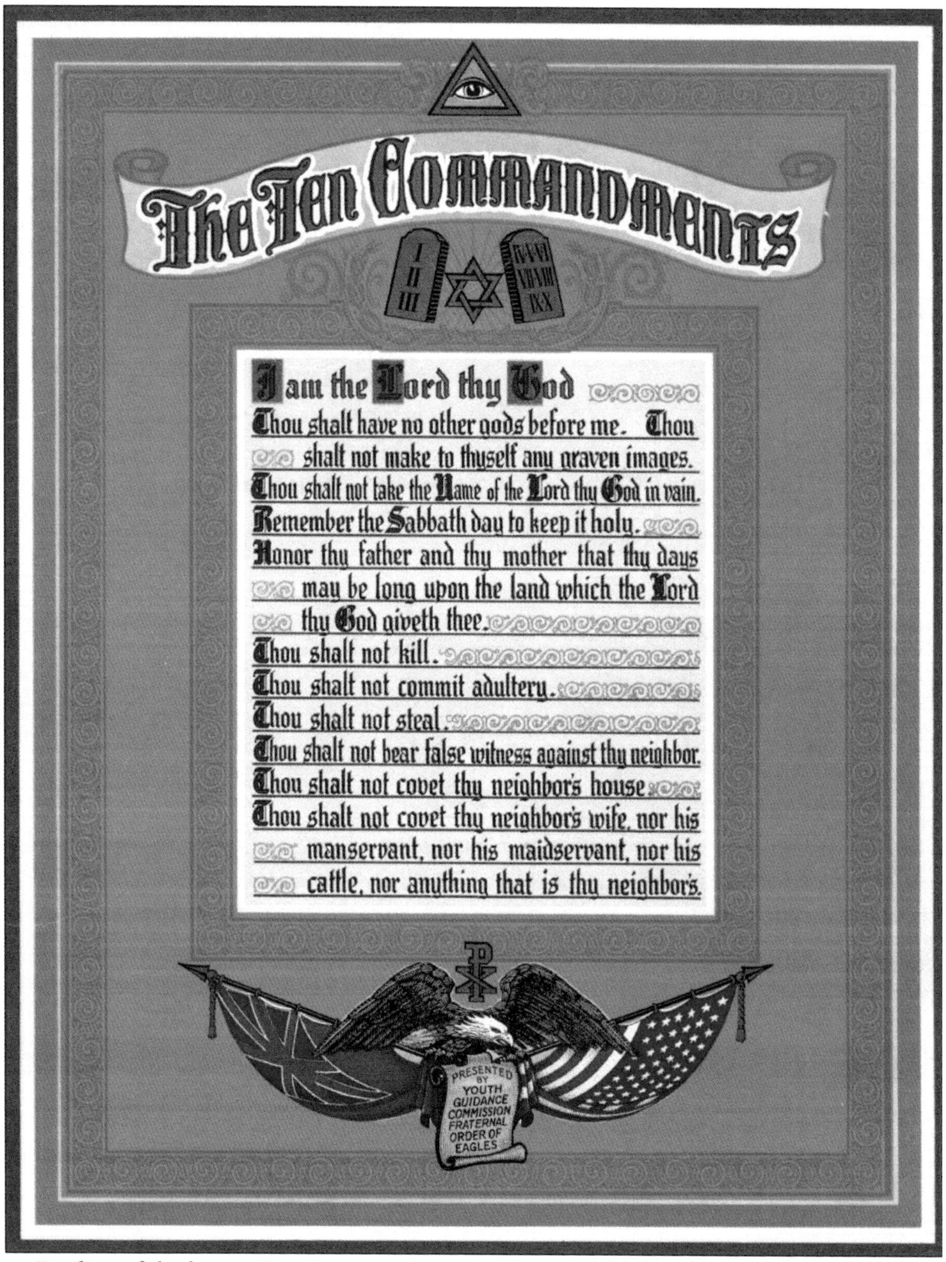

Replica of the larger Ten Commandments print on eight-by-eleven inch cardstock

The Ten Commandments

Presented to Moses on Mount Sinai by the hand of God on two stone tablets, the Ten Commandments stand today after more than 3500 years as God's law to the human race. The first three are our obligations to God—the last seven our obligations to our fellow men. They are a pattern for our human relations. All the laws of the Country dealing with human relations are based upon the Ten Commandments.

Since the establishment of the Youth Guidance Commission by the Grand Aerie of the Fraternal Order of Eagles, numerous successful projects have been undertaken throughout the country. There has always been the challenge that a single project, designed to be acceptable to all Eagle Aeries in the jurisdiction and one which would promote a practical program of youth Guidance be conceived and sponsored on the national level. After several years of careful study the Minnesota Youth Guidance Committee concluded that there can be no substitute, no more defined, nor better program of youth guidance than the original program presented by God, The Ten Commandments, since echoing down the ages we hear the words: "My son, forget not the law, but let thine heart keep my Commandments, for length of days and long life and peace shall they add to thee."

After consultation over a period of years with the clergy of many denominations, noted artists were employed to produce this illuminated print, incorporating a universally acceptable translation of the Ten Commandments from the Old Testament, ornated in multi-color and including many significant symbols. Included in the art scheme is the American Emblem, the emblem of the Fraternal Order of Eagles; the two tablets of the Ten Commandments; the All Seeing Eye of God, superimposed on the triangle; the Stars of David; the Greek Letters Chi Rho, being the first two letters of Christ. This latter symbol also having the appearance of the intersecting letters PX has been interpreted as an abbreviation of Pax, meaning peace.

This program was first initiated on the state level by the Minnesota State Aerie for the purpose of testing its universal acceptance, and after the presentation of more than 7000 copies, principally by aeries within the state, but also with some active participation by aeries outside of Minnesota, the project was in December 1953 adopted as a national youth guidance project.

Presentations of the Ten Commandments are being made by local aeries or individual members thereof to Juvenile, District, Municipal and other courts, to churches, schools, civil and fraternal organizations and other agencies and individuals serving youth. It is the further aim of this great fraternity that ultimately every Eagle home may be identified by the display therein of the Ten Commandments.

The Constitution of the United States and the Declaration of Independence show concrete evidence that the authors, the founders of this great nation, were inspired by a belief in God and his Commandments.

It is a pleasure therefore to present to you this beautiful illuminated version of the Ten Commandments. May it inspire in all who see it renewed respect for the Law of God, which is our greatest strength against the forces that threaten our way of life. It furnishes a means of reaffirming our faith in the fundamental precepts of democracy and freedom.

If we work upon marble, it will perish;
If we work upon brass, time will efface it,
If we rear temples they will crumble into dust,
But if we work upon immortal souls,
If we imbue them with principles,
With the just fear of the Creator and love of fellow men,
We engrave on those tables something
Which will brighten all eternity.

YOUTH GUIDANCE COMMISSION
FRATERNAL ORDER OF EAGLES

E. J. RUEGEMER,
Chairman, Judge District Court, St. Cloud, Minnesota.

The Ministerial Association of St. Cloud heartily endorses the project of the Fraternal Order of Eagles in their publicizing of the Ten Commandments. We feel that the nationwide response to this project is indicative of its validity, and we are of the definite opinion that the distribution of copies of the Ten Commandments, as well as erection of granite monoliths, even on public property, does not in any way nullify the principle of "separation of church and state." Since our country was founded upon religious principles and the law of God, we consider this method of publicizing the Ten Commandments to be worthy of the support of all good citizens.

Rev. Ray Boehlke and Rev. Harry S. Dodgson, *Past Presidents*
Special Committee on "Ten Commandments"
Ministerial Association, St. Cloud, Minnesota

One can only write words of commendation to the Fraternal Order of Eagles for their worthy project of keeping before the minds of the American people, the Ten Commandments of God. The Divine Law as expressed in the commandments is the basis of all law. Respect and obedience to this Divine Law gives birth to respect for human law, which in turn develops good citizenship in our nation. As a Catholic bishop, I give my blessing to this project and trust that much spiritual and moral good shall come to our people in this nation for this worthy effort.

✠ P. W. BARTHOLOME, D. D.
Bishop of St. Cloud

There is great wisdom in the conclusion of the Minnesota Youth Guidance Commission, i. e., that there can be no substitute and certainly no more defined nor better program of youth guidance than the original program presented by God, the Ten Commandments. In my opinion this is indeed a wonderful project and I shall deem it an honor to add my indorsement. My every good wish is extended to you in this noble undertaking.

FULTON OURSLER,
Author of the Greatest Story Ever Told,
Author of The Greatest Book Ever Written

The Fraternal Order of Eagles is rendering a significant service to our country in its project of encouraging obedience to the will and law of God as declared in the Ten Commandments. We adults can place before our youth no finer example than by indicating our belief that our lives should be guided by the Divine Law.

LUTHER W. YOUNGDAHL,
Judge of the United States District Court, Washington, D. C.

I think you could not have had a greater idea for Youth Guidance than to re-state and re-affirm God's ageless patern for human conduct. Every constitution conceived by man has found the need for amendment, but the Ten Commandments have stood unaltered, not only as a guide for youth, but as a path to be followed by all men of good will—a path which could lead us to Peace on Earth.

CECIL B. De MILLE,
Paramount Pictures Corporation

I would like to see the Ten Commandment scroll posted in every school and library in the country. Its message is sadly needed in the instruction of our children and young people so many of whom have but slight acquaintance, if any, with them, (the commandments). All thoughtful people will thank you and the Order for this contribution to the Youth of America.

ANGELO PATRI,
Educator and Author

The program of the Fraternal Order of Eagles to distribute illuminated prints of the Ten Commandments to our country's youth in order to foster observance of God's Laws is a most worthy one and merits sympathetic and zealous support.

JOHN EDGAR HOOVER,
Director Federal Bureau of Investigation

By placing the Ten Commandments so attractively within the easy reading view of all the children of America, the Fraternal Order of Eagles puts the imperishable first and helps to arm our beloved country against the Godlessness of communism.

GAREY CLEVELAND MYERS,
Editor of Highlights For Children,
Author of The Modern Parents and numerous other books,
Writer of Daily Syndicated Newspaper column

Presented to..

By..

Backside of the Ten Commandments print

According to Meyers, "Garry Cleveland Myers, author of a daily syndicated column of advice to parents on the rearing of children, and of several books on that subject, was inspired to devote one of his newspaper articles to the Eagles' program. 'If all we parents and our children were to keep these Commandments in our hearts and really live them, we soon would need no police or prisons, and our nation would become so strong that we would lose our fears of the Communistic portion of the world.'" Dr. Myers and his wife, Caroline Clark Myers, were the founders of *Highlights for Children* in 1946. *Highlights* is still in publication today.

On a special ministerial mission, Msgr. T. Leo Keaveny, Diocesan Director of Catholic Education, presented a Fraternal Order of Eagles' Ten Commandments print to Pope Pius XII. He also distributed scrolls to various orphanages in Italy, France, and Ireland.

In Zanesville, Ohio, 1,300 Ten Commandments scrolls were presented to all of the town's children. The Aerie planned to distribute scrolls to all students in the county.

In 1954, the Youth Guidance Commission saw the distribution of over 18,000 prints of the Ten Commandments which were placed in Eagle homes, many state capitols, and in county and local government offices. Some had even been presented to members of the US Senate and House of Representatives.

Photo courtesy of the Stearns History Museum, Saint Cloud, Minnesota

Barrister Harry Goodman, center, gave a Canadian flag to Saint Cloud, Minnesota and received a Ten Commandments scroll for his Aerie

How the Scrolls Are Prepared

THE TASK OF PREPARING for shipment the framed copies of the Ten Commandments distributed under Eagle auspices is under the supervision of another widely known St. Cloud Eagle, the agile Al Schmitt, past president of Minnesota State Aerie, past regional vice-president of the Grand Aerie, secretary of the National Youth Guidance Committee, and one of the program's most ardent boosters.

The scrolls are printed on the largest press in the world at Brown-Bigelow in St. Paul. Eagles and members of their families at the printing plant work on every step of the process.

The attractive and impressive framed copies of the Ten Commandments may be obtained by writing to Albert Schmitt, Box 557, St. Cloud, Minnesota. The uniform copies are available at cost, $1.50, plus packaging costs and postage, which amounts to $2.25 per copy.

It is hoped that every Aerie will display a framed copy in a prominent place in its Aerie home. The cost to individuals who desire a copy to grace their own homes is the same as for an Aerie.

Except for the printer, who must make a reasonable margin of profit to remain in business, there is no profit-making involved in this Eagle effort to spread the most workable philosophy of living ever given to mankind.

PRESSMAN RICHARD GEISBAUER, left, and salesman Harry Cater of St. Cloud, Brown and Bigelow employees, examine with pride the Ten Commandments' Scroll that they helped produce.

SANDING AND FILLING frames for the world's most honored of all codes of law, the Ten Commandments, are Eagle member Edw. Love and Brown and Bigelow employe, Victoria Schroeder.

EAGLE VOLUNTEER, after inserting glazier's points, inspects Commandments Scroll, noting perfection of workmanship.

EAGLE DAUGHTERS, Connie Kappahan and Ann Ruegemer, are proud of being selected to play a part in the project.

SECRETARY AL SCHMITT of the National Youth Guidance Commission lends a hand in packaging the finished product.

Photo courtesy of *The Eagle Magazine* (July 1954)

NEW EAGLE AL SCHRIVER starts to process rough lumber as a first step in making frames for Commandment Scroll.

EAGLE BROTHERS, Walter Anderson and Al Schriver, operate shaper to form the frame from carefully selected woods.

EAGLE MEMBERS, Miles G. Steidl and Harold Danzel, assemble and sand frames in project that they are proud to work on.

THAT THE GOOD WORDS may gleam more brightly, Kathy Weisbrick and assistant wash the glass that covers the scroll.

WIFE OF CHAIRMAN, of the Ten Commandment project, Agnes Ruegemer, examines the glass to see that it is good.

AFTER READING the glorious words, Victoria Schroeder inserts glass, the printed scroll, and the backing into the frame.

AT THE ST. CLOUD POST OFFICE, Al Schmitt, Secretary of the Youth Guidance Commission; Eagle Tom Sloan, train-master; and Dombrovski, railroad employee, unload precious packages.

FINAL INSPECTION is made by Veteran Eagle Koshiol, post office official Ruegemer, postmaster Mrs. Glaesgens, and postal official Barrett, past president of Aerie 622. Scrolls are on way.

Photo courtesy of *The Eagle Magazine* (July 1954)

There were approximately 4,000 framed prints that lined the basement walls of the Ruegemer home. Eagle friends, family members, and neighbors chipped in to help with the process of making the frames, washing the glass, assembling the photos, and boxing them up for shipment. Most of the prints were personalized with dedication information prior to the final assembly.

In Carnegie, Pennsylvania, according to *The Eagle Magazine* (date unknown):

Aerie 1134 presented a copy of the Ten Commandments to the Carnegie Council. A. J. Sgro, Aerie president, was surrounded by Carnegie Borough officials as he presented the scroll bearing the Ten Commandments to Burgess T. T. Coyne. Eagles present at the impressive ceremony at the Council Chambers included Past President Paul Grandinetti, Secretary Morris L. Speizer, and Charles Skirpan. The presentation inspired a commendatory editorial in Carnegie's newspaper, *The Signal-Item*, warmly endorsing the Eagles for their public spirit. The editorial lauding the presence of the Ten Commandments in the Council Chamber said, "Just as the Pledge of Allegiance reminds one of democracy's values, so the copy of the Ten Commandments brings to the attention of all the timeless concepts and intrinsic values of our priceless Judeo-Christian heritage."

Photo courtesy of Richard Hernandez, Yuma, Arizona
Arizona Governor Howard Pyle receiving Ten Commandments Print from Aerie 398 President Earl Steven

Photo courtesy of *The Eagle Magazine* (August/September 1954)
Carlisle, Pennsylvania Eagles Aerie 1299 presented a Ten Commandments scroll in a black walnut frame to Judge Dale F. Shughart of the Juvenile Court of Cumberland County, on left. Presenting it is Paul Coleman, Aerie secretary/treasurer and chairman of the Aerie's committee on combating juvenile delinquency. Also at the ceremony are President N. D. Krawciw, Chaplain Frank Darr, and Probation Officer Irvin Groniger.

The Ten Commandments Project was "swinging into high gear." According to Al Schmitt, who was secretary to the Youth Guidance Commission, "The response has been tremendous." The committee was kept busy filling orders. According to *The Eagle Magazine* (May 1954), "Eagles get the benefit of a large quantity contract, and can buy the scrolls framed and ready for hanging at actual cost price of $1.50 a piece. Judge E. J. Ruegemer envisions a handsome Eagle scroll of the Decalogue in every court, school, and public building in the nation."

Also in the *The Eagle Magazine*, it was reported that on behalf of Bethlehem, Pennsylvania Aerie 284, State President Al Williams presented a framed copy of the Ten Commandments to Judge William Barhold. The scroll was placed in the juvenile court room at the North Hampton County Courthouse.

Probate Judge Peter R. Dufresne of Wallace, Idaho, was presented a framed copy of the Ten Commandments according to *The Eagle Magazine* (July 1954) by the Wallace Aerie. When juvenile offenders appeared before Dufresne, they not only got to hear kind words of advice, but they were also read the words of the Ten Commandments.

Photo courtesy of *The Eagle Magazine* (April 1955)

In Coeur d'Alene, Idaho, people handing scrolls to school principals are from left: E. B. Christian, Bill Ahern, J. L. McDaniels, Bill Turner, Ed Cry, P. C. Olson, Fred Suter, Don Lovett, and Larry Cleveland. Receiving the scrolls are A. C. Lunden, Dwain Harrison, Dallas Ator, Glen and Betty Satchwell. The Past Presidents of Coeur d'Alene, Idaho Aerie 486 are fulfilling a pledge to place a framed scroll of the Ten Commandments in every school in Kootenai County.

The Past Presidents made the framed scrolls themselves to distribute to the twenty-five schools in Kootenai County, Idaho. Along with the above presentation of Ten Commandments scrolls to the principals:

> Coeur d'Alene children and the students from Kootenai County schools participated in a big Flight for Freedom balloon launching sponsored by Aerie 486. The students released twenty-one balloons, each balloon representing a separate school in the area. The Coeur d'Alene high school band and the girls' drill team from the Immaculate Heart of Mary Academy took part in the program which was attended by Chief of Police Arnold Engen, Fire Chief Wallace Swofford, State Policeman Lt. J McGinnis, and Peter Wilson, commander of the American Legion Post. Main speakers at the program included Mayor L. L. Gardner and Aerie President Frank Secaur. Clifford Parks was chairman of the balloon-launching program. P. C. Olson and E. B. Christian had charge of circulating the Freedom Scrolls.

The Eagle Magazine (November 1954) reports:

> Santa Cruz Aerie 460 members have been revisiting their old schools to present them with Ten Commandments scrolls. Plaques have also been distributed to the local churches, libraries, and public institutions. A total of twenty-five scrolls have been given out by Aerie members. Club members worked long hours making frames for the scrolls from wood taken from an old Philippine mahogany and oak bar. Members helping to pass the plaques around the city include Charter Member Charles J. Gillen, Treasurer Ed Blaisdell, Secretary John DeMello, President Paul Niswender, Past President Ernie Graft, Vern Fulton, Louis Lippi, Walter Bettencourt, Vic Marini, Augie Meschi, Enrico Brunetti, and Ben Partlow.

Photo courtesy of *The Eagle Magazine* (October 1954)

Santa Cruz librarian, Geraldine Work, receives a scroll of the Ten Commandments for the library from Police Chief Eagle Al Huntsman. Aerie members Charlie Gillen, Ed Blaisdell, and Ben Partlow watch.

Photo courtesy of the Stearns History Museum
Saint Cloud, Minnesota

Staples, Minnesota Aerie 1553 present a copy of the Ten Commandments to Judge E. J. Ruegemer by Frank King. Hugo Klang watches as George Johnstone presents a copy to Judge Ruth Tronsrue

Photo courtesy *The Eagle Magazine* (June 1954)

Judge Frank Carden of Glendale, Arizona (seated) was presented a framed Ten Commandments scroll by Osborn Aerie Eagles. Left to right: Robert Miller, Vernon Croaff, and Tom Croaff

In 1955, the Fraternal Order of Eagles united with the National Conference of Service, Fraternal, and Veterans Organizations on juvenile delinquency created in Washington, DC under a resolution of the Subcommittee of the Judiciary Committee of the United States Senate studying the problem of juvenile delinquency. The efforts of the Eagles in regard to youth guidance attracted nationwide attention because of their sound approach of taking into account all factors that enter human behavior when it comes to young people. In comparison to the other organizations that were affiliated with this Subcommittee, the Eagles offered the only complete program to the National Conference. It was at this time that the Youth Guidance Commission, after a thorough restudy of certain legislative changes that were made, presented a newly-created 1955 edition of the Youth Guidance Handbook to the attendees of the 1955 Fraternal Order of Eagles International Convention held in Milwaukee, Wisconsin.

According to *The Eagle Magazine* (July 1956), there was a noticeable decrease in juvenile crimes as stated by E. A. Prochaska, Commissioner of Public Safety for Cedar Rapids, Iowa. The credit for the decline was attributed to Aerie 2272 and Sid Water, who was chairman of the state youth guidance program and youth activities director for the Aerie. "We've got a fine group of kids in this city, and it's up to the adults to give the kids a chance to have clean fun in decent surroundings."

Photo courtesy of *The Eagle Magazine* (July 1956)
Framed scrolls of Ten Commandments were presented by Cedar Rapids Aerie to all high schools in town. Past President Orville Dorland makes the award.

How did they do it? According to *The Eagle Magazine*:

> On the fourth Friday of each month, a teenage dance for youngsters thirteen-to-nineteen is held at the Eagles club.
>
> Admission and checkroom facilities are free. During intermission, milk and sandwiches are sold at a nominal charge. The local Musicians' Union, No. 137, provides live music. The only requirement is that the boy or girl is teen-age and comes in and acts like a lady or gentleman. Eagles and their wives serve as chaperons. Fred Peterson, an Eagle member of the city's auxiliary police, attends dances in uniform as a representative of the law. He donates his time.
>
> Upon entering the club, each teenager is given a ticket, and during intermission, door prizes are drawn. Prizes have ranged from pizza pies to fine Cashmere sweaters and a portable radio. Through these admission tickets, an accurate attendance count can be made. One recent dance was attended by 278 teenagers.

Those were the days, my friend – reminiscent of *Happy Days*, Richie Cunningham, and the Fonz – in the Midwest.

Photo courtesy of *The Eagle Magazine* (March 1959)

George Wilson, Aerie president of Fargo, North Dakota, presented framed copies of the Ten Commandments on behalf of the Youth Guidance Committee to Fargo public schools. Receiving them on behalf of their respective schools were principals: Lowell J. Mitchell, Earl Torgerson, Melvin Stutrud, Clyde Wilman, Jeanette Stone, Robert Brown, Armond Larson, Glen Melvey, Vincent Dodge, and Vivian Mero. Unable to attend was Nellie Minnis. Superintendent Hamilton Vasey was also presented with a copy. Others present were Al Velline, Youth Guidance chairman, and John Hanson, chairman of the Bi-state Aerie.

In the midst of the Cold War in September 1959, Soviet Premier Nikita Khrushchev and President Dwight D. Eisenhower were planning a summit in Washington, DC to discuss issues of trade, cultural exchanges, and especially the policies regarding Berlin. Just prior to this historic meeting, the Fraternal Order of Eagles held their International Convention in Toronto, Canada. One of the main events was the presentation by Circuit Judge of Milwaukee, Judge Robert C. Cannon, of the Ten Commandments Award. It was being presented to Cardinal Francis Spellman of New York because of his "annual visits to American soldiers on the battlefields all over the world, his defense in the fight against Communism, and his leadership in strengthening the moral and spiritual fabric of American life." In his acceptance speech, His Eminence is quoted as saying:

> I have been asked, not only here in Toronto, but also in New York before I left, to comment on the visit of Mr. Khrushchev to President Eisenhower, and I have not made any comment.
>
> But I think tonight, after listening to the significance of the Award, the Ten Commandments, the spirit of the judge with the boy who said he never heard of them – I think it would be a wonderful thing if Mr. Khrushchev would have an opportunity of reading, studying, meditating, and with unusual, extraordinary Grace of God, believing and practicing the Ten Commandments. I think it would be wonderful.
>
> What a tremendous transformation would take place in this war-ravished, poverty-stricken, fear-enshrouded world. A miracle such as has not taken place since the time of Christ Himself would be worked, and the hearts of suffering human beings everywhere would be uplifted.

Photo courtesy of *The Eagle Magazine* (unknown issue)

Police Chief Cornelius W. Olsen, second from left, and County Judge Eugene McEssey, third from left, received Ten Commandments Awards during special ceremonies conducted in the Branch 3 Court Room at the Municipal Building in Fond du Lac, Wisconsin. The presentations were made by Past State President Lloyd M. Hawes on behalf of Fond du Lac Aerie, and were given in recognition of the dedicated guidance and outstanding contributions both men constantly made to youth programs in the community. With the recipients are County Supervisor William Bormann, Village President Frank Spangle, Past Wisconsin State President Lloyd M. Hawes, and his son, Lloyd F. Hawes.

What I find in the total insanity of all of those who "have their knickers in a knot," is that during the time that the thousands, upon thousands, upon thousands of Ten Commandments scrolls handed out to children with their individual names on them, to teachers, principals, police chiefs, mayors, governors, lawyers, judges, congressmen, senators, (in all local, state, and federal jurisdictions), presidents, and even the Pope – where were the naysayers? There were only three documented Protestant ministers between 1953 and 1958 who objected over the numbering of the Ten Commandments on the scrolls and prints. But where were the church/state sympathizers? Where were the First Amendment activists? But after there are 184 known Ten Commandment monoliths, and only a handful of complainants, America gets turned upside down?

What I find in the total insanity of all of those who "have their knickers in a knot," is that during the time that the thousands, upon thousands, upon thousands of Ten Commandments scrolls handed out to children with their individual names on them, to teachers, principals, police chiefs, mayors, governors, lawyers, judges, congressmen, senators, (in all local, state, and federal jurisdictions), presidents, and even the Pope – where were the naysayers?

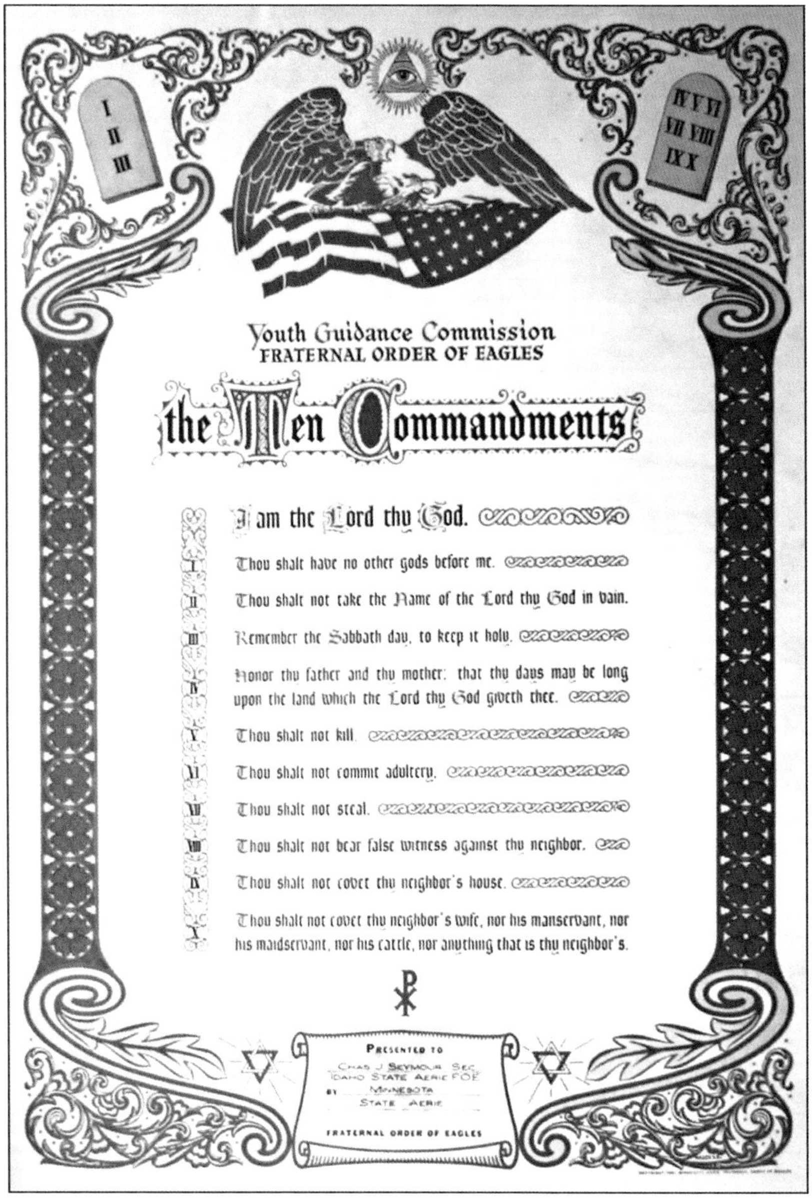

Photo courtesy of Heather Callahan, Coeur d'Alene, Idaho
Twenty-by-twenty-six inch Ten Commandments print

On Eagle Wings

One of my many prized possessions from the Ten Commandments Project was given to me by Chuck Cunningham who is currently the Fraternal Order of Eagles' Grand Aerie Secretary. While on my very first adventure seeking the stories behind the Ten Commandments monoliths, and after purging files for two hours at the Eagles' Headquarters when it was located in Milwaukee, Wisconsin, Cunningham handed me this and said, "I think that you will appreciate this." He continued to explain that *On Eagle Wings* was one of the National Youth Guidance Commission's programs back in the late 1950s. What I have come to realize is that this ninety-six-page illustrated, comic-like, book encapsulates the whole idea behind the Ten Commandments Project regarding our nation's youth.

Front and back cover of an original copy of *On Eagle Wings*

Studying the book today, its simplistic pictures and bright colors may not be very appealing to the digitally-crazed young people who need this kind of guidance. Its language is slightly archaic, one of the main characters smokes a pipe, and there is even an episode of corporal punishment that would not be universally accepted by some individuals. But this endearing book was perfect for teenagers in the 1950s and 1960s, and its universal truths still ring true today.

Cover introduction and Page 1 of *On Eagle Wings*

Sometime between 1956 and 1957, Judge E. J. Ruegemer acquired the printing plates from Rev. Louis Gales of the Catechetical Guild. The book was originally printed for one of the Guild's programs, but the program was discontinued. With a few alterations to update the plates to make them more compatible with the Youth Guidance Commission, a total of 250,000 illustrated books were printed for youth organizations across the country. The program was made available in 1957, and in 1958, every attendee of the Grand Aerie International Convention was able to take one of these books back to their Aeries to share as a possible local program.

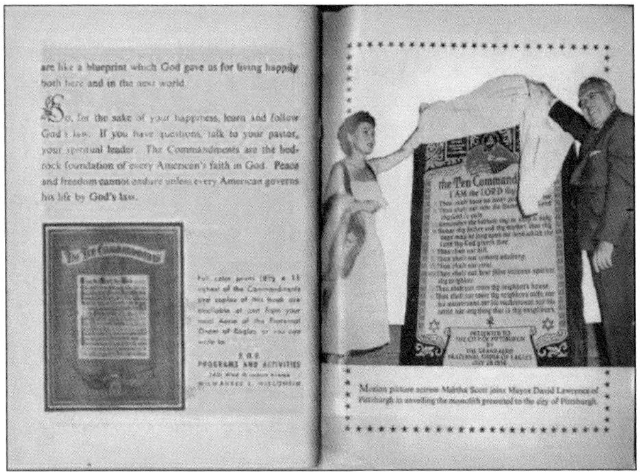
Last page and inside back cover of *On Eagle Wings*

As much success as *On Eagle Wings* may have had, the printing costs, as well as its references to numbered Commandments, may have given it an earlier demise than it deserved. The original book measured seven-by-five inches. My personal copy is very much yellowed with age and the cover has been repaired with tape. It is a snapshot into yesteryear of the way things may have been, and it is a great representation of one of the many programs of the Eagles' Youth Guidance Commission.

Judge E. J. Ruegemer sent a copy of *On Eagle Wings* to Angelo Patri (who was retired at the time) to share what he was doing with the Youth Guidance Commission and the Ten Commandments Project. Patri immigrated to New York from Italy when he was five years of age. He truly lived the American dream as he first became a teacher, then a principal, and then the first Italian director of a school district in the United States. He later became an advisor for children's educational television. Patri was a follower of John Dewey and a firm believer of social justice and change through liberal-minded progressive education.

This is only being mentioned to point out the absurdity of the angst of like-minded people today who have the same ideological mindset as Patri did back then. Why is it that the Ten Commandments Project was considered wonderful in the 1950s and is now held in contempt today? Patri wrote back to Ruegemer on January 16, 1958, and said, "I have at last read, several times over, the booklet, *On Eagle Wings*. I think that it should be helpful as a means of reinforcing the instruction of parents, teachers, and youth leaders." He goes on to say, "You have my wholehearted congratulations for the work you are doing in this field. It's a fine contribution to the country's welfare. The spread of the Ten Commandments is a wonderful help."

Why is it that the Ten Commandments Project was considered wonderful in the 1950s and is now held in contempt today?

Through the courtesy of Chuck Cunningham and the Fraternal Order of Eagles, it is a privilege to share my copy of *On Eagle Wings* as a digital copy that can be acquired only if this book was purchased through CreateSpace or a Kindle version through Amazon (please see the ordering information provided in the Addendum). Please note that the Catechetical Guild, when they created this book for a program that they had developed for young Catholic boys and girls, that they, too, did not "get the memo from God" regarding the numbering of the Ten Commandments. The life lessons learned by Nicholas Aloysius "Lucky" Sevan are, in no way, impacted by the "controversial" numbering system. What "Lucky" learned, as illustrated by this book, were instrumental life lessons written by the hand of God. Isn't that what is most important regarding the Ten Commandments?

Written In Stone

Judge E. J. Ruegemer not only believed that the Ten Commandments are "the oldest code of conduct handed down to man," but he also felt that the Fraternal Order of Eagles was destined to have the Ten Commandments put in every juvenile courthouse across the country. From his position as a juvenile court judge, he saw on a daily basis what the results were of not having a moral code introduced at a young age. In his heart of hearts, he "just wanted people to know the Ten Commandments." He also felt that it was his obligation to share what the Eagles were doing through the Youth Guidance Commission regarding the distribution of Ten Commandments scrolls and prints in every venue possible. The Judge was definitely the P. T. Barnum of the Ten Commandments Project, and who better than the Judge to be the face and voice for the Youth Guidance Commission?

The Judge knew that if he could find a way that would further along the Youth Guidance Commission's task of spreading the Ten Commandments scrolls and prints, he could make it happen. It was not a coincidence that Cecil B. DeMille had first-hand knowledge of the Eagles' Ten Commandments Project. When DeMille called Judge E. J. Ruegemer that "fateful" day in 1953, he knew full well that the Judge wanted to continue to spread the Eagles' program across the nation. DeMille wanted to congratulate the Judge and the Fraternal Order of Eagles for such an exceptional program and to wish him well in his endeavors. With almost one million members willing to carry out the Ten Commandments Project in scrolls and prints, perhaps the Judge could consider doing something more permanent by the means of bronze plaques at the juvenile court level.

A "light bulb must have turned on" in Judge E. J. Ruegemer's head because his thoughts verbalized as, "God did it in stone – so should we." The first granite Ten Commandments monolith was created in 1954 in time for the Chicago Fraternal Order of Eagles International Convention. The rest is *almost* history because this story has been so maligned regarding the business relationship between the Eagles and Cecil B. DeMille.

On July 14, 1955, in a letter from Art Arthur of Paramount Pictures to Judge E. J. Ruegemer, on behalf of Cecil B. DeMille, a Ten Commandments tablet (Commandments 5 through 10) was sent to the Judge. The letter granted the Judge permission to refer to Mount Sinai and the granite used in the tablet when talking about the Ten Commandments Project and the placing of granite Ten Commandments monoliths. The Judge was also allowed to refer to *The Ten Commandments* movie when publicizing the Ten Commandments scrolls, prints, and monoliths.

Contained on the next page, in its entirety, the Resolution from the Report of the Youth Guidance Commission at the Fraternal Order of Eagles' Fifty-Eighth Annual International Convention in Pittsburgh, Pennsylvania in July 1956 clarifies *exactly* what the connections were between DeMille and the Fraternal Order of Eagles.

The Resolution reiterates the information from Art Arthur's letter that the Fraternal Order of Eagles was given permission to use the format of the tablet in the creation of the Ten Commandments monoliths. Charlton Heston and Martha Scott participated at the dedications at the International Peace Garden in North Dakota and in Pennsylvania in 1956. In addition to what was stated in either the Resolution or the letter, artifacts from *The Ten Commandments* movie were on display at a county fair in 1956 along side of a monolith on the verge of a dedication, and Yul Brynner attended the rededication of a Wisconsin monolith in 1957.

RESOLUTION

WHEREAS, Mr. Cecil B. DeMille, of Paramount Pictures, is striving in his production of the film, *The Ten Commandments*, to achieve the same objective as the Fraternal Order of Eagles in their Youth Guidance Program, by the recognition that there can be no better nor more defined program of youth guidance and prevention of delinquency than the program handed down by God Himself, in the presentation to Moses more than 3,500 years ago, of the Ten Commandments; and

WHEREAS, we have during the time that our program has been in the process of development, simultaneously with the ten-year period that *The Ten Commandments* picture has been in the making, had the benefit of many valuable suggestions, a beautiful article in *The Eagle Magazine*, "I Bear Thee on Eagles' Wings," by Cecil B. DeMille, written in the heights of Mount Sinai while filming portions of the motion picture, and for his gift to the Eagles of a replica of one of the sacred and invaluable tablets of the Ten Commandments, hewn from Mount Sinai granite, copies of which replica now being incorporated among the other symbols in our granite monoliths, all culminating in the erection of granite monoliths of the Ten Commandments upon state capitol grounds, courthouse grounds, public parks, etc.; and

WHEREAS, Mr. Cecil B. DeMille has sent as his representative to the International Peace Garden on the occasion of the dedication of a granite monolith of the Ten Commandments, Mr. Charlton Heston, starring as Moses in *The Ten Commandments* picture; and during the Pittsburgh convention at the unveiling of a similar monolith, Martha Scott, starring in the role of the mother of Moses, each of whom addressing throngs of members of our Order including the general public, and each lending dignity to the occasion;

NOW, THEREFORE, BE IT RESOLVED, that this Grand Aerie session express its sincere thanks and appreciation to Mr. Cecil B. DeMille for his valuable contribution of this worthy cause, to Charlton Heston for his participation in the dedication of the Ten Commandments monolith at the International Peace Garden on June 10, 1956, to Martha Scott for her address to the delegates and Auxiliary delegates at the convention, for her participation in the dedication of the monolith as the Grand Finale in the Eagles Tribute to Pittsburgh;

BE IT FURTHER RESOLVED, that all Aeries and the entire membership of the Fraternal Order of Eagles be urged to support the forthcoming film production, *The Ten Commandments*, and, timed with its showing in the various cities, to carry on our program of presenting to courts, schools, churches, and all agencies where youth gather, framed prints of the Ten Commandments, including, where feasible, the erection of granite monoliths upon state capitol grounds, courthouse lawns, and public parks.

AND BE IT FURTHER RESOLVED, that a copy of this resolution be sent to Mr. Cecil B. DeMille, to Mr. Charlton Heston, and to Miss Martha Scott of Paramount Pictures.

Signed: Members of Resolutions Committee
Resolution submitted by Youth Guidance Commission:
E. J. Ruegemer, Chairman
Thomas J. O'Connor
Carl L. Anderson
Darrell Maxson
G. R. Benden
M. C. Dufek
Albert W. Schmitt, Secretary

In 1957, Mr. Weiss of Paramount Pictures authorized that in every city where *The Ten Commandments* film was shown that there was an Eagles' Aerie, the local theaters were asked to designate **one night** as "Eagles' Night." The local Aeries were given a certain number of tickets to sell to their own Eagle members for that one night, and a designated portion of the proceeds of those particular tickets were to be returned back to the Aeries for their individual campaigns of the Ten Commandments Project – be it for prints, scrolls, or monoliths.

To make it perfectly clear once and for all, leaving no doubt in anyone's mind, the contributions of Cecil B. DeMille and Paramount Pictures to the Fraternal Order of Eagles' Ten Commandments Project were based solely on DeMille's personal high regards of the Eagles' Youth Guidance Commission's work. In the closing paragraphs of his article in *The Eagle Magazine* in 1955, "I Bear Thee on Eagles' Wings," DeMille wrote:

> . . . The scene below my window here at Sinai is unlike anything that could be seen in America. Yet people are much the same everywhere; and, when you stop to think of it, these young people and our American youth have fundamentally the same questions in their minds, the same problems to face as they grow into adulthood. In a thousand external details of life they differ as much as it could be possible to differ. But strip away the external differences and, whether at Sinai or Seattle, the great basic questions by which men and woman guide their lives are much the same.
>
> What is the final purpose of life? How can I behave towards my fellowmen, first those in my own family and then all those in the world around me? What about sex? What about money, or whatever it is that represents material values for me? What about honor, sincerity, truthfulness? What shall I put first, my own temporary advantage or the permanent value there is in being a man whose word is his bond? What about the government of my mind itself, the hidden places of the heart where my actions are first born of my desires? How shall I reveal myself?
>
> Those are questions everyone has to answer. They are not limited to any country or way of life. The way a boy or girl learns to answer those questions determines the kind of man or woman that boy or girl will be.
>
> We have a veritable army of juvenile court judges and officials, probation officers, psychologists, and others trying to do repair work on young lives because, somewhere along the line in those lives, fundamental questions were answered wrong or left unanswered by those who were responsible for the guidance that youth needs but does not always get.
>
> Some of the saddest words ever written are those in the Book of Common Prayer: "We have left undone those things which we ought to have done." It might be salutary, if something cruel, to inscribe those words on the walls of our juvenile courts, facing the place where parents sit. But it would be more salutary if our schools and homes – and our minds and hearts – were deeply inscribed with certain other words which are the answer to those questions. There are such words. They are the Ten Commandments. They are older than Moses, older than this mountain, because they are not laws – they are *the* law.
>
> To guide young people in today's complex world we need all the light that expert knowledge and advance scientific techniques can give. But most of all we need the Divine Code of guidance which was given to the world. This is why I am so enthusiastic about the Fraternal Order of Eagles' project of circulating the erecting copies of the Ten Commandments everywhere that the Order's widespread influence reaches. The many young people who will know the Commandments better because of the Eagles' work may well apply to themselves the words the Lord spoke here at Sinai long ago: "I bear you on eagles' wings, and brought you unto myself."

And what did Cecil B. DeMille and Paramount Pictures receive in return for all of the above? **A promise** "that all Aeries and the entire membership of the Fraternal Order of Eagles be urged to support the forthcoming film production, *The Ten Commandments*, and, timed with its showing in the various cities, *to carry on our [Eagles] program* of presenting to courts, schools, churches, and all agencies where youth gather, framed prints of the Ten Commandments, including, where feasible, the erection of granite monoliths upon State Capitol grounds, courthouse lawns, and public parks."

To make it perfectly clear once and for all, leaving no doubt in anyone's mind, the contributions of Cecil B. DeMille and Paramount Pictures to the Fraternal Order of Eagles' Ten Commandments Project were based solely on DeMille's personal high regards of the Eagles' Youth Guidance Commission's work.

The ability for the Eagles to have at their disposal a distinguished movie producer, two famed actors and an actress, Mount Sinai artifacts, a designated percentage of the proceeds of a movie to promote the Youth Guidance Commission's Ten Commandments Project, and bragging rights of all of the above, leads me to believe that the Fraternal Order of Eagles were given more than enough support to continue with their work for years to come. Unfortunately, it wasn't enough to keep the wolves at bay – the American Civil Liberties Union (ACLU) was champing at the bit to twist this story every which way but loose.

As of the 1956 Fraternal Order of Eagles International Convention, the Grand Aerie presented monoliths to the cities of Chicago, Milwaukee, and Pittsburgh, and they had the commitment for the presentation to Boys Town, Nebraska. The dedication at the International Peace Garden in North Dakota was highly covered by NBC, CBC, and CBS, not to mention the local radio and television station WDAY. The Youth Guidance Commission reiterated again, "There can be no substitute and certainly no more divine nor better program of Youth Guidance than the Ten Commandments handed down to Moses, as a guide to the human race."

All of the years spent handing out thousands, upon thousands, of prints and scrolls to individuals, from children to presidents, basically went out the window with all of the perceived Hollywood hoopla. To this day, the importance of the DeMille connection is horribly taken out of context. That was NOT the story of the Youth Guidance Commission's Ten Commandments Project. That was NOT what Cecil B. DeMille envisioned with his "help." This became a total travesty, not because of what DeMille did, but because of what some inane individuals and organizations have done with misinformation and lies.

There truly was a much simpler story to the Ten Commandments Project when they erected the granite monoliths. Most of the Ten Commandments monoliths were placed in small communities with only the local people taking center stage during the dedications. There were various reasons why each community wanted a monolith, including honoring an event or person, or making a declaration of historic significance regarding the codes of law. Any time that an Aerie wanted to gift a monolith to a town or government entity, they always asked two questions:

1. Do you WANT a monolith?
2. If you do, where do you want it placed?

The town or city, after getting appropriate permissions and permits, would then receive a Ten Commandments monolith at no cost to them. The monolith was paid for by the local Aerie who would have a fund-raising campaign doing activities like car washes, dances, bake sales, Ten Commandments pin sales, requesting donations, etc.

The dedications, or unveilings, of these monoliths were big celebrations in the towns. Some of the dedications took place on special holidays like Memorial Day, Fourth of July, Veterans Day, Mother's Day, etc. There were always local political dignitaries, Eagle dignitaries, and representatives from each of the major religions – Protestant, Catholic, and Jewish. Youth organizations were involved and sometimes military or veterans' groups. There may have been parades, picnics, speeches, etc. When these memorable dedication ceremonies occurred, sometimes whole towns came out for the celebration. These monoliths, at the time of the dedications, meant a great deal to the people who were involved and their fellow citizens.

Mihelich Monument Company of Saint Cloud, Minnesota, originally manufactured the Ten Commandments monoliths for the Youth Guidance Commission. When changes were made to the original design of the monoliths, they could not compete against the proposed pricing from Granit-Bronz, Inc., a subsidiary of Cold Spring Granite Company in Cold Spring, Minnesota.

A number of artists contributed to the design of the Ten Commandments monoliths. Many attributes of the paper versions were used including the American flag, an eagle, two tablets of the Ten Commandments at the top, the All-Seeing Eye of God super-imposed on a triangle, two Stars of David, and the Greek letters of Chi Rho. At the base was an engraved section that mentioned who, or what, the monolith was dedicated to, by whom, and the year of dedication. Carnelian granite, thought to be the closest type of granite to that found on Mount Sinai where Moses received the original tablets, was used in making some of the original monoliths.

PRICE LIST
for
MONOLITHS

*GRANITE MONOLITHS	32" x 8" x 54", Shipping weight 1600 lbs. Price F. O. B. St. Cloud, Minn. $200.00 42" x 8" x 72", Shipping weight 2500 lbs. Price F. O. B. St. Cloud, Minn. $325.00 Quotations on larger monoliths available upon request to the Program and Activities Dept.
FRAMED TEN COMMANDMENT SCROLLS	12" x 16" Framed in Honduras blonde mahogany, single order $2.25, postage paid. In lots of ten or more, price is $1.50 plus shipping costs.
UNFRAMED SCROLLS	8½" x 11" .10 cents each 12" x 16" .30 cents each presentation certificate completed. 16" x 22" .30 cents each with blank presentation certificate.
*GRANITE TEN COMMANDMENT PLAQUES	25" x 16½"x 7/8" including rosetts of bronze, F. O. B. St. Cloud, Minn. $100.00

Please address all requests for Ten Commandment's material to:

PROGRAM & ACTIVITIES DEPARTMENT
2401 WEST WISCONSIN AVENUE
MILWAUKEE, WISCONSIN

*Made by Cold Spring Granite Co., Cold Spring, Minnesota

Courtesy of the Fraternal Order of Eagles

One of the first known and most complete pricing lists for the Ten Commandments Project

E. J. RUEGEMER, Chairman

ALBERT W. SCHMITT, Secretary

Fraternal Order of Eagles

National Youth Guidance Commission

ST. CLOUD, MINNESOTA

LIBERTY TRUTH JUSTICE EQUALITY

F. O. E.

Dear Brothers:

We are most grateful to the many Aeries and Auxiliaries who have cooperated with our program of erecting Ten Commandments monoliths throughout our great land.

It is the hope of the Youth Guidance Commission "THAT HEREAFTER THE HOST AERIE OF EVERY STATE CONVENTION WILL ERECT A TEN COMMANDMENT MONOLITH". This recognition of the Natural Law will be a fitting remembrance of the convention. These may also be ordered for your own special dedication programs.

A picture of the revised monolith is enclosed with an order blank. Retain these until such a time as you may need them. Place order directly with Granit-Bronz, Inc., Cold Spring, Minnesota.

The tablet is formed with the traditional arch at the top. The face of the monolith is given high finish, including full polish to bring out the wealth of lettering and symbolic ornaments. Included in the art scheme is the American emblem; the All Seeing Eye of God, superimposed on the triangle; the Stars of David and the Greek letters Chi Rho, being the first two letters of Christ, also interpreted as meaning Peace. The back is clean surfaced in a rubbed and sanded finish; the sides and top are rough-hewn. Bronze dowels 5/8" in diameter tie the tablet to the base on which it is to be set.

The Monolith and Base are fabricated from 8 inch thick Carnelian granite, similar to Mt. Sinai. Overall sizes and prices are as follows and can be purchased with or without the base:

NEW PRICES F.O.B. COLD SPRING, MINNESOTA

	SMALL SIZE			LARGE SIZE	
Monolith:	32 x 56"	$305.00	Monolith:	42 x 74"	$495.00
Base:	40 x 14"	60.00	Base:	56 x 16"	85.00
		365.00			580.00

Sincerely and Fraternally,

EAGLES NATIONAL YOUTH GUIDANCE COMMITTEE

E. J. Ruegemer, Chairman

Albert W. Schmitt, Secretary

Courtesy of the Fraternal Order of Eagles

This very specific letter with the attachments shown on the next page, was sent to the Aeries sometime in 1958 with the new designs regarding the Paleo-Hebrew tablets, no numbering, and the addition of a Commandment. It included an order form and a picture with clear definitions regarding size, decorative emblems, and surface polishes. Some Aeries chose to disregard these instructions and "did their own thing."

The monoliths were supposed to be one of two different sizes, but the end results show that the monoliths range from three-to-six feet tall (some even larger), not including the base, and they were manufactured out of red, brown, peach, or gray granite. Although Cold Spring Granite Company made many of the monoliths, the individual Aeries sometimes had them made locally. It was not until after a few of the monoliths were placed that some criticism surfaced because of the different versions of the Ten Commandments and their numbering. Changes were made after the first series of distributions including removing the numbering and changing the wording of the Ten Commandments. Some Aeries still chose to keep the numbering system even after the changes were offered.

The prices of the granite monoliths went steadily up as the years passed by, as did everything else. The first known price list quoted $325 for a six-foot monolith (shipping weight was 2,500 pounds). The 1958 letter quoted $495 (not including the base). Very shortly thereafter, the price for the same monolith increased to $630. Considering that the Grand Aerie paid $6,880 for their monolith (not including the base) in 2005, prices of granite well surpassed the rate of inflation. The equivalent cost, had all things remained equal, should have been $2,316.

Not all granite Ten Commandments were large. There are no available records as to how many of the smaller granite plaques were made, but there were indeed several. One known Ten Commandments plaque was displayed in the Allen County Public Library in Fort Wayne, Indiana. When Judy Pankow attempted to acquire a photo in 2012, for some unknown reason, not only was the plaque no longer exhibited, but no one in

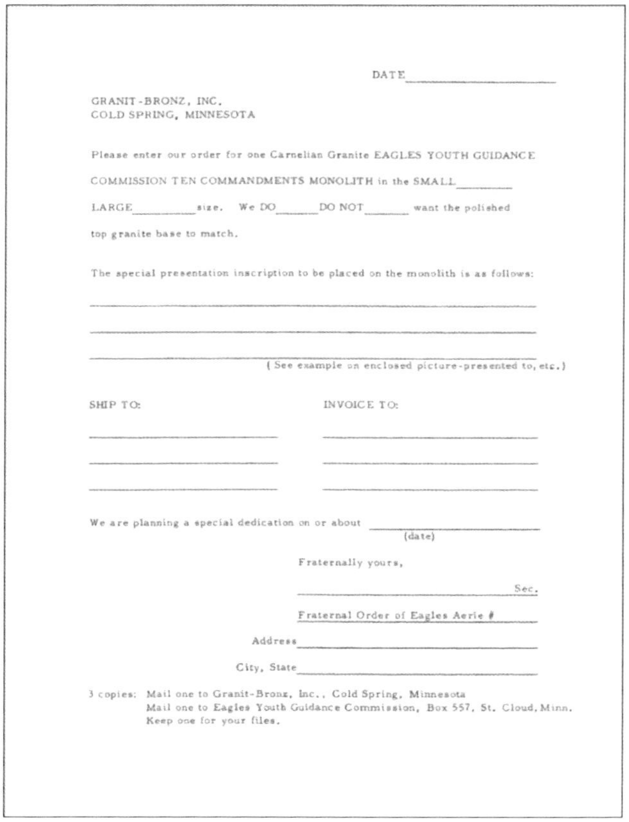

DATE ____________

GRANIT-BRONZ, INC.
COLD SPRING, MINNESOTA

Please enter our order for one Carnelian Granite EAGLES YOUTH GUIDANCE COMMISSION TEN COMMANDMENTS MONOLITH in the SMALL ______ LARGE ______ size. We DO ______ DO NOT ______ want the polished top granite base to match.

The special presentation inscription to be placed on the monolith is as follows:

____
____
____
(See example on enclosed picture-presented to, etc.)

SHIP TO: | INVOICE TO:

We are planning a special dedication on or about ____________ (date)

Fraternally yours,

____________ Sec.

Fraternal Order of Eagles Aerie # ______

Address ____________

City, State ____________

3 copies: Mail one to Granit-Bronz, Inc., Cold Spring, Minnesota
Mail one to Eagles Youth Guidance Commission, Box 557, St. Cloud, Minn.
Keep one for your files.

FRATERNAL ORDER OF EAGLES
OFFICIAL TEN COMMANDMENTS MONOLITH AND BASE

SMALL SIZE
Monolith: 32 x 56"
Base: 40 x 14"

LARGE SIZE
Monolith: 42 x 74"
Base: 56 x 16"

Granit-Bronz, Inc
Cold Spring, Minn.

the entire facility had any recollection of when it was removed or where it currently was being stored. The Ten Commandments plaque obviously just vanished and left no traces as to its new whereabouts.

During an official visit to Milwaukee, Wisconsin, Grand Worthy President Lawrence Leahy presented a Ten Commandments plaque to past national president Judge Robert W. Hansen.

Leahy said, "Judge E. J. Ruegemer of Minnesota has given us impetus in bringing to our court rooms, our schools, our public buildings, the primary, and the fundamental, Laws of God. The effort of the Fraternal Order of Eagles will have been well worthwhile if one of the unfortunate people appearing before Judge Hansen receives from this plaque of the Ten Commandments an inspiration to better him or herself."

Photo courtesy of Stearns History Museum, Saint Cloud, Minnesota
Eagles National Project Originates Here – Judge E. J. Ruegemer presents on behalf of the Eagles Local Aerie 622 a granite monolith of the Ten Commandments to Bishop Peter W. Bartholome. In the picture are (left to right): Bishop Bartholome, A. W. Schmitt, Herschel L. Holmes, Harold Kunkel, president, and E. J. Ruegemer, chairman and originator of the project.

Photo courtesy of Stearns History Museum, Saint Cloud Minnesota
A granite monolith of the Ten Commandments was presented to the Ministerial Association here [Saint Cloud, Minnesota] by E. J. Ruegemer, chairman of the program for the Eagles. Pictured are (left to right): Judge Ruegemer, A. W. Schmitt, Herschel L. Holmes, Rev. Robert Waggoner, secretary, and Rev. Ray Boehlke, president.

Photo courtesy of *The Eagle Magazine* (December 1956)
Lawrence Leahy presents to Judge Bob Hansen a plaque of Ten Commandments to display in his court room

Communities all across the United States have been deluged with lawsuits regarding their Ten Commandments monoliths over the past several decades. Their struggles, losses, and successes, are addressed in subsequent chapters. Also addressed in those chapters are references to faith and religion, and what legal objections have been used to have the monoliths removed. While Judge E. J. Ruegemer was struggling over what, if any, numbering system should be used to keep various religious groups happy in 1956 and 1957, the American Civil Liberties Union (ACLU) was hard at work to find a way to prevent any more Ten Commandments monoliths from being dedicated.

This is the place where we need to open the discussion regarding the "elephant in the room." Many of the condemnations against the Ten Commandments monoliths come back to this time frame in 1958. This is when the first known widespread attack from the Minnesota Branch of the ACLU became public knowledge. The 1958 letters between the ACLU and the Fraternal Order of Eagles continue to be held as a "warning" of why these monolith dedications should have ceased at that time.

On February 18, 1958, Donald G. Paterson from the Minnesota Branch of the ACLU wrote a letter to Ross Schmidt, Minnesota State President of the Fraternal Order of Eagles. It states:

> Complaints have been received by our organization that the constitutional principle of separation of church and state is being violated in Duluth and in other localities of Minnesota due to the activity of your fraternal group in persuading governmental officials to erect the Ten Commandments on public property. We are certain that the motives behind these actions are laudable as being a sincere attempt to aid in the fight against juvenile (and adult) delinquency.
>
> As soon as a governmental agency invokes a religious sanction in its attempts to prevent lawlessness, another evil may arise. We refer to the breeching, in the words of Thomas Jefferson, of the wall of separation between church and state. Furthermore, one also gets into theological difficulties because of the religious sanction one happens to adopt. This is true of the Ten Commandments in the Bible. There are also three versions of the Ten Commandments, Protestant, Catholic, and Jewish. Which one is to be used? Who decides which one to use? Can one version be adopted without giving serious offense to the sensibilities of those whose version is thus discriminated against? Our Committee on Separation of Church and State (consisting of a Roman Catholic, a Jew, a Presbyterian, a Lutheran, a Seventh Day Adventist, and a philosopher) has considered the specific mentioned at the beginning of this letter and recommended to our Board of Directors that appropriate action be taken.
>
> . . . We are enclosing a copy of President Pemberton's Memorandum to Members of the 1957 Legislature. We are also enclosing a copy of *Memorandum on Display of Crosses, Crucifixes, Creches, and Other Religious Symbols on Public Property.* This Memorandum has been endorsed in principle by our Board of Directors. . . .

It is so questionable how the ACLU can "laud" the motives of the Fraternal Order of Eagles without full understanding of the entire Ten Commandments Project. In the next breath, they ask the insufferable question regarding the multiple versions of the Ten Commandments. Please refer to Chapter 5 for the definitive answer to that question.

Thanks to the research of the great nephew of Judge E. J. Ruegemer, Joseph Haker (a Ph.D. candidate in American history at the University of Minnesota who wrote a dissertation on the history of public Ten Commandments displays), an added development arose when he discovered that additional information was also sent to the Judge. According to Haker, *The Memorandum of Law in Opposition to the Display of the Ten Commandments on Public School Premises*, written by Leo Pfeffer who was an attorney with the American Jewish Congress (AJC), was a determining factor regarding the decision to try to remove Ten Commandments displays. Haker wrote:

> [*The Memorandum*] served as the backbone of the ACLU stance toward religious displays. The ACLU and AJC objected to such displays as the Eagles' on constitutional grounds – they believed it violated the separation of church and state – but also, very interestingly, on theological and religious grounds as well.
>
> Pfeffer suggested that the actual text and organization of the Ten Commandments mattered very profoundly and was, in fact, sacred to a great many people. The very real differences between the versions of the Ten Commandments "cannot be brushed aside by a secular authority as inconsequential," and a non-sectarian version was, therefore, a "profane and sacrilegious use of one of the most deeply felt spiritual and religious symbols." To treat the Ten Commandments as little more than a secular "adjunct of sociology [or] community relations," and not something that is inherently and inextricably sacred, he [Pfeffer] suggested, "would be to denigrate their authentic purpose, to divest them of their transcendental meaning, and to reduce them to the level of moral teaching to be compared and equated with other comparable moral teachings." Thus, he argued, any attempt to make a version that was suitable for state use did actual damage to the religious scruples of individual citizens, many of who were forbidden by Catholic or Jewish law from taking into cognizance any other version. By forcing citizens to recognize a vague, state-sponsored religion (instead of their denominationally-specific content), the state was infringing on freedom of conscience.
>
> In other words, the ACLU and the AJC objected, in significant part, to the very idea that you could even have a "non-sectarian" version of the Ten Commandments without violating the sanctity and integrity of the various religions themselves, or in some way forcing religious individuals to sublimate their own beliefs to those that fit into a "non-sectarian" framework.

Haker believes that this memorandum caused a few of the rabbis who were originally in support of the Fraternal Order of Eagles Ten Commandments monoliths in Portland, Oregon and in Minnesota to withdraw their backing.

Haker found Pfeffer's argument "compelling," and I have to admit, just reading his findings got "my dander up." I am so grateful that Haker found this information because I find it so hypocritical and sanctimonious of Pfeffer and his ilk. The American Jewish Congress (AJC) and Pfeffer (who joined the AJC in 1946, became the director of the AJC Commission on Law and Social Action in 1957, served as general counsel for a time, and in 1964, served as special counsel) should be ashamed of themselves. They tout themselves as representatives of what all Jewish people should stand for, and yet they use their religious credentials to twist and manipulate people and laws to their advantage. Their knowledge of the law and what it could do for their organizations, trumped their knowledge of God's law.

I learned at an early age that a man is known by the company he keeps, and although Pfeffer was Jewish and regularly attended synagogue, his lawyering days were spent in endless battles against church and state. His affiliation with the ACLU was legendary. Pfeffer even joked at a speech that he gave at the Freedom from Religion Foundation's (FFRF) Eighth National Convention in 1985 in Minneapolis, Minnesota, "The Orthodox consider me to be the worst enemy they've had since Haman in the Purim story!"

To put this into context, in Chapter 7 of the Book of Ester, Haman sold out the Jewish people to be "destroyed, killed and annihilated." When this was discovered, King Xerxes ordered that Haman suffer the same death that Haman had planned for Mordecai, so Haman was impaled on a seventy-five-foot pole.

The FFRF hails Pfeffer's book, *Church, State, and Freedom,* as "the ultimate sourcebook for the history of the evolution of the all-American principle of the separation of church and state." Pfeffer was named the Humanist of the Year in 1988 by the American Humanist Association (AHA). His funeral in 1993 relays the sadness of it all – "although it was held in a synagogue, it was secular in content."

Back in 1958, only a few of the rabbis who worked with Judge E. J. Ruegemer and the Youth Guidance Commission spoke out against the misconceptions of Pfeffer, the AJC, and the ACLU. We should all be proud of their ability to stand against organizations like AJC and the ACLU – it had to be difficult back in those days. But what about today? So many individuals and organizations, especially our politicians, personally believe one thing and then do something else. How long did it take someone of the Catholic faith to finally confront Congresswoman Nancy Pelosi who claims to be "a devout Catholic," but is openly pro-choice? On June 20, 2013, according to Billy Hallowell of *The Blaze*:

> [Democratic Representative Nancy Pelosi] recently rebuffed a reporter and used her faith to defend her policy views on abortion. It seems at least one priest is calling for her to either comply with – or renounce Catholicism. In an open letter, Fr. Frank Pavone, national director for Priests for Life, a pro-life organization, made known his discontent with Pelosi's most recent comments about abortion. "Whatever Catholic faith you claim to respect and practice, it is not the faith that the Catholic Church teaches. And I speak for countless Catholics when I say that it's time for you to stop speaking as if it were."

It is not always easy to always walk out your faith – been there, done that. In the same spectrum, in James 5:19-20 (ESV), "My brothers, if anyone among you wanders from the truth and someone brings him back, let him know that whoever brings back a sinner from his wandering will save his soul from death and will cover a multitude of sins." We are called to help others to see the truth if they should wander. There are enough individuals out there who are not of God. If someone claims to have God in his heart, and he walks a stray path, we need to call that to his attention, grab him by the hand, and lovingly steer him in the right direction. God will handle those who are not believers – we have plenty to worry about, starting with each of us.

Though I digressed, it is important to know who is behind some of these legal papers and memorandums and where they come from in their personal beliefs. Haker went on to explain that the hoopla of these letters in 1958 against the dedications of the Fraternal Order of Eagles Ten Commandments monoliths died down for a few years because, "They [ACLU and the AJC] had limited resources and decided it wasn't a particularly pressing issue. In the late 1950s and early 1960s, more and more of the ACLU resources were being channeled into fighting for the Civil Rights Movement, and the resources they did allocate to church/state issues generally went to much larger issues like school prayer or parochaid." This just emphasizes that the ACLU is just an opportunist organization that follows the cultural heartbeat and the money that it can bring in to further its own interests and atheist agenda.

According to a letter dated March 11, 1958 to the Honorable Robert W. Hansen, Judge E. J. Ruegemer stated, "He [Rabbi A. Krantz] emphatically could see no objection to the erection of this [Ten Commandments] monolith [dedicated in Fargo, North Dakota], and that the Rabbi insisted that the New York Board of Rabbis is but one of many such groups and they do not necessarily express the views of others."

In a letter that crossed paths with the above letter from Hansen to both Ruegemer and F. C. Schroeder (legal counsel for the Fraternal Order of Eagles) dated March 12, 1958, Hansen expressed:

> The opposition to the display of the Ten Commandments on public property came, I believe, from the Civil Rights Advisor of the American Jewish Committee, 386 Fourth Avenue, New York City. This is a group with which we have had close personal and organizational contact. Two years ago, we discussed this matter with some of their staff members. They had a very firm opinion that this sort of display would be the opening wedge for the introduction of religious objects, etc., that would be offensive and humiliating to Jewish children.
>
> . . . The subsequent brief from the American Jewish Congress (a different organization), the position of the American Civil Liberties Union (ACLU), and the action of the New York Education Commissioner, all stem from this initial American Jewish Committee statement of policy. I certainly have no objection to exhausting the possibilities of conciliation and compromise with the groups involved but it is my firm opinion that they will not be moved and must be accepted as dissenters to this program. I do not think that this is as harmful as it might at first seem. The complete lack of discipline and social and moral chaos in the New York City schools is a direct result of this type of brittle intellectual thinking which, consciously and subconsciously seeks to minimize the role of religion and eliminate the disciplinary codes or sanctions of our society.

To the best of my knowledge, there are no known Ten Commandments monoliths in the State of New York.

In a letter dated July 25, 1958 from the Special Committee of the Saint Cloud Ministerial Association regarding their evaluation of the Eagles' Ten Commandments Project, they stated:

> The Program as presently being conducted merits the support of God-fearing men of all faiths. It is our conviction that the program does not infringe upon the spirit of the First Amendment to the Constitution of the United States, for the Constitution does not deny the existence of almighty God and His moral laws in the universe. There is no sectarianism in the Ten Commandments, per se. They represent not a religious creed but are the natural, moral laws of God. It is our feeling that the program will result in greater appreciation of respect for law and order in all our relationships for this code of moral law, the Ten Commandments, is the essential foundation of all common law.
>
> Further, you would be interested to know that we have prepared a comprehensive statement reaffirming our previous endorsement of the Eagles' Ten Commandment Project. This statement will be submitted to the Saint Cloud Ministerial Association.
>
> Respectfully submitted by Ray Boehlke, Pastor of the Grace Evangelical United Brethren Church, and Harry S. Dodgson, Minister of the First Presbyterian Church for the Saint Cloud Ministerial Association.

This letter, read at the 1958 Fraternal Order of Eagles International Convention was understood by many, including Judge E. J. Ruegemer, as a statement that the "matter" of the Duluth, Minnesota's Ten Commandments monolith, as well as others in that state as mentioned by the ACLU, would now go by the wayside.

In a letter dated March 28, 1958 to the Honorable Robert W. Hansen, E. J. O'Donnell, S. J. I., of Marquette University in Milwaukee, Wisconsin, offered a list of thirteen instances in which the "religious basis of our American way of life was pointed out." Some of these included the Northwest Ordinance, the Declaration of Independence, President Washington's Farewell Address, and quotes from Thomas Jefferson, Alexander Hamilton, and President Eisenhower, along with several court cases.

March 28, 1958

References to printed material in which the religious basis of our American way of life was pointed out:

1. The Northwest Ordinance. Documents of American History, Ed. by Henry Steele Commager (New York: F.S.Crofts & Col., 1946), p. 131.

2. The Declaration of Independence. Ibid., p. 100.

3. President Washington's Farewell Address. Ibid., p. 173.

4. Jefferson's statement: "The God who gave us life gave us liberty at the same time." Benjamin Wright, American interpretations of the Natural Law (Cambridge: Harvard Univ. Press, 1931), p. 88, note 105.

5. Jefferson' Statement: "Can the liberties of a nation be thought secure when we have removed their only firm basis, a conviction in the minds of the people that their liberties are the fits of God?" Thomas Jefferson, Notes on the State of Virginia. Ed. by William Peden (Chapel Hill: The Univ. of North Carolina Press, 1955), p. 163.

6. Alexander Hamilton: "The sacred rights of mankind are not to be rummaged for among old parchments of musty records. They are written, as with a sunbeam, in the whole volume of human nature, by the hand of Divinity Itself, and can never be erased or obscured by mortal powers."

7. President Eisenhower, February 20, 1955: "Without God there could be no American form of government, nor an American way of life. Recognition of the Supreme Being is the first--the most basic-- expression of Americanism. Thus the founding fathers saw it, and thus, with God's help, it will continue to be."
He said, moreover, that the "founding fathers expressed in words for all to read the ideal of government based upon human dignity," and the "recognition of God as the author of individual rights."
Man's fundamental rights are from God--not from the state. For, said the President, "if the state gives rights, it can--and inevitably will--take away those rights." The New York Times, Feb. 21, 1955.

8. McCollum v. Board of Education, 333 U.S. 203 (1948), Justice Reed's dissenting opinion.

9. Zorach v. Clauson, 343 U.S. 306 (1952). We are a religious people whose institutions presuppose a Supreme Being.

10. Story, Joseph, Commentaries on the Constitution of the United States (Boston: Hilliard, Gray, 1833), III, pp. 724-726.

11. Terrett v. Tyler, 9 Cranch (U.S.) 43 (1815). The meaning of the religious clauses of the First Amendment.

12. Vidal v. Gigard's Executors, 2 How.127 (1844). Christianity is part of the common law.

13. Church of Holy Trinity v. United States, 143 U.S. 457 (1892). This is a Christian nation.

Courtesy of the Fraternal Order of Eagles

Attachment to the letter dated March 28, 1958 from Marquette University

There also was the blessing bestowed by Rabbi Krantz at the Ten Commandments monolith dedication in Fargo, North Dakota, and the speech offered by Rabbi Cashdan at the Ten Commandments monolith dedication in Jefferson City, Missouri, that same year. One would hope that all matters regarding the separation of church and state, and the above ACLU complaint, would be declared dead and never be resurrected again.

Blessing by Rabbi Krantz, Fargo, North Dakota (March 8, 1958)

Lord God of the expanding universe and the diminishing world of people, look with favor upon the efforts of this day. Grant that dedicated men may pursue to fruition and completion of their plans for the elevation of man, his health, his dignity, his mature development.

For these pursuits do we fulfill their destinies as partners, children of God, committed to aiding in the moral completion of that world and the enablement of man.

May it by Thy will to please us, to sustain us, and to allow us to gather together again in the future when the promises of today will have become the reality of tomorrow.

Partial Speech Given by Rabbi Cashdan, Jefferson City, Missouri (June 28, 1958)

. . . It is on the wings of Eagles through the generosity of the Fraternal Order of Eagles and their concern for the moral welfare of His blessed country that they have brought the monolith of the Ten Commandments to this state capitol, and for this we are truly grateful.

. . . The scientific achievements of our age have succeeded in doing physically what the teachings of the Ten Commandments seek to do spiritually. Today, men and nations are physically closer to each other than ever before in history. We are near to each other as the distance of a guided missile can travel, but only the universal and humanitarian teachings of the Ten Commandments can produce guided men and women to the love of God and fellow-man in their hearts.

. . . In this country, man is free to live in accord with the religion of his choice, and we as individuals have the freedom to follow the Laws of God or to be indifferent to them. In our decision is our destiny and the destiny of mankind, for the Ten Commandments must survive if humanity is to endure. The Ten Commandments make us the heirs of the past and the trustees of the future, and that their essence and their lesson contain the greatest common denominator of all religions, the teaching, "Thou shalt love the Lord thy God with all thy heart, with all thy soul, and with all thy might. And thou shalt love they neighbor as thyself."

The Fraternal Order of Eagles continues dedicating Ten Commandments monoliths throughout the country through their local Aeries. The ACLU, as well as many other organizations, continues their fight to have them removed.

Chapter 5

Those Are Not My Ten Commandments

The Fraternal Order of Eagles' Ten Commandments monoliths have "offended" people for years because they are "perceived" to be the exclusive beliefs of a particular religion, negating all other beliefs, and for that reason, they need to be removed. The alleged problem is not only that they are on public property, but that they are on public property and seemingly tout a singular, rather than universal, message. This ostensibly is a most horrific offense.

In June 1999, with a seventy percent majority, the US House of Representatives voted to allow the Ten Commandments to be posted in schools and other government buildings. Representative Jerrold Nadler of New York questioned, "Whose Ten Commandments? The Catholic version, the Protestant version, or the Jewish version? They are different, you know."

"Whose Ten Commandments? The Catholic version, the Protestant version, or the Jewish version? They are different, you know."

In October 1999, when the Family Research Council in Washington, DC, provided framed copies of the Ten Commandments to forty-one members of Congress at a news conference, Steve Benen of Americans United for Separation of Church and State (AU) demanded to know, "Which version of the Ten Commandments was given to the representatives?"

In a letter to the *Pittsburgh Tribune-Review*, Joseph Forbes wrote the following regarding the Ten Commandments on the Allegheny County Courthouse, "I cannot help noting that it is a Protestant version of the Ten Commandments that is being displayed. Seeing only the Protestant version on public display makes me feel that I am to some extent a second-class citizen because I am Catholic rather than Protestant."

These comments from educated individuals display a true lack of knowledge of religion in general, and the Bible in particular. In regard to the history behind the Ten Commandments monoliths, a discussion concerning religion from an historic perspective must take place. To discuss religion from an emotionless, non-faith-based perspective is difficult. We have been taught through the years not to discuss religion and politics in public unless we were willing to lose friends and family members in heated arguments. Looking at religion strictly from a scholarly viewpoint, based on facts of religion itself, should help in understanding the historic background of the Ten Commandments monoliths.

To share ideas about religion without being offensive requires that a distinction be made between religion and faith. Religion is defined by doctrines and rules that have been written down through the ages on which individuals choose to base their beliefs and actions. Faith may be based on those doctrines, but faith is actually the relationship between individuals, their perceived God, or in some vernacular Higher Power. It is the discussion of faith that gets everyone in an uproar because that is very personal. Religion, on the other hand, is indisputable because the doctrines are in written form and can be researched and studied in the public forum.

A few generic examples to distinguish between religion and faith are as follows:

In the Catholic religion, birth control is not allowed, yet there are Catholics who practice birth control. Their religion says that it is unacceptable, but their faith, that relationship between them and God, seeks an acceptance.

In the Jewish religion, it is unacceptable to eat unclean foods such as pork, and yet there are Jews who love pepperoni pizza. Eating pepperoni may be against Jewish kosher laws, but their faith (again, that relationship between them and God), will seek to work out the discrepancy.

There are religions which proclaim that their faith comes from the Bible, and yet they are dependent on writings of men and women, who professed to be latter-day prophets, to clarify how they walk out their faith. The Church of Jesus Christ of Latter Day Saints (LDS, or the Mormon Church) relies heavily on The Book of Mormon. The Seventh Day Adventist Church (SDA) gives credence to the writings of Ellen G. White. Both religions have similarities to many Christian churches to the extent that their weekly worship services are lock-step with their Bible-believing brethren. Their doctrinal stances stray enough from common Biblical practices to form a distinctive, and decisive, alienation from those same Christian churches. Both of these religions encourage acceptance of the principles behind the Ten Commandments.

These are just a few examples out of hundreds that can be used to show the difference between religion and faith. The very personal relationship between man and God should not be up for discussion in the public forum, but religion, on the other hand, should always be up for debate. It is not my intention to promote any specific religion over another, but it is necessary concerning the Ten Commandments monoliths to understand how religion has become a contentious issue in regard to deciding whether the monoliths may be allowed to remain on public property.

It must also be understood that any time that the Ten Commandments are listed, or displayed, they are only a representation of what is stated in the Bible.

It must also be understood that any time that the Ten Commandments are listed, or displayed, they are only a *representation* of what is stated in the Bible. They never have the entire text listed on them, and they may not even be in a language that is universally understood. They may even just contain symbols or lettering, but when they are viewed, the general public "just knows" that they are the Ten Commandments despite their professed religion or belief system.

Problems arise in three different areas when referring to the Fraternal Order of Eagles' Ten Commandments monoliths:

- Religions use different versions of the Bible, so how can any one version of the Ten Commandments be the "right" one and be expected to be acceptable to everyone?

- Because the Ten Commandments are found in several places in the Bible and the verbiage differs in each location, which set should be used for everyone?
- Different religions have "different" Commandments (or at least "different" numbering schemes), so if only one numbering version is used, does that not exclude all other religions?

Are any of these concerns legitimate when it comes to the validity of Fraternal Order of Eagles' Ten Commandments monoliths being erected on public property? It is time to talk about religion.

Religion 101

So, where DID those Ten Commandments come from? The obvious answer is from the Bible, but from that point, all of the questions arise. Let us first look at the Bible in general.

The original Bible texts were written between 1450 and 400 Before Common Era (BCE) in Hebrew. Certain parts of the books of Daniel and Ezra were written in Aramaic. These original texts were written with no spacing, no punctuation, and definitely no chapter and verse markings. Around 500 BCE, the Masoretes developed a system of vowels and accents that broke up the texts and made them easier to read. The Old Testament (which is the entire Jewish Bible referred to as the Tanakh), contained thirty-nine separate books.

Around 200 BCE, the first five books of the Old Testament (the Torah) were translated into Greek for the Jewish community in Alexandria. This translation was called the Septuagint (Latin for seventy) because legend has it that there were six elders from each of the twelve tribes of Israel on the translation committee. By its completion, the Septuagint contained not only the thirty-nine original books which were translated from Hebrew, but also fourteen Apocrypha books.

During the last few centuries before the Common Era (CE), Jews around Judea had problems reading the Hebrew texts, so first the Torah, and then the rest of the books, were translated into Aramaic. These translations were called the Targums.

By the end of the first century, twenty-seven books of the New Testament were completed in Greek. There were several other books written, and a decision had to be made as to what constituted the "official" books of the Bible. The Council of Laodicea in 363 CE, along with making many major decisions regarding church doctrine, finalized which books would make up what we call today the Bible. Other highlights regarding major changes in translating the Bible include:

- 382 CE – Jerome's Latin Vulgate manuscript contained all eighty books of the Bible (thirty-nine Old Testament, fourteen Apocrypha, and twenty-seven New Testament books) (revised in 405 CE).
- 600 CE – Latin was the only language allowed for Scripture (which held true until 1582 CE).
- 1455 CE – Johannes Gutenberg invented the printing press and the first book in print was Vulgate's Bible (up until this time, all manuscripts were written by hand).
- 1516 CE – Desiderius Erasmus translated a Greek/Latin parallel New Testament.
- 1522 CE – Martin Luther translated the New Testament into German.
- 1526 CE – William Tyndale translated the New Testament into English.
- 1535 CE – Myles Coverdale translated the first complete Bible (all eighty books) into English.
- 1560 CE – The Geneva Bible is the first English Bible to have numbered verses in each Chapter which were devised by Robert Stephanus in 1550 CE.

- 1609 CE – The Douay-Rheims Bible combined the Douay Old Testament with the Rheims New Testament (from 1582) to create the first English Catholic Bible.
- 1611 CE – The King James Bible was printed to include all eighty books (considered to be the first Protestant Bible).
- 1885 CE – The King James Bible removed the Apocrypha and the Protestant Bible was reduced to sixty-six books.

As an example, out of at least 213 English versions of the Bible in use today, the following is a breakdown of three different Bibles used by three different religions by comparing their books:

ESV Bible	**Douay Rheims Bible**	**JPS Bible**
Old Testament	**Old Testament**	
Genesis	Genesis	**The Law**
Exodus	Exodus	Genesis
Leviticus	Leviticus	Exodus
Numbers	Numbers	Leviticus
Deuteronomy	Deuteronomy	Numbers
Joshua	Josue	Deuteronomy
Judges	Judges	**The Prophets**
Ruth	Ruth	Joshua
1 Samuel	1 Kings	Judges
2 Samuel	2 Kings	1 Samuel
1 Kings	3 Kings	2 Samuel
2 Kings	4 Kings	1 Kings
1 Chronicles	1 Paralipomenon	2 Kings
2 Chronicles	2 Paralipomenon	Isaiah
Ezra	1 Esdras	Jeremiah
Nehemiah	2 Esdras	Ezekiel
	Tobias *	**The Minor Prophets**
	Judith *	Hosea
Esther	Esther	Joel
Job	Job	Amos
Psalms	Psalms	Obadiah
Proverbs	Proverbs	Jonah
Ecclesiastes	Ecclesiastes	Micah
Song of Solomon	Canticles	Nahum
	Wisdom *	Habakkuk
	Ecclesiasticus *	Zephaniah
Isaiah	Isaias	Haggai
Jeremiah	Jeremias	Zechariah
Lamentations	Lamentations	Malachi
	Baruch *	**The Writings**
Ezekiel	Ezechiel	Psalms
Daniel	Daniel	Proverbs
Hosea	Osee	Job
Joel	Joel	**Megilot**
Amos	Amos	Song of Songs
Obadiah	Abdias	Ruth

ESV Bible	**Douay Rheims Bible**	**JPS Bible**
Jonah	Jonas	Lamentations
Micah	Micheas	Ecclesiastes
Nahum	Nahum	Esther
Habakkuk	Habacuc	Daniel
Zephaniah	Sophonias	Ezra
Haggai	Aggeus	Nehemiah
Zechariah	Zacharias	1 Chronicles
Malachi	Malachias	2 Chronicles
	1 Machabees *	
	2 Machabees *	
	Apocrypha	
New Testament	**New Testament**	
Matthew	Matthew	
Mark	Mark	
Luke	Luke	
John	John	
Acts	Acts of Apostles	
Romans	Romans	
1 Corinthians	1 Corinthians	
2 Corinthians	2 Corinthians	
Galatians	Galatians	
Ephesians	Ephesians	
Philippians	Philippians	
Colossians	Colossians	
1 Thessalonians	1 Thessalonians	
2 Thessalonians	2 Thessalonians	
1 Timothy	1 Timothy	
2 Timothy	2 Timothy	
Titus	Titus	
Philemon	Philemon	
Hebrews	Hebrews	
James	James	
1 Peter	1 Peter	
2 Peter	2 Peter	
1 John	1 John	
2 John	2 John	
3 John	3 John	
Jude	Jude	
Revelation	Apocalypse	

*Seven extra Books and the Apocrypha are found in Catholic Bibles that are not found in Protestant Bibles

The first Bible featured in the list is the *English Standard Version Bible* (ESV) which is considered to be a non-denominational, or Protestant, Bible. The ESV Bible is copyrighted by Crossway Bibles in 2001 CE, states:

> . . . Each word and phrase in the ESV has been carefully weighed against the original Hebrew, Aramaic, and Greek, to ensure the fullest accuracy and clarity and to avoid under-translating

> or overlooking any nuance of the original text. . . . The ESV is an "essential literal" translation that seeks as far as possible to capture the precise wording of the original text and the personal style of each Bible writer. As such, its emphasis is on "word-for-word" correspondence, at the same time taking into account differences of grammar, syntax, and idiom between current literary English and the original languages.

The second Bible featured on the list is the *Catholic Douay-Rheims Bible* which is still used today. It dates back to 1609 CE and states:

> The New Testament of Jesus Christ translated faithfully into English, out of the authentical Latin, according to the best corrected copies of the same, diligently conferred with the Greek and other editions in diverse languages. With arguments of books and chapters, annotations, and other necessary helps for the better understanding of the text, and especially for the discovery of the corruptions of diverse late translations, and for clearing the controversies in religion of these days (printed at Rhemes by John Fogny in 1582). The Holy Bible faithfully translated into English, out of the authentical Latin, diligently conferred with the Hebrew, Greek, and other editions in diverse languages. With arguments of the books and chapters, annotations, tables, and other helps for better understanding of the text, for discovery of corruptions in some late translations, and for clearing controversies in religion (printed at Doway by Laurence Kellam in 1609 and 1610).

The third Bible on the list, *Tanakh, the Holy Scriptures, The Jewish Bible*, is the Jewish Publication Society's (JPS) Bible copyrighted in 1985 and states:

> The Tanakh is an entirely original translation of the Holy Scriptures into contemporary English, based on the Masoretic text. It was made directly from the traditional Hebrew text into the idiom of modern English. It represents the collaboration of academic scholars with rabbis from the three largest branches of organized Jewish religious life in America. Begun in 1955, the ongoing translation was published in three main stages: The Torah in 1962, The Prophets in 1978, and The Writings in 1982. These three volumes, with revisions, are now brought together in a complete English Tanakh, the latest link in the chain of Jewish Bible translations.

In comparing these three Bibles' book contents from three different religions, it is easy to see that in the overall picture, the books are pretty universal. The ESV is standard among the Protestant listing of books within the Bible. The Catholic Douay-Rheims Bible contains the same books, with some names slightly altered (although they are same books as in the ESV). Douay-Rheims also added seven additional books plus the Apocrypha. The Apocrypha (meaning "hidden things" in Greek) are books of the Bible that are considered good for historical significance but were not accepted as Canon (inspired by God) by other religions. The JPS has the same books as the ESV and the Douay-Rheims in the Old Testament except that they are in a different order. There are no New Testament books in a Jewish Bible.

Bibles also contain additional information. Some Bibles contain footnotes of explanation at the bottom of each page. These explanations may be directly connected to the religion that sponsors a particular version of the Bible. A lot of Bibles contain ancient maps and places to note family births, deaths, and marriages. Some Bibles have explanations on Biblical weights and measures, as well as concordances and cross references.

Critics of the Ten Commandments monoliths have spent countless pages in newspaper articles and court documents trying to explain the differences between the Catholic, Protestant, and Jewish versions of the Ten Commandments. If an individual were to ask a priest, a pastor, and a rabbi where the Ten Commandments originate from, all of the religious leaders will direct him to the Bible. Again, all visualizations of the Ten Commandments, whether they are posters, monoliths, cards, or whatever, are only a representation of what is in the Bible.

Following is a verse-by-verse comparison of the three Bibles from Deuteronomy 5:6-22. To put it into context, the book of Deuteronomy (meaning "Second Law") is the retelling by Moses of the teachings and events of Exodus, Leviticus, and Numbers. Moses is giving his farewell address to a new generation of Israelites who are waiting to enter the Promised Land. The purpose of doing this line-by-line comparison of three different versions of the Bible is to demonstrate that as much as they are different, they are even more similar. This section of the Bible is also one of several areas where the Ten Commandments are listed. Please note that there are no enumerations of the Ten Commandments and it takes several verses in some instances to state a Commandment. Some Commandments are contained within one verse. As you can see, the verses' numbers have no relationship to the perceived breakdown of each Commandment:

> 6 I am the Lord your God, who brought you out of the land of Egypt, out of the house of slavery.
>
> 6 I am the Lord your God, who brought you out of the land of Egypt, out of the house of slavery.
>
> 6 I am HaShem thy G-d, who brought thee out of the land of Egypt, out of the house of bondage.
>
> 7 You shall have no other gods before me.
>
> 7 Thou shalt not have strange gods in my sight.
>
> 7 Thou shalt have no other gods before Me.
>
> 8 You shall not make for yourself a carved image, or any likeness of anything that is in heaven above, or that is on the earth beneath, or that is in the water under the earth.
>
> 8 Thou shalt not make to thyself a graven thing, nor the likeness of any things, that are in heaven above, or that are in the earth beneath, or that abide in the waters under the earth.
>
> 8 Thou shalt not make unto thee a graven image, even any manner of likeness, of any thing that is in heaven above, or that is in the earth beneath, or that is in the water under the earth.
>
> 9 You shall not bow down to them or serve them; for I the Lord your God am a jealous God, visiting the iniquity of the fathers on the children to the third and fourth generation of those who hate me,
>
> 9 Thou shalt not adore them, and thou shalt not serve them. For I am the Lord thy God, a jealous God, visiting the iniquity of the fathers upon their children unto the third and fourth generation, to them that hate me,
>
> 9 Thou shalt not bow down unto them, nor serve them; for I HaShem thy G-d am a jealous G-d, visiting the iniquity of the fathers upon the children, and upon the third and upon the fourth generation of them that hate Me,
>
> 10 but showing steadfast love to thousands of those who love me and keep my commandments.
>
> 10 And showing mercy unto many thousands, to them that love me, and keep my commandments.
>
> 10 and showing mercy unto the thousandth generation of them that love Me and keep My commandments.

11 You shall not take the name of the Lord your God in vain, for the Lord will not hold him guiltless who takes his name in vain.

11 Thou shalt not take the name of the Lord thy God in vain: for he shall not be unpunished that taketh his name upon a vain thing.

11 Thou shalt not take the name of HaShem thy G-d in vain; for HaShem will not hold him guiltless that taketh His name in vain.

12 Observe the Sabbath day, to keep it holy, as the Lord your God commanded you.

12 Observe the day of the sabbath, to sanctify it, as the Lord thy God hath commanded thee.

12 Observe the sabbath day, to keep it holy, as HaShem thy G-d commanded thee.

13 Six days you shall labor and do all your work,

13 Six days shalt thou labour, and shalt do all thy works.

13 Six days shalt thou labour, and do all thy work;

14 but the seventh day is a Sabbath to the Lord your God. On it you shall not do any work, you or your son or your daughter or your male servant or your female servant, or your ox or your donkey or any of your livestock, or the sojourner who is within your gates, that your male servant and your female servant may rest as well as you.

14 The seventh is the day of the sabbath, that is, the rest of the Lord thy God. Thou shalt not do any work therein, thou nor thy son nor thy daughter, nor thy manservant nor thy maidservant, nor thy ox, nor thy ass, nor any of thy beasts, nor the stranger that is within thy gates: that thy manservant and thy maidservant may rest, even as thyself.

14 but the seventh day is a sabbath unto HaShem thy G-d, in it thou shalt not do any manner of work, thou, nor thy son, nor thy daughter, nor thy man-servant, nor thy maid-servant, nor thine ox, nor thine ass, nor any of thy cattle, nor thy stranger that is within thy gates; that thy man-servant and thy maid-servant may rest as well as thou.

15 You shall remember that you were a slave in the land of Egypt, and the Lord your God brought you out from there with a mighty hand and an outstretched arm. Therefore the Lord your God commanded you to keep the Sabbath day.

15 Remember that thou also didst serve in Egypt, and the Lord thy God brought thee out from thence with a strong hand, and a stretched out arm. Therefore hath he commanded thee that thou shouldst observe the sabbath day.

15 And thou shalt remember that thou was a servant in the land of Egypt, and HaShem thy G-d brought thee out thence by a mighty hand and by an outstretched arm; therefore HaShem thy G-d commanded thee to keep the sabbath day.

16 Honor your father and your mother, as the Lord your God commanded you, that your days may be long, and that it may go well with you in the land that the Lord your God is giving you.

16 Honour thy father and mother, as the Lord thy God hath commanded thee, that thou mayst live a long time, and it may be well with thee in the land, which the Lord thy God will give thee.

16 Honour thy father and thy mother, as HaShem thy G-d commanded thee; that thy days may be long, and that it may go well with thee, upon the land which HaShem thy G-d giveth thee.

17 You shall not murder.

17 Thou shalt not kill.

17 Thou shalt not murder.

18 And you shall not commit adultery.

18 Neither shalt thou commit adultery.

18 Neither shalt thou commit adultery.

19 And you shall not steal.

19 And thou shalt not steal.

19 Neither shalt thou steal.

20 And you shall not bear false witness against your neighbor.

20 Neither shalt thou bear false witness against thy neighbour.

20 Neither shalt thou bear false witness against thy neighbour.

21 And you shall not covet your neighbor's wife. And you shall not desire your neighbor's house, his field, or his male servant, or his female servant, his ox, or his donkey, or anything that is your neighbor's.'

21 Thou shalt not covet thy neighbour's wife: nor his house, nor his field, nor his manservant, nor his maidservant, nor his ox, nor his ass, nor any thing that is his.

21 Neither shalt thou covet thy neighbour's wife; neither shalt thou desire thy neighbour's house, his field, or his man-servant, or his maid-servant, his ox, or his ass, or any thing that is thy neighbour's.

22 These words the Lord spoke to all your assembly at the mountain out of the midst of the fire, the cloud, and the thick darkness, with a loud voice; and he added no more. And he wrote them on two tablets of stone and gave them to me.

22 These words the Lord spoke to all the multitude of you in the mountain, out of the midst of the fire and the cloud, and the darkness, with a loud voice, adding nothing more: and he wrote them in two tables of stone, which he delivered unto me.

22 These words HaShem spoke unto all your assembly in the mount out of the midst of the fire, of the cloud, and of the thick darkness, with a great voice, and it went on no more. And He wrote them upon two tables of stone, and gave them unto me.

The Ten Commandments are also found in the previous chapters of Exodus. To put it in context, the people of Israel were wandering around in the desert and they came to Mount Sinai. Moses went up the mountain where God talked to him, and then he came back down the mountain and told the people what God said. Then Moses went back up the mountain and told God what the people said. Moses then came back down the mountain and told the people to get ready because God now wanted to talk to them. Moses went up the mountain again while the people waited, came back down, got Aaron, and went back up the mountain. At this point, in Exodus 20, God *spoke* the Ten Commandments directly to the people of Israel.

All of the darkness, thunder, lightning, and trumpet sounds terrified the people and they were afraid to listen to God directly. So Moses went closer to the darkness and God continued with Commandments regarding altars, slaves, hitting people, curses, restitution, and the list goes on.

God continued talking from Chapter 20 through Chapter 31 and a lot of time had passed. When God was done speaking, according to Exodus 31:18 (ESV), "He gave to Moses, when he had finished speaking with him on Mount Sinai, the two tablets of the testimony, tablets of stone, written with the finger of God." Exodus 32:15 (ESV) states, "Then Moses turned and went down from the mountain with the two tablets of the testimony in his hand, tablets that were written on both sides; on the front and on the back they were written."

Moses broke the tablets in Chapter 32, spent some time at the base of Mount Sinai, and in Chapter 34:1 (ESV), God said, "Cut for yourself two tablets of stone like the first, and I will write on the tablets the words that were on the first tablets, which you broke." With that said, Moses went back up the mountain, and God continued to talk with Moses and giving more laws. Exodus 34:28 (ESV) continues, "So he was there with the Lord forty days and forty nights. He neither ate bread nor drank water. And he wrote on the tablets the words of the covenant, the Ten Commandments."

That is what is said in the Bible. Anything outside of that is up for debate. What was exactly inscribed on those tablets is not known. *What is known for sure is that when any form of the Ten Commandments is seen today, it is only a representation of what might have been on those tablets.* Again, any religious leader, when asked where the Ten Commandments came from, would reply that they came from the Bible. These specific Ten Commandments have been referred to as only a representation of all that God has asked of us. The Jewish religion claims 613 Commandments (603 plus the Big Ten). The New Testament has 772 Commandments. Although people tend not to think of the New Testament as having Commandments, there are 772 do's and do not's. Can a specific version of the Bible be used as the only source for the Ten Commandments?

According to Wycliffe International in 2012, out of over 6,800 languages spoken worldwide, there are currently fewer than 2,000 of those languages without any part of the Bible translated. There are 518 languages that have adequate Old and New Testament translations, and 1,275 languages that have only adequate New Testament translations. Wycliffe has participated in work for over half of all languages receiving translated Scripture.

Also, if we question why there are over 213 English versions of the Bible alone, we find that the translations are done in different reading levels – from third grade to twelfth grade (keeping in mind that most newspapers are done at a sixth-grade reading level). Bibles are also translated in word-for-word direct translations out of the Greek and Hebrew (which makes for difficult word flow and readability), thought-by-thought, and paraphrase, all of which may alter original intent and meaning.

Regarding the Ten Commandments monoliths, those individuals who are scrutinizing the Bible for discrepancies between the different versions for the intent of demonstrating that the monoliths are inconsistent and discriminatory to all religions, will find those discrepancies. They will also miss the intent of what the monoliths were meant to be. To pull a Bible off of a shelf and question whether that one version, out of the 213 English versions that are available, was meant to be THE Bible for every person is quite ludicrous. Which version of the Bible an individual reads for spiritual growth is personal. The version may be directly related to his church affiliation, what reading level he is comfortable with, whether he would like a close-as-possible direct translation of the original Hebrew and Greek texts, or whether a paraphrase is more suitable.

If an individual takes the spiritual aspect (faith) out of reading the Bible, then the only things that individual will see and experience are words and stories that have no relationship or meaning to him personally.

Ted Turner has been quoted as saying that he has "read the Bible cover-to-cover more than once" and he is still not sure what it means. The Bible was never intended to be scrutinized for the purpose of taking the content out of context. The original authors were trying to educate future generations. If an individual takes the spiritual aspect (faith) out of reading the Bible, then the only things that individual will see and experience are words and stories that have no relationship or meaning to him personally.

That brings us back to religion. If different versions of the Bible are similar enough so that there is no known break in the Commandments or the exact wording cannot be determined based on the 213 English versions of the Bible, then why do there appear to be different versions of the Ten Commandments based on religion? Generally speaking, if the primary religions are all using the same Bible (initiating from the original Hebrew and Greek texts), than how can there be "different" Commandments?

Religion has been debated through the ages and it will do no good to try to debate it here. Unfortunately, the individuals and groups who wish to remove the monoliths try to make religion one of the major reasons for removal. This may be an unorthodox thought, but where religion is concerned, if the Bible is considered as the main source of Judeo-Christian beliefs regarding religion, any alterations to that main source become man-made rules, and therefore, open to error.

According to *ReligiousTolerance.org*, there are approximately forty main organized world religions. An in-depth look into those religions reveals thousands upon thousands of religions that have broken from the main religions. In every religion, breaks have been made between conservative and liberal factions. There will always be, within any organization (religious or otherwise), individuals who will want to be better, different, more in tune, less restrictive, etc., and will break off and start something new. It only takes one person to say, "I think this is wrong. It must be done this way. I am going to do it on my own. Come follow me because I have the right way." Bingo! A new religion is born. With that new religion, a new man-made interpretation of what the Bible states is also devised.

One example of a man-made change from the original Hebrew and Greek texts was altering the Sabbath from Saturday (Friday sundown to Saturday sundown) to Sunday. It may be argued that the Christians went from Friday to the "Lord's Day," but the bottom line remains that this change was a definitive way to separate the Jews from the Christians. The Muslims also got in on this by making their Sabbath on Friday so that they were neither like the Christians or the Jews.

Some religions have tried to honor what is within the original Hebrew and Greek texts by creating new regulations that will protect the original rules. This is called "building fences." One example of this comes from the Jewish faith. The Bible states in Exodus 23:19 (ESV) that, ". . . You shall not boil a young goat in its mother's milk." To honor and protect that Commandment, kosher law states that meat and dairy cannot be consumed at the same time.

Another example of building fences is taking words from the Bible and creating sacraments, or specific holy rites, in order to protect those words. In 1 Corinthians 11:27 (ESV), "Whoever, therefore, eats the bread or drinks the cup of the Lord in an unworthy manner will be guilty concerning the body and blood of the Lord." Certain denominations of the Lutheran religion, in order to honor and protect those words, exclude people from participating in communion unless they are believers of the same Lutheran denomination.

These are only three examples out of thousands of possibilities, mentioning only three religions that demonstrate what man can do, with good intentions, to revere what is held as sacred and worth defending. This does not make it wrong, nor does it make other practices or rituals wrong. It is just an observation.

In relationship to the Ten Commandments taken right from the pages of the Bible, these words have no numbering sequence. The wording is slightly different in different parts of the Bible. Nonetheless, religious groups have chosen to make mountains out of molehills and vice versa for the sake of ease and clarity for their parishioners. For example, the First Commandment for Catholics, taken from the Catechism of the Catholic Church, reads as follows:

> I am the Lord your God, who brought you out of the land of Egypt, out of the house of bondage. You shall have no other gods before me. You shall not make for yourself a graven image, or any likeness of anything that is in heaven above, or that is in the earth beneath, or that is in the water under the earth; you shall not bow down to them or serve them. It is written: You shall worship the Lord your God and him only shall you serve.

The First Commandment is then broken down into four parts and additional explanations:

- YOU SHALL WORSHIP THE LORD YOUR GOD AND . . . (faith, hope, charity)
- HIM ONLY SHALL YOU SERVE (adoration, prayer, sacrifice, promises and vows, the social duty of religion, and the right to religious freedom)
- YOU SHALL HAVE NO OTHER GODS BEFORE ME (superstition, idolatry, divination and magic, irreligion, atheism, and agnosticism)
- YOU SHALL NOT MAKE FOR YOURSELF A GRAVEN IMAGE

Despite the ongoing critical comments that Catholics removed the Second Commandment regarding graven images, it is definitely included in the First Commandment from a learning perspective in the Catholic faith. They have made the First Commandment so extensive with detailed explanations (longer than a full page), that for print purposes, and also for memorization, it was just summarized into one line.

The Lutheran religion goes in the opposite direction from the Catholic religion. When Martin Luther wrote Luther's Small Catechism, which was meant as a book of instruction for the family, Luther states, "As the head of the family should teach them in a simple way to his household (referring to the Ten Commandments)." The First Commandment, to keep it simple, is:

- "Thou shalt have no other gods."
- And then it questions: What does this mean? Answer – We should fear, love, and trust in God above all things.

This Commandment, as in the Catholic religion, includes graven images because "no other gods" means NO OTHER GODS.

In keeping true with the concept that religions must differentiate themselves from each other, even when it comes to the Ten Commandments, the Catholics and the Lutherans reversed the Ninth and Tenth Commandment from each other in order to mark their differences. There is no intent to single out or ridicule Catholics or Lutherans. There are non-Biblically based doctrines, rules, sacraments, etc., in ALL religions.

Numbering Explanation

The ongoing mantra of people who agonize over the Fraternal Order of Eagles' monoliths and continue to question, "Whose Ten Commandments?" need to step back for a moment, take a deep breath, and offer some grace. It appears that the initial monoliths that were gifted to communities across the United States favored Catholics and Lutherans, which allegedly offended everyone else who had other religious belief systems or no belief structure at all.

It appears that the initial monoliths that were gifted to communities across the United States favored Catholics and Lutherans, which allegedly offended everyone else who had other religious belief systems or no belief structure at all.

The idea of putting the Ten Commandments into the hands of our nation's youth initiated with Judge E. J. Ruegemer. The Judge was a practicing Catholic. Others who were involved with the original design had similar religious backgrounds.

When individuals with these backgrounds think of the Ten Commandments, they instinctively revert back to their Catechism classes of young adulthood and the memorization that was required at that time. "Going with what you know," the last time that I checked into it, was not a criminal offense.

The original design had curled decorations to fill in any spaces just like the cardstock prints and framed versions of the Ten Commandments.

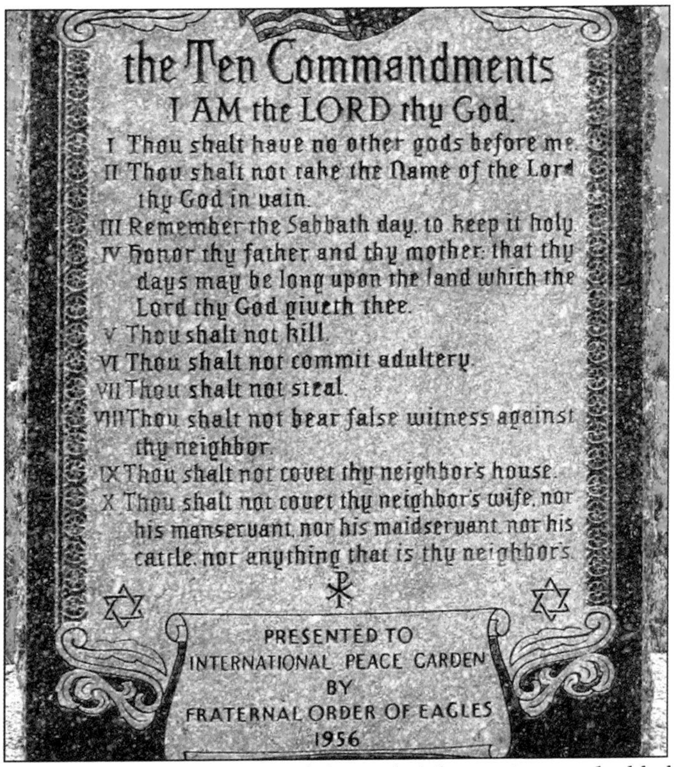

The second design removed the curled decorations and added the DeMille Paleo-Hebrew tablets at the top, but the Ten Commandments remained numbered.

For those individuals who have had a religious upbringing (by attending church or synagogue weekly, participating in Saturday or Sunday school, being confirmed or becoming a bar or bat mitzvah, having to memorize Bible verses or sections of Torah, attending religious or parochial schools, etc.), the "Sunday School Effect" is always close at hand. The constant repetitions of the Lord's Prayer, the Sh'ma, Apostles' Creed, Ten Commandments, liturgy, etc., all become a matter of rote.

Anyone who was ever involved, or who is now involved, in religious training understands that learning a religion as a child means that there are specific things that need to be memorized. Most of those doctrines that required memorization are NOT direct Bible translations, but shortened versions of the "real" thing. All memorization work, when it starts in early childhood, is age-appropriate, and that means taking items of Scripture and doctrine and condensing it into child-size sound bites. Because most vigorous religious training ends by the time a child reaches young adulthood, the shortened versions of doctrine are the ones that "stick." As noted above, each religion has a way of taking what is contained in Scripture and making it their own. The religion that the child was involved with will determine what was memorized.

When the first wave of monoliths was dedicated, people who were not Catholic or Lutheran were quick to point out that the numbering sequence was inconsistent with their religious background. To some individuals, the monoliths seem to be missing a Commandment. By the time the monoliths were being dedicated, thousands of prints and scrolls of the Ten Commandments had already been gifted by the Fraternal Order of Eagles to people all across the country with no known negative consequences. The monolith design was based on the prints.

When the Fraternal Order of Eagles became aware that there were some individuals who took offense to the wording and numbering, they went into action because they never had any desire to offend anyone. Although they were not complacent in this area, the Eagles did remain baffled regarding intermittent uproars over the numbering.

They had to again seek guidance from leaders of various religious organizations to develop a universally acceptable set of Ten Commandments. They referenced the 1958 Interdenominational Public School Format as a guide. The individual Aeries were then given the option to remove the numbering and add additional wording in future monoliths so that people could visualize any numbering system that would seem appropriate to them.

THE TEN COMMANDMENTS

Interdenominational Public School Format as Stated in 1958
The Foundation of Law and Order
Dr. William Bennett

<table>
<tr><th>Episcopal</th><th>Catholic</th><th>Lutheran</th><th>Jewish</th><th>Protestant</th><th>Commandments</th></tr>
<tr><td rowspan="2">1</td><td rowspan="3">1</td><td rowspan="3">1</td><td rowspan="2">1</td><td>Preface</td><td>I am the Lord thy God who brought you out of the house of bondage.</td></tr>
<tr><td>1</td><td>Thou shalt not have other gods before Me.</td></tr>
<tr><td>2</td><td>2</td><td>2</td><td>Thou shalt not make unto thee any graven image.</td></tr>
<tr><td>3</td><td>2</td><td>2</td><td>3</td><td>3</td><td>Thou shalt not take the name of the Lord thy God in vain.</td></tr>
<tr><td>4</td><td>3</td><td>3</td><td>4</td><td>4</td><td>Remember the Sabbath day to keep it holy.</td></tr>
<tr><td>5</td><td>4</td><td>4</td><td>5</td><td>5</td><td>Honor thy father and thy mother.</td></tr>
<tr><td>6</td><td>5</td><td>5</td><td>6</td><td>6</td><td>Thou shalt not murder.</td></tr>
<tr><td>7</td><td>6</td><td>6</td><td>7</td><td>7</td><td>Thou shalt not commit adultery.</td></tr>
<tr><td>8</td><td>7</td><td>7</td><td>8</td><td>8</td><td>Thou shalt not steal.</td></tr>
<tr><td>9</td><td>8</td><td>8</td><td>9</td><td>9</td><td>Thou shalt not bear false witness against thy neighbor.</td></tr>
<tr><td rowspan="2">10</td><td>10</td><td>9</td><td rowspan="2">10</td><td rowspan="2">10</td><td>Thou shalt not covet thy neighbor's house.</td></tr>
<tr><td>9</td><td>10</td><td>Thou shalt not covet thy neighbor's wife.</td></tr>
</table>

The Ten Commandments of any religion may be read in the above unnumbered format.
The format as displayed on classroom posters does not have the numbering as itemized above.
The above breakdown is for the information of the reader of this reprint.

In a letter dated January 21, 1958 to the Honorable Robert W. Hansen, Judge E. J. Ruegemer wrote:

> I am enclosing a photograph of one of the newer monoliths. From examination you will discover a few changes have been made upon the recommendation of our Ministerial Association and our Catholic Bishop with the hope of overcoming any possible objection to the version of the Ten Commandments. First of all, we have deleted the numbers and secondly, we have added some words to the First Commandment. In the way the artist has set this up, the denominations that choose to call the Fourth Commandment the Fifth Commandment may do so. Those who object to the division of the last two may combine them, and even our Jewish friends may regard the words 'I am the Lord thy God' as the First Commandment.

The following design did take away the numbering which had caused a lot of grief. The addition of "Thou shalt not make unto thyself any graven images" was intentionally indented so that it seems to be a part of the Commandment above it, as stated in the Judge's letter ("we have added some words to the First Commandment"). It was unfortunate that someone within the Eagles made the determination not to align these words to the left to signify a different Commandment based on his (or her) view of how the Commandments should, or should not, be numbered. Ironically, only one of the Ten Commandment monoliths was ever corrected in future engravings regarding the indentation.

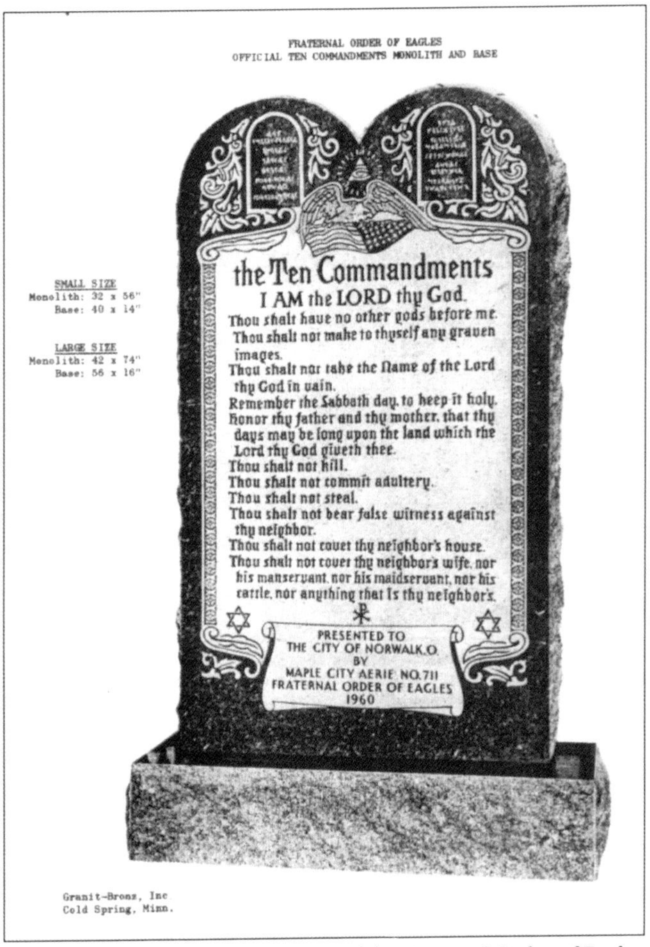

Courtesy of the Fraternal Order of Eagles

Copy of the attachment to letters sent to the Eagle Aeries which was used to promote the newly revised monolith

With that said, there are a few Ten Commandments monoliths throughout the country that have the original numbering and wording on them. This is where grace enters the picture regarding these earlier monoliths.

With the grace aspect in mind, I have developed the "Oh" factor. An individual's understanding (or lack thereof) of the original intent of the Fraternal Order of Eagles' Ten Commandments Project will be revealed by which "Oh" factor is used when he approaches a numbered Ten Commandments monolith. There are basically four "Oh" factors that will also reveal how the presence of such a monolith would be explained to others and what the appropriate reactions should be based on that "Oh" factor. The "Oh" factors are for amusement purposes only. But then again, there are some obvious, universal truths exposed in the "Oh."

With the grace aspect in mind, I have developed the "Oh" factor.

"Oh, how nice" is symbolic of those individuals having come from similar backgrounds as the individuals who originally placed the monoliths. They understand, from their world view, the basic concept of these Commandments as they were given from God, and that following these concepts would create a better world in which to live. They would encourage others to appreciate their significance and have no qualms as to the location of the monoliths.

"Oh, how interesting," if uttered, may appear that these individuals are familiar with these words in stone, and may even follow their guidance, but they note something is a little amiss (the numbering, or the "appearance" that a Commandment is missing). They may also wonder about the monoliths being on public property, but continue on their way. They may possibly enter into conversations regarding the exact wording or the location of the monoliths, but they are comfortable enough with the intent of the message as to not "rock the boat." These individuals would also attempt to explain to others the similarities, and the differences, to their own beliefs, and use these monoliths as an educational tool.

"Oh, how stupid," if an individual actually mocks the monolith's presence and therefore the belief systems from which the monolith came, would lead one to believe that these individuals are just experiencing a lack of education, or showing ignorance, regarding religious beliefs of fellow citizens. Although this "Oh" factor may be annoying to those people in the previous two "Oh" categories, this ignorance, or even lack of judgment, may, and should, be overlooked. These individuals may not have been exposed to various religions, or have walked away from those concepts at the earliest opportunity in their upbringing. Their ridicule just stems from the lack of appreciation, tolerance, or acceptance of others, who believe differently.

The last "Oh" factor, "Oh, how disgusting," is the utterance at the beginning of the thought process about how these monoliths should be removed. These individuals do not have the same convictions as those in the above categories, nor do they care about those convictions. They are not ignorant, nor are they lacking the educational background. Instead, they have formed a near hatred for those beliefs. They are fully aware of the origins of the monoliths, the stories involved with them, the exact locations, etc., and they have made a specific choice, a direct decision, to be intolerant to the extent that the monoliths cannot be allowed to exist AND that everyone should be in agreement that the monoliths should be extinct. This total condemnation disallows the opportunity, even the need, for any possibility of diversity.

With all of these temperamental world views, various interpretations of Biblical texts and Bible translations, and just hard-core gut feelings, it is no wonder that the Fraternal Order of Eagles' Ten Commandments monoliths have created such intense controversies on both sides of the issue.

CHAPTER 6

TAKE THEM DOWN

The simple phrase, "Take Them Down," is difficult for me, at best. The two allegedly problematic issues of forced religious connotations of the Ten Commandments monoliths, and the misunderstood numbering, have been the largest stumbling blocks to keeping the monoliths where they were originally placed. Unfortunately, these issues are not the only concerns of those individuals who want the monoliths removed.

For most individuals, the entire discussion of wanting to remove the Ten Commandments monoliths is incomprehensible. There are several schools of thought as to why they should remain where they stand, but the primary justifications are the historical and cultural aspects that the monoliths have come to represent.

If we look at the timeframe of when the Fraternal Order of Eagles began the discussions of gifting Ten Commandments prints to youth organizations, we are looking at a totally different culture in the United States. This was a time that, albeit not perfect, is referred to as "Norman Rockwell's America."

Rockwell "told stories through his illustrations that reflected idealized views of American life and showed ordinary people doing ordinary things." Rockwell said, "The view of life I communicate in my pictures excludes the sordid and ugly. I paint life as I would like it to be." Robert Stern, a New York-based international architect said, "Rockwell's art mirrors our world – or at least an ideal, slightly lost version of that world. . . . Mom and apple pie are very good institutions, and so was Rockwell's America – despite the presumed shortcomings of its seeming simplifications. Rockwell was really a very fine artist. He captured in ways no one else has how America was, and how a large part of it wants to be."

All across the United States during the 1950s, students were able to see the Ten Commandments posted on their classroom walls as they began the day with the Pledge of Allegiance, prayer, and Bible readings.

The 1950s were a time of post-World War II ideologies: men were working in factories and women were home raising the children. The goals were simple: a three-bedroom/one-bathroom home, a car in the driveway, and the family looking forward to attending church or synagogue once a week. This was a time when blue laws were still on the books that restricted tobacco and alcohol purchases on Sundays. People's habits were changing from listening to live broadcasts on the radio to tuning in to the very large television box with the small screen in the living room.

All across the United States during the 1950s, students were able to see the Ten Commandments posted on their classroom walls as they began the day with the Pledge of Allegiance, prayer, and Bible readings. Children were sent to the principal's office for a paddling if they did not adhere to those Commandments. It goes without saying that it was not all good, perfect, and fair, but this was the norm, and this is what was expected in the school systems. There were complaints and questions regarding some of these established practices, but more for clarification of the guidelines rather than attempting to change the status quo.

This was also the time when patriotism flowed through the bloodstream of almost every American. Fourth of July picnics, Veterans Day parades, Memorial Day observances – these were not days for rushing off to the shopping malls – these were days for national observance and family time. People clambered to have time with their loved ones. Families were not spread out all across the United States. For the most part, children not only grew up with their immediate family, but they had cousins to play with and grandparents to spoil them on a regular basis.

On June 14, 1954, President Dwight Eisenhower signed a bill that would add the phrase "One nation, under God" to the Pledge of Allegiance. On July 11, 1955, the President signed into law that all forms of American currency would display, "In God We Trust" as soon as the printing facilities could update the presses. The first time this was put into practice was when it appeared on the one-dollar silver certificate bill in 1957. Between March 1964 and September 1966, all paper bills being printed declared, "In God We Trust." On July 30, 1956, President Eisenhower approved a Joint Resolution of the Eighty-Fourth Congress which made the national motto of the United States, "In God We Trust."

By the time the Fraternal Order of Eagles began placing Ten Commandments monoliths at courthouses, in parks, and by the entrance ways at city halls, there were little, if any, concerns regarding the words, "I AM the LORD thy God" emblazoned at the top of the Ten Commandments. People came out in droves to the dedications to celebrate and honor these gifts, and felt blessed to have the monoliths in their communities.

It truly was another time in our society, but it is not one that we should try to cover up by removing the signs of those days gone by. Perhaps instead, we should try to protect that part of our heritage and remember what we were a part of at one time. As an alternative to removing the monoliths from the public's eyes, maybe we should share that heritage with our children and grandchildren before there are no memories of a simpler, humbler time.

As our culture has changed, so have the views of having God in the midst of our lives. People have started to question not only the faith of our forefathers, but that of our parents and our peers. Every aspect of our lives is up for scrutiny and challenge, and even the smallest of details is being torn apart to look for ulterior motives and hidden agendas. With that said, this brings us to a few more reasons why "the monoliths must be taken down" in the minds of a few.

Publicity Stunt

One of the many complaints about the monoliths being on public property is the allegation that this was a promotional publicity stunt for Cecile B. DeMille and the film, *The Ten Commandments.* If the timeframes of the movie's creation, production, and opening galas are carefully compared to when the monoliths began appearing in cities across America, the numbers do not match up.

Of the 184 known monoliths, only forty-four were placed prior to 1958. The movie debuted in October 1956, and ran its course over the next year (although it still claims a large television audience on an annual basis). Publicity stunts tend to appear prior to a movie's release and over the first few weeks after the first screening. Even with statistical proof against the accusation of a publicity stunt, it is still worth contemplating the thought process of Cecil B. DeMille when he placed that initial phone call to Judge E. J. Ruegemer.

Just as the Judge was the P. T. Barnum of the Ten Commandments Project, DeMille was the P. T. Barnum of the movie industry. He seemed larger than life with his abilities to not only make memorable epic movies, but also in the promotion of his own masterpieces. It is this side of DeMille that is being portrayed by individuals who claim that DeMille did everything from helping with financing, to coercing acceptance, to promoting the Fraternal Order of Eagles in their endeavors of placing Ten Commandments monoliths in the public arena.

There is no doubt that DeMille was a phenomenal promoter. He went above and beyond all measures during his lifetime to catch the public's eyes, ears, and hearts when it came to his written works, plays, films, and radio broadcasts. He knew the ins-and-outs of managing people on, and off, the stage and screen. His charismatic demeanor drew people to him, and his integrity and goodwill preceded him in his adventures. His political and patriotic stance offended some, and was heralded by others. DeMille seemed to relish his role as the defender of those who had been wronged in the entertainment community when it came to questionable union tactics and blacklisted individuals.

DeMille also had one of the largest studios behind him with Paramount Pictures making and distributing his films. Paramount produced some of the biggest stars of the 1940s and 1950s during a time when studios went from having contract players continually under their wings, to being able to acquire individual artists for their movies. In making a movie like *The Ten Commandments*, the most expensive film ever done to that date ($13.3 million in 1956 which is equivalent to $112.5 million in 2013), Paramount Pictures demonstrated their undeniable trust in Cecil B. DeMille to make a film that would have legions of movie goers to guarantee the financial success of this movie.

Photo courtesy of the DeMille Office

Cecil B. DeMille, an avid Bible reader, often consulted Scripture to ensure the accuracy of his Biblical epics.

The Ten Commandments had everything going for it – a world-renowned director, established and well-loved actors and actresses, innovative special effects, a seemingly unlimited budget which allowed for massive set designs, 15,000 extras, 12,000 animals, detailed props, authentic costuming, masterfully-executed music, and filming in the Beni Yousef Desert in Egypt, as well as massive sound sets in Hollywood. This astronomical production was destined to greatness from its humble beginnings as a 308-page script lined with Bible verses in its margins, to its three hours and forty minutes of visual excellence when it was released on October 5, 1956.

Based on who the public perceived the great Cecil B. DeMille to be based on his life and accomplishments up until the release of *The Ten Commandments* as a director, producer, writer, actor, etc., it would be an easy assumption to make the connection between the movie and the monoliths for financial purposes. It would be naïve NOT to visualize the win/win situation. But when did a win/win situation get to be an undesirable event? And when did the normal course of doing business within the movie industry create such a negative connotation? Movie directors promote their films; stars are sent world-wide to opening-night screenings; and towns hold special promotion events where there are multiple financial benefactors within that community.

Why would a man such as Cecil B. DeMille, with all of the fame and fortune one could desire at that point in time, contact an unknown judge in a small Minnesota town just to promote a movie extravaganza like The Ten Commandments?

Why would a man such as Cecil B. DeMille, with all of the fame and fortune one could desire at that point in time, contact an unknown judge in a small Minnesota town just to promote a movie extravaganza like *The Ten Commandments*? The bottom line is that he would not do such a thing. DeMille had no need, or desire, to promote his latest movie project when he initiated that telephone conversation with Judge E. J. Ruegemer back in 1953.

I would like to suggest an alternate, speculative view based on a man, in the twilight of his years, contemplating the true meaning of his life and legacy.

A politician, when his term in office comes to a close, reflects on his accomplishments and what will be perceived as his greatest contributions to the citizens that he represented. A company CEO, when contemplating his upcoming retirement, takes pride in the direction his organization followed because of his vision and managerial skills. When an individual sees his life coming to a foreseeable end, he usually takes stock of his time here on earth, and he wonders how he will be remembered by those whose lives he has touched.

DeMille was a man who was facing the end of his years and was reflecting inward. The proof of that comes from his writings and words. When DeMille suffered that near-fatal heart attack after climbing a 107-foot ladder to the top of the Per Rameses gate on location in Egypt, his life became more meaningful. He was seventy-three and directing his seventieth, and last, film – he knew he had an opportunity, perhaps a perceived obligation, not only with his film, but with his words. What man would not take a reflective look at his life and make the most of what was left of it?

In an article that was published in 1955 that he wrote for *The Eagle Magazine*, DeMille asked, "What is the final purpose of life?" He questioned his behavior towards his fellow men and his family. He compared material values versus honor, sincerity, and truthfulness. DeMille expressed his enthusiasm for the Fraternal Order of Eagles and their Ten Commandments Project.

When DeMille was addressing the crowd at the New York City opening of *The Ten Commandments* in 1956, he said, "The Ten Commandments are the principles by which man may live with God and man may live with man. They are the expressions of the mind of God for His creatures. They are the charter and guide of human liberty, for there can be no liberty without the law. . . . What I hope for our production of *The Ten Commandments* is that those who see it shall . . . not only be entertained and filled with the sight of a big spectacle, but be filled with the spirit of truth."

These are not the words of a man solely concerned with money-making promotions, but they are the words of a man who has the opportunity to leave a legacy through a film that is filled with hope and promise. With speculation based on Cecile B. DeMille's own writings, it is appropriate and justified to assume that when he contacted Judge E. J. Ruegemer, it truly was in concern for the youth of our country. He was very sincere in his belief that, "The many young people who will know the Commandments better because of the Eagles' work may well apply to themselves the words the Lord spoke here at Sinai long ago: 'I bear you on eagles' wings, and brought you unto myself.'"

Hidden Meanings

The original design of the Ten Commandments prints was created by Brown & Bigelow located in Saint Paul, Minnesota. Their website defines their business as follows: "We have been partnering with businesses for over 100 years. We built our reputation on manufacturing and distributing world class calendar advertising and are one of the promotional product industry's most respected and innovative firms."

After several months of discussions between the Eagles and Brown & Bigelow designers, the Ten Commandment prints were made with the following remarks on the reverse side:

> Your committee, therefore, decided after consultation over a period of several years with the clergy of many denominations, to employ the artists of Brown & Bigelow to prepare an illuminated version of the Ten Commandments, suitable for framing, incorporating a universally acceptable translation of the Ten Commandments from the Old Testament, ornated in multi-color, and including in the art scheme among the symbols and emblems, the American Emblem; the emblem of the Fraternal Order of Eagles; the two tablets of the Ten Commandments; the All-seeing Eye of God, super-imposed on the triangle; the Star of David; the Greek letters of Chi Rho, being the first two letters of Christ. This latter symbol also has the appearance of the intersecting letters PX has been interpreted as an abbreviation of Pax, meaning peace. All this is beautifully carried out in this twenty-by-twenty-six inch illuminated print. At the bottom is a flexible presentation certificate to permit presentation by individual members of the Order, by the subordinate and state Aeries, even inter-fraternal and other groups, through arrangement with the FOE.

The most suggested, and prominent, "conspiracy" symbol on the monoliths appears to be the All-seeing Eye of God. This symbol was taken from the reverse side of the Great Seal of the United States which was first used on the one-dollar Federal Reserve note in 1935, and is still used today on the one-dollar bill. Today, the Great Seal, which is permanently displayed in the Exhibit Hall at the Department of State, is used after the President and the Secretary of State sign the following documents: ratification and proclamations of treaties and other international agreements, and the commissioning of ambassadors, Foreign Service officers, consular officers, and Cabinet officers. The Great Seal is also affixed to envelopes that accredit and recall our ambassadors to foreign countries, and for other ceremonial correspondence from the President to other heads of state of foreign governments. The Department of State is the official keeper of the Seal. The following renderings feature both the front and reverse sides of the Great Seal. The use and explanation of the All-seeing Eye of God is taken directly from the United States Department of State:

Reverse Side of the Great Seal

> The pyramid signifies strength and duration: The eye over it and the motto, Annuit Coeptis (He [God] has favored our undertakings), allude to the many interventions of Providence in favor of the American cause. The date underneath is that of the Declaration of Independence and the words under it, Novus Ordo Seclorum (A new order of the ages), signify the beginning of the new American era in 1776.

Official renderings of the Great Seal of the United States

These renderings were extracted from a PDF version of "Symbols of the Great Seal" poster which was part of a US Diplomacy Center (State Department) Exhibition on the 225th Anniversary of the Great Seal. All materials that were in the exhibit are in the public domain and can be reproduced without permission.

The Fraternal Order of Eagles recognizes "the importance of Divine guidance in favor of the American cause," and thought it would be appropriate to convey this message with the Ten Commandments monoliths.

According to the Fraternal Order of Eagles, "the floral designs and scrolls were considered pleasing to the eyes, easy to replicate on paper and granite, and suitable as decorations no matter where the monoliths were placed."

There are a few individuals who are convinced that the Fraternal Order of Eagles' Ten Commandments monoliths are overflowing with hidden meanings and satanic symbols. They further believe that these symbols were intentionally intertwined to not only fool the general public, but also to bring evil upon this country while demonizing certain groups of people and showering distain upon specific religious organizations. The floral designs at the top and bottom of the monoliths are being touted as Easter lilies that represent Christ's resurrection, hence promoting Christianity. The Eagles have been accused of misusing the federally-protected 4H emblem with the flowers that run along each side of the monoliths because they appear to be four-leaf clovers. Other floral designs purportedly reflect Knights Templar symbols used during the Crusades and currently, with Freemasons and other Masonic organizations.

These conspiracy theories cannot be totally disclaimed, nor can they be held up as being applicable today. All of the people involved with the design of the paper scrolls and prints have passed away. The monoliths are granite replicas of the original prints. If someone chose to independently wreak havoc by including hidden messages in the design of the monoliths, then like so many other pieces of art throughout the centuries, it would be acknowledged as a lone statement of potentially malicious intent.

It was discovered that Michelangelo's frescoes in the Sistine Chapel's ceiling in Rome may include symbols that have secret, negative connotations. There will be no call to repaint the ceiling to cover up the insults to the Pope of Michelangelo's day. The frescoes are what they are. Without meaning to imply that the monoliths are cut from the same artistic cloth as Michelangelo's frescoes, if it is possible that someone at Brown & Bigelow chose to manipulate the artistic design of the Ten Commandments scrolls, and hence the monoliths themselves, then it is as it is. Although it is very improbable, it would still not justify the removal of the monoliths from public land.

Regarding the Fraternal Order of Eagles, in all of the historical documents that have been scrutinized again and again regarding their Ten Commandments Project, no evidence has ever been unearthed that they were involved in any satanic plots, or ritualistic endeavors, through the creation of these monoliths. Although other organizations may use similar symbols that are altered to fit their organizational doctrines and beliefs, the Fraternal Order of Eagles has historically separated themselves from those organizations. The Eagles have also evolved, and removed themselves, from the influences of those other organizations over the years so that they truly are the service organization that they claim to be. This does not mean that the Eagles have turned their backs on meaningful rituals and practices, but it does mean that the shadowing of secret traditions is not a part of who, or what, they are today.

A Few Individuals and Organizations

The intention of this book, from its conception, is to be an overview of events that have happened since the Fraternal Order of Eagles began its Ten Commandments Project in 1948. It is a gathering place in which parts of a puzzle come together to try to tell a story. Unfortunately, there are pieces of this particular puzzle that are missing and may never be found. This part of the story, however, sharing the names of some of the individuals and organizations who have tried to take away a small part of our American heritage, was never intended to be a part of this puzzle. It became very evident early on in this endeavor just how difficult it was going to be to just focus on the facts and not revert back to thirteen years of personal opinions on my part regarding certain individuals and organizations.

After reading hundreds of blogs and articles concerning these monoliths, and after being amazed, flabbergasted, angered, and bewildered by what I read, it became increasingly, and unmistakably, apparent that this is an ongoing problem throughout the journalistic world. There is so much pent-up emotion surrounding these monoliths, both for and against them, that it is extremely difficult not to include personal prejudices when putting thoughts on paper. Facts just seem to get slanted, one way or another, based on which side of the argument an individual chooses to be on.

And yet, it still is important to share some of the names of these individuals and organizations. The clearest way to do this is to disclose information that can be found by anyone using the Internet. The following information is taken directly from the organizations' websites which will almost guarantee that it will be shared in the manner in which the organizations intended. Of course, actually going online will expand your knowledge in more ways than what time and space will allow to be shared within these pages. My intent is to be fair, informational, and without bias, while still presenting two sides of the Ten Commandments Project.

Thomas Van Orden (Austin, Texas)

The most highly visible confrontation with an exacting result regarding the Ten Commandments monoliths occurred in Austin, Texas in June 2005. Thomas Van Orden sued Rick Perry, et al, for having a monolith on the State Capitol grounds. Van Orden was dubbed the "homeless attorney," a name that he despised.

He was indeed homeless, destitute, and lived in a tent in the woods. Van Orden's career once included working in the Army's Judge Advocate General's Office during the Vietnam War, practicing as a criminal defense attorney, getting his pilot's license, and then becoming a flight instructor. Unfortunately, suffering from deep depression, he lost not only his career, but his family as well. Van Orden had his attorney license suspended in 1985, 1989, and 1999 for taking money and never performing the work promised, and for failing to pay fines. He put those days in the past when he gained a new passion. He truly believed that the Ten Commandments monolith did not belong on the Texas State Capitol grounds.

Carrying around a duffle bag with a broken zipper, using reading glasses that he found in a parking lot, taking notes with pens and papers that he found in the trash, Van Orden spent two years studying case law in the State Law Library in the Supreme Court Building in Austin. This was also a place of solitude that granted him refuge from the elements.

Although Van Orden chose to represent himself in his earlier lawsuits, Erwin Chemerinsky, from Duke University during the time of the case lawsuit, was the counsel of record for Van Orden during the US Supreme Court case. The US Supreme Court ruled that the monolith could remain on the Texas State Capitol grounds in Austin. Thomas Van Orden died in 2010 at age sixty-six, and received a military graveside service prior to his burial in a veterans' cemetery.

Red River Freethinkers (Fargo, North Dakota)

According to Judy Keen from *USA Today* in July 2007, "A Ten Commandments monument will remain on the lawn outside City Hall in Fargo, North Dakota, for now, but the City Commission's recent vote to keep it there won't end controversy over the marker."

The Red River Freethinkers, a group of about 100 people who believe that the monument violates the constitutional separation of church and state, will continue to press commissioners to allow them to erect a new marker nearby which would read:

THE GOVERNMENT OF THE UNITED STATES OF AMERICA IS NOT,
IN ANY SENSE FOUNDED ON THE CHRISTIAN RELIGION
From the Treaty of Tripoli, Approved Unanimously by the United States Senate, June 7, 1797
~ Signed by President John Adams ~

Jon Lindgren, a Freethinker and a former Fargo mayor for sixteen years, said the group will "try to figure out a way to bring it up again. We do not want to go to court." He continued, "[The Freethinkers' proposed monument] would balance the Ten Commandments, which is quite provocative from our point of view."

In April 2008, the Red River Freethinkers again requested to place a monument next to the Ten Commandments monolith in Fargo via a lawsuit filed in federal court. The civil suit argued that the city of Fargo violated the Freethinkers' constitutional rights in 2007 when it refused to allow the group to place a monument near the Ten Commandments monolith on city property.

American Atheists (Cranford, New Jersey)

According to their website, "American Atheists, a nationwide movement which defends the civil rights of nonbelievers, works for the separation of church and state, and addresses issues of First Amendment public policy." They have also been pursuing the removal of the Fraternal Order of Eagles' Ten Commandments monoliths for years.

In 1997, Dan Foster, the Idaho State Director for American Atheists in Caldwell, Idaho, proposed that a monument be placed next to the Ten Commandments monolith with the following words:

> An Atheist loves himself and his fellowman instead of a god. An Atheist knows that heaven is something for which we should work now – here on earth – for all men to enjoy. An Atheist thinks that he can get no help through prayer but that he must find in himself the inner conviction and strength to meet life, to grapple with it, to subdue, and enjoy it. An Atheist knows that a hospital should be built instead of a church; a deed done instead of a prayer said. An Atheist strives for involvement in life and not escape into death. He wants disease conquered, poverty vanquished, war eliminated. He wants man to understand and love man. He wants an ethical way of life. He knows that we are our brothers' keeper and keepers of our lives; that we are responsible persons, that the job is here and the time is now.

Foster received the Outstanding Member Award for his local activism and efforts challenging the Ten Commandments monolith according to *The American Atheist Volume 36 No. 1.*

Madalyn Murray O'Hair founded the Society of Separationists in 1963, and later, also founded American Atheists. In 1964, Life magazine referred to O'Hair as the "most hated woman in America" for successfully having prayer and Bible reading removed from public schools the year before. In August 1995, O'Hair, Jon Garth Murray (her son), and Robin (her granddaughter who was the daughter of her other son, Bill Murray), disappeared, along with $600,000 from the American Atheists Trust Fund. Despite speculations and conspiracy theories that surrounded the disappearance of the trio, the American Atheists organization continued to move forward with its message. Five and one half years later in January 2001, on a ranch near Camp Wood, Texas, the O'Hairs' dismembered bodies were found. Sadly, their demise was a horrific plot by an ex-employee and an accomplice who forced O'Hair and her family members to withdraw the funds from the organization. The founding members of these two atheist organizations were then brutally murdered and callously disposed of.

Since that time, there have only been a handful of people who have led the American Atheists. Besides Madalyn Murray O'Hair and her son, Jon, Ellen Johnson was appointed after the Murray O'Hairs' disappearance. She created the Godless Americans Political Action Committee and worked to organize the Godless Americans March on Washington, DC. One of her achievements is the television show, *The Atheist Viewpoint*. Johnson was deposed of her office as president of American Atheists in May 2008.

Frank Zindler served as interim president from May until September 2008, when Dr. Ed Bucker was chosen to lead the organization. In 2010, David Silverman took over as president.

In June 2013, the American Atheists established the first atheist-sponsored monument on US government property at the Bradford County Courthouse in Starke, Florida. They placed an engraved 1,500 pound bench near a Ten Commandments monument which was donated by the Community Men's Fellowship (which is unrelated to the Fraternal Order of Eagles' Ten Commandment monoliths) on National Day of Prayer in May 2012.

Millionaire atheist Todd Stiefel of the Stiefel Freethought Foundation, funded the $6,000 bench after settling a lawsuit filed against Bradford County. American Atheists dropped the lawsuit in May 2013 because they were allowed to place their own monument near the Ten Commandments monument with certain restrictions regarding the content of the engraving. Unfortunately, being totally honest, and keeping historical information in context, was not part of the stipulations.

One of the engravings on the bench references the often misinterpreted Treaty of Tripoli between the United States and the Muslim Barbary nations. President George Washington and his American envoys construed several treaties to try to stop the attacks against American cargo ships that had no means to protect themselves. According to David Barton of WallBuilders:

> The 1797 treaty with Tripoli was one of the many treaties in which each country officially recognized the religion of the other in an attempt to prevent further escalation of a "Holy War" between Christians and Muslims. Consequently, Article XI of that treaty stated: "As the government of the United States of America is not in any sense founded on the Christian religion as it has in itself no character of enmity [hatred] against the laws, religion or tranquility of Musselmen [Muslims] and as the said States [America] have never entered into any war or act of hostility against any Mahometan nation, it is declared by the parties that no pretext arising from religious opinions shall ever produce an interruption of the harmony existing between the two countries."

Other engraved quotes on the American Atheists' bench that are not appropriately put into context are taken from the Bible. When being interviewed by the *Christian Post*, their public relations director, Dave Muscato, stated, "It also includes a ten-point list that parallels the Ten commandments monument, specifying the Biblical punishment prescribed for violating each Commandment, with Biblical citations. Several of the punishments are simply execution."

Summum (Salt Lake City, Utah)

The Summum have lost several city, state, and federal court cases between 2002 and 2010 trying to place monuments of The Grand Principles of Creation next to Ten Commandments monoliths in Duchesne City (which is the only monolith not connected with the Fraternal Order of Eagles), Ogden, and Pleasant Grove City, Utah. They contended that not being able to place their monuments violate their rights based on the First Amendment of the US Constitution in regard to freedom of speech.

In 2012, the Summum went back to court, this time claiming that their rights are being violated regarding the Establishment Clause of the Utah State Constitution. Civil rights attorney, Brian Barnard, had been championing the Summum cause for all of those years, but he died suddenly in his sleep in September 2012. After Summum's losses at the Utah state level, in March 2014, arguments were again heard in the Utah Supreme Court. What is expected to be the final judgment in the Summum v. Pleasant Grove saga will be announced in the summer of 2014 (after this book is published) without the ever-present Barnard. Jay Sekulow, Francis Manion, and Edward White with the American Center for Law and Justice (ACLJ), have litigated all of the Summum cases, and will be there to finalize this last chapter in the Summum case log.

The monument that the Summum would like to place next to The Ten Commandments monolith would be of comparable size engraved with the following Grand Principles of Creation stating Summum's Seven Aphorisms as follows:

THE GRAND PRINCIPLE OF CREATION
"NOTHING AND POSSIBILITY come in and out of bond infinite times in a finite moment." Summum

"The Principles of knowing Creation are Seven; those who know these possess the Magic Key to whose touch all locked doors open to Creation." Summum

THE PRINCIPLE OF PSYCHOKINESIS
"SUMMUM is MIND, thought: The Universe is a Mental Creation." Summum

THE PRINCIPLE OF CORRESPONDENCE
"As above, so below; as below, so above." Summum

THE PRINCIPLE OF VIBRATION
"Nothing rests; everything moves; everything vibrates." Summum

THE PRINCIPLE OF OPPOSITION
"Everything is Dual; everything has an opposing point; everything has its pair of opposites; like and unlike are the same; opposites are identical in nature, but different in degree; extremes bond; all truths are but partial truths; all paradoxes may be reconciled." Summum

THE PRINCIPLE OF RHYTHM
"Everything flows out and in; everything has its season; all things rise and fall; the pendulum swing manifests in everything; the measure of the swing to the right is the measure of the swing to the left; rhythm compensates." Summum

THE PRINCIPLE OF CAUSE AND EFFECT
"Every Cause has its Effect; every Effect has its Cause; everything happens according to Law; Chance is just a name for Law not comprehended; there are many fields of causation but nothing escapes The Law." Summum

THE PRINCIPLE OF GENDER
"Gender is in everything; everything has its Masculine and Feminine Principle; Gender manifests on all levels." Summum

Summum was founded in 1975 by a man born as Claude "Corky" Rex Nowell, (whose last name was changed to King when his mother remarried in 1948, and then changed back to Nowell around 1964), aka, Summum Bonum Amon Ra, who was raised in The Church of Jesus Christ of Latter Day Saints. The facility where the followers of Summum meet is the Summum Pyramid that was completed in 1979 in Salt Lake City, Utah. It is used as a classroom, to create and store the Summum Nectar Publications (sacramental nectars/wines that are used to develop mystical incites and for meditation), and as a place to hold sacred initiations. Summum philosophy states:

> The purpose of Summum is to help you realize your prison and become aware of the blocks you use to build and maintain it. Summum provides tools and an environment to assist you in coming to know and understand yourself. Summum promotes the self-study of your own personal psychology and behavior at the deepest of levels. Through the understanding that you gain, you can free yourself from what you believe to be your mind. You can free yourself from the confining and incarcerating influences of your fears, habits, tendencies, and propensities that you have for so long developed.

The Summum have mummified cats, dogs, and birds, but the founder of Summum, also known as Corky Ra, died at the age of sixty-three in 2008, and became the first human to be mummified in the Summum Pyramid. The process began by soaking his body in mummification solution. For seventy-seven days after his death, Corky Ra was visited in the Summum Pyramid by at least one of his officers who sat with him to read his 'spiritual will' that he wrote prior to his passing which allegedly served as a guide of where his spirit wanted to go. After being soaked, his body was cleaned, covered with lotion, and wrapped in cotton gauze. Then a series of layers were applied to his body including a polyurethane membrane, fiberglass, resin, a bronze mummiform, amber resin, and then a gold leaf coating reflecting a facial likeness and various ancient, Egyptian-like, symbols. Corky Ra is the first known modern mummy and was placed standing on display in the Summum Pyramid.

Freedom from Religion Foundation (FFRF) (Madison, Wisconsin)

In 1989, the Freedom from Religion Foundation (FFRF) went to the Colorado State Court to remove the Ten Commandments monolith that was on Capitol grounds in Denver, Colorado. In 1992, the trial judge ruled that the Ten Commandments were the basis of constitutional law and the monolith could remain. In 1993, the FFRF won the case before the Colorado Court of Appeals to have the monolith removed. The State Supreme Court, in November 1994, reversed the appeals court ruling, and the US Supreme Court, in 1995, refused to take the case, hence leaving the Ten Commandments monolith on the capitol grounds in Denver.

In 1996, attorney Robert R. Tiernaney, past president of the Denver, Colorado, chapter of the FFRF, requested that a monument be placed next to Denver's Ten Commandments monolith that stated:

There are no gods,
no devils, no angels,
no heaven or hell.
There is only
our natural world.
Religion is but
myth and superstition
that hardens hearts
and enslaves minds.

According to Freedom from Religion Foundation, Inc., it is "an educational group working for the separation of state and church." Its purposes, as stated in its bylaws, are "to promote the constitutional principle of separation of state and church, and to educate the public on matters relating to nontheism."

Founded by Anne Nicol Gaylor and her daughter, Annie Laurie Gaylor, FFRF began in 1978 in Wisconsin, and consists of people who consider themselves "freethinkers: atheists, agnostics, and skeptics of any pedigree." They believe that there should be an equal representation of their beliefs next to every Ten Commandments monolith. They have also been cited in lawsuits in La Crosse, Wisconsin (1985), Milwaukee, Wisconsin (2001), and Connellsville and New Kensington, Pennsylvania (2013). Dan Barker and Annie Laurie Gaylor (a husband and wife team), are currently the co-presidents. The twosome host a weekly broadcast on Freethought Radio, and publish *Freethought Today* ten times a year.

Rev. Fred Phelps (Topeka, Kansas)

Rev. Fred Phelps, Sr. was the founder and pastor of the Westboro Baptist Church in Topeka, Kansas since 1955. He repeatedly insisted that a monument needs to be placed next to every

Ten Commandments monolith regarding a young man who was brutally murdered for his sexual orientation in Casper, Wyoming. The monument would have a photo and the following words:

> MATTHEW SHEPARD entered Hell October 12, 1998, in defiance of God's warning at age twenty-one: "Thou shalt not lie with mankind as with womankind; it is abomination." ~ Leviticus 18:22

Rev. Phelps was quoted as saying:

> We adhere to the teachings of the Bible, preach against all forms of sin (e.g., fornication, adultery [including divorce and remarriage], sodomy), and insist that the sovereignty of God and the doctrines of grace be taught and expounded publicly to all men. In 1991, WBC took our ministry to the streets, conducting over 34,000 peaceful demonstrations (to date) opposing the fag lifestyle of soul-damning, nation-destroying filth.

Rev. Phelps, and members of his congregation, have continually protested at various Ten Commandments sites in Casper, Wyoming, and Boise and Nampa, Idaho, to name a few. When the Casper City Council met in October 2003 regarding establishing an historic monuments plaza for placing the Ten Commandments monolith, as well as other historical markers, then-Mayor Barb Peryam stated:

> And for those outsiders who think they can run our city, I say, "Thank you, thank you very, very much." Because, you know what, if you think that we are going to put our monument someplace in cold storage, I've got another thought for you. We are going to put it where it will be more noticed, more taken advantage of, and used for learning purposes by all families. . . . If we are going to be taken to court for this action, then so be it. . . . Bring it on, because this is a battle I firmly believe we can win.

In March 2006, members of Westboro Baptist Church picketed the funeral of Lance Corporal Matthew A. Snyder in Westminster, Maryland, who died in Iraq. His father won a $10.9 million lawsuit against Rev. Phelps and a few members of the Phelps' family in 2007 because the picketers had invaded the family's privacy and inflicted emotional distress during the funeral. Unfortunately, after litigating through the appeal process up to the United States Supreme Court, the decision was reversed in 2011 in favor of Phelps much to the outrage of people all across the United States.

Rev. Fred Phelps, Sr. died on March 20, 2014 at the age of 84 at the Shawnee Mission Medical Center outside of Topeka, Kansas. No public funeral or service marked his life or his passing.

Stephen Michael Schroeder (Indianapolis, Indiana)

Stephen Schroeder damaged the Fraternal Order of Eagles' monolith on five different occasions while it was on the Indiana State House lawn because he maintained that the monolith was "a sneaky pagan plot." In 1991, Schroeder finally broke the monolith in two pieces, and after refusing to pay the $2,500 fine, he spent ninety days in jail. The monolith was repaired in 1998 and rededicated at Aerie 174, but it has since been destroyed and never replaced. Schroeder founded the Protestant Separatist Organization and has stated:

> Just because I challenge Masonic politicians at the State Capitol on their authority to "modify" the Ten Commandments to give preference to Roman Catholics over Protestants (by removing

the second Commandment forbidding graven images), doesn't mean that I am anti-Masonic, for it is their own religious dogma that has identified us as their enemy, the enemy of Freemasonry, we being guilty of religious bigotry for our exclusionary claim of only one way to heaven, only one way to the Father and that is through the only-begotten Son of God, the Word of God. Thus, the Protestant Separatist Organization was born out of necessity in Indianapolis.

American Humanist Association (AHA) (Washington, DC)

According to their website, the American Humanist Association (AHA), founded in 1941, advocates for "progressive values and equality for humanists, atheists, freethinkers, and the non-religious. The AHA has over 20,000 members and supporters and over 160 local chapter groups across the country. With our extensive local and national media contacts, our lobbying and coalition efforts on Capitol Hill, and the efforts of our grassroots activists, we ensure that the humanist point of view is represented – the idea that you can be good without a belief in a god."

"Fair is fair," declared Mel Lipman, a constitutional lawyer and past-president of the AHA. "If Pleasant Grove, Utah, keeps its Ten Commandments monument on the pretext of [US] Supreme Court rulings that allow such religious expressions on public property when included with others, then Pleasant Grove will have to allow others. On the other hand, if the city is willing to give up its Ten Commandments monument, then it can reject the Summum monument."

In 1988, Ted Turner claimed that an alternative to the Ten Commandments was in order so he developed the Ten Voluntary Initiatives. "In anticipation of a Supreme Court victory for Summum, the American Humanist Association is now pursuing the idea of placing stone monuments of Ted Turner's 'Ten Voluntary Initiatives' in every public park that has a Ten Commandments monument. Turner received the Humanist of the Year Award from the American Humanist Association in 1990 and the organization had widely publicized the humanist principles stated in what has been nicknamed, 'The Ted Commandments.'"

Ted Turner's Ten Voluntary Initiatives*

1. I promise to care for planet earth and all living things thereon, especially my fellow human beings.
2. I promise to treat all persons everywhere with dignity, respect, and friendliness.
3. I promise to have no more than one or two children.
4. I promise to use my best efforts to help save what is left of our natural world in its undisturbed state, and to restore degraded areas.
5. I promise to use as little of our non-renewable resources as possible.
6. I promise to minimize my use of toxic chemicals, pesticides and other poisons, and to encourage others to do the same.
7. I promise to contribute to those less fortunate, to help them become self-sufficient and enjoy the benefits of a decent life including clean air and water, adequate food, health care, housing, education, and individual rights.
8. I reject the use of force, in particular military force, and I support United Nations arbitration of international disputes.
9. I support the total elimination of all nuclear, chemical and biological weapons, and ultimately the elimination of all weapons of mass destruction.
10. I support the United Nations and its efforts to improve the conditions of the planet.

*Conceived in 1988/Modified in 2003

Ted Turner, who once called Christianity a "religion for losers," created a $200 million partnership in April 2008 with Lutherans and Methodists to fight malaria in Africa, apologizing for his past criticism of religion, and calling faith a "bright spot" in the world.

American Civil Liberties Union (ACLU) (New York City, New York)

The American Civil Liberties Union (ACLU) made the decision that there should not be any monoliths in Utah. They found eight monoliths, but assumed there was a ninth, so they issued an "action alert" asking for help to find the last monument. They urged the people of Utah to "go visit your local public parks and city buildings to see if the monument is there." The ACLU very proudly announced that "several cities voluntarily removed monuments from public land after receiving our letters and noting the court ruling, and costs, in other Utah cases."

According to the ACLU website in May 2013, with over 500,000 members and supporters, almost 200 staff attorneys, as well as "thousands" of volunteer attorneys, and "constant" lobbying efforts not only in Washington, DC, but also at the state level, their claim to be the "nation's guardian of liberty" is well-founded. The ACLU has done exceptional work protecting people's civil liberties since its founding in 1920, especially fighting for the rights of those individuals who cannot fend for themselves. At times, just a piece of simple correspondence from the ACLU strikes fear and trembling into the heart of the recipient, which is exactly what happened in Utah regarding the removal of several Ten Commandments monoliths. ACLU continues its fight against the monoliths in spirit, as well as in actual campaigns of elimination.

In Frederick, Maryland, Blake Trettien, who was an Urbana High School student in 2002, contacted the ACLU, and with their encouragement and guidance, wrote a letter to the city commissioners requesting that the Ten Commandments monolith be removed from the old Memorial Park. He was quoted as saying, "A lot of people took it very personally, which I guess I didn't expect," after 100 people protested the possible removal, and over 2,000 signatures were obtained to keep the monolith in the park. After that, Trettien enrolled in Johns Hopkins University with nearly a full scholarship as an economics and political major. He was president of the JHU chapter of the ACLU. Trettien won the Student Activist Award, along with a $1,000 check, at the 2002 annual convention of the Freedom from Religion Foundation (FFRF), and he also won the 2006 Abell Foundation Award in Urban Policy for a paper on Baltimore's alleged failed police strategies. Treittien worked as a policy researcher and a community organizer prior to graduating from NYU Law School in 2010. As of May 2013, he was employed as an advocacy and communications officer with the International Legal Foundation.

Americans United for Separation of Church and State (AU) (Washington, DC)

According their website, Americans United for Separation of Church and State (AU), ". . . represents members and supporters in all fifty states and the District of Columbia. We come from different religious, political, and philosophical viewpoints, but we share a common commitment to church/state separation and individual freedom." Its roots sprouted in 1947 with a wide variety of religious, civic, and educational leaders. They have been very active fighting against school vouchers, prayers in political and educational settings, keeping religious symbols off of public property, and anything that may appear to be a "wall of separation between church and state" issue. They have a strong desire to fight "the religious right's courtroom agenda," as well standing against any perceived right-wing organization. Rev. Barry Lynn, an ordained minister in the United Church of Christ, has led this organization since 1992. He is well known in the political realm, as well as in the media, for his commentary and publications.

Ayesha N. Khan, Legal Director for the AU, has filed several lawsuits on behalf of the AU, including the *Amicus Curiae* filed in August 2005 in the Tenth Circuit Court of Appeals for the Society of Separationists against Pleasant Grove, Utah and their Ten Commandments monolith.

Jesse Card received a variation of the Student Activist Award in July 2004 when he was named "Young Activist" at the Freedom from Religion Foundation (FFRF) conference, and was awarded $1,000. Card was the sole plaintiff and original complainant in a federal lawsuit filed by the AU in July 2003 challenging placement of a Ten Commandments monument near the city council chambers by the Fraternal Order of Eagles in Everett, Washington. His acceptance speech included the following:

> . . . After high school, I was coming into work every day on the bus, and the bus stop that I go to is right in front of the police station. So, every day I'd go past and I noticed the Ten Commandments marker. Well, that didn't look right, that's the City Hall, it says on the side. So just a couple of days later, I emailed Americans United for Separation of Church and State. They said they were already aware of it and just that "we're thinking about it." Then, a few months later, they said, "Oh, yeah, well, about that. We are going to do this case, and we'd like you to sign on as a co-plaintiff." So they sent me the papers and I signed on as co-plaintiff, and then I find out that I'm the only plaintiff. A little bit of a surprise, but it worked out fine, because I didn't really care. So long as it gets removed.

The Everett, Washington suit explained that, "Mr. Card is offended by the Ten Commandments display in front of the old city hall because it conveys a message of state endorsements of religion in general, and a specific religious viewpoint in particular, and thereby ostracizes citizens who do not conform to the religious beliefs that the monument expresses."

Center for Inquiry (CFI) (Amherst, New York)

In June 2008, the "Brief of the Center for Inquiry (CFI) and the Council for Secular Humanism as *Amici Curiae* in Support of Neither Party" in the case of Pleasant Grove City v. Summum, stated that, "The Center for Inquiry (CFI) is a nonprofit educational organization dedicated to promoting and defending reason, science, and freedom of inquiry. The Council for Secular Humanism (CSH) is an affiliate of the CFI. Through education, research, publishing, social services, and other activities, including litigation, CFI and CSH encourage evidence-based inquiry into science, pseudoscience, religion, and ethics. CFI and CSH believe that the separation of church and state is vital to the maintenance of a free society that allows for a reasoned exchange of ideas, and have participated as *Amici Curiae* in several Establishment Clause cases before this Court." Their claim is that due to the First Amendment right of freedom of speech, the Summum should be allowed to place their monument next to the Ten Commandments monument in Pleasant Grove City, Utah.

According to Paul Peters of the *Missoula Independent* in 2007, Dan Kelleher of Creston is:

> . . . a Montana man on a mission to keep Christianity out of government, public, and educational institutions. Kelleher makes frequent appearances at events where he believes the line between church and state is being blurred, including Christian seminars held on school property and National Prayer Day events. When he attended the rededication of the [Ten Commandments] monolith near his hometown [Kalispell, Montana], he made sure that he had his opportunity to denounce the event and pointed out that the Commandments "represented just one religion." He has written dozens of letters to Flathead Valley newspapers in support of

atheism and in opposition to what he sees as the encroachment of Christianity on the state. Kelleher has formed the Flathead Free Thought Forum, a social group for local atheists and agnostics, and he had served as a board member of the CFI.

Avrahaum Segol (New York City, New York)

Avrahaum Segol, a native of Wisconsin who has changed his birth name and now has dual Israeli-American citizenship, has been problematic during my research for the Fraternal Order of Eagles' Ten Commandments monoliths. He would be pleased that I mention him, but it is an admitted personal struggle to do so.

I was first approached by Segol through a phone call in which he stated that he was calling from Israel and was doing research regarding religious symbols on government buildings and their meanings, etc. He claimed that he was interested in the Ten Commandments monoliths and would like some information and photos so that he could add the monoliths to his studies. In the early beginning of my research, I was very open with the information that had been entrusted to me. Any requests would be dutifully answered with the hope that the shared information would be educational and assist individuals in coming to an understanding of the historic significance of the monoliths.

Information went back and forth through the mail and using email. There were many conversations with shared family stories and well-wishes granted on both of our accounts. I was interested in Segol's work which, over the phone, seemed upbeat and enlightening. When he finally sent me a part of what he was working on, I was dismayed to learn that everything that I had shared with him was being twisted and taken out of context.

With the maligned works in hand, he was contacting everyone from the Fraternal Order of Eagles' legal department to heads of state demanding that the monoliths be removed because of their supposed hidden meanings in regards to anti-Jewish and pagan symbolism. His rants were not necessarily new, but the way in which he demonized people and organizations were somewhat frightful. When I informed him that our working relationship was over, he went on a full rampage of harassing phone calls and threatening demands. Everything escalated when I reported him to authorities, including Homeland Security.

Segol has since continued his writing campaign with horrific comments and slander. He has attempted to change people's hearts regarding the Ten Commandments monoliths with his hateful speech and twisted lies. It has been a very draining, and time-consuming, effort on my part to do damage control. Segol has temporarily moved on to "bigger fishes to fry." He continues to live with his family in New York City, and perhaps elsewhere as well. He also carries on with his inventions that lead to patents, and works in his garment business.

Jefferson Madison Center for Religious Liberty (Falls Church, Virginia)

Robert V. Ritter was the Counsel of Record for the Appignani Humanist Legal Center and the American Humanist Association (AHA) when the US Supreme Court heard the Pleasant Grove City v. Summum case based on the perceived violation of the Establishment Clause in 2008. This loss has set Ritter on a downward spiral of sheer abhorrence of Judge E. J. Ruegemer and the Fraternal Order of Eagles' Ten Commandments monoliths.

Under the guise of preserving religious liberty, proclaiming the United States is a secular nation, and championing the causes of any removal of God from the public forum, Ritter (founder and president of The Jefferson Madison Center for Religious Liberty) has obsessed over the Ten Commandments monoliths. The home page of his website is dedicated to a continual working draft of his "Supreme Scandal: How the Supreme Court Blessed the Ten Commandments," and his despicable commentary referring to the monoliths as "tombstones" and the US Supreme Court's decision in Austin, Texas in 2005 as "Black Friday." For a person who has never met Judge E. J. Ruegemer, sat in the Judge's court room, or been privy to the dozens of awards and accolades that the Judge received for his exemplary service as a judge and outstanding member of his community, Ritter's degrading, inflammatory statements regarding Ruegemer are unfounded and slanderous. His inferences that Ruegemer may have committed perjury in his affidavits, and that the Eagles' Ten Commandments Project was a charade, along with his insatiable desire to destroy every monolith, belies any dignity of Ritter's legal stature.

After several phone conversations with Ritter, and his off-handed offer of funds for information regarding monolith locations, it became very apparent that this individual will not cease from this path of destruction until all of the parties involved with the Ten Commandments monoliths have been torn apart through legal actions, even if those actions are based on figments of his own very active imagination.

Could there be an Alternative Solution?

From the time that I first viewed a photo of a monolith located in Indiana in a magazine, it became obvious that these monoliths needed to be protected not just on a local level, but from the highest court in the land. I could feel Judge E. J. Ruegemer's pain when the US Supreme Court refused to hear the case in Elkhart, Indiana. This meant that the decision stayed and the monolith had to be removed. There had to be some kind of legal precedent that would shield these monoliths from a change in our nation's culture.

Some towns were already beginning to regret the hasty decisions that were made to tear them down without making attempts at alternative solutions to keep them on public land. Other towns were grateful that they had avoided the high cost of looming court battles. Citizens were at odds with the local officials. Trying to make everybody happy was making no one happy. It was, and still is, a mess. The Ten Commandments monoliths went back to the US Supreme Court in the fall of 2008, and there is no question that they will probably end back there again. If the US Supreme Court does not address all of the Fraternal Order of Eagles' monoliths that are currently on public land, then the battles will continue, and each town will face lawsuit after lawsuit just like Pleasant Grove City, Utah.

The pursuit for the perfect alternative solution ended for me when an Internet search provided a paper written by a then-Valparaiso University law student, Julie Van Groningen, for the *Valparaiso Law Review* in 2004 entitled: *Thou Shalt Reasonably Focus on its Context: Analyzing Public Displays of the Ten Commandments.* This brilliant paper, in all of its legalese, is the answer, not only to the Ten Commandments monolith displays, but to all questionable religious displays (i.e., crèches and menorahs) that have brought copious numbers of lawsuits over the past sixty years. Van Groningen wrote this paper during her second year in law school, has since graduated, and began her legal career as a research attorney and law clerk for the Michigan Court of Appeals.

I am humbled by her attention to detail and the great lengths she went to in making logical, clear-cut points. They are exceptional, well-thought out, and meticulously explained methods of determining the constitutionality of some religious displays versus others. Van Groningen has done a superior job with notes and court cases throughout her paper to explain the legal determinations. The following outline is taken directly from her sixty-two page document so as to not alter any of its meaning. It has been shortened to make it more readable for the lay person by removing the court references. According to Van Groningen:

> When a lawsuit comes before a judge to make a determination whether a religious display is constitutional or not, the judge makes the decision by contemplating what a "reasonable observer" would think when he or she sees the display. The "reasonable observer" factor is different in every judge's mind. This is why a monolith in one town is allowed to stay on public land, and the exact same monolith is ordered to be removed in another town. Judges continually disagree on what the "reasonable observer" sees when looking at monoliths, and this creates inconsistent rulings.
>
> In addition, by just applying the "reasonable observer" standard to public displays of the Ten Commandments, courts have often ignored the civic significance of long-standing displays by focusing primarily on the context of the display. This also prohibits the government from recognizing the Ten Commandments as one of the foundations of American law and leaves that determination in the hands of the "reasonable observer."

Van Groningen proposed a new test to objectively analyze the displays instead of depending on the inconsistent and subjective "reasonable observer" test. She recommends that the judge should first look at the type of display based on the following four categories, and then make the appropriate ruling based on the test for the category that the display fits into. The following information is taken as closely as possible out of Van Groningen's work:

> Category 1. *A newly erected stand-alone display that contains the text of only the Ten Commandments and has **not** gained local civic significance.* A newly erected stand-alone display shall be presumed unconstitutional unless the government can show that several elements in the display, or its context, negate the religious nature of the Ten Commandments.
>
> Elements which could negate the religious nature of the Ten Commandments include: the display's location, the integration of symbols from different religions on the monument, and a plaque recognizing the donor of the monument and stating the purpose in displaying the monument.
>
> Category 2. *An already existing stand-alone display is a display that contains the text of only the Ten Commandments **and** has gained local civic significance.* An already existing stand-alone display shall be presumed constitutional unless it is shown that the religious significance of the display significantly outweighs the civic significance. By presuming that an already existing display is constitutional, this proposed test allows government to recognize the civic significance of the display.
>
> Possible ways to show that the religious nature significantly outweighs the civic nature could include showing that the public controversy regarding the display has not dissipated since the display was erected, or showing that local citizens see the display as a place of worship.
>
> By presuming this display to be constitutional, this proposed test rejects the argument that any display on government property is a per se violation of the Establishment Clause. In addition, by presuming this display to be constitutional, the danger of creating a "jurisprudence of minutiae" is removed. Courts no longer have to analyze where the monument is located in relation to the center of the archway or to the front door of the municipal building.
>
> Category 3. *Originally as part of a historical display when the display contains the text of the Ten Commandments and other historical legal documents and when the first time the disputed*

> *Ten Commandments display was erected, it was within the historical display.* A Ten Commandments monument originally part of a historical display shall be presumed constitutional unless it can be shown that the government lacked any intent to display the Ten Commandments as a historical document. By presuming that a historical display is constitutional, this proposed test allows the government to recognize the historical significance of the Ten Commandments without first determining if a reasonable observer would be able to establish a historical connection between the documents.
>
> Historical displays are granted a presumption of constitutionality because the context of the Ten Commandments – surrounded by historical legal documents – negates the religious nature of the Ten Commandments. In addition, by presuming that the other historical legal documents have negated the religious nature of the Ten Commandments, a court is prevented from declaring a historical display unconstitutional merely because it believes that government did not include the necessary documents.
>
> The context of the display, however, may also be strong evidence to support the opponent's argument that government acted with no intention to display the Ten Commandments as a historical document. For example, the opponents of the display could prove that government had no intention to acknowledge the historical value of the Ten Commandments by showing that the Ten Commandments are double the size of any other document.
>
> Category 4. *As part of a historical display after originally being a stand-alone display when the display contains the text of the Ten Commandments and other historical legal documents and when the disputed display of the Ten Commandments became part of a historical display after it had previously been a stand-alone display.* A Ten Commandments display that is part of a historical display after originally being a stand-alone display shall be presumed constitutional unless it can be shown that the context of the historical display has not significantly negated the religious nature of the Ten Commandments.
>
> This proposed test provides a presumption of constitutionality for these displays to maintain consistency with all historical displays; in appearance there are no differences between historical displays when the Ten Commandments were originally part of the display and when they were not. Though the Ten Commandments were originally displayed as a religious document, the new context negates the religious nature of the Ten Commandments by surrounding them with historical legal documents.
>
> However, because government may have acted with an impermissible purpose in erecting the first display of the Ten Commandments, thereby including the display's history in the context of the historical display, government must put the Ten Commandments in a context that will significantly negate the religious nature of the Ten Commandments and erase any reminders that the Ten Commandments once stood as a stand-alone display. To do this, government may have to change the location of the Ten Commandments monument rather than erect the other monuments at the location of the original Ten Commandments display, or reframe the Ten Commandments to match the other framed documents.

Also according to Van Groningen, although most Ten Commandments displays can easily be placed into one of the four categories, a few clarifications and warnings need to be given:

> First, while stand-alone displays contain the text of only the Ten Commandments, they may also contain engravings and plaques.
>
> Second, a historical display may be a single monument with texts of various documents engraved on it, a series of framed documents, or a series of monuments.

> Because the provided definitions offer no guidelines for when a stand-alone display has gained civic significance, courts will struggle in determining when a stand-alone display has gained local civic significance. Without a doubt, not all cases will be as clear as the Fraternal Order of Eagle displays, many of which stood for thirty-to-forty years without being challenged. On the other end of the spectrum, Judge Roy Moore's monument was surrounded by controversy for the entire two years of its existence.
>
> Although courts may struggle with this issue, a set arbitrary time period for when a display has gained civic significance should not be stated because each display and community is unique and courts need to consider the characteristics of each display and its community. The courts could use the following factors to determine if a display has civic significance: the age of the display, the number of times the display has been relocated, the amount of present controversy regarding the display, the donor of the display and his or her relationship to the community, and any designations labeling the display or its location a historical landmark.

I would like to acknowledge Julie Van Groningen as my personal hero. I have no idea how she was graded on this paper or if it was ever meant to see the light of day in a court room. What I do know is that if her four tests were applied to the Fraternal Order of Eagles' monoliths starting today, there would be no more court battles because the monoliths pass all aspects of constitutionality. In addition, because of the civic and historical context of the monoliths, there would be no mandate to place any other monuments near them from any other organization based on freedom of speech. Thank you, Ms. Van Groningen.

Another means to constitutionally display the Ten Commandments was developed by The Rutherford Institute. According to their website, the Institute was founded in 1982 by constitutional attorney and author John W. Whitehead. It is "a civil liberties organization that provides free legal services to people whose constitutional and human rights have been threatened or violated. . . . It has a twofold mission: to provide legal services in the defense of religious and civil liberties, and to educate the public on important issues affecting their constitutional freedoms."

In a paper prepared by The Rutherford Institute in 2004 entitled, "Affirming Religious and Traditional Heritage: Constitutional Guidelines for Displaying Religious Documents on Public Property," a case was outlined with a five-point plan that should pass all constitutional concerns if the Ten Commandments were displayed with other historical and traditional documents. These points are as follows:

1. The posting is done for an express and legitimate secular purpose, such as affirming the country's diverse civic heritage.
2. The Ten Commandments should not be placed in a position that is more prominent than other documents, such as in height, size, or visibility.
3. Arrangements should include at least several other documents that are predominately nonreligious, such as the Declaration of Independence, portions of the US Constitution including the Preamble, selected Articles, and/or the Bill of Rights, the Magna Carta, state constitutional provisions, the Gettysburg Address, and other federal and state historical documents.
4. Whenever possible, donated private funds should be used for the display.
5. The arrangement as a whole should not appear to create a symbolic union with governmental authority, particularly by being located in close proximity to signs or symbols of governmental authority, such as in entrance areas of government buildings, executive offices, and hearing chambers.

Several cities, in an attempt to appease those who objected to their Ten Commandments monoliths, went through the expense of creating wonderful displays of American heritage using the above guidelines.

In Conclusion

There has been a significant societal switch and unfortunately, we will not be returning to Norman Rockwell's America. There cannot be one man, the likes of Judge Roy Moore in Montgomery, Alabama, making such a strong, and personal, religious stand from his position of authority without severe consequences such as losing that status. It does not matter how many individuals publicly, and privately, supported him. We cannot have protestors like the people in Boise, Idaho willing to serve jail time by attempting to physically stop the court-ordered removal of a monolith. It does not help the cause to have people so wrapped up in their personal convictions that they are willing to disobey the law.

On the other hand, we cannot have one or two individuals like Blake Trettien in Frederick, Maryland, and Jesse Card in Everett, Washington, use their misguided understanding of who and what America was, to sway the courts to remove monoliths against the wishes of the majority of the people in the communities where they stand. It also seems highly inappropriate to have large, anti-religious organizations not only help these individuals, but also threaten other small communities with financial ruin if they choose to keep their Ten Commandments monoliths. These strong-arm tactics coming from out-of-state institutions used in small towns like Roy, Utah and Mishawaka, Indiana seem so incomprehensible.

If our nation as a whole has made such a radical change of beliefs so that it no longer believes that our laws were based on the moral code that is found in the Ten Commandments, than the least we can do is try to protect the heritage and culture that once existed. We owe that to our children, and to our children's children. Somehow over the past few decades, the majority appears to have lost its fight in the cultural battle of what it means to live in America, but that does not mean that we have to remove all vestiges of those days gone by. We can, and must, protect our nation's past. Take them down? I think not.

Somehow over the past few decades, the majority appears to have lost its fight in the cultural battle of what it means to live in America, but that does not mean that we have to remove all vestiges of those days gone by.

Chapter 7

Statistics and Comparisons

Just the Known Facts

When Scott Meyer asked why part of a Commandment was missing on one of the Paleo-Hebrew tablets on a Ten Commandments monolith that he had seen, I was at a loss for words. He sent a photo of what he was referring to, and the monolith on his photo differed slightly than the photo that I was using for reference. That was the beginning of not only trying to locate Fraternal Order of Eagles monoliths, but also attempting to compare them in detail to see how many differences I could find. Although the Fraternal Order of Eagles' Ten Commandments monoliths have many similarities, there are enough differences to keep them as individually unique as the towns in which they appear.

There are the obvious differences, one being their size – the monoliths range from as small as three feet in height up to well over six feet tall. Their widths and depths fluctuate not only in conjunction with their height, but also apparently on a whim. Some monoliths seem to have a slender depth compared to their height, while others appear slightly chunky. The roughness of the granite in the contour around the edges and sides varies from a chiseled effect to a highly polished surface.

Although the Fraternal Order of Eagles' Ten Commandments monoliths have many similarities, there are enough differences to keep them as individually unique as the towns in which they appear.

Several colors of granite have been used, but the colors may be directly related to the types of granite found in the local areas where they were manufactured. In reading several newspaper articles regarding the dedications of monoliths, there have been quite a few references to the monoliths being made of marble. One known monolith is made of concrete, but all of the others are made from granite with varying degrees of color and quality. Photos of the monoliths do not always tell the whole story of their color because of the time of day when the photo was taken, whether it had just rained, or it might even depend on the film and photo processing used at the time.

The engraving of the Ten Commandments monoliths vary from the words used, to the decorations, and even to the accuracy. Even though it has been mentioned previously, and it will be mentioned again, there are errors on the monoliths that are just going to remain. It is not like they can be fixed without doing major damage to the surfaces. These errors could have been made by people who work at the granite companies, but once an error occurred, it was probably duplicated by people taking photos of a monolith and then telling other granite companies to make a monolith "just like the one in the picture." As new Ten Commandments monoliths are created, checking every little detail regarding the monolith before it actually gets engraved – from the Commandments themselves, the numbering, spelling, the Paleo-Hebrew, and even the dedication information (dedication dates would really be helpful) would be a good safeguard.

In looking at the Ten Commandments monoliths from a statistical point of view, the following information is for those individuals who like numbers and comparisons – the "who, where, and how many" of it all.

Over the past thirteen years, I have been able to document and locate 184 known monoliths. Out of those monoliths, four are totally missing (Chicago, Illinois; Great Bend, Kansas; Sparks, Nevada; and Rock Springs, Wyoming), and two are broken (Connersville, Indiana and Murray, Utah), leaving 178 full monoliths in existence. If the documents that I have from the 1950s are accurate, there should be monoliths in Boys Town, Nebraska (1956), Philadelphia, Pennsylvania (1957), Baltimore, Maryland (1957), Morgantown, West Virginia (1957), Youngstown, Ohio (1957), Topeka, Kansas (1957), Bend, Oregon (1957), Miami, Florida (1958), East Grand Forks, Minnesota (1958), Michigan City, Indiana (1958), and Shelbyville, Indiana (1958). I made the error of assumption by physically going to Morgantown, West Virginia and searching for the monolith – big mistake in wasting time and energy.

All of the cities that should have monoliths have been deluged with phone calls, letters, emails, etc., trying to gain cooperation in locating monoliths to no avail. The exception to the lack of support was Laura Shields, Director of the Michigan City Old Lighthouse Museum, and Fern Eddy Schultz at the La Port County Historical Society in Indiana. They went above and beyond trying to locate a Ten Commandments monolith somewhere around Michigan City, Indiana. So, yes, there are more monoliths out there, but I have to have a closing point for this journey, and that is now, so the following information is based on those 184 known monoliths.

Monolith Dedications:

1954-1957	44
1958-1959	24
1960-1964	32
1965-1969	38
1970-1979	35
1980-Present	11

Monoliths were dedicated to:

City	131
County	26
State	7
Honored Person	5
Other	13
Unknown	2

Monoliths were dedicated by:	
Local Aeries	94
Aeries/Auxiliaries	17
States	43
State Aeries/Auxiliaries	21
Grand Aerie	5
Other	2
Unknown	2

Monolith Sizes:	
Small (between three and four feet)	12
Medium (around five feet)	95
Large (around six feet)	68
Extra Large (over six feet)	6
Unknown size	3

Monolith Colors:	
Brown/Brown	4
Brown/Peach	151
Gray	20
Rose	6
Black	1
Unknown color	2

Monolith Types:	
Original (Roman numerals in the mini-tablets)	11
New Style without "graven images" (Paleo-Hebrew mini-tablets)	27
New Style with "graven images"	134
Different style	10
Unknown type	2
Numbered Commandments	47
Commandments not numbered	135
Unknown numbering	2

Where the Monoliths are located:	
State capitals	5
County courthouses	31
Police stations	8
Fire stations	1
City parks	37

Where the Monoliths are located (continued):	
Personal/private	4
Churches	13
Cemeteries	7
Museums	3
Eagle Aeries	19
County libraries	1
City libraries	1
City halls	11
City municipal buildings	7
Down/waiting for a home	2
Other	30
Missing	4

Paleo-Hebrew issues in the mini-tablets:	
Switched Second and Third Commandments	71
Missing Third Commandment	1
Missing Eighth Commandment	1
Missing "No" in the Ninth Commandment	40
Missing "No" in the Tenth Commandment	5
Missing space markers in the Commandments	39
Other miscellaneous errors	20

Miscellaneous:	
Used the word "Lodge"	2
Extra support used for stabilization	8
Missing	4
Partial monolith	2
Relocated by choice or "force"	76
Next to lakes or rivers	9
Lawsuits or serious threats	54
Closed Aeries that gave monoliths	26
Polished backs	6
Smithsonian Institute Research Information System (SIRIS)	3
Explanation signs	9
Plaques	6
British flags	6
Lights	14
Time Capsules	3
No contrast in the engraving	51

Miscellaneous (continued):	
Eagles with dark heads	37
Eagles with light heads	82
Eagle heads with no contrast	62
Eagles with dark bodies	78
Eagles with light bodies	41
Eagle bodies with no contrast	62
Flags carried on pole naturally	100
Flags forced to fly upright	79
No flags	3
Stripes with contrast	115
Stars with contrast	120

This has been just a listing of fun facts to illustrate the incredible amount of minute differences among the Ten Commandments monoliths.

Mini-Tablets and Their Significance

There are some things that are just better off left to the experts. I have been truly blessed to have made the acquaintance of Scott E. Meyer who is a Development Research Analyst in the Office of Alumni Relations and Development at Northwestern University in Evanston, Illinois. Meyer has been researching all aspects of Ten Commandments tablets in print and movies for years. He also has had the privilege of being able to sort through items in the DeMille Archives located at Brigham Young University in Provo, Utah which gives him a truly well-rounded viewpoint of all things having to do with the tablets from *The Ten Commandments* movie and DeMille's personal collection of tablets.

Because the mini-tablets within the Fraternal Order of Eagles' Ten Commandments monoliths are full of interesting stories, Meyer has taken the time and effort to answer copious amounts of questions, along with providing photos and charts for clarification. It was Meyer who shared the following information regarding several flaws contained not only in the mini-tablets, but also in the actual tablets used in *The Ten Commandments* movie. The following information is just a fraction of the work that Meyer has done in tracing the various forms of Moses' tablets through generations of interpretations.

Cecil B. DeMille, who craved authenticity in his historical epics, engaged scholar Ralph Marcus from the University of Chicago's Oriental Institute to help with the design of the tablets for Moses. Marcus turned to archeological artifacts of the ancient near east assuming that the original tablets of law would have followed the conventions of their time and place. Evidence suggested that the monumental tablets would have been inscribed on arched-topped tablets of stone large enough to be seen from a distance, but small enough to be lifted.

According to Meyer's research, DeMille's head researcher noted that the writing was of "an early Canaanite type which came about in the general area of Canaan during the late Bronze Age, which was the era of Moses." Despite that statement, there are no known examples of Israelite writing from that era (1318 BCE to 1234 BCE). The Paleo-Hebrew script that was used on the tablets was found on some of the oldest known examples of Israelite artifacts dating from a more recent period.

Another discrepancy between the tablets from *The Ten Commandments,* and possibly the real tablets, relate to the stone material itself. The movie tablets were inscribed on rock taken from Gebel Musa, one of the several sites believed to be the original site of Mount Sinai. Though the granite in that location is red, legal documents would likely have been inscribed on black tablets. Some now think that red might have been reserved for documents relating to music. Of course, God would use whatever color of rock He would want to use despite what man would do with the color choices available.

As far as the actual text on the tablets, the movie tablets had text that was right aligned with ragged left alignment and blank spaces between the words. Text written in the time of Moses would have been done in a full-justified style, aligned on both the left and the right, and the spaces (if any) between the words would have been taken up by dots to prevent extra letters from being engraved in there which could alter the meaning.

Photo courtesy of Scott E. Meyer
One of many sets of tablets used in *The Ten Commandments*

But the most grievous issue with *The Ten Commandments* tablets concerned the actual wording. Sometime before the movie was released in 1956, but after the first tablets were made for the production of the movie, an error was discovered in them. The tablets were missing the Commandment, "Thou shalt not take the name of the Lord thy God in vain." The movie and all of the publicity shots were already completed with the error on the tablets. Ralph Marcus, who originally designed the tablets, died in December 1956, only two months after the release of the movie.

Photo courtesy of Scott E. Meyer
Cecil B. DeMille's original mini-tablets

Several mini-tablets were also created to resemble the tablets used in *The Ten Commandments.* These miniature versions were given as gifts. One set was given to Barney Balaban who was the president of Paramount Pictures. Judge E. J. Ruegemer received one tablet (fifth through the tenth Commandments). There are currently two and one half sets in the DeMille Archives which leads one to believe that one set was broken up so that Ruegemer could be gifted with his own personal tablet from the original production of the mini-tablets.

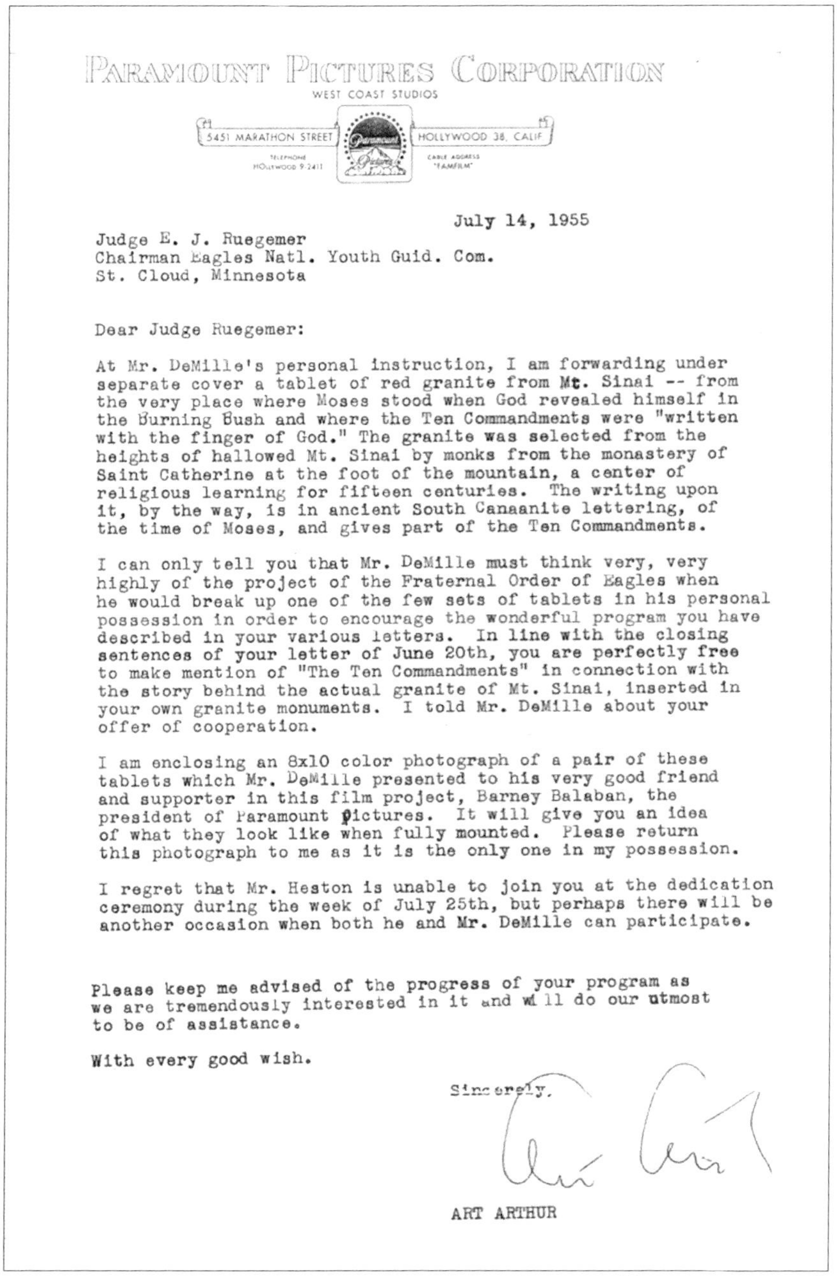

PARAMOUNT PICTURES CORPORATION
WEST COAST STUDIOS
5451 MARATHON STREET HOLLYWOOD 38, CALIF
TELEPHONE HOLLYWOOD 9-2411
CABLE ADDRESS "FAMFILM"

July 14, 1955

Judge E. J. Ruegemer
Chairman Eagles Natl. Youth Guid. Com.
St. Cloud, Minnesota

Dear Judge Ruegemer:

At Mr. DeMille's personal instruction, I am forwarding under separate cover a tablet of red granite from Mt. Sinai -- from the very place where Moses stood when God revealed himself in the Burning Bush and where the Ten Commandments were "written with the finger of God." The granite was selected from the heights of hallowed Mt. Sinai by monks from the monastery of Saint Catherine at the foot of the mountain, a center of religious learning for fifteen centuries. The writing upon it, by the way, is in ancient South Canaanite lettering, of the time of Moses, and gives part of the Ten Commandments.

I can only tell you that Mr. DeMille must think very, very highly of the project of the Fraternal Order of Eagles when he would break up one of the few sets of tablets in his personal possession in order to encourage the wonderful program you have described in your various letters. In line with the closing sentences of your letter of June 20th, you are perfectly free to make mention of "The Ten Commandments" in connection with the story behind the actual granite of Mt. Sinai, inserted in your own granite monuments. I told Mr. DeMille about your offer of cooperation.

I am enclosing an 8x10 color photograph of a pair of these tablets which Mr. DeMille presented to his very good friend and supporter in this film project, Barney Balaban, the president of Paramount Pictures. It will give you an idea of what they look like when fully mounted. Please return this photograph to me as it is the only one in my possession.

I regret that Mr. Heston is unable to join you at the dedication ceremony during the week of July 25th, but perhaps there will be another occasion when both he and Mr. DeMille can participate.

Please keep me advised of the progress of your program as we are tremendously interested in it and will do our utmost to be of assistance.

With every good wish.

Sincerely,

ART ARTHUR

Courtesy of the Ruegemer Family

Copy of the letter from Paramount Pictures, dated July 14, 1955, gifting a Ten Commandments mini-tablet to Judge E. J. Ruegemer

After moving from Milwaukee, Wisconsin to Grove City, Ohio, the Fraternal Order of Eagles' Grand Aerie created a museum-like historical display in the new Headquarters lobby. They unboxed a set of mini-tablets that was dusty and dirty from sitting on top of a file cabinet for years back in Milwaukee. Other than realizing that they were old, and probably related to the Ten Commandments Project from the 1950s, no one really knew how they were actually acquired or from whom. The mini-tablets were cleaned up and placed in the lobby display cabinet.

In gold paint on the back side, one states, "Presented by Fraternal Order of Eagles." The other one states, "To Yul Brynner."

Chuck Cunningham, (who was Assistant to the Grand Aerie Secretary at the time and has since become Grand Secretary), along with many other duties, was responsible for trying to catalogue documents, items, photos, etc., for preservation and posterity, came across the photo below and realized that the mini-tablets were gifted during Law Enforcement Week in Milwaukee, Wisconsin in February 1957. The inscriptions on the reverse side of the mini-tablets, if put together, read, "Presented by Fraternal Order of Eagles To Yul Brynner."

Photo courtesy of the *The Eagle Magazine* (September 2001)

Yul Brynner (Rameses II), during Law Enforcement Week in February 1957 in Milwaukee, Wisconsin, stated, "Man has made 32,600,000 laws. God made only ten, and yet there is no law among all these millions man has made that is not covered with the Divine ones you can count on the fingers of your hands."

Photo courtesy of the Fraternal Order of Eagles

Yul Brynner, Judge. E. J. Ruegemer, and Milwaukee Mayor Frank Ziegler during Law Enforcement Week, Milwaukee, Wisconsin in February 1957

In reference to the mini-tablets that are currently at the Grand Aerie in Ohio, Yul Brynner either did not take his mini-tablets with him when he left Milwaukee in February 1957, or he returned them at a later date. What is interesting to note is that Brynner's mini-tablets were manufactured for the Fraternal Order of Eagles as granite bookends that were to be given to outstanding community leaders per an article from a *Special to the Minneapolis Tribune* (published sometime prior to 1958).

There are a few differences between the Eagles' mini-tablets and DeMille's. The first sets of mini-tablets created for DeMille were done on red granite from the area around Mount Sinai. Judge E. J. Ruegemer's lone mini-tablet is one from the original sets that were missing a Commandment. Corrected versions were made of DeMille's mini-tablets after post production.

Photo courtesy of the Fraternal Order of Eagles

Judge E. J. Ruegemer explaining the Mount Sinai granite used in the creation of Cecil B. DeMille's mini-tablets

The mini-tablets at the Grand Aerie are shaped slightly differently (even though they were about the same size as the original mini-tablet sets), done in a different color of granite, and have all Ten Commandments listed on the two tablets. The writing was also different from DeMille's original mini-tablets – the lines of text were centered and the letters themselves were of a slightly different style of script hinting of a more recent timeframe, still being a Paleo-Hebrew type. There was also one omitted character on line six of the left-handed side tablet.

What is the relevance of all of this information? At some point in time, it was someone's idea to use the design of the mini-tablets at the top of the Ten Commandments monoliths instead of Roman numerals that represented the Ten Commandments. There is no known documentation of who made this decision or exactly when it did occur. It could have been Cecil B. DeMille's idea, or Judge E. J. Ruegemer could have requested permission to use the mini-tablets as an example. The letter dated July 14, 1955 from Art Arthur of Paramount alludes to that possibility, but there is no record of the exact details. What is known is that a new design was created for the Ten Commandments monoliths that not only included the addition of *The Ten Commandments* mini-tablets, but it also marked the time when the change in the wording of the Ten Commandments, and the removal of the numbering, occurred.

The following photo break down, line by line, is the transliterations and English meanings of the Paleo-Hebrew writings on the FOE mini-tablets. This becomes interesting because it is from these specific mini-tablets that a new design was created for the Ten Commandments monoliths.

MINI TABLETS EXPLANATION

Hebrew is read from right to left

The second tablet comes first when displayed on the monoliths

"H*" represents the guttural sound that is similar to that found in the German expression, "ach"

TABLET 2

Paleo-Hebrew Writing	Hebrew Transliteration	Literal English Translation	Non-Denominational Commandment
	Kabed	Honor	5
	et aviH*a v'et imeH*a	Your father and your mother ["your father" is one word] ["your mother" is one word]	5
	Lo tirtzaH*	No murder	6
	Lo tinaf	No adulter	7
	Lo tignov	No steal	8
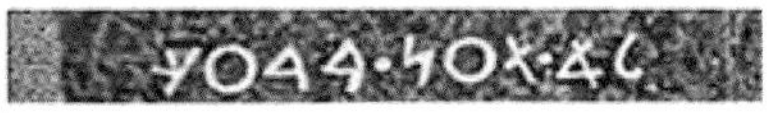	Lo taane v'reaH*a	No false witness bear	9
	ed shaker	against neighbor	9
	Lo tH*mod bet reeH*a	No covet house neighbor	10

TABLET 1

Paleo-Hebrew Writing	Hebrew Transliteration	Literal English Translation	Non-Denominational Commandment
	AnoH*i	I am ["I am" is one word]	1
	YHVH eloheH*a	YHVH your God ["your God" is one word]	1
	Lo yihiye l'H*a	No there will be to you ["there will be" is one word] ["to you" is one word]	1
	elohim aH*erim	gods after me	1
	Lo taase l'H*a pesel	No make for you idol	2
	Lo tisa	No take	3
	et shem YHVH	Name YHVA	3
	ZaH*or et yom	Remember the day	4
	hashabat l'kadsho	the Sabbath to holy ["to holy" is one word]	4

It might prove to be interesting to include Paleo-Hebrew text in a monument, but it did create replicating problems for the engravers of the monoliths. Even though there were photos of the mini-tablets for the engravers to go by, errors continued to be made. Would anyone even notice if there were mistakes in the Paleo-Hebrew characters on top of Ten Commandments monoliths? Unless the mini-tablets on the monoliths are compared character by character, the errors would probably go unnoticed – until now.

Human error is a wonderful thing, and once it is "written in stone," there is not a lot that anyone can do about it. As far as the mini-tablets are concerned, there are a lot of errors – everything from switching the second and third Commandments, omitting Commandments, to taking the word "No" out of the last few Commandments. There are also added spaces and missing spaces. Because the set of mini-tablets that was used as a model is missing an explicit character, that same character is missing on all of the monoliths with mini-tablets.

What is important to take note of is that after all of these years have passed is that these errors cannot be fixed. This also means that the local Aeries who purchased these monoliths are in no way responsible for these engraved inaccuracies. Maybe even the granite manufacturers cannot be held liable because they were only engraving characters that they were given. Unless they were knowledgeable in Paleo-Hebrew, they would have no inkling as to the errors that they were creating. This also, in no way, takes away from the actual intent of the gifting of these Ten Commandments monoliths. For those of us who are detail oriented and fascinated by comparisons, the explanation of the mini-tablets just adds to the ongoing saga of this statistical journey.

Monolith Comparisons – No, They Are Not All Alike

The following photos are meant to illustrate the differences in the Ten Commandments monoliths. Not only will colors, font differences, and quality of granite be noticeable, but there will also be photos of brokenness, errors, and oddities. This is not meant to criticize or embarrass those who have these monoliths in their possession because there may not be a definitive person or organization to blame. Even if there was, it really should not be an issue after all of these years – the monoliths are what they are.

As I have mentioned before, human error, vandalism, time, or whatever, has caused some of these issues. That is what makes these specific Ten Commandments monoliths so interesting. If they were all identical and perfect, then this God-given journey would have been boring. Just like each of us, with all of our faults and frailties, so are these Ten Commandments monoliths.

Beautiful granite coloration

Backs

The following pages are just some samples of some of the differences located on the backs of the monoliths.

Vandalism at a Police Department

Natural stone look

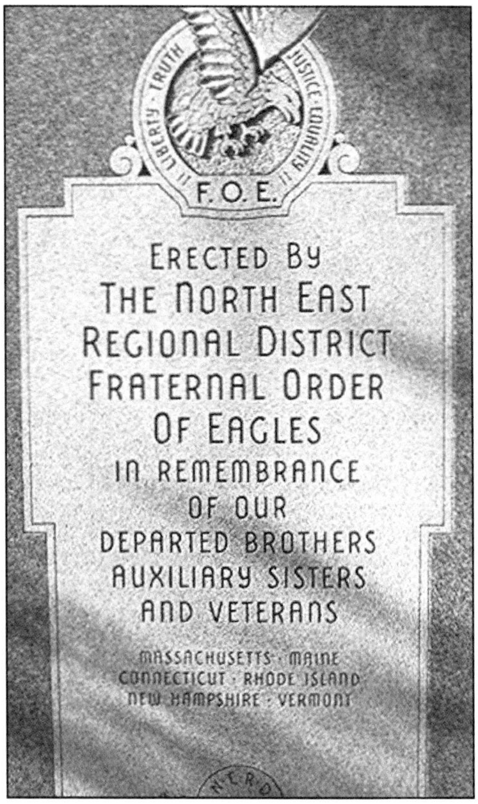

Written words

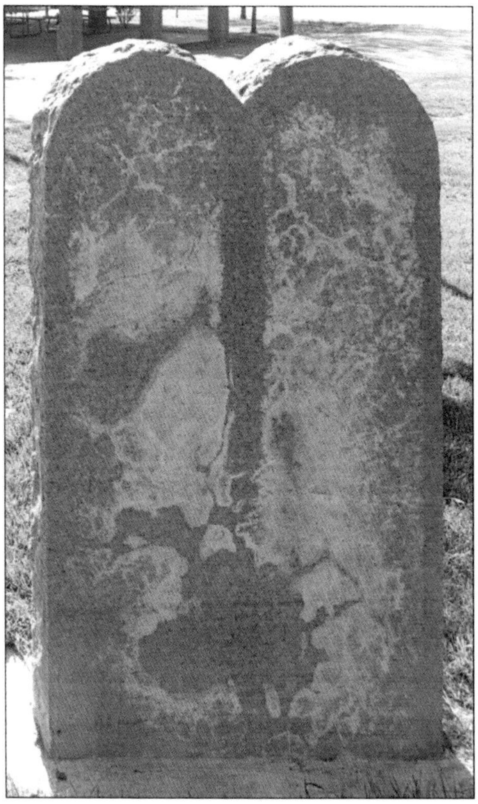

Could be the granite, but more likely from being laid down

Written words

Highly polished back

Vandalism and granite coloring

Paint to possibly cover up vanalism

Vandalism and interesting colorization

Written words

Beautiful granite coloring

This vandalized monolith had to be sandblasted leaving visible lines

Beautiful vein of color within the granite

This used to be the front with the Ten Commandments until is was broken

Bases

It was amazing to discover all of the ways that Ten Commandments monoliths can be displayed. These are only a few of the examples. What stood out regarding these bases was not only the different kinds of materials used (granite, concrete, bricks, stone, etc.), but also the sizes of some of bases – everything from being nonexistent to being over a foot tall. The landscaping surrounding the monoliths either added, or detracted, from the overall look of the Ten Commandments monoliths.

FRATERNAL ORDER OF EAGLES
NOVEMBER 1957

DSB

FRATERNAL ORDER OF EAGLES
APRIL 28, 1973

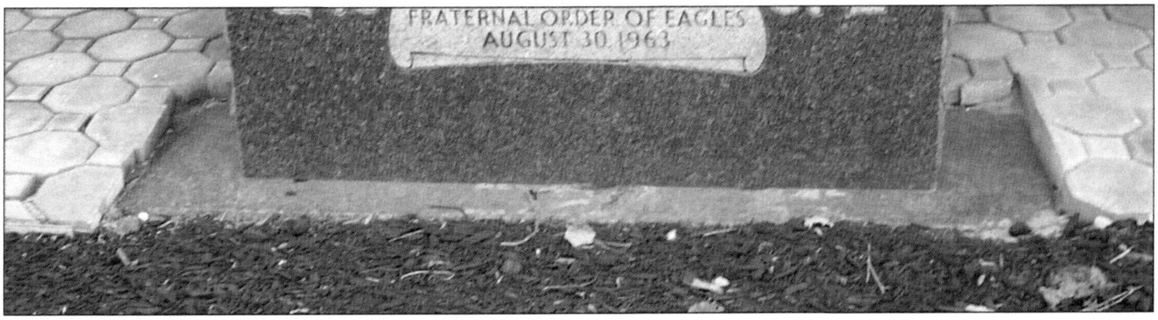
FRATERNAL ORDER OF EAGLES
AUGUST 30 1963

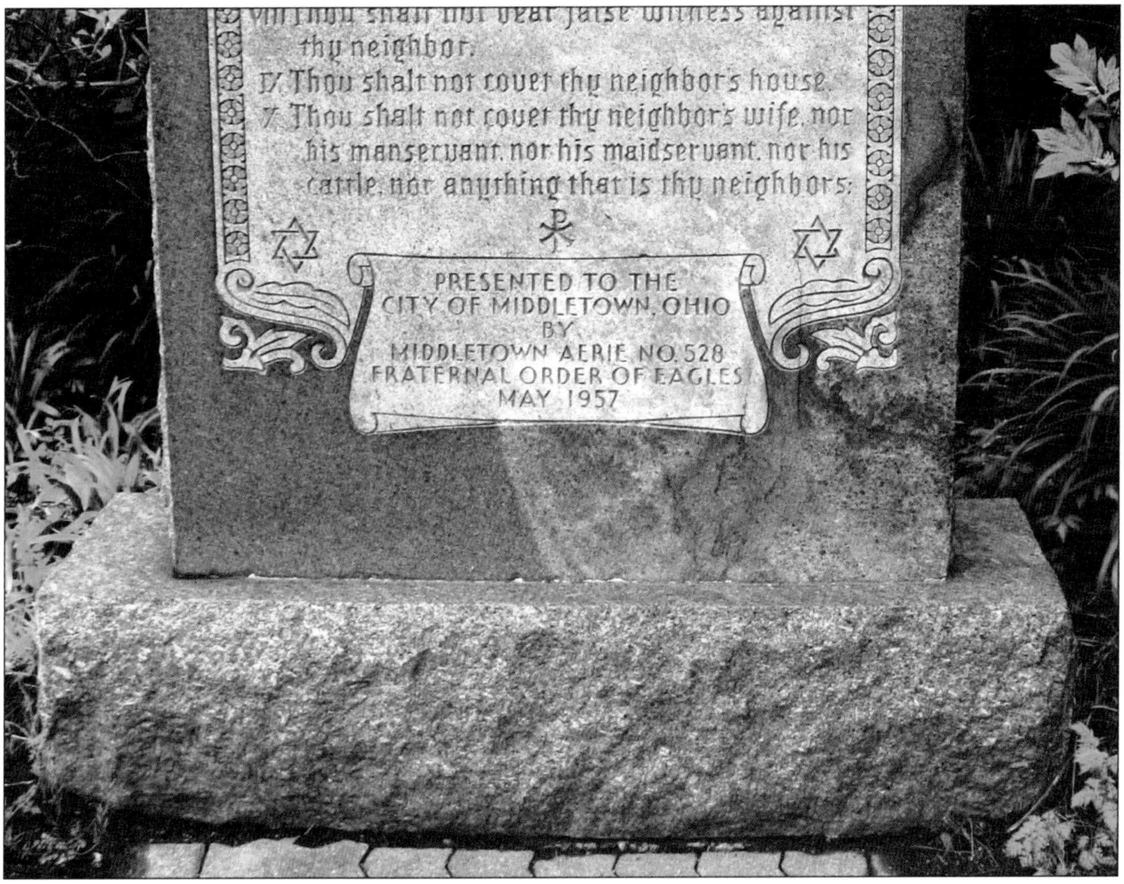
thy neighbor.
IX Thou shalt not covet thy neighbor's house.
X Thou shalt not covet thy neighbor's wife, nor his manservant, nor his maidservant, nor his cattle, nor anything that is thy neighbors.
PRESENTED TO THE
CITY OF MIDDLETOWN, OHIO
BY
MIDDLETOWN AERIE NO. 528
FRATERNAL ORDER OF EAGLES
MAY 1957

CHAMPION
FRATERNAL

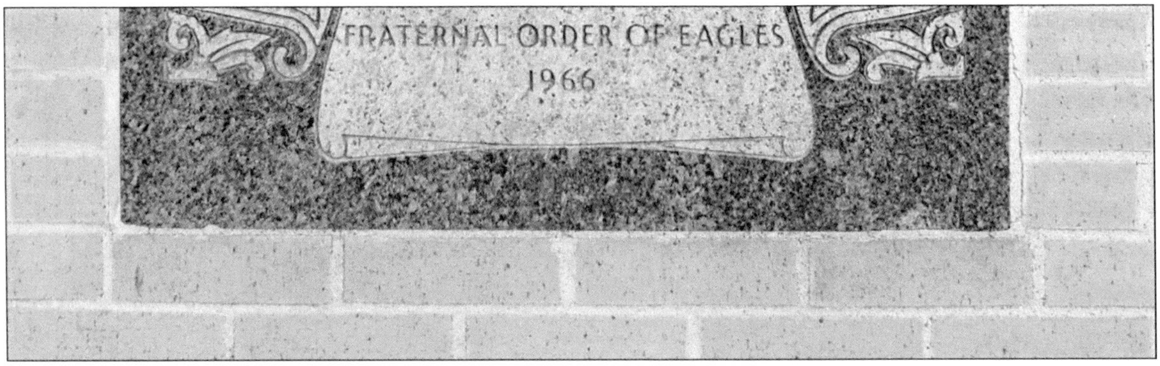
FRATERNAL ORDER OF EAGLES
1966

DEDICATED JUNE 29, 1958

FRATERNAL ORDER OF EAGLES
1967

BY
STATE COUNCIL OF THE
FRATERNAL ORDER OF EAGLES
JULY 15, 1967

VII Thou shalt not steal.
VIII Thou shalt not bear false witness against thy neighbor
IX Thou shalt not covet thy neighbors house
X Thou shalt not covet thy neighbors wife, nor his manservant, nor his maidservant, nor his cattle, nor anything that is thy neighbors.
PRESENTED TO SUNSET MEMORIAL PARK BY FRATERNAL ORDER OF EAGLES OCTOBER 1956

FRATERNAL ORDER OF EAGLES
OF ARIZONA
1964

FRATERNAL ORDER OF EAGLES

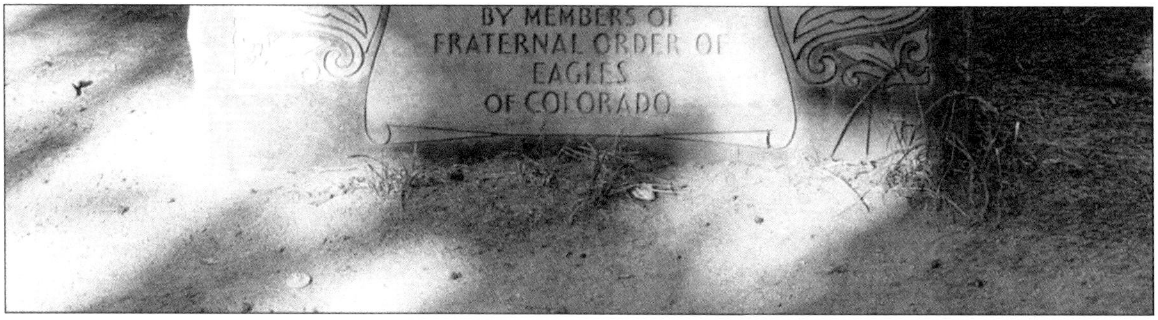
BY MEMBERS OF
FRATERNAL ORDER OF
EAGLES
OF COLORADO

PRESENTED TO
IDAHO YOUTH RANCH BY
IDAHO STATE AERIE AND
IDAHO STATE AUXILIARY
FRATERNAL ORDER OF EAGLES
JUNE 1969

cattle, nor anything that is thy neighbors.
PRESENTED TO THE CITY OF
GLENWOOD SPRINGS
BY
GLENWOOD SPRINGS AERIE NO. 215
FRATERNAL ORDER OF EAGLES
OCTOBER 5, 1957

FRATERNAL ORDER OF EAGLES

FRATERNAL ORDER OF EAGLES
1972

FRATERNAL ORDER OF EAGLES

FRATERNAL ORDER OF EAGLES
1990

MAY 12, 1957

FRATERNAL ORDER OF EAGLES

FRATERNAL ORDER OF EAGLES
JUNE 1972

FRATERNAL ORDER OF EAGLES
SEPTEMBER 1957

FRATERNAL ORDER OF EAGLES
1983

FRATERNAL ORDER OF EAGLES
JUNE 1976

FRATERNAL ORDER OF EAGLES
JUNE 1971

FRATERNAL ORDER OF EAGLES
1963

Broken Monoliths

Murray Park Arboretum Monument Vandalism 1980s

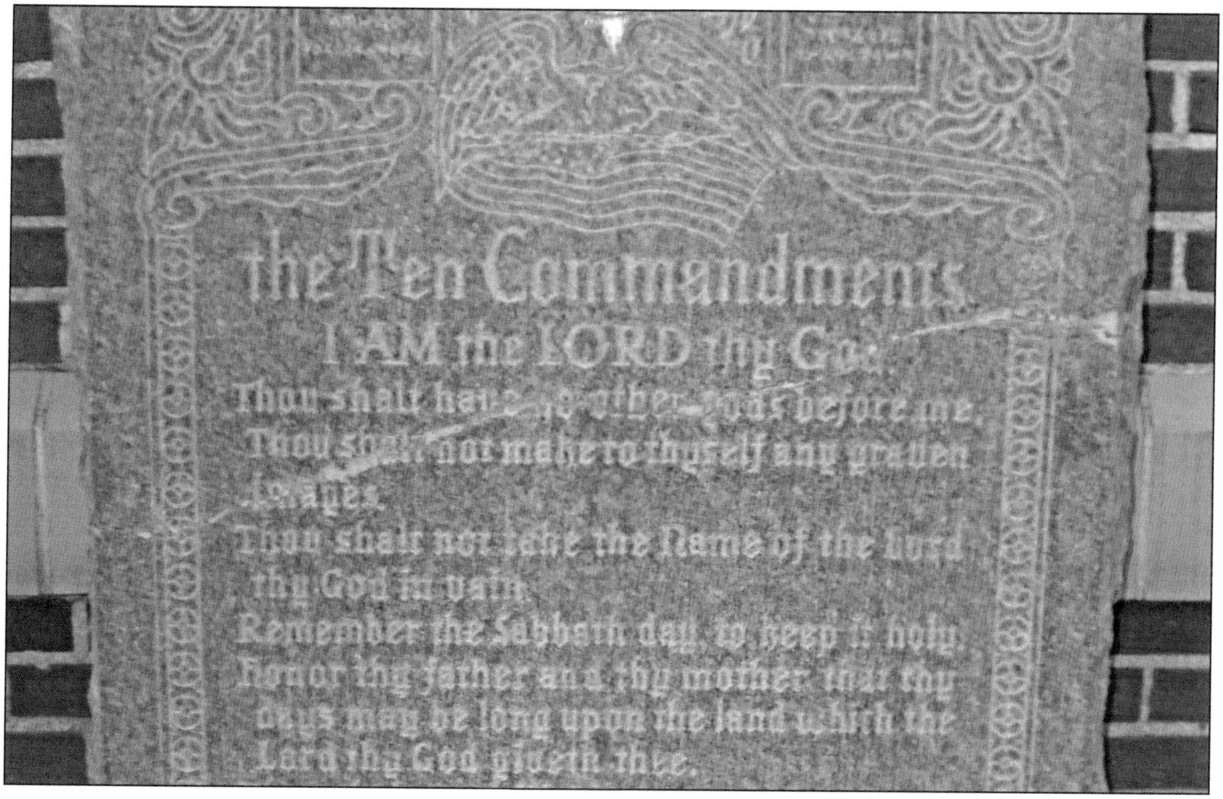
the Ten Commandments
I AM the LORD thy God
Thou shalt have no other gods before me.
Thou shalt not make to thyself any graven images.
Thou shalt not take the Name of the Lord thy God in vain.
Remember the Sabbath day, to keep it holy.
Honor thy father and thy mother that thy days may be long upon the land which the Lord thy God giveth thee.

PRESENTED TO
AND BARTON COUNTY

Eagles

The differences in the eagles on the Ten Commandments monoliths were amazing. How these photos were cropped not only shows the eagles, but also the flags and the All-Seeing Eye of God. The eagles are everything from majestic to almost bizarre. The heads of these eagles have some really drastic differences in how they were etched into the granite that varies the size and look of the actual head of the eagle. They have dark heads and light bodies, light heads and dark bodies, all dark, all light, no contrast, etc. The wings can be slightly flattened to flaring. The flags range from having no contrast, to having only the stripes contrasted, or only the stars contrasted, or any mixture in between. The flags have varying numbers of stripes and stars. The eagle either carries the flag naturally on a pole, or the flag has been forced into an upright position. Some monoliths have both the British flag and the American flag, or none at all. The All-Seeing Eye of God varies in contrast and sunbursts. I found it all very entertaining and fascinating.

en Commandm

en Commandm

en Commandm

TEN COMMANDME

e Ten Commandmen

en Commandm

en Commandm

en Commandm

en Commandm

en Commandm

en Commandm

Explanation Signs

Several monoliths had explanation signs and these are just samples of some of the words that were used. The signs were made out of several different kinds of materials such as granite, metal, wood, and plastic. They were located in front of, or next to, the monoliths.

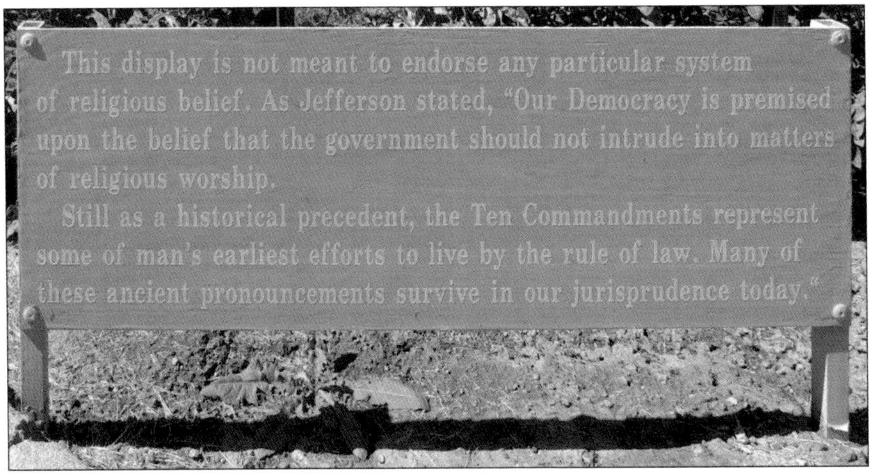

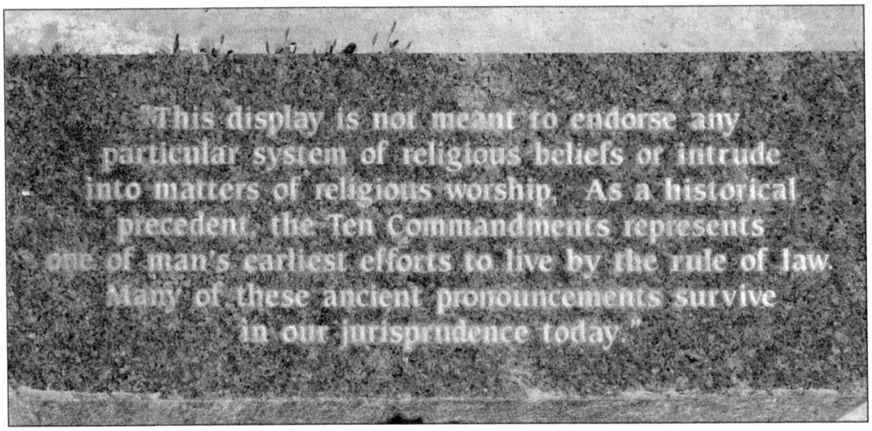

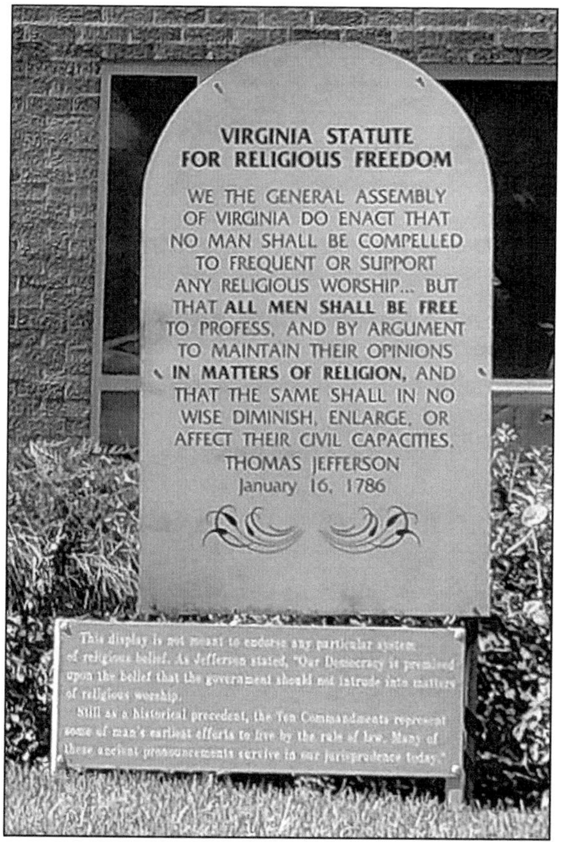
VIRGINIA STATUTE
FOR RELIGIOUS FREEDOM
WE THE GENERAL ASSEMBLY OF VIRGINIA DO ENACT THAT NO MAN SHALL BE COMPELLED TO FREQUENT OR SUPPORT ANY RELIGIOUS WORSHIP... BUT THAT ALL MEN SHALL BE FREE TO PROFESS, AND BY ARGUMENT TO MAINTAIN THEIR OPINIONS IN MATTERS OF RELIGION, AND THAT THE SAME SHALL IN NO WISE DIMINISH, ENLARGE, OR AFFECT THEIR CIVIL CAPACITIES.
THOMAS JEFFERSON
January 16, 1786
This display is not meant to endorse any particular system of religious belief. As Jefferson stated, "Our Democracy is premised upon the belief that the government should not intrude into matters of religious worship.
Still as a historical precedent, the Ten Commandments represent some of man's earliest efforts to live by the rule of law. Many of these ancient pronouncements survive in our jurisprudence today."

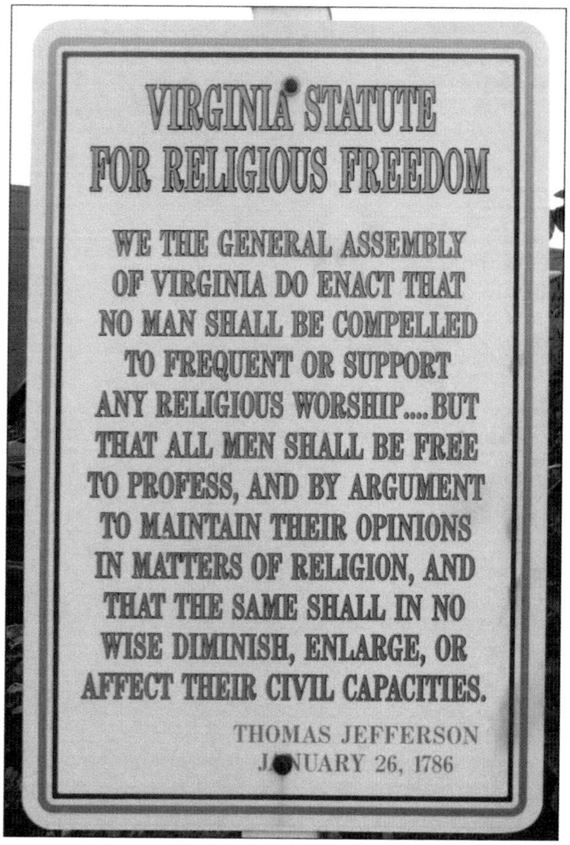
VIRGINIA STATUTE
FOR RELIGIOUS FREEDOM
WE THE GENERAL ASSEMBLY OF VIRGINIA DO ENACT THAT NO MAN SHALL BE COMPELLED TO FREQUENT OR SUPPORT ANY RELIGIOUS WORSHIP....BUT THAT ALL MEN SHALL BE FREE TO PROFESS, AND BY ARGUMENT TO MAINTAIN THEIR OPINIONS IN MATTERS OF RELIGION, AND THAT THE SAME SHALL IN NO WISE DIMINISH, ENLARGE, OR AFFECT THEIR CIVIL CAPACITIES.
THOMAS JEFFERSON
JANUARY 26, 1786

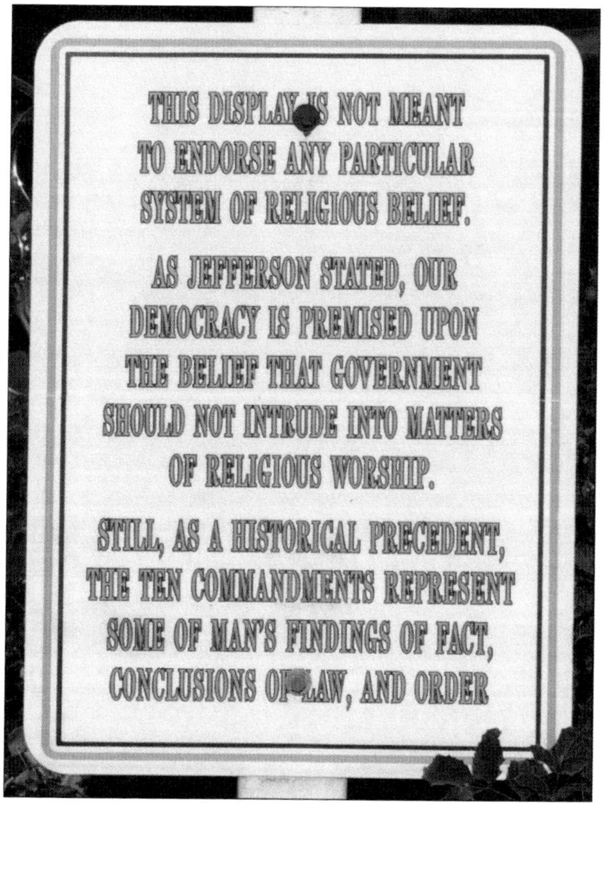
THIS DISPLAY IS NOT MEANT TO ENDORSE ANY PARTICULAR SYSTEM OF RELIGIOUS BELIEF.
AS JEFFERSON STATED, OUR DEMOCRACY IS PREMISED UPON THE BELIEF THAT GOVERNMENT SHOULD NOT INTRUDE INTO MATTERS OF RELIGIOUS WORSHIP.
STILL, AS A HISTORICAL PRECEDENT, THE TEN COMMANDMENTS REPRESENT SOME OF MAN'S FINDINGS OF FACT, CONCLUSIONS OF LAW, AND ORDER

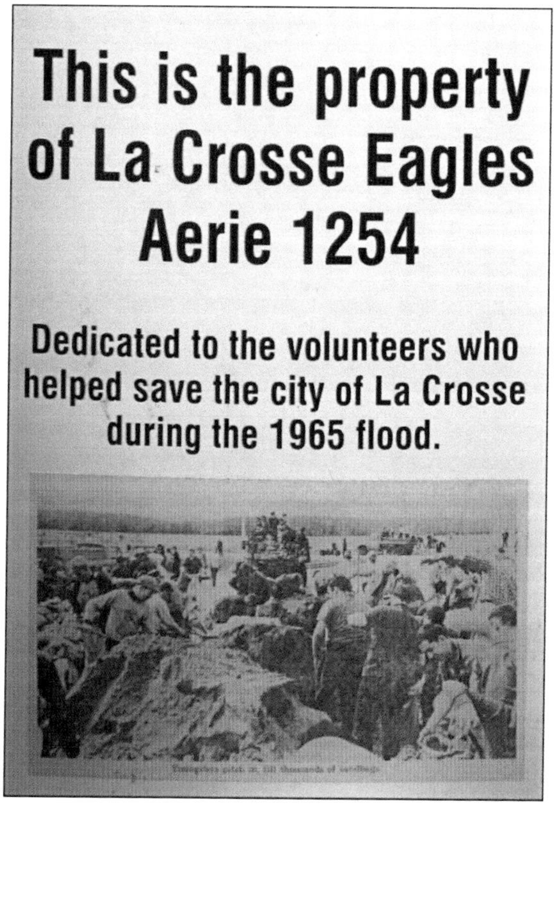
This is the property of La Crosse Eagles Aerie 1254
Dedicated to the volunteers who helped save the city of La Crosse during the 1965 flood.

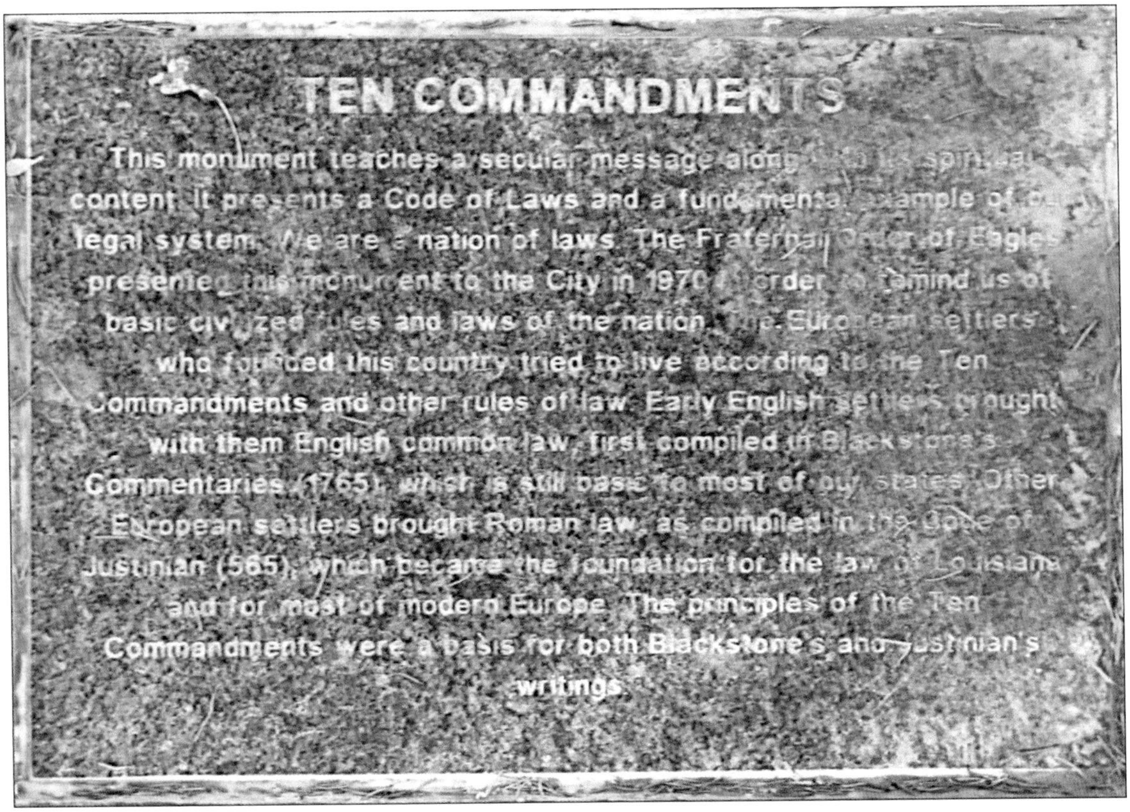
TEN COMMANDMENTS
This monument teaches a secular message along
content. It presents a Code of Laws and a fundamental
legal system. We are a nation of laws. The Fraternal Order of Eagles
presented monument to the City in 1970 order remind us of
basic civ zed les and laws of the nation. European settlers
who ded this country tried to live according the Ten
Commandments and other rules of law. Early English brought
with them English common law, first compiled in Blackstone's
Commentaries (1765), which is still basic to most of our states. Other
European settlers brought Roman law, as compiled in the of
Justinian (565), which became the foundation for the law of Louisiana
and for most of modern Europe. The principles of the Ten
Commandments were a basis for both Blackstone's and Justinian's
writings.

SEAL OF THE CITY OF CASPER, WYOMING
WELCOME TO HISTORIC MONUMENTS PLAZA
THE FOUNDING FATHERS OF THE UNITED STATES UNDERSTOOD THAT SOCIETIES CANNOT EXIST WITHOUT LAW. BUT THEY ALSO UNDERSTOOD THAT THE POWER TO ENFORCE LAW COULD BE SUBVERTED INTO A MEANS OF OPPRESSION. THE AMERICAN SYSTEM SOUGHT TO BALANCE THIS CONFLICT BY BUILDING A LEGAL SYSTEM UPON THE PRINCIPLES OF EQUALITY BEFORE THE LAW, INDIVIDUAL RIGHTS, AND GOVERNMENT FOR THE GOOD OF THE PEOPLE. THESE PRINCIPLES ARE WOVEN THROUGHOUT THE CONSTITUTION AND THE OTHER FOUNDING DOCUMENTS OF OUR NATION.
HISTORIC MONUMENTS PLAZA SEEKS TO HONOR THESE PRINCIPLES BY TRACING THEIR ORIGINS THROUGH TIME. ALL GREAT IDEAS EVOLVE, AND THESE PRINCIPLES ARE NO EXCEPTION.
THE CASPER CITY COUNCIL WOULD LIKE TO EXTEND ITS THANKS TO THE CITIZENS OF THE CITY OF CASPER, WITH PARTICULAR THANKS TO THE SPONSORS, FOR THEIR SUPPORT OF THIS PLAZA AND ITS EDUCATIONAL

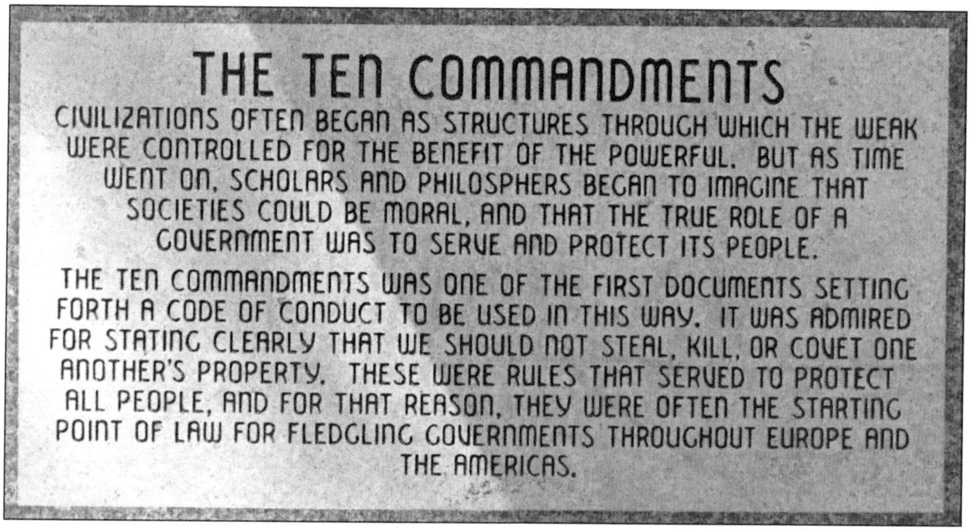
THE TEN COMMANDMENTS
CIVILIZATIONS OFTEN BEGAN AS STRUCTURES THROUGH WHICH THE WEAK WERE CONTROLLED FOR THE BENEFIT OF THE POWERFUL. BUT AS TIME WENT ON, SCHOLARS AND PHILOSPHERS BEGAN TO IMAGINE THAT SOCIETIES COULD BE MORAL, AND THAT THE TRUE ROLE OF A GOVERNMENT WAS TO SERVE AND PROTECT ITS PEOPLE.
THE TEN COMMANDMENTS WAS ONE OF THE FIRST DOCUMENTS SETTING FORTH A CODE OF CONDUCT TO BE USED IN THIS WAY. IT WAS ADMIRED FOR STATING CLEARLY THAT WE SHOULD NOT STEAL, KILL, OR COVET ONE ANOTHER'S PROPERTY. THESE WERE RULES THAT SERVED TO PROTECT ALL PEOPLE, AND FOR THAT REASON, THEY WERE OFTEN THE STARTING POINT OF LAW FOR FLEDGLING GOVERNMENTS THROUGHOUT EUROPE AND THE AMERICAS.

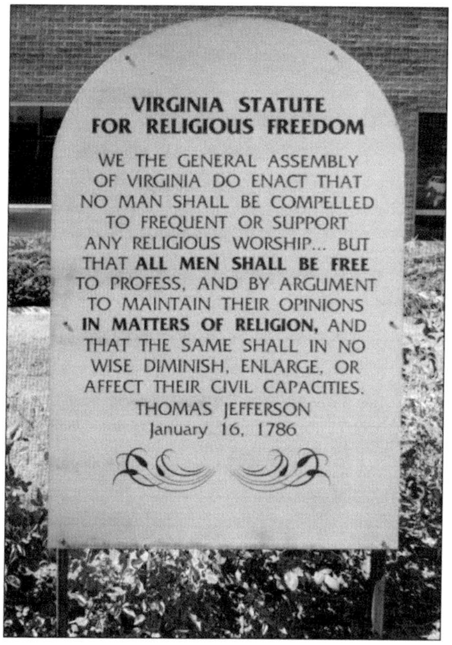
VIRGINIA STATUTE FOR RELIGIOUS FREEDOM
WE THE GENERAL ASSEMBLY OF VIRGINIA DO ENACT THAT NO MAN SHALL BE COMPELLED TO FREQUENT OR SUPPORT ANY RELIGIOUS WORSHIP... BUT THAT ALL MEN SHALL BE FREE TO PROFESS, AND BY ARGUMENT TO MAINTAIN THEIR OPINIONS IN MATTERS OF RELIGION, AND THAT THE SAME SHALL IN NO WISE DIMINISH, ENLARGE, OR AFFECT THEIR CIVIL CAPACITIES.
THOMAS JEFFERSON
January 16, 1786

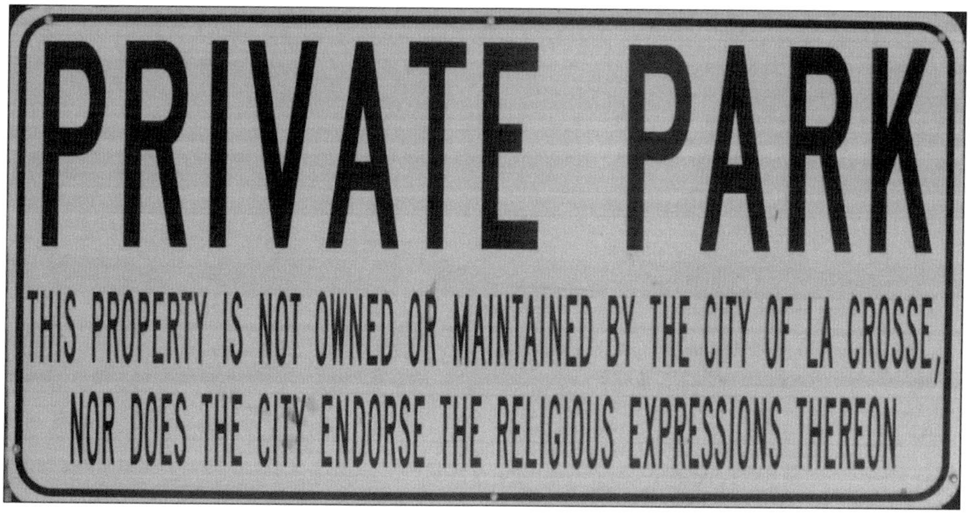
PRIVATE PARK
THIS PROPERTY IS NOT OWNED OR MAINTAINED BY THE CITY OF LA CROSSE,
NOR DOES THE CITY ENDORSE THE RELIGIOUS EXPRESSIONS THEREON

Property of
GITT-MOUL
Historic Properties
PUBLIC WELCOME

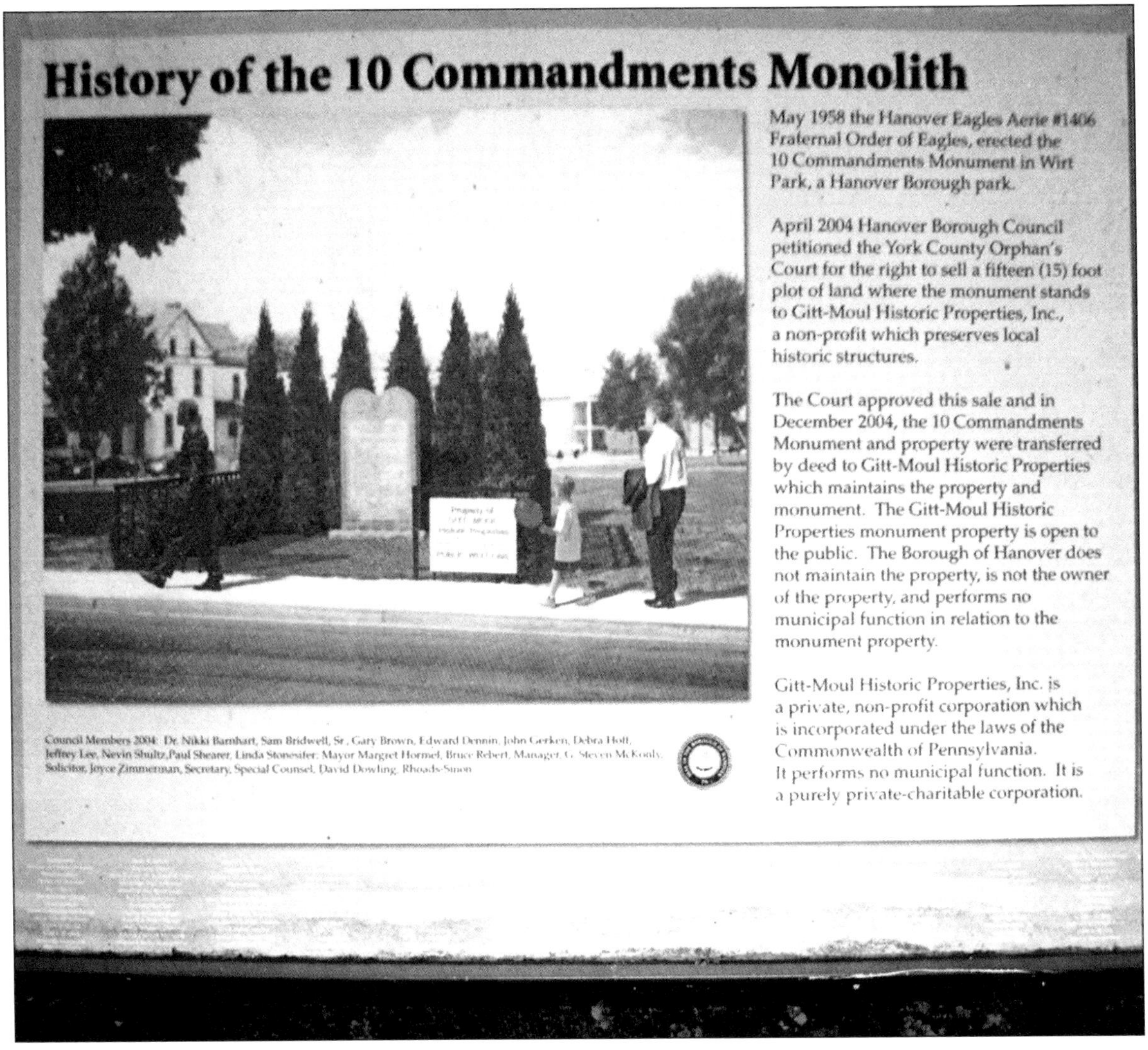
History of the 10 Commandments Monolith
May 1958 the Hanover Eagles Aerie #1406 Fraternal Order of Eagles, erected the 10 Commandments Monument in Wirt Park, a Hanover Borough park.
April 2004 Hanover Borough Council petitioned the York County Orphan's Court for the right to sell a fifteen (15) foot plot of land where the monument stands to Gitt-Moul Historic Properties, Inc., a non-profit which preserves local historic structures.
The Court approved this sale and in December 2004, the 10 Commandments Monument and property were transferred by deed to Gitt-Moul Historic Properties which maintains the property and monument. The Gitt-Moul Historic Properties monument property is open to the public. The Borough of Hanover does not maintain the property, is not the owner of the property, and performs no municipal function in relation to the monument property.
Gitt-Moul Historic Properties, Inc. is a private, non-profit corporation which is incorporated under the laws of the Commonwealth of Pennsylvania. It performs no municipal function. It is a purely private-charitable corporation.
Council Members 2004: Dr. Nikki Barnhart, Sam Bridwell, Sr., Gary Brown, Edward Dennin, John Gerken, Debra Holt, Jeffrey Lee, Nevin Shultz, Paul Shearer, Linda Stonesifer. Mayor Margret Hormel, Bruce Rebert, Manager, G. Steven McKonly, Solicitor, Joyce Zimmerman, Secretary, Special Counsel, David Dowling, Rhoads-Sinon

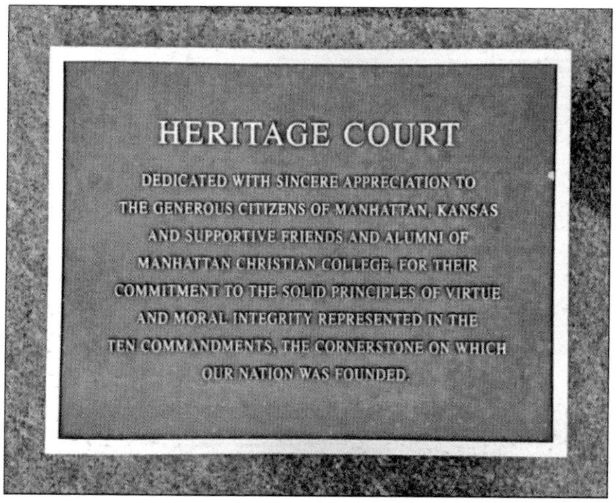
HERITAGE COURT
DEDICATED WITH SINCERE APPRECIATION TO THE GENEROUS CITIZENS OF MANHATTAN, KANSAS AND SUPPORTIVE FRIENDS AND ALUMNI OF MANHATTAN CHRISTIAN COLLEGE, FOR THEIR COMMITMENT TO THE SOLID PRINCIPLES OF VIRTUE AND MORAL INTEGRITY REPRESENTED IN THE TEN COMMANDMENTS, THE CORNERSTONE ON WHICH OUR NATION WAS FOUNDED.

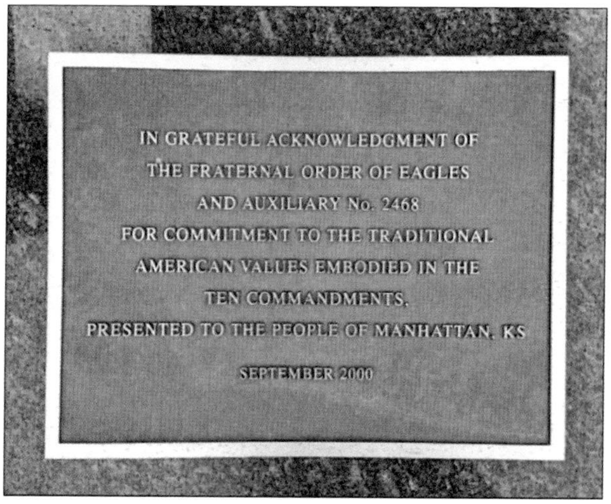
IN GRATEFUL ACKNOWLEDGMENT OF THE FRATERNAL ORDER OF EAGLES AND AUXILIARY No. 2468 FOR COMMITMENT TO THE TRADITIONAL AMERICAN VALUES EMBODIED IN THE TEN COMMANDMENTS.
PRESENTED TO THE PEOPLE OF MANHATTAN, KS
SEPTEMBER 2000

TEN COMMANDMENTS
THE FIRST MONUMENT TEACHES A SECULAR MESSAGE ALONG WITH ITS SPIRITUAL CONTENT. IT IS A FIRST CODE OF LAWS, A FUNDAMENTAL EXAMPLE OF OUR LEGAL SYSTEM. WE ARE A NATION OF LAWS. THE FRATERNAL ORDER OF EAGLES PRESENTED THIS MONUMENT TO THE CITY IN 1958 IN ORDER THAT OUR NATION'S YOUTH WOULD BE REMINDED OF BASIC CIVILIZED RULES.
THE EUROPEAN SETTLERS WHO FOUNDED THIS COUNTRY TRIED TO LIVE ACCORDING TO THE TEN COMMANDMENTS. IN ADDITION, THE EARLY ENGLISH SETTLERS BROUGHT WITH THEM THE ENGLISH COMMON LAW FIRST COMPILED IN BLACKSTONE'S COMMENTARIES (1765). THE ENGLISH COMMON LAW IS STILL BASIC TO MOST OF OUR STATES. OTHER EUROPEAN SETTLERS BROUGHT ROMAN LAW AS COMPILED IN THE CODE OF JUSTINIAN (565), WHICH BECAME THE FOUNDATION FOR THE LAWS OF LOUISIANA AND FOR MOST OF MODERN EUROPE. THE PRINCIPLES OF THE TEN COMMANDMENTS WERE A BASIS FOR BOTH BLACKSTONE'S AND JUSTINIAN'S WRITINGS.

Extra Support Used for Stabilization

Some monoliths are no longer stable. The following monoliths are fortunate to have some help, but there are some out there that need to be attended to because they are kind of wobbly.

Lights

PRESENTED TO
THE CITY OF GLENDALE
BY THE
FRATERNAL ORDER OF EAGLES

FRATERNAL ORDER OF EAGLES
1971

PRESENTED TO THE CITY OF
MANHATTAN, KANSAS
BY
FRATERNAL ORDER OF EAGLES

FRATERNAL ORDER OF EAGLES
JUNE 1975

Thou shalt not covet thy neighbor's house
his manservant, nor his maidservant, nor his
PRESENTED TO
THE CITY OF MONONGAHELA
BY

Oops, we're in trouble!

Why are you behind the fence that's supposed to keep you out?

You're in lockdown? And what's a Burning Man?

Where's your hardhat? Can't you see this is a construction zone?

Plaques

The following plaques were permanently attached to the Ten Commandments monoliths.

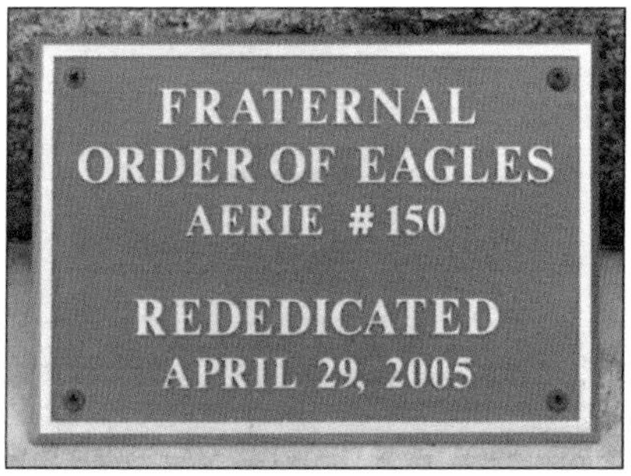

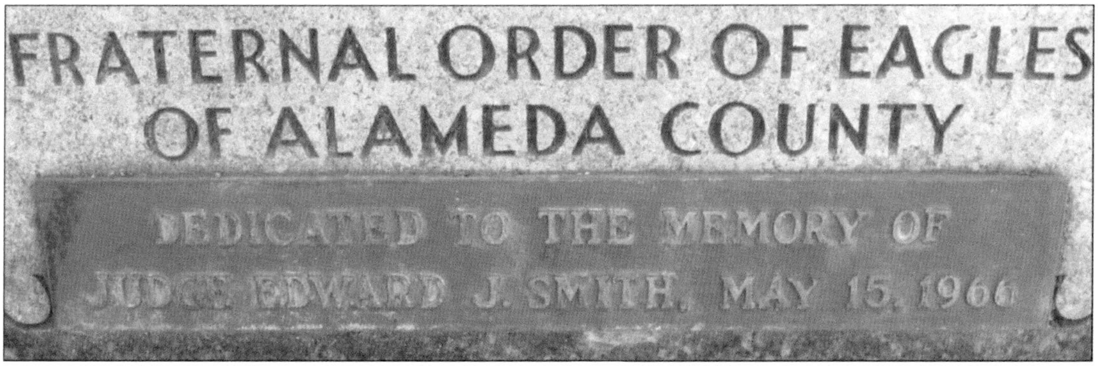

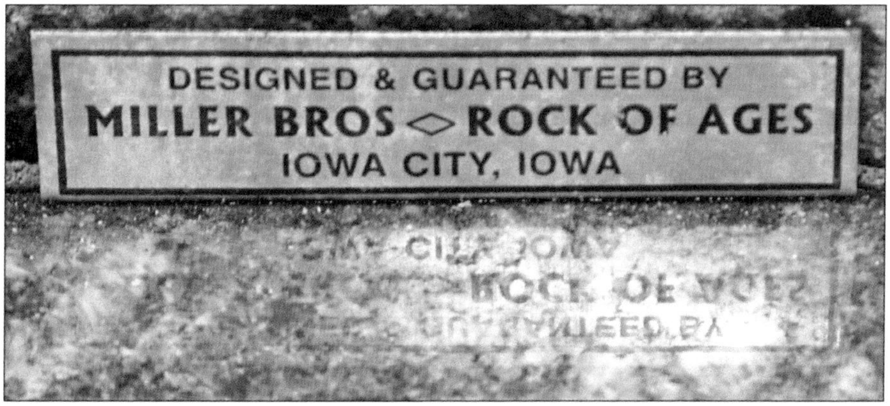

Time Capsules

Tops

The tops of the Ten Commandments monoliths show the differences in not only the curvature of the specific monoliths, but also in the floral decorations, contrast, shading, engraving and coloring distinctions. These are only a few samples of the different monoliths.

the Ten Commandments
I am the Lord thy God

the Ten Commandments

THE TEN COMMANDMENTS
I AM THE LORD THY GOD.

the Ten Commandments

the Ten Commandments

the Ten Commandments

the Ten Commandments
I am the Lord thy God

I AM the LORD thy God

the Ten Commandments

Covered in spider webs

The FOE Auxiliary dedicated this monolith near the
Ten Commandments monolith in a city park.

Whitened Paleo-Hebrew and Stars

These are just a few of the Ten Commandments monoliths that someone had purposely painted the Paleo-Hebrew and/or stars to make them stand out.

This one was painted in brown

Word Issues

These errors are just that. Perhaps the receivers of these monoliths got major discounts to keep them as is, or perhaps no one just ever noticed.

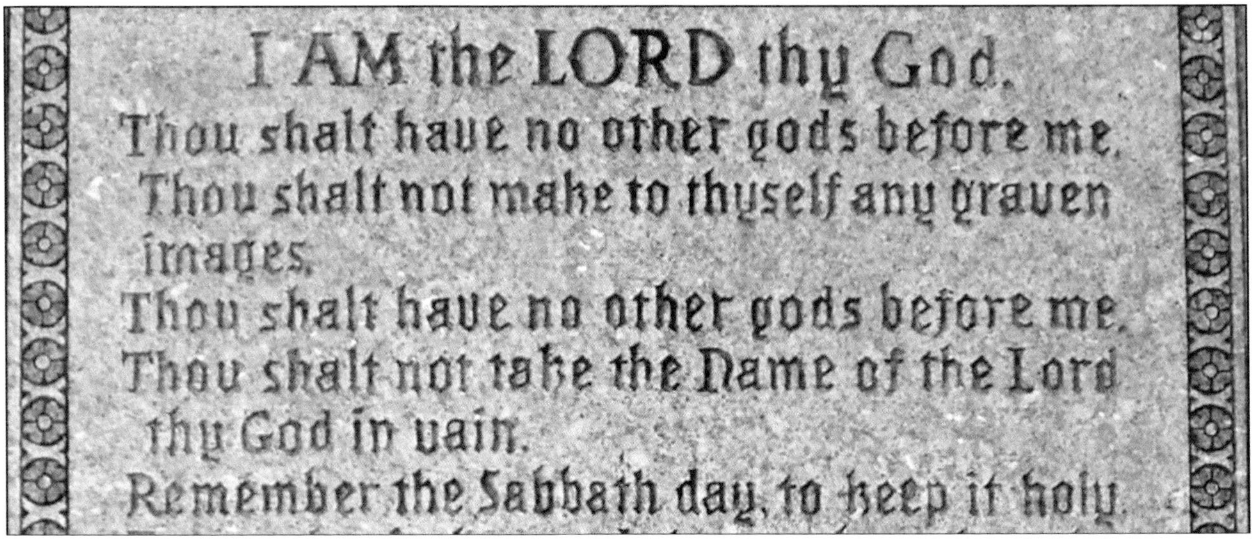

Repetitive Commandments

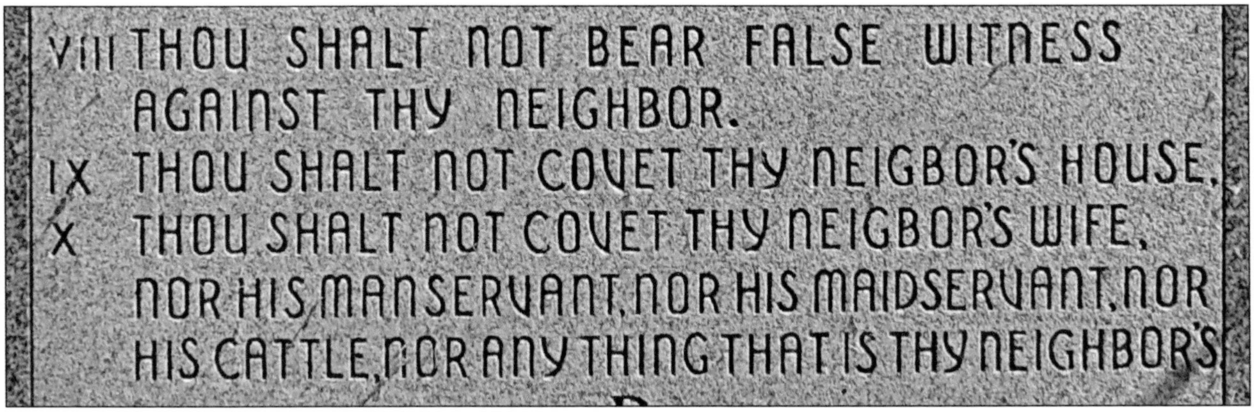

VIII THOU SHALT NOT BEAR FALSE WITNESS
AGAINST THY NEIGHBOR.
IX THOU SHALT NOT COVET THY NEIGBOR'S HOUSE.
X THOU SHALT NOT COVET THY NEIGBOR'S WIFE,
NOR HIS MANSERVANT, NOR HIS MAIDSERVANT, NOR
HIS CATTLE, NOR ANY THING THAT IS THY NEIGHBOR'S

Spelling issue

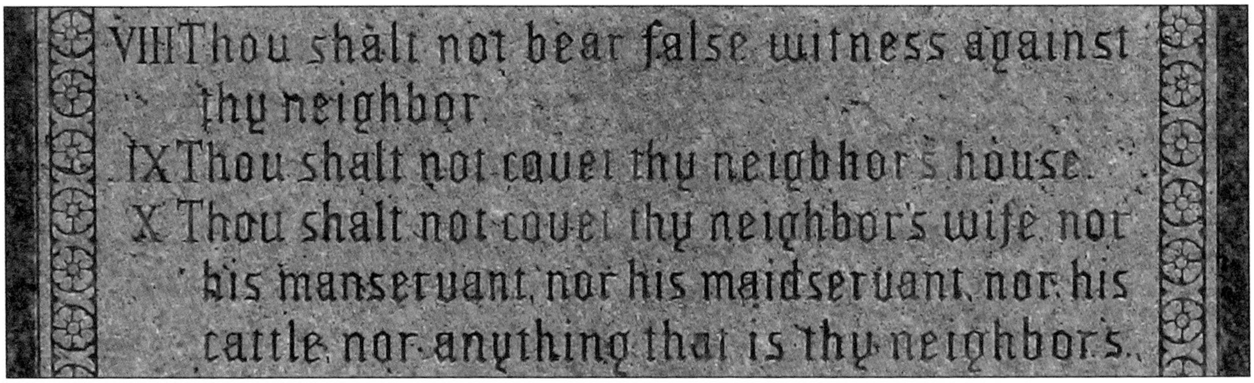

Spelling issue

Totally Different Monoliths

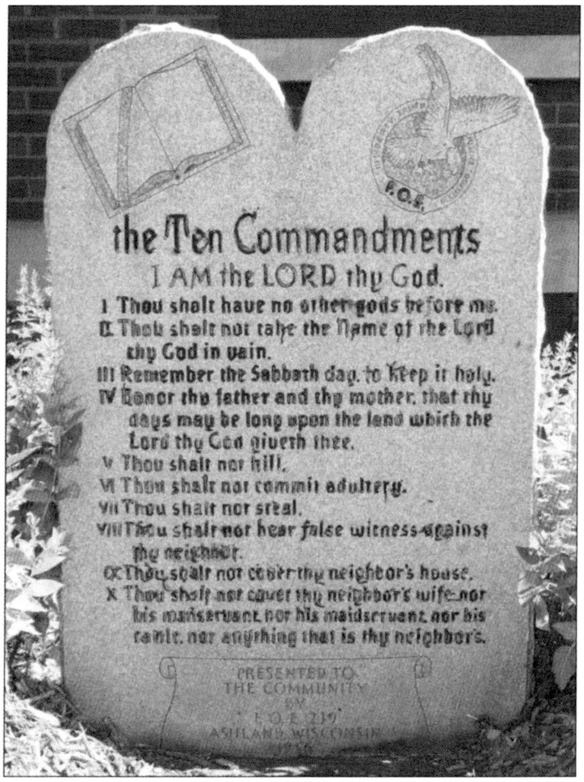

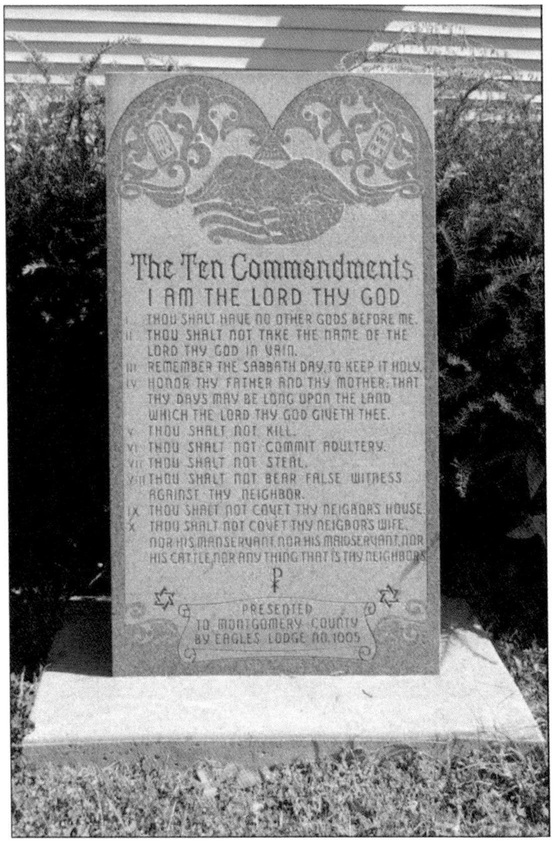
The Ten Commandments
I AM THE LORD THY GOD
I THOU SHALT HAVE NO OTHER GODS BEFORE ME.
II THOU SHALT NOT TAKE THE NAME OF THE LORD THY GOD IN VAIN.
III REMEMBER THE SABBATH DAY, TO KEEP IT HOLY.
IV HONOR THY FATHER AND THY MOTHER: THAT THY DAYS MAY BE LONG UPON THE LAND WHICH THE LORD THY GOD GIVETH THEE.
V THOU SHALT NOT KILL.
VI THOU SHALT NOT COMMIT ADULTERY.
VII THOU SHALT NOT STEAL.
VIII THOU SHALT NOT BEAR FALSE WITNESS AGAINST THY NEIGHBOR.
IX THOU SHALT NOT COVET THY NEIGBOR'S HOUSE.
X THOU SHALT NOT COVET THY NEIGBOR'S WIFE, NOR HIS MANSERVANT, NOR HIS MAIDSERVANT, NOR HIS CATTLE, NOR ANY THING THAT IS THY NEIGHBOR'S.
PRESENTED
TO MONTGOMERY COUNTY
BY EAGLES LODGE NO. 1005

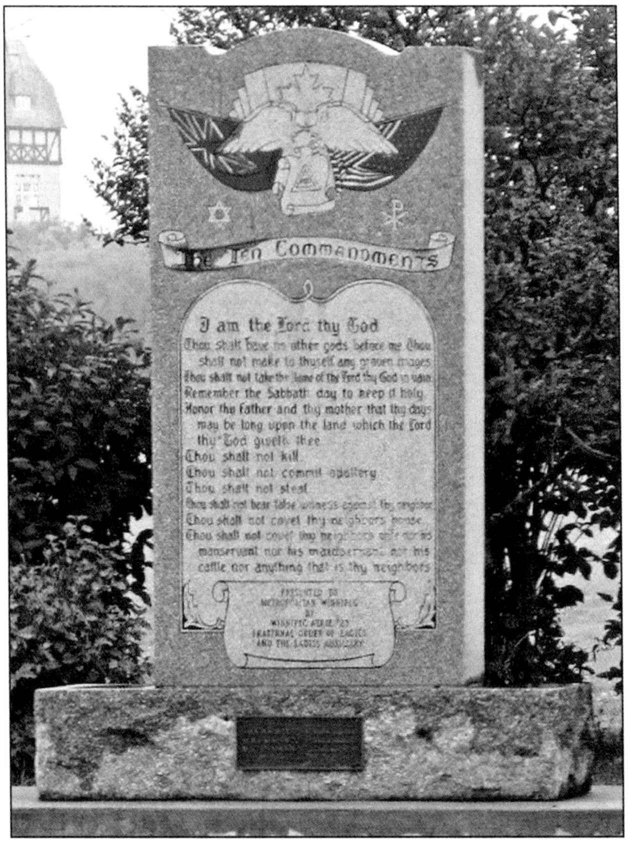
The Ten Commandments
I am the Lord thy God
Thou shalt have no other gods before me Thou shalt not make to thyself any graven images
Thou shalt not take the Name of the Lord thy God in vain
Remember the Sabbath day to keep it holy
Honor thy father and thy mother that thy days may be long upon the land which the Lord thy God giveth thee
Thou shalt not kill
Thou shalt not commit adultery
Thou shalt not steal
Thou shalt not bear false witness against thy neighbor
Thou shalt not covet thy neighbor's house
Thou shalt not covet thy neighbor's wife nor his manservant nor his maidservant nor his cattle nor anything that is thy neighbors

the Ten Commandments
I AM the LORD thy God
I Thou shalt have no other gods before me
II Thou shalt not take the Name of the Lord thy God in vain
III Remember the Sabbath day to keep it holy
IV Honor thy father and thy mother that thy days may be long upon the land which the Lord thy God giveth thee
V Thou shalt not kill
VI Thou shalt not commit adultery
VII Thou shalt not steal
VIII Thou shalt not bear false witness against thy neighbor
IX Thou shalt not covet thy neighbor's house
X Thou shalt not covet thy neighbor's wife nor his manservant nor his maidservant nor his cattle nor anything that is thy neighbor's
PRESENTED TO

The stripes are not reflections, but altering colors of ingrained granite

The only known monolith made out of concrete

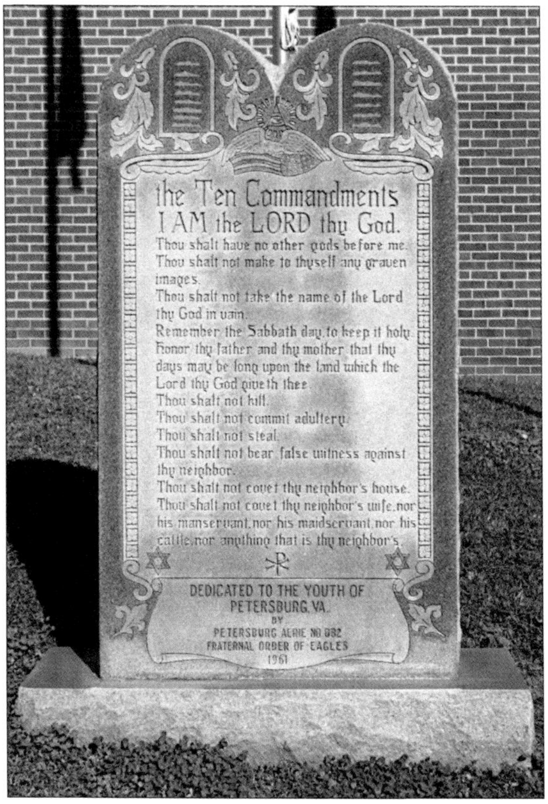

The only known monolith that blurs the Paleo-Hebrew in the mini-tablets and has ALL of the lines of the Commandments aligned left

CHAPTER 8

THE TEN COMMANDMENTS MONOLITHS

The following pages contain photos, documents, and stories of the Ten Commandments monoliths based on the only information that has been made available to me. Through the diligent efforts of a handful of people, this is the best that can be put together. Are there more monoliths? Without question. Are there more photos? Definitely. Are there people out there who have more information than what is presented here? Of course, but the numbers are dwindling as time marches on. As my God-given journey delivers slightly more than a glimpse into the Ten Commandments Project, it is my desire that someone else might take on this adventure and continue to unwrap the mystery of the monoliths. Until that happens, this is what is known so far, and it is with great pleasure that I let the following stories speak for themselves.

1954-1957

The Grand Aerie Convention held in Chicago, Illinois in 1954, introduced the Eagles' Ten Commandments Monoliths Project to its members. The very first granite monolith created was presented to the Chicago Park District at the Convention.

Bill McFetridge, who was Chairman of the Chicago Park District at the time, suggested that the monolith should be placed on Michigan Avenue in Grant Park between Randolph and Twelfth Streets. He said, "On behalf of the Park District and the City of Chicago, we are sincerely grateful for this presentation by your Organization, an honor to Chicago, by so fitting a tribute as the Ten Commandments. No one can truthfully say that if we would take just a look at the Commandments, all of us, say once a week, much less once each day, we would all be better men and women."

To this day, members of the Chicago Park District, as well as other city employees, have no idea of the current location of this Ten Commandments monolith. It continues to remain a mystery whether the monolith was ever dedicated, or even placed, in the city of Chicago.

YOUTH GUIDANCE AIMS GAIN IMPETUS FROM TEN COMMANDMENTS PLAN

THROUGHOUT THE LAND the Eagles, through the efforts of the Youth Guidance Commission headed by Judge E. J. Ruegemer, St. Cloud, Minn., have been instrumental in influencing young people by means of introducing them to God's law through placing the Ten Commandments in courts, schools and other public places.

Hundreds of Aeries have presented the scrolls to judges, educators and other public officials, said Judge Ruegemer in a moving report to the Grand Aerie Convention. "If all of us, youngsters and adults as well, would heed ten simple laws that were handed down to Moses over thirty-five hundred years ago on Mt. Sinai, we would not today have to be talking about juvenile delinquency, or crime and its prevention," said the judge.

One of the highlights of the presentation of the Youth Guidance Commission was the giving to the Chicago Park District of a monolith into which were hewn the Ten Commandments. The granite replica will be placed in a prominent spot in one of the parks within the city of Chicago, as a gift of the Eagles.

Judge E. J. Ruegemer reports on youth guidance.

Photo courtesy of *The Eagle Magazine* (October 1954)

Photo courtesy of *The Eagle Magazine* (October 1954)

Judge Duncan explains the Ten Commandments to the granddaughter of Al DiPalma of Scranton Aerie 314 at the 1954 Grand Convention in Chicago, Illinois. This is the only known photo of this Ten Commandments monolith.

The very first Ten Commandments monolith that was dedicated and *placed* is located in P. J. Caul Memorial Park in Ambridge, Pennsylvania. ➡

Photo by Sue A. Hoffman (October 2008)

Photo by Sue A. Hoffman (October 2008)

Ambridge, Pennsylvania (1955)

Photo courtesy of the Fraternal Order of Eagles

Milwaukee, Wisconsin (1955)

Although Milwaukee, Wisconsin's Ten Commandments monolith was dedicated in 1955 during the Grand Aerie Convention, it was not placed until two years later. Yul Brynner, who played Pharaoh Rameses II in the movie, *The Ten Commandments* was the guest speaker at the outside rededication ceremony during Law Enforcement Week in February 1957.

Forty-four years later, the Freedom from Religion Foundation (FFRF) threatened to sue the City of Milwaukee if they did not remove the monolith. The city did not want to go through a lawsuit, nor did they want to incur the costs associated with it. Frank Zeidler, namesake of the Frank P. Zeidler Municipal Building, was eighty-eight years of age at the time the city decided to remove the monolith. He said, "I would have urged the city to resist moving the monument. It was not a religious group that put it up – it was a fraternal organization. Is it a religious statement or a standard of conduct?"

Photo by Sue A. Hoffman (August 2001)
Judy Pankow standing in front of the Frank P. Zeidler Municipal Building, Milwaukee, Wisconsin

Photo by John Pankow (Judy Pankow's son) (August 2012)
Madelyn and Grant Pankow (grandchildren of Judy Pankow standing in the opposite photo) in the "Garden of Healing" at Saint Joseph's Hospital, Milwaukee, Wisconsin

On March 27, 2002, the city removed the monolith and relocated it in the "Garden of Healing," which is on the grounds of Saint Joseph's Hospital in Milwaukee.

The Fraternal Order of Eagles, either the national, state, or local groups, has taken on various charities as special projects through the years. In Ohio, the Boys Village in Wooster has been the beneficiary of several fundraisers held by Eagle members.

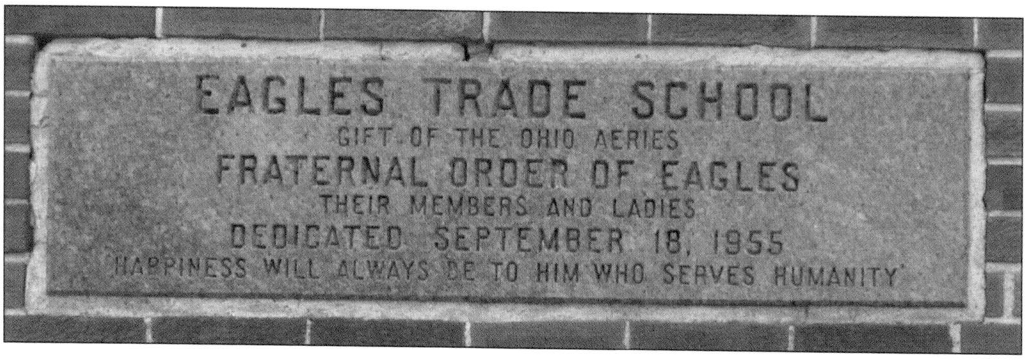

Photos by Karen Madsen (April 2010)

Boys Village, Wooster, Ohio (September 1955)

Photo courtesy of the Fraternal Order of Eagles

Judge E. J. Ruegemer, Lyman Cover, Paul Squire, Edward Burk, Doc Reynolds, and Palmer Albin were in attendance during the Fraternal Order of Eagles' Forty-Eighth State Convention

Photo by Sue A. Hoffman (May 2010)
Dedicated in 1955

Photo courtesy of the Fraternal Order of Eagles

Photo by Tom McGrath (March 2011)

This Ten Commandments monolith was registered with the Smithsonian Institution Research Information System (SIRUS) in 1977.
Dedicated in 1955

All known monoliths that were created in 1954 and 1955 were of the old style, having tablets with Roman numerals representing the Ten Commandments.

The early monoliths had many similarities – there were curls for all of the spaces, the tops were comparable, and they were all of the smaller size. The Ten Commandments were numbered on all of them, and some of the dedication information seemed rather lengthy on a few of them.

The monoliths with red granite were distinctly red in color. This was an intentional effort to try to match the granite that was found in Israel at the time.

Starting in 1956, the new style of Ten Commandments monoliths came into being, and so did the controversies (not that one had anything to do with the other, and in some cases, it took years before anything erupted).

Photo by Sue A. Hoffman (September 2012)

The only known monolith with the Latin notation,
"Anno Domini" (Year of our Lord)
Dedicated in 1955

The Posey County Courthouse in Mount Vernon, Indiana was the recipient of a Ten Commandments monolith which was placed in the Mount Vernon Public Square. The dedication program was held on the courthouse lawn and was attended by several hundred people. In addition to the Ten Commandments monolith, Ten Commandments scrolls were donated to every child in the Posey County school system – both public and parochial.

Photo courtesy of *The Eagle Magazine* (August/September 1956)
Seated: County Commissioners William Holler and Kyle Rigg
Standing: Charles Moye, Eldon Crawford, Judge Francis Knowles, Hugh Price, William Watson, Earl Young, Charles LaFollette, Carl Kreiger, Thomas Parker, and Milburn Bradley

Unfortunately, a teen-aged person did not appreciate the monolith's existence in March 2005, and was able to break the piece of granite into three pieces. Because of the upcoming US Supreme Court case in June regarding the monolith in Austin, Texas, County Attorney Hank Hudson, and the Posey County officials, hesitated on what to do concerning the monolith. The local Aerie decided to take the monolith off of their hands, had it restored, and then rededicated it on their property. In 2006, the trustees of Old Beech Cemetery presented a new Ten Commandments monolith to the Posey County Courthouse to replace the one that had been destroyed.

Photo by Sue A. Hoffman (May 2010)
Mount Vernon, Indiana (May 1956)

Aerie 1717 has a beautiful, historical building that if you stand on their front porch, you can look across the Ohio River and see the farmlands of Kentucky. Between the eagle on top of their flag pole, and the two majestic eagles guarding their entrance steps, there is no doubt that this where they hold their events. Their front lawn is the final resting place of the once proud monolith that stood on the grounds of the Posey County Courthouse.

The first Fraternal Order of Eagles' Ten Commandments monolith placed on state capitol grounds was in Denver, Colorado. The monolith is located in Lincoln Park on the west lower Capitol lawn, a block away from the very impressive Capitol Building. The park, on a Saturday night at dusk in the heat of the summer, is a gathering place for a few unsavory individuals, as well as the homeless, teenagers looking for something to do, and those who have chosen to drink more than the legal limit.

Photo by Jeffrey Hoffman (September 2012)

In 1987, Bill Talley, a self-appointed atheist, and lawyer Robert Tiernan and the Freedom from Religion Foundation (FFRF), started a string of lawsuits to remove the Denver monolith. In addition to their first attempt in 1987, they tried again in 1989, 1993, 1995, and in 1996. Denver District Court's Judge Robert Fullerton decreed that the monolith was not an endorsement of religion in the 1989 case. In 1992, a trial judge ruled that "the Ten Commandments were the basis of constitutional law." The Colorado Court of Appeals reversed that verdict in June 1993 with a three-to-zero decision, and declared the monolith unconstitutional.

In June 1994, the Colorado Supreme Court reversed the Appeals Court decision in a four-to-three vote to keep the monolith. In September 1995, the FFRF filed a petition with the US Supreme Court to hear the case, but it was denied. In June 1996, Robert Tiernan requested that he be able to place a counter monument near the monolith, and that was also denied.

Photo by Jeffrey Hoffman (September 2012)

Denver, Colorado (June 1956)

When Charlton Heston assisted in the dedication of the Ten Commandments monolith at the International Peace Garden in Dunseith, North Dakota, he was quoted as saying, "The Ten Commandments have become the basis for the whole code of human law. . . . It is appropriate that on the border between two countries, the United States and Canada, the Ten Commandments have an important place to show how men can live in peace."

Photo courtesy of the Ruegemer Family

Charlton Heston (Moses in *The Ten Commandments*) and Judge E. J. Ruegemer (directly behind the monolith) at the dedication at the International Peace Garden

The dedication festivities began earlier in the day when Charlton Heston's four-seat chartered plane taxied onto the grassy pasture outside of Dunseith and was enthusiastically hailed with a huge welcome banner by the Dunseith Chamber of Commerce. After being greeted by Eagles and Dunseith townspeople, Heston was "whisked away" to a chicken dinner served by the Dunseith civic boosters.

The Ten Commandments monolith was draped with both the American and Canadian flags. Judge E. J. Ruegemer presented the monolith to D. G. McKenzie, the Canadian president of the International Peace Garden. After Heston spoke, many dignitaries took their turn at the microphone: Lieutenant Governor C. P. Dahl of North Dakota; Mayor Hershel Lashkowitz of Fargo, North Dakota; John Stormon, chairman of the Peace Garden Board; Father Elwood Cassedy, director of the Bi-State-Aerie-maintained Boys Home on the Range; as well as many others. When all of the speeches concluded, Charlton Heston was presented with an honorary lifetime membership in the Peace Garden Aerie of the Fraternal Order of Eagles in Bottineau, North Dakota. ". . . An honor," Heston stated, "that rounds out my day."

Photo courtesy of the Fraternal Order of Eagles

It was estimated that over 5,000 people from all over the world were present at the dedication of this Ten Commandments monolith

The construction of the International Peace Garden began in 1934 by the US Civilian Conservation Corps under the direction of the National Park Service. The first building created by the Corps in the late 1930s was the Historic Lodge. It was built out of logs donated by Manitoba, Canada from the Riding Mountain National Park, and the stones came from North Dakota. The monolith is located next to the Historic Lodge in the International Peace Garden.

Photo by Karen Madsen (July 2012)

International Peace Garden, Dunseith, North Dakota (June 1956)

Photo courtesy of *The Eagle Magazine* (July 1957)

Ten Commandments monolith dedication with Eagle members Ed Kline, Matt Michels, Bud Bergeson, Ivan Plaggemeyer, Father Cassedy, Phil Bighley, and other local leaders

This monolith was placed in a city park across the street from the local high school. When the school was torn down in 2006, the Ten Commandments monolith was moved to the center of the park and nestled between majestic pine trees. To this town's credit, according to the local Eagle members, this monolith has never been damaged or defaced.

Photo by Karen Madsen (July 2011)

Dedicated in June 1956

Such a glorious beginning – a famous movie star, a parade, a super-hyped movie waiting in the wings, and the Grand Aerie International Convention celebration – all of this ending in such a sad current state of affairs. Dedicated in the summer of 1956, the Ten Commandments monolith was part of quite a party thrown by the Fraternal Order of Eagles in Pittsburgh, Pennsylvania.

Photo courtesy of the Fraternal Order of Eagles

Martha Scott (Moses' mother in *The Ten Commandments*),
Mayor David Lawrence, and Judge E. J. Ruegemer
Pittsburgh, Pennsylvania (July 28, 1956)

This is one of the three monoliths that have been referred to in litigations to have the monoliths removed because of the connection between Hollywood's release of Cecil B. DeMille's *The Ten Commandments* movie and the Eagles' monoliths. As discussed previously, this win-win connection and timing makes for interesting press and may have produced a few raised eyebrows. The reality is that the coincidence created a winning situation by both parties involved. Although it is unknown what happened to the monolith immediately after all of the hoopla, it was eventually placed on a pathway at the National Aviary which is located in Pittsburgh's oldest municipal park, Allegheny Commons.

Unfortunately, this famous monolith endured several years of abuse and vandalism. After several attempts by the City of Pittsburgh to keep it standing and in one piece, it was decided to remove the monolith and place it in storage with the Department of Public Works – where it has been located for over four years at the time of this writing. The monolith will obviously break in two pieces,

Photo by Jeffrey Hoffman (June 2012)
Mike Salem, Department of Public Works, City of Pittsburgh

if it hasn't happened already, upon trying to lift it off of the floor. This kind of damage usually occurs when a monolith has been tipped over. Although the City of Pittsburgh should be commended for trying to preserve it, they should also be questioned as to why they allow the monolith to take up space on the floor of a warehouse located in downtown Pittsburgh under a main bridge.

Would the monolith, and the city, be better served by giving it to an organization that could have it repaired and placed on private property? With a little bit of "granite glue" to hold it together, this Ten Commandments monolith would be "as good as new" and could be placed in any number of locations within the Pittsburgh area. There are at least twelve local Eagle Aeries within twenty miles of downtown Pittsburgh, along with an abundance of churches and veterans groups. And yet, for the past four years, the City Attorney continues to mull over the rules regarding how to dispose of city-owned property that was originally gifted to them.

There is nothing grander than an old-fashioned County Fair – especially when Paramount Pictures pitches a circus-sized tent featuring the Fraternal Order of Eagles' Ten Commandments monolith.

The movie company provided detectives to guard the exhibit 24/7 because it also included several artifacts used in *The Ten Commandments* film, along with the movie's original Ten Commandments tablets held by Moses (who was played by Charlton Heston).

Photo courtesy of *The Eagle Magazine* (February 1957)
Eagles' Membership Department's Otto Miller presents the Ten Commandments monolith

Over 11,000 Ten Commandments scrolls were handed out during the run of the County Fair. At some point after the County Fair closed, the monolith was given a more permanent home.

For such a famous monolith, it took some exceptionally sly investigative work to discover its exact locale. Many thanks to the following very special people who were so diligent in their pursuit: Amie Downs, Andy Baechle, Joe Olczak, Jim Flynn, the Regional History Center, and the photographer who had the proof, Margaret Stanley. It was a pleasure working with such extraordinary, like-minded people.

Photo by Jeffrey Hoffman (June 2012)
Dedicated in September 1956

Photo by Karen Madsen (September 2008)
Kate Shepherd (Karen Madsen's daughter) in Helena, Montana

Currently among many other art and memorial pieces, the Ten Commandments monolith in Helena, Montana was the first monolith to show the eagle carrying both the American flag and the British flag. It also encapsulated the Ten Commandments and used unique floral designs.

In September 2004, the Capitol Complex Advisory Council, consisting of Martz Administration and the Montana Historical Society, recommended that the monolith be allowed to stay at its current location on the lawn of the Capitol Building. The committee remarked that the monolith was part of the Capitol area when the Capitol was added to the National Register of Historic Places.

Photo by Karen Madsen (September 2008)

Basking in the shadow of the State of Montana's Capitol Building
Helena, Montana (September 1956)

Photo by Karen Madsen (July 2011)

It was very uncommon for an organization, other than the Fraternal Order of Eagles, to purchase a monolith and give credit elsewhere. Sunset Memorial Park and Funeral Chapel did just that by incurring the cost of the monolith, even though the dedication states that it was presented by the Eagles. Officials came from both Minneapolis and Saint Paul to attend a very impressive ceremony when the monolith was placed.

Photo by Karen Madsen (July 2011)

Sunset Memorial Park and Funeral Chapel, Minneapolis, Minnesota (October 1956)

Although the terrain may have been much different over fifty years ago, the monolith is currently very difficult to locate within the Park. It is pressed against a grove of trees and quite a distance from the road. As you drive along, you can barely catch a glimpse of the Ten Commandments monolith just for a second before you go immediately under a bridge.

When Darrel Russelburg from Fort Branch, Indiana, was charged with aiding and abetting, and indecent exposure (topless dancing and table dances), at his Old Hickory Barbecue restaurant, he came across the Ten Commandments monolith when he made his first court appearance at the Gibson County Courthouse. Together with Deborah Nally in September 2003, he joined forces with Kenneth Falk of the Indiana Civil Liberties Union (ICLU) and sued Gibson County for the removal of the monolith.

David Tanner, Russelburg's attorney for the aiding and abetting charges, commented, "This action is not designed to make him popular – if he wanted to gain the hearts and minds of the public, he would have left well-enough alone."

Photo by Sue A. Hoffman (May 2010)
Princeton, Indiana (1956)

US District Court Judge Richard L. Young gave a court order that the monolith must be moved within sixty days as of January 31, 2005. US Representative John Hostettler proposed the Ten Commandments Amendment to a key spending bill, HR 2862, which passed in the House in early 2005 that utilized Article 1, Section 8 (power of the purse) of the US Constitution to prevent any funding from being used by the US Marshall's service to remove the monolith.

Photo by Sue A. Hoffman (May 2010)
Gibson County Courthouse, Princeton, Indiana

In June 2005, Russelburg and Nally dropped their case. The same judge reversed his decision in September 2005 stating that the monolith can remain at the Gibson County Courthouse. County Attorney Jerry Stilwell expected this decision based on the outcome of the earlier decision by the US Supreme Court in Austin, Texas in June of that year. The Ten Commandments monolith is one of nine monuments displayed at the Courthouse.

Photo courtesy of *The Eagle Magazine* (January 1957)
Trenton, New Jersey Aerie 100 presents monolith to the City of Trenton in front of City Hall with Steve Voorhees, Rev. F. M. Adams, Mayor Donal Connolly, and Foster Voorhees III

This rose-colored Ten Commandments monolith has very visible, natural peach streaks throughout the granite which are also visible in the black and white photo.

Photo by Tom McGrath (April 2011)
Trenton, New Jersey (1956)

Photo by Bill Collins (September 2012)
Dallas, Texas (1956)

It is currently unknown where the Dallas, Texas Ten Commandments monolith was originally dedicated and placed, but it spent several years in storage before it ended up in Fair Park at the Texas State Fair sometime in the 1990s.

Photo courtesy of the Fraternal Order of Eagles
Ashland County Courthouse
Ashland, Wisconsin (1956)

A very unique Ten Commandments monolith was dedicated in front of the Ashland County Courthouse in 1956. It featured an opened Bible and the eagle symbol of the Fraternal Order of Eagles. Judge E. J. Ruegemer was present, along with many other city officials and dignitaries.

While the monolith was in front of the Courthouse, it became the target of multiple acts of vandalism. After being tipped over yet again in November 1998, it was placed in the County Highway Garage in Highbridge. The Kelly-Johnson American Legion Post 90 and the Chequamegon Memorial VFW Post 690, who share a facility on Main Street East in downtown Ashland, requested the monolith. The Law Enforcement Committee recommended that this request be approved, and the Board of Supervisors of Ashland County agreed to let the American Legion and the VFW acquire the monolith in December 1999.

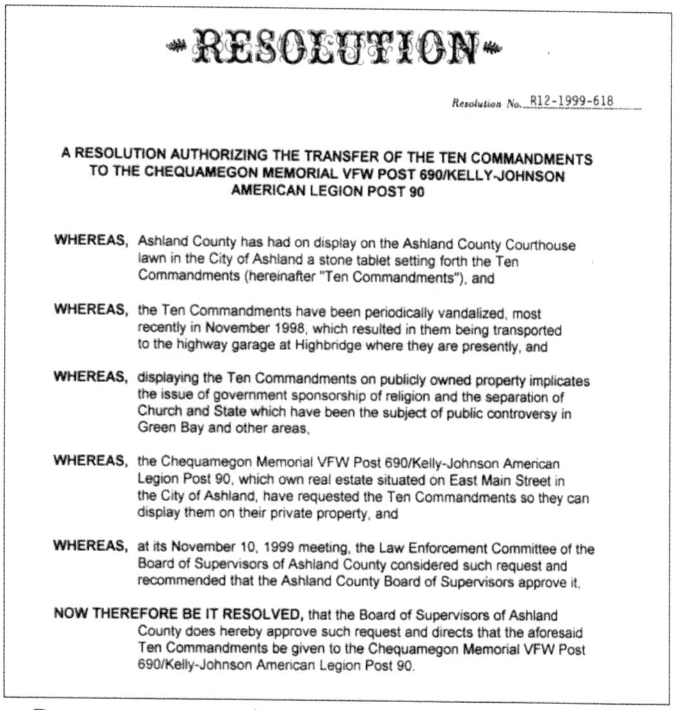

RESOLUTION

Resolution No. R12-1999-618

A RESOLUTION AUTHORIZING THE TRANSFER OF THE TEN COMMANDMENTS TO THE CHEQUAMEGON MEMORIAL VFW POST 690/KELLY-JOHNSON AMERICAN LEGION POST 90

WHEREAS, Ashland County has had on display on the Ashland County Courthouse lawn in the City of Ashland a stone tablet setting forth the Ten Commandments (hereinafter "Ten Commandments"), and

WHEREAS, the Ten Commandments have been periodically vandalized, most recently in November 1998, which resulted in them being transported to the highway garage at Highbridge where they are presently, and

WHEREAS, displaying the Ten Commandments on publicly owned property implicates the issue of government sponsorship of religion and the separation of Church and State which have been the subject of public controversy in Green Bay and other areas,

WHEREAS, the Chequamegon Memorial VFW Post 690/Kelly-Johnson American Legion Post 90, which own real estate situated on East Main Street in the City of Ashland, have requested the Ten Commandments so they can display them on their private property, and

WHEREAS, at its November 10, 1999 meeting, the Law Enforcement Committee of the Board of Supervisors of Ashland County considered such request and recommended that the Ashland County Board of Supervisors approve it,

NOW THEREFORE BE IT RESOLVED, that the Board of Supervisors of Ashland County does hereby approve such request and directs that the aforesaid Ten Commandments be given to the Chequamegon Memorial VFW Post 690/Kelly-Johnson American Legion Post 90.

Documentation marking the approval of transferring the Ten Commandments monolith in December 1999 to the Kelly-Johnson American Legion Post 90 and Chequamegon Memorial VFW Post 690

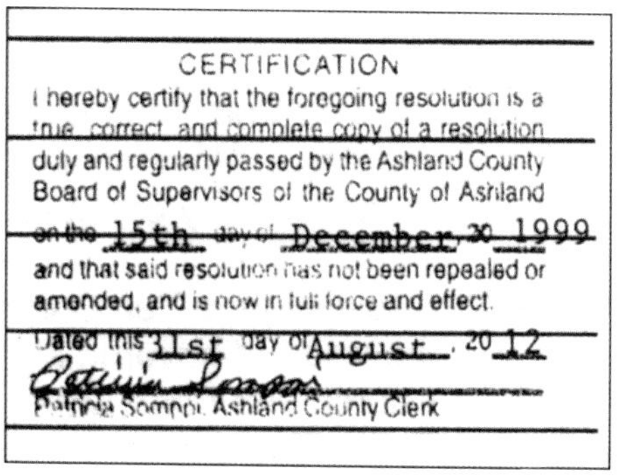

CERTIFICATION

I hereby certify that the foregoing resolution is a true, correct, and complete copy of a resolution duly and regularly passed by the Ashland County Board of Supervisors of the County of Ashland on the 15th day of December, 20 1999 and that said resolution has not been repealed or amended, and is now in full force and effect.

Dated this 31st day of August, 20 12

Patricia Somppi, Ashland County Clerk

Joan Haukaas, Edward Monroe, and Danielle Vanderscheuren of the Ashland Historical Museum, were key players in locating and documenting the Ashland, Wisconsin Ten Commandments monolith's travels. Many thanks for their sincere efforts and wonderful civic pride.

Photo by Edward Monroe (August 2012)

American Legion and the VFW, Ashland, Wisconsin

Photo by Sue A. Hoffman (October 2008)

Dedicated in May 1957

Photo courtesy of the Fraternal Order of Eagles

C. P. Clark, Fred Cappadona, Rabbi Louis Feigon,
and John Christensen, Jr.
Dedicated on Memorial Day in 1957

Photo by Joe Bundy Smith (May 2008)

Tyler Smith, Lauren Ball, and Alisa Sharp (Junior Eagles)

According to a newspaper account reflecting the town's historical past, the Ten Commandments monolith was considered to be placed on "prime property." At that time, it was called the Municipal Building, and on Mother's Day in 1957, it hosted the likes of Willard Biddle, John (Casey) Burnette, Ernest Scotillo (who erected the monolith), Amos Roebuck, and Steve Patrick.

Photo by Sue A. Hoffman (October 2008)

Dedicated on Mother's Day in May 1957

Photo courtesy of the Fraternal Order of Eagles

The Ten Commandments monolith's original location Middletown, Ohio (May 1957)

The Ten Commandments monolith in Middletown, Ohio was originally placed at City Building. When the city decided to move its facilities to another location in 1976, the monolith was placed in the vestibule at Holy Trinity Catholic Church. At some point, the church was remodeling its entryway and decided that the monolith needed a new home. Today, the monolith is located at the Woodside Cemetery and Arboretum next to a memorial site dedicated for babies.

Photo by Karen Madsen (April 2010)

Woodside Cemetery and Arboretum, Middletown, Ohio

Photo by Karen Madsen (October 2008)

Dedicated in 1957

Photo courtesy of *The Eagle Magazine* (October 1957)
Vernon Smith, Sr., Rev. Vernon Bowers, Rabbi Stampfer, Mayor Hugo Parenti, Vernon Smith, Jr., Robert Huscroft, Father Martin O'Toole, Evelyn Huscroft, Rev. John Govrusik (Eastern Orthodox faith), Joseph Martz, Eagle Scouts Steve Bezuska and John Dragon, and Leo Dopler
Dedicated in 1957

Photo by Sue A. Hoffman (October 2008)
Dueling monoliths (one from the Aerie and the other from the Auxiliary)
The flag pole is still behind the Aerie's Ten Commandments monolith fifty-one years later.

Jackie Jameson was born and raised in this town and remembers seeing the Ten Commandments monolith when she went to school years ago. When Jeffrey and I asked about the monolith at the local Eagles' Aerie, she had a notion of its location. Jackie, and her husband Dave,

Photo by Jeffrey Hoffman (June 2012)
Jackie and Dave Jameson

hopped in their truck and went on a mission. Others felt that we were a little off base and were doubtful that we had a clue of what we were talking about. We were tired, it was dark, and it was late. If Dave and Jackie weren't standing in the street yelling and waving us down, we would have driven right by and headed due east of there.

According to Jackie, this monolith was originally located in the playground alongside of the elementary school. When schools in the district combined five-to-seven years prior, the monolith was moved to what is now considered the back of the building, even though it is now facing towards a very prominent street and kitty-corner to multiple county offices.

Photo by Jeffrey Hoffman (June 2012)
Dedicated in 1957

The monumental "Flood of 2008" wreaked havoc with the city of Cedar Rapids, Iowa, as well as crippling several other towns along the path of the Cedar River. It put most of its historical downtown under water, including the government offices on Mays Island. Dedicated at Linn County

Courthouse in 1957, the Ten Commandments monolith, at some point in time and for reasons unknown, had been moved and was facing Cedar Rapids City Hall along the banks of the Cedar River on the Island. The torrential waters flattened the monolith in place.

When Karen Madsen visited Cedar Rapids and witnessed all of the devastation in September of that year, she was able to see the monolith within a fenced area still flat on its back and covered with mud. Cedar Rapids had a long way to go, with thousands of buildings throughout the area rendered useless due to flooding. The monolith was understandably low on the list of priorities.

Photo by Judy Pankow (September 2012)
Ten Commandments monolith was covered in spider nests and webs
Cedar Rapids, Iowa (June 1957)

Photo by Judy Pankow (September 2012)
Ten Commandments monolith huddled in the trees near the Veterans Memorial Building (site of the old City Hall)

Karen returned in June 2012 and saw that the monolith had been moved and put in an upright position, but still within a fenced area that was under construction. With a lot of volunteer help, including Coonrod Wrecker and Crane Service, Iowa Valley Monument Company, and Marion Aerie 4522, Cedar Rapids Aerie 2272 was able to re-erect the Ten Commandments monolith with hopes of a future rededication along the newly-designed park beside Cedar River. The banks of the river had been shored up and the government buildings were slowly becoming habitable.

Judy Pankow also went to this site in September 2012, snuck behind the fence with the help of new-found friends, and took some quick photos as a police officer stood by to keep them out of harm's way.

Photo by Judy Pankow (September 2012)
To the right of Steve Langton, and his mother Betty, was the old site of the Ten Commandments monolith that was at least four feet under water in 2008.

Photo by Sue A. Hoffman (October 2008)
Dedicated on the Fourth of July 1957

Photo by Karen Madsen (April 2010)
Dedicated in 1957

Dedicated in July 1957, records concerning this Ten Commandments monolith were lost when the Aerie's building went up in flames. Only one original member who was involved with the erection and dedication of the monolith remains, but he is very elderly and in ill health. In September 1995, city councilmen and county commissioners were concerned about the American Civil Liberties Union's (ACLU) investigation into the possible violation of this monolith in regards to the Establishment Clause. Both the city and county officials offered their full support and determination to defend their Ten Commandments monolith at the County Courthouse.

Dr. Jeffrey M. Davis, if nothing else, was persistent considering that he filed complaints on at least three separate occasions regarding the Ten Commandments monolith in Cumberland, Maryland. Although a resident of Swanton in Garrett County, he was an emergency room physician with the Western Maryland Health System in Cumberland and stated, "I've always been very adamantly opposed to any mixing of religion and government."

Allegany County Administrator at that time, Vance Ishler, was probably of the same mindset, although his executive decision, along with the approval of three other county commissioners, was "just attempting to preclude any lawsuits." His unprecedented act of secrecy to move the monolith across the street to private property behind the C. William Gilchrist Gallery was witnessed on Friday, October 8, 2004 by Ron May (a security officer at the courthouse annex). The work was being done thirty yards from the monolith's dedication cite, at the edge of an alley against a wall, surrounded on three sides with high hedges and a narrow, gated archway. May stated, "I watched them work with a Bobcat and a dump truck. They cut trees and took truckloads of brush and debris out. I thought they were just cleaning it up." Another security officer, J. "Bob" Krampf observed the commotion and noticed that the work was being performed by county workers and an inmate work-release detail from the Allegany County Detention Center.

Photo by Jeffrey Hoffman (June 2012)
Cumberland, Maryland (August 1957)

When May came into work before 7:30 AM on Monday the eleventh (which was Columbus Day and all of the offices were closed because of the Federal holiday), the monolith was gone and tucked away from public view. It didn't take long for the community to hear about it and take action. Krampf was perturbed to say the least. "Who made the decision and when? It's a black Monday for Allegany County and the American people and the people that believe in God." Ron Yost, pastor of the Cumberland Community Church said, "We can't even show our kids the Ten Commandments in front of our courthouse. And that's what the law being used inside the court is based on. The county commissioners did this under the cover of darkness, but what they did was wrong. Nothing can undo this except to pick it up and put it back." Pastor Yost later said, "We need to tell the commissioners that what they did was foolish. Cumberland needs to stand up for this. We never take a stand for something until it's taken away."

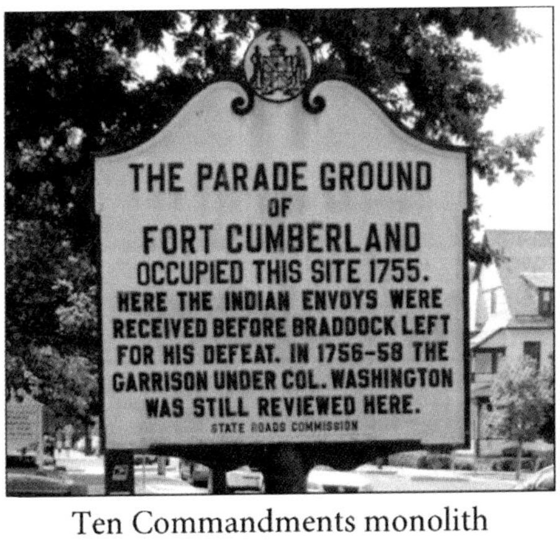

Ten Commandments monolith proudly stands on Fort Cumberland's Parade Ground

Ed Taylor, Jr., who was president of the Cumberland Historic Cemetery Organization, and about fifty others, demonstrated in front of the courthouse on the very next day. Thelma Galford, age

Photo by Jeffrey Hoffman (June 2012)
Ten Commandments monolith is situated at the far right of the Old Allegany County Courthouse (above the blue/gray car in this photo)

seventy-two and owner of the beauty salon in town, spread the news through her customers. Another retired business woman, Anna M. Sheetz who, at age sixty-eight, had never protested before, found herself milling around with the demonstrators. She quit going to church years before, but the removal of the Ten Commandments monolith was just the catalyst to make her step up and have her voice heard.

With all of the publicity and public outcry, the monolith was returned in less than a week to its original place in front of the courthouse. County Commissioners Jim Stakem, Robert Hutcheson, and Barbara Roque "just happened" to be out of town that week and unavailable for comment. Dr. Jeffrey Davis continued to harass Allegany County in 2008 when he requested that the Citizens for a Secular Government be allowed to place a monument honoring the US Constitution next to the monolith or remove the monolith within two months. The Ten Commandments monolith remains unscathed, and Dr. Davis continues to write letters to the editor, and other various public officials, about various church/state issues.

Photo by Jeffrey Hoffman (June 2012)
Dedicated in 1957

The Ten Commandments monolith once stood in front of the Public Works Building, which has since been torn down. Now all that is left is a parking lot for businesses on the other side of the block in the middle of this busy shopping district.

In August 2001, this monolith was spray painted with the words, "Not on Public Land." The monolith had to be sandblasted to remove the paint. It was promptly cleaned up and it now has new plants and fresh stones around the foundation thanks to a local organization.

Photo courtesy of the Fraternal Order of Eagles
Dedicated in 1957

Photo by Sue A. Hoffman (September 2012)

According to the Historical Preservation Commission's Catherine Hostetler, volunteers from a local landscaping company took it upon themselves to, "Raise awareness around the community about really improving green spaces around town and making everyone aware. Just a little volunteer project can go a long way." The volunteers chose the Ten Commandments monolith for a much-needed facelift. Good Friday and Earth Day fell on the same day in April 2011. The owner of the landscaping company said, "Doing good deeds on Good Friday, so we're out here to do our part and make this town a more beautiful place."

If I had to rely on the young president of the Fraternal Order of Eagles' Glenwood Springs, Colorado Aerie, the Ten Commandments monolith would have remained missing. Between his condescending attitude and lack of response to all of the information that I forwarded to him, I was almost willing to let this one remain unknown. Fortunately, the February 1958 article in *The Eagle Magazine* was too important to let slide, and there was a willing Aerie trustee who seemed a little more interested in the Aerie's past to make our trip to Glenwood Springs worthwhile.

Amazing metal sculpture on the front door of Aerie 215
Glenwood Springs, Colorado

When the monolith was dedicated on October 5, 1957, it was a part of the annual State President's Ball and Inter-Aerie meeting. Mayor Jack C. Mitchell accepted the monolith, and representatives from all religious groups and churches participated in the activities. The main speaker for the dedication was Robert W. Atkinson, a representative of the Grand Aerie. The high school band and the Glenwood Springs Boy Scout Troop were in attendance, as well as representatives from the Pueblo, Colorado Springs, Aspen, Grand Junction, Lamar, and Denver Aeries.

Every school child and teacher in Glenwood Springs, and the surrounding areas, received a beautifully colored, ready-to-frame, personalized copy of the Ten Commandments. Over 1,200 Ten Commandments scrolls were distributed by the Glenwood Springs Aerie. The Eagles' goal at the time, according to State President E. C. Rowe, was "to place the Ten Commandments in every American home."

Robin Unsworth and Ann Green were instrumental in looking into the history of Glenwood Spring's Ten Commandments monolith. It possibly was dedicated at the Chamber of Commerce, but "someone complained," so sometime in the late 1980s, it was moved to the Church of the Nazarene. The building eventually was sold to a different congregation, so the Eagles requested that it be placed at Saint Stephen Catholic Church. The base that the monolith was mounted on is still visible at the old location of the Church of the Nazarene.

Photo by Jeffrey Hoffman (September 2012)
Glenwood Springs, Colorado (October 1957)

In the small town of Monongahela, Pennsylvania, a Ten Commandments monolith rests in the community park between a Veterans' War Memorial and a band stand – the very epitome of Americana at its best.

Sign in Chess Park near the band stand – a glimpse into Monongahela's historic past

Photo by William Pankow (brother of Sue A. Hoffman) (May 2013)

Monongahela, Pennsylvania (October 1957)

Photo by William Pankow (May 2013)

Veterans' War Memorial in Chess Park

On the outskirts of Lawrence, Kansas, the O'Connell Youth Ranch, established in 1975 and currently directed by Deanie Hayes, is 120-acre haven gifted by Mrs. Elsie O'Connell and her late husband, Dan. It was created "to give young boys a second chance for a fresh start in life."

Photo by Judy Pankow (September 2012)
Entrance to the O'Connell Youth Ranch, Lawrence, Kansas

Photo by Judy Pankow (September 2012)
Picnic area with Ten Commandments monolith in the background

Photo by Judy Pankow (September 2012)
Lawrence, Kansas (October 1957)

The Ten Commandments monolith, originally dedicated at the Topeka Municipal Auditorium, was removed at some point in time, placed in city storage for some unknown reason, and left there for some amount of time. Gordon and Mary Garber, active members of Aerie 4319's youth activities, paid a monument company to erect the monolith behind one of the youth residences at the O'Connell Youth Ranch in the early 1990s. Ron and Linda Flinner were instrumental in gathering information about the past history of the Ten Commandments monolith and their efforts are greatly appreciated.

The monolith is currently nestled in the trees in a meditation area near the campfire and picnic area where the staff gathers in their spare time. It is unknown what the original engraved dedication information stated.

According to Mike Flaherty, the Duluth, Minnesota's Ten Commandments monolith did not have to be removed from in front of Duluth City Hall and be put into storage on May 14, 2004. "The interesting thing about this particular monument is that it sits within the Duluth Civic Center Historic District. This district, including the Ten Commandments monument, was listed on the National Register of Historic Places on November 6, 1986." He lamented that, "Since the Federal Government recognizes this district as historic; the monument is historic rather than religious. Also, if the City of Duluth was ordered to remove the monument, Duluth would be in violation of the NHPA Act since the city receives federal funds."

Photo courtesy of *The Eagle Magazine* (June 1958)

The Duluth Aerie presented a Ten Commandments monolith to the city with Judge Mark Nolan (Master of Ceremonies), Mayor Eugene Lambert, Judge Bob Cannon, and Aerie President George Muckart in attendance.

As a side note on the adjacent photo – two judges, and a mayor, do not see any problem having a Ten Commandments monolith on city property. As a matter of fact, they were instrumental during the dedication. When did the tides turn, not only in Duluth, Minnesota, but all across America? At what point did the judicial system change the interpretation of the First Amendment? When did we, as Americans, decide that it was not appropriate to see the Ten Commandments in the public square? For Duluth, it happened in 2004.

Unfortunately, the Minnesota Civil Liberties Union (MCLU) and ten Duluth residents, including Bill Van Druten, didn't quite see it like that when they filed a lawsuit in February 2004. They contended that the monolith "violated the establishment clause of the First Amendment, which states that Congress shall make no law respecting an establishment of religion, or prohibiting the free exercise thereof." Rev. Dale Nau, chancellor of the Catholic Diocese of Duluth, said in an article in the *Duluth News Tribune*, "The framers of the Constitution didn't want to remove all traces of religion from the public arena. They just didn't want to exclude any religions."

Saint Louis County offered to take the monolith AND the lawsuit off of the city's hands. Gary Doty (former Duluth mayor) and Dr. Steven Peterson (physician at Saint Mary's Hospital) organized a campaign to save the monolith. They raised over $20,000 to help cover legal fees for the first go-round of litigation. They also gathered 5,400 signatures out of the required 6,000 necessary to put the measure up for a vote on the city ballot in November. In March, with assumed time to continue their efforts, the City Council voted five-to-four to remove the Ten Commandments monolith and Mayor Herb Bergson signed the resolution. All but $6,000 of the over $20,000 was returned to the donors, and the rest stayed with Save the Ten Commandments Committee for costs related to the effort.

At what point did the judicial system change the interpretation of the First Amendment? When did we, as Americans, decide that it was not appropriate to see the Ten Commandments in the public square?

In June 2004, the city of Duluth decided to auction off the Ten Commandments monolith to the highest bidder even though it was gifted to the city. Dr. Peterson's group hoped to buy the monolith. There was a demonstration against the sale, but evangelist Lowell Lundstrom's Celebration Church in Lakeville, Minnesota purchased the monolith for more than $15,000. They were able to then place the Ten Commandments monolith on private property next to Canal Park by October 2004 in a very public location near the finish line of Grandma's Marathon. This international race, which began in 1977 and was named after the only sponsor at the time, Grandma's Saloon and Grill, begins in the town of Two Harbors and ends in Duluth in Canal Park. The Ten Commandments monolith's international prominence brings an actual sense of victory to those trying to preserve this part of our American heritage, contrasted with the perceived, but shallow, victory of the Minnesota Civil Liberties Union as far as visibility to the general public.

Photo courtesy of the Fraternal Order of Eagles
Canal Park, Duluth, Minnesota (October 1957)

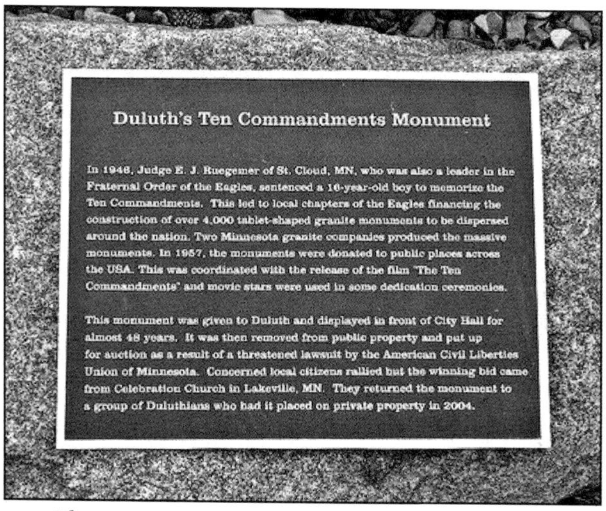

Plaque next to Ten Commandments monolith explaining the monolith's existence

Once located between the Pennington County Courthouse and City Auditorium, the Ten Commandments monolith has been relocated between the United Methodist Church and the head of River Walk that leads down to the water front. Although it is unknown when, or why, the monolith was moved, the setting is not only more visible to the general public, but it is beautifully placed overlooking Red Lake River.

Photo by Karen Madsen (July 2011)

Entry to the River Walk, Thief River Falls, Minnesota

Photo by Karen Madsen (July 2011)

Thief River Falls, Minnesota (1957)

Photo by Sue A. Hoffman (September 2012)
Odessa, Texas (November 1957)

Originally dedicated at the Ector County Courthouse, Odessa's monolith was moved at some point to the Medical Center Hospital. It is in a curious location such that it is surrounded by mechanical boxes in an area that can be seen through the glass walkway into the hospital, but there is no way to approach the monolith. It is protected by a low stone wall, trees, stone landscaping, and artificial grass that is so hot in the afternoon sun that it cannot be walked on.

On September 14, 2012, Freedom from Religion Foundation (FFRF) filed a lawsuit to force Valley High School in New Kensington, Pennsylvania to remove its Ten Commandments monolith that was dedicated in 1957 (the school was dedicated in 1956). FFRF member Marie Schaub, and her child (Doe 1 in the lawsuit), Doe 2 (a student at Valley High School), and Doe 3 (parent/guardian of Doe 2), filed the case in US District Court, Western District of Pennsylvania. According to the lawsuit, "Both parent plaintiffs have felt stress and anxiety over concern that they and their children would continue to encounter the religious monument at the school." FFRF is insisting on a permanent injunction for removal, reasonable costs and attorneys' fees, and damages paid to the plaintiffs.

Photo by Sue A. Hoffman (October 2008)
New Kensington, Pennsylvania (1957)

This lawsuit occurred because Staff Attorney Patrick Elliott sent a letter in March 2012 to District Superintendent George Batterson demanding that the Ten Commandments monolith be removed because, "it violates the Establishment Clause of the First Amendment." According to FFRF, the school not only did not remove the monolith, but it also failed to issue an official response. Local clergy did respond after the second letter in September by holding a rally in front of Valley High School to gather support for the school's monolith. Batterson said, "We've decided to take a hard line on this. We have legal counsel, and we are not going to remove the Ten Commandments."

The school district has received over 1,000 emails and calls in support of the Ten Commandments monolith and only three messages against. "We don't promote any religions or push any religions," according to Batterson. "We don't think having the Ten Commandments monument in front of our high school is influencing them to become Christian, Jewish, or any other religion. I've had parents call me, students email me, and graduate students reach out. There has been tremendous support for what we're trying to do." School Board President Robert Pallone took to social media and posted, "Keep the Ten Commandments at Valley High School."

Photo by Sue A. Hoffman (October 2008)
Standing at the front entrance of Valley High School, looking across the park-like setting where the Ten Commandments monolith is, there is a walkway and foot bridge to the parking lot near the main road that passes by the school

There was an effort to have the case dismissed in November 2012 by the school district's attorneys Anthony G. Sanchez and Amie A. Thompson. They contend that it has been over fifty years since the Ten Commandments monolith has been placed and it is now considered "a secular and historical touchstone rather than a religious endorsement." In December 2012, Marcus B. Schneider, representing FFRF and the plaintiffs, responded that it was too early to dismiss the case because the discovery phase, when each side exchanges information and establishes the facts, has not yet occurred. US District Judge Terrence F. McVerry agreed with the plaintiffs, and the case will continue on past the deadline phase of publishing this book. Unfortunately, this is where we have to leave New Kensington, Pennsylvania – unresolved.

Photo courtesy of The Eagle Magazine (July 1957)
While hosting a District Convention, this Aerie presented a Ten Commandments monolith to the city with Judge E. J. Ruegemer (presenter), Rev. Wayne Van Kirk (Ministerial Association), Lyle Zick, Mayor Frank Ducan, and a color guard from a neighboring Aerie.

Photo by Karen Madsen (July 2011)

After the previous photo's monolith was dedicated in 1957, it was placed at the local library.

Photo by Judy Pankow (October 2012)

Dedicated in 1957

Photo courtesy of *The Eagle Magazine* (1964)

Don Gunter and Congressman Basil Whitener during a 1964 Eagle Convention

Photo courtesy of the Fraternal Order of Eagles

The county received several anonymous letters in the early 1990s requesting that the Ten Commandments monolith be removed, and yet it still stands.

Photo by Sue A. Hoffman (September 2012)

Dedicated in 1957

1958-1959

Fargo, Fargo, Fargo – What did you do to deserve such wrath from your former mayor and those Red River Freethinkers who just won't leave you alone? This poor North Dakota town has been harassed relentlessly since 2001, and the good people of Fargo just keep fighting back against the continued onslaught of totally ridiculous lawsuits that continue to waste taxpayer dollars.

The problems started in 2001 when five Red River Freethinkers threatened to sue Fargo over the placement of their Ten Commandments monolith. North Dakota Family Alliance circulated petitions in August 2001 to keep the monolith. In September 2001, a few hours before the Fargo City Commission met to discuss the status of the monolith, someone dumped what appeared to be motor oil on the monolith. The Commission voted four-to-one to let the monolith stay in front of City Hall.

Wesley Twombly, et al, also sued the City of Fargo to have the Ten Commandments monolith removed. They were represented free-of-charge by student attorneys from the University of North Dakota. Twombly might have done better had he gotten attorneys who had successfully passed the bar.

The Red River Freethinkers then wanted to place their own monument next to the Ten Commandments monolith that would state, "The government of the United States of America is not in any sense founded on the Christian religion." The Fargo City Commission rejected the idea of a "sister" monument and voted to remove the monolith in June 2007 and donate it to a private entity. Fargonians were not pleased with that decision and they gathered 5,265 signatures to keep their monolith – so the decision was reversed and the monolith remained as of July 2007.

In April 2008, the Red River Freethinkers again requested to place a monument next to the Ten Commandments monolith in Fargo via a lawsuit filed in federal court. The civil suit argued that the City of Fargo violated the Freethinkers' constitutional rights in 2007 when it refused to allow the group to place a monument near the Ten Commandments monolith on city property.

US District Judge Ralph Erickson dismissed the lawsuit in 2010 on a recommendation from US Magistrate Judge Karen Klein that the suit did not have merit. Erickson declared, "The monument celebrates both religious and secular ideals and does not violate the Constitution."

In May 2012, the Eighth US Circuit Court of Appeals, in a two-to-one vote, allowed the Red River Freethinkers to continue with its lawsuit against Fargo having a Ten Commandments monolith on government property. It contended that the Red River Freethinkers' constitutional rights were violated. The case has been sent back to district court and is not settled at the time this book is being published. Bruce Schoenwald, the lawyer representing the Red River Freethinkers, stated, "Of course we're elated and we're planning to go forward with the case. I assume it will go to trial at some point if we can't get it resolved some other way."

Photo by Karen Madsen (July 2012)

Mayor Herschel Lashkowitz accepted the Ten Commandments monolith in 1958. Judge E. J. Ruegemer and Senator Langer were at the dedication. The monolith was in storage from 1958 until it was installed in 1961 "Commemorating the first Urban Renewal Project in North Dakota dedicated to the State's future development and a better way of life for all its people."
Fargo, North Dakota (1958)

This Ten Commandments monolith was dedicated "In memory of the war survivors and those who did not survive." When it was requested that the monolith be removed in the 1990s, the former mayor told the group to "go jump in a lake." The subsequent mayor had the same response to the unnamed atheist organization.

Photo by Karen Madsen (December 2010)

Dedicated in 1958

On Memorial Day 1958, Elkhart, Indiana's City Hall was graced with a Ten Commandments monolith, but sadly, that is not where it remained. The state director of Indiana American Atheists, Michael Suetkamp, was "offended" when he saw the Ten Commandments monolith on public property in 1998. The monolith also "bothered" William Books. Together with the Indiana Civil Liberties Union (ICLU), they sued the City of Elkhart. The US District Court initially ruled that the monolith was to remain at City Hall. In December 2000, the Seventh District Court of Appeals (which includes Indiana, Illinois, and Wisconsin) ruled that the monolith "violated the constitutional separation of church and state and suggested that some faith traditions were officially favored."

Jay Sekulow and the American Center for Law and Justice (ACLJ) took the case and at least seven states filed petitions with the US Supreme Court. Dr. Laura Schlessinger rallied for the Ten Commandments monolith on national radio, and over 60,000 people nationwide signed letters to maintain the monolith at Elkhart City Hall. The US Supreme Court refused to hear the case in May 2001, which meant that the monolith had to be removed.

Chief Justice William H. Rehnquist, a dissenter in the case, stated that the Ten Commandments had played a "foundational role . . . in secular, legal matters" that can be featured in a city's "celebration of its cultural and historical roots" without becoming "a promotion of religious faith." Justice Rehnquist was joined by Justices Clarence Thomas and Antonin Scalia, who made it clear that "the court should have overturned the ruling, clearing the way for government at all levels to display the Ten Commandments."

The *Falwell Confidential Newsletter* bemoaned, "People of faith across the nation were disheartened" by the US Supreme Court's decision to not hear the Elkhart case. Rev. Jerry Falwell went on to say, "Activist judges are deliberately ignoring the actuality of America's founding an actuality of dependence on the Bible and Judeo-Christian values."

Pat Robertson of the 700 Club called the ruling, "the craziest thing." He insisted, "There's nothing in the Constitution that ever intended this." He called for Congress to take away the Justices' money. He said, "They can also take away their appellate jurisdiction if they so choose, because the Constitution gives that power."

Jay Sekulow remarked that, "The court action against a government display of the Ten Commandments could put the country on a 'slippery slope' toward moral ruin."

In March 2002, the US District Court said that the monolith may stay **if** four other monuments were added nearby (the Bill of Rights, the Preamble to the US Constitution, the Declaration of Independence, and the Magna Carta). Elkhart might have considered this, but in August 2002, the US District Court ordered the City of Elkhart to pay $63,000 in legal expenses and remove the monolith. The Ten Commandments monolith was taken down and then placed prominently on private property at the entrance of Elkhart's famed River Walk.

This legal action gave fuel to the many other organizations who want the monoliths removed across the United States. The Books v. Elkhart decision was the case that broke the heart of Judge E. J. Ruegemer.

Photo by Sue A. Hoffman (September 2012)

Elkhart, Indiana (May 1958)

Photo by Lisa D. Lind (July 2013)
(Sue A. Hoffman's daughter)
Amelia and Levi Lind in
Somersworth, New Hampshire
(Grandchildren of Sue A. Hoffman)

This town couldn't be more proud of its Ten Commandments monolith. It sits next to City Hall, the VFW is across the street, and the Police Station and the Post Office are on the same street. Michael Carnevale and Dennis Rhoades are greatly appreciated for verifying the monolith's existence in June of 2008. The monolith was dedicated, "In memory of Departed Brothers."

Photo by Lisa D. Lind (July 2013)
Somersworth, New Hampshire (May 1958)

The Borough of Hanover, Pennsylvania was elated in 1958 when it received its Ten Commandments monolith in Wirt Park. In 2003, Americans United for Separation of Church and State (AU) made a challenge to remove the monolith.

Photo courtesy of the Fraternal Order of Eagles
Celebratory event in Hanover, Pennsylvania in which the "pre-monolith" was present for viewing

The City Council of Hanover planned to move the monolith to a private site in 2004, but over 10,000 signatures were gathered to keep the monolith right where it was. The Hanover Area Heritage Association raised more than $30,000 to fight the lawsuit. In April 2004, the York County Orphans' Court allowed the Hanover Borough to sell a fifteen-by-fifteen foot parcel of land to Gitt-Moul Historic Properties, Inc. (a non-profit organization which preserves local historic properties and structures) in Wirt Park for $900. In December 2004, the deed was handed to Gitt-Moul.

The Borough Council agreed to enclose the area with a gate, plant trees, and lay a brick area that would lead from the sidewalk to the monolith. The Council has made it very clear that the Borough of Hanover "is not the owner of the property, does not maintain the property, and performs no municipal function in relation to the monument property."

Photo by Karen Madsen (October 2011)
Hanover, Pennsylvania (1958)

According to the *Great Bend Sunday Tribune* (June 8, 1958), the dedication of the Ten Commandments monolith was the highlight of the three-day Fortieth Kansas State Convention of the Fraternal Order of Eagles. The governor, the lieutenant governor, state, county, and local representatives, as well as Mayor R. E. "Bud" Morrison, were all on hand for the unveiling that Saturday, June 7. Three motorcycles led the procession from the Eagles Aerie to the Barton County Courthouse.

Photo courtesy of *The Eagle Magazine* (November 1958)

A host of officials representing all levels of government and the Fraternal Order of Eagles were present for the dedication of an eight-foot stone monolith of the Ten Commandments, unveiled in front of the courthouse Saturday afternoon. From the left are Eagles' State President Claude Roberts of Hutchinson; Fred J. Cappadona, Galveston, Texas, representing the National Eagles lodge; Robert Lathrop, Great Bend, State FOE trustee; State Senator Glee Smith, Larned; Dedication speaker Ray S. Schulz, Great Bend; Lieutenant Governor J. W. Henkle, Sr., Great Bend; Congressman J. Floyd Breeding, Rolla; Harry Searles, local FOE president; and Govenor George Docking. On the other side of the monolith, County Commissioners Wilfred Marquis, Wilbur Bryant; Probate Judge Robert Bates (holding a framed plaque presented for the probate court); State Representative Tony Schartz; and Commissioner Gary Brown.
Great Bend, Kansas (June 1958)

Ray Schulz, a Great Bend attorney, "presented a brief address on the Ten Commandments and the story behind the Eagles' gift to the city. He pointed out that the Ten Commandments have served as a code for over 3,000 years, and are accepted by Jews, Christians, and Muslims. Yet, only one person in seven can recite the Commandments from memory." The Great Bend newspaper also stated that "Judge Morgan C. Harris of Cumberland, Maryland, suggested that a granite monolith be built in front of every courthouse to display the Ten Commandments."

The Great Bend Eagles also presented copies of the Ten Commandments to each school child in grades one through nine. Every person who attended the dedication ceremony received a scroll of the Ten Commandments.

Soon after the dedication, letters were written to the Great Bend Tribune objecting to the wording and the numbering of the Ten Commandments on the monolith. A committee got together, made up of a Protestant minister, a Catholic priest, and a Jewish rabbi. They were satisfied with the version that was presented on the monolith. The individuals who objected to anything regarding the separation of church and state were not satisfied with the committee's ruling, so they continued to complain.

On Thursday, March 18, 1971, shortly before noon, winds reaching more than fifty mph toppled the Ten Commandments monolith. Vibrations from the fall rattled the Barton County Courthouse. When the monolith blew over, it broke into two pieces and was taken away and stored at an unknown location. The Street Scape Renovation of Downtown Great Bend (1989-1992) motivated some individuals to initiate a petition drive to return the Ten Commandments monolith back to the Barton County Courthouse based on its historical significance to the county. For some unknown reason, the Ten Commandments monolith had disappeared and was never resurrected in Great Bend, Kansas.

Photo, as well as other historical data, courtesy of Joe Boley, Great Bend, Kansas

Photo by Karen Madsen (December 2012)

Jefferson City, Missouri (June 28, 1958)

In 2003, when asked if the American Civil Liberties Union (ACLU) had any desire to remove the Ten Commandments monolith at the State Capitol Building in Jefferson City, Missouri, Dan Viets, an ACLU counselor and Columbia attorney said, "Neither I nor the ACLU have, at this point, committed to taking any specific action regarding the issue." The Attorney General's Office offered that it had not received any lawsuits regarding the monolith.

Program

DEDICATION OF THE FRATERNAL ORDER OF EAGLES MONOLITH, "THE TEN COMMANDMENTS" ON THE CAPITOL GROUNDS JEFFERSON CITY, MISSOURI

12:00 Noon, Saturday, June 28, 1958

DR. R. R. McDERMOTT .... Presiding
Immediate Past President of the Missouri State Aerie

HON. JOHN M. DALTON .... Master of Ceremonies
Attorney-General of the State of Missouri

1. Advance of Colors .... Color Guard, Roy Sone Post No. 1003, V. F. W.
   WARREN ROARK, HENRY ELLS, JR., EUGENE PERKINS, ROBERT B. TOLIN, SIDNEY FERGUSON, JEROME HAAR
   Jefferson City, Missouri
2. Musical Selection .... "The Mellokats"
   Jefferson City, Missouri
3. Pledge of Allegiance to the Flag .... Boy Scout Troop
   Jefferson City, Missouri
4. Invocation .... The Rev. Russell Lytle
   Pastor of the First Methodist Church of Jefferson City
5. Address of Welcome .... Hon. Arthur W. Ellis
   Mayor of the City of Jefferson City
6. Remarks on Youth Guidance .... Judge Robert W. Hansen
   Past Grand Worthy President F. O. E., Milwaukee, Wisconsin
7. Dedication Address .... Rabbi Louis Cashdan
   B'nai Jehudah Temple, Kansas City, Missouri
8. Unveiling of the Monolith ...... A. J. Schwaller, State President; Lester J. Mueller, State Trustee
   Jefferson City, Missouri
9. Presentation .... Dr. R. R. McDermott
   Kansas City, Missouri
10. Acceptance .... Hon. James T. Blair
    Governor of the State of Missouri
11. Benediction .... Msgr. Paul U. Kertz
    Pastor of Immaculate Conception Church, Jefferson City, Missouri
12. National Anthem .... By the Band

HOST AERIE No. 2693—JEFFERSON CITY

Courtesy of the Fraternal Order of Eagles
Page from the Jefferson City, Missouri Dedication Program

Photo courtesy of the Fraternal Order of Eagles
Lieutenant Governor Edward V. Long, who later became a US senator, presided over the dedication ceremony. Judge Robert Hansen and Arthur Ellis were in attendance. There are several dedicated monuments and statues on the Capitol grounds.
Jefferson City, Missouri

About 300 people are buried in Bentz Street Graveyard Memorial Ground in Frederick, Maryland. It used to be the church graveyard of the Evangelical Reform Church, which donated the property in 1924 to the city and county. At some point, the name was changed to Old Memorial Park, but that changed in 2002.

Urbana High School senior, Blake Trettien, wrote a letter to city and county officials in March 2002, stating, "The government's endorsement of one belief over another creates an environment that is hostile to those who do not hold the same beliefs. This is offensive; governments simply should not display religious symbols in a way that divides us." The American Civil Liberties Union (ACLU) came along side of Trettien and sued giving the city until August 1 to remove the monolith.

About 100 supporters rallied in front of Frederick City Hall in support of the monolith at Old Memorial Park in April 2002. Pastor Robinson presented a petition with over 2,000 signatures of those who wanted the monolith to remain in the park. In an act of desperation, the Frederick Board of

Aldermen voted unanimously to rededicate Old Memorial Park as an historic cemetery in August 2002, returning it to its former name of Bentz Street Graveyard Memorial Ground to help thwart the legal action of the ACLU. Heather Smith, Frederick's Chief Legal Services Officer at the time, confirmed that, "The site has historical, archeological, and cultural significances."

Stacy Mink, mouth-piece for the Maryland branch of the ACLU, didn't buy the move by the Board of Aldermen. She commented, "The rededication of the park as a Christian burial ground does not make for a better land classification. It is still unconstitutional." In November 2002, the ACLU forced the hand of the Board to sell a ten-by-fifty foot parcel of land that the Ten Commandments monolith rests on for $6,700 to the Fraternal Order of Eagles against the wishes of the Friends of Frederick Foundation.

Roy Chambers and the Americans United for Separation of Church and State (AU) then sued the City of Frederick in 2003. The American Center for Law and Justice (ACLJ) agreed to represent the Fraternal Order of Eagles in January 2004. In June 2005, the US District Court for Maryland, and Judge William Quarles, found that the sale of the land and the monolith to the Eagles was constitutional.

Photo by Carol Carman (June 2012)

The Ten Commandments monolith was originally dedicated at the Frederick County Courthouse, which then changed to the Frederick City Hall in 1983. The monolith was moved to Old Memorial Park in 1985.
Frederick, Maryland (June 1958)

In December 2005, Winona, Minnesota's Ten Commandments monolith was sprayed with black paint referencing someone's problem regarding "state/church issues." Mayor Jerry Miller said that this was the first time that any controversy had ever been displayed against the monolith. The paint was able to be removed, leaving no trace of the vandalism.

Photo by Karen Madsen (July 2011)

Winona, Minnesota (June 1958)

Photo by Stephanie Pankow Wood (May 2013)
(Sue A. Hoffman's niece)

Dedicated in 1958

A Ten Commandments monolith was dedicated at Indiana's Montgomery County Courthouse in September 1958. Indiana Civil Liberties Union (ICLU) filed a lawsuit in October 2001. The county commissioners voted three-to-zero to remove the monolith instead of fighting to keep it, and it was promptly removed and placed in front of Eagles' Aerie 1005. Greg Colburn was able to get several photos of Ten Commandments monoliths in the early stages of this journey, not only in Crawfordsville, but several other locations as well. His efforts are very much appreciated.

Photo by Sue A. Hoffman (September 2012)

Crawfordsville, Indiana (September 1958)

Businessman Earl Myler offered to buy a small piece of land at the Montgomery County Courthouse so that the Ten Commandments monolith could be returned. Ken Lewis from Colorado pledged to outbid any offer that Myler would make. The county commissioners decided to put the whole thing on hold until the US Supreme Court decision was made in June 2005 regarding the Ten Commandments monolith in Austin, Texas. The matter is still on hold, as of this report, nine years later.

In a confusing tale of two intertwining monoliths, the Indiana State Fraternal Order of Eagles placed one of the largest Ten Commandments monoliths made in the United States at the Indiana State House in 1958. It was unusual in that it had a center piece that had a cross at the top, two Stars of David, and then the Ten Commandments. The left side listed all of the Indiana Aeries, and the right side listed all of the Indiana Auxiliaries.

Stephen M. Schroeder of Indianapolis damaged the Ten Commandments monolith on five different occasions while it was on the Indiana State House lawn because he maintained that the monolith was "a sneaky pagan plot." He saw himself as a "Christian, Protestant, anti-Catholic, and anti-Mason." He also firmly believed that Indianapolis "is the supreme capital of pagan worship." In 1991, Mr. Schroeder finally broke the monolith into two pieces, and after refusing to pay the $2,500 fine, he spent ninety days in jail. The broken Ten Commandments monolith was removed from state property.

Enter then-Indiana State Representative Brent Steele. He thought that if the Ten Commandments monolith could be repaired, then Indiana courts would have no problem having the monolith returned back to the State House lawn. When he found the monolith, he commented,

It looked more like six Commandments." Steele created a non-profit organization, Ten Commandments Foundation, Inc., that commissioned a new, four-sided, Ten Commandments monolith that included the Bill of Rights and the 1851 Indiana Constitution Preamble. One side of the new monolith mentioned the donation from the Indiana Limestone Industry and the following words: "This monument replaces the one donated by the Aeries and Auxiliaries of the Indiana Fraternal Order of Eagles on October 25, 1958."

Photo courtesy of the Fraternal Order of Eagles

Indianapolis, Indiana (October 1958)

In the meantime, the original Ten Commandments monolith was able to be repaired. Anderson Aerie 174 (about thirty miles away from the State Capital) placed a new plaque on the monolith and rededicated it in 1998 in front of their Aerie.

When then-Governor Frank O'Bannon announced that he would install the newly commissioned monument at the State House, the Indiana Civil Liberties Union (ICLU) sued on July 27, 2001. They got a federal court injunction to block the placement of the new Ten Commandments monolith stating that the destroyed monolith could not be replaced because the new monolith had no historic credence. In October, the Lawrence County Commissioners unanimously voted to put the new monument on the Lawrence County Courthouse lawn where it lasted only a few days before the ICLU sued again. The new Ten Commandments monolith was placed in storage.

Coincidentally, Kim Henderson, owner of a new Subway restaurant, was getting ready to reopen her shop across the street from the County Courthouse in 2002 after it had been destroyed by a fire. The new 13,700 pound Ten Commandments monolith was dedicated in front of Subway during the Limestone Heritage Festival during the week of July 4, 2002.

In March 2004, a "Jeep Cherokee filled with young white males" drove into the original Ten Commandments monolith at the Anderson Aerie breaking it into twelve pieces rendering it useless. The vandal driving the Jeep who destroyed the monolith stepped forward, sued against having the new replacement Ten Commandments monolith placed on Indiana's capitol grounds, and won. He did have to pay a fine for destroying the original Eagles' Ten Commandments monolith.

And the new Ten Commandments monolith? It was removed from its location at Subway in 2009 for repair work and refurbishing due to skateboard scratches and miscellaneous stains, and it will not be returned. It was given a new home at the Thirty-Ninth Street Christian Church in Bedford, Indiana.

Photo courtesy of *The Eagle Magazine* (April 1959)

Members of the Indianapolis Auxiliary drill team acted as escorts at the Ten Commandments monolith presentation to the State of Indiana. Among those present were William Curley, grand conductor.From right are: Friar Albert Ajamie, Mayor Philip Boyt, and Judge Donald Bowen representing former Governor Handley.

Photo by Judy Pankow (September 2012)

Junction City, Kansas (November 1958)

Michael Brown and Tyrel Brown attended the October 2004 meeting of Junction City's Commissioners' meeting. They requested that the Ten Commandments monolith be removed. If the monolith remained, a statute of Buddha had to be placed adjacent to the monolith. In July 2005, the City Manager basically considered it a done deal that the Ten Commandments monolith will remain unaccompanied.

Photo courtesy *The Eagle Magazine* (June 1959)

A Ten Commandments monolith was presented to Junction City, Kansas. From the left are: Lieutenant Governor J. Hinkle of Kansas, Joseph Domme, past state president; Rev. Charles Cook; Carl Swenson, Aerie vice president; Joe Hood, Aerie president; Byron Boger, Kenneth Eddy, past presidents; Mayor Thomas Fegan; Clifford Harris, past president; Jess Filby, city commissioner, Guy Beam, Aerie member; Carl Deppish, city commission; Virgil Basgall, city manager; Robert Schonberner, state chaplain; Loy Hale, past state president; Floyd Searls, past president; and Ernest Taylor, finance committee chairman.

Photo by Dan Tate (May 2009)

A broken monolith is found.

Dan Tate is an Indiana realtor by trade and a Wayne County historian out of pure passion. The two combined one fateful day while Dan was surveying some property of a defunct monument company that was up for sale. His story is as follows:

A Wayne County Indiana monument company closed its doors several years ago and left behind its unsold, scrapped, and damaged stones. These scrapped stones were piled at the rear of the property and were fast becoming a part of the landscape. Trees, weeds, and shrubs have almost concealed these unused granite markers (not to mention overflowing vines of poison ivy).

Early in 2009 while investigating this site, I noticed an odd shaped monument – it was barely

Photo by Dan Tate (September 2009)
Stone Plans (brothers Ganesh and Senthil Murguathur) volunteered their time and equipment to help with the move.

visible from beneath its camouflage of small saplings and other bits and pieces of monuments piled close-by. I pulled the weeds and debris from the top of the stone and immediately realized it was one of the original Ten Commandment stones from the 1950s and 1960s! Unfortunately, a large piece of the stone was missing from the bottom of the monument, but the text of the Ten Commandments had survived the damage and remained, for the most part, intact.

During a conversation with Pastor Robert Johnson, he indicated that his church would like to have the old monument. I contacted the owners of the property and they agreed to give it to the church. Stone Plans, a local monument company, graciously volunteered to donate the use of their equipment and labor to relocate the approximately 2,000 pound stone.

Located at the North 27 Worship Center, the salvaged Ten Commandments monument is now visible to northbound and southbound traffic on US 27, north of Richmond, Indiana.

It was a real pleasure meeting Dan Tate and Pastor Johnson. I am truly grateful, along with many others, for all of their efforts to find a good home for this monolith. A more permanent and stable base will be designed in the future, and a rededication will be planned to honor the occasion.

Based on all of the records that I have at my disposal, it is my best assumption that this broken Ten Commandments monolith belonged to the good people of Connersville, Indiana – a town approximately twenty-five miles southwest of Richmond. The Connersville monolith was dedicated in 1958. According to Karen Madsen who visited the town, the Aerie burned down in 1961 and all of the records were destroyed at that time. Karen talked to people at the Aerie, library, courthouse, and local historical museum, and no one had any recollection of this monolith, so it must have been destroyed many years ago. Dan Tate noted the obvious – the monolith had lost its dedication information – almost as if the act of vandalism had an intentional purpose. How it ended up in a monument graveyard is anyone's guess.

Photo by Dan Tate (September 2009)

Photo by Jeffrey Hoffman (June 2012)
Pastor Robert Johnson and Dan Tate

Photo by Sue A. Hoffman (May 2010)
Vincennes, Indiana (1958)

Kenneth Falk and the Indiana Civil Liberties Union (ICLU) gave Vincennes, Indiana just ten days to remove its Ten Commandments monolith in front of the Knox County Courthouse in June 2001. After visiting one of the most patriotic towns of Middle America that I have ever been in, I don't think that Falk knew what he was in for. Vincennes is Norman Rockwellville times ten. Just for the day that I was there, I felt proud to be an American – the beautiful huge, old homes, US flags flying everywhere, clean streets, people greeting each other with a smile and "How ya doing?"

Vincennes did not remove their monolith and the ICLU sued. Hundreds of residents protested the lawsuit by placing Ten Commandments signs in their yards. The county attorney requested assistance from the American Center for Law and Justice (ACLJ). The case was dropped in September 2001 because the two plaintiffs refused to reveal their names and they withdrew from the case.

The town must have seen the "writing on the wall" and decided to be proactive against any further litigation. It took five years, a complete do-over on the Knox County Courthouse lawn, and a lot of money, but what was created is a testament to American fortitude and civic pride.

Photo by Sue A. Hoffman (May 2010)
Knox County Courthouse with several Veterans memorials

The Ten Commandments monolith presided at the side of Manhattan City Hall in Manhattan, Kansas from the time of its dedication in 1958 until 1998 when there was a major renovation. Gary Greer, the city manager, wrote a memo in October 1998 to the City of Manhattan to assure them that the monolith was not in violation of the Constitution and could remain on City Hall grounds. In a three-to-two vote, the Manhattan City Commission voted to not only keep the monolith on the grounds, but have it reset at the front doors of Manhattan City Hall.

Moving the Ten Commandments monolith caught the attention of the American Civil Liberties Union (ACLU) of Kansas and the Americans United for Separation of Church and State (AU). Together, along with seven local citizens, a lawsuit was filed for the removal of the monolith on April 7, 1999.

Photo by Judy Pankow (September 2012)

Manhattan, Kansas (1958)

Wasting no time at the April 27, 1999 City Commission meeting, with a new commissioner in place (Carol Peak), after four hours of public commentary and less than one hour of discussion, the vote was recast and a decision was made to remove the Ten Commandments monolith. Not only that, the City of Manhattan, in a four-to-one vote, also agreed to pay approximately $12,000 in court costs to the ACLU, giving more credence to future litigations.

The very next day, on April 28, the city "dumped" the monolith behind Eagles' Aerie 2468. It took two years, but the Ten Commandments monolith was enthusiastically rededicated at Manhattan Christian College on May 4, 2001 with over 200 people in attendance. College President Kenneth Cable said, "The College is humbled to have been given the privilege of providing a place to display the monolith in a manner worthy of the values and traditions embodied in the Ten Commandments. I wish to express our heartfelt appreciation to the Fraternal Order of Eagles. We will strive to preserve the monolith in a manner that befits such a community treasure."

Photo courtesy of *The Eagle Magazine* (September 2001)

City Commissioner Roger Raitz, Manhattan Christian College President Kenneth Cable, Past Worthy President Bill Ellis, and City Commissioner Ed Klimek at the Rededication of the Ten Commandments monolith on May 4, 2001

Photo donated by John Ellzey, Yazoo City, Mississippi
Photo from Yazoo City High School's 1962 Yearbook

On April 17, 1959, a Ten Commandments monolith was placed at the Yazoo City High School in Yazoo City, Mississippi. When a new high school was built, the building became the temporary home for the junior high school.

At some point, the junior high school students moved on, and the building became the new home of the Boys & Girls Club where the Ten Commandments monolith still stands.

John Ellzey, who is with the B. S. Ricks Memorial Library, was fundamental in securing information regarding this monolith's location. Vay, an erstwhile town historian, was able to take one photo of the Ten Commandments monolith proving that the monolith needed to be stabilized a bit after all of these years.

It was a pleasure dealing with people in Mississippi – their southern charm and hospitality really came through. At one point, there were twelve Fraternal Order of Eagles' Aeries in the state, and now there are none.

Scan donated by John Ellzey, Yazoo City, Mississippi
Mingo Chito 1961 – Cover of the Yazoo City High School Yearbook

Photo donated by John Ellzey, Yazoo City, Mississippi
Snow in Mississippi in 1963 as pictured in the Mingo Chito, Yazoo City High School Yearbook

Photo by Karen Madsen (April 2010)

Logan, Ohio (1959)

According to *The Eagle Magazine* (August/September 1959):

Many state, county, and city officials were present for the dedication of the Ten Commandments monolith to the city by Logan, Ohio Aerie. Guest speakers were William G. Watson, Grand Secretary, and Paul N. Hoffmann, Grand Trustee, representing the Grand Aerie, and Harry Veddern, Past Ohio State President.

The program for the afternoon consisted of the Advance of Colors by Logan VFW Post; musical selection by the Logan High School Band; Oath of Allegiance; invocation by Rev. R. B. Wilson; address of welcome by Mayor Francis Myers; remarks by Harry Veddern, Past State President; dedication address by William G. Watson, Grand Secretary; unveiling of the monolith by Robert Kern and Lawrence Ellinger; presentation remarks on the Ten Commandments by Rev. J. Carl Plummer, Rev. D. S. Dunkle, Rev. Roy Klinger, Rev. P. O. Householder, Rev. Earl Edwards, Rev. Peyton D. Reed, Rev. Charles V. Turner, Rev. Paul Sellers, Rev. Marvin Franklin, and Rev. Earl F. Schottke, each speaking briefly about each Commandment.

Introduction of dignitaries was given by Glen A. Gartner, Master of Ceremonies. James C. Cottril acted as program chairman for the dedication. The program was brought to a close with benediction by Rev. Father Charles P. Foy, and the National Anthem by the Logan High School Band.

Photo by Sally Widener (November 2012)
Dedicated in 1959

After over a year of planning, the dedication ceremony for this monolith was at hand. "Erection of the monolith . . . will present a pleasing and reverent touch to the grounds of the Memorial Building." The high school band performed and the Presentation and the Retreat of Colors was provided by members of the Post of the Veterans of Foreign Wars, the American Legion, and the County Post. The Pledge of Allegiance was led by a Methodist pastor; the Invocation was led by a Catholic priest; two short addresses on the Ten Commandments were given by a Lutheran pastor and a pastor from the United Church of Christ, Evangelical and Reformed; the mayor accepted the monolith for the town; and the Benediction was given by a different Lutheran pastor. I would say that all of the bases were covered at this celebration of the unveiling of the Ten Commandments monolith.

The Ten Commandments monolith in Mishawaka, Indiana was dedicated on October 8, 1959 at City Hall. In 1986, the City Hall relocated and took the monolith with it.

David Hoffman, a non-practicing local attorney and college teacher, filed a lawsuit in November 2001, along with the Indiana Civil Liberties Union (ICLU), protesting that the Ten Commandments monolith stood on government property. Rather than fight the

Photo by Sue A. Hoffman (September 2012)
Mishawaka, Indiana (October 1959)

lawsuit, the city decided to cut its costs and removed the monolith in November 2002. The Ten Commandments monolith was rededicated at First United Methodist Church in November 2002 – just two weeks after it was removed from City Hall.

City Hall in Everett, Washington needed more room to install a War Memorial, so they had to move the Ten Commandments monolith a tad bit to the left in 1988. It had been planted in its spot since it was dedicated in December 1959. The City Hall building then became the Everett Police Department, but the monolith and the other memorials stayed.

Americans United for Separation of Church and State (AU) had been on a letter-writing campaign against the City of Everett since 1993. In June 2001, the City Attorney finally made it known that the monolith was not going anywhere. When a twenty-year-old Mormon-turned-agnostic student, Jesse Card, contacted AU regarding the Ten Commandments monolith in Everett, they couldn't wait to file a lawsuit. Card said, "I walk past this thing, and it just doesn't seem right to me whatsoever, to have this giant granite marker with the Ten Commandments on it. Those aren't universal values." Together, they sued the City of Everett for one dollar in damages in July 2003.

Photo by Lynn Thompson (February 2013)
Karen Madsen and Sue A. Hoffman
The only time that these friends were together visiting the same Ten Commandments monolith at the same time
Everett, Washington (December 1959)

In August 2003, the Snohomish County Council unanimously passed a resolution supporting the City of Everett's decision to maintain the Ten Commandments monolith in its current location. Everett turned down an offer from the Christian Coalition of America to help fight the court battle in 2004 to distance itself from appearing to support religion in an attempt to keep the monolith. Card received $1,000 at the Freedom from Religion Foundation (FFRF) Mini-Convention of the Pacific Northwest on July 10, 2004 for his "outstanding efforts."

After running up a $125,000 tab for legal fees, US District Judge Robert Lasnik declared that Everett had won the battle and the Ten Commandments monolith could stay at the Everett Police Station. Unfortunately, the case went back on appeals. On March 26, 2008, after spending another $65,000, a three-judge panel of the US Ninth Circuit Court of Appeals upheld the 2005 ruling claiming that, "The monument doesn't violate the constitutional separation of church and state." Jesse Card and the Americans United for Separation of Church and State (AU) lost their battle in Washington State, and perhaps someday, they will lose the war.

Photo by Jeffrey Hoffman (June 2012)
Richmond, Indiana (1959)

The Indiana Civil Liberties Union (ICLU) and William Roha did not like seeing a Ten Commandments monolith at the Wayne County Courthouse in Richmond, Indiana that had been there since 1959. They filed a lawsuit in the US District Court in January 2002.

The Ten Commandments Action Committee proposed that the monolith be secularized by permanently covering the two Stars of David, the Greek letters Chi and Rho, and the American eagle holding the flag. This did not seem to go over very well with the general public, so Wayne Bank and Trust Company requested to be the recipient of the Ten Commandments monolith if it had to be removed.

Roha requested reimbursement of $9,200 from Wayne County, plus court costs, when all was said and done. The monolith was removed on January 3, 2003. Rev. Gene Calicott addressed the attendees at the rededication ceremony in June 2003 at the Wayne Bank and Trust Company.

The citizens of Springfield, Ohio take their Ten Commandments monolith very personally. From the very beginning, it was all about the people who really cared to have a monolith in their community.

Monies were raised by a raffle for an afghan made by Helen Johnson (wife of Worthy President Clarence Johnson). Louis French sold the most raffle tickets and he, and Helen Johnson, were honored by cutting the ribbon at the monolith dedication ceremony in the late summer of 1959.

An anonymous letter threatening a lawsuit was sent in 1993 to the Clark County Commissioners with a few follow-up letters through 1995. Springfield's local Channel 7 reported that there had been anonymous letters, and numerous newspaper articles were written along with letters to the editor of the *News-Sun Times*. Almost all of the letters and editorials were supportive of keeping the monolith at the Clark County Courthouse except those written by one out-of-town attorney, Derrick Stroble, an out-of-town pastor, G. Weir Hartman, and an out-of town writer, Steven Shimits.

A petition with over 2,200 names was presented at a hearing at the commissioners' meeting requesting that the monolith remain in its current location. Louis French wrote a letter to the commissioners that he read at the meeting and it was also aired on the local radio station. The commissioners responded with a letter stating, "Rest assured, this County Commission has no plans to relocate this monument now or in the future." Someone else had other plans.

Around 2:30 AM on Halloween night in 2009, a driver in a red truck (according to witnesses) plowed into the Ten Commandments monolith and sped off leaving the monolith in two pieces. It was removed from its location and placed in the Clark County engineers' office while they decided what should come next. The town wanted its Ten Commandments monolith back in one piece. County officials said the support to have the monolith returned had been "amazing." They wanted to avoid future litigations if the County put up a new version of the monolith. According to Clark County Commissioner John Detrick, "If it's the same stone, then we have no issue. It's still grandfathered."

Photo by Sue A Hoffman (September 2012)

Springfield, Ohio (1959)

Drake Monument offered to repair the monolith, but the face was so damaged that it would require actual removal of the words by grinding them off of the face. Then, after putting the two pieces back together, old photos would have to be used to replicate the Ten Commandments on the other side of the stone. According to County Facilities Director Jackie Ashworth, "Only four quarries nationwide have the ability to fix the stone. The pins it sits on were destroyed when the monument was ripped from its base." The monolith was sent to Georgia and it was repaired for $10,250 (about twice the cost of replacing it). The insurance covered $7,750 of that cost.

The foundation had to be repaired by the county, and Drake Monument agreed to place the Ten Commandments monolith at its old location. The Alliance Defense Fund had volunteered as legal counsel should anyone try to take the monolith down based on separation of church and state. The whole idea behind repair versus replacement was to avoid future lawsuits.

On Wednesday, July 28, 2010, the Ten Commandments monolith was placed back at Clark County Common Pleas Court.

The Ten Commandments monolith in Grand Junction, Colorado changed locations four times between 1958 and 2000. The fourth move was after City Hall was rebuilt in 2000 and the city officials moved the monolith to the corner of the property.

In February 2001, rumblings were being heard of an impending lawsuit by the American Civil Liberties Union (ACLU) against the City of Grand Junction regarding the Ten Commandments monolith. The American Center for Law and Justice (ACLJ) agreed to provide free legal assistance to Grand Junction. On March 6, a public hearing in the council chambers overflowed with crowds numbering in the four hundreds to keep the monolith. The city officials were bombarded with phone calls, letters, and emails demanding that the Ten Commandments monolith stay. In a five-to-two vote on March 16, the council voted to not only keep the monolith, but appropriated $50,000 to incorporate other monoliths to create the "Cornerstones of Law and Liberty." They also added a disclaimer that read:

> It is the intent of the City Council to recognize our cultural past. We do not endorse, in any way, any religion.
>
> We respect the good intentions of the Fraternal Order of Eagles in presenting the Ten Commandments monument to our residents during the decade of the 1950s when Congress adopted our national motto, "In God We Trust." That same decade Congress included "Under God" in the Pledge of Allegiance. During those 1950s, the Cold War prompted many changes in our national spirit.
>
> We are mindful that this twenty-first century brings a new diversity of citizens. We must necessarily strive to make our government sensitive to the values of Americans with minority views, whether religious, political or otherwise.

Photo by Jeffrey Hoffman (September 2012)

Grand Junction, Colorado (1959)

Kathryn Christian, Jill Havens, Jeff Basinger, Clare Boulanger, and Sarah Swedberg, along with the American Civil Liberties Union (ACLU) Foundation of Colorado and their team of Baker and Silverstein, and affiliated ACLU attorney Neville Woodruff, filed a lawsuit in Federal District Court in Denver in April 2001 stating that displaying a granite Ten Commandments monument in a prominent location at the entrance to City Hall unconstitutionally promoted religion. They also contended that,

"It was unwelcoming to members of minority religious groups, nonbelievers, and political community outsiders. It was also an attempt by the government to establish religion."

In June 2001, US District Judge Wiley Daniel refused the request of the ACLU to have the Ten Commandments monolith removed based on a 1973 ruling in Utah. Jay Baker, attorney for the ACLU, asked that the case be dismissed in the US District Court in Denver after the dedication of the "Cornerstones of Law and Liberty" in October 2001.

Photo by Jeffrey Hoffman (September 2012)

Cornerstones of Law and Liberty, Grand Junction City Hall

1960-1964

Atheist Rob Sherman has had a very busy life being an agitator in the Chicago area. Encouraged by a speech that Madalyn Murray O'Hair gave in 1981, Sherman not only joined American Atheists, but became the Illinois director and a national mouthpiece of the organization for a brief time. He was quoted as saying, "My notoriety comes from attacking virtually every church/state separation violation within shouting distance of Chicago. Victories include: removal of Christian crosses from city seals in numerous nearby municipalities, ending Buffalo Grove, Illinois, Police Department exclusion of atheists from their public education program, ending forced acknowledgement of the Judeo-Christian God in compulsory recitation of Pledge of Allegiance in Illinois public schools, and removal of Christian crosses that adorned the Kane County, Illinois Government Center."

Starting in 1986, Sherman's activism made him front page fodder for the Chicago Tribune. His atheistic crusading not only gave him face time on Chicago's 10 o'clock news, but also on Oprah Winfrey, Phil Donahue, and Larry King. His star lost some shine in July 1998 when he was convicted of domestic battery for striking his sixteen-year-old son when his son did not want to babysit his younger sister so that Sherman could host his radio show. He not only served two jail terms for refusing to complete his court-ordered domestic violence counseling, but he lost his radio show for a short time when the advertisers pulled out. His "Rob Sherman Travel Agency" business also declined. He has since tried to "revive his career as the self-described Jesse Jackson of atheists," and has created "Rob Sherman Advocacy" and "Rob Sherman News."

Sherman was not happy about coming in contact with Waukegan, Illinois's Ten Commandments monolith as he "made one too many visits to criminal court in the Lake County Building in downtown Waukegan, Illinois." Even though he was miles away from his hometown, he made countless treks to protest at the Waukegan City Council meetings between 1986 and 1994. He said, "I think the city should be neutral" and that "the matter should be handled quietly and discreetly." He let it be known that he had no problem initiating a lawsuit. The city attorneys made it crystal clear so that Rob Sherman *finally* acknowledged that, "the city of Waukegan has the obligation not to promote religion, but at the same time it must protect religion."

Photo courtesy of the Fraternal Order of Eagles
P. Haney, Rabbi Albert Taab, Rev. Alden Salstrom, Rev. Paul Cull, and Judge E. J. Ruegemer presided at the dedication.

The Ten Commandments monolith was dedicated in 1960 (the specific month is in dispute as the monolith states April but there are records – and clothing in the photo – that point to January) at the Jane Dowst Memorial Emergency Hospital which opened its doors in 1934. The first aid hospital served Waukegan area physicians and emergency patients. When the hospital shut its doors, the Dowst family gifted the building to the city, and the Police Department used it for training purposes. To make room for the new Waukegan City Hall, the building was torn down and the monolith was temporarily put into storage. In 2003, Ray Vukovich, director of governmental services, said that the Ten Commandments monolith was offered to a nearby church, but they declined the gift. He said, "We'd like to find it a good home – to a not-for-profit or church. I'm sure the City Council would be receptive to it."

Photo by Karen Madsen (April 2010)
Waukegan, Illinois (June 1960)

When the US Supreme Court sided with Perry in the Austin, Texas Ten Commandments monolith case in 2005, Vukovich said, "It appears that we could remount and display the monument on city property. I know that there will be a cost involved with the installation." He discussed the possibility of reinstituting the monolith, and brought the matter up at the next City Council meeting. The Ten Commandments monolith now resides in front of the Waukegan Police Department.

Photo by Karen Madsen (June 2012)

Dedicated in 1960

Photo by Karen Madsen (October 2008)

Hastings, Nebraska (June 1960)

The Ten Commandments monolith sat undisturbed at the Hastings Museum of Natural and Cultural History in Hastings, Nebraska since 1960. The museum was in the midst of building an IMAX theater and the monolith "seemed" to be in the way. The Nebraska American Civil Liberties Union

(ACLU) threatened a lawsuit in August 2000. A decision was quickly made to give the Ten Commandments monolith to Parkview Cemetery. It holds an honored position right inside the massive gates and across from the Veterans' Memorial.

In a special session of the County Board of Commissioners, this Ten Commandments monolith met the legal criteria of being allowed to stay on the courthouse grounds.

Photo by Karen Madsen (July 2011)

Dedicated in 1960

Photo by Carla Pearson (September 2012)

Dedicated in 1960

Freedom from Religion Foundation (FFRF) originally asked that the Ten Commandments monolith be removed from Lincoln Park in Monroe, Wisconsin in 1983. For reasons unknown, the Monroe City Council voted in April 2002 to have the monolith removed. It was given to Green County Family YMCA in June 2002.

Photo by Judy Pankow (December 2012)
Monroe, Wisconsin (October 1960)

The Eagle Magazine (January 1961) printed the following article that relayed the events of the dedication:

> [The] Aerie recently dedicated a Ten Commandments monolith which will be located on the front lawn of City Hall. The program opened with the posting of colors by the Ladies Auxiliary and the Fireland's Cadets, sponsored by the Aerie. The National Anthem was presented by the High School Band. Rev. Paul Carpenter gave the invocation, followed by the singing of *America*. Presentation of distinguished guests included State Vice President Ludwig Hoge, who gave the main address.
>
> Then came the presentation and unveiling of the monument by Aerie President Ed McManus. The monolith was accepted by Mrs. Helen Lippert, City Auditor. The address was given by Rabbi Lawrence Montrose, with remarks from the president of the Chamber of Commerce, Curt Casper. Also present was Louis Nardecchia, representing Organized Labor. The main address was given by Eagle Mayor, with Rev. George Jaeger giving the benediction.
>
> The monument was paid for from the individual contributions of one dollar or more from Aerie members. The names of all contributors were sealed in a metal box and encased in the base of the monolith. The dedication was followed by a lunch and entertainment at the Aerie home for all in attendance.

Photo courtesy of *The Eagle Magazine* (January 1961)
President Ed McManus presented the monolith to Mrs. Helen Lippert, City Auditor, who accepted on behalf of the city.

Photo by Sue A. Hoffman (September 2012)

Dedicated in 1960

Only two questions come to mind – why was Organized Labor pointed out as being represented and what ever happened to the sealed metal box? We may never know, but what we do know is that when City Hall was remodeled, the Ten Commandments monolith was moved to the left front corner of the building.

Photo by Karen Madsen (July 2011)

Moorhead, Minnesota (1960)

Fargo, North Dakota Eagles presented to Clay County this Ten Commandments monolith shown with, from left, Commissioner Thornley Wells, Judge E. J. Ruegemer, Moorhead Mayor I. T. Stennerson, and Fargo Eagle President Morrill Olson. Program was planned by Aerie's Youth Guidance Committee consisting of Chairman Leonard W. Caverly, Donald E. Nelson, and Past Presidents John W. Hanson and George H. Wilson.

Photo courtesy of *The Eagle Magazine* (February 1961)

Photo by Beth Dachenhaus (May 2008)

Dedicated in 1961

Photo by Sue A. Hoffman (September 2012)
Cheviot, Ohio (January 1961)

Photo by Karen Madsen (September 2008)
Nebraska City, Nebraska (May 1961)

Somewhere along the line, Otoe County Courthouse, home of a Ten Commandments monolith that was dedicated in May 1961, was threatened with a lawsuit.

To avoid any possible lawsuit, Otoe County sold a thirty-by-thirty foot plot of land to Aerie 968 for one dollar in 2001. A chain link fence now runs along the back and sides of the Ten Commandments monolith.

Retired Major Paul Madsen (1926-2010), the father of Karen Madsen, along with his wife, Rose, raised a most wonderful daughter. With a wink and a smile, he once told me that he was very proud of "how Karen turned out." Major Madsen retired from the US Air Force after twenty years of service and then worked for the Veterans Administration. It was both a pleasure and an honor to have made his acquaintance.

On June 5, 2001, the Unified Board of Commissioners in Kansas City, Kansas announced that the Ten Commandments monolith would have to be moved from the Wyandotte County Courthouse. This decision was based on the US Supreme Court's stayed decision in Elkhart, Indiana. In a change of heart, the same Unified Board of Commissioners declared that the monolith will remain at the Courthouse as of June 20, 2001.

In July 2001, the American Civil Liberties Union (ACLU) smacked Wyandotte County with a lawsuit in the US District Court in Kansas City. In an eight-to-zero decision, the municipal government decided, in July 2003, to move the monolith 150 feet across the street to Saint Mary's-Saint Anthony's Catholic Church.

Photo by Karen Madsen (September 2010)

Kansas City, Kansas (November 1961)

Photo by Karen Madsen (April 2010)

Lorain, Ohio (May 1961)

Photo by William Shepherd (Karen Madsen's son) (October 2010)
Dedicated in 1961

Photo by Karen Madsen (September 2008)
Fremont, Nebraska (1961)

In 2003, Matthew Layman was sentenced to sixty days in jail, fined $400, and had his driver's license suspended for six months because he crashed his car into the Ten Commandments monolith in Memorial Park and knocked it off of its base. He pleaded guilty to driving while intoxicated even though he refused to submit to a chemical test. Drinking thirteen beers just prior to the crash may have had something to do with the collision with the monolith. Although the pins were sheared off, it was able to be repaired.

The American Civil Liberties Union (ACLU) "advised" Fremont officials not to reinstall their monolith, or be prepared to move it if they chose to put it back into Memorial Park. As of 2008, the Ten Commandments monolith remains in the park.

At one time, there were seventeen monuments and twenty-one historical markers on the Texas State Capitol grounds in Austin. Homeless and unemployed lawyer Thomas Van Orden passed by the Ten Commandments monolith for six years with no apparent personal harm, injury, or offense. What happened to alter that is unknown, but what is known is that Van Orden got it in his mind, in July 2001, to sue and to sue big – a habit that he continued to 2005.

Photo by René Guggisberg (January 2013)
Austin, Texas (1961)

In the initial case of Van Orden v. Perry, et al, in 2002, Van Orden was denied his request to have the Ten Commandments monolith removed from the Capitol grounds. US District Court Senior Judge Harry Lee Hudspeth explained in a fourteen-page ruling that no reasonable person would consider the display a religious endorsement. Van Orden appealed, and in October 2004, the US Supreme Court agreed to hear the case. The ultimate ruling on June 27, 2005 found that, "A Ten Commandments monument erected on the grounds of the Texas State Capitol did not violate the Establishment Clause because the monument, when considered in context, conveyed a historic and social meaning rather than an intrusive religious endorsement." This ruling changed the course for several Ten Commandments monoliths that were in the process of being removed from government property at that time.

Photo courtesy of *The Eagle Magazine* (February 2006)
Dick Berry, Sandra Lowery, Tom Weaver, Barney Leddy, Rosalyn Andrews, and Mike Lundie presenting a check for $20,000 to the Southside Virginia Chapter of the American Red Cross for the Hurricane Relief Fund.

In 2008, I stumbled upon a photo in *The Eagle Magazine* that pictured Aerie 882 donating money for hurricane relief. They were standing next to a Ten Commandments monolith that I didn't know existed in Petersburg, Virginia.

The Worthy Secretary sent a nice photo with several different people standing next to their Ten Commandments monolith after I requested some information. The specific photo led to more questions, so I needed additional photos to verify a few things that seemed slightly different than on other monoliths.

Photo by Gregory A. Jastrzemski (October 2012)

Petersburg, Virginia (1961)

After several phone calls requesting updated photos went unanswered, it was wonderful to discover that there is extended family out there ready for an adventure. And yes, there are a few quirks regarding the Petersburg Ten Commandments monolith that make it unique – one of a few that are gray, all the lines of the Ten Commandments are aligned left, and the Paleo-Hebrew in the mini-tablets is blurred.

Photo by Sue A. Hoffman (October 2008)

Dedicated in 1962

Among the hills and pine trees of Rindge, New Hampshire, Sanderson "Sandy" Sloane was supposed to build a home, get married, and have children. His parents had purchased 128 acres of land in 1937 that they envisioned would be shared by Sandy and his other three siblings. Unfortunately, as Sandy proudly served his country as a B-17 bomber pilot, his plane was shot down over Germany in 1944. His parents, Sibyl and Douglas Sloane III, founded Cathedral of the Pines in 1945 as a memorial to those men and women, including their son Sandy, who had sacrificed their lives in World War II. There are several monuments located throughout the memorial park including a Ten Commandments monolith.

Photo courtesy of the Fraternal Order of Eagles
Rindge, New Hampshire (May 1962)

The Northeast Region Eagles (Connecticut, Maine, Massachusetts, New Hampshire, Rhode Island, and Vermont) hold an annual remembrance to the families, loved ones, and friends of their departed Aerie Brothers, Auxiliary Sisters, and Veterans on Memorial Day. It has become a time-honored tradition filled with remarks from dignitaries, music, and prayer.

PROGRAM

OPENING REMARKS .... Joseph F. Pannone, P.S.P.
Master of Ceremonies

GREETINGS .... Dr. Douglas Sloane
Founder of Cathedral of the Pines

INVOCATION .... Protestant Chaplain,
Fort Devens, Mass.

SOLO (God Bless America) .... Lillian Vegiard

— REPRESENTING NORTHEAST REGION —

NORTHEAST REGIONAL PRESIDENT .... Michael Quarry
Portland, Maine

REMARKS .... William E. Tyler,
Conn. State Chairman

REMARKS .... Mrs. Louise McElroy
Past Grand Madam Chaplain

PRAYER .... Catholic Chaplain,
Fort Devens, Mass.

REMARKS .... Willie J. Regnaiere
Pres., R. I. State Aerie

PROGRAM

REMEMBRANCE *CANDLE CEREMONY*

WARWICK AERIE NO. 1313 AUXILIARY

Madam President .... Florina Champlin
Past Madam President .... Gertrude Costa
Madam Vice President .... Lucy Gauthier
Madam Chaplain .... Stella Neary
Chairman .... Dorothy Bettencourt

— SPEAKERS —

Louise McElroy	Florina Champlin	Gertrude Costa
Lucy Gauthier	Dorothy Bettencourt	Evelyn Chapdelaine

— GUARDS —

Yvonne Regnaiere	Mary Brouchu	Mary Serpa
Dorothy Rathbun	Karen Couture	Ann Shipley

SOLO (Lord's Prayer) .... Lillian Vegiard
REMEMBRANCE DAY ADDRESS .... Representative,
Grand Aerie, F.O.E.
EAGLE EULOGY .... Gustave Jodoin
SOLO (The Old Rugged Cross) .... Lillian Vegiard
ORGANIST .... Beatrice Blais

PLACING OF WREATHS AT THE MONOLITH
By Representatives

Bristol Aerie	East Providence Aerie	Providence Aerie
Central Falls Aerie	Woonsocket Aerie	West Warwick Aerie

VOLLEY .... Firing Squad from Fort Devens
TAPS .... Bugler from Fort Devens

— ONE MINUTE OF SILENCE —

Courtesy of the Fraternal Order of Eagles
Inside one of the many programs from the Memorial Day Services at
Cathedral of the Pines, Rindge, New Hampshire

Special thanks go out to Marty Wiley, County Natural Resources/Parks Recreation Director, who personally went on a treasure hunt to find this Ten Commandments monolith. "Stormy" Jacobson also did some valuable work concerning this mystery.

Photos by Karen Madsen (July 2012)

Dedicated in 1962

Photo by Lyle Frost (July 2008)

Dedicated in 1963

This Aerie was in the process of celebrating its sixteenth anniversary with a two-day celebration when torrential rains delayed the dedication of the Ten Commandments monolith. This may have been a foretelling of what was to come.

When the monolith was finally dedicated, Rabbi David Daro gave the Invocation and the presentation address was given by Rev. H. B. Kildahl. Father William Fahnlander provided the closing prayer and Benediction.

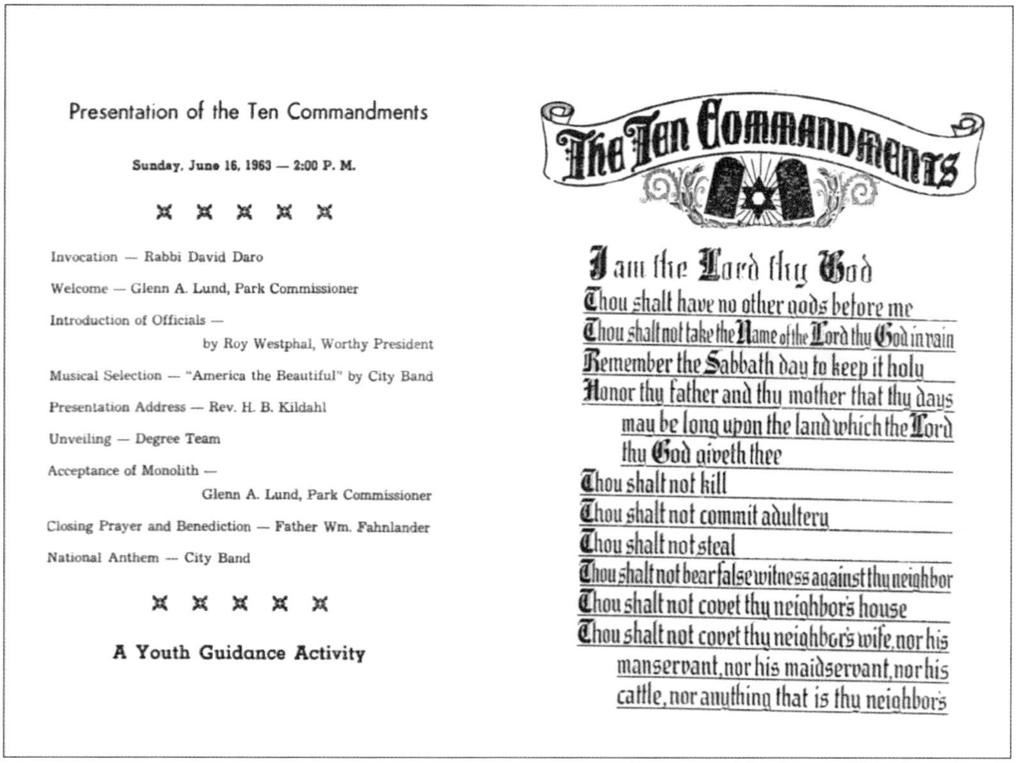
Presentation of the Ten Commandments

Sunday, June 16, 1963 — 2:00 P. M.

Invocation — Rabbi David Daro

Welcome — Glenn A. Lund, Park Commissioner

Introduction of Officials —
by Roy Westphal, Worthy President

Musical Selection — "America the Beautiful" by City Band

Presentation Address — Rev. H. B. Kildahl

Unveiling — Degree Team

Acceptance of Monolith —
Glenn A. Lund, Park Commissioner

Closing Prayer and Benediction — Father Wm. Fahnlander

National Anthem — City Band

A Youth Guidance Activity

The Ten Commandments

I am the Lord thy God

Thou shalt have no other gods before me

Thou shalt not take the Name of the Lord thy God in vain

Remember the Sabbath day to keep it holy

Honor thy father and thy mother that thy days may be long upon the land which the Lord thy God giveth thee

Thou shalt not kill

Thou shalt not commit adultery

Thou shalt not steal

Thou shalt not bear false witness against thy neighbor

Thou shalt not covet thy neighbor's house

Thou shalt not covet thy neighbor's wife, nor his manservant, nor his maidservant, nor his cattle, nor anything that is thy neighbor's

Courtesy of the Fraternal Order of Eagles

Program from the Dedication

The Ten Commandments monolith was completely refurbished in the spring of 2003, but the flood in 2012 not only caused damage to the area surrounding the monolith, but the entire territory.

Photo by Karen Madsen (July 2012)

Devastation after the Flood of 2012

Photo by Karen Madsen (April 2010)
Ashland, Ohio (1963)

Eagles' Aerie 2178 wanted to have a Ten Commandments monolith, but they didn't have any room to put it at their facility. They asked the City of Ashland, Ohio, if they wanted it "temporarily," so the monolith was dedicated and placed in the corner of Kinnamon Park at Center and Main Streets where it stayed for forty years before it was reclaimed and removed.

During the Ashland City Council Meeting in July 2004, Bob Valentine (Ward 1) questioned Mayor Stine about the reason for the removal of the monolith from Kinnamon Park. He felt that it should have stayed there. Mayor Stine said that the Aerie contacted him requesting that the monolith be returned to the Aerie to be placed in front of their "new" (seven-year-old) building. This came at a time that there were lawsuits being filed all across the country to have the Ten Commandments monoliths removed from public property. Perhaps the Aerie wanted to prevent the city from bearing any possible legal action or expense, or they may just have figured that it was time to have the monolith relocated to their "new" facility. Either way, they wanted it back and Mayor Stine allowed it to be removed from Kinnamon Park.

The best headline ever by Irv Oslin of the *Times-Gazette*, albeit sad, stated, "Someone has violated the Ten Commandments. Literally." On a Friday night in May 2008, someone had gone right up in front of the Aerie and painted through each line of the Ten Commandments monolith.

Anthony Karper reported the vandalism to the police, but he had no idea who would have done such a thing. He hoped that it would able to be repaired, but as of April 2010, the damage remained.

Photo by Karen Madsen (April 2010)
Vandalized in May 2008
Ashland, Ohio

Somerset's Ten Commandments monolith has always been located at Aerie 1801. The Aerie moved to a new facility and took their monolith with them where it is prominently displayed out front. A special thank you goes out to Patricia Cox who originally provided location photos. Aerie 1801, close to financial ruin and due to close in 2013, has been revitalized and brought back from the brink with hopes of a bright future in the Somerset community.

Photo by Sue A. Hoffman (October 2008)

Somerset, Pennsylvania (August 1963)

Photo courtesy of The Eagle Magazine (1964)

From the left are Aerie President Alfred Frombaugh, Rev. James L. Lumadue, Grand Conductor Steven V. Thomas, Judge Thomas Lansberry, Monolith Chairman Joseph Livengood, Master of Ceremonies A. M. Matthews, and Council Member John Wilson, all of whom took part in the Ten Commandments monolith dedication at Somerset, Pennsylvania. The monolith, dedicated to Somerset County youth, is placed on the Aerie's lawn.

Aerie 515 was celebrating its sixtieth anniversary in October 1963 when it dedicated the Ten Commandments monolith to the City of Dover, Ohio. At some point, and for reasons unknown to this author, it was moved to Grace Evangelical Lutheran Church.

Photo by Randy Wenger (May 2010)

Dover, Ohio (October 1963)

Photo courtesy of *The Eagle Magazine* (1964)

Present at the dedication of a huge granite Ten Commandments monolith presented to the City of Dover, Ohio were from the left: Father Johnson, Kenneth Amsbaugh, Mayor C. Lemoyne Luthy, Worthy President Richard Frey, Rev. Alto Taylor, and John Stoller. The monolith was placed in City Square.

All Aerie 2212 has left of their Ten Commandments monolith is an old newspaper photo taken when the monolith was in storage at the City Department Garage in Hastings, Minnesota pinned to the Aerie bulletin board. It's not that the monolith doesn't exist anymore, but it has been moved so many times that the Aerie had problems keeping tabs on it.

Their frustration lies in the fact that they really wanted a Ten Commandments monolith for the youth of Dakota County. They worked really hard and did a lot of fundraisers to make it happen. The monolith was originally dedicated in 1963 in front of the Dakota County Courthouse that was on Fourth Street.

The Ten Commandment monolith was moved to Roadside Park in 1993 when the courthouse was renovated and became the new Hastings City Hall. In 1997, Roadside Park was being renovated so the monolith was moved again - this time into storage at the City Department Garage.

The Hastings mayor and the city council voted to put the monolith back into Roadside Park, but the legal department ruled against it. The monolith was rededicated in July 2002 at Saint John's Lutheran Church.

Photo by Sue A. Hoffman (July 2002)
Hastings, Minnesota (1963)

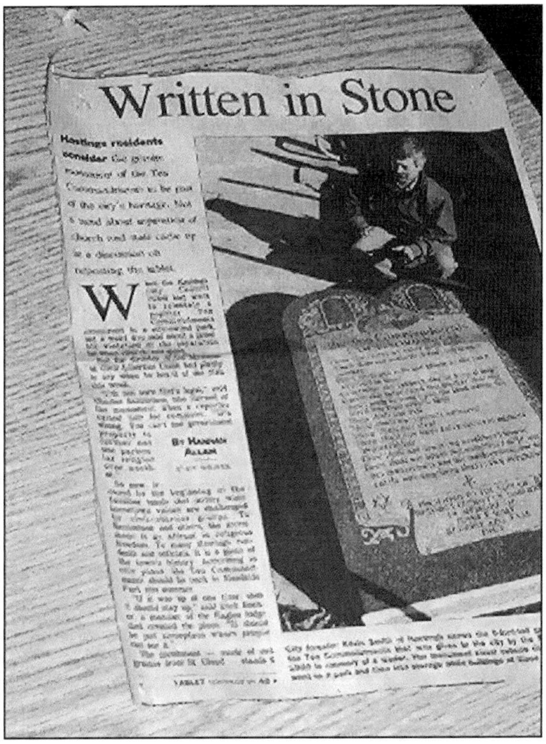

Old article from the Pioneer Press that hangs on Aerie 2212's bulletin board

The original dedication of the Ten Commandments monolith in Providence, Rhode Island was scheduled for November 24, 1963. Two days prior to the dedication, President John F. Kennedy was assassinated. The ceremony was rescheduled for December 8, 1963 with Walter Reynolds and John Flynn in attendance.

Committee

LADD LYON
P. W. P., State Trustee

GEORGE J. COSTA
P. W. P., State Trustee

NICOLA GUERCIA
P. W. P.

GUSTAVE L. JODOIN
P. S. P., State Treasurer

GEORGE NAJJAR

JOSEPH F. PANNONE
P. S. P., State Secretary

OSWALD A. THOMAS
W. P.

DONALD TURNBULL
P. S. P.

DR. RAYMOND A. THOMAS
W. S. P. (Ex-Officio)

HON. JOHN R. FLYNN
Chairman of Board of Park Commissioners

RALPH J. HARTMEN
Superintendent of Parks

Rhode Island State Aerie

Fraternal Order of Eagles

Dedication Exercises

Ten Commandments Monolith

Roger Williams Park

Providence, Rhode Island

Sunday, December Eight

Nineteen hundred and sixty-three

Program

Greetings	LADD LYON *Chairman*
Opening Remarks	DR. RAYMOND A. THOMAS *State President, Master of Ceremonies*
Invocation	REV. PETER HOBEIKA *Pastor, St. George R. C. Church, Providence*
Remarks	HON. JOHN R. FLYNN *Chairman of Board, Park Commissioners*
Introduction	HON. WALTER H. REYNOLDS *Mayor, City of Providence*
Remarks	MAJOR GENERAL LEONARD HOLLAND *Adj. Gen., State of Rhode Island* *Representing the Jewish Community*
Representing the Grand Aerie	ANDREW J. HALLORAN, P.G.W.P. *Framingham, Mass.*
Placing of Flowers	MRS. RAYMOND P. McELROY, P.G.M.C.
Closing Prayer	THE VEN. WILLIAM L. KITE *Archdeacon, Episcopal Diocese of R. I.*

The Ten Commandments

I am the Lord thy God.
Thou shalt not make to thyself any graven images.

Thou shalt not take the Name of the Lord thy God in vain.

Remember the Sabbath day to keep it holy.

Honor thy father and mother, that thy days may be long upon the land which the Lord thy God giveth thee.

Thou shalt not kill.

Thou shalt not commit adultery.

Thou shalt not steal.

Thou shalt not bear false witness against thy neighbor.

Thou shalt not covet thy neighbor's house.

Thou shalt not covet thy neighbor's wife, nor nor his manservant, nor his maidservant, nor his cattle, nor anything that is thy neighbor s.

Courtesy of the Fraternal Order of Eagles

The Dedication Program for the Ten Commandments monolith on Sunday, December 8, 1963 at Roger Williams Park in Providence, Rhode Island. The city park was named after Roger Williams who was an ordained minister who started the first Baptist Church in America and initiated the State Charter for Rhode Island.

Photo by Karen Madsen (October 2011)
Karen Madsen's husband, Bill Shepherd, is standing in the doorway.
Providence, Rhode Island (1963)

The Aerie that originally donated the monolith closed its doors, so the monolith was re-etched on its back side to reflect the rededication in 1980.

The Ten Commandments monolith was threatened with a lawsuit in April 2003 by former lawyer, and chair of the Rhode Island American Civil Liberties Union (ACLU), Greg Frazier. He waited twenty-four years from first seeing the monolith before he requested that the city remove the monolith or face legal action.

Volunteers from Aerie 1313 removed the monolith in September 2004 under pressure from the city that they would lose their chance to have it placed at their Aerie if they did not act quickly. City council members thought that the city solicitor's office acted too hastily in forcing the removal of the monolith, so the Council introduced a resolution for the return of the monolith back to the city in June 2005.

The ACLU is committed to fight any attempt to have the monolith returned to the original park or any other location on public property. In March 2006, citizens still upset over the quick removal of the monolith, contacted the Grand Aerie regarding the possibility of replacing the monolith with private funds in a "memorial park" setting. A replacement of the monolith has not occurred.

According to *The Eagle Magazine* (October 1963):

> Provo, Utah Aerie was host to more than 400 delegates and guests during the 1963 State Convention. Highlight of the convention was the presentation of a granite Ten Commandments monolith to Provo Memorial Park. Prior to the convention, then Grand Worthy President Carl Thacker traveled to Salt Lake City where he presented a Ten Commandments award to David O. McKay, president of the Church of Jesus Christ of Latter Day Saints. Thacker then attended the state convention in Provo. State President Willard MacFarlane made the presentation of the Ten Commandments monolith to Provo Mayor Verl G. Dixon for Memorial Park. Master of Ceremonies at the dedication service was William K. Wotherspoon, manager of the Chamber of Commerce, City of Provo.

In 2003, the City of Provo chose to move the Ten Commandments monolith even though they had not received any complaints regarding its location in Memorial Park, which also has a Veterans' memorial. Their decision was based solely on the letters that were sent to Salt Lake City, Ogden,

Tooele, Roy, and Murray government officials from Summum's attorney, Brian Barnard. Thomas Lee, a professor of law at Brigham Young University added his "two cents" by commenting, "The monument of a specific religion on public property is a violation of the Establishment Clause." Michael Mower, Provo city spokesman stated, "The goal was to show our community's support for the display of the Ten Commandments without causing contention because they were located in a public park. We wanted to avoid giving people who opposed the Ten Commandments monument a cause to complain."

Photo by Sue A. Hoffman (September 2012)

Provo Utah (1963)

Provo wanted it moved, and moved quietly, so the move was organized by Provo city officials, the LDS Church, and the Fraternal Order of Eagles. They decided to put it on the corner of Center Street and University Avenue, which just happens to be the most prominent intersection in Provo. The monolith sits across from the joint Utah County and Provo City Building. The corner spot where it rests is actually part of the Provo Mormon Temple property which was surrounded in construction chain link fence. The Temple had a fire in December 2010 which did not completely destroy the 125-year-old structure. It was in the process of being rebuilt, with the completion date set for 2015, as this book was written. Once the fence is removed, the Ten Commandments monolith will be a formative corner stone for the LDS Temple property.

Frank W. Clark was ecstatic about the Ten Commandments monolith. In a letter to Robert W. Hansen at the Grand Aerie on August 22, 1964, Clark said, "Iowa City Aerie has raised the money and purchased a large granite slab engraved with the Ten Commandments on one side. Our local Johnson County supervisors have agreeably allowed us to erect this beautiful monolith on the front lawn of our county courthouse. We plan to formally present this to the county from Iowa City

Aerie on September 12 at 11 AM." The letter goes on to request a representative from the Youth Guidance Commission to be present at the unveiling.

A lawsuit was originated, and then dropped, in 1978. Unfortunately, the Iowa Civil Liberties Union (ICLU) threatened lawsuits in 2000 and 2001. The Board of Supervisors unanimously agreed to remove the Ten Commandments monolith on March 15, 2001.

Michael Duehr was quoted as saying, "We need to go to the largest hill and tell people that we support the Ten Commandments. We need to say that we support putting prayer back in school, and that we oppose the desecration of the American Flag."

The Ten Commandments monolith now proudly resides at the Iowa City Fraternal Order of Eagles Aerie.

Photo by Karen Madsen (September 2008)
Joe Roe and the Ten Commandments monolith
Iowa City, Iowa (September 1964)

Photo courtesy of *The Eagle Magazine* (October 1964)
Herschel McWilliams dedicated the monolith to the City of Tooele, Utah.
The Boy Scouts formed the color guard for the event.

At this particular Utah State Convention, the first order of business was to dedicate the Ten Commandments monolith to the City of Tooele, Utah.

Threatened by the Society of Separationists and Brian Barnard, the City of Tooele wasted no time in finding a new home for the Ten Commandments monolith at Tate Mortuary.

Photo by Sue A. Hoffman (September 2012)

Tooele, Utah (1964)

Photo courtesy of *The Eagle Magazine* (October 1964)
Governor Paul Fannin and Joseph Burtle at the presentation of the Ten Commandments monolith at the State Capitol Building

In a ceremony at the Phoenix, Arizona State Capitol Building, representatives from Catholic, Protestant, and Jewish faiths were in attendance when a Ten Commandments monolith was given to the State of Arizona from the Past Presidents' Club in 1964. According to *The Eagle Magazine* (October 1964), "The dedication, attended by numerous government and Eagle dignitaries, was covered by television, radio, and newspapers." In 1974, the monolith was moved from the Capitol Building to a state park just east of the Capitol.

Monty Gaither, state director the American Atheists, threatened a lawsuit in 1992. The Arizona Civil Liberties Union threatened a lawsuit in August 2001 and July 2003. Instead of moving the monolith again, it was decided to create Wesley Bolin Memorial Plaza where there are twenty-seven memorials to various individuals, events, and organizations.

Photo by Sue A. Hoffman (September 2012)

Phoenix, Arizona (May 1964)

Photo by Tom McGrath (June 2008)

This Ten Commandments monolith is the only monolith known to be dedicated in honor of a president – John F. Kennedy. It was moved once in order to be placed closer to the military monuments.

Dedicated in 1964

Photo by Karen Madsen (April 2010)
This county received anonymous letters in the early 1990s requesting that this monolith be removed.
Dedicated in 1964

1965-1969

In 1965, thanks to then Parks Commissioner, Harry Hatt, the Ten Commandments monolith was placed in a prominent location east of the intersection of Front and Jefferson Streets in front of Memorial Auditorium in Burlington, Iowa. City Manager Jane Wood did not care for the monolith, so it was then put into hibernation in a hanger at the Burlington Airport.

Photo courtesy of *The Eagle Magazine* (August 2005)
The 104th Anniversary for Aerie 150 in April 2005

After hearing complaints from several citizens that the Ten

Commandments monolith disappeared, the monolith was placed near the Burlington Depot and the antique locomotive. After issues surfaced in Iowa City with their monolith, Aerie 150 and the City Council agreed that the monolith should be placed on Eagle property to avoid any possible legal entanglements in the future.

Leyda Burris & Metz dismantled and moved the monolith to the Aerie facility. Aerie 150 rededicated the monolith in April 2005 in conjunction with the grand opening of their newly-remodeled Aerie home.

Photo by Karen Madsen (October 2008)
Burlington, Iowa (March 1965)

Portland, Oregon is a large metropolitan city built on hills with crowded, busy, winding one-way streets which are flooded with bicyclists. In trying to find the Ten Commandments monolith, the GPS had us on the wrong side of Interstate 5 with no guidance in maneuvering us to the other side where Sunset Memorial Park is located. In all things, God has a way of making lemonade out of lemons.

Photo by Jeffrey Hoffman (September 2008)
Synagogue in Portland, Oregon

It was Yom Kippur, the most holy of Jewish holidays, when we were in this community, quite lost, but able to see an amazing display of Ten Commandments on the local synagogue. Clearly not thinking the situation through, we drove into the overly-crowded parking lot within minutes of the beginning of the sacred service. September 11, 2001 changed a lot of things, and one of them was the high security this Jewish holiday brought to all synagogues across the United States. There were police vehicles at all of the entrances, people scurrying into the building before the first call to worship began, and we were trying to find a spot in the parking lot which was teeming with vehicles. It probably wasn't the most ingenious of ideas to try to photograph a synagogue on Yom Kippur during the service under high security, but after spending years of looking at Ten Commandments monoliths, this set of tablets was amazing.

Photo courtesy of *The Eagle Magazine* (June 1965)
Portland, Oregon (May 1965)

It took "the cooperation of countless individuals to make possible the placement of the impressive Ten Commandments monolith on this Saturday in May," according to *The Eagle Magazine* (June 1965), including the likes of Glenn Anderson, Kay Peterson, and Joe Caputo. The Portland General Electric Company donated the use of a truck crane to lift the Ten Commandments monolith into place. Vern Weifle, who was a new member of the Portland Aerie, arranged for the planting of flowers.

Photo by Jeffrey Hoffman (September 2008)

Photo by Jeffrey Hoffman (September 2008)
Garden of Eagles (where there are 653 allotted cemetery plots for departed Fraternal Order of Eagles Brothers and Sisters plus an Urn Garden) in Sunset Hills Memorial Park, Portland, Oregon

What a convoluted mess poor La Crosse, Wisconsin had to go through these past few decades. The La Crosse Eagles simply wanted to permanently honor the youth of their community for all of their help during a major flood in the spring of 1965. During the dedication of the Ten Commandments monolith in Cameron Park, Alvin A. Watson, past president of the Aerie, stated, "The flood volunteers [are] gallant fighters, tireless workers, and true children of the pioneer spirit. We worry not about our children or their future. They have displayed their ability to meet life's greatest obstacles and hazards." Others in attendance were: Rev. Stefan Guttormsson of the Evangelical Lutheran Church; J. Philip Bigley, past grand president; Fred Affeldt, monolith fund raising chairman; George Felton, Aerie president; Paul Marcou, city park board chairman; and Judge Lincoln Neprud.

In 1985, retired school teacher Phyllis Grams had a friend who saw the Ten Commandments monolith in Cameron Park and told Grams about it. Grams went to see it for herself and decided that the Ten Commandments monolith shouldn't be in the city park. She called Anne Gaylor with Freedom from Religion Foundation (FFRF). They both wrote letters to Mayor Patrick Zielke, the Common Council of La Crosse, and to the City of La Crosse claiming that the Ten Commandments monolith was viewed by them as a message from the city about what kind of beliefs the citizens should have. The Common Council held a public meeting, and because of the support of the Ten Commandments monolith voiced by those present at the meeting, decided not to take any action regarding the letters from Grams and the FFRF.

FFRF and Grams filed a lawsuit in the US District Court for the Western Division of Wisconsin to have the Ten Commandments monolith removed. The Court found that Grams and the FFRF failed to "meet case or controversy." Grams could not prove that she paid municipal taxes in the City of La Crosse, therefore her money did not support the monolith, or that she suffered any alleged injuries because of the monolith. Grams also couldn't prove that the monolith was in close proximity to anything that she did around town, so she would not, in the normal course of living her life, ever come in contact with it. The court also felt that the FFRF had "no standing or jurisdiction" in the case. The lawsuit was dismissed in 1987. Judge Barbara Crabb said, "It [the monolith] was not hurting anybody." For all of her efforts, Phyllis Grams was given the 1987 Freethinker of the Year Award from the FFRF.

Starting in June 2001, everything started falling apart for the supporters of the monolith. The FFRF wrote a letter to the City of La Crosse again requesting that the Ten Commandments monolith be removed. The City Council refused to do so.

In September 2001, the Eagles wrote to the City Attorney and offered to take the monolith off of the city's hands and prominently display it on private property. The city declined. In March 2002, a local Episcopal church offered to take the Ten Commandments monolith. The city passed on the offer.

In April 2002, the La Crosse City Council addressed the Ten Commandments monolith controversy and passed a resolution stating the following:

1) There was a threat of a renewed lawsuit by the Foundation.
2) The monument was given to the City to honor the flood-fighting effort of area youth.
3) The Council believed the monument did not violate the Constitution.
4) The monument deserved to remain in its current location.
5) The Council would take the necessary steps to keep the monument in its current location.

Their resolution, in June 2002, was to offer to sell to the Eagles a twenty-by-twenty-two foot parcel of land that surrounds the Ten Commandments monolith.

Photo by Karen Madsen (July 2011)

La Crosse, Wisconsin (June 1965)

In July 2002, the FFRF and two fictitiously-named plaintiffs filed a lawsuit, but the court denied them to proceed because the plaintiffs were not willing to use their real names. One person dropped out of the case and the other person "became known" and then considered dropping out. Also in July, by a five-to-two vote, the City Council approved the sale of the parcel of land to the Eagles for $2,640.

In August 2002, the FFRF added an additional twenty plaintiffs to the initial complainant and filed another lawsuit. All twenty-one had the same complaint: "They are all residents of La Crosse and claim that they avoid [Cameron] Park because of the presence of the monument, or that they are emotionally disturbed or distressed when they travel to one of the commercial businesses surrounding the park because of the presence of monument."

In October 2002, the Eagles erected a four-foot high steel fence around their mini-park. They also installed a light that went from the Aerie building to across the street that lit up the Ten Commandments monolith at night. One month later, the City of La Crosse put up their own four-foot high wrought-iron fence encircling the Eagles' fence.

This pretty much ticked off the FFRF and the Appellees. They amended their complaint twice – once when the sale of the land was processed, and then again when the fences were installed. They said that even though the Eagles own the land, the Ten Commandments monolith was still in Cameron Park and its presence still violated the Establishment Clause.

The district court agreed with the FFRF and in July 2003, granted summary judgment in favor of the Appellees and stated that the Ten Commandments monolith had to be removed from Cameron Park and the plot of land had to be returned to the City of La Crosse.

Photo by Karen Madsen (July 2011)

Not only is the Ten Commandments monolith double fenced, but it has protective posts standing guard.

Since the Eagles had never been named in any of the lawsuits, they decided that since this land belonged to them, that they should have some say in any decisions regarding their property. The district court agreed and held off on their original judgment until the Eagles were able to collect and present their case.

In February 2004, after hearing what the Eagles had to say, the district court denied the Eagles motion for vacating the decision, and decreed that the land had to be returned to the city and the Ten Commandments monolith had to be removed.

That didn't go over very well with the Eagles, so with the help of the American Center for Law and Justice (ACLJ), they filed an appeal with the Seventh Circuit US Court of Appeals, and the court reversed the decision in January 2005 in a two-to-one vote. This allowed the Eagles to keep their Ten Commandments monolith within their private fenced mini-park.

Even though they eventually lost, the FFRF threw a "thank you" dinner party in La Crosse on June 15, 2005 to "honor" the La Crosse residents who signed on as plaintiffs against the Ten Commandments monolith. They were awarded with the "Friend of Freedom" award which is a replica of the Statute of Liberty with their names inscribed on it. The following individuals who were bestowed with a statute include: Sue Mercier (original plaintiff), Elizabeth J. Ash, Angela Belcaster, Janet Bohn, Julie Chamberlain, Maureen Freedland, David Goode, Betty Hammond, Curt Leitz, Constance R. Long, David W. Long, Myrna D. Peacock, Becky Post, James L. Reynolds, Ellen Dodge Severson, Eric Severson, Leslie Slauenwhit, Herman S. Wiersgalla, Howard Wiersgalla, James E. Wiffler, Robert Wingate, and Henry Zumach.

City Park in Casper, Wyoming seemed to be a fitting place for a Ten Commandments monolith in 1965. In September 2003, Freedom from Religion Foundation (FFRF) sent a threatening letter demanding to have the monolith removed from City Park because of the Establishment Clause, and then sued the City of Casper in October 2003 when it failed to act. Duane Buchholz, a retired judge and Wyoming State Director of the American Atheists in Sheridan, Wyoming, also worked toward the removal of the monolith from City Park.

Photo by Karen Madsen (October 2008)
Casper, Wyoming (June 1965)

The City Council agreed to create a Historic Monument Plaza with five other monuments with a five-to-four vote in October 2003 for a cost of no more than $11,500. "If you think that we are going to put our monument someplace in cold storage, I've got another thought for you," said then-mayor Barb Peryam at the Council's October 28 meeting. "We are going to put it where it will be more noticed, more taken advantage of, and used for learning purposes by all families."

The Ten Commandments monolith was moved into storage in November 2003. The new monuments were paid for by four private sponsors at $2,500 each, and the city paid the remaining $1,650. The sponsors that stepped forward were First Interstate Bank, Reliant Federal Credit Union, Hilltop Bank, and Five Trails Rotary Club.

Historic Monument Plaza has five other monuments which include the Declaration of Independence, the Preamble to the US Constitution, the Mayflower Compact, the Bill of Rights, and the Magna Carta. Mayor Kate Sarosy dedicated the new Historic Monument Plaza in July 2007, which is located in a small park behind the Nicolaysen Art Museum.

The only known Ten Commandments monolith located in Canada is at Assiniboine Park in Winnipeg, Manitoba. It was the most publicized monolith dedication in 1965.

Photo by Karen Madsen (July 2012)

Winnipeg, Canada (1965)

Fred Phelps, of Westboro Baptist Church in Topeka, Kansas which is known for its "God hates fags" rhetoric, threatened a lawsuit if he could not install an anti-gay monument in Julia Davis Park in Boise, Idaho near the Ten Commandments monolith.

The Boise city officials voted to remove the monolith in January 2003. Keep the Commandments Coalition filed a lawsuit to keep the monolith where it was. In January 2004, the City Council directed the Parks and Recreation Department to help return the monolith to the possession of the Fraternal Order of Eagles "and aid them and assist them in whatever manner we can."

Photo by Jeffrey Hoffman (April 2012)
Boise, Idaho (1965)

The US District Court denied the Keep the Commandments Coalition's request to stop the City of Boise from getting rid of the Ten Commandments monolith in February 2004. Eleven protesters, including a former state representative, were each sentenced to twenty-five hours of community service for illegally blocking the removal of the monolith in March 2004. The Ten Commandments monolith was moved to Saint Michael's Cathedral Church, which is directly across from the State Capitol Building.

After a long battle, it was decided that the voters should decide whether or not to move the monolith *back* to Julia Davis Park. Keep the Commandments Coalition turned in 18,507 signatures (nearly 10,000 more than what was needed) to put the monolith decision on the ballot. In November 2006, fifty-three percent of the voters decided NOT to move the monolith back to its original location.

Marlene Duvall had been volunteering her time and talents with Easter Seals Camp Sunnyside near Des Moines, Iowa since 1978. Camp Sunnyside sits on eighty-eight acres and was "designed, built, and staffed to meet the recreational needs of campers with all types of disabilities." There was a tiny, dilapidated chapel with a Ten Commandments monolith standing near its doors. When the chapel had to come down, a new children's playground was created which was also near the Child Development Center.

Sometime around 2005, in the height of church/state issues, complaints surfaced regarding the children being "unnecessarily exposed" to the Ten Commandments. Easter Seals, which is dependent on donations, grants, and gifts from all sectors of society, not wanting to risk the generosity of others because of some offense that might be taken, banished the monolith to languish behind the storage shed. Attempts were made to find a new home for the monolith, but it remained there for quite some time.

Photo by Charlie Scarlett (2012)
Des Moines, Iowa (1965)

Marlene, having family members with heavy equipment and the wherewithal to literally "lift this heavy burden" from Camp Sunnyside, "rescued" it, and took it home. The Ten Commandments monolith was placed in her yard where it could be seen from the road and by all who came to visit. When she moved in the fall of 2012, she took her monolith with her and will place it in her yard when the landscaping is complete. Perhaps a possible future donation to a church might be planned, but Marlene would like the monolith to stay with the family.

Although her volunteer work has been with Camp Sunnyside all of these years, Marlene Duvall was named Easter Seal's National Volunteer of the Year in 2008. As of this writing, she, as well as several members of her family, continues to offer her time and talents to Easter Seals Camp Sunnyside.

The American Civil Liberties Union (ACLU) Nebraska Foundation, and atheist John Doe, filed a lawsuit against the City of Plattsmouth, Nebraska in May 2001 after their request to remove the Ten Commandments monolith in the summer of 2000 was not granted. The American Center for Law and Justice (ACLJ), and Senior Attorney Francis Manion, represented the City of Plattsmouth.

A US district judge ruled in favor of the ACLU in February 2002 that the monolith must be removed. Nebraska Attorney General Don Stenberg said, "It is hard to understand a federal government which prints 'In God We Trust' on its money, but orders the removal of religious symbols from city parks and state capitols."

In a two-to-one vote, a three-judge panel of the Eighth US Circuit Court of Appeals upheld the decision in February 2004 that the Ten Commandments monolith must be removed. In April 2004, the full Eighth Circuit Court of Appeals (which includes Nebraska, North Dakota, South Dakota, Minnesota, Iowa, Missouri, and Arkansas) agreed to review the earlier decision.

Photo by Karen Madsen (December 2008)
Plattsmouth, Nebraska (1965)

Photo by Karen Madsen (December 2008)
Rose Madsen (Karen Madsen's mother) in Memorial Park, Plattsmouth, Nebraska

In July 2005, a judge declined the request from the ACLU to stop the *Omaha World Herald* from publically naming atheist Ron Larsen who brought the suit against the City of Plattsmouth. In August 2005, the full Eighth Circuit Court of Appeals reversed its decision with an eleven-to-two ruling and declared that the monolith could stay in Memorial Park.

In 1911, Edward and Emma Lievens emigrated from Belgium and homesteaded land near Sentinel Butte, North Dakota. In 1949, Rev. Father Elwood E. Cassedy spoke in front of the Bi-State Convention of the Fraternal Order of Eagles in Deadwood, South Dakota about his dream for a boys' ranch. The Eagles donated the first $123 at the Convention and a committee of Eagle members was established to help Father Cassedy establish his dream. The Lievens read an article in the *Bismarck Tribune* about Father Cassedy, and since they were getting close to retirement, decided to deed their property over to Father Cassedy for the ranch.

In December 1949, a 940-acre ranch called Home on the Range was incorporated under the laws of North Dakota to be established as a home and agricultural and trade school for delinquent boys. In January 1950, the Bismarck Eagles donated $5,000 for the construction of a new dormitory. In 1957, the Eagles held a "Buck a Brick Fundraiser" to build Eagle Hall.

Today, Home on the Range has grown to 1,500 acres of land that supports horses, chickens, and cattle, three dormitories, facilities for administrative staff, social workers, and support staff, mechanic shop, carpentry shop, public school classrooms, and all kinds of buildings associated with running a farm, including a meat processing plant. There are programs that include learning skills that help strengthen families, provide drug and alcohol education, cognitive principles

Photo by Karen Madsen (June 2012)
Entrance to Home on the Range, Sentinel Butte, North Dakota

Photo by Karen Madsen (June 2012)
The Ten Commandments monolith was dedicated in memory of
Rev. Father Elwood E. Cassedy (1908-1959).
Home on the Range, Sentinel Butte, North Dakota (1965)

and restructuring programs, how to handle stress, life skills, spiritual guidance, character enrichment, equine-assisted treatment groups, and a canine intervention program which helps train puppies and dogs to be service animals. The Fraternal Order of Eagles has been a continual source of financial support for Home on the Range since its inception.

Brigham City, Utah's Ten Commandments monolith was the last one on the American Civil Liberties Union's (ACLU) agenda for Utah. It was removed from public land and placed at the Eagles' Aerie.

Photo by Karen Madsen (October 2008)
Brigham City, Utah (1965)

While playing tennis with a friend as a young man in high school, Dr. Dale Hansen wondered how long it would take for someone to question the existence of the Ten Commandments monolith near the tennis courts at Les Gove Park in Auburn, Washington.

When the City of Auburn built a new library, the Ten Commandments monolith was in the way. The curator of city-owned Mountain View Cemetery requested that the monolith be placed there, and since no else seemed to have wanted it, that's where it ended up.

Photo by Sue A. Hoffman (May 2008)

Auburn, Washington (1965)

Photo courtesy of John Elizondo, Oakland, California

John Elizondo, Worthy President, John Seulberger, President of the Park Board, Andre Fontes, President of the Board of Trustees of the Oakland Park Board, and Sam B. Goodman, General Chairman, uncrating the Ten Commandments monolith that was presented to the Zoological and Botanical Society of the East Bay near the Snow Building.

John Elizondo could not be more thrilled that his Aerie was providing a Ten Commandments monolith for the Oakland Park Zoo in California. The presentation was made to honor the memory of the late Judge Edward Smith who fostered the idea of the monolith's placement in 1961. Civic and religious leaders were present at the dedication.

On the other hand, when the new CEO and president of the Oakland Park Zoo, Dr. Joel Parrott, came onboard, his thrill level was quite less than that of John Elizondo's. The level was so much lower, in fact, that Parrott had no qualms about removing the Ten Commandments monolith at the slightest threat of an atheist demonstration. Joey Piscitelli of the East Bay Atheists, and the America Atheists, Inc., scheduled a protest for late June 2012 to have the monolith removed.

Photo by Karen Madsen (June 2012)

Oakland, California (May 1966)

Piscitelli, a self-proclaimed pagan, had rented the Snow Building at the Oakland Zoo in May 2008 for his daughter's wedding. The best location for taking photos overlooking the Bay area was the spot where the Ten Commandments monolith rested. Piscitelli said that his guests were "shocked" to see the "religious display." He wrote letters to the city and to Mayor Jean Quan in 2008, and again in May 2012. He called the Ten Commandments monolith "prejudicial" and stated that it "denigrates the views of non-Christian zoo visitors." Supervising Deputy City Attorney Mark Morodomi sent Piscitelli a letter defending the Ten Commandments monolith stating that the US Supreme Court ruled that a similar monument on public property was constitutional.

Days before the alleged protest was supposed to begin, Parrott tore down the monolith on July 25, 2012 and is holding it in storage at an unknown location. He has made no known attempts to find a new home for it, and calls made to his office for information have not been productive or informative as of this writing. Parrott said that the threatened weekend protests by the atheists had nothing to do with his decision to remove the Ten Commandments monolith, stating that it was in the works to be removed anyway. "We had wanted to do it for a long time. Now, it just seemed like it was the proper time." He said, "We try to be very sensitive to the community so that we can be inclusive. This wasn't the right location for that type of thing." He said that sensitivity for visitors was the only reason for its removal. "It was never unconstitutional or illegal, and it wasn't removed for legal reasons." Parrott even confessed that he (meaning the publically-owned Oakland Zoo) didn't even have ownership of the Ten Commandments monolith. To have one man with the tenacity to make such a major, hasty decision regarding the removal of donated public property without public input is frightening to say the least.

To have one man with the tenacity to make such a major, hasty decision regarding the removal of donated public property without public input is frightening to say the least.

Photo by Karen Madsen (September 2008)

Cody, Wyoming (June 1966)

A Ten Commandments monolith was dedicated at the Ogden City Municipal Building in the Municipal Gardens north of the courthouse in 1966. The Freedom from Religion Foundation (FFRF) sued the City of Ogden in 1998 on the basis of "separation of church and state." Their request to have the monolith removed was denied.

Summum and R. L. Zefferer sued in 1999 and in 2002 on the basis of freedom of speech and stated that they wanted to place a monument etched with the Seven Aphorisms near the Ten Commandments monolith. The District court denied both lawsuits.

In July 2002, the US Court of Appeals for the Tenth District Circuit Court reversed the original decision and ruled that the city cannot have the monolith displayed unless it displayed the other monument for the Summum. The City Council chose to remove the monolith in December 2002 and returned it back to the Eagles.

Photo by Sue A. Hoffman (September 2012)

Ogden, Utah (July 1966)

Photo by Karen Madsen (November 2008)

Dedicated in 1966

Photo by Karen Madsen (October 2008)

Dedicated in 1966

According to *The Eagle Magazine* (September/October 1966):

> The Ten Commandments monolith dedication was the highlight of the 1966 Convention. Clergymen from the Catholic, Protestant, and Jewish faiths were on hand for the unveiling of the monolith which was erected on the courthouse lawn. Monolith plaques were also presented to the Rt. Rev. Msgr. C. W. Trautner, Senior High School Principal Russell White, and the Junior High School Principal Ernie Edwards. A civic service award was presented to the Mayor. The Home on the Range for Boys at Sentinel Butte was gifted with a check for $13,149.32 that was accepted by Father William Fahnlander.

Photo by Karen Madsen (July 2012)

Dedicated in 1966

One of those memorable moments occurred while being extremely tired, knowing that the GPS has taken you the long way around to somewhere that you have never been before, and also knowing deep down inside there must be a reason why you needed to be right where God has placed you. From just out of nowhere I saw something that was incredibly unbelievable.

Driving through another quaint town in Ohio, I was surprised to see an Eagles' Aerie off to the right, and what appeared to be a poster or sign of a Ten Commandments monolith. I just had to get a photo. No, it wasn't a sign – it WAS a Ten Commandments monolith – stuck in the front of the Eagles' building. Someone had literally carved the brick front of the building so that a 2,000 pound monolith could be fitted into it. Truly amazing. The funny thing was that no one inside at the time knew it was there, and a few even came out to check what I was talking about. Someone in Mansfield, Ohio must know where the monolith was originally placed, and why and when it was moved. After several attempts to find out the history of its mysterious placement, the questions remain unanswered.

As a side note, this Aerie used to own the building next door but lost it a few years back. The front cornerstone reads "FOE AD 1912."

Photo by Sue A. Hoffman (September 2012)

Mansfield, Ohio (1966)

Photo by Karen Madsen (June 2012)

Great Falls, Montana (May 1967)

The Ten Commandments monolith was unveiled during the 1967 Fraternal Order of Eagles Montana State Convention in Great Falls, Montana. D. D. Billings, Judge Lawrence Leahy, Juanita Dix, and Katy Shaw were present at the dedication according to *The Eagle Magazine* (August/September 1967). In June 2012 when the photo was taken, the monolith appears to have been re-veiled with greenery.

Photo by Karen Madsen (September 2008)

Dedicated in 1967

Grand Aerie representatives D. D. Billings and Paul Shaver were invited to the New Mexico State Council in July 1967 when the Aerie presented the Ten Commandments monolith to the City of Clovis, New Mexico.

Photo by Sue A. Hoffman (September 2012)

Clovis, New Mexico (July 1967)

Andrew Albanese asked Bannock County to remove their Ten Commandments monolith which was located about forty feet from the front doors of their courthouse in Pocatello, Idaho in 1992. The county officials responded in 1993 by placing a sign next to the monolith with words from the Virginia Statute for Religious Freedom which quoted Thomas Jefferson on January 16, 1786: "We, the General Assembly of Virginia, do enact that no man shall be compelled to frequent or support any religious worship . . . but that all men shall be free to profess, and by argument to maintain, their opinions in matters of religion, and that the same shall in no wise diminish, enlarge, or affect their civil capacities."

Photo by Sue A. Hoffman (August 2012)

Pocatello, Idaho (1967)

The county also posted a sign that read: "This display is not meant to endorse any particular system of religious belief. As Jefferson stated, 'Our Democracy is premised upon the belief that the government should not intrude into matters of religious worship. Still as a historical precedent, the Ten Commandments represent some of man's earliest effort to live by the rule of law. Many of these ancient pronouncements survive in our jurisprudence today.'"

Sometime during the lawsuit, Albanese withdrew from the legal battle when he left the area for a job in another state. This infamous case continued to bear his name. A few others enlisted in the case allowing the American Civil Liberties Union (ACLU) to continue to pursue it.

A few reasons why the US Federal District Court ruled in 1995 that the Ten Commandments monolith did not violate the Establishment Clause and that the monolith could stay in place were: the litigants could not prove a religious-based reason for Bannock County originally accepting the gift from the Fraternal Order of Eagles, the county officials put permanent explanations next to the Ten Commandments monolith explaining their stance on the gift, and because of the distance between the front doors and the monolith, visitors did not have to come into direct contact with the Ten Commandments monolith.

What does Burning Man in Black Rock City, Nevada have in common with the Ten Commandments monolith in Lovelock, Nevada? Bad timing. The reaction to strangers taking photos outside of the courthouse was met with the same concern as having someone from Burning Man making threats against the Pershing County Courthouse which caused it to be on lockdown. The security people were not too fond of either at the moment.

Photo by Sue A. Hoffman (August 2012)

Lovelock, Nevada (1967)

Burning Man is like Woodstock in the desert – envision about 50,000 people coming from all over doing whatever their hearts desire for a week. Then imagine a few people disgruntled with law enforcement making threats against "the establishment." Then comes along a couple of "old ladies" gawking at the Pershing County Courthouse (it is only one of handful of round courthouses in the United States) taking photos and making notes. Not a good plan on our part, but also we had no idea that Burning Man was about to begin and that the courthouse was on lockdown. Silly us.

There was "picture proof" of Murray, Utah's Ten Commandments monolith through the Murray City Museum. Museum Assistant Bunny Ankney was extremely helpful with historical trivia regarding the monolith and its first location in the Murray Park Arboretum when the monolith was dedicated in 1967. The monolith had been knocked over and vandalized numerous times over a several-year period. The Society of Separationists, and lawyer Brian Barnard, also threatened a lawsuit against the City of Murray for having a Ten Commandments monolith on public property.

Used by permission. Murray City Collections, all rights reserved.

Murray Park Arboretum Monument in 1969

After writing to Murray's Mayor Daniel C. Snarr requesting information regarding their Ten Commandments monolith, I received a very terse piece of correspondence from G. L. Critchfield who is the Deputy City Attorney for the City of Murray. It stated, ". . . In 2002, the Board of Trustees for the Fraternal Order of Eagles, Aerie 1760 (Murray Eagles), requested that the Ten Commandments monument previously given to the City be returned to it. The monument was returned and beyond that, the City has no knowledge of what happened to the monument."

The attorney was kind enough to attach a copy of the October 10, 2002 letter from the Murray Eagles addressed to Daniel C. Snarr, Mayor, but it only stated, ". . . We have spoken to Mr. Chad Wilkinson, the Principal of Murray High School, to ask if the LDS Seminary there would like to have the monument. We have at this time not heard back from him. We would like to donate it to them. If not, or if it is in conflict for them also, please return the monument to us, the Murray Eagles. We will display it in front of our building." This was signed by the Board of Trustees, and the secretary, Billie Bell. This letter was a request for the Ten Commandments monolith, but the City of Murray could not come up with any follow-up correspondence as to what happened after this request was made in 2002.

Mary Ann Kirk, a member of the Murray Arts Advisory Board who works in the Parks Department, was told "by someone who was involved with the move," that the Ten Commandments monolith was delivered to a church just outside of town, but that church may not exist any longer. She had no further specific details. This is in direct conflict with Murray's deputy city attorney's statement that the monolith was returned to the Eagles.

Photo by Sue A. Hoffman (August 2012)
Murray, Utah (1967)

Karen Madsen, on one of her many treks in search of Ten Commandments monoliths, visited the Mayor's office and was told that the monolith was removed from the city park perhaps around 2005 or 2006. Karen then talked with Billie Grey, a member of the Eagles, who was going to do a little research regarding this matter. Timing is everything, and God's timing is always perfect.

In December 2010, Jessie Ogden, the current secretary of Murray Aerie 1760, and also a state officer for the Fraternal Order of Eagles, received a phone call from a jogger in Draper, Utah. Mike Draper, who used to pass by the Ten Commandments monolith on his bicycle when he was a child growing up in Murray, was jogging in his neighborhood in the town of Draper when he passed by a house that had a Ten Commandments monolith leaning on a tree.

Upon closer observation, he realized that the monolith belonged to the Murray Aerie and contacted Jessie Ogden. Together, they went out to inspect the Ten Commandments monolith and discovered that the house was inhabited by renters who said that the monolith was there when they moved in and that they had no idea of how, or when, it got there. Mike Draper, a descendant of the Drapers who founded the town of Draper, made an additional trip to verify location and photograph the monolith to help in the efforts of this monolith journey.

Burning questions remain regarding the City of Murray officials stating that they gave the Ten Commandments monolith back to the Eagles (even though they didn't have any recollection or proof of doing so), the Parks Department commenting that it was delivered to a church but they don't recall when and which one, and the Murray Eagles saying that they never received it. When, why, and how did a 2,000 pound monolith end up in another town approximately eleven miles away, broken and placed in a yard in a neighborhood that is located off of any main roads? And where did the rest of the monolith go? Yet another mystery left unsolved in the case of the missing, and now found, Ten Commandments monolith.

When, why, and how did a 2,000 pound monolith end up in another town approximately eleven miles away, broken and placed in a yard in a neighborhood that is located off of any main roads?

Photo by John Pankow (August 2012)

South Milwaukee, Wisconsin (1967)

David A. Ulrich often "credited his successes to failure." According to a tribute upon Mr. Ulrich's death in the Tri City National Bank's history section of their webpage:

> Growing up on Milwaukee's West Side, Dave failed two years at Saint Anthony of Padua Grade School in Wauwatosa. Years later, Dave returned to the school to thank the school's sisters of Saint Francis for turning his life around. "Whatever I amount to, I owe an awful lot to those sisters," Dave would often say. Dave's unique view of business, his wisdom, his entrepreneurial zeal, his brand of success, his sense of humor, and his ready smile were lost to the world when he died after a courageous battle with cancer.

Ulrich was also a philanthropist who appreciated a good education and gave countless amounts of monies towards scholarships for students at Pius XI High School. He also donated funds to build a community center where he lived. It is no wonder that when the Ten Commandments monolith in South Milwaukee needed to find a new home that Tri City National Bank, one of the forty-three branches that Mr. Ulrich founded since 1963, was more than willing to prominently display it.

Photo by Karen Madsen (October 2008)

Green River, Wyoming (June 1968)

When Green River City Hall was relocated and a new county courthouse was built in 1970, the Ten Commandments monolith was moved to Riverview Cemetery. Thanks to James Mauch who helped with the background and the original photos verifying Green River's monolith.

Even though the Ten Commandments monolith is placed in this very picturesque setting at the Range Riders Museum next to a memorial that is "dedicated to Miles City's spiritual history," it is a far cry from its previous notorious location in front of Custer County Courthouse.

In 1997, a group of disgruntled citizens not only complained about the Ten Commandments monolith that graced the lawn of the courthouse, but they were also not pleased with the Nativity scene sitting nearby. The two displays were seen by them as an egregious violation of their interpretation of separation of church and state. They contacted the American Civil Liberties Union (ACLU) of Montana and initiated a lawsuit against the county in 1999.

In October 2000, the county commissioners agreed to a consent decree that they would move the Ten Commandments monolith to a less prominent location by the courthouse and add Evolution of Law monuments next to the monolith. If they could not make this happen within a reasonable amount of time, the county would have the monolith removed.

In September 2003, the Ten Commandments monolith was moved to the Range Riders Museum. County Commission Chairwoman Janet Kelly voted to have the monolith removed and said, “I’m pleased that ‘the issue’ has been resolved.” On the other hand, Commissioner Duane Mathison, who wanted to keep the Ten Commandments monolith in front of the courthouse, said, “We had no choice. It had to be moved.” The reason for removing the monolith was that it would be too expensive to create the Evolution of Law display.

Photo by Karen Madsen (June 2012)
Miles City, Montana (1968)

Photo by Sue A. Hoffman (September 2012)
Santa Fe, New Mexico (July 1968)

Fire Station 3 in Santa Fe, New Mexico ran out of room for the growing needs of the community, so a new fire station was built right next door at one of the entrances to Ashbaugh Park, and the old facility was turned into a museum. The Fire Department relocated the Ten Commandments monolith in front of their new facility.

Photo by Sue A. Hoffman (August 2012)

Dedicated in 1968

Charles E. Epler was a willing accomplice on this journey in 2008 and originally found this monolith and provided photos. He said in reference to his home state, "The Monolith Project was started in the early 1960s and was originally designed to present a monolith to every city in which the State Aerie and Auxiliary held their State Convention which is held every June, if that city would accept it. Later, the project expanded to try to place one in each city that had an Eagles Aerie."

Photo by Jeffrey Hoffman (September 2012)

Aspen, Colorado (1968)

Photo by Sue A. Hoffman (September 2012)
Yerington, Nevada (1968)

Friends of Karen Madsen, Jim Funfar and Patty Evoy, saw this Ten Commandments monolith while traveling through Mandan, North Dakota in August 2011 and contacted Karen. They got the original photos and measurements to add to this ongoing adventure.

Photo by Karen Madsen (June 2012)
Mandan, North Dakota (1968)

Yuma City-County Library Park, Yuma, Arizona, was gifted with a Ten Commandments monolith by the State Past Presidents of the Fraternal Order of Eagles in September 1968. Mayor Thomas F. Allt, State Past President James Day from Phoenix, and local and county officials were present for the dedication. According to the local newspaper, "Accepting the monolith on behalf of the city, Mayor Allt called the impressive monument to the word of God 'a rare thing' as he expressed his thanks to the past presidents and other Eagles present."

Photo by Sue A. Hoffman (September 2012)

Yuma, Arizona (September 1968)

Senator Harold Giss also thanked the Eagles by saying, "This monolith is especially significant to me because of its meaning to my forefathers." The dedication ceremony ended with a prayer by Rev. Father Anthony Tomicich of the Immaculate Conception Parish, who also gave the Invocation. Also in attendance were Yuma council members Mrs. Jo Ochsner, Henry Mitchell, and Walter Duncan.

Noel Hail moved and installed the Ten Commandments monolith. Gary Cardenas framed and poured the concrete base. Many thanks go out to Richard Hernandez who provided historical documentation and photos for Yuma's monolith.

At one point, the City of Yuma asked the Eagles to move the monolith because the street needed to be widened, but the Eagles contended that the city now owns the monolith, so it was up to them if they needed it moved. The federal government refused to allow any library property to be taken for street widening which solved the problem of ownership moving responsibilities, and the Ten Commandments monolith remains in its original location.

The local newspaper has never commented on any of the Ten Commandments monolith lawsuits nationwide. The monolith is located at the 1912 Chicago, Burlington, and Quincy Railroad Depot. The original 1892 wooden depot is still there.

Photo courtesy of Roger Calkins (May 2008)

Dedicated in 1969

This Ten Commandments monolith is registered with the Smithsonian Institution Research Information System (SIRIS). There were several dignitaries present at the monolith unveiling ceremony including Mayor Eddie Pedersen, Pastor Jack Nitz, and Governor John Evans.

Photo courtesy of LeRoy Bledsoe

At the Ten Commandments monolith dedication in June 1969, from left to right: Evan Pierce, Lloyd Brown, Darrell Greenhaugh, Governor John Evans, Stan Burgard, Jim Kenney, Ernie Luthy, and an unknown person

Photo by Deborah Arnett (August 2012)

Dedicated in 1969

It probably wasn't the wisest thing to enter a taped-off construction zone during noon-time traffic with heavy construction vehicles present without a construction helmet. Kudos to Deborah Arnett for the tenacity to get up close and personal to the Ten Commandments monolith to get the photos and measurements necessary for this journey.

People around the United States are starting to wake up to the fact that elections have consequences. No matter what your political stance is, the people that you elect into public office will impact your way of life in one way or another for a long time to come. These effects may be even greater on a local level verses a federal level. This has never been more evident in a Ten Commandments monolith situation than the travesty that occurred in Kalispell, Montana.

The Ten Commandments monolith was originally dedicated in June 1969 to the people of Flathead County. Douglas Renick and Rev. William Fahnlander (superintendent of the Home on the Range for Boys at Sentinel Butte, North Dakota) presided over the dedication.

Americans United for Separation of Church and State (AU) threatened legal action if the monolith was not removed in a letter sent to the Flathead County officials in mid February 2004. Quickly responding in late February 2004, Governor Judy Martz defended the monolith at a press conference by saying, "People who are offended by the Ten Commandments have a deeper problem than the stone that it is written on, I think. Anybody that has trouble with the Ten Commandments, I think that they have something going on inside of them that would need a little help anyway."

County Commissioner Gary Hall decided to fight the threat from the atheist contingent and raised over $11,000 from private funds with the help of two other county commissioners and towns people like Fred Bryant (retired US Navy and member of the Eagles for almost forty years). The Liberty Council offered their services if further litigation was needed. Their combined determination warded off the pending litigation of the AU. Once the "Cornerstone of Law" was in place, it appeared that the Ten Commandments monolith had been tampered with, so Flathead county workers installed security lights that illuminated the monolith.

Unfortunately, those patriotic elected officials were no longer in office when the historic courthouse was renovated in 2011. Without any public forewarning, the "Cornerstone of Law" was

Photo courtesy of Fred Bryant (May 2008)

The proud display of the Ten Commandments monolith, along with the Magna Carta, Mayflower Compact, Declaration of Independence, Preamble to the Constitution, Bill of Rights, and the Preamble to the Montana Constitution in front of the Old Flathead County Courthouse, Kalispell, Montana

in the way of some construction work. The monuments all ended up *behind* the Flathead County Courthouse in a corner next to a stairwell by the juvenile detention center – a far cry from the prominent position they once had.

Fred Bryant, along with members of the American Legion and Veterans of Foreign Wars, was outraged. In response to this secretive relocation, Bryant requested that the City of Kalispell take possession of the "Cornerstone of Law" and place it in Depot Park in Kalispell with the rest of the veterans' monuments. He told the *Beacon*, "These are things that veterans have fought for and quite a few of them have died for. Up there [at Depot Park], they would be more visible."

County Commissioner Cal Scott said, "At first blush, I think it's an excellent idea. If the county will remit [the monuments] to the city and they are put up at the Veterans' Memorial, I think that'd be a good fit. Sitting back here in the back corner doesn't really do them, or the community, justice."

Photo courtesy of Fred Bryant (May 2008)

Flathead County Commissioner Gary Hall and Fred Bryant

The City of Kalispell might have gone with the idea, but the Flathead Area Secular Humanist Association (FASHA) strongly fought the relocation specifically because of the Ten Commandments monolith, even though putting the Ten Commandments monolith within an historical context has been universally accepted at all levels of litigated confrontations.

FASHA, and specifically Ian Cameron, Jesse Ahmann, Kristin Hargrove, Shawn Hargrove, Doug Bonham, Frank Jeniker, Susan Miller, Bob Beck, and others, penned a letter to Kalispell city staff and council members. The letter stated:

> We see absolutely no justification for including a Ten Commandments monument – there is no known reference to the Ten Commandments in US law or founding documents. So, in placing the Ten Commandments monument in a prominent public display on public land, the City of Kalispell is at risk of being perceived (and is perceived by members of FASHA) as taking a "theological" position rather than presenting an historically accurate one, and endorsing one religion over another. There are also potential legal consequences which we will pursue if needed.

FASHA continued to expose their radical point of view by requesting that other forms of free speech be allowed on public land. They purported that "The Enlightenment Thinkers" were "hugely influential for Thomas Jefferson, Benjamin Franklin, Thomas Paine, and James Madison in drafting the US Constitution." Obviously, FASHA has little knowledge of either American history or the law when it comes to our Founding Fathers and the current Ten Commandments court cases.

Photo by Karen Madsen (June 2012)

Kalispell, Montana (June 1969)

As of October 2012, FASHA not only stopped the City of Kalispell from placing the "Cornerstone of Law" in Depot Park, but they made it clear that they want all of the monuments removed from the back of Flathead County Courthouse and returned to the Fraternal Order of Eagles.

According to their website, "The Idaho Youth Ranch program in Rupert, Idaho provides long-term residential care to young people who are traumatized by abuse and/or neglect or an adverse experience, and as a result, this trauma interferes with their ability to control behavior and manage emotions. The program is based on an early intervention model to help at-risk youth who are in the beginning stages of behavior problems."

Methodist minister, Rev. James Crowe, wanted to help troubled youngsters in a working ranch environment. In 1952, he began the paperwork process, and then President Harry Truman signed an act that would provide the Idaho Youth Ranch with four square miles of land at the price of one dollar per acre, per year, for twenty-five years. "The Ranch has expanded in size with facilities catering to residents, horses and cows, and services designed to meet the specific needs of at-risk boys and girls who benefit from the unique attributes of a ranch environment. In 1983, a thrift store was opened to generate revenue for The Ranch from the sale of donated clothing and household items. Today, an integrated network of twenty-seven stores, located throughout Idaho, provides substantial revenue, work opportunities, and goodwill for The Ranch and its nearby citizens and communities."

Photo by Karen Madsen (October 2008)
Crowe Chapel, Idaho Youth Ranch
Rupert, Idaho (June 1969)

Tia Bland, Public Information Director for Bernalillo County in Albuquerque, New Mexico knew exactly who she had to talk with in order to get the details regarding the Ten Commandments monolith that was dedicated at the Bernalillo County Courthouse on July 12, 1969 during a Fraternal Order of Eagles State Convention. Ray Lopez, the County Facilities Maintenance Supervisor was there in 2001 when a donated crane from a local refrigeration company loaded the Ten Commandments monolith on the back of a City of Las Vegas, New Mexico truck. Finding out where the monolith went from there took a little bit more effort.

When Bernalillo County built a new county courthouse in 2000, the question regarding what to do with the Ten Commandments monolith remained. Had the county known that their monolith was registered with the Smithsonian Institution Research Information Center (SIRIS) as a "saved" outdoor sculpture, they may not have been so quick to dispose of it. They thought about moving the monolith to the new District Attorney's Office where there was a small space for a park and some benches, but by then, it was 2001 and there were lawsuits in the air regarding the Ten Commandments monoliths. It seemed that no one in Bernalillo County wanted it, even though it was given specifically to the county. The monolith crossed county lines as it traveled to Las Vegas, New Mexico.

Photo by Sue A. Hoffman (September 2012)
Originally located in Albuquerque, New Mexico
Las Vegas, New Mexico (July 1969)

Carole Gonynor, Office/Finance Manager for the Chamber of Commerce of Las Vegas/San Miguel County, had an inkling of where the Ten Commandments monolith ended up, but it was hard to explain and even harder to find up in the hills just outside of Las Vegas. After talking with Rick Jaramillo, president of the Las Vegas Eagles' Aerie, everything snowballed. Benerito Valdez knew that the Ten Commandments monolith was placed at a church. Sandra Mares went to work on the Internet and found the newspaper articles relating to the monolith move. Denise Gibson went to the church and took photos. As for Rick, he did what he had to do, including emailing detailed maps and directions on how to find the "church with no name" on a dirt road in a very small community.

It truly was a team effort with the county folks in Albuquerque, the Chamber of Commerce, and the Fraternal Order of Eagles in Las Vegas, to find the Ten Commandments monolith. What a great group of individuals to work with and a beautiful part of the country to visit.

When Eagles' Aerie 453 wanted to donate a Ten Commandments monolith to the City of Waukesha, Wisconsin, the city "refused to accept it." No problem for them – it looks beautiful on the front lawn of their newly-remodeled facility.

Photo by Judy Pankow (September 2012)

Waukesha, Wisconsin (1969)

1970-1979

Photo courtesy of the Fraternal Order of Eagles
Taken in 1982

Photo courtesy the Fraternal Order of Eagles
Dale Chadwick

Photo by Jeffrey Hoffman (September 2008)
Dedicated in 1970

Photo by Sue A. Hoffman (September 2012)
Dedicated in 1970

In a letter written in December 1994 to then-Mayor Randal Owensby, the Freedom from Religion Foundation (FFRF), along with one complainant, requested that the Ten Commandments monolith be removed from in front of city hall in this city. The local newspaper immediately ran an editorial, "Getting Religion at City Hall," in support of the monolith. The newspaper continued to run several front-page articles about outraged local citizens who wanted the monolith left alone.

When the city hall moved to its new facility, the monolith was placed in the city garage to be cleaned of the mineral deposits from the town's hard water. Mayor Gary Don Reagan promised that the monolith would be located in front of the new city hall as soon as the base was prepared. Reagan kept his promise. Gilbert SaLoga is credited with gathering this information and getting the original photos of the monolith in front of the old city hall. His efforts in this journey are greatly appreciated.

The Ten Commandments monolith was removed from Soroptimist Park in Bozeman, Montana in July 2006. It was held by the Salvation Army across the street while renovations were being done in the park. Charles Swart volunteered to personally pay the costs to put the monolith back in the park when the landscaping was just about completed in order to save the city from any possible future litigation by outside organizations that were threatening other cities around the country. The city manager polled the commissioners and they agreed to let the monolith go back into the park.

Photo by Chuck Beers (June 2008)

Bozeman, Montana (1970)

Bill Halpin, owner of Greenspace Landscaping, went fishing for three weeks and did not know that the city put the Ten Commandments monolith back into Soroptimist Park. Upon his return from the fishing excursion, Halpin removed the monolith from the park *again*. In December 2006, in a four-to-one vote, the city agreed to put the monolith back into the park.

Photo courtesy of the Fraternal Order of Eagles

Sparks, Nevada (1970)

In July 1970, a Ten Commandments monolith was dedicated at the Metropolitan Hall of Justice in Salt Lake City, Utah. Six months after the unveiling, four citizens filed the first lawsuit charging that the city and county were "foisting religious beliefs on those who did not choose to be receptive" because they illuminated the monolith after dark and erected a stone bench next to the monolith so that passers-by could sit next to it. In the now infamous case of Anderson v. Salt Lake City Corp. in September 1972, US Circuit Court, and Chief Judge Willis Ritter, agreed that that the message conveyed by the monolith was "clearly religious in character" and called for its removal.

There was "overwhelming approval of the monolith's location by thousands of individuals and long lists of local organizations. Newspaper, television, and radio editorials deplored the judicial verdict to have the monolith removed." The Tenth District Court of Appeals, and Judge Murrah, in March 1973, were "brought to the conclusion that the monolith is primarily secular, and not religious in character; that neither its purpose or effect tends to establish religious belief," and reversed the prior decision.

Photo by Karen Madsen (October 2008)

Salt Lake City, Utah (July 1970)

In 1994, the Summum asked Salt Lake County to allow them to place a stone monument with the Seven Aphorisms next to the Ten Commandments monolith. The county officials denied the request because they claimed that the county was possibly going to create a new jail on that site and that "it would not be prudent to engage in any construction or development, of any kind, on that site at this time."

This infuriated the Summum and they filed a federal case in 1996 alleging that the county had violated its speech and religious liberty rights. The US District Court dismissed the Summum's suit declaring that the Ten Commandments monolith "was primarily secular in nature and therefore the county had not created a forum for religious expression."

In an appeal in November 1997 (Summum v. Callaghan), Judge Stephanie K. Seymour stated, "The courthouse lawn cannot be characterized as a purely nonpublic forum reserved for specific official uses. By allowing access to the Eagles, the county has opened the forum to at least some private expression, clearly choosing not to restrict the forum to official government uses. Allowing government officials to make decisions as to who may speak on county property, without any criteria or guidelines to circumscribe their power, strongly suggest the potential for unconstitutional conduct, namely favoring one viewpoint over another." The appeals court panel then sent the case back to the district court "for determination as to whether the county had acted reasonably and not arbitrarily in denying the Summum's request."

The monolith was removed in Salt Lake City in 1998 after a three-judge panel of the Tenth US District Court of Appeals reversed an earlier district court's dismissal of the Summum's claim of free speech rights. Commission Chairwoman Mary Callaghan said that the action was taken for "practical" reasons. "First of all," she said, "We are in the process of vacating the block. We felt we needed to be careful in separating church and state. If we didn't remove it or moved it to another location, how large would the forum have to be to provide space for all different views?"

Salt Lake City and Ogden together paid the American Civil Liberties Union (ACLU) approximately $80,000 in court costs but still did not get to keep their monoliths on public property. Salt Lake County put the monolith in a shed in 1998. Disgusted by the course of events, the then-Aerie manager, using his farm equipment, picked up the monolith and put it in his barn. Aerie 67 reinstalled the Ten Commandments monolith on their property in October 2008.

Leland Duck was also on a journey when he began a six-year effort to bring the "Little Sister of Liberty" to Lions Park in Cheyenne, Wyoming. When he was fifteen-years-old, he initiated an Eagle Scout project that helped launch a nationwide effort to locate the 200 Statue of Liberty copper replicas that were dedicated across the United States by the Boy Scouts between 1949 and 1952.

On May 27, 1950, nearly 1,000 Boy Scouts marched from downtown Cheyenne to the Capitol Building for the dedication of the Statue of Liberty and to hear a speech by Governor Arthur Crane. Since that time, between harsh weather conditions and vandalism, the statue was no longer presentable and was removed from the Capitol grounds. Leland Duck wanted to have it repaired and again put up in all its glory, but the cost of repairs would be more than the cost to have a new statue recast in bronze which would be more suitable to Wyoming's climate.

Leland then proceeded to raise $2,500 towards the $8,500 cost to recast the 300 pound "Little Sister of Liberty," and the City of Cheyenne picked up the tab for the remainder of the cost. Mayor Jack Spiker allotted $41,422 from the city's budget to create the Liberty and Law Square in

Photo by Karen Madsen (October 2008)

Cheyenne, Wyoming (1970)

Lions Park, and $20,658 was donated by churches, organizations, and individuals to complete the project. The "Little Sister of Liberty" stands tall surrounded by the Preamble to the US Constitution, Bill of Rights, Mayflower Compact, Declaration of Independence, Magna Carta, and the Ten Commandments monolith.

After the City of Cheyenne was threatened by Rev. Fred Phelps of Topeka, Kansas, and also the American Civil Liberties Union (ACLU), the City Council voted to keep the Ten Commandments monolith in Lions Park. The monolith was temporarily removed and put into storage while the Liberty and Law Square was being developed. God's timing, the city's tenacity, and the power of one individual, Boy Scout Leland Duck, created the beautiful Liberty and Law Square. Never underestimate the power of what one individual can accomplish, even at the young age of fifteen.

Once known as the "richest place on earth," Virginia City, Nevada has moved its Ten Commandments monolith at least once. It may have been located elsewhere in the town, but at one point, it was sitting centered on a light pole in front of the public restroom in a parking lot near Nevada Centennial Marker 13.

Photo by Sue A. Hoffman (September 2012)

Virginia City, Nevada (1971)

The monolith now sits in a beautifully revamped roadside park overlooking the mountains. We wish that there had been more time to spend in this historic town where the Comstock Lode Silver Strike occurred in 1859. Virginia City was also the first place that Samuel Clemens, a promising young reporter for the *Daily Territorial Enterprise* newspaper, used his pen name, Mark Twain in 1863. Ben Cartwright and his sons' Little Joe, Hoss, and Adam roamed the streets of Virginia City when they came to town from their ranch in the famed *Bonanza* television series that ran from 1959-1973. In a town filled with old stories of saloons and friendly prostitutes, the Ten Commandments monolith seems to hold an obscure place in the historical context of miners and rags-to-riches stories.

Photo by Jeffrey Hoffman (September 2008)

Dedicated in 1971

Photo by Karen Madsen (October 2008)

Dedicated in 1971

Photo by Sue A. Hoffman (September 2012)

Carson City, Nevada (1971)

Dedicated in 1971, the Ten Commandments monolith was unveiled at the Capitol Building in Carson City, Nevada. At some point, for reasons unknown, it was moved to the Old Civic Auditorium which was then turned into the Regional Children's Museum of Northern Nevada.

The ongoing saga of Pleasant Grove, Utah and its Ten Commandments monolith continues to befuddle the imagination. In September 2003, Summum wrote its first letter to the mayor of Pleasant Grove requesting its monument with Seven Aphorisms be placed in Pioneer Park next to the monolith. This request was denied two months later.

In May 2004, the Society of Separationists sued Pleasant Grove City, et al, demanding the removal of the Ten Commandments monolith because it violated the "law of separation of church and state." The State District Court judge threw out the lawsuit because complaints must be answered by an appeals court.

Summum again requested that they be able to erect a monument in Pioneer Park in May 2005, and when this letter was ignored, they initiated a lawsuit in the US Federal District Court.

In August 2005, the Society of Separationists failed to state a claim that they should be granted relief after presenting letters in March and July 2005. They asked to drop their lawsuit in February 2006 but retain the right to raise the issue again.

A three-judge panel of the Tenth Circuit Court of Appeals ruled in favor of Summum and their monument in April 2007, but in May, it was requested that the decision be reheard. In August 2007, the full Tenth Circuit Court of Appeals ruled in a split six-six vote not to rehear the case which allowed the decision to stay and that the Summum could erect their monument.

The American Center for Law and Justice (ACLJ) filed for *Writ of Certiorari* to the US Supreme Court in November 2007, and in March 2008, the US Supreme Court decided to hear the case of Pleasant Grove City v. Summum in the fall of 2008. Chief Counsel Jay Sekulow argued the case in November 2008 on behalf of Pleasant Grove.

In a nine-to-zero decision in February 2009, the US Supreme Court ruled that Pleasant Grove does not have to allow the Summum to place their monument next to the Ten Commandments monolith in Pioneer Park. Justice Samuel Alito wrote, "A public park, over the years, can provide a soapbox for a very large number of orators, but it is hard to imagine how a public park could be opened up for the installation of permanent monuments by every person or group."

According to Geoffrey Surtees of the ACLJ:

> After Summum lost on its free speech claim, it went back to the federal trial court to argue that the city's decision violated another provision of the First Amendment: the Establishment Clause. In an argument all but identical to its free speech claim, Summum argued that the city's display of the Ten Commandments, but not the Seven Aphorisms, was an impermissible endorsement of religion.
>
> The district court was not persuaded by Summum's attempt to put a new label on its defunct free speech claim. In his opinion, Judge Dale Kimball wrote, "There is no evidence that anyone in Pleasant Grove government had any idea what Summum's religious beliefs were, and thus it cannot be said that the Pleasant Grove government demonstrated a preference for one religion over another." Summum's case against Pleasant Grove was dismissed from federal court once and for all.

Perhaps the Summum were finished with the federal court system, but they decided to try again in the Utah state court in 2012. They claimed that the city's decision to not allow them to have their Seven Aphorisms monument next to the Ten Commandments monolith violated the Establishment Clause of the Utah State Constitution (versus that of the US Constitution which they have lost repeatedly). After months of briefing and oral arguments, the trial court ruled against the Summum and in favor of the city. Judge Howard wrote, "The benefit described by the Plaintiff . . . of one group being allowed to erect a monument while another group is denied the same privilege, simply does not exist." Unfortunately, again, in May 2013, the Summum filed with the Utah Supreme Court asking that it reverse Howard's ruling and "force Pleasant Grove to display a monument it does not wish to display."

Photo by Sue A. Hoffman (August 2012)
Pleasant Grove, Utah (1971)

Geoffrey Surtees and the ACLJ continue this fight as this book goes into publication. May this be the last battle that the Ten Commandments monolith and the City of Pleasant Grove, Utah have to face against the Summum and their Seven Aphorisms monument.

The Ten Commandments monolith that was dedicated at the Capitol Building in Frankfort, Kentucky in 1971 was put into storage in 1984 during a construction project on the State Capitol grounds.

The General Assembly passed a measure calling for the monolith to be returned to the Capitol grounds in 2000, but the American Civil Liberties Union (ACLU) threatened a lawsuit. US District Judge Joseph Hood ruled that displaying the monolith on government property was an unconstitutional religious endorsement, so the Ten Commandments monolith remained in storage.

Photo by Sue A. Hoffman (May 2010)

Frankfort, Kentucky (1971)

The State of Kentucky paid $121,524 in legal fees in July 2003 when it lost its attempt to put the monolith back on the Capitol grounds in Adland v. Russ. Hopkinsville Aerie 3423, which is 215 miles from Frankfort, spent about $2,500 in transportation and set-up costs to retrieve the monolith. It is unknown why the Hopkinsville Aerie was able to get the monolith from Frankfort considering that the monolith was "Presented to the Commonwealth of Kentucky by Kentucky State Aerie." It is conjectured that Hopkinsville requested the monolith from Frankfort and had the means to come and get it. Since the State wanted to get rid of the monolith, this seemed to be the most convenient way to have it taken off of their hands.

In March 2006, the House voted ninety-one-to-three, and the Senate voted thirty-seven-to-one, passing a bill that would require that the Ten Commandments monolith be returned to State Capitol grounds and be placed with other historical monuments. Governor Ernie Fletcher signed into law a measure that directed the Historic Properties Advisory Commission to replace the monolith.

In June 2006, the ACLU wanted to go back to court because they believed that state officials should be held in contempt of court if they tried to replace the monolith on Capitol grounds. The US District Court prevented the return of the monolith until the court reviewed the state's plan for the display. Since that time, there have been elections in the State of Kentucky, and those elections had consequences. The newly-elected officials have not required the Hopkinsville Aerie to return the monolith, or that a new Ten Commandments monolith be placed on Capitol grounds to replace the one that was removed.

Photo by Jeffrey Hoffman (September 2008)

Dedicated in 1972

There are conflicting stories of where this monolith originally came from, but it was moved to Aerie 2957 in 2007.

Photo by Sue A. Hoffman (September 2012)

Phoenix/Sunnyslope, Arizona (1972)

Situated with the Fallon Veterans Memorial and a tribute to those who lost their lives in the Global War on Terror, the Ten Commandments monolith stands in a very special setting that also has a "United We Stand" Memorial Wall featuring a piece of steel gifted by New York City from 9/11.

Photo by Sue A. Hoffman (August 2012)

Fallon, Nevada (1972)

Plaque honoring those who lost their lives in Somerset County, New York City, and Washington, DC on the "United We Stand" Memorial Wall

"United We Stand" Memorial Wall with a piece of steel donated by the people of New York City to the City of Fallon in remembrance of September 11, 2001

Rock Springs, Wyoming had a Ten Commandments monolith, perhaps dedicated in 1972, but the details are sketchy because this is one of the three missing monoliths. Aerie 151's best recollection is that the monolith was moved from its original location and placed in Bunning Park. At some point, it was moved again to the end of an underground sidewalk that went under the railroad tracks in town. At some point several years ago, a car probably ran into the monolith destroying it, and then the monolith was presumably thrown away.

Located in Triangle Park, Kemmerer, Wyoming, the Ten Commandments monolith is located next to the Kemmerer/Diamondville Chamber of Commerce. It is also a stone's throw away and across the street from the very first JC Penney Store on one side, and the home of its founder, James Cash Penney, Jr., across, and down the street, on the other side.

Special thanks to Tommy Woolsey who was able to help with the original photos and information regarding Kemmerer, Wyoming

Photo by Sue A. Hoffman (August 2012)

Kemmerer, Wyoming (June 1972)

Photo by Sue A. Hoffman (September 2012)

Roswell, New Mexico (April 1973)

Photo by Jeffrey Hoffman (April 2012)

Coeur d'Alene, Idaho (June 1973)

The Ten Commandments monolith in Coeur d'Alene, Idaho had been vandalized in 2008 when Cher Rhoads took a photo of it sitting in front of the Kootenai County Courthouse. Someone had sprayed yellow paint across the words, "The Ten Commandments." By the time Karen Madsen visited the monolith five months later, there were no signs of the paint.

In 2011, the county commissioners decided to move the Ten Commandments monolith to an area between the Kootenai County Administrative Building and the Courthouse in the Veterans Memorial Plaza. Dan Green, one of the commissioners said, "We moved it 100 yards to what we think is a more appropriate place, that's all. We had some picnic benches and some bike racks kind of scattered around the campus. We also brought them here. It is just more of a place for people to relax, reflect." He also added that the area is now easier to maintain with all of the monuments in one area and that it had "nothing to do with the federal mandate." What federal mandate?

Photo by Sue A. Hoffman (September 2012)

Dedicated in 1973

In April 2006, Marine Corps veteran and atheist, Joe Dickson, was "offended" by the Ten Commandments monolith's location based on his interpretation of separation of church and state. When the monolith was challenged, City Manager Doug Selby stated that there were no plans to remove it and that the city was unaware of any previous complaints.

The American Civil Liberties Union (ACLU) is "concerned" about this monolith, but they are not going to pursue its removal. Why is it that the ACLU actively "pursues" only certain monoliths?

Photo by Sue A. Hoffman (October 2008)

Clearfield, Pennsylvania (1973)

Photo by Sue A. Hoffman (September 2012)

Phoenix/Glendale, Arizona (1974)

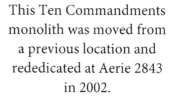

This Ten Commandments monolith was moved from a previous location and rededicated at Aerie 2843 in 2002.

Resting on the banks of Orange Lake in New Port Richey, Florida, in May 2011, the Ten Commandments monolith had to be moved for reasons unknown. It was placed behind Community Congregational Church. The church sits on the road that encircles Orange Lake. Instead of placing the Ten Commandments monolith facing the road that is well used by people taking advantage of the lake, the congregation chose to put it behind the church where the parishioners park. This seems to be such a missed opportunity of sharing their beliefs with those who are seeking the Truth. It is odd that they appear to have chosen to "preach to the choir."

Photo by David Cox (August 2011)
New Port Richey, Florida (1974)

The following is a note from someone working for the City of Worland, Wyoming regarding their Ten Commandments monolith:

> The monolith is located on the grounds of the US Post Office, but the PO relocated and the building now houses a City Hall Water Department. Landscaping is being redone so the monolith has been removed and put elsewhere for safekeeping until the landscaping is completed. Problem: Don't know where to put it now because the City Attorney is arguing with the City Council and telling them it cannot be located on city property according to federal law. The City Attorney, as you might guess, is up for re-election in four weeks. At the meeting, the city churches were very upset and quite vocal regarding the City Attorney. No decision was made at the meeting as to what the city is going to do. The City Attorney is doing all the advising. One lady even wanted to put it in her back yard.

Photo by Karen Madsen (September 2008)
Worland, Wyoming (June 1974)

The Worland, Wyoming Ten Commandments monolith is now located at the First Baptist Church.

Photo by Karen Madsen (October 2008)
Dedicated in 1975

Rev. Fred Phelps attempted to force this town's City Hall to place an anti-gay display next to the Ten Commandments monolith in February 2004. The mayor chose to ignore the request and the monolith stayed.

Once located at the county courthouse, the Ten Commandments monolith got moved to the front of City Hall. County Manager Richard Primrose personally drove around town trying to find the new location of the monolith in an effort to help on this journey prior to our visit, which is greatly appreciated.

Photo by Sue A. Hoffman (September 2012)
Dedicated in 1975

Photo by Karen Madsen (September 2008)

Dedicated in 1975

None of the wonderful people who have been such a blessing by taking photos in an effort to ease the travel burden for this journey are professional photographers. Out of the kindness of their hearts, be they family, friends, or new acquaintances, they have given of their time, efforts, and finances "to donate to the cause."

There was a time that I considered using photos by people with specific photography skills, whether it was their profession or their passion. It was discovered that lawyers love to take photos of courthouses and Ten Commandments monoliths, and they are quite skilled at it. For some unknown reason, the few lawyers that were contacted for permission to use their photos declined to be a part of this endeavor. One photo that I was interested in was exceptionally beautiful. When I asked this particular lawyer if I could use it, there was no problem initially. A few days later, I received this email:

> Dear Sue,
>
> An unfortunate problem has been brought to my attention. I am an elected public official, as well as an attorney admitted to the bar. Since the Supreme Court has ruled against religious monuments upon public property, it became awkward for me to be credited towards a project that appears to take the opposite position. I must therefore, unfortunately, decline to be included in your project. I am certain that there must be someone in the area who could take a fine photograph of the monument for your book. Again, I am truly sorry to be in the position of having to decline, and I wish you the very best for completion of your heartfelt objectives.
>
> [Lawyer's name withheld], Chelan, Washington (May 8, 2008)

Photo by Sue A. Hoffman (August 2012)

Dedicated in 1975

It appears that some lawyers have taken a personal position that Ten Commandments monoliths should not be placed on public property despite the US Supreme Court decisions that counter their misguided opinions. It never occurred to me that a photo would make a political statement one way or another, and that lawyers would be concerned about how that might reflect on them.

The Ten Commandments monolith was originally placed in Downtown Square in Moscow, Idaho in June 1975. In less than a year, it had been vandalized several times. The city had the monolith repaired and moved it to East City Park, where, unfortunately, the vandalism continued.

In 1979, the Ten Commandments monolith was moved to Saint Mary's Church. There are no photos or records of the dedication because the Aerie's records were lost in a fire in 2000.

Photo by Karen Madsen (November 2008)

Moscow, Idaho (June 1975)

Photo by Karen Madsen (October 2008)

Dedicated in 1976

Photo by Karen Madsen (October 2008)

West Valley City, Utah (1977)

Photo by Karen Madsen (September 2008)

Dedicated in 1978

Basin, Wyoming had already seen its Ten Commandments monolith get moved once in 2001 when it was placed in front of the Big Horn County Jail. Sheriff Dave Mattis said that he liked it in front of the jail and wished that it didn't have to be moved. County Commissioner Don Russell wasn't quite as enthusiastic. He said, "No one has really complained yet. . . . [But] there's no doubt about it, it is sitting on county property." Trying to beat the national trend of having to remove the monolith under duress, the county chose a preemptive move and looked for a willing recipient.

Photo by Karen Madsen (September 2008)

Basin, Wyoming (May 1978)

Ann Brundage, owner of Wheeler's IGA, was glad to have the Ten Commandments monolith placed in the parking lot of her store. It was a major community effort with everyone donating their time and equipment. The Town of Basin donated their machinery and labor, including a front-end loader that lifted and carried the monolith. Members of the American Legion dug and set the posts. Lamax Construction donated and poured the concrete around the base of the monolith. Machinery Power and Equipment Company donated the saw that helped dislodge the monolith from its previous base so that it could be moved to IGA. It was a three-day process to complete the move, but the Ten Commandments monolith was given a new home.

1980-PRESENT

It is unknown when, or even if, this Ten Commandments monolith was ever moved, but it was likely on government property prior to being placed in front of the Lemhi County Historical Museum. Doris Huntington was very helpful in locating this monolith, as well as several other monoliths, when the search began anew in 2008.

Photo by Sue A. Hoffman (September 2012)

Salmon, Idaho (1981)

On the south side of Buffalo, Wyoming, Willow Grove Cemetery hosts this lone Ten Commandments monolith. This is another case where a monolith may have been on government property prior to its present location.

Photo by Karen Madsen (September 2008)

Buffalo, Wyoming (June 1981)

Photo by Karen Madsen (November 2008)
Dedicated in 1982

Photo by Karen Madsen (October 2008)
Dedicated in 1983

Once accommodating the working residents of City Hall, this building is now used for Developmental Services. The Ten Commandments monolith was threatened in July 1997 by the American Atheists as it appeared to be "a clear violation of the Establishment Clause of the First Amendment." They were requesting to position their own monument next to the monolith with a ceremony to mark its placement. The city justified the Ten Commandments monolith by placing two signs explaining why the city felt it is appropriate to leave the monolith where it is.

Photo by Sue A. Hoffman (July 2002)
Mary Rednour, Post Falls, Idaho

Dick Rednour was instrumental in working with city officials in Post Falls, Idaho when it came to dedicating a Ten Commandments monolith at City Hall. One of the many fundraisers that he organized to fund the monolith was selling Ten Commandments pins. His wife, Mary, was the very first person from an Aerie that actually offered encouragement when I began this journey. She explained how hard everyone worked to help get the monolith placed. She kindly gave me one of the beautiful Ten Commandments pins that were part of the fund-raising event. Her husband had passed away by the time that we met, but his memory lives on through the work that he did with the Eagles.

Photo by Sue A. Hoffman (July 2002)
Old City Hall, Post Falls, Idaho

When Post Falls moved to its brand new City Hall building, they took the Ten Commandments monolith with it and gave it a place of honor on the main street which winds past the building.

Photo by Jeffrey Hoffman (September 2008)

Post Falls, Idaho (1985)

Photo by Jeffrey Hoffman (April 2012)

Dedicated in 1986

Photo by Sue A. Hoffman (August 2012)

Dedicated in 1988

Photo by Sue A. Hoffman (August 2012)

Dedicated in February 1990

Photo by Jeffrey Hoffman (April 2012)

Hayden, Idaho (June 1993)

City Park is right next to City Hall in Hayden, Idaho. The park is home to many different plaques and memorials.

Photo by Jeffrey Hoffman (August 2005)
Grove City, Ohio (August 2005)

One of my greatest pleasures was to be invited to the Fraternal Order of Eagles dedication of their own Ten Commandments monolith at their International Headquarters in Grove City, Ohio in August 2005. Representatives from each state were gathered for various meetings and functions over a period of a couple of days, but everyone assembled out on the lawn for this momentous occasion.

Between speeches, prayers, song, and the official unveiling, lunch was a welcomed treat amidst the pomp and circumstance under the noon-day sun.

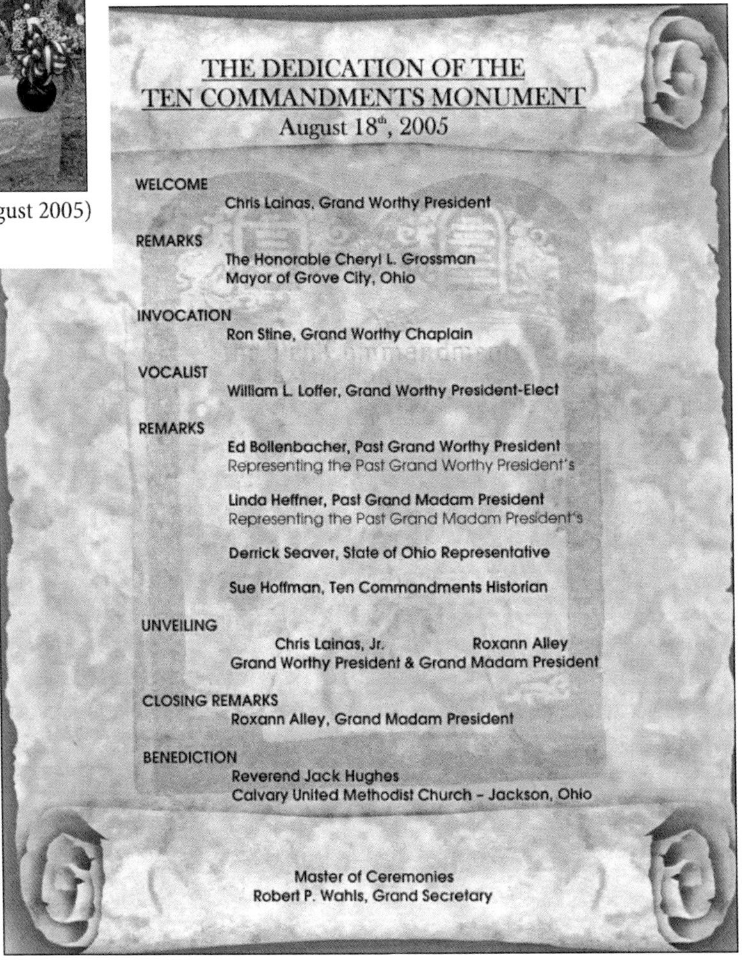

THE DEDICATION OF THE
TEN COMMANDMENTS MONUMENT
August 18th, 2005

WELCOME
Chris Lainas, Grand Worthy President

REMARKS
The Honorable Cheryl L. Grossman
Mayor of Grove City, Ohio

INVOCATION
Ron Stine, Grand Worthy Chaplain

VOCALIST
William L. Loffer, Grand Worthy President-Elect

REMARKS
Ed Bollenbacher, Past Grand Worthy President
Representing the Past Grand Worthy President's

Linda Heffner, Past Grand Madam President
Representing the Past Grand Madam President's

Derrick Seaver, State of Ohio Representative

Sue Hoffman, Ten Commandments Historian

UNVEILING
Chris Lainas, Jr. Roxann Alley
Grand Worthy President & Grand Madam President

CLOSING REMARKS
Roxann Alley, Grand Madam President

BENEDICTION
Reverend Jack Hughes
Calvary United Methodist Church - Jackson, Ohio

Master of Ceremonies
Robert P. Wahls, Grand Secretary

Program from the Ten Commandments Monolith Dedication
(August 18, 2005)

"In Remembrance of Our Sisters and Brothers," Addison County Aerie 3801 developed a thirty-by-seventy-five foot Memorial Park for a Ten Commandments monolith that was dedicated on September 6, 2010.

Photo by Tom McGrath (March 2011)

Vergennes, Vermont (September 2010)

Photo by Tom Cole (May 2008)

Roy Historical Museum, Roy, Utah

Tom Cole must have heard God whisper in his ear to give me a call just a few days before this book had to be delivered to the publisher. In May 2012, the Roy Historical Museum in Utah was closed due to lack of funding from the city. This museum had a special place in my heart because the Ten Commandments monolith was located in its basement. Cole sent me photos in May 2008 when I had called Aerie 3355 inquiring about the monolith.

The Ten Commandments monolith had been dedicated at the Roy City Hall and Fire Station in 1972 with Mayor Charles Hull. A lawsuit was threatened by the Society of Separationists and their lawyer, Brian Barnard. City Manager Chris Davis said that the city leaders decided to remove the monolith from city property when they received a copy of the lawsuit even though the lawsuit was never actually filed.

Photo courtesy of the Fraternal Order of Eagles

Roy, Utah (1972)

Photo courtesy of Tom Cole (June 2013)

Taking the Ten Commandments monolith for a leisurely stroll

Together with a team of architects, engineers, and heavy equipment operators, Tom Cole, operating as the crew leader, was able to organize an impromptu move of the Ten Commandments monolith from the Roy History Museum to Aerie 3355. Fred Welty (truck driver), Jim Gallegos (handy man), and Dick Jarman (quality control advisor) were all essential in this mammoth project. The management and employees of the Roy Water Conservancy were invaluable in their assistance. Cole shared the following photos that were taken in June 2012.

Aerie Secretary Jim Gallegos prepares a place for the Ten Commandments monolith (upper left)
Lowering the Ten Commandments monolith into position (upper right)
Tom Cole, Dick Jarman, and Chuck Perry – Job well done! (bottom)

Roy, Utah's Ten Commandments monolith found its final resting place at Aerie 3355. With the help of many hardworking individuals, another saga of the "brotherhood of the traveling monoliths" has come to a close.

EPILOGUE

According to Guy Tressler, the timing was right when Aerie 493 in Connellsville, Pennsylvania received a letter from the Fraternal Order of Eagles' Grand Aerie in 1956 inquiring if they would be interested in displaying a Ten Commandments monolith in their town at no cost to them. Tressler was president of the Aerie in 1957 when the monolith was dedicated at Connellsville Joint High School next to the auditorium.

Photo courtesy of Guy Tressler (president of FOE Aerie 493) who, unfortunately, missed the dedication ceremony because he had to be at work

Dr. Ned Culler (supervising principal), Mayor Abe Daniels, Rev. R. A. Nelson (pastor of Albright Evangelical United Brethren Church in South Connellsville), Frances Balsely (school board member), John Moore of Toledo, Ohio (1919 graduate of Connellsville High School), James Pujia (FOE state president), George Strine of York (FOE Grand Aerie representative and guest speaker for the dedication), William Dolde (school principal), C. V. Payne (school board member), and Robert Beard (Joint Board president)
Connellsville, Pennsylvania (June 3, 1957)

When the school board was approached regarding the Ten Commandments monolith, they were more than happy to accept it. Tressler stated, "The board accepted it with love and compassion. The biggest thing was that it was put there for the good of the community so the people could go by and read what it meant. More people go to school than to church, and I thought the children who need it could stand by and read it."

Photo courtesy of Guy Tressler

Officers of FOE Aerie 493 in Connellsville, Pennsylvania in 1957
Standing L to R: Frank Pierson, John Ross, Zebe Riley, Don Boyd, Jim Pujia, and Biz Bieshada
Seated L to R: Sidney Riordan, Charles Jammison, Reed Kuhn, Guy Tressler (who grew a beard for Connellsville's 150th Anniversary Celebration in August 1956), Jim Quinn, Ted Mickey, and August Sidow

Just like Ten Commandments monolith dedications all across the country, the town of Connellsville was no exception when it came together to celebrate and honor the event. On Monday at 10:15 AM, June 3, 1957, the entire high school student body was dismissed from classes in order to join with the citizens of Connellsville to take part in the festivities on the school grounds. The invocation (as well as the benediction) was offered by Rev. R. A. Nelson. Ray Barr, the high school vocal music instructor, led everyone in group singing. Supervising Principal Dr. Ned Culler introduced James Pujia, State President of the Fraternal Order of Eagles, who served as Master of Ceremonies. Mayor Abe Daniels extended the formal welcome, and Principal William Dolde spoke briefly to all of the guests. Guest Speaker George Strine, Fraternal Order of Eagles Grand Aerie Representative, made the formal presentation of the monolith. Robert Bear, president of the Connellsville Joint School Committee, accepted the monolith and introduced all of the school directors. This was a major event, and all of the town's dignitaries and officials were present to celebrate this grand affair.

Guy Tressler was interviewed in *The Daily Courier* in June 1957, and said that the Ten Commandments monolith was gifted to the community to, "Inspire all who pause to view the Ten Commandments with a renewed respect for the law of God, which is our greatest strength against the forces that threaten our way of life." As the "lone survivor" from that era, celebrating his ninetieth birthday in September 2012, Guy was recently interviewed by several local news organizations regarding the Connellsville monolith. Guy became very disturbed at the news of an attempt to have this piece of history removed from its original dedication site. He told Natalie Bruzda of *HeraldStandard.com*, "I've left a lot of footprints in the sand in this town," letting her know that he was not going to stay silent and let some out-of-town organization tell Connellsville what to do. Tressler got involved by telling anyone who would listen regarding the history of the monolith and what it means to his community.

Guy D. Tressler, Jr.
February 2013

In an August 1, 2012 letter to Dr. Daniel Lujetic, Superintendent of Connellsville Area School District, and to Richard Evans, Principal of Connellsville Junior High East, the Americans United for the Separation of Church and State (AU) in Washington, DC required a response within thirty days regarding *one* complaint that they had received about the Ten Commandments monolith. The letter stated that the monolith violated the Establishment Clause of the First Amendment to the US Constitution and that it should be removed promptly.

This letter listed several court cases regarding Ten Commandments on public property, most of which allowed the Ten Commandments to remain where they were placed based on historical significance except for the three Supreme Court cases that follow. It was interesting, in light of the demand to remove the monolith, to see how the judicial system had treated similar church/state situations when one individual was offended.

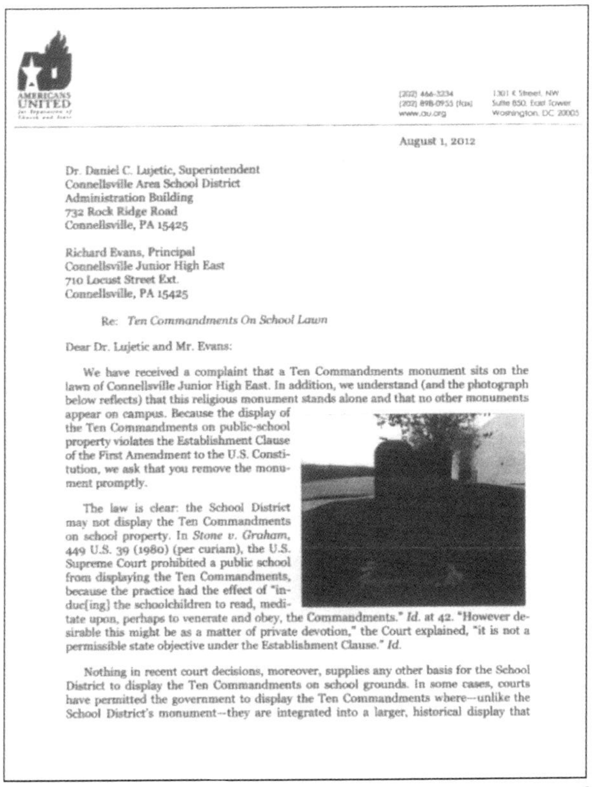
AMERICANS UNITED

(202) 466-3234
(202) 898-0955 (fax)
www.au.org

1301 K Street, NW
Suite 850, East Tower
Washington, DC 20005

August 1, 2012

Dr. Daniel C. Lujetic, Superintendent
Connellsville Area School District
Administration Building
732 Rock Ridge Road
Connellsville, PA 15425

Richard Evans, Principal
Connellsville Junior High East
710 Locust Street Ext.
Connellsville, PA 15425

Re: *Ten Commandments On School Lawn*

Dear Dr. Lujetic and Mr. Evans:

We have received a complaint that a Ten Commandments monument sits on the lawn of Connellsville Junior High East. In addition, we understand (and the photograph below reflects) that this religious monument stands alone and that no other monuments appear on campus. Because the display of the Ten Commandments on public-school property violates the Establishment Clause of the First Amendment to the U.S. Constitution, we ask that you remove the monument promptly.

The law is clear: the School District may not display the Ten Commandments on school property. In *Stone v. Graham*, 449 U.S. 39 (1980) (per curiam), the U.S. Supreme Court prohibited a public school from displaying the Ten Commandments, because the practice had the effect of "induc[ing] the schoolchildren to read, meditate upon, perhaps to venerate and obey, the Commandments." *Id.* at 42. "However desirable this might be as a matter of private devotion," the Court explained, "it is not a permissible state objective under the Establishment Clause." *Id.*

Nothing in recent court decisions, moreover, supplies any other basis for the School District to display the Ten Commandments on school grounds. In some cases, courts have permitted the government to display the Ten Commandments where—unlike the School District's monument—they are integrated into a larger, historical display that

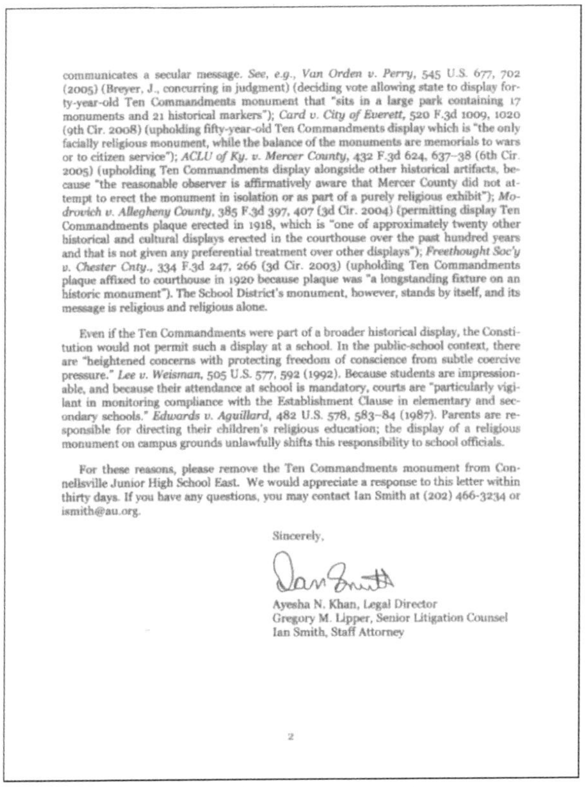
communicates a secular message. *See, e.g.*, *Van Orden v. Perry*, 545 U.S. 677, 702 (2005) (Breyer, J., concurring in judgment) (deciding vote allowing state to display forty-year-old Ten Commandments monument that "sits in a large park containing 17 monuments and 21 historical markers"); *Card v. City of Everett*, 520 F.3d 1009, 1020 (9th Cir. 2008) (upholding fifty-year-old Ten Commandments display which is "the only facially religious monument, while the balance of the monuments are memorials to wars or to citizen service"); *ACLU of Ky. v. Mercer County*, 432 F.3d 624, 637–38 (6th Cir. 2005) (upholding Ten Commandments display alongside other historical artifacts, because "the reasonable observer is affirmatively aware that Mercer County did not attempt to erect the monument in isolation or as part of a purely religious exhibit"); *Modrovich v. Allegheny County*, 385 F.3d 397, 407 (3d Cir. 2004) (permitting display Ten Commandments plaque erected in 1918, which is "one of approximately twenty other historical and cultural displays erected in the courthouse over the past hundred years and that is not given any preferential treatment over other displays"); *Freethought Soc'y v. Chester Cnty.*, 334 F.3d 247, 266 (3d Cir. 2003) (upholding Ten Commandments plaque affixed to courthouse in 1920 because plaque was "a longstanding fixture on an historic monument"). The School District's monument, however, stands by itself, and its message is religious and religious alone.

Even if the Ten Commandments were part of a broader historical display, the Constitution would not permit such a display at a school. In the public-school context, there are "heightened concerns with protecting freedom of conscience from subtle coercive pressure." *Lee v. Weisman*, 505 U.S. 577, 592 (1992). Because students are impressionable, and because their attendance at school is mandatory, courts are "particularly vigilant in monitoring compliance with the Establishment Clause in elementary and secondary schools." *Edwards v. Aguillard*, 482 U.S. 578, 583–84 (1987). Parents are responsible for directing their children's religious education; the display of a religious monument on campus grounds unlawfully shifts this responsibility to school officials.

For these reasons, please remove the Ten Commandments monument from Connellsville Junior High School East. We would appreciate a response to this letter within thirty days. If you have any questions, you may contact Ian Smith at (202) 466-3234 or ismith@au.org.

Sincerely,

Ayesha N. Khan, Legal Director
Gregory M. Lipper, Senior Litigation Counsel
Ian Smith, Staff Attorney

2

Americans United for the Separation of Church and State Letter (August 1, 2012)

The first case listed in the letter, Stone v. Graham (1980), concerned a statute that required the posting of the Ten Commandments (which were privately funded) on the wall of each public classroom in the State of Kentucky. At the bottom of each poster, the following words were imprinted, "The secular application of the Ten Commandments is clearly seen in its adoption as the fundamental legal code of Western Civilization and the Common Law of the United States." Despite that required wording, the decision was made by the US Supreme Court that these posted Ten Commandments had no secular legislative purpose, and therefore, the requirement to post them in the classrooms was unconstitutional.

Justice William Rehnquist offered the dissent on this case, and stated:

> The Court rejects the secular purpose articulated by the State because the Decalogue is "undeniably a sacred text." It is equally undeniable, however, as the elected representatives of Kentucky determined, that the Ten Commandments have had a significant impact on the development of secular legal codes of the Western World. The trial court concluded that evidence submitted substantiated this determination. . . . The Establishment Clause does not require that the public sector be insulated from all things which may have a religious significance or origin. This Court has recognized that religion has been closely identified with our history and government, and that the history of man is inseparable from the history of religion.

Justice Rehnquist then referred to the case of McCollum v. Board of Education where Justice Robert Jackson said, "The fact is that, for good or for ill, nearly everything in our culture worth transmitting, everything which gives meaning to life, is saturated with religious influences, derived from paganism, Judaism, Christianity – both Catholic and Protestant – and other faiths accepted by a large part of the world's peoples. One can hardly respect the system of education that would leave the student wholly ignorant of the currents of religious thought that move the world society for a part in which he is being prepared." One wonders why the wisdom of these justices did not prevail in this Kentucky case.

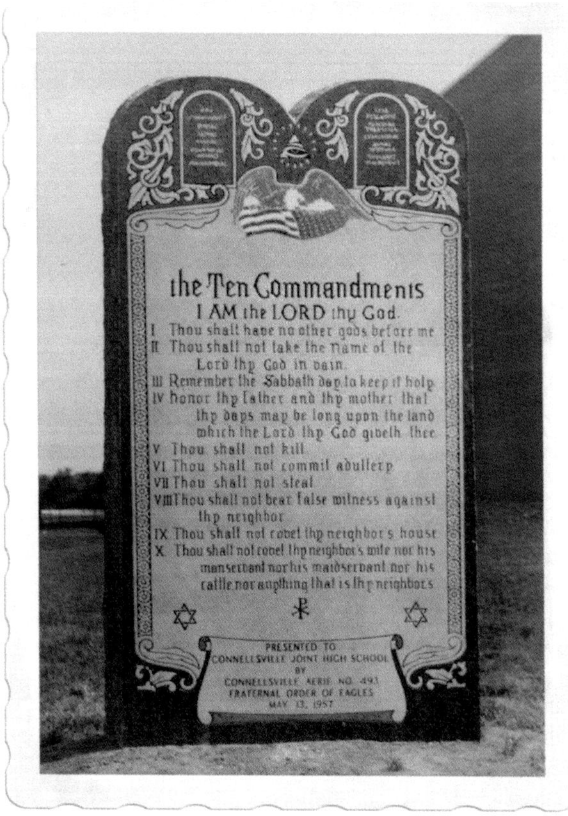

Photo courtesy of Guy Tressler

The letter also cited the Lee v. Weisman case that was decided in 1992 by the US Supreme Court in a five-to-four decision regarding prayers at a middle school graduation that were given by an invited rabbi. Although the decision held because the prayers were not sectarian enough, Justice Antonin Scalia, in his dissent, stated, "In addition to this general tradition of prayer at public ceremonies, there exists a more specific tradition of invocations and benedictions at public school graduation exercises." Historical context should have counted in this decision, as well as an inkling of common sense, but political correctness had already invaded even our highest Court of the land. The prayers of Rabbi Leslie Gutterman of Temple Beth El in Providence, Rhode Island, probably blessed most of the students at the graduation ceremonies at Nathan Bishop Middle School in 1989. They are worthy of being shared again, since this case was brought up by the AU, to also encourage the students at Connellsville Junior High East:

INVOCATION

God of the Free, Hope of the Brave: For the legacy of America where diversity is celebrated and the rights of minorities are protected, we thank You. May these young men and women grow up to enrich it. For the liberty of America, we thank You. May these new graduates grow up to guard it. For the political process of America in which all its citizens may participate, for its court system where all may seek justice, we thank You. May those we honor this morning always turn to it in trust. For the destiny of America, we thank You. May the graduates of Nathan Bishop Middle School so live that they might help to share it. May our aspirations for our country and for these young people, who are our hope for the future, be richly fulfilled. AMEN.

BENEDICTION

O God, we are grateful to You for having endowed us with the capacity for learning which we have celebrated on this joyous commencement. Happy families give thanks for seeing their children achieve an important milestone. Send Your blessings upon the teachers and administrators who helped prepare them. The graduates now need strength and guidance for the future; help them to understand that we are not complete with academic knowledge alone. We must each strive to fulfill what You require of us all: to do justly, to love mercy, to walk humbly. We give thanks to You, Lord, for keeping us alive, sustaining us, and allowing us to reach this special, happy occasion. AMEN.

The last case in this letter, Edwards v. Aguillard, a case that was also decided in a five-to-four decision by the US Supreme Court in 1987, was to determine if Louisiana's "Creationism Act" was constitutional. The Act stated that if the theory of evolution in public elementary and secondary schools was taught, it must also be accompanied by the theory of creation science. Again, Justice Scalia offered the dissent, because in order to claim that those who taught creation science would teach it strictly from a religious viewpoint, would question their personal motivation. He noted that:

> After seven hearings and several months of study, resulting in substantial revision of the original proposal, they approved the Act overwhelmingly, and specifically articulated the secular purpose they meant it to serve. Although the record contains abundant evidence of the sincerity of that purpose (the only issue pertinent to this case), the Court today holds against this requirement essentially on the basis of "its visceral knowledge regarding what must have motivated the legislators." This kind of decision process relates less to the historical context as than it reflects the absurdity that some individuals, or organizations, who claim to know the intent of the original leaders who initiated not only the "Creationism Act," but also the Ten Commandments Project so many years before.

The AU wrote a very authoritarian-sounding piece of correspondence. Their act of regurgitating court cases to the Connellsville School authorities appeared to be a feeble attempt to intimidate them into a knee-jerk reaction that would initiate the removal of the Ten Commandments monolith. Their plan almost worked.

The next letter (dated August 29, 2012) was sent by certified mail to Dr. Daniel Lujetic, superintendent of the Connellsville Area School District. It came from the Pittsburgh-based firm of Steele Schneider Attorneys at Law who represented the Freedom from Religion Foundation (FFRF), a notorious anti-religion organization from Madison, Wisconsin, as well as the parent (identified only as an atheist) of a Connellsville Area School District student (identified only as being non-religious). The letter claimed, that in no uncertain terms, the Ten Commandments monolith "is in clear violation of the Establishment Clause of the First Amendment to the United States Constitution" and that "[It] will not withstand judicial scrutiny." This letter also contained an enclosure that listed multiple court cases in an attempt to prove the justification of permanently removing the monolith as their clients demanded. Again, another very pertinacious letter from a law office was sent with menacing verbiage of unending litigation and financial woes if demands were not met. This attempt almost worked, too, but the townspeople of Connellsville had other plans.

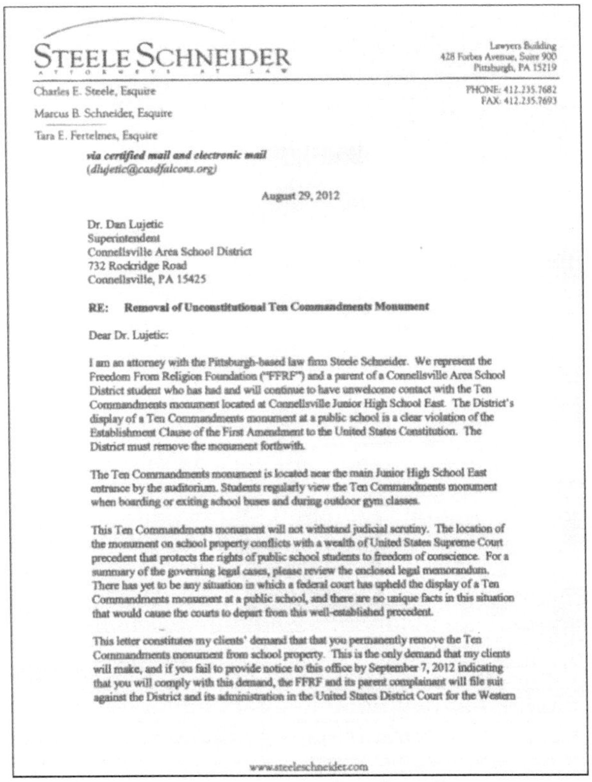

STEELE SCHNEIDER
ATTORNEYS AT LAW

Lawyers Building
428 Forbes Avenue, Suite 900
Pittsburgh, PA 15219

PHONE: 412.235.7682
FAX: 412.235.7693

Charles E. Steele, Esquire
Marcus B. Schneider, Esquire
Tara E. Fertelmes, Esquire

via certified mail and electronic mail
(dlujetic@casdfalcons.org)

August 29, 2012

Dr. Dan Lujetic
Superintendent
Connellsville Area School District
732 Rockridge Road
Connellsville, PA 15425

RE: Removal of Unconstitutional Ten Commandments Monument

Dear Dr. Lujetic:

I am an attorney with the Pittsburgh-based law firm Steele Schneider. We represent the Freedom From Religion Foundation ("FFRF") and a parent of a Connellsville Area School District student who has had and will continue to have unwelcome contact with the Ten Commandments monument located at Connellsville Junior High School East. The District's display of a Ten Commandments monument at a public school is a clear violation of the Establishment Clause of the First Amendment to the United States Constitution. The District must remove the monument forthwith.

The Ten Commandments monument is located near the main Junior High School East entrance by the auditorium. Students regularly view the Ten Commandments monument when boarding or exiting school buses and during outdoor gym classes.

This Ten Commandments monument will not withstand judicial scrutiny. The location of the monument on school property conflicts with a wealth of United States Supreme Court precedent that protects the rights of public school students to freedom of conscience. For a summary of the governing legal cases, please review the enclosed legal memorandum. There has yet to be any situation in which a federal court has upheld the display of a Ten Commandments monument at a public school, and there are no unique facts in this situation that would cause the courts to depart from this well-established precedent.

This letter constitutes my clients' demand that that you permanently remove the Ten Commandments monument from school property. This is the only demand that my clients will make, and if you fail to provide notice to this office by September 7, 2012 indicating that you will comply with this demand, the FFRF and its parent complainant will file suit against the District and its administration in the United States District Court for the Western

www.steeleschneider.com

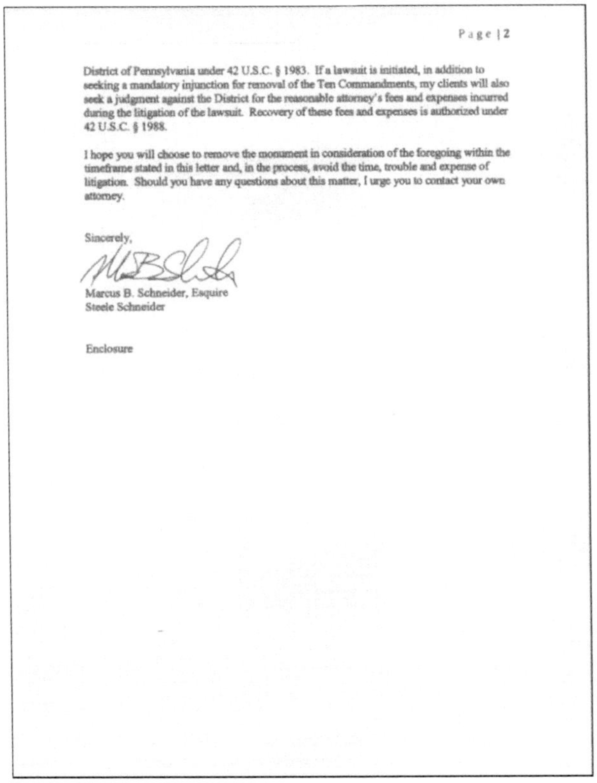

Page | 2

District of Pennsylvania under 42 U.S.C. § 1983. If a lawsuit is initiated, in addition to seeking a mandatory injunction for removal of the Ten Commandments, my clients will also seek a judgment against the District for the reasonable attorney's fees and expenses incurred during the litigation of the lawsuit. Recovery of these fees and expenses is authorized under 42 U.S.C. § 1988.

I hope you will choose to remove the monument in consideration of the foregoing within the timeframe stated in this letter and, in the process, avoid the time, trouble and expense of litigation. Should you have any questions about this matter, I urge you to contact your own attorney.

Sincerely,

Marcus B. Schneider, Esquire
Steele Schneider

Enclosure

Steele Schneider Attorneys at Law Letter (August 29, 2012)

Understandably, the Connellsville Area School District officials were shaken by these two letters. They agreed that the best thing for the school district would be to quietly remove the Ten Commandments monolith by September 7 to avoid any legal expenses. They had the monolith covered in plastic which mysteriously disappeared in the dead of night on several occasions over the next couple of days while they researched a possible new home for the large piece of granite. Because of the depth of the monolith footers, the planned removal received a temporary reprieve for two weeks.

In order to keep the monolith in exile, it was covered with plywood and banded with metal straps. These, too, had to be replaced several times because they kept getting removed.

On Sunday, September 9, one of the days that the monolith's words were exposed, three American flags were placed at its base as members of the Church of God voted to accept the Ten Commandments monolith. The church was approached by Jon Detwiler, president of the Connellsville Area School Board, as a possible site for the relocation of the monolith. Although he received multiple phone calls to fight the removal of the monolith, and even admitted, "It's not really the worst thing in the world to have our kids reading," he thought it would be best to give the monolith to a private organization which just happened to be adjacent to Junior High East. By placing the monolith on the corner of the church's property, which is at the entrance of the school complex at the soccer fields, more students would be exposed to the monolith than at its current location which is near the staff parking lot. Also, the church owns the property and allows the school district to use it. Rev. Nelson Confer was pleasantly surprised and overwhelmed by phone calls from local organizations calling the Church of God and offering to purchase park benches and landscaping items to enhance the beauty of the monolith's proposed new site. The church was also looking into illuminating the Ten Commandments monolith at night.

The very next day, Monday, September 10, three of Connellsville area pastors led over 150 local townspeople in a prayer rally at the Ten Commandments monolith to encourage the Connellsville Area School District to keep the monolith where it stood. Pastor Ewing Marietta, pastor of Liberty Baptist Church in nearby Uniontown, urged those who were present to "take a stand and be courageous." He continued, "We are upset that this would ever be considered to be removed. There is no doubt in my mind that we can win this case."

The school board held an open agenda meeting that same evening and over 100 citizens from Connellsville anxiously waited for an opportunity to voice their opinions regarding the Ten Commandments monolith. Many people came forth with their support of the monolith. Students, as well as adults, pledged to hold future rallies at the monolith. After an hour and a half of public comments demanding that the monolith not be moved, Director Paul Means asked that a motion be put on that coming Wednesday's school board agenda that would delay any further action regarding removing of the monolith.

Another rally was held on Wednesday, September 12, with community members and students holding signs in support of the monolith. After the rally, they walked to the Connellsville Area District Board Meeting to join approximately 100 cohorts. After two hours of discussions held in support of retaining the Ten Commandments monolith, the unanimous decision was announced stating, "Request approval to delay any further action concerning moving the monument from its current location at Connellsville Junior High until further notice and pending further legal action." People rose to their feet as the room erupted in a joyous clamoring of approval.

A Connellsville businessman, Gary Colatch, pleased with the school board's decision to keep the Ten Commandments monolith, put his money where his beliefs were to insure that the people would continue the fight. "I'm Catholic, and I really haven't been to church that much lately," he said. "But we needed to do something here, and we needed to drum up support. If we don't get support, the school board is going to fold." He distributed Ten Commandments tablets around town and went on local talk radio. "In my opinion, an extremist group is taking advantage of a way to manipulate and bully a little community like Connellsville. I just don't think this should be tolerated." Colatch even offered personal funds to help pay the school district's legal fees.

Many others in the community chose to voice their support and lend their talents to save the Ten Commandments monolith. John Orr used social media as he posted an online petition to the Connellsville School Board:

> Leave the Ten Commandments Monument Stand
>
> The monument that stands on the property of Junior High East has stood for fifty-five years having been donated by the Connellsville Eagles and is a valued part of our local history. The Ten Commandments aside from faith has had a profound effect on the United States and our system of law and should be revered for that reason. We also believe that it is profitable for a community to be able to freely, but respectfully, express their religious beliefs in public and it is always acceptable as long as it is not being funded by taxpayer dollars. We also believe that to remove a discreet historical monument due to religious affiliation when only opposed by a small group would be an oppressive act against our freedom of religion.

When the petition was presented to the school board, it was signed by 1,034 individuals.

Pastor Marietta was so energized by the school board's decision to not move the monolith that he initiated the "Thou Shall Not Move" organization which has since met several times at the Connellsville Eagles' Aerie. They not only want to keep the Ten Commandments monolith at the school, but they have also sold over 4,100 cardboard Ten Commandments signs in hopes of generating money for Ten Commandment monuments to be prominently displayed all over Connellsville. As of March 2013, they have enough funds to purchase eleven monoliths with twenty-two churches wanting them. Other businesses have contacted Pastor Marietta requesting how to place monoliths at locations other than churches. There are Ten Commandments signs all over Connellsville – from private yards to businesses of all sizes.

Freedom from Religion Foundation (FFRF) was thrown into a tizzy. With a high majority of Connellsville-ites outwardly protesting attempts to remove the monolith, and with Ten Commandments signs, posters, and tablets popping up all over town, what's an anti-religion organization supposed to do? They smacked the Connellsville Area School District with a lawsuit. According to Pittsburgh attorney Marcus B. Schneider, who is working with the FFRF on the case, stated that even *if* the monolith got moved to the local church, students who play athletics on the school's soccer fields still would not be able to "avoid" the Ten Commandments.

Freedom from Religion Foundation (FFRF), along with female Doe 4 and female parent Doe 5 (who is also a member of FFRF), filed suit against Connellsville Area School District on Thursday, September 27, 2012. Doe 4 and Doe 5 claimed that the Ten Commandments monolith cited views contrary to their family's personally-held nonreligious views. The monument also excluded them, and others in the community, who do not follow the beliefs stated on the monolith, and that they were becoming stressed. They also claimed that the monolith endorsed a specific religion that the district favors, and if they chose to have a different god, or many gods, or no gods at all, that the school district should not have the right to instruct its "captive audience of impressionable students" in a way that would be considered contrary to Doe 5's parental authority.

Attorney John Smart of Andrews & Price in Pittsburgh, Pennsylvania, on behalf of the Connellsville Area School District, contended that, "Even if the religious aspects of the monument's appearance and history indicate that it has some religious meaning, the district is not bound to display only symbols that are wholly secular, or to convey solely secular messages." He filed a Motion to Dismiss on December 4, 2012, stating that the Ten Commandments monolith "was not promoting any one religion and was the gift of a secular fraternal organization." Because of the looming legal action, the only Ten Commandments in town that was not visible in public was the monolith located at Junior High East. Sadly, it was fully covered in a wooden box and metal straps were welded in place.

On March 7, 2013, US District Judge Terrence McVerry of the Western District of Pennsylvania, denied the dismissal of the case to remove the Ten Commandments monolith from Connellsville Junior High East, and ruled that all the parties of the lawsuit should be ready for the initial Case Management Conference on April 11, 2013, which would be held prior to "going to court."

On May 24, 2013, the judge granted the request of the FFRF for female Does 4 and 5 to be able to remain anonymous during all of the litigation proceedings. They were concerned about retribution from the community for their desire to remove the Ten Commandments monolith. As the attorneys spent their time gathering information and going through depositions, the court prepared for the case that began on August 23, 2013.

Photo courtesy of Guy Tressler

In the interim, on June 29, 2013, Connellsville Aerie 493 accepted a Ten Commandments monolith from the Shall Not Move Committee and Pastor Marietta in recognition of the Fraternal Order of Eagles' great history regarding the Ten Commandments. Although he was unable to make the first Connellsville dedication because of work obligations fifty-six years prior, Guy Tressler was there to assist with the unveiling and say a few words. Unfortunately, Pastor Marietta purposely designed the Ten Commandments monoliths for Connellsville based on the Protestant numbering of the Ten Commandments with full knowledge of the dismal historic uproar this kind of numbering has created in the past. History may repeat itself – even as with "the best laid plans of mice and men" – this, too, may go astray. Sadly, it seems that even members of the clergy have a difficult time accepting that God did not number His Commandments. With time constraints and publishing deadlines, this is where this saga has to come to a close.

Just like today in Connellsville, Pennsylvania, back on Thursday, June 12, 2003, the people of Carson City, Nevada were attempting to make a similar decision whether or not to allow a Ten Commandments monolith to stay in the place that it was dedicated so many years before. The City Assembly was called to order and the roll was taken. There seemed to be no better way to bring the collection of events to a temporary close other than to utter the prayer that was offered by Chaplain Beverly Mobley on that day in Carson City over ten years ago.

Let us pray.
Dear Lord, You have changed the seasons for us since we first came into these chambers – winter to spring, and soon spring to summer. We have enjoyed the new environments You have given us. This body, too, is contemplating a change, and we ask that You give them the wisdom and courage to make sound judgments. Your words in Exodus inspired a motion picture, *The Ten Commandments*. Give us patience, Lord, as we wait for these creators of law to proclaim the words from the silver screen, "So let it be written, so let it be done!" AMEN.

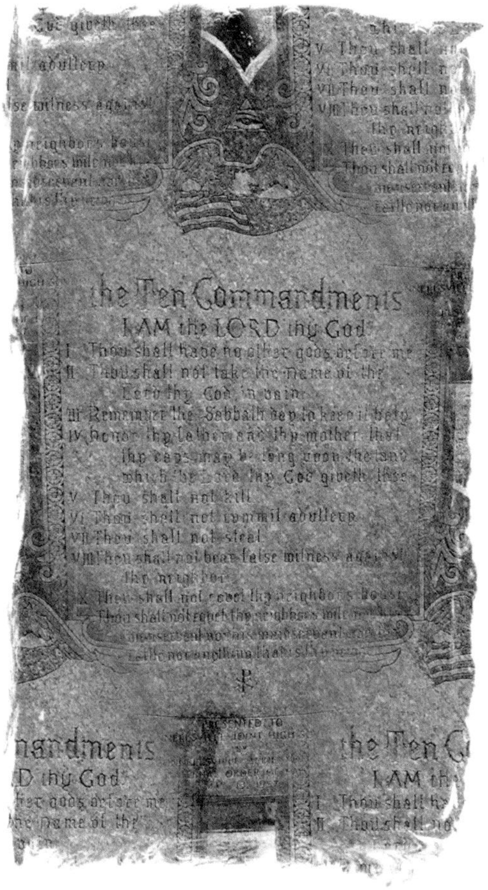

To be continued another day . . .

ABOUT THE AUTHOR

"I know a little bit about a lot of things." ~ Sue A. (Pankow) Hoffman

Raised in a small town between Niagara Falls and Buffalo, New York, Sue met her future husband, Jeffrey, while living in the Town of Wheatfield. She worked as a secretary for a year after graduating from high school in 1973, and then enlisted in the US Army as a medical specialist as the Vietnam War came to a close.

After graduating from high school in 1971, Jeffrey joined the US Air Force. While Sue was stationed at Fort Lewis, Washington, she married Jeffrey in 1976, and together, they had joint military assignments in Hawaii for the next three years. They began their civilian lives in Western Washington. Sue worked for the Air Force at Boeing for three years while Jeffrey began his career at The Boeing Company (where he is still employed at the time of this writing with dreams of retiring soon). Jeffrey's career took them to Sanaá, Yemen in 1983 for one year where Sue worked for the United States Agency for International Development (USAID).

Jeffrey and Sue then became proud parents to a wonderful daughter, Lisa, in 1984. Sue eventually went back to work as a part-time admitting clerk in a hospital emergency room. Easily bored, Sue then became a financial planner and insurance advisor for several years. After that, she did a few odd jobs, a few years at a time for each, to include customer service at a battery company, office assistant for other insurance representatives, word processing business owner, and also did some summer-time acting, etc., just to mention a few. Sue also went to college intermittently and earned an Associate of Arts Degree and an Associates' Degree in Law Enforcement.

Through a combined program at Green River Community College and Seattle Pacific University, Sue was able to earn her teaching certification. After two years in substitute and part-time positions, Sue began full-time instruction at West Seattle High School teaching computer classes and four-year planning to ninth graders for the next five years.

It was during this time that Sue was diagnosed with multiple sclerosis. Although making a valiant effort to continue teaching to retirement age, it was not meant to be. She medically retired from the Seattle School District in 2003, and has since spent her time trying to unravel the tale of the Ten Commandments monoliths. She has also been an active member of her church, the Assistance Dog Club of Puget Sound, her neighborhood homeowner's association, and the Moms' Group.

As each day offers unique and entertaining medical challenges, Sue relishes her time that she has with family and friends. Her greatest pleasures come from being a wife, mom, and grandmother. Sue gives all glory to God for His faithfulness in each new day and for His continued blessings.

ADDENDUM: HOW TO OBTAIN A FREE DIGITAL COPY OF *ON EAGLE WINGS*

Starting June 14, 2014, and only through June 30, 2015, if you have done any of the following:

- Purchased this book through **www.createspace.com/4615643** for $49.95, paid taxes, shipping, and handling, AND have a receipt or other form of Proof of Purchase
- Purchased the Kindle version of this book through Amazon, paid taxes, AND have a receipt or other form of Proof of Purchase
- Purchased this book at a book-signing event with the Author, filled out a submission form, AND either turned it in at the event or made other arrangements with the Author

You may receive a FREE digital copy of the 96-page illustrated 1957 *On Eagle Wings* Flipbook sent as an attachment via Dropbox™ to your personal email account for your PC or Mac computer.

Just email a copy of your Proof of Purchase as an attachment with your full name and phone number (in case there are email or Dropbox™ issues) to **tencommandmentsjourney@outlook.com.** You will then receive an email with instructions on how to retrieve *On Eagle Wings* via Dropbox ™. If you already have a free account with Dropbox™, then it will be in your folder. If not, instructions will come with your email regarding opening a free account.

Thank you for supporting IN SEARCH OF GOD AND THE TEN COMMANDMENTS.

All glory to God!

Romans 8:31

30068745R00195

Made in the USA
Charleston, SC
31 May 2014

AQA English Literature B

AS

Exclusively endorsed by AQA

2nd Edition

Adrian Beard
Alan Kent

Nelson Thornes

First edition published in 2008 by Nelson Thornes Ltd.
This edition published in 2012 by:
Nelson Thornes Ltd
Delta Place
27 Bath Road
CHELTENHAM
GL53 7TH
United Kingdom

12 13 14 15 16 / 10 9 8 7 6 5 4 3 2 1

A catalogue record for this book is available from the British Library

ISBN 978 1 4085 1533 4

Cover photograph by Photolibrary
Page make-up by The OKS Group
Printed and bound in Spain by Graphycems

Contents

AQA introduction

Nelson Thornes has worked in partnership with AQA to ensure this book offers you the best support for your GCE course.

All resources have been approved by senior AQA examiners, so you can feel assured that they closely match the specification for this subject and provide you with everything you need to prepare successfully for your examinations.

How to use this book

This book covers the specification for your course and is arranged in a sequence approved by AQA. The introduction to the book explains what will be required of you as an English Literature student. There are two units in the book. Unit 1 will prepare you for the examination and deals with various aspects of narrative that you may choose to write about in your answers. Chapter 7 draws these aspects together to show how you might construct a response for the examination that covers all of these aspects, while Chapter 8 deals specifically with preparation for the examination itself.

Unit 2 is a guide to your coursework study, based on a study of aspects of comedy. This unit takes you through comedic conventions, concepts and theories from Ancient Greek comedy to modern comedy, using key extracts from Shakespeare and other playwrights. Chapter 16 explains in detail how to prepare for, write and create a commentary on your coursework.

Definitions of any words that appear in **bold** can be found in the glossary at the back of this book.

Learning objectives

At the beginning of each section you will find a list of learning objectives that contain targets linked to the requirements of the specification.

The features in this book include:

Key terms

Terms that you will need to be able to define and understand. These terms are coloured blue in the textbook and their definition will also appear in the glossary at the back of this book.

Hint

Useful suggestions for study.

Remember

Reminder of key terms and ideas that you have already come across earlier in the textbook.

Link

Links to other areas in the textbook that are relevant to what you are reading. Links can also refer you to longer extracts to be used in activities; these can be found in the Extracts section at the back of the book.

Further reading

Suggestions for other texts that will help you in your study and preparation for assessment in English Literature B.

Activity

Activities that develop the skills you will need for success in your English Literature B course.

Extension tasks

Tasks that take your learning further to increase your skills and give you even more knowledge and understanding. You should complete these tasks when you have extra time after completing the activities.

Commentaries

Examples of answers you might give to the activities. Commentaries sometimes appear directly after the activity and sometimes at the end of the chapter in the section headed Commentaries. They may also appear in the main text with the corresponding activity in the margin.

Did you know?

Interesting facts to extend your background knowledge.

AQA Examiner's tip

Hints from AQA examiners to help you with your study and to prepare for your examination.

Summary

A summary of what is covered in each chapter of the book.

Introduction to this book

Aims of the chapter:

- Presents your AS Level English Literature course.
- Explains how your work for each of the two units of the course will be assessed.

Welcome to AS Level English Literature. It is worth reading this first chapter at the start of your course, when it will give you some ideas about what is to come, and then you can return to it when you have had more experience of reading your texts and working with this book.

The course at a glance

AS Level English Literature has two units: Unit 1 is taken as a formal examination; Unit 2 is coursework. How the work is divided up in terms of time, and among your teachers, will depend very much on the circumstances in the institution you attend – so you could prepare for Unit 1 first and then do Unit 2, or you could prepare for them both simultaneously, or you could do them in reverse numerical order.

It is always worth remembering that across the course as a whole you will do much more reading and preparation than the examination/coursework can possibly assess. This means that the assessment is a snapshot of what you have been doing, rather than the whole process. As we move on to look at how the assessment works, try to see it as a shaping mechanism rather than the be-all and end-all of what AS Level English Literature is all about.

Unit 1: Aspects of Narrative

The full implication of this unit's title will be explained in the next chapter. In outline, though, you will do the following in preparation for this unit:

- you will read and study two novels from a set text list
- you will read and study two poetry texts from a set text list.

You can take all four texts into the examination with you, but you are not allowed to make any annotations in them beforehand. In many cases the overall poetry 'text' is made up of a number of separate poems.

The following box outlines the ways in which Unit 1 will be assessed.

Assessment of Unit 1: Aspects of Narrative

Examination: 2 hours (open-book)
60% of total AS marks
30% of total A Level marks

Four texts for study:
Two novels (at least one post-1990)
Two poetry texts (1800–1945)

Two sections:

Section A

- Involves close analysis of narrative method in **one** text
- Contains specific questions on each of the set texts
- Two questions to be answered on your chosen text
- Short answer required for each of the two questions

Section B

- Involves comparing an aspect of narrative across **three** texts
- Contains two questions, wide-ranging in scope
- Essay required on the three texts you have not covered in Section A

Unit 2: Dramatic Genres

The **genre** referred to in the unit's title is comedy. The full implications of this unit will be explained later in the book. In outline, though, you will do the following in preparation for this unit:

- you will read and study a Shakespeare play that can be labelled a comedy
- you will read and study another play that can also be labelled a comedy.

After you have studied the texts, you will produce a portfolio of coursework consisting of two written responses, one on each text. In each piece of work your response will involve thinking about the play within the broader generic frameworks of drama and comedy.

Key terms

Genre: a type of text (e.g. a crime novel, a narrative poem). Texts can be grouped and labelled for various reasons, such as their content, their intended audience (e.g. a children's novel) and how readers respond to them.

In this unit there is also the possibility of writing a **re-creative response**. If you intend to use this method, you will need to negotiate the task carefully with your tutor. You will also need to provide a commentary to go with the response, in which you can explain the thinking behind your approach, and what it has shown you about the original text.

Key terms

Re-creative response: a piece of writing that throws light on the original text in a creative rather than an analytical way.

The box below outlines the ways in which Unit 2 will be assessed.

Assessment of Unit 2: Dramatic Genres (Aspects of Comedy)

Coursework
40% of total AS marks
20% of total A Level marks

Minimum **two** texts for study within dramatic genre of comedy
A portfolio of **two** pieces of written coursework (one may be re-creative), **1,200–1,500 words** for each piece:

1. An aspect of dramatic/comedic genre with regard to a Shakespeare play
2. An aspect of dramatic/comedic genre with regard to another play

Assessment Objectives

As part of the process by which all specifications are regulated, English Literature is broken down into four Assessment Objectives, or AOs.

These AOs do not specify the content of your course as such, but they do specify the skills and approaches that you are required to cover. As a student you do not need to worry about covering them, provided you answer the question, whether it be an examination or coursework. The question will be designed to cover the skills and approaches – your job is to answer its requirements exactly.

None the less it is useful for you to have an understanding of what these AOs actually say. The following box gives them in their official format. But what are their implications in more practical terms?

AO1
Articulate creative, informed and relevant responses to literary texts, using appropriate terminology and concepts, and coherent, accurate written expression

AO2
Demonstrate detailed critical understanding in analysing the ways in which structure, form and language shape meanings in literary texts

AO3
Explore connections and comparisons between different literary texts, informed by interpretations of other readers

AO4
Demonstrate understanding of the significance and influence of the contexts in which literary texts are written and received

AO1

Two key elements combine here: the quality of your writing and your knowledge of the necessary terminology that goes with this subject. All AS Level subjects have their own specialist language and their own academic conventions when it comes to writing. The specialist terminology that you need will emerge as you go through the book and can be checked in the glossary at the end of the book.

Below are some of the types of writing you could come across during your AS course:

- short answers, which require no introduction or conclusion
- essays in examinations, but with text available
- a coursework essay
- a piece of re-creative writing.

Each of these is subtly different, but each needs to be practised and improved. English Literature is all about reading, but it is assessed totally by writing. You therefore need to prepare for your AS assessments by working at your writing skills, making sure that you know exactly what is required.

AO2

This is concerned with how texts work, how they are constructed – what authors do with language when they write. The best order in which to take the three key terms is as follows: **form**, **structure**, **language** – that is, the biggest unit first and the smallest last.

Key terms

Form: the aspects of a text in its totality that enable it to be identified as a novel, a poem, an epistolary novel (i.e. a story told in the form of letters), a sonnet (a poem of 14 lines), and so on.

Structure: how the significant parts of a text work together to form a whole (e.g. the connection between chapters in a novel, or the way time is organised, or the connection between verses in a poem).

Language: in this context, generally refers to specific words or phrases in the text.

Of the three terms, looking at the use of language in a text can sometimes be useful in poetry, but it tends to have less significance in novels and plays.

As you work through this book you will acquire considerable expertise in how to analyse texts in order to meet the requirements of AO2.

AO3

AO3 has two parts to it. It requires that you make connections and comparisons across texts and that when you make these connections you are aware that you are not dealing with absolutes – there are other ways in which the texts can be interpreted, in which case different connections might be made.

At the heart of this idea of interpreting texts through connecting them with others is the idea of genre, or type of text. Generic labels help us to identify what a text is like, but we need to be aware that although it has some qualities in common with the other texts, it may also be different from them.

In this AO, then, we look for similarity and difference across the texts we are studying, and we will probably find people disagreeing about whether various categories apply. This means that when we are studying literature we are not dealing with fixed and known interpretations.

AO4

AO4 follows naturally from AO3, because how you categorise a text depends on various factors, or **contexts**, which shape your response. Contexts can arise from circumstances to do with the way the text was produced, called **contexts of production**, and contexts to do with the way it is received now, called **contexts of reception**.

Key terms

Context: the circumstances surrounding a text (e.g. where it first appeared, social attitudes today) which affect the way it is understood. The word is formed from *con* (= with) + *text*, so literally it means 'what goes with the text'.

Contexts of production: the circumstances that might affect a text at the time of its writing.

Contexts of reception: the circumstances that might affect a text at the time of its being read.

Being aware of the context of a text, and its interpretation, is always important, but if you are not careful you can allow context to become more important than the text itself. That is why this course tends to focus rather more on contexts of reception: you are unlikely in this specification to be asked specifically about historical contexts, although they may of course be referred to when relevant.

AQA Examiner's tip

You have heard it stated many times, but the key to doing well in your examination is answering the question exactly as it is worded. It is the examiners' job to make sure that all the technical requirements of the course are met through the questions. It is your job to do exactly as the question states – no more, no less!

Summary

This introduction has outlined the content of the course and the way in which it will be assessed, and has raised some issues regarding the course overall. You will find it useful to refer back to it occasionally to keep yourself informed of the overall design of the course.

1 Aspects of Narrative

Introduction to Unit 1

This chapter:

- Introduces Unit 1, Aspects of Narrative.
- Considers some of your workload requirements.
- Gives answers to some of the key questions you are likely to face as you start the course.

A couple of points should almost go without saying: you cannot study literature if you have not read the books, and ways of reading the books differ considerably. Novels need to be read privately, and then discussed in class with reference to key passages. Poems, on the other hand, need to be both read and heard, and are much more amenable to collaborative working throughout.

Reading and studying the novels

When we read for pleasure most of us read with various levels of intensity and with enough sense of recall for us to get to the end without having to keep stopping to remember who people are and what they did earlier. We then move on to the next novel and our short-term memory quickly fades.

Studying a novel is different. Its very length means that it cannot be returned to endlessly, yet you are required to have a very good knowledge of the text so that you can access it quickly in an examination. The fact that the examination is open-book makes no difference here. The open-book examination allows the examiner to set specific questions on chapters of novels, but you do not have time then to actually read the chapter – a skim-reading and recognition of its key features is all you will have time for.

Your knowledge of the book also has to be such that you can discuss aspects of it in any chronological order – if Chapter 14 is the most relevant, and it connects in various ways with Chapter 8, then you need to be able to make the links and sift through the novel to pick out relevant sections.

How then should you read the set-text novels? The following are some common questions and answers.

How many times should I read the novels?

It would be easy to come up with a high figure, but the reality is that you have lots of reading to do, and not just in this subject. The minimum would be once through before you start studying the novel in class, and once as you prepare for the examination – at other times you will be accessing parts of the novel and rereading them. When you are reading and working through this textbook, you will find frequent points when you are asked to go back to your novels for evidence of a particular point that is being made. The advantage of working in a class or group is that the burden of this, and other work, can be shared.

Of the two novels you are studying, you might focus on one in more detail than the other.

Do I need to read the novels before we start studying them in class?

Absolutely. If you are 'reading as you go' you will never see the whole text, and you will inevitably force your teacher into the chapter-by-chapter approach, which is not very helpful to your learning.

Do I just read the novels, or do I make notes?

This in part depends on how many times you intend to read the novels. If you think you can only manage to read them twice, then you need to make the most of each reading. Certainly at some point you will need to come up with a chapter-by-chapter synopsis – or use one provided by somebody else. Again tasks can be shared across a class or group. Typically a group might share the following tasks and present them to the class – you are then in a position to add your own details when it comes to revision:

- a synopsis of each chapter
- a 'tree' of how characters and actions connect
- a 'map' of various locations and settings
- a timeline of key events and where they are placed in the novel.

AQA Examiner's tip

When you write about the novels, remember that:

- your markers have read them, but not quite as closely as you have
- they are interested in your arguments but need you to prove them
- they need reminding of key moments rather than being told about them in detail.

Reading and studying the poetry

Depending on the choices that are made from within the selected set texts, the word 'poetry' will have a slightly different meaning. Sometimes the poetry counting as a set text will consist of several poems by the same author. In other cases it will be fewer but longer poems, and in one or two cases it might even be a single long poem.

Clearly the ways in which we read and study poems differ from the ways we read and study novels. Poems have both a visual and an aural dimension: they can be read silently and privately, but they can also be heard publicly. When you study the poems it is likely that you will do so in a group or class context, with the poems being heard. Private revision, on the other hand, requires you to 'hear' the poems in your head if you are to fully appreciate how they work.

Reading poetry aloud does not come naturally to many, and indeed some poetry readings can sound very artificial. (Strangely, sometimes the very worst readers are the poets themselves.) Even if you are not that good at reading aloud, you really ought to try to work at reading these poems aloud, because by doing so you will be forced to find meanings in them. This requires help, patience, practice and confidence. The end result of this, though, is that when you turn to a poem in the examination, you not only see it, you also hear it in your head, and by hearing it you make meanings.

How then should you read the set-text poetry? The following are some common questions and answers.

Do I need to read the poems before we start studying them in class?

It always helps to have some prior knowledge, but in this instance much of the reading will also be done in class.

How many times should I read the poems?

Obviously it takes less time to read the poems, but their meanings and techniques tend to be much more condensed. You will therefore need to read them several times to explore and understand them. Each time you read them you will be looking for something specific: the ways in which people are presented, for example, or the different voices that the poem contains.

Hint

Reading poems aloud helps you to 'hear' as well as 'see' them, and so helps you to understand and appreciate them more fully than if you only read them silently.

Remember

Every time you read a set text, you do so with a research purpose in mind: you are looking for specific meanings or techniques.

What is special about poetry?

As mentioned above, poetry is a condensed form of expression, with many more patterns to it than prose fiction. These patterns can include:

- repetition of structure (e.g. verses)
- repetition of metaphorical language (e.g. imagery and symbolism)
- repetition of sound (e.g. rhyme and rhythm)
- repetition of voice (e.g. speakers identified by certain speech habits).

If commentating on such patterns, though, you must do much more than simply identify them. You must show how these patterns contribute to the telling of the story.

The poems you are studying have been selected because in various ways they provide examples of narratives – they tell stories. The mixture of condensed language and patterning, though, means that these stories need to be uncovered by close reading strategies, sometimes closer than those that apply to novels.

Do I just read the poems, or do I make notes?

You definitely make notes, but, as always, be selective in what you write down, focusing on the key issues of narrative rather than on what could be incidental detail.

Should I learn quotations?

Because this is an open-book examination, you will have the texts in front of you. This means that you may not need to commit so much to memory, but you will need to know where to find the right quotation without delay. So it is probably worth knowing some key quotations, but you also need to know how to navigate your way around the poems quickly.

Link

See Chapter 2 for an explanation of metaphorical language and symbolism.

AQA Examiner's tip

It is possible to read the set texts endlessly and convince yourself that you are doing quality revision. In fact, though, you need to do more than this: you need to reread the texts with research questions in mind, making notes as you go. Reading on its own will not achieve much; reading with a purpose will achieve much more. Many students have found it useful to keep an exercise book for notes on each of their texts. You could also keep your own computer-based notes.

Summary

This chapter has introduced you to some key features of Unit 1 and looked at some of the most important questions that arise when preparing for your study of the texts themselves.

1 Introducing narrative

This chapter:

- Presents some key terms to do with narrative.
- Explains that stories are representations of the world, not the world itself.
- Describes the key aspects of narrative.

Unit 1 of your AS course is entitled 'Aspects of Narrative'. In the next chapters you will be shown ways to look in detail at this key concept in the study of literature. It is important to understand that this book helps you to work on skills rather than set books. Examples from literature will be used because they help to show a point. Sometimes they will be examples from the current set-text list, but not always – and anyway it might not be a text that you are doing.

We are surrounded by storytelling, and on a basic level it forms an essential part of how we live. All cultures have storytelling as a vital part of human connection, and children, of course, are taught how to live within their culture by being told stories from a very young age.

Activity 1

On a piece of paper note down all the stories you have come into contact with in the last 24 hours. Then share one of them with your class as a whole.

Key terms

Story: all the various events that are going to be shown.

Plot: the chain of causes and circumstances that connect the various events and place them into some sort of relationship with each other.

Narrative: involves how the events and causes are shown, and the various methods used to do this showing. Exploring aspects of narrative involves looking at what the writer has chosen to include or not include, and how this choice leads the reader to certain conclusions.

AQA Examiner's tip

Learn the distinction between the three key terms defined above and always use them accurately when writing about your set texts.

Commentary on Activity 1

It is likely that you came up with plenty of examples of stories. The ones most people start with when doing this activity are the set pieces, coming from quite formal sources such as newspapers and magazines, and much more informal sources such as conversations about nights out with friends. You may, though, have spread your net more widely. It can be argued that many of the visual texts that surround us wherever we go, advertising all sorts of products and services, tell us stories about our lives and our desires. And even the simplest of SMS texts from a friend might well be part of a bigger story.

Story/plot/narrative

In everyday use it does not really matter how we use the term 'story' because, after all, these stories flash past us at a rapid speed. We take from them as much as we want at any given time, and then pass on to the next one.

When it comes to studying stories in a more academic way, however, it is useful to sort out some key terms and agree that they will be used in quite specific ways. As is always the case with such terminology, it is not important as such, but using it consistently helps to establish a common way of thinking and explaining – in this case about how literature works. Understanding the difference between the terms **story**, **plot** and **narrative** can help you to see where to focus your attention when reading the set texts for this unit.

Representation

You will notice above that the word 'shown' has been used to describe the events in a story. This is because all stories are a form of representation. In terms of studying literature at AS Level there can be no more important concept to grasp than that of representation. Although when you read a text, or watch a film, or listen to a friend telling you about a night out, you might for part of the time believe you are watching or hearing about something 'real', when what you are actually doing is taking part in a constructed process. You are being shown something, being given a version. A film may seem incredibly realistic, but in the end it is still a film. Even a report of an event on a news broadcast, although originating in a real event, is a version of that event, shown by various narrative methods. The same goes for a friend telling you about a night out – even they are giving a version of events, almost certainly seen from their own perspective.

The logic of the paragraph above should be clear, then, for students of literature. Characters in literary texts, whether novels, plays or poems, are not real. Nor are the things that the characters do or say. They are representations of people living in a representational world. So, when studying literary texts, especially if you are looking at aspects of narrative, bear in mind the following simple rule:

It is the author who controls the characters and events in a story. Characters cannot do or say anything other than what the author makes them do.

For this reason, when asked to explore aspects of narrative in examinations, it is vital to keep the authors, and their methods of working, at the heart of what you say.

Remember

Characters and events in stories are representations of reality, not real themselves, and are completely controlled by the author. Always bear in mind the author's role when you write about narrative in examinations.

A true-life narrative

From what you have seen so far, it should be clear that while a story can be based on real events, when it comes to telling the story we are dealing with a representation of what happened, rather than the actual event itself. However, this does not stop the producers of stories, whether in print or in film, from labelling their products as though they are 'real' or 'true'. After all, there is seemingly something more immediate and believable about a story that is trailed as having an intimate connection with the real world.

One genre that can be found easily on any magazine rack is the real-life story. Looking at an example from this genre is useful in setting out some of the aspects of narrative that you need to look at when studying literary texts.

Remember

A genre is a type of text (e.g. a crime novel, a narrative poem).

Activity 2

1. Look at the opening paragraphs of a story taken from *Woman's Own* on page 7. From your knowledge of other stories, and working with a partner if possible, try to list some of the ways in which the story is 'shown' to the reader. Remember: we are not dealing here with what happened, but with the methods the writer uses to represent events to the reader.
2. What do you think the overall message or moral of this story might be?

'He died a hero'

It was meant to be a relaxing family holiday by the seaside, but then tragedy struck ...

Patricia Mangle took one last look at the paramedics trying to revive her husband. As a wife and mother, she had to make an agonising decision. She wanted to go with him in the helicopter, but her children needed her, too. As Steven was airlifted to hospital, she turned away, blinded by tears.

It would be the last time she saw her husband of 20 years alive.

Just an hour or so earlier, Patricia, a supermarket cashier, and Steven, 50, who worked for a refuse collection company, were happily relaxing outside the caravan in Skegness that they'd rented for four days. With them were their two youngest children, Mark, 16, and Laura, 12, with two of their friends, Josh, 16, and Laura-Beth, 13.

'It was teatime on 19 July, the hottest day of the year, and Steve and the kids were keen to get down to the beach,' says Patricia.

'I needed to stay and tidy up a bit, so they all went on ahead.

'From what Laura and Mark have told me since, Steve and the four children were splashing about in the water, when the sea suddenly changed and became choppy.

'Concerned for everyone's safety, Steve ordered the four youngsters out of the water, swimming with them towards the shore.

Then behind him, he suddenly heard screams for help. A young girl was caught in the waves.'

Eyewitnesses have told how Steven managed to swim against the tide, then reach the girl, aged 13, before pushing her to safety in shallower water. But the current was too strong for him.

'He was pulled under and didn't resurface. Two men on the beach raced to his aid and pulled him out of the sea, but by then it was too late,' says Patricia, her voice strained with emotion ...

Woman's Own, 30 October 2006

Commentary on Activity 2

Looking closely at aspects of narrative involves understanding that the same story can be told in a number of ways. In working out how an author has told the story, you then inevitably think about why the author might have done it this way, what effects the author has possibly been aiming for, and whether you as a reader find these effects interesting and convincing.

Each chapter in this unit will discuss one of the main aspects, or 'building blocks', of narrative that feature in this article. These are summarised below.

The building blocks of narrative

Scenes and places

This refers to where the action is set, and its significance beyond just being a place where something happens. So although this story is set in the seaside town of Skegness, there is wider significance to the scene. This involves the idea of the family holiday, of getting away from work – but also the hidden and sudden tragedy that can come out of any happy moment.

Time and sequence

The order in which events are shown is a key part of how narrative works. While time in the real world is represented by clocks and calendars that tick over at the same regular rate, time in stories is manipulated so that some points in time go slowly, others accelerate and others are missed out altogether. In this story we move very quickly to 'teatime on 19 July' before slowing right down as the tragedy unfolds.

Sequence meanwhile refers to the order in which events are told. Although at a very simple level all narratives involve a movement from a beginning to an end, they are rarely told in strict sequence. So here the first paragraph begins towards the end of the story, the third moves us back an hour. The reason for this should be obvious: if as readers we are to be interested in the story we need some action at the start.

Characters

Character in this sense refers not just to the people in the story but, much more importantly, to their character traits and how they are revealed: this is known as characterisation. It would be fair to say that here there are two main characters, Patricia Mangle and Steven Mangle. They are frequently referred to in terms of family relationships: 'husband', 'wife', 'mother', for example. Patricia is forced to make an 'agonising decision' based on the fact that she is both wife and mother. While Patricia tidies up, Steve is more active – they are cast in typical gendered roles. Steve is also a man with a sense of duty, who looks after all children, not just his own.

Meanwhile there is also a cast of more minor characters: their children who are named, and the young girl who is rescued who is not named.

Woman's Own is a magazine with a certain presumed readership – women who have children. Not surprisingly in a magazine that constructs its readers as women in family relationships, this story, despite being 'tragic', is very positive about notions of family, duty and heroism.

Voices in the story

One way in which we get information in a story is through what we are 'told' by characters involved. There are various ways of showing this, which will be looked at in detail later, but here we hear directly from Patricia – 'It was teatime on 19 July ...' – and more indirectly from her children: 'From what Mark and Laura have told me since'. Note too that although we are not given their precise words, what 'eyewitnesses' have reported is also given to us. These are not the actual words they would have spoken though – they are a tidied-up version of them, a representation of what they probably said.

Voices in stories can help to establish character traits, and so are part of characterisation, but they also enable authors to give information.

Point of view

In the section above one key voice in the text has not been mentioned: the voice of the narrator, standing outside the story. Although we are not told who wrote this story, it is told in the voice of a third person; it is a **third-person narrative**. One option available to the magazine was to tell the story entirely through the voice of Patricia. In this case it would have been a **first-person narrative**. The term 'point of view' is used to help with the idea that a story is told from a certain standpoint or perspective. (You might notice here that the words used to describe narrative are often derived from visual metaphors.)

Key terms

Third-person narrative: a story told through the voice of a narrator who is not one of the characters in the story.

First-person narrative: a story told through the voice of one of the characters, using 'I'.

Just as the voices in the text are created voices, so are narrative voices. It is tempting, especially in poems, to confuse the voice that speaks a poem with the voice of the actual author. Avoid doing this at all times! You will find that questions in the examination sometimes refer to the **speaker** of the poem – this is a useful term that is well worth using.

Destination

So far you have looked at some of the ways in which stories can be told. But for this storytelling process to have any real purpose, you need to understand that the whole process is designed to make readers think, to make them respond to what has been said, to make them see the point or points. You have been taken on a journey in the story, and when you reach the end, you have reached a destination.

Although you have not been given the full story here, it is easy enough to work out what the destination, or morals, of the story could be:

- Tragedy is potentially everywhere.
- Love endures and alleviates at least some pain.
- Family ties are the strongest of all.

In working out that the story has moral messages, ideas that we are expected to believe in, we can see that the **ideology** of the story needs to be uncovered and explored. It is the assumptions made by the author that can often be the most interesting to find in texts: here for example we are expected to believe in the notion of the family, so this belief is never actually stated.

There are two final points to make here. As individual readers you may have seen some different points to the story from those given here. And although you may understand what you are meant to think, you may want to resist the most obvious message for various reasons. This means that in applying an analysis of narrative methods (AO2) you have come up with different interpretations (AO3) depending on the contexts in which you have read the story (AO4). In other words, you have made all the necessary connections that are involved in reading texts.

Making a building out of the blocks

Each of the next six chapters explores one of the aspects set out above, using **prose** and poetry as examples. It is important to remember, though, that all these aspects work together to form a complete narrative: separating them out at this stage can help you to understand how narrative works, but when it comes to examinations you will be expected to draw on your knowledge of all the aspects, and decide which ones are most relevant in writing about your chosen text. To make sure that this is clear, each chapter concludes by looking at the same text, Robert Browning's poem *The Patriot*. At the end of the work on Unit 1, these aspects can be combined to look at the poem overall.

Summary

This chapter has introduced you to the key aspects of narrative, and to the fundamental point that when stories are told, they are representations of the world, not the world itself. Once you have grasped this key point, it is then possible to explore and analyse the ways in which stories are told, whether they are oral stories, popular journalism or literature.

Key terms

Speaker: the person whose voice is heard in a poem, as opposed to the author.

Ideology: the attitudes, values and assumptions that a text contains.

Prose: 'normal' speech in paragraphs and not poetry.

Link

Assessment Objectives (AOs) 1–4 are explained in full in the Introduction to this book.

AQA Examiner's tip

Try to develop a specialist vocabulary for English Literature that looks at large issues, rather than tiny (and sometimes irrelevant) details. It is no doubt true that using the correct terminology makes you seem well-informed and in the know. But equally important is the fact that using terminology accurately lets you write much more quickly and economically about your ideas and interpretations.

2 Scenes and places

This chapter:

- Explains the importance of places in stories.
- Shows that because stories are representational, the places in stories can take on an added significance.
- Demonstrates that in fictional worlds *something* significant happens *somewhere* significant.

Fictional stories, if they are to represent in some ways the real world, need to be set in significant places. These places can vary in size: they can be rooms, houses, gardens, streets, towns, regions, countries, worlds and even universes. They can be recognisable as places we already know, based on places we know, but also clearly fictional or completely invented 'new' worlds.

These places though, all share something in common: they are representations of places, not actual places. At one end of the spectrum, a highly realistic description of an actual place that can be found on a map is still a version of the place in words, a depiction by an author of some aspects of the place but not others. At the other end of the spectrum, a completely invented place, that cannot possibly exist in our real world, will none the less have all sorts of features from our world that we can recognise. Between these two extremes, authors take bits of real places and alter them to suit their purposes.

Stories are condensed versions of reality, shaped to present actions and ideas that tell us something about the lives we lead. Stories need to be set in places if they are to persuade us of their connections with our lives, but at the same time these places can be more than just settings where events happen. Scenes and places frequently carry a significance that goes way beyond being where something merely happens. In their use of scenes and places, authors are taking advantage of the possibilities of creating meanings.

Activity 1

From your own knowledge, and using research facilities such as the internet, histories of literature, and so on, make a list of novels that have a place as a major part of their title. Does the name of this place carry connotations of meaning? You could then extend the search to include films and television programmes, especially soap operas, and again consider the possible significance of the places.

There is no commentary on this activity.

Place and significance

Robert Frost's poem *Stopping by Woods on a Snowy Evening* tells an apparently simple story. In the poem Frost describes places, with the woods as the main but not only place mentioned.

Key terms

Significance: when this specification uses the word significant it does so in the literary sense of the word. Significance is to do with signification, the making of meanings, so when asked to find significance you are being asked to think about potential meanings.

Activity 2

Read the poem at least twice, and with this poem in particular it helps to hear it read aloud. Then consider the following questions:

- What sort of places does Frost describe and what details does he provide?
- Is it possible to find potential **significance** in the places that give the story some potential meanings?

Stopping by Woods on a Snowy Evening

Whose woods these are I think I know.
His house is in the village, though;
He will not see me stopping here
To watch his woods fill up with snow.

My little horse must think it queer
To stop without a farmhouse near
Between the woods and frozen lake
The darkest evening of the year.

He gives his harness bells a shake
To ask if there is some mistake.
The only other sound's the sweep
Of easy wind and downy flake.

The woods are lovely, dark, and deep,
But I have promises to keep,
And miles to go before I sleep,
And miles to go before I sleep.

Robert Frost, 1923

Commentary on Activity 2

It is important, when analysing narrative, to have a clear sense of what story is being told. Here the **narrative persona** is riding his horse (home?) and stops in a snowy wood to soak up the atmosphere. He is tempted to stay, but has made promises and has a long journey ahead of him.

Details of the woods are very limited. We know that they are remote, that their owner lives some way away, and that they are 'lovely, dark, and deep', but beyond that not much more.

Other places are both mentioned and implied, though they gain significance by being set against the woods. The village where the owner lives could be seen as a more civilised place than this. And although we do not know where the rider is going, he clearly has a destination too, where he will 'sleep'.

It would be tempting to take the idea of sleep literally were it only mentioned once, but the haunting repetition of the last line does give it added significance. Is Frost using the idea of sleep as death, in which case the journey the rider is on also assumes greater significance?

As with all the examples you look at in this book while learning about aspects of narrative, your attention is being drawn to one aspect at a time. Inevitably, though, there are other aspects of narrative at work here too. If you return to this poem once you have read all the chapters on narrative, you will notice that it has other aspects of narrative that contribute to its overall narrative structure and meanings.

A short walk or a whole life?

We have seen above that places can be used as locations for stories, but also as contributors to the wider significances of the stories being told. This section looks at a variant on the idea of the significance of place, and one that was hinted at in the previous poem – the recurring **metaphor** that our life is a journey.

Key terms

Narrative persona: a useful term used to describe the unnamed 'I' who sometimes narrates a story. Be aware that the 'I' is rarely the author, so the term persona is a helpful point of reference.

Metaphor: metaphor involves the transfer of meaning, with one thing described as another. When one thing is described as being *like* another it is known as a simile.

AQA Examiner's tip

When answering an examination question, make sure you do exactly what is asked:

- In Section A you will be asked to look in detail at how the story is told in one of your set texts.
- In Section B the questions are much broader, asking you to write about an aspect of narrative across the other three texts you have studied.

These questions require different approaches.

Activity 3

Draw up a list of phrases that are commonly used to describe what happens in a lesson or lecture, and that refer metaphorically to a journey. Here are three to get you started:

- A lesson begins
- Pupils make progress
- Pupils get stuck.

Link

For a Commentary on Activity 3, see the end of this chapter (p17).

In their book *Metaphors We Live By* (1980), George Lakoff and Mark Johnson show how metaphors are not just used in literature, but also in our everyday speech and thinking. In some ways, reality itself is defined by the metaphors we commonly use to describe it; but because these metaphors are so common, we are often not even aware that we are speaking metaphorically.

One of the most ubiquitous of all metaphorical fields involves describing change and development in terms of a journey.

This same metaphor of the journey exists in many literary texts as well as films. So called 'road' novels and films are a distinct genre in themselves. Frequently the road and the journey serve as literal settings for action to take place, but as the journey progresses we are frequently aware that the main character (or characters) is learning from their experiences and becoming a new and altered person, usually wiser and more knowledgeable. As the journey develops, so does the individual.

In his much anthologised poem *The Road Not Taken*, the poet Robert Frost gives a variant on the road theme: he gives us a person standing at a crossroads, deciding which path to take. The idea of the crossroads is, of course, a common one in everyday life – we frequently refer to ourselves and others as being at a crossroads, when we are referring to potentially life-changing decisions.

Activity 4

Read the poem below and see if you can find different possible meanings for the way Frost uses the 'two roads' in this poem.

The Road Not Taken

Two roads diverged in a yellow wood,
And sorry I could not travel both
And be one traveler, long I stood
And looked down one as far as I could
To where it bent in the undergrowth.

Then took the other, as just as fair,
And having perhaps the better claim,
Because it was grassy and wanted wear;
Though as for that the passing there
Had worn them really about the same.

And both that morning equally lay
In leaves no step had trodden black.
Oh, I kept the first for another day!
Yet knowing how way leads on to way,
I doubted if I should ever come back.

I shall be telling this with a sigh
Somewhere ages and ages hence:
Two roads diverged in a wood, and I –
I took the one less traveled by,
And that has made all the difference.

Robert Frost, 1920

Commentary on Activity 4

If you read this poem a number of times, its apparent simplicity becomes, if anything, ever more complex. Clearly one way to read the poem is to stick with the idea that it is about having the nerve to make the unconventional life choice, but the more you read the poem, the more of a problem that simple reading can become.

Where poems are so clearly structured in their verse patterns, it can often help to take one verse at a time and see how the argument moves forward. Here we have four verses of five lines each.

Verse 1: Here the dilemma is set up: there are two paths, and although the speaker (whom we will assume is male) would like to travel down both, he knows that he can only choose one. None the less he takes his time and tries to peer ahead down one route (that is, into the future) to see if it is worth taking.

Verse 2: Somewhat surprisingly, he chooses the one he has not considered much. This one is the one that is less worn – but actually it is a close-run thing between the two. The choices are not that different.

Verse 3: Again he tells us that there is not much to choose between the two paths, and that on that morning they were in fact identical! He decides to keep one for another day (so it is not a major decision), while at the same time knowing that he will probably never come back to take the other path.

Verse 4: We now come to the final verse and the lines we quoted out of context. They are put in a different context by the two lines that precede them. The chronology of the poem, its time sequence, makes reference to both the present, the future and, in the last lines, a sort of future/past. Out of context, of course, the final three lines look sure and definitive, but in context there is much more **ambiguity**. The fact that the speaker knows he will be 'telling this with a sigh' makes the choice seem far less obviously 'right'. A sigh seems to suggest possible regret, for example.

Not surprisingly this poem has received a huge amount of criticism. Whatever the reading of the poem, most critics see the crossroads as highly symbolic. Just to add to the ambiguity, though, Frost himself denied that the poem was meant to have huge significance. He claimed the poem was about his friend and fellow poet Edward Thomas, who was horribly indecisive and could not even make up his mind about which path to take without making a fuss about it!

Link

For more on time and chronology, see Chapter 3.

Key terms

Ambiguity: part of the drama which might have two or more possible meanings or interpretations.

Places in prose fiction

Places have a significant role in prose fiction. In a poem, with its concise narrative, specifics of a place can be given without all the detail of precise location. In the poem above, we do not know where the paths actually are, in which village. Indeed, the absence of any precise location helps us to think that the paths could be anywhere, which makes the significance more widely applicable.

In prose fiction, though, there is a greater expectation that places will be filled out in detail. There is more room in novels and short stories, and readers have the expectation that places will be described more fully. In novels and short stories people's lives are examined in detail, and although these lives are fictional, in most cases we expect them to be 'realistic', to represent a world we recognise. (There are, of course,

AQA Examiner's tip

You are encouraged at AS Level to consider different possible interpretations of the same piece of text. Meanings are not fixed, and you are not expected to say that one interpretation is 'right'. It is perfectly acceptable, though, to give a personal preference.

always exceptions to rules about literature: science fiction and fantasy, for example, tend to describe weird and exotic places, even if in some ways such genres still comment on the actual world as we know it.)

Not surprisingly, then, there is a tradition in English literature of novelists who centre their work on one particular place or area. Dickens frequently writes about London, representing real places with their actual names. Hardy does something slightly different: although his novels are largely set in the area around Dorset, he uses the older name of Wessex for the area, and changes the names of towns, with Dorchester becoming Casterbridge, for example.

Key terms

Dialect: regional and sometimes social variations in language.

Eye-dialect: the representation of the vocabulary, grammar and sound of dialect in a way the reader can understand, in contrast to the phonetic representation (with special symbols) that a linguist would use.

When authors set a novel in a known geographical area, they also have the opportunity to represent people who live in that area by giving a version of their **dialect**. In this case the dialect can refer to grammar, vocabulary and pronunciation.

At the start of the novel *Fingersmith* by Sarah Waters, set in London in 1862, the narrator Susan describes how Flora and she went pickpocketing and brought back some stolen perfume to the woman who looks after them, Mrs Sucksby.

> 'What you get? A couple of wipers was it? A couple of wipers, and a lady's purse?'
> Flora pulled the strand of hair to her mouth and bit it. 'A purse,' she said, after a second. 'And a bottle of scent.'...
> Mrs Sucksby sniffed.
> 'Pretty poor poke,' she said, 'ain't it?'
> Flora tossed her head. 'I should have had more,' she said, with a look at me, 'if she hadn't started up with the sterics.'
> Mrs Sucksby leaned and hit her again.
> 'If I had known what you was about,' she said, 'you shouldn't have none of it at all. Let me tell you now, you want an infant for prigging with, you take one of my other babies.'

Sarah Waters, Fingersmith, *2003, pp4–5*

Here Sarah Waters uses occasional items of vocabulary and grammar to represent local speech and also social class. So in vocabulary there is 'poke' for 'smell', 'sterics' for 'hysterics', 'prigging' for 'stealing'. And in grammar there is 'ain't it' for 'isn't it', 'you was' for 'you were' and the double negative 'shouldn't have none'. There is no attempt as such to represent the accent, though, the distinctive local sounds – the word 'bottle', for example, is written in standard form, and it is left to the reader to imagine how this might sound.

Link

For more on the importance of how characters speak in a story, see Chapter 4.

This literary representation of talk can be taken further by adding some sense of sound. This involves using what is known as **eye-dialect**.

In Thomas Hardy's *Tess of the D'Urbervilles*, a local woman meets a stranger to the area:

> 'Well, I suppose you'll want a dish o' tay, or victuals of some sort hey?'

Emily Bronte's use of the servant Joseph in *Wuthering Heights* takes this method to a greater extreme:

> 'If Aw wur yah, maister, Aw'd just slam t'boards I' their faces, all on em'.

The gap

Although locations in fiction are necessary arenas for people and their actions to take place in, these locations can also carry greater significance, much as we saw in the poems earlier. The places are not only venues where things happen; they throw extra light and significance on events, people and relationships.

In his story *Abyss*, the American writer Richard Ford writes about Howard and Frances, two estate agents who are having an affair while attending a conference. Instead of attending the conference, they decide to bunk off and instead visit the Grand Canyon in Arizona. The Grand Canyon is described as follows on its national park website:

> The Grand Canyon is more than a great chasm carved over millennia through the rocks of the Colorado Plateau. It is more than an awe-inspiring view. It is more than a pleasuring ground for those that explore the roads, hike the trails, or float the currents of the turbulent Colorado River.
>
> This canyon is a gift that transcends what we experience. Its beauty and size humbles us. Its timelessness provokes a comparison to our short existence. In its vast spaces we may find solace from our hectic lives.

Did you know?

The Grand Canyon, in the US state of Arizona, is a vast and colourful gorge cut by the Colorado River over a period of about 6 million years. It is 277 miles (446 km) long, between 4 and 18 miles (6.4 to 24 km) wide, and more than a mile (1.6 km) deep.

Figure 2.1 *The Grand Canyon*

Activity 5

Read the tourist information extract again, which gives the 'official' version of how tourists should perceive the Grand Canyon, and study the photo. Then consider the following questions:

1. Given that Ford could have chosen any location in which to set his story, what might happen in the plot to make his choice of the Grand Canyon especially significant?
2. What effects might the 'awe-inspiring' view of the canyon have on the two characters? How might they respond to the almost religious experience that the tourist hype suggests?

Activity 6

Now read the extract from Richard Ford's story *Abyss* on the next page. At this point in the story Frances and Howard actually reach the Grand Canyon. The story is told in the third person, but here it is very much told from the point of view of Howard. Answer the following questions:

1. In what ways do Howard and Frances react differently to their first experience of the Grand Canyon?
2. In the light of what you have discussed already about the significance of place, what use does Ford make of the Grand Canyon in this extract?

Link

For a Commentary on Activity 5, see the end of this chapter (p17).

Link

For more on point of view, see Chapter 6.

Link

For a Commentary on Activity 6, see the end of this chapter (p17).

And then, all at once, just very suddenly, he was there; at the Grand Canyon, beside Frances who had her camera up to her face. And there was no way really not to be surprised by it – the whole Grand Canyon just all right there at once, opened out and down and wide in front of you, enormous and bottomless, with a great invisible silence inhabiting it and a column of cool air pushing up out of it like a giant well. It was a shock.

'I don't want you to say one single thing,' Frances said. She wasn't looking through her camera now, but had begun to stare right into the canyon itself, like she was inhaling it. Sunlight was on her face. She seemed blissed.

He did, however, expect to say *something*. It was just natural to want to put some words of your own to the whole thing. Except he instantly had the feeling, standing beside Frances, that he was already doing something wrong, had somehow approached this wrong, or was standing wrong, even looking at the goddamned canyon wrong. And there was something about how you couldn't see it at all, and then you completely did see it, something that seemed to suggest you could actually miss it. Miss the whole Grand Canyon!

Of course, the right way would be to look at it all at once, taking in the full effect, just the way Frances seemed to be doing. Except it was much too big to get everything into focus. Too big and too complicated. He felt like he wanted to turn around, go back to the car and come up again. Get re-prepared.

Though it was exactly, he thought, staring mutely out at the flat brown plateau and the sheer drop straight off the other side – how far away, you couldn't tell, since perspective was screwed up – it was exactly what he'd expected from the pictures in high school. It was a tourist attraction. A thing to see. It was plenty big. But twenty jillion people had already seen it, so that it felt sort of useless. A negative. Nothing like the ocean, which *had* a use. Nobody *needed* the Grand Canyon for anything. At its most important, he guessed, it would be a terrific impediment to someone wanting to get to the other side. Which would not be a good comment to make to Frances, who was probably having a religious experience. She'd blow her top on that. The best comment, he thought, should be that it was really quiet. He'd never experienced anything this quiet. And it was nothing like an airport. Though flying in that little plane was probably the best way to see it.

Richard Ford, Abyss, *1996, pp270–1*

The Patriot

As mentioned in Chapter 1, each of the chapters that looks at a different aspect of narrative concludes by looking at the same text, *The Patriot* by Robert Browning.

Link

To complete Activity 7 you will need to use *The Patriot*, which is printed in the Extracts section at the back of this book, Extract 1 (p132).

For a Commentary on Activity 7, see the end of this chapter (p18).

Activity 7

Read the poem and answer the following questions:

1. This poem has a setting. What details are you given about that setting?
2. Can you say precisely where that place is?

Extension tasks

1. Rewrite the extract taken from the short story *Abyss*, this time describing the Grand Canyon from the point of view of Frances. How does your version differ from the original?
2. Consider the novels that you are studying, and discuss the following issues:
   - What are the major locations where the novels are set?
   - How much space, roughly, do the authors give to describing places?
   - Do any of the places seem to be especially significant, and, if so, how?
   - Is speech used to represent the way local people might talk?
3. Now consider the poetry text or texts that you are studying and discuss the following:
   - Are scenes and places of any particular significance? If so, in what ways?
   - How have the authors signalled this significance to the reader?

Commentaries

Commentary on Activity 3

Among the other possibilities are:

- Going round in circles
- Moving ahead of the rest
- Finishing early
- Being lost
- Following an argument
- Straying from an argument
- Covering a lot of ground
- Going back over the same material
- Getting off the point
- Well on your way to making good progress
- Lagging behind the others
- Going off in the wrong direction.

Commentary on Activity 5

1 The title of the story gives a clue – an abyss is a huge hole, a gap, which is exactly what the Grand Canyon is. This idea of a gap in nature can easily be transferred to a gap in the relationship between the two characters.

2 The awe with which one is expected to view the canyon could go in a number of ways: the two characters could find perfect harmony or, far from bringing them together, the experience could drive them apart. Again, the title of the story gives a clue as to which is likely to be the case. If one or both of the characters does not respond to the almost religious experience that the tourist hype suggests, the location could be used to highlight something *not* happening, making a sort of contrast.

Commentary on Activity 6

1 Howard arrives at the canyon after Frances. She is clearly overwhelmed by the experience, or so Howard thinks. She tells him, 'I don't want you to say a single thing', and to Howard she 'seemed blissed'. Notice that although they do not say anything, Howard did

expect to 'say something'. He seems to want to share the experience; she wants to experience it alone.

For Howard, therefore, the experience is unsettling, and in various ways unsatisfactory. Annoyed by being shut out by Frances, he is as bothered by her as he is by the canyon. He considers it possible to miss the whole thing, while on the other hand it is impossible to get it all into focus. Because so many others have seen it, he finds it 'sort of useless'. All he can think of is that it stops you getting to the other side, whereas Frances seems to be finding it 'a religious experience'.

In other parts of the story Ford switches his perspective to Frances – we get a sense here that were she to be telling the story it would be very different.

2 What should be clear is that Ford has used the Grand Canyon as a vehicle to show the two lovers drifting apart, that what lies ahead of them, in terms of their relationship, is an abyss, a chasm. Ford needs to set the story of this failing relationship somewhere, because stories need to be placed. But in choosing this venue, he has given himself the opportunity to make the place stand for more than just a location. The alert reader recognises the connections between where a story is set and what the story is saying.

Commentary on Activity 7

1 There are a few details about the setting. It seems to be a walled town or even a city, given that we are told there are 'church-spires' in the plural. The reference to 'house-roofs' might imply a place of some grandeur.

2 Although the brief references to setting may remind you of a certain type of city – York maybe – in fact there is nothing very precise about the location. Not even the country is specified.

Summary

This chapter has explored the significance of places in stories. Even if the places actually exist, in the representational world of stories certain details will have been selected to help make a point. Looking at the significance of places is therefore one way to explore narrative technique.

3 Time and sequence

This chapter:

- Describes the importance in stories of time and sequence.
- Explains that because stories are representational, time in stories needs to be compressed.
- Shows how time in stories can be rearranged, repeated, speeded up and slowed down.
- Demonstrates that in fictional worlds things happen only when the writer chooses.

All stories, however fantastic their genre, need to have aspects of time. The word 'aspects' is in the plural because even in this broad sense time can work in at least two ways:

1 The time covered by the events within the story.
2 The broader time that surrounds the story, the time in which the story is set.

For example, if a contemporary novelist writes a love story, the time covered by events might be from the time the couple meet to the time they marry (or divorce?). But if the author wants to write a love story set in Victorian times, then other aspects of time are involved – if the story is to appear believable then the author will have to incorporate aspects of Victorian life and attitudes (which probably would not lead to divorce!). In a general sense, then (general because, as always, these aspects of narrative overlap), how the author manages time *within* the story is covered by AO2, which looks at aspects of form, structure and language, in this case with a special focus on structure. Meanwhile, how the author manages time that *surrounds* the story is covered by AO4, which looks at contexts.

So if the story is to involve a sequence of events, how the sequence is presented to the reader can be of considerable importance.

Remember

AO2 and AO4 are two of the four Assessment Objectives discussed in the Introduction to this book.

Chronology

If we were all to write our stories, whether 'real' or 'imagined', in strict **chronological order**, two main issues would arise:

1 Telling a story in strict chronological order can be very dull – one of the first lessons children have to learn when writing stories is not to start at the beginning (and maybe not even end at the end).
2 Is it actually possible with a complex story to say definitively that it has a beginning and an end anyway? In a complex world, such hard-and-fast distinctions are not always possible – and writers, of course, are aware of this.

Key terms

Chronological order: the sequence of events as they happen, in a timeline that goes from A, the start of events, to, say, E, the end.

Imagine, as an example, that you are going to write a piece of crime fiction, which will have a murder as its main 'crime'. Immediately you are faced with all sorts of narrative questions, but for the moment concentrate on aspects of sequence. Questions you will have to consider include:

- Does the story start with the body being discovered?
- Does the story start with the murder itself?
- Does the story start with the planning of the murder?
- Does the story start with the detective being called to the case?

If you think this through, it should be clear to you that how you answer this question potentially points to the type, or sub-genre, of crime fiction you are going to write. If you start with the discovery of the body, you might be writing a forensic novel where the perpetrator is uncovered through evidence; if you start with the planning of the murder, then the murderer will be known to the reader but not to the detective.

Remember

A genre is a type of text, such as a crime novel or a narrative poem, so a sub-genre is a particular type of text within that genre.

And when you have sorted this out, you have to ask yourself: what comes next?

Activity 1

Look at the three different comic-strip chains below, showing how the same murder story can be told in different sequences. Then write an outline for a crime story of your own, and work out different chronological sequences for the key events. How would your story's genre change depending on the sequences you choose? If you are working in a class setting you can also compare stories with a partner.

There is no commentary on this activity.

If we take as an example a typical plot line from a detective story, its chronological sequence might be something like this:

1 A murder is planned for a certain motive.
2 A body is found that yields evidence.
3 The detective pursues a number of clues and identifies the killer.
4 A violent shoot-out leads to the death of the villain.
5 This leads to another revenge killing.

It is easy to conceive, however, other ways of presenting this sequence – for example it could go 4, 1, 2, 3, 5 or 2, 1, 3, 4, 5. In each case something different would be foregrounded by the chronology. Chronology, then, is one way in which the writer of a narrative can influence the way a reader responds to it. This can lead to a focus on suspense, where the action and its results are foregrounded, or on character, where feelings are foregrounded, or sometimes both.

Figure 3.1

Key terms

Establishment: refers to how texts begin, the work the author does for the reader at the beginning of the text. Establishment can involve introducing people, places, time, and so on.

Aspects of time in poetry and novels

Your work for this unit on Aspects of Narrative includes looking at both novels and poems. Poems, by definition, tend to be briefer exercises in narrative than novels. Whereas in a novel we expect some detailed **establishment**, in terms of place, time, people, and so on, in poems we tend to be straight in and out of the story with much less detail. Indeed the effects of the poem are often emphasised by what is not given, by what can be called meaningful absence.

We will begin by looking at examples of time and sequence in poems.

Time and sequence in poetry

O What Is That Sound?

O what is that sound which so thrills the ear
  Down in the valley drumming, drumming?
Only the scarlet soldiers, dear,
  The soldiers coming.

O what is that light I see flashing so clear
  Over the distance brightly, brightly?
Only the sun on their weapons, dear,
  As they step lightly.

O what are they doing with all that gear,
  What are they doing this morning, this morning?
Only the usual manoeuvres, dear,
  Or perhaps a warning.

O why have they left the road down there,
  Why are they suddenly wheeling, wheeling?
Perhaps a change in their orders, dear,
  Why are you kneeling?

O haven't they stopped for the doctor's care,
  Haven't they reined their horses, their horses?
Why, they are none of them wounded, dear,
  None of these forces.

O is it the parson they want with white hair,
  Is it the parson, is it, is it?
No, they are passing his gateway, dear,
  Without a visit.

O it must be the farmer who lives so near.
  It must be the farmer so cunning, so cunning?
They have passed the farm already, dear,
  And now they are running.

O where are you going? Stay with me here!
  Were the vows you swore deceiving, deceiving?
No, I promised to love you, dear,
  But I must be leaving.

O it's broken the lock and splintered the door,
  O it's the gate where they're turning, turning;
Their boots are heavy on the floor
  And their eyes are burning.

W.H. Auden, 1934

Commentary on Activity 2

1 We are told that the poem was written in 1934, and that perhaps alerts us to the fact that it was written at a time of growing dictatorships and fascism in Europe. Yet at the same time the poem does not seem to be set in 1934: the soldiers drumming, the soldiers' uniforms, the suggestion that they might be carrying swords all suggest an earlier, less mechanised time. So to this extent the poem has no specific time reference. It also has no specific reference to place.

Activity 2

In W.H. Auden's ballad-type poem *O What Is That Sound?* two voices take it in turns to speak. Here they have been distinguished by different typefaces, although that is not always the way the poem is presented. Read the poem at least twice, preferably aloud, and then answer the following questions:

1 When is this poem set in terms of its 'surrounding' time?

2 Is the action of the poem chronological?

3 Does the action of the poem have a clear beginning and end?

4 How do your answers to the questions above contribute to your understanding of the poem's overall meanings and effects?

AQA Examiner's tip

It is always worth thinking about the differences in the ways in which novels and poems can tell stories.

2 The action of the poem is indeed chronological, narrated from the watching perspective of the two speakers.

3 There is no beginning to the story: who are these people, where are they staying, why are they there? There is also no ending. Although the soldiers have arrived and broken down the door, we do not know if one of the lovers gets away or not, or what happens to the other one.

4 Because there is so much absence of detail here, the poem opens up many possible meanings. Is it about oppression, with its insistent patterns of sound drumming out a warning about the individual's plight in the face of military might? Is it a spy story, with the spy getting away and leaving his lover to face the music? Is it a love story? The strength of the poem is that it sets up possibilities and ambiguities that make the reader work hard and return to the poem again and again. While novels can often also have their absences and ambiguities, it is fair to say that they tend to operate with less intensity than here.

Time and sequence in the modern novel

Unit 1 of your AS examination involves reading at least one modern novel – modern in that it was written since 1990 (another way in which literature can be viewed according to time!). However, just because a novel is written post-1990, that does not mean that it has to be set in that period of time. The novel *Birdsong* by Sebastian Faulks begins with a page saying:

> PART ONE
> France 1910

Here the author establishes three things with a minimum of fuss: that the novel is set in France, that the time is 1910 (even though the novel was published in 1993) and that time is unlikely to remain at that point, the implication being that part two will move to another year.

Key terms

Prologue: an introduction to a play.

Andrea Levy in *Small Island* takes a less straightforward approach to time – remember, there is nothing that says a story has to be told chronologically. The first chapter of *Small Island* is called '**Prologue**'. This is followed by a chapter entitled '1948'. Two chapters after this comes a chapter labelled 'Before'. So within 30 or so pages we have the following headings:

> Prologue
> 1948
> Before

Each one potentially deals with a different point of time, but with the implication that events are connected.

Activity 3

Sebastian Barry's novel *The Secret Scripture* is about a woman, Roseanne McNulty, who is nearing her 100th birthday in the hospital she was committed to as a young woman. The hospital is soon to be closed and one of the psychiatrists, Dr Greene, is intrigued by the story she tells of her life. What do you notice about the treatment of time as the novel begins?

CHAPTER ONE

Roseanne's Testimony of Herself

(Patient, Roscommon Regional Mental Hospital, 1957–)

The world begins anew with every birth, my father used to say. He forgot to say, with every death it ends. Or did not think he needed to. Because for a goodly part of his life he worked in a graveyard.

**

That place where I was born was a cold town. Even the mountains stood away. They were not sure, no more than me, of that dark spot, those same mountains.

There was a black river that flowed through the town, and if it had no grace for mortal beings, it did for swans, and many swans resorted there, and even rode the river like some kind of plunging animals, in floods.

The river also took the rubbish down to the sea, and bits of things that were once owned by people and pulled from the banks, and bodies too, if rarely, oh and poor babies, that were embarrassments the odd time. The speed and depth of the river would have been a great friend to secrecy.

That is Sligo town I mean.

Sebastian Barry, The Secret Scripture, 2008, p3

Commentary on Activity 3

- Although there is plenty you could also say about place, there are several issues about time too. Part of the headings which represent this as the doctor's file on his patient include a date. '1957–'. We presume this is the time Roseanne has been in the hospital, but that still leaves the mystery of when 'now' is. So although precise details of time are given, they do not at this stage mean much to the reader.
- The opening sentences about birth and death, and references to her dead father, all give dimensions of time.
- As Roseanne's testimony begins properly (her words transcribed by the doctor?), we begin with reference to her birth. But this is soon taken over by references to the mountains that have been there much longer than she has. And as we move on to the river there is also a sense of timelessness, of the river having a long-established role in things. This, though, is then cut into by two verb tenses that suggest something else: 'would have been' suggests a past that is different from now; 'is' suggests something more immediate.
- Overall, then, the subtle and shifting references to time here seem to have significance, but we are clearly going to have to read more to find out what they are. This is typical of first-person narratives, especially from characters who are old and maybe struggling to remember.

Time frames

Timescales can be deliberately manipulated by writers to help them create subtle effects and meanings. One way of doing this is to create what is often called a time frame, putting one story inside another. This 'frame' appears at the beginning of the story, and sometimes – but not always – at the end, and there can even be reminders of the different timescales elsewhere in the story.

The gaps between the timescales can vary. In her novel *Frankenstein*, Mary Shelley's timescales are quite close together. In his poem *Godiva*, Tennyson separates events from over one thousand years. The legend of Godiva centres on the town of Coventry, where Lady Godiva acted against her husband in defence of the poor.

Activity 4

Read the opening lines of Tennyson's poem *Godiva* and answer the following questions:

1. What timescales does Tennyson use in the poem, and how does he indicate these to the reader?
2. What meanings does Tennyson make through this use of a time frame?

Godiva

I waited for the train at Coventry;
I hung with grooms and porters on the bridge,
To watch the three tall spires; and there I shaped
The city's ancient legend into this: —

Not only we, the latest seed of Time,
New men, that in the flying of a wheel
Cry down the past, not only we, that prate
Of rights and wrongs, have loved the people well,
And loathed to see them overtax'd; but she
Did more, and underwent, and overcame,
The woman of a thousand summers back,
Godiva, wife to that grim Earl, who ruled
In Coventry: for when he laid a tax
Upon his town, and all the mothers brought
Their children, clamouring, 'If we pay, we starve!'
She sought her lord, and found him, where he strode
About the hall, among his dogs, alone,
His beard a foot before him and his hair
A yard behind. She told him of their tears,
And pray'd him, 'If they pay this tax, they starve.'
Whereat he stared, replying, half-amazed,
'You would not let your little finger ache
For such as these?' – 'But I would die,' said she.

Alfred Tennyson, 1842

Did you know?

In the legend of Lady Godiva her husband said he would grant her request to cut taxes if she would ride naked through the streets of Coventry. She did this clothed only in her long hair, while the townspeople stayed inside. Her husband kept his word.

Commentary on Activity 4

1. Writing in the first person, the narrator compares himself on a bridge at Coventry station with events in the town 'a thousand summers back'. By referring to the station he is deliberately using something very modern (at least to Victorians) and he reinforces this by references to 'new men' and 'the flying of a wheel'.

   Once he begins to tell the story of Godiva, though, other aspects of time can be noticed. He begins the story with Godiva telling her husband of the people's poverty, and the verb tense 'would' suggests something possibly to happen in the future.

2. Various effects can be seen in this use of a time frame. The story is given a context, which allows Tennyson to use rather **archaic** vocabulary to simulate ancient times. The most significant meaning, though, is not about the past, as such, but about Tennyson's view of the present. He is saying here that his own age may think itself sophisticated, as exemplified by train travel, but the legend of Godiva gives a purer moral picture. While modern men 'prate/Of rights and wrongs', Godiva 'did more, and underwent and overcame'. People in those times were 'overtax'd', not just financially but by the burdens of life itself.

Key terms

Archaic: belonging to a much earlier period; archaic vocabulary is 'old' words deliberately used to suggest an earlier time.

Time and cause

A tendency in modern fiction, or at least in the sub-genre called 'literary fiction', has been to show that meaning is relative, that even the most simple of incidents has a string of causes and motives that cannot easily be untangled. One way of highlighting this position is to consider aspects of time – although, as has been suggested many times already, there are other aspects of narrative involved too.

Activity 5

Read the opening of Ian McEwan's novel *Enduring Love*. It is narrated by Joe Rose, a middle-aged man who is a science journalist. He is having a picnic with his girlfriend Clarissa, when he sees a child in a hot air balloon. Read the extract carefully, and make notes in response to the following questions:

1. What references to time can you find here, and what might they tell you about the novel's ideas?
2. What is significant, do you think, about the last sentence in this extract?

> The beginning is simple to mark. We were in sunlight under a turkey oak, partly protected from a strong, gusty wind. I was kneeling on the grass with a corkscrew in my hand, and Clarissa was passing me the bottle – a 1987 Daumas Gassac. This was the moment, this was the pinprick on the time map: I was stretching out my hand, and as the cool neck and the black foil touched my palm, we heard a man's shout. We turned to look across the field and saw the danger. Next thing, I was running towards it. The transformation was absolute: I don't recall dropping the corkscrew, or getting to my feet, or making a decision, or hearing the caution Clarissa called after me. What idiocy, to be racing into this story and its labyrinths, sprinting away from our happiness among the fresh spring grasses by the oak. There was the shout again, and a child's cry, enfeebled by the wind that roared in the tall trees along the hedgerows. I ran faster. And there, suddenly, from different points around the field, four other men were converging on the scene, running like me.
>
> I see us from three hundred feet up, through the eyes of the buzzard we had watched earlier, soaring, circling and dipping in the tumult of currents: five men running silently towards the centre of a hundred-acre field. I approached from the south-east, with the wind at my back. About two hundred yards to my left two men ran side by side. They were farm labourers who had been repairing the fence along the field's southern edge where it skirts the road. The same distance beyond them was the motorist, John Logan, whose car was banked on the grass verge with its door, or doors, wide open. Knowing what I know now, it's odd to evoke the figure of Jed Parry directly ahead of me, emerging from a line of beeches on the far side of the field a quarter of a mile away, running into the wind. To the buzzard Parry and I were tiny forms, our white shirts brilliant against the green, rushing towards each other like lovers, innocent of the grief this entanglement would bring. The encounter that would unhinge us was minutes away, its enormity disguised from us not only by the barrier of time but by the colossus in the centre of the field that drew us in with the power of a terrible ratio that set fabulous magnitude against the puny human distress at its base.

Link

For a Commentary on Activity 5, see the end of this chapter (p27).

What was Clarissa doing? She said she walked quickly towards the centre of the field. I don't know how she resisted the urge to run. By the time it happened – the event I am about to describe, the fall – she had almost caught us up and was well placed as an observer, unencumbered by participation, by the ropes and the shouting, and by our fatal lack of co-operation. What I describe is shaped by what Clarissa saw too, by what we told each other in the time of obsessive re-examination that followed: the aftermath, an appropriate term for what happened in a field waiting for its early summer mowing. The aftermath, the second crop, the growth promoted by that first cut in May.

I'm holding back, delaying the information. I'm lingering in the prior moment because it was a time when other outcomes were still possible; the convergence of six figures in a flat green space has a comforting geometry from the buzzard's perspective, the knowable, limited plane of the snooker table. The initial conditions, the force and the direction of the force, define all the consequent pathways, all the angles of collision and return, and the glow of the overhead light bathes the field, the baize and all its moving bodies, in reassuring clarity. I think that while we were still converging, before we made contact, we were in a state of mathematical grace. I linger on our dispositions, the relative distances and the compass point – because as far as these occurrences were concerned, this was the last time I understood anything clearly at all.

What were we running towards? I don't think any of us would ever know fully. But superficially the answer was, a balloon. Not the nominal space that encloses a cartoon character's speech or thought, or, by analogy, the kind that's driven by mere hot air. It was an enormous balloon filled with helium, that elemental gas forged from hydrogen in the nuclear furnace of the stars, first step along the way in the generation of multiplicity and variety of matter in the universe, including our selves and all our thoughts.

We were running towards a catastrophe, which itself was a kind of furnace in whose heat identities and fates would buckle into new shapes. At the base of the balloon was a basket in which there was a boy, and by the basket, clinging to a rope, was a man in need of help.

Even without the balloon the day would have been marked for memory, though in the most pleasurable of ways, for this was a reunion after a separation of six weeks, the longest Clarissa and I had spent apart in our seven years.

Ian McEwan, Enduring Love, 1997, *pp1–3*

The Patriot

We return to *The Patriot*, a poem by Robert Browning, written in the mid 19th century. The poem is narrated by a man about to be hanged.

Link

To complete Activity 6 you will need to use *The Patriot*, which is printed in the Extracts section at the back of this book, Extract 1 (p132).

Activity 6

1. Is it possible to say when this poem is set in terms of historical time?
2. What meanings can you find in the subtitle of the poem, 'An Old Story'?
3. What specific references to time are made in the poem?
4. How does understanding the poem's use of time and sequence open up possible meanings in the poem?

Link

For a Commentary on Activity 6, see the end of this chapter (p27).

Extension tasks

1. Consider the novels that you are studying, and for each novel discuss the following issues:
   - What timescale is covered by the novel?
   - At what point in the timescale does the novel open in the first chapter?
   - Map out an outline of the sequence of events in the novel. To what extent are they chronological?
   - At what point in time does the novel end? Would you say this is the 'end' of the story and everything is complete?
   - How significant overall is time to the way the story is told and to what its meanings are?

2. Consider the poetry texts that you are studying, and for each discuss the following issues:
   - To what extent do the poems show aspects of time?
   - What is the significance of time in the poem or poems?
   - Does the poet use aspects of time to reflect on aspects of human existence?
   - Is there any ambiguity about the time in which the poems are set? If so, what is the effect of this?

Commentaries

Commentary on Activity 5

1 The first sentence is 'spoken' by Joe, but clearly Ian McEwan is immediately making a point here. Saying that 'The beginning is simple to mark' sounds very confident and assured, but by the end of this extract it is clear that the 'beginning' is not simple, and perhaps never can be. Causes of events, however strange and serious, are more complex than this. There is never really a 'pinprick' of time that is 'the moment'.

There are plenty of chronological time references as he races across the field, such as 'next thing' and 'suddenly', but then the action stops and we are brought forward in time to 'knowing what I know now'. But even that certainty is made more doubtful by references to 'an obsessive re-examination' in the 'aftermath' of what happened.

Meanwhile, partially hidden in the unfolding drama of the balloon is an event of much more significance as far as Joe is concerned: his encounter with Jed Parry, whose significance, when it happened, was blocked by 'the barrier of time'. And as Joe ponders on this, time almost stops altogether.

2 The gap between the end of the first section and the start of the second is a sort of pause, and then as Joe continues he begins to chip away at what he claimed at the start. The story whose beginning was so easy to mark has already gone back 'six weeks' and then 'seven years'.

Commentary on Activity 6

1 In terms of actual historical time there are few clues. The occasional reference, such as to 'Shambles' Gate', and the occasional archaism, such as 'trow', suggest quite a distant past, but in contextual terms there is no specific period of time.

2 The subtitle, which could suggest that the story is set in the distant past, is subtly ambiguous. Is this an old story because it is historical, or is it an old story because it is one told many times, with as much reference to now as to any other time?

3 There is a clear and precise timescale to the poem. The voice narrating the poem compares his public reception a year ago with his reception now. He is on his way to the scaffold, near the Shambles (where butchers traded), where a vast and aggressive crowd waits. It was at this point where a year ago he was feted with flowers. The

Remember

The term 'archaic' was defined earlier in this chapter. An archaism is a word used to suggest an earlier time.

preciseness of the time here, exactly a year, helps to highlight the difference between then and now.

4 Once we establish that the poem revolves around this difference in time, we can begin to explore what exactly is different in his reception, and wonder why. Is it the narrator who has changed, or the public? Although he says he has committed 'misdeeds', this may be ironic – it could be how the public perceives what he has done.

Titles of poems are usually highly significant. If we consider that the narrator a year ago was 'a patriot', but now he is to be hanged, could it be that it is the public who have changed, not him? That we send men off to fight, and at first glorify what they do, but when they return we want nothing to do with them?

Summary

This chapter has explored the significance of time in stories. In the representational world of stories, time needs to be compressed and altered. Looking at how authors do this, and to what effect, should be central to the way you analyse your chosen set texts. Looking at the significance of time and chronology will take you to the very heart of what the author is doing and the meanings that are being conveyed.

4 Characters and characterisation

This chapter:

- Establishes the importance of characters in stories.
- Explains that people in stories can have various levels of significance.
- Shows that all people in stories are there for a specific purpose.

Key terms

Characterisation: the way in which an author creates and uses characters, and why.

AQA Examiner's tip

Never write about people in stories as though they are real. The more you can mention the author when talking about characters in texts, the better: this means that you will be writing about the characteristics people are given by authors, and how authors establish these characteristics.

People in stories

Stories are about people doing things and having things done to them. (There are sometimes stories, especially those written for children, where animals replace people, but they still have distinctly human qualities.) When looking at aspects of narrative, though, you are not concerned with the characters as such, but with aspects of **characterisation**. Reminding yourself that a character is not real, does not actually exist outside the confines of the novel or poem, reminds you that you are looking at how authors achieve effects.

This is not to say that as keen readers we do not lose ourselves in a book, and talk and think about characters as though they are real. But that reality is an illusion, a representation of people rather than the people themselves. Studying literature is not the same as just reading it – in studying literature you need to **analyse** rather than describe.

Starting with a name

One of the first things we are given after we are born is a name: in our own culture the first part of an individual's name is a choice our parents make from a limited collection; the second part is a family name. Most of us have no choice about this and quite a few of us wish we could change what we have been given. Although the names we have can tell quite a bit about our cultural origins, it feels as though there is something random about what we end up with.

There is nothing random, though, about the names of characters in literature, because of course they do not really exist. They have been invented by the author, and this offers the author a chance to signal to the reader what sort of person the character is. Names can carry a great deal of significance, in the process saving the author a lot of time and work. There are varying degrees of subtlety in this, depending in part on the genre of the text, but look closely and it is possible to see something significant in even the most ordinary of names – the ordinariness itself sometimes carrying significance. And when there are virtually no names at all – as in Cormac McCarthy's *The Road* – that too is significant.

The process of signification, though, is a cultural one. In other words, the meanings and associations we find in names are not there as of right; they are implied by the author and understood by those readers who have enough knowledge of the culture to make the connections. So when you read a fictional text that comes from a culture other than your own, you may miss the significance of all sorts of things, without necessarily losing the point of the text altogether. Two obvious ways that cultural references can be lost are through geography and through time. Texts from countries we are not fully familiar with, and texts from earlier times, require a special effort when reading, and an understanding on our part that we may not quite be getting the whole point.

One author who created a huge cast of characters was Charles Dickens. He often created names that were memorable (important in a complex plot) and at the same time pinned down the character to a certain

Activity 1

Below are some more names created by Dickens. Put them into two lists, one for good characters and one for bad. Then have a guess at what characteristic might be implied by the name of each character.

Thomas Gradgrind

Mr McChoakumchild

Stephen Blackpool

Josiah Bounderby

Charles Cheeryble

Sir Leicester Dedlock

Uriah Heep

Krook

Seth Pecksniff

Wackford Squeers

Miss Flite

Noddy Boffin

Esther Summerson

Ada Clare

Link

For a Commentary on Activity 1, see the end of this chapter (p34).

physical or emotional characteristic. So, for example, Silas Wegg (in *Our Mutual Friend*) has a wooden leg and is unpleasantly devious and greedy. While there is no reason in principle why a character called Silas Wegg could not be heroic, it somehow seems unlikely that an author would give a hero such a name.

Figure 4.1 *One of the Dickens characters listed in Activity 1. Which one do you think it is? For the answer, see the end of this chapter (p35)*

Making an appearance

You have seen above that a fictional name can say a great deal about a fictional person. The same goes for the appearance of characters: what they look like, how they dress, their physical gestures, and so on. Characters in fictional texts are usually described early on, as part of the establishment of the text. Obviously in novels there is plenty of space to do this, whereas in narrative poems a couple of features are often enough to pin down not just what a character looks like, but what a character is like in a broader sense. Just as a name can conjure up ideas about a character's moral qualities, so can a description of their appearance.

Activity 2

Look at the description below of the Mayor of Hamelin in Robert Browning's poem *The Pied Piper of Hamelin*. Based on these lines alone, what can you work out about the characteristics that he may show later in the story?

(With the Corporation as he sat,
Looking little though wondrous fat;
Nor brighter was his eye, nor moister
Than a too-long-opened oyster,
Save when at noon his paunch grew mutinous
For a plate of turtle green and glutinous)

Robert Browning, The Pied Piper of Hamelin, *1842*

Did you know?

Hamelin is a town in Lower Saxony, Germany, best known for the events narrated in Browning's poem, which took place in medieval times and are re-enacted every Sunday throughout the summer as a tourist attraction.

Commentary on Activity 2

There are a number of suggestions here that can be taken from this short extract, based on the fact that authors often use **cultural stereotypes** as a short route to creating meanings. Here are the physical features that Browning describes:

Stature – small but fat

Eyes – dull and dry

Stomach – noisy when hungry, wanting glutinous food

It would be strange if any reader found this description anything other than repulsive, and a repulsive outside, in literary texts, often means an unpleasant 'inside' too. Browning here prepares us for the fact that the Mayor is both greedy and untrustworthy. Why untrustworthy? Because of his eyes, the eyes always being a key part of a character's description, carrying considerable significance beyond their literal description.

We have noticed above the importance of cultural significance. In many cultures the physical description involved in eyes and seeing comes to represent the internal process of knowing and understanding. In English, to say 'I can see' carries both the external and internal sense of the word. No wonder then that literature is full of references to eyes and seeing, especially when the eyes are also seen as 'the window to the soul'. The dull and dry eyes of the Mayor represent a man of little vision.

Key terms

Cultural stereotype: used here to suggest that authors present characters with features that we are conditioned to recognise as having a certain meaning. Bright eyes, for example, will often suggest wisdom and creativity.

Activity 3

Look at the opening verses of Samuel Taylor Coleridge's narrative poem *The Rime of the Ancient Mariner*. What details about the appearance of the Ancient Mariner are given here? What do they suggest about him as a character?

> It is an ancient Mariner,
> And he stoppeth one of three.
> 'By thy long grey beard and glittering eye,
> Now wherefore stopp'st thou me?
>
> The Bridegroom's doors are opened wide,
> And I am next of kin;
> The guests are met, the feast is set:
> May'st hear the merry din.'
>
> He holds him with his skinny hand,
> 'There was ship,' quoth he.
> 'Hold off! Unhand me, grey-beard loon!'
> Eftsoons his hand dropt he.
>
> He holds him with his glittering eye –
> The Wedding-Guest stood still,
> And listens like a three years' child:
> The Mariner hath his will.
>
> The Wedding-Guest sat on a stone:
> He cannot choose but hear;
> And thus spake on that ancient man,
> The bright-eyed Mariner.

Samuel Taylor Coleridge, The Rime of the Ancient Mariner, *1798*

Commentary on Activity 3

The Ancient Mariner has a long grey beard (signifying age) and a skinny hand (signifying age, but also perhaps a life devoid of pleasures such as food). But it is again the eyes that are most highlighted. They are mentioned three times: 'glittering eye' is mentioned twice and 'bright-eyed' once. It would appear that his eyes belie his physical appearance. He may be old and decrepit but inside he burns fiercely in his desire to endlessly tell his story. He is a man possessed by a mission.

Did you know?

Khaled Hosseini was born in Afghanistan and moved to the USA in 1980. *The Kite Runner* is his first novel.

Activity 4

Look at the paragraphs on the right which introduce the boy Hassan. Based on these descriptions, what can you work out about the characteristics that the author is establishing?

Link

For more on eye-dialect, see Chapter 2.

Characters in novels

As we saw above, novels can take a more leisurely look at appearance, especially when an important character is being portrayed. The example below is taken from Khaled Hosseini's novel *The Kite Runner*. Near the start of the novel the narrator, Amir, looks back to his childhood and begins to build up a picture of his friend Hassan, who is the Kite Runner of the title. Hassan is the son of a family servant, but a playmate of Amir. Later in the novel Amir betrays his friend, an action that lives with him for the rest of his life.

> I can still see Hassan up on that tree, sunlight flickering through the leaves on his almost perfectly round face, a face like a Chinese doll chiseled from hardwood: his flat, broad nose and slanting, narrow eyes like bamboo leaves, eyes that looked, depending on the light, gold, green, even sapphire. I can still see his tiny low-set ears and that pointed stub of a chin, a meaty appendage that looked like it was added as a mere afterthought. And the cleft lip, just left of mid-line, where the Chinese doll maker's instrument may have slipped, or perhaps he had simply grown tired and careless.
>
> Sometimes, up in those trees, I talked Hassan into firing walnuts with his slingshot at the neighbour's one-eyed German shepherd. Hassan never wanted to, but if I asked, *really* asked, he wouldn't deny me. Hassan never denied me anything.

Khaled Hosseini, The Kite Runner, *2003, pp3–4*

Commentary on Activity 4

Unlike the description of the Mayor in *The Pied Piper of Hamelin*, this time we are meant to form a positive picture of the character. His face is 'almost perfect' and there is a sense here that the slight imperfection, the lip, makes him even more attractive. The eyes are again given prominence, but this time they shine, with not one colour but three. The poetic comparison, the way the boy is in harmony with his surroundings, is also a hint that here is someone special by character, if not by social status.

Hassan's loyalty to his friend is then shown, which takes on much greater significance once we know that his friend will betray him.

It is how you say it

Obviously what characters have to say is of huge importance to how a text works, but authors can also signal aspects of character by giving their creations distinctive speech manners or mannerisms. Sometimes these can be used to represent social class: working-class characters, for example, might be given a certain identity through the use of eye-dialect, thus linking character with setting and place.

In the following example the effect is rather more subtle, with the speech going against what we might initially expect. In this extract from a poem by Browning, the speaker has actually murdered his wife.

Here, in monologue form, the speaker of the poem *My Last Duchess* talks about the woman he has killed, while looking at a painting of her. He is speaking within the poem to an employee of the family who are going to provide the next Duchess.

> ... Oh sir, she smiled, no doubt,
> Whene'er I passed her; but who passed without
> Much the same smile? This grew; I gave commands;
> Then all smiles stopped together. There she stands
> As if alive. Will't please you rise? We'll meet
> The company below, then. I repeat,
> The Count your master's known munificence
> Is ample warrant that no just pretence
> Of mine for dowry will be disallowed;
> Though his fair daughter's self, as I avowed
> At starting, is my object ...

Robert Browning, My Last Duchess, *1842*

Browning here uses the speaker's voice to alert the hearer/reader outside the text to the appalling nature of this character. The formal words, some linked to money – 'munificence', 'ample warrant' – do not mask the fact that this insanely jealous man, who could not bear his wife to smile at anyone but himself, is currently undertaking another business venture to do the same to his next wife. And even more scary is that he is not interrupted.

Browning also uses the condensed form of poetry to chilling effect. Look how much is packed into the following lines, with the suggestion that it is all of the same importance to the speaker, who of course knows what he has done to the last duchess.

> There she stands
> As if alive. Will't please you rise? We'll meet
> The company below, then.

The ins and outs of characterisation

So far you have seen three ways of creating characters, all of which are external: names, physical appearance and speech habits. You have also seen that poetry, which often works in briefer and more symbolic ways, makes particular use of these short cuts.

There are, though, other ways in which characters are presented, some of which are also external, and some of which are more to do with the internal workings of the characters – their thoughts and motives. Again, the poem can do less with these than the novel, which is not necessarily a drawback. Hinting at thoughts and motives, rather than following them carefully, can create an unsettling effect.

AQA Examiner's tip

Do not take dialogue and speech for granted. They can tell you a great deal about how the story is being constructed and shaped.

Activity 5

Below is a list of some of the ways in which characters can be presented by the author – in other words, some of the ways in which we get to know about a character. As you consider this list, see if you agree with the external/internal labels that have been attached. Is anything missing from the list?

How the character is named	external
What the character looks like	external
The character's speech habits	external
What the character does, their actions	external
The character's motives for what they do	internal
What the character has to say	external/internal
What the character thinks	internal
What others say about the character	external/internal
What others think about the character	internal/external

There is no commentary on this activity.

Link

The last four aspects listed in Activity 5 lead to the next chapter, which looks at voices in texts.

Link

To complete Activity 6 you will need to use *The Patriot*, which is printed in the Extracts section at the back of this book, Extract 1 (p132).

The Patriot

As in previous chapters, we conclude by looking at *The Patriot*.

Activity 6

This chapter has looked at some of the ways authors use external features of characterisation, such as naming, appearance, actions, to develop their stories. Now look again at *The Patriot* and answer the following questions:

1. What people are included in the poem?
2. What external clues are given to the identity of these people?
3. Are actions important in this poem?

Extension tasks

1. Consider the novels that you are studying and discuss the following issues:
   - Can you find significance in the way any of the characters are named?
   - Can you find any significance in the way characters are described externally? This need not be limited to their physical characteristics, but could also include the jobs they do, and so on.
   - Are any of the characters given any noticeable features of speech that help you to remember them and their specific traits?
   - Are there any other aspects of the author's methods of characterisation that you can identify?
2. Consider the poetry texts that you are studying and discuss the following issues:
   - To what extent do the poems show aspects of individual characters?
   - What methods does the poet use to create characters?
   - Does the speaker of the poem have a discernible character? If so, how is it created?

Commentaries

Commentary on Activity 1

Good

Esther Summerson (because of summer)

Ada Clare (sweetness)

Noddy Boffin (eccentricity)

Miss Flite (lightness?)

Charles Cheeryble (humour)

Stephen Blackpool (more open to question, but solid and dependable)

Bad

Thomas Gradgrind (hard-sounding)

Mr McChoakumchild (a teacher – who chokes the child's creativity)

Josiah Bounderby (cad)

Uriah Heep (a creep)

Krook (a thief)

Seth Pecksniff (two unpleasant words together)

Sir Leicester Dedlock (intransigent and unmoveable)

Wackford Squeers (a different kind of teacher)

Illustration of Dickens character

The illustration is of Uriah Heep, from *David Copperfield*.

Commentary on Activity 6

1. There is the patriot himself who narrates the poem, and the people of the city.
2. The patriot has a label: he is 'The Patriot', but has no name. The people of the city are described a year ago, when they were enthusiastic about what The Patriot was doing, but now they are absent, waiting offstage somewhere else to see him hanged. Only 'a palsied few' remain in the town itself, presumably because they cannot move.
3. Actions are implied rather than seen. In his year away The Patriot has lived life to the full – 'Naught man could do, have I left undone' – but we are given no actual details about whether this refers to public actions in war or more private actions.

Summary

This chapter has looked at some of the ways in which people in texts are created and given characteristics. The focus has been on some of the external methods of characterisation, and your attention has been drawn to some of the differences between poetry and novels.

5 Voices in texts

This chapter:

- Explains the different kinds of voices in texts: characters and narrator.
- Shows ways of identifying the different voices in texts.

The idea of voices in texts is closely linked to the aspect of characters and characterisation discussed in the previous chapter. Voices in texts can be the actual 'voices' of characters who get to speak in the text, and they can also be the thoughts of characters and the voice of the narrator. Identifying voices in texts can be a complicated business, but at AS Level there are some basic issues to understand that will help you think about how narratives work. In the real world, we can shut out the extraneous noise of people talking, and we certainly cannot hear people thinking. In fictional worlds, when somebody talks we take notice, and sometimes we can also access what they are thinking.

Direct speech and attribution

Activity 1

Look at the following extract from *Small Island* by Andrea Levy. Here Hortense, newly arrived in London from Jamaica in 1948 and accompanied by her landlady Mrs Bligh, tells of going to buy some food. The first person to speak is the shopkeeper, who has red hair.

1 How many speaking voices can you identify in this extract?

2 What information relating to their speech is given in addition to the actual words they say? Is this significant?

> 'What can I do you for?' he asked me directly. A red Englishman!
>
> 'He wants to know if you'd like anything,' Mrs Bligh told me.
>
> I obliged her concern by making a purchase. 'A tin of condensed milk, please,' I asked him.
>
> But this red man stared back at me as if I had not uttered the words. No light of comprehension sparkled in his eye. 'I beg your pardon?' he said.
>
> Condensed milk, I said, five times, and still he looked on me bewildered. Why no one in this country understand my English? At college my diction was admired by all. I had to point at the wretched tin of condensed milk, which resided just behind his head.
>
> 'Oh, condensed milk,' he told me, as if I had not been saying it all along.
>
> Tired of this silly dance of incomprehension, I did not bother to ask for the loaf of bread – I just point to the bread on the counter.

Andrea Levy, Small Island, *2004, pp331–2*

Key terms

Direct speech: the actual words spoken by characters in a narrative.

Attributed: describes direct speech that is identified (i.e. the reader is told who is speaking).

Commentary on Activity 1

1 Three people's words are quoted here, in what we call **direct speech**. The speakers are the unnamed shopkeeper, Mrs Bligh and Hortense herself.

2 Every time someone speaks their contribution is **attributed**. So for the first three speeches we get:

- he asked me directly
- Mrs Bligh told me
- I asked him.

Note that a variety of words can be used to attribute speech instead of the straightforward 'said'. Are they just used to give variety? Possibly, but to be 'told' something might indicate that you are being treated as an inferior. In addition, if the attribution includes *how* someone speaks, then further information is given. The shopkeeper 'asked directly'. Does that hint at a certain rudeness perhaps, especially as he has made a sort of joke?

There is also, though, another voice in the text, 'speaking' to the reader. Because the narrative is first person, we can confidently say that voice belongs to Hortense, not speaking in the story but speaking *in the telling* of the story.

If we want to make this a little more complicated, we can find her using a range of voices. Sometimes she tells the story, at other times she reflects on its significance to her at the time of the event. So in the line:

> Condensed milk, I said, five times, and still he looked on me bewildered

we have Hortense telling the story. However, in the line

> Why no one in this country understand my English?

Hortense is *thinking* about what is happening and trying to find a reason. This thought, though, is not attributed: it is **free**. The fact that she thinks in a slightly non-British standard form of English adds to our awareness that she is not being understood by others in the story, but she is of course being understood by us the readers.

What we have seen in the activity above is that speaking and thinking can both lead to 'voices', and that sometimes these voices are attributed and sometimes free. An example of free speech from the same novel is given below. Here Hortense, recently arrived in England, talks to her husband who has lived there for some time. Hortense speaks first – an important point when you are having to follow a sequence without being told who is speaking:

> 'Who is that woman downstairs?'...
> 'Oh, Queenie – she own the house.'
> 'You know her?'
> 'Of course. She own the house. She is the landlady.'
> 'She married?'
> 'Her husband lost in the war.'
> 'She on her own?'
> 'Yes.'
> 'You friendly with her?'

Andrea Levy, Small Island, *2004, pp28–9*

Sometimes writers use free speech to give variety, maybe to hurry the action a bit. The effect of this stretch of free speech is more specific, though: it sounds very much as though Hortense is suspicious of her husband and is conducting some sort of interrogation. (There comes a point with free speech, incidentally, when the reader can lose track – we are all familiar with having to go back to the beginning to work out who is talking.)

Remember

A first-person narrative is a story told through the voice of one of the characters, using 'I', as opposed to a third-person narrative in which the story is told by a narrator who is not one of the characters. In this case Hortense is part of the story (which makes her what is sometimes called a **homodiegetic narrator**), but her knowledge of the story she tells is incomplete (which makes her an **intradiegetic narrator**).

Key terms

Free: in a technical sense, describes thought or speech that is not attributed (i.e. the reader is not told specifically who is speaking or thinking).

Homodiegetic narrator: the narrator who is part of the story they describe.

Intradiegetic narrator: the narrator who is not omniscient and does not know everything, usually because they are part of the story rather than in control of it.

AQA Examiner's tip

It is well worth using some of the technical terms defined above when analysing the ways in which authors create speaking and thinking voices. The terminology is not essential, but it helps you to deal with the analysis quickly and accurately.

Key terms

Indirect speech: speech that is reported by the narrator, giving a version of the words spoken rather than the words themselves.

Speech marks: inverted commas used to indicate the start and end of direct speech.

Indirect speech

In addition to giving the actual words spoken, a narrator can report what was said in what we call **indirect speech**. An example from *Small Island* is given below. This time the narrator is Mrs Bligh, whose neighbour and her husband have objected to Mrs Bligh having a black lodger.

Activity 2

Read the extract below and answer the following questions:

1. Identify the direct speech.
2. Identify the indirect speech.
3. For the indirect speech write out a direct speech version.
4. Is there any thought presented here?

> But Blanche, or Mrs Smith as she now wanted me to call her, put her house up for sale. Furious with me. Told me it wasn't so much her as her husband. 'This is not what he wanted, Mrs Bligh. He's just back from fighting a war and now this country no longer feels his own.' What was it all for? That's what it left Morris wondering. And she told me she had her two little girls' welfare to think of.

Andrea Levy, Small Island, *2004, p117*

Commentary on Activity 2

1 There is one piece of direct speech, the sentences beginning 'This is not what he wanted...' We are helped in identifying this by the use of **speech marks**; although they are the traditional way of marking direct speech, in modern novels they are not always used.

2 and 3 Indirect speech is as follows, with a possible direct speech version following:

Mrs Smith as she now wanted me to call her
'I want you to call me Mrs Smith'

Furious with me
'I am furious with you'

Told me it was not so much her as her husband
'It's not me, it is my husband,' she told me.

What was it all for? That's what it left Morris wondering.
'Morris has been left wondering what it is all for.'

And she told me she had her two little girls' welfare to think of
'I have my two little girls' welfare to think of,' she told me.

4 There are a few structural points to note here. Note that pronouns and verb tenses change when moving from direct to indirect speech, as does word order. Also, note, it is possible to have attributed indirect speech and free indirect speech. Where the indirect speech is free, it merges seamlessly into the narrative. The same goes for indirect free thought. The sentence 'Furious with me' has been assumed to be spoken in the list above, but it could be thought only – Mrs Bligh's interpretation of her neighbour's words, rather than the actual words being spoken. The use of free indirect thought and speech allows authors to create a certain ambiguity when telling the story.

Did you know?

Speech marks can be 'single' or "double", depending on the style – and country – of the publication. In America the style is generally double, whereas many British publications (including this book) use single speech marks.

Remember

With attributed speech the reader is told who is speaking; with free speech there is no such indication.

So what is gained by using indirect speech? Well again, in the long run, authors will use it for variety. Here, though, it may serve another purpose: in not being given many of Mrs Smith's actual words, they are being downgraded, rendered less powerful.

To recap on what we have found so far: one way in which we get information in a story is through what we are 'told' by the characters involved. Areas to consider include:

- Who speaks, to whom and when?
- What are they talking about?
- What information does the talk give to (a) other characters and (b) the reader?
- Is the speech direct or indirect?
- Is the speech attributed or free?
- If attributed, is the attitude towards the character contained in the attribution?
- Whose thoughts are accessed?
- Are these thoughts attributed or free?
- Voices in stories can help to establish character traits, so are part of characterisation, but they also enable authors to provide information.

Although there are always exceptions to every rule in literature, it is largely true to say that novels do not provide the so-called small talk that is such a feature of our everyday 'real' lives. This is because narrative is about information, and small talk, while being very important socially, does not tell a story as such.

Thought in novels

One of the distinctive features of the novel form is that it can give us the detailed thoughts of characters as the story progresses. This is possible up to a point in poetry, but much more problematic in drama, where artificial means have to be used if characters are going to 'speak' their thoughts. The fact that the novel as a form allows thought to be given makes it interestingly different from real life: in real life we can think ourselves but cannot access the thoughts of others, unless they choose to give us a version of them. Not surprisingly, novelists make full use of thoughts to give their characters distinctive voices and thus character traits.

In Chapter 3 we saw the opening action of Ian McEwan's *Enduring Love*. Soon after the event, where a boy is eventually rescued in the balloon accident but a man dies, the first-person narrator of the novel, Joe Rose, reflects on what had happened the previous day. This is done by the use of indirect thought, so we do not get the actual words he thought and speech marks are not used.

Link

Reread the extract from *Enduring Love* in Chapter 3 (p25) to remind yourself of what happened there.

Activity 3

Read the extract on the next page and answer the following questions:

1. Identify the points where McEwan makes it clear that Joe is thinking here.
2. What do you notice about the references to time near the beginning of the extract?
3. What contribution to the novel as a whole might this extract be serving? Think in terms of the characterisation of Joe and the issues raised by what he thinks.

I had left Clarissa sleeping and brought with me my coffee, the paper and my pages from the night before.

But instead of reading myself or others I thought about John Logan and how we had killed him. Yesterday the events of the day before had dimmed. This morning the blustery sunshine illumined and animated the whole tableau. I could feel the rope in my hands again as I examined the welts. I made calculations. If Gadd had stayed in the basket with his grandson, and if the rest of us had hung on, and if we assumed an average weight of a hundred and sixty pounds each, then surely eight hundred pounds would have kept us close to the ground. If the first person had not let go, then surely the rest of us would have stayed in place. And who was this first person? Not me. Not me. I even said the words aloud. I remembered a plummeting mass and the sudden upward jerk of the balloon. But I could not tell whether this mass was in front of me, or to my left or right. If I knew the position, I would know the person.

Could this person be blamed? As I drank my coffee the rush hour below began its slow crescendo. It was hard to think this through. Phrases, well-worn and counter-weighted, occurred to me, resolving nothing. On the one hand, the first pebble in an avalanche, and on the other, the breaking of ranks. The cause, but not the morally responsible agent. The scales tipping, from altruism to self-interest. Was it panic, or rational calculation? Had we killed him really, or simply refused to die with him? But if we had been with him, stayed with him, no one would have died.

Ian McEwan, Enduring Love*, 1997, pp55–6*

Commentary on Activity 3

1 McEwan makes it clear at various points that Joe is thinking rather than speaking (although there is one point where he speaks to himself – an advanced form of thinking perhaps!). We are given the following attributions as part of indirect thought:

> I thought
> I could feel
> I remembered
> It was hard to think this through
> Occurred to me.

It could also be argued that the many question marks also signify a thought process.

2 The references to time at the beginning of the extract are as follows:

> the night before
> yesterday
> this morning.

They show a subtle shift from a distant past (*the night before* instead of *last night*) to a more recent past (*yesterday* instead of *the previous day* and *this morning* instead of *that morning*). This subtle shift brings the thought processes a little closer to the reader.

3 In terms of its wider contribution this extract establishes certain character traits that can be seen in Joe. He is considerate and concerned, worried about the accident and its causes. He is also very rational, teasing out reasons for what happened. We are also meant to see him as an intelligent man, whose thoughts, as given to us here, sound like formal writing. Although all thoughts in a novel

are written down, authors can try to represent them in various ways as more random and chaotic than those given here. Even the questions, which in part represent the flow of ideas, suggest a questioning of events in a scientific way.

What we see here, then, is that thought can be as significant as talk in helping an author tell a story. Add thought to talk and action and you have three of the key ingredients to storytelling and narrative.

Third-person narrative

In the extract from *Enduring Love* we have seen an example of how thought can be used within a first-person narrative. It can also be used within third-person narratives, and often with a wider frame of reference: a third-person narrative can access a much wider number of characters and their thoughts, and in the process shift the point of view. Where free thought is used, it can also form part of the overall narrative, making it difficult to see whether it is a character's thoughts we are being given, in which case the information is open to question, or whether it is the voice of the more authoritative narrator.

In real life, of course, there is no narrator to oversee our thoughts and actions. In a philosophical sense there is no definitive truth about something, only the aggregation of all our thoughts and words on it. So if the owner of a house thinks it looks lovely from the outside and a passer-by thinks it looks tatty, we cannot say that either is right. Modern novelists in particular work with the idea that there cannot be absolute truths, only the words, thoughts and actions of people, and they try to reflect this lack of certainty in their novels.

Link

See Chapter 6 for a discussion of point of view.

Voices in poetry

Narrative poems also have voices within them that help tell the story. How many voices, and what use is made of the voices, can vary, though. Some of the narrative poems in your AS course selection are quite short, so are likely to have fewer voices than the extended narrative poems that are another option. Read Activity 4 first, before looking at the following extracts.

Activity 4

The following extracts have already been seen in previous chapters. For each one, identify:

- how many voices there are
- whether the voice presents speaking or thinking
- whether the voices are attributed or free
- what effects the poet is achieving through using voices in this way.

1 *The Rime of the Ancient Mariner* (opening lines)

It is an ancient Mariner,
And he stoppeth one of three.
'By thy long grey beard and glittering eye,
Now wherefore stopp'st thou me?

The Bridegroom's doors are opened wide,
And I am next of kin;
The guests are met, the feast is set:
May'st hear the merry din.'

He holds him with his skinny hand,
'There was ship,' quoth he.
'Hold off! Unhand me, grey-beard loon!'
Eftsoons his hand dropt he.

Samuel Taylor Coleridge, 1798

Link

For each poem in Activity 4 there is a short commentary at the end of this chapter (p43).

2 *O What Is That Sound?* (opening lines)

O what is that sound which so thrills the ear
  Down in the valley drumming, drumming?
Only the scarlet soldiers, dear,
  The soldiers coming.

O what is that light I see flashing so clear
  Over the distance brightly, brightly?
Only the sun on their weapons, dear,
  As they step lightly.

W.H. Auden, 1934

3 *Godiva* (opening lines)

I waited for the train at Coventry;
I hung with grooms and porters on the bridge,
To watch the three tall spires; and there I shaped
The city's ancient legend into this: —

  Not only we, the latest seed of Time,
New men, that in the flying of a wheel
Cry down the past, not only we, that prate
Of rights and wrongs, have loved the people well,
And loathed to see them overtax'd; but she
Did more, and underwent, and overcame,
The woman of a thousand summers back,
Godiva, wife to that grim Earl, who ruled
In Coventry: for when he laid a tax
Upon his town, and all the mothers brought
Their children, clamoring, 'If we pay, we starve!'
She sought her lord, and found him, where he strode
About the hall, among his dogs, alone,
His beard a foot before him and his hair
A yard behind. She told him of their tears,
And pray'd him, 'If they pay this tax, they starve.'
Whereat he stared, replying, half-amazed,
'You would not let your little finger ache
For such as these?' – 'But I would die,' said she.

Alfred Tennyson, 1842

The Patriot

As in previous chapters, we conclude by looking at *The Patriot*.

Link

To complete Activity 5 you will need to use *The Patriot,* which is printed in the Extracts section at the back of this book, Extract 1 (p132).

Activity 5

This chapter has looked at some of the ways in which authors use voices in narratives. Now look again at *The Patriot* and answer the following question:

- What voices are in the poem and how are they presented?

Extension tasks

1. Consider the novels that you are studying. Choose a representative section (say a chapter) and discuss the following issues:
   - How is speech used in this chapter of the novel?
   - Is attribution used to indicate aspects of character?
   - Is thought given in this chapter? Whose thoughts are given?
   - Are there points in the chapter where who is speaking/thinking is deliberately ambiguous?

2. Consider the poetry texts that you are studying, and discuss the following issues:
   - To what extent do the poems contain direct speech? What is the effect of this?
   - Do the poems have a range of speakers?
   - Who is heard and who is not? Is this significant?

Commentaries

Commentary on Activity 4

1 The Rime of the Ancient Mariner

There are three voices: the narrator, the Mariner and the Wedding-Guest. It would seem that all voices are spoken rather than thought. The Wedding-Guest's speech is free (so in fact more than one guest could be speaking). The Mariner's is attributed. Coleridge establishes right at the start that this is a narrative poem with a mix of narrative and speech. It is also dramatic and rather strange.

2 O What Is That Sound?

Here there are two free voices, each speaker signalled by a different font. The fact that they are not attributed means we do not know who they are, creating a deliberate ambiguity – they could be any people under threat from forces of repression at any time.

3 Godiva

There are three direct speaking voices here, all attributed. They are the poor mothers, Lady Godiva and her husband. The fact that they are all attributed means that Tennyson's method is different from Auden's. He wants to be clear about the specifics and tells the story conventionally, even if it is probably in fact a legend.

The other voice is the first-person narrator, which, because of the opening time frame, seems like a representation of Tennyson himself. Whether this is thought or spoken is not clear; nor is who it is addressed to.

Commentary on Activity 5

The dominant voice is that of The Patriot, who sounds as though he is making a final speech before his execution. The voice is resigned and thoughtful rather than aggressive and angry, which presumably it could be, given his treatment.

There is one other brief piece of reported speech, the collective 'cries' of the people celebrating his return. There are also some short pieces of direct speech, but they are slightly different from others we have seen. Within the world of this story they are not words that have been spoken, they are words that might have been spoken. So in the first instance he pretends to ask for the impossible and the grateful crowd is willing to give him anything. This make-believe exchange heightens the sense of love and gratitude that the people have for their hero.

The second imaginary piece of direct speech involves God, who makes the moral point that earthly riches are nothing compared with eternal ones.

Summary

This chapter has looked at some of the ways in which authors use speaking and thinking voices in texts. One result of this process has been to see that it contributes to the point of view of the story, an idea that is developed further in the next chapter.

6 Points of view

This chapter:

- Explains that stories are told from certain viewpoints.
- Shows how these viewpoints are carefully managed by authors to convey meanings.
- Demonstrates that the words we use to explain how a story is told are the same words used to examine the ideas that the story presents.

Visual and spatial metaphors

The term 'point of view' is very important when studying aspects of narrative, but it is hard to define, partly because it is a metaphor based on a visual and spatial idea. If you are at a football match and you stand behind the goal, that is your point of view of the game. If you are on the side of the pitch, that is a different point of view, as is the view from the other end of the ground. And it can easily be argued that where you stand affects how you see the game. It depends on your position, your standpoint. Behind the goal where your own team scores gives a different perspective from being at the far end of the pitch. Digital television coverage nowadays even allows you to change the angle you are watching from.

So where, as readers, we are 'placed' in the telling of the story is vital to the way we interpret it, in just the same way as where we stand in the football ground affects how well we think our team has played.

Remember

Metaphor (a key term used in Chapter 2) involves the transfer of meaning, with one thing described as another (e.g. life is a journey).

While this football analogy should be clear, you may have noticed that in explaining point of view, other metaphorical terms were used, which also depend on visual and spatial concepts. So we can say:

- It depends on your point of view.
- It depends on where you stand – your standpoint.
- It depends on what perspective you take.
- It depends on your position.
- It depends on the angle you take.

These terms can have another level of meaning too. Here we are not just talking about your physical position, we are also talking about your position in terms of the beliefs you hold, the ideas you have. To continue with the football analogy, we might say something like, 'Whether or not Bobby Smith should be sacked as manager depends on your point of view, but I think he's doing a good job.'

For our purposes, then, looking at point of view is important because it allows us to analyse narratives technically and also in terms of their ideas and views: how they see the world. Point of view is therefore both the technical description to do with how a text works and an indication of the ideology in a text. By exploring both these elements we are able to arrive at a more complete reading of the text.

Figure 6.1 *Different points of view*

Remember

The ideology of a text (a key term used in Chapter 1) is the attitudes, values and assumptions that the text contains.

The narrator – first person or third person?

We have already used the terms 'first person' and 'third person' in earlier chapters. They are the starting points for a more sophisticated way of looking at narratives, and it is useful to consider in a broad sense what they allow writers to do.

Activity 1

Imagine you are going to write a story about two people meeting and falling in love.

1. Consider telling it in the first person, through one of the two people meeting. What are the advantages and disadvantages of this?
2. Now consider telling it in the third person. What are the advantages and disadvantages of this?
3. Can you think of any other ways the story could be told?

Commentary on Activity 1

1. An advantage of the first-person method is that it can be intimate, close to the action, have a very personal narrative voice. But within this advantage lies a distinct disadvantage: the narrator can only report on what they themselves think and feel, and only on action that takes place when they are present. There are ways round this of course: other characters can tell you what they did, what they think, and you can use devices like letters, diaries, emails, and so on, to provide further information. There are times, though, when the narrator can seem almost required to be the novelist, to give the reader necessary information – and at times such as these the first-person method is at its least effective.
2. The advantage of the third-person narrative is that it offers the author the possibility of taking the narrative anywhere, of observing everything and everyone – but the downside is that this can feel quite remote to the reader and it can lack the personal nature of the first-person method.
3. In reality, authors do not necessarily have to stick rigidly to one method, and there are many ingenious ways to overcome narrative problems. For example, there can be more than one first-person narrator in a novel, with the switch clearly marked in the chapter headings. Or there can be a third-person narrative, but one that changes the point of view, often getting very close to different characters, one at a time. Using indirect free thought can be a great help here.

99 Ways to Tell a Story

One way to understand how the narrative can shift across characters is to see this represented visually. In his comic book *99 Ways to Tell a Story*, Matt Madden tells the same story in 99 different pages of drawings. The first he calls 'Template', which is reproduced on p46.

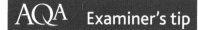

AQA Examiner's tip

When answering questions in Section A of your examination, always give prominence to the point of view that you are being given in the telling of a story.

Link

See Chapter 5 for a discussion and examples of first- and third-person narratives.

Link

See Chapter 5 for more on indirect free thought.

Activity 2

Look at 'Template' and answer the following questions:

1. Write out the story, frame by frame.
2. Now write out the plot using a third-person narrative.
3. What narrative methods that you have already learned about (e.g. treatment of time, use of different voices) are used here?

Link

For a Commentary on Activity 2, see the end of this chapter (p51).

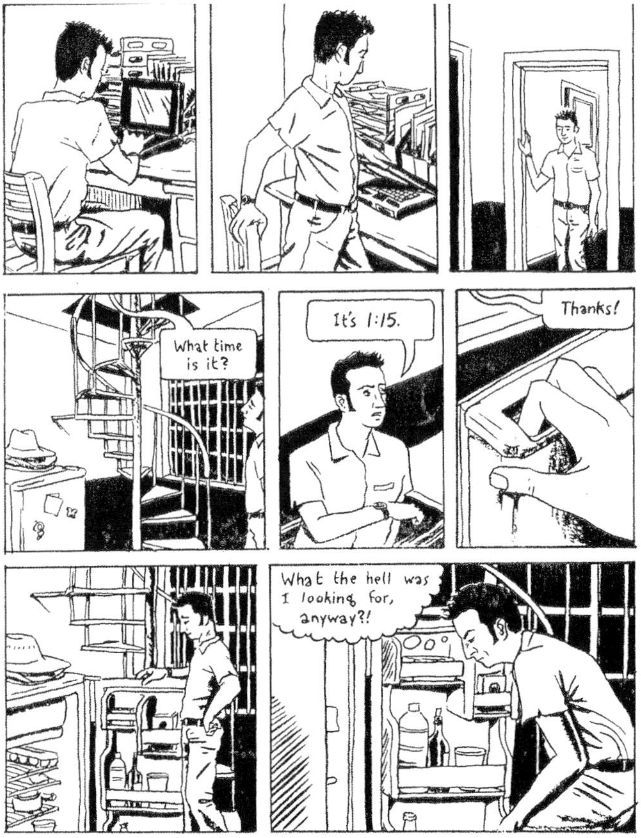

Figure 6.2 *'Template'*

Activity 3

1. Now look at the same story but this time labelled 'Upstairs'(Figure 6.3). What extra information are we given by 'going upstairs'?
2. What are the crucial differences between this drawing and the previous one called 'Template'?

Link

For a Commentary on Activity 3, see the end of this chapter (p51).

Figure 6.3 *'Upstairs'*

Proximity to the action

Another way in which the narrative point of view can be varied is by how close to the action we as readers are allowed to get. Is it viewed from a certain distance or is it viewed in close-up? What is our proximity? If you look at the 'Template' drawings you will see that Madden uses a sort of zoom effect when the man's hand goes to the fridge door (frame 6). This is much closer to the action than frame 3, which seems the most distant.

Activity 4

Here are the opening sentences of each of the first five paragraphs of *Birdsong* by Sebastian Faulks. The novel begins in France in 1910. What do you notice about the focus of each of the paragraphs? How does each paragraph connect with the one before? The paragraphs have been numbered for ease of reference.

1 The boulevard du Cange was a broad, quiet street that marked the eastern flank of the city of Amiens. The wagons that rolled in from Lille and Arras to the north made directly into the tanneries and mills of the Saint-Leu quarter without needing to use this rutted, leafy road. The town side of the boulevard backed on to substantial gardens which were squared off and apportioned with civic precision to the houses they adjoined …

2 Behind the gardens the river Somme broke up into small canals that were the picturesque feature of Saint-Leu; on the other side of the boulevard these had been made into a series of water-gardens, little islands of damp fertility divided by the channels of the split river …

3 The Azaires' house showed a strong, formal front towards the road from behind iron railings. The traffic looping down towards the river would have been in no doubt that this was the property of a substantial man. …

4 Inside, the house was both smaller and larger than it looked. It had no rooms of intimidating grandeur, no gilt ballrooms with dripping chandeliers, yet it had unexpected spaces and corridors that disclosed new corners with steps down into the gardens …

5 Stephen Wraysford's metal trunk had been sent ahead and was waiting at the foot of the bed. He unpacked his clothes and hung his spare suit in the giant carved wardrobe …

Sebastian Faulks, Birdsong, 1993, *pp3–4*

Commentary on Activity 4

In each paragraph the focus gets tighter, zooming in from a broad starting point and getting more and more specific. It goes something like this:

1 We see a quite distant view of a town, region, district and main street, followed by houses and gardens.

2 Then we get closer by seeing the already mentioned gardens and what lies behind them.

3 This is followed by a closer view, of a single house belonging to a well-off family.

4 Next we go inside the house, looking round in general.

5 And finally we go to a specific room inhabited by a specific man – clearly an Englishman who has come to stay, for an as yet unspecified reason.

Both distance and proximity can be useful: among other things distance tends to let us judge characters and their actions, see the importance of places, while proximity allows us to be more involved with characters, their relationships, their emotions.

Shifting perspectives

This chapter is headed 'Points of view', because perspectives frequently shift and move within texts – this is certainly the case in novels, but can be seen in poems too. Sometimes, to highlight the different perceptions of characters, and perhaps misunderstandings between them, essentially the same incident is seen twice, first from one character's point of view, then from another's. The following extracts from *Small Island* come early in the novel, when Hortense has arrived in London in 1948 from Jamaica, to be reunited with her husband Gilbert, who has lived in London for some time – and has failed to meet her at the dock. Hortense has just seen the room they are to live in and is horrified at how small it is. Gilbert, on the other hand, is aware that living in London means you live in small rooms. We, as readers, understand their misunderstanding in a way that the two characters do not.

Activity 5

How does Andrea Levy show the differing perceptions of the two characters in each of the extracts? Can you see a third point of view here, which involves what the reader could think about this exchange?

Hortense

'Well,' I said, 'show me the rest, then, Gilbert'. The man just stared. 'Show me the rest, nah. I am tired from the long journey.' He scratched his head. 'The other rooms, Gilbert. The ones you busy making so nice for me you forgot to come to the dock.'

Gilbert spoke so softly I could hardly hear. He said, 'But this is it.'

'I am sorry?' I said.

'This is it, Hortense. This is the room I am living.'

Three steps would take me to one side of this room. Four steps could take me to another. There was a sink in the corner, a rusty tap stuck out from the wall above it. There was a table with two chairs – one with its back broken – pushed up against the bed. The armchair held a shopping bag, a pyjama top, and a teapot. In the fireplace the gas hissed with a blue flame.

'Just this?' I had to sit on the bed. My legs gave way. There was no bounce underneath me as I fell. 'Just this? This is where you are living? Just this?'

Gilbert

'Is this the way the English live?' How many times she ask me that question? I lose count. 'This the way the English live?' That question became a mournful lament, sighed on each and every thing she see. 'Is this the way the English live?'

'Yes', I tell her, 'this is the way the English live … there has been a war … many English live worse than this.'

> She drift to the window, look quizzical upon the scene, rub her gloved hand on the pane of glass, examine it before saying once more, 'This the way the English live?'
>
> Soon the honourable man inside me was shaking my ribs and thumping my breast, wanting to know, 'Gilbert, what in God's name have you done? You no realise, man? Cha, you married to this woman!'

Andrea Levy, Small Island, *2004, pp20–21, 22*

Commentary on Activity 5

Hortense's point of view is given through a number of methods, beyond the obvious one that it is her first-person narrative. Her imperative way of speaking, giving orders, is contrasted with Gilbert's softly spoken words. The detail of what she sees, especially things that are broken and out of place, suggests someone seeing something for the first time with a critical eye. The repetition of 'Just this' and the giving way of her legs focus on her shock and surprise.

Whereas repeated words from Hortense show her amazement, when Gilbert reports her repetition he does so with increasing irritation, until we are given, in direct thought, the idea that he is wondering if he should regret his marriage.

As readers we probably do not take sides in this misunderstanding, but we are being offered a third, more indirect point of view to consider – provided, that is, that we pick up the potential meanings on offer. Hortense has supposedly come from a small island, Jamaica, but it is she who is shocked by the squalor she finds in England, when she expected to be impressed. To her, Britain is the small island. One detail in Gilbert's narrative highlights this: when Hortense rubs the window, he does not comment on its significance, and because it is not in her narrative nor does she. But attentive readers will note that she is wearing a glove, a sign of social standing, and after rubbing the dirty window, which soils her (white?) glove, she repeats her question. The **semiotics** here suggest that how you view a culture depends on your point of view, and in this novel English readers are being asked to examine the assumptions they make about cultural superiority over others.

What this shows is that while there can be points of view directed through characters, readers too are involved in the process, sometimes finding meanings that the characters themselves do not.

Points of view in poetry

Although poems sometimes give multiple points of view, more frequently they keep to one or two. Poetry tends to condense narratives, which may in part account for this. If only one point of view is given, there is potential for ambiguity – what would the story be like if it were told by another voice that is not heard? Some of the best examples of re-creative responses to literature look at a text from the point of view of a voice that is absent from the original text. This process does two things:

- It provides scope for a piece of creative writing.
- It sheds potentially new light on the original text, perhaps making us less sure of the 'truth' behind the story we have been given.

Key terms

Semiotics: relates to the meanings of signs. Signs can be visual (a red light on a traffic light means stop) and signs can be verbal (a white glove could signify innocence, for example). Semiotics, then, looks at the significance of connotations.

AQA Examiner's tip

If the text you are writing about has shifting perspectives, try to say what they contribute to the story overall.

Link

For a Commentary on Activity 6, see the end of this chapter (p51).

Activity 6

Read carefully the poem *Sister Maude* below. Then answer the following questions:

1. What would you say is the plot of this poem?
2. How would you describe the poem's point of view?
3. Whose voices are absent in the poem?
4. What might these voices have to say?
5. How does considering question 4 throw new light on the poem?

Sister Maude

Who told my mother of my shame,
Who told my father of my dear?
Oh who but Maude, my sister Maude,
Who lurked to spy and peer.

Cold he lies, as cold as stone,
With his clotted curls about his face:
The comeliest corpse in all the world
And worthy of a queen's embrace.

You might have spared his soul, sister,
Have spared my soul, your own soul too:
Though I had not been born at all,
He'd never have looked at you.

My father may sleep in Paradise,
My mother at Heaven-gate:
But sister Maude shall get no sleep
Either early or late.

My father may wear a golden gown,
My mother a crown may win;
If my dear and I knocked at Heaven-gate
Perhaps they'd let us in:
But sister Maude, oh sister Maude,
Bide you with death and sin.

Christina Rossetti, 1860

Link

To complete Activity 7 you will need to use *The Patriot*, which is printed in the Extracts section at the back of this book, Extract 1 (p132).

The Patriot

As with other chapters, this one closes by looking at the poem *The Patriot*, this time focusing on its point of view.

Link

For a Commentary on Activity 7, see the end of this chapter (p52).

Activity 7

1. How do we know that the narrative in this poem is from the point of view of The Patriot? Are there any places in the poem where the narrative may be from a different perspective?
2. Write (in prose, or poetry if you wish) versions of this story as they might be told by others who are mentioned in this poem.

Extension tasks

1 Consider the novels that you are studying. Choose a representative section (say a chapter) and discuss the following issues:

- What is the point of view in this section of the novel? How close or distant is it from the action? Can you find an ideological point of view?
- Does the point of view remain constant or does it shift?

2 Consider the poetry texts that you are studying, and discuss the following issues for various poems:

- What is the point of view in the poem? How close or distant is it from the action? Can you find an ideological point of view?
- Does the title have the same point of view as the rest of the poem?
- Do a re-creative exercise, where you rewrite a poem, or part of a poem, from a different point of view. You can do this in verse or prose. What do you learn about the original in doing this?

Commentaries

Commentary on Activity 2

1 You will have given a frame-by-frame account of what you can see.

2 You will almost certainly have connected different frames and begun to develop a sort of plot. You may have written something like this:

A man is working at his computer. He gets up to go to the fridge, but on his way to the kitchen is interrupted by a voice upstairs asking him what time it is. By the time he opens the fridge door he has forgotten what he was looking for in the first place.

3 Narrative methods that you may have noticed include: a character is created; there is a sense of place; there is a chronology to the story; there is a plot of sorts; there is speech, some of which is attributed (his) and some of which is not (the voice upstairs); there is thought. There is also the expectation that the reader will fill in the gaps (literal gaps here between the images) to create a continuous plot and narrative.

Commentary on Activity 3

1 We now find out that the voice upstairs belongs to a woman – we might assume she is the man's wife or partner. She is drawing something, which might be a comic strip, but we do not get close enough to see. We find out that it is 1.15 at night, not during the day. From the look on her face she might have asked about the time because she is bored.

2 The most obvious crucial difference is that this time the story is drawn from her point of view, and given that she is not the main participant, we cannot make up a plot from this in the way we could before. We can only see what she sees, which is not much.

Commentary on Activity 6

1 Some aspects of the plot are clear, others less so. The narrator of the poem has had an illicit affair with a man who has been killed. The narrator blames her sister Maude for informing about the affair, and hints that Maude may have betrayed her sister through sexual jealousy. Among various hints and possibilities brought about by words like 'may' and 'if', the final lines are certain – Maude will go to hell for what she has done.

2 The poem is told entirely from the point of view of the narrator. Some or even all of the poem is spoken directly to Maude, which accounts for the uncertainties the reader faces; while they both know, within their fictional world, the details of what happened and who they are, we as readers are less certain. It is tempting to believe everything you are told by the main narrative voice, as they are in control of the story, but it is possible for narrators to tell only part of the story, and for what they say to be in various ways unreliable.

3 Because we only hear from the (unnamed) narrator, lots of voices are absent, most especially that of sister Maude, the father/mother and the dead lover. The implication is that Maude did what she did out of jealousy and spite – but the narrator would say that, wouldn't she?

4 A very different story about duty, morality, family shame, Victorian moral customs, and so on, could be told.

5 Thinking about other ways of telling the story highlights how important it can be to consider point of view. We can never, in one sense, get the 'whole story', only a version – and that can set us thinking about other possible ways of seeing what happens both in life and in stories. Re-creative writing of literary texts can stem from this line of thought.

Commentary on Activity 7

1 Pronouns always tell you a lot about narrative point of view. In this poem the dominant pronouns belong to the first person – 'I' and 'me'. The narrative voice that speaks the poem refers to the people who have rejected him with the pronoun 'they', which puts a distance between him and his opponents. However, when the narrator says, 'And you see my harvest', who is being referred to as 'you'? Is it another person within the fictional story being told, or is it more a sort of 'you as reader'?

There are, though, two places where it can be argued that the narrative is not in the first person – these are the title and the subtitle. We cannot be sure, of course, but if the two titles are narrated by a different source than the rest of the poem, then they contain more potential significance: they indicate what we are meant to think about the story we are about to be told. If, on the other hand, they are narrated by the same voice as the poem, then they are just part of his version of events.

2 Because the narrative of the poem itself is in the first person, Browning is able to create considerable ambiguity by his character hinting at events, without giving them the objective detail that would come with a third-person narrative. These hints and ambiguities will have allowed you to give various other interpretations when you have creatively reconstructed the narrative in question 2.

Summary

In this chapter you have considered aspects of point of view, and seen how words to describe point of view are also used to describe ideological perspectives. This means that thinking about where the story is coming from, whose views are allowed to dominate and whether we accept/approve of these views, is a vital part of the reading process.

7 Destination

This chapter:

- Looks at different aspects of narrative in order to consider the narrative as a whole.
- Explains that all parts of the narrative process contribute to the overall effects and meanings of the story being told.

This chapter looks at aspects of narrative in a more holistic way, drawing together the different aspects you have studied in earlier chapters, to consider the narrative as a whole. In the real world our experiences can seem quite random, shapeless, without any overarching point or meaning. In the fictional world of stories, though, there is usually a greater sense of wholeness and completion.

Reading as a journey

As we have worked our way through different ways of looking at aspects of narrative, we have noticed metaphors that often derive from visual sources, such as point of view, perspective, and so on. In this chapter, the metaphor changes to one involving a journey of discovery and exploration. We have explored aspects of narrative in the texts we are studying, and looked at how various methods are used – but where does it get us in the end? What have we ultimately found out about the text? What interpretations can be made from what we have seen? What is our destination?

Put another way, much can be gained and enjoyed from looking at how texts work in terms of their narratives, but if we then stop at that point, it is rather like giving up on a journey before you actually get anywhere important. We need to come to some wider conclusions based on what we have seen in detail along the way. In terms of studying AS Level English Literature you need to consider the following:

- What have I seen about the methods used and how does this help me come to an interpretation?
- Is there contextual material worth considering in helping me come to an interpretation?
- Are different interpretations now possible? Is one more convincing than another?

In other words – and this time using the official language of the Assessment Objectives – having done the exploratory work, which has looked in detail at the ways in which form, structure and language shape meanings in literary texts (AO2), you will now broaden your horizons by showing your understanding of the significance and influence of some of the contexts in which literary texts are written and received (AO4) through making connections and comparisons between different literary texts, informed by possible interpretations of other readers (AO3). In order to do this well you will need to write informed and relevant responses to literary texts, using appropriate terminology and concepts, and coherent, accurate written expression (AO1).

Bringing all four Assessment Objectives together in this way, you will be illustrating that Unit 1 is a comprehensive unit that covers all the main elements of AS Level study of English Literature. You have begun with the analysis of textual detail before moving on to look at wider implications.

Link

See the Introduction to this book for more on the Assessment Objectives.

Remember

The word 'text' refers to a whole text, which in terms of poetry may be a long single poem or a collection of shorter ones.

Wider implications

What exactly are these wider implications, as suggested by AOs 3 and 4? They can be subdivided into the following categories:

- If you are looking at part of a text, what is its relationship with the whole text? What is its relationship with the other texts being studied? What common ground can be found?
- What is the relationship between the opening of the text and its closure? How do these two vital parts of the text relate to each other?
- Are there relevant ideas that arise out of the writer's life and times that may be helpful when considering the text? These can be called contexts of production.
- Are there relevant ideas that arise out of contemporary ideas and situations that may affect the way the text can be read? These can be called contexts of reception.
- Can different critical methods be applied to the text? What ambiguities and uncertainties arise from studying it? Can these ambiguities be seen positively?

Examination questions

Clearly, how the examination questions are worded will depend in part on the actual texts you are studying; there will be four in total: two novels and two poetry texts. Section A of the examination will focus on single texts, while Section B will ask you to write about three others. The following sample questions show you how the paper is designed: as with all sample questions, try to see beyond the set texts themselves into a broader scheme of enquiry.

Link

See the Introduction for more detail on the examination requirements.

In Section A you will write about one set text, so there will be considerable choice available to you.

Examples of questions from Section A

1 Poetry: Robert Browning, named poems

(i) Write about the ways Browning tells the story of the Pied Piper of Hamelin in Chapter VII (7) of the poem.

(ii) *The Pied Piper of Hamelin* is subtitled 'A Child's Story'. Is it simply a child's story?

2 Novel: Khaled Hosseini, *The Kite Runner*

(i) Write about the ways Hosseini opens the story in Chapter 1.

(ii) Some readers see the title *The Kite Runner* as representing a journey. What meanings can you find in the title of the text?

In Section B the questions are more general, and although there is some choice, there will be less than in Section A.

Examples of questions from Section B

1. Write about the importance of places in the telling of the stories in three texts that you have studied.
2. Write about some of the ways in which characters have been created in the three texts you have studied.

AQA Examiner's tip

It is always useful to have a working knowledge of what your examination paper will be like. Bear in mind, though, that examination questions are not written to absolute formulae, and ultimately your job is to answer the question exactly as required.

The Patriot

In a book such as this one it is often necessary to look at parts of texts for illustrative purposes. The longer study of complete texts needs to be done by you in the light of what this book is saying. To consider how the idea of destination works we will use the single poem *The Patriot*, which we have already looked at in previous chapters.

The Patriot
An Old Story

I

It was roses, roses, all the way,
  With myrtle mixed in my path like mad;
The house-roofs seemed to heave and sway,
  The church-spires flamed, such flags they had,
A year ago on this very day.

II

The air broke into a mist with bells,
  The old walls rocked with the crowd and cries.
Had I said, 'Good folk, mere noise repels --
  But give me your sun from yonder skies!'
They had answered 'And afterward, what else?'

III

Alack, it was I who leaped at the sun
  To give it my loving friends to keep!
Naught man could do, have I left undone:
  And you see my harvest, what I reap
This very day, now a year is run.

IV

There's nobody on the house-tops now --
  Just a palsied few at the windows set;
For the best of the sight is, all allow,
  At the Shambles' Gate – or, better yet,
By the very scaffold's foot, I trow.

V

I go in the rain, and, more than needs,
  A rope cuts both my wrists behind;
And I think, by the feel, my forehead bleeds
  For they fling, whoever has a mind,
Stones at me for my year's misdeeds.

VI

Thus I entered, and thus I go!
  In triumphs, people have dropped down dead.
'Paid by the world, what dost thou owe
  Me?' – God might question; now instead,
'Tis God shall repay: I am safer so.

Robert Browning, 1985

So far we have found out the following by looking at some of the building blocks of narrative.

Setting (places)

There are a few details about the place. It seems to be a walled town or even a city, given that we are told there are 'church-spires' in the plural. The reference to 'house-roofs' might imply a place of some grandeur. Not even the country is specified.

Time and sequence

In terms of actual historical time there are few clues. The subtitle, which could suggest that the story is set in the distant past, is subtly ambiguous. Is this an old story because it is historical, or is it an old story because it is one told many times, with as much reference to now as to any other time?

There is, though, a clear and precise timescale to the action of the poem. The voice narrating the poem compares his public reception a year ago with his reception now. The preciseness of the time here, exactly a year, helps to highlight the difference between then and now.

Is it the narrator who has changed, or the public? Although he says he has committed 'misdeeds', this may be ironic – it could be how the public perceives what he has done.

Characters and characterisation

There is the patriot himself who narrates the poem, and the people of the city. The patriot has a label: he is 'The Patriot', but has no name. The people of the city are described a year ago, when they are enthusiastic about what The Patriot is doing, but now they are absent, waiting offstage somewhere else to see him hanged. Only 'a palsied few' remain in the town itself, presumably because they cannot move.

Voices

The dominant voice is that of The Patriot, who sounds as though he is making a final speech before his execution. The voice is resigned and thoughtful rather than aggressive and angry, which presumably it could be, given his treatment.

There is one other brief piece of reported speech, the collective 'cries' of the people celebrating his return. There are also some short pieces of direct speech that *might have been* spoken. In the first instance he pretends to ask for the impossible and the grateful crowd are willing to give him anything. The second imaginary piece of direct speech involves God, who makes the moral point that earthly riches are nothing compared with eternal ones.

Point of view

In this poem the dominant pronouns belong to the first person – 'I' and 'me'. There are, though, two places where it can be argued that the narrative is not in the first person – these are the title and the subtitle.

Because the narrative of the poem itself is in the first person, Browning is able to create considerable ambiguity by his character hinting at events, without giving them the objective detail that would come with a third-person narrative.

These reminders should help us as we now widen our consideration by looking at aspects of context and interpretation. We will begin by looking at some issues to do with key aspects of the text itself.

Activity 1

This poem has both a title, *The Patriot*, and a subtitle, 'An Old Story'. Both these phrases carry possible cultural associations; in other words, when you read them, you may be aware that they have various possible meanings, both for you and for others.

Working in a group if possible, and using reference works such as a dictionary and a dictionary of quotations, make a list of your initial responses to these titles.

Commentary on Activity 1

The main title uses the definite article 'The', whereas the subtitle uses the indefinite article 'An'. This suggests that the poem is about someone specific (*the* patriot) on the one hand and yet tells one of a number of stories (*an* old story) on the other.

The word 'patriot' derives originally from the Greek word *patrios*, meaning 'of one's father'. A patriot, then, loves the fatherland, but for many readers, certainly within British culture, to be a patriot is not necessarily a good thing. Dr Johnson famously wrote that 'Patriotism is the last refuge of a scoundrel'. There is a long tradition in British culture of the word being used to suggest either foolishness or cunning – as bald a title as *The Patriot* hints that this poem is not going to end happily.

Did you know?

Dr (Samuel) Johnson (1709–84) wrote the first standard dictionary of the English language, which took him eight years to complete and was first published in 1755.

As we have already seen when considering aspects of time in the poem, 'An Old Story' can be read in different ways. The phrase could refer to the fact that this is a poem set in past times, or it could suggest that it is an old story because it is telling the same old story – in other words, there have been many such stories and they all turn out the same.

Activity 2

Make a list of what Browning allows you to find out about the actions of the narrator of the poem and then make a list of what you do not know – and what, if you did, would make the poem more straightforward in its meaning.

Commentary on Activity 2

What we find out

A year ago he was a hero.
He received a rapturous reception.
He tried to help his friends.
He is now going to the scaffold.
Only a few watch now.

What we are not told

What he had done to be so popular.
Where the action is set.
In what time the action is set.
What he has done in the intervening year.
Why he is being executed.

In many ways what we are not told makes the more interesting list. By being so inexact about many of the core things that make up the narrative, Browning is deliberately making us look beyond the specifics of a story and inviting us to consider wider significances.

So one possible reading is that the patriot in this poem is presented as both wise and foolish. When describing the entry to the city, he provides an imaginary conversation with the crowd ('Had I said'). He knows that if he had asked for the sun, they would have offered it and more – and yet it would have been an impossible thing to ask for. He knows that the crowd is fickle, and will promise anything because they are swept up in the occasion

Activity 3

Look at the final verse of the poem. What sort of conclusion does it give to the poem? Compare this ending to way that the poem begins.

Key terms

End-stopped: a line of poetry where a grammatical unit of sense, usually a sentence, is completed at the end of a line.

in a way that he was not. And yet for 'my loving friends', friends whom he knows will be disloyal, he 'leaped at the sun' and ruined everything.

Even as he walks to the scaffold he is detached enough to know where the best views of hanging are. His line 'Thus I entered and thus I go' is resigned rather than bitter, the resignation stressed by the way Browning uses repetition in both vocabulary and syntax.

He is presented, then, as someone who now knows the world and the people in it.

Commentary on Activity 3

The opening line of the poem 'It was roses, roses, all the way' is exceptionally rhythmic, with its uncomplicated vocabulary and its repetition. By the end of the poem, though, things are a good deal more complicated. The verse begins with two **end-stopped** lines, 'Thus I entered and thus I go!' followed by, 'In triumphs, people have dropped down dead'. Both lines carry the suggestion of someone resigned to his fate, aware that triumph and death are always close. The last three lines, however, are much more enigmatic, and the verse form emphasises this, with its more fractured use of lines.

There is a sustained metaphor of paying, owing, repaying that runs through the last three lines, but its precise meaning seems elusive. If the patriot is 'safer', safer than what? Safer in the hands of God than men?

Contexts of production

While all texts have to be read within a contextual framework – there can be no such thing as a text existing in a world of its own – how much context you apply to your answers, and what sort of context, involves making careful, thoughtful choices. This poem does not appear to have any connection to Browning's own personal experience, for example, so there is no real point in going into authorial biography to help us.

However, there are some more literary contexts to do with the time of writing that might help when considering the poem as a whole.

Dramatic monologues

Browning is renowned for his writing of dramatic monologues. Dramatic monologues are narrated by a single voice, often of a central character in a story. As we have already seen, though, first-person narratives are subjective, so the reader has to work out that there is more to the story than the speaking voice knows or is willing to acknowledge.

This information is useful for us here up to a point, in that as readers we certainly have to work hard to find meanings because so much vital information is missing. It would be hard, though, to say that this poem is 'dramatic', because the narrator does not appear to be talking to anyone else within the world of the poem.

Victorian poetry

Victorian poetry is sometimes seen as rather sentimental, milking emotion out of stories of lost love and medieval romance. There is certainly a medieval feel to the setting of this poem, albeit in general terms. So here we have two historical strands: a Victorian text, with its contexts of Victorian times, is itself representing an even earlier age.

On the other hand, the poem is marked by surprisingly little emotion – the narrator seems to be completely resigned to his fate, and although there are expressions of regret they are not sentimentally overemphasised.

So what we can see here is that contexts of production need to be evaluated carefully and always measured against the core text itself. For our purposes, both here and in an examination, we are concerned with this poem, not with other poems by Browning or indeed with other poems written when Browning was alive.

Contexts of reception

It was noted above that there were two historical strands when looking at contexts of production. But if we now consider contexts of reception there is another obvious question to ask: why are we studying a poem written over 150 years ago? Is it just interesting as an old text, or are we studying it because it says something to us now, because in a sense it has outgrown its original contexts and can now be seen to work within new contextual frameworks? Or put another way, although we considered that the text could be looked at through thinking about contexts at the time of production, surely what has happened after the text was written, and indeed what is happening now, also need to be considered?

Figure 7.1 *A recruitment poster from World War One*

When talking about historical contexts, especially with texts that are 'old', there is an inevitable, and not always very helpful, tendency to generalise: to say that all Elizabethans were racist/sexist/homophobic, and so on, is neither helpful nor true. When looking at contemporary contexts, in the circumstances that affect our readings in the here and now, we can be much more specific about the contexts we are applying, and much more receptive to views other than our own.

The 20th century and the first years of the 21st century have seen warfare, sometimes on a mass scale, with millions involved in worldwide conflict, and sometimes on a smaller scale, yet still with horror and suffering. Whether it be to recruit new forces to replace the dead, or to keep public opinion in favour of a war that on television looks awful, countries and their politicians have needed to ensure that there is public support for war. One way in which they have done this is to invoke notions of patriotism: our country is right and good, the enemy is wrong and evil.

We are all familiar with images of mass propaganda and recruitment from World War One, for example. In more recent times there have been wars that have been highly controversial, with many objectors claiming that they should not be fought at all. In these wars in particular, when public opinion is much more divided, notions of patriotism are invoked both by those who support the cause and by those who deny it.

The problem with notions of rightness and goodness, wrong and evil, is that they are shifting terms. What happens when the war is over, when forms of peace are made? What do we do with those who fought for the cause and who survived, but who may be injured or embarrassing to have around for various reasons?

Activity 4

Now considering the poem overall, and the contextual material presented on the previous pages, what ideas would you say are most important in the poem *The Patriot*? What in the end is the poem saying? Why should we still read it now?

Evidence would suggest that those whom the Americans call 'vets' (veterans) are not always welcomed, back. They find it difficult to settle, they behave in unorthodox ways, they have lived through incredible stress. Is that what this poem is about – the universally fickle way in which societies treat their heroes?

Commentary on Activity 4

What we are ideally doing in answering this question is incorporating our work on narrative with a sense of wider context. We have noticed much that is absent here that we might expect to find in a story: details of time and place, motivation of character, and so on. This, while not necessarily appealing to everyone, can be justified by showing that in deliberately not being specific, Browning is being universal. He is talking about a number of issues that seem to have universal meanings. These could include:

- the briefness of success and popularity
- the manipulation of mass groups
- the fickle ways in which heroes are first loved and then ignored
- that with celebrity can come excess
- that patriotism is a shifting concept
- that heroes become villains when the cause is finished.

The last bullet point seems to resonate the most. It is possible in the same American city, for example, to see heroic receptions for soldiers returning from Iraq and street beggars who fought in Vietnam. What Browning is saying, it seems, is that there will be times when your country needs you, followed by times when it does not.

You may notice in the paragraph above that the most favoured issue has been given as a personal preference. There often comes a point in weighing up different interpretations when you want to give your own preferred reading, while acknowledging that there are others. At this point in your answer it is fully acceptable to refer to yourself as 'I/me'.

Conclusion

The word 'narrative' has its origins in the Greek word for knowledge. Ultimately, then, looking at narrative involves looking at knowledge. Put this another way and you can ask yourself the following questions, taking the idea of 'knowing' here in its broadest sense. For any text, at any point in the text, you can ask:

- Who knows what?
- When do/did they know it?
- How do they know it?

But there is one further point to make here. Because this is literature, and so representational, we are not dealing with the real world, we are dealing with a fictional world designed for readers. So now we can slightly reconfigure the questions above and also ask of any text at any point:

- What does the reader know?
- When does/did the reader find this out?
- How did they find it out?

Bear these questions in mind and they will prove invaluable as you tackle questions in the examination.

8 Preparing for the examination

This chapter:

- Enables you to be well prepared for your examination.

AQA Examiner's tip

Always make sure that your preparation and revision involve a specific task, with a specific amount of time allocated and a clear end result. Revision involves looking over something you have done already, which is important, but it is equally important to do something new, to prepare some thoughts and ideas on topics that have not been covered so far.

Link

See the Introduction to this book for an outline of the examination requirements.

AQA Examiner's tip

Always make sure that your focused stint of work leaves you better informed about the key topic – in this case narrative – than you were before you started. Also make sure that you have a written record of what you have prepared so that you can glance over it in the final few days before the examination.

This short final chapter in this unit gives you some hints on final preparation for your AS Level English Literature examination – some of which apply to all your examinations, whatever the subject. These hints are based on the assumption that you have worked hard up to this point and that you have read the texts and know them well.

Using this book

One obvious way of preparing for the examination is to use this book. Take each chapter in turn and apply its focus to the actual set texts you are studying.

You might also, along with your teacher, think of some ways of focusing more specifically on some of the four texts you have studied for this unit. Here are some points to consider, bearing in mind that this is an open-book examination:

- This unit is organised under the title 'Aspects of Narrative'. This means that you do not need to know everything there is to know about these texts: your starting point for revision will be ideas about narrative.
- Remember that in Section A of the examination you will be required to write in some detail on one of the four texts. Which text will it be? How many of the four do you intend to prepare in this way?
- Remember that in Section B you will need to write in a much more general way about the three other texts you have studied (i.e. not including the one you have used in Section A). Do you have a good overview of them, and can you find significant parts of them without delay?
- What use do you expect to make of the open-book facility? Section A will ask you to look at a specific section of a text, but you will not necessarily have time to read it all. How well do you know your text so that a skim reading will suffice?

Short answers

Both parts of Section A involve short answers – you will have about half an hour for each one. Short answers differ from essays in that you do not need to provide introductions and conclusions. You simply get on and answer the question directly.

You will need to practise this sort of writing. The odd-numbered part of your question in Section A will always ask a variant of the question, 'How does the author tell the story in this part of the text?' It makes sense, therefore, to highlight early in your answer exactly what part of the story is being told at this point. Do not waste time re-telling the story; but engaging initially and briefly with the story in that section will lead you into talking relevantly about narrative.

So if asked the question 'How does Fitzgerald tell the story in Chapter 1 of *The Great Gatsby*?' you might begin your answer with something like:

> Here Fitzgerald establishes a number of things. We are introduced to Nick Carroway through his own voice and to the social world he and the novel move in – a rich but rather empty world of rumour

> and dishonesty. We are also given occasional references to Gatsby, until finally we see him briefly and mysteriously from a distance.

In writing this you have given a brief overview of the opening chapter's content and also its method. Now you can now go on to look in detail at establishment, Carroway as narrator, place and time, the delayed introduction of Gatsby, and so on.

One way to revise effectively would be to practise this method on other chapters, other poems, and so on.

The essay

In Section B you will be writing an essay on an aspect of narrative across three texts. What, in outline, will this involve?

- You will need to write a short introduction, giving an overview of the topic as it affects your chosen texts.
- You will need to provide some evidence from each of the three texts, but with limited time you cannot be expected to say everything.
- You will need to write approximately the same amount on each text, but there is no rule that says they have to be exactly equal.
- You will need to tie your ideas together at the end with a brief conclusion.

You will need to practise this sort of writing.

AQA Examiner's tip

At some points in your preparation programme, actually write some sample answers and show them to your teacher for feedback and guidance.

Learning to quote and refer

How are you going to prepare for giving textual evidence? One form of evidence is direct quotation.

Quotation can involve quoting chunks of text, but it can also involve integrating words or phrases into your own syntax. So while you could quote from *The Patriot* by writing:

> Browning begins his poem with his narrator describing past glories:
> 'It was roses, roses, all the way,
> With myrtle mixed in my path like mad'

You could also write:

> In his opening lines Browning's references to 'roses' and 'myrtle' placed in the patriot's 'path like mad' help to create an initial mood of celebration.

The second method is often better, as it lets you get on with your argument while at the same time showing that you know the text well. Practise this method of quoting and you will soon find that you become adept at it.

Equally effective, though, can be reference, especially when you are writing about a novel. Reference is when you show awareness of an event, a character, a place, and so on, by referring to it with knowledge rather than using the exact words the author uses. Keeping for the moment to the lines above, if you refer to them you would write something like:

> Browning's references to flowers being thrown in the path of the patriot give an immediate sense of celebration.

To summarise, here is a list of points to bear in mind when you are using quotation and reference:

- You should support your arguments with frequent and relevant textual evidence.
- Quotations should be brief.
- Quotations should be accurate.
- The best quotations are embedded in your own sentences.
- Reference to the text can also help to give evidence: close references can often work better than quotation.
- Quotations and references should never stand alone: they should be used in support of specific points you are making.

So how much learning do you need to do for an open-book examination? Probably more than you might imagine. If you have to stop at every point to check even the smallest detail, you will lose momentum and continuity. In the end you need to be able to refer to the texts with appropriate detail depending on the question. Only practice in answering such questions will show you how much you really need to do.

The examination itself

It is common among students to talk of dreading examinations, but this can sometimes be overplayed. Examinations are a fact of the system we are all in, so we might as well make the most of them.

If you are well prepared then examinations should be seen, in part anyway, as a chance to show what you know. And the nature of English Literature as a subject also means you should find some space in your head to think in the examination itself.

It is never really appropriate to say 'good luck' to someone before an examination, because examinations are not about luck. They are about being well prepared in advance, and thoughtful on the day itself.

Hint

As a general rule, short, concentrated bursts of work followed by periods of relaxation are much better than long stretches of time that deliver little in terms of end product.

AQA Examiner's tip

The very highest marks usually go to students who show that they are thinking about the topic rather than repeating what they have said before. Amidst all the pressure of the event itself, try to find time to think clearly and say exactly what you want to say.

2 Dramatic Genres: Aspects of Comedy

Introduction to Unit 2

This chapter:

- Introduces Unit 2, Dramatic Genres: Aspects of Comedy.
- Considers some general ideas about the study of your coursework texts.
- Specifies what you need to submit for your coursework.

'Comedy' is a complex form of theatre, and in this unit you will explore several aspects of comedy that will lead into your coursework. The specification asks for the compulsory study of at least one Shakespeare play, so it should come as no surprise that the works of William Shakespeare are seen as central to our understanding of comedy. In addition to your Shakespeare play you will also study another play that falls into the comedy genre. The range of plays that could be chosen for this study is wide and varied, with many time periods and sub-genres of plays available. However, the play you will study will ordinarily be chosen for you by your teacher. Because the range of plays is so wide it is important that you do not skip activities in this book or texts that you are not studying, since all the activities will help you develop your understanding and skills that you can apply to your own coursework texts.

Please note that the Shakespearean extracts that support the activities in chapters 10–13 are not provided in the back of this book. You will need to have access to a copy of the relevant play to complete these activities.

Reading and studying plays

Drama: a difficult genre

When dealing with plays, you should remember that the texts you are reading were not written to be read, but to be performed. Much can be learned by reading the words on the page, but that is not the entire text. Drama texts consist not only of language, but also of visual aspects, including set, movement and sound. While English Literature focuses on the written text, you should be aware of these other aspects and of the different interpretations of the text that these can give. For example, the same words might be spoken by an actor using different facial expressions to give a different meaning, or the atmosphere of a play might be altered significantly by the amount of light on the stage. A comedy might once have been imagined in a particular era, but could be re-staged in a new one, and this will have an impact on the way we respond to it. Comedies are often staged to make them more relevant to present-day audiences. Your job is to be aware of the different interpretations they could create.

Active reading

As with Unit 1, it is important that you read each text at least once to get an overview of the plot. When you have chosen a title for your coursework, you will find it beneficial to read your text through again, focusing specifically on the question you have chosen. As you go along, make notes of key moments, quotations and points you could use in your work. Since you will be able to use your notes when writing your coursework, these notes will form the basis of your plans. It will be much easier to spot important quotations when you are reading through your text than to search through the whole text looking for something relevant. Some students find that keeping a reading journal is useful. This might be a notebook or folder in which you write down your observations. Other readers find it helpful to place sticky notes in the text to mark key moments.

With the genre here being drama, you will benefit much from actively reading and performing these works in your classroom. Even if you do not consider yourself a great performer, it is often beneficial to organise or direct a scene from a comedy. Other students in your class may be happier to act. Often this will give you much greater insight into how the drama operates, and may actually open your eyes to some of the comedy, which might not come across if it is studied without any performance. It will also allow you to better understand what the actors performing the characters have to do and what the intentions of the dramatist were in constructing the text.

Assessment of Unit 2

This unit will be assessed by the production of a coursework portfolio of two pieces of work:

1 A study of an aspect of the comic genre with regard to a Shakespeare play (1,200–1,500 words).
2 A study of an aspect of the comic genre with regard to another play (1,200–1,500 words).

One of the two pieces can be in the form of a creative (or, more accurately, a re-creative) exercise – you will look at this in more detail in Chapter 16. At the end of each of Chapters 9–15 we offer you and your teacher some suggestions for coursework tasks, related to what you have studied in that chapter.

The examination board offers your teacher the opportunity to consult with an adviser about the suitability of your coursework tasks. This may help sharpen your chosen task and therefore make for a better essay.

Summary

This chapter has introduced you to some key features of Unit 2 and looked at some of the most important questions which arise when preparing for your study of the texts themselves.

9 Introducing comedy

This chapter:

- Introduces comedy as a literary genre.
- Considers a range of examples of other forms of comedy.
- Sets out the differences between literary comedy and popular (everyday) forms of comedy.

Key terms

Disorder: inversion (turning upside down) of the normal order in a society.

Charade: an absurd pretence.

Folly: a foolish act.

Caricature: an exaggerated portrayal of a person or type of person for comic effect.

Figure 9.1 *The masks of Tragedy and Comedy*

What is comedy?

An easy definition might be to say that comedy is drama that makes us laugh. However, we need to understand why it makes us laugh. Usually, it is because it is about people caught in difficult situations that we find funny. We know that the situation they are in will most likely be resolved, but we enjoy seeing how they cope with the difficulties. As an audience, we put ourselves in their place and wonder what we would do in the same situation. In early and traditional dramatic comedies (like those written by William Shakespeare), the play usually ends with a marriage or similar celebratory event, sometimes accompanied by music and dance. Marriage is important because it suggests that a harmony has been reached and that the marriage might result in children for the future, so that society can continue to develop and grow.

Very often at the heart of a comedy is **disorder**. Disorder is an inversion of the normal order so that everything in the society moves out of harmony. This disorder can be funny and amusing, but it can also be threatening and dangerous. Only when this is overcome can things return to normality. We may go further and argue that comedies are not just about laughter. At the centre of them is a key premise suggesting that human life and experience are actually a **charade** and that whenever civilisation reaches a point of order, human beings seemingly have a natural ability to be foolish and act stupidly. This characteristic is called **folly**.

You may be under the impression that comic dramatists might write comedy to help human beings try to change their behaviour. Stand-up comedians often do this in live performances to expose how silly people are. However, over time many dramatists have shown that actually the human race is unlikely to change, and that human weakness will continue.

Comedy is one of the oldest forms of drama. You are probably aware of the two masks representing drama: Tragedy and Comedy. While tragedies show over and over again that people can face unalterable problems, comedies highlight that human beings are in fact ridiculous and cannot change. Comedies, therefore, often confirm our view of the world.

Characteristics of dramatic comedy

We might expect to see the following characteristics in dramatic comedy:

- Love is often a motivating force, and occasionally when people are in love or infatuated with someone else, they do foolish things.
- Comedy shows that people do face difficult situations and serious problems, but also that human beings have a tendency to take themselves too seriously.
- Some dramatic comedy intends to poke fun at the folly of human beings by using **caricature**.
- Human endeavour is often seen as being pretentious and ludicrous, and therefore it should be exposed as foolish.

- Comedies often expose the foolishness of society's customs and manners or an era's rules and laws. Characters very often say one thing about these customs and rules but undermine them with their own behaviour.
- Exaggerations of stereotypes are often used.
- Sometimes characters are placed in bizarre and absurd situations that they are unable to escape from. This reflects how we all feel sometimes – that the order of the world is a veneer that can easily be removed.
- The Seven Deadly Sins (in particular pride, lust and greed) are all prime targets for satire within comic writing.

Comedy and dramatic structure

All dramatic comedies have the same basic structure to them. This is a tripartite structure of exposition, complication and resolution. The exposition prepares the audience for what will happen, probably by showing us some alteration in the lives of the characters. The complication stage occurs when the dramatist develops the problems that the characters face. Usually as part of the complication, a sense of disorder and anarchy prevails, often resulting in the lives of the characters being 'turned upside down'. Occasionally, this can result in the wrong pair of lovers being placed together, confusions in identity or sexuality, and people generally getting hold of the 'wrong end of the stick'. Disguise, foreign or new locations and mishearing key information all contribute to this disorder. At the end of the play the complications and disorder are resolved and a new order is generated. The main characters usually come to realise their mistakes and then try to deal with the new situation.

AQA Examiner's tip

For the purposes of your coursework we see dramatic comedies as purely that. Bear in mind that Unit 2 is called Dramatic Genres, so the focus is on drama. However, within that we are studying Aspects of Comedy. We do not see Dramatic Genres as an opportunity for you to explore, for example, stand-up comedy, as that is an entirely separate genre. Our main view of Dramatic Genres: Aspects of Comedy is that you will be studying plays. There will, however, be occasions when the television genre does overlap with dramatic genres.

No laughing matter: comedies in context

One important thing to say about comedy is that it is often serious. There are moments in everyone's life when absurd or puzzling things happen that we have to cope with. We know that events in life do not always go according to plan. Comedy understands this and uses these difficulties to show us the folly of human beings and their behaviour. This is its very serious intent. By laughing at the misfortunes of other characters on stage, we contemplate our own weaknesses and realise we might do exactly the same thing.

This same pattern is found in all dramatic comedies. What makes a comedy interesting is how the dramatist finds a new or novel way of developing this structure. Thus the huge complexities of human beings' experiences are considered within what is actually a very tightly organised format. If you bear in mind this same order, you can more easily spot what makes a comedy so individual and innovative.

One important way of thinking about comedies is to know how they are different from tragedies. Generally, in comedies the complications are eventually resolved, but in tragedies the complications are not resolved, usually resulting in the death of one or more characters. In tragedies the resolution can only come after the death of key characters. Some comedies come very close to being tragedies, and we will explore some of these in this unit.

Activity 1

Working with a partner, write down a list of all the events, plays, stories, films, songs, television programmes and computer games you can think of that involve aspects of comedy. Share some of these with others in your class and answer the following questions:

- What common features can you identify?
- What makes the storylines particularly comic?
- What kinds of comedy appeal most to young people?

There is no commentary on this activity.

Some examples of comedies

Plays

In Activity 1, you and your partner have probably developed a long list of texts that involve aspects of comedy. You will have instantly thought of plays that you have read or heard of before, especially the comedies by William Shakespeare such as *A Midsummer Night's Dream*, *Twelfth Night*, *As You Like It*, *Much Ado About Nothing* and *The Comedy of Errors*. There may be other Shakespeare plays you have heard of that have comic elements, but that seem to have more serious subject matter. These might include *The Merchant of Venice* and *Measure for Measure*. These are often known as the dark comedies or are labelled **tragi-comedies**. You may also have heard of a few more modern comedies, such *The Importance of Being Earnest* by Oscar Wilde and Samuel Beckett's *Waiting for Godot*. The British playwrights Alan Ayckbourn and Alan Bennett have also written a number of comedies. Although some plays by writers such as Harold Pinter, Caryl Churchill and Jez Butterworth are serious dramas, they also have many comic ingredients.

Key terms

Tragi-comedies: comedies that have more serious subject matter.

Motif: a recurring element in a story that has symbolic significance.

Protagonist: in dramatic terms, this refers to the first major character who offers a particular view.

Antagonist: this refers to the second character, who usually disagrees in some way with the protagonist. Some comic dramas also have a third actor – the tritagonist.

Repartee: the ability to make witty replies and remarks. It is often a key component of both Shakespearean and Restoration comedy.

Parody: a comic or grotesque imitation of another text.

Television programmes and computer games

More likely, though, you will have thought of texts that feature lots of mix-ups and confusion surrounding the main characters. Television and radio soap operas such as *Coronation Street*, *Eastenders* and *The Archers* very often incorporate comic elements into their storylines. There has also been a range of classic television comedy produced in Britain, including *Hancock's Half Hour*, *Dad's Army*, *Fawlty Towers*, *Only Fools and Horses*, *Last of the Summer Wine*, *Blackadder*, *Little Britain* and *The Office*. Many computer games use comic sequences, such as *The Sims*, *Monkey Island* and *Crash Bandicoot*. Several are also based on comic television programmes and films.

Films

Film is a particularly rich area to consider since many plots use **motifs** and ideas loosely from the comic genre. The early films of comedians such as Charlie Chaplin or Harold Lloyd may come to mind, but as film has developed through the 20th and 21st centuries, it has borrowed conventions from dramatic comedy.

An established classic contemporary film comedy is *Anchorman* (2004), which is a tongue-in-cheek take on the 1970s American news format. In the film, the actor Will Ferrell plays Ron Burgundy, the television station's anchorman. Burgundy is the drama's **protagonist** and he clashes with Veronica Corningstone (played by Christina Applegate). Corningstone is the **antagonist** here and although initially they disagree, eventually they fall in love. There are lots of absurd and difficult situations in which the characters become embroiled, but they are able to cope with events by using wit and **repartee**. These are typical aspects of the comic genre.

Did you know?

Another useful film to consider is *Paul* (2011), a buddy road-trip movie that satirises any aspects of science fiction and road-trip movies with in-jokes and spoof sequences. In some senses *Paul* is a **parody** of other science-fiction films, such as *Close Encounters of the Third Kind*.

Other popular comedies of recent years have included *Hot Fuzz*, *Shaun of the Dead*, *The Hangover*, *Mr Bean*, *Ali G Indahouse*, *Borat: Cultural Learnings of America for Make Benefit Glorious Nation of Kazakhstan*, *Tropic Thunder* and *Bruce Almighty*.

Very often comic films mix genres and re-work established plot-lines for new audiences. The comedy *She's the Man* (2006) was essentially a re-working of Shakespeare's *Twelfth Night*. Although comic films are amusing to watch, they very often have a more serious message to convey about what it means to be human. Very often comic films are about a coming-of-age moment when characters grow up or mature through events that occur.

The development of dramatic comedy

In the 5th century BCE, Greek writers wrote a number of comedies that seemed to establish some of the rules for comedies, influencing their long-term development in European culture. Indeed, the Greek word *κομος* (*komos*) means a **revel** or celebration. This revel was often led through the countryside. Early plays by writers like Aeschylus and Sophocles often featured satyrs (pagan gods with long ears generally depicted as being half-goat), who offered primitive stories in the same environment, usually deceiving or outwitting a god. They were probably very **pantomime**-like and were performed to offer a contrast to the more serious tragic dramas. One of the surviving comedies from this period is *The Frogs* by Aristophanes, which contains lots of dancing and satire. Aristophanes is considered the greatest of the Greek comic writers since his dramas featured a number of high-and-mighty characters who are made to look unimportant. His plays have storylines that actually feel quite modern: public figures were often ridiculed, similar to the way in which modern newspaper cartoonists draw politicians.

The critic F.L. Lucas (in *Greek Drama for the Modern Reader*) has summarised the values of these kinds of play:

1 Some character has a bright idea: a man thinks of stopping a war by flying to heaven on a dung-beetle, or a woman tries to stop it by organising a woman's sexual strike.
2 A **chorus**, sympathetic or hostile, enters.
3 There follows a debate about the proposal.
4 The chorus turns and addresses the audience directly.
5 A series of **farcical** episodes arises from putting the original idea into practice.
6 All ends in a scene of revelling, such as a feast for a wedding: a further relic of the primitive merry-making.

Commentary on Activity 2

It is clear that these values are still highly relevant when looking at later or contemporary comedy. Maybe you thought of films or television shows where a character has a mad-cap idea to change the world and make it a better place. A second character usually either supports or disagrees with them – this is a bit like the Greek dramatic chorus. A debate is set up in a comedy because we as the audience watch the development of events and have to decide whose side we are on. We are generally sympathetic to the mad-cap character, although we realise their idea may be foolish.

The chorus might turn to the audience directly. In some modern comedies this is direct address (used very well in BBC television's *Miranda*) and the farcical episodes are very characteristic of modern comedy (you may have thought of *Only Fools and Horses* or *Dad's Army*). It seems likely that these dramas emerged from periods in the year when rituals or celebrations happened, and weddings and feasts were important occasions. Lots of modern dramatic comedy ends with a feast or celebration.

AQA Examiner's tip

In order to understand the different aspects of comedy, keep a notebook and write down typical comic storylines from films, television and plays that you watch. Try to work out what structural elements they have in common.

AQA Examiner's tip

In order to write your coursework for AS English Literature you do not always need to refer back to older ideas about dramatic comedy, but it may be useful to have some awareness of the historical roots of the genre.

Activity 2

Although these values are from a long time ago, see if any of them can be applied to comedies you know well. What connections can you see? Discuss the six statements opposite with a partner and consider whether they are still relevant.

Key terms

Revel: a lively festival often incorporating dancing and disguise.

Pantomime: in modern culture, a play generally based on a fairy-tale or folk-tale, often performed around Christmas. In theatre, pantomime has a long tradition of a variety of styles.

Chorus: in Greek dramas, this was usually a number of performers who comment with a collective voice on the play's action. In later dramas, the chorus could be a solitary performer, who assists the audience with narration and understanding.

Farcical: a method of entertaining an audience that uses improbable situations and useless pretence.

Did you know?

Mummers' plays are a form of traditional folk drama found all over the islands of Britain. They were usually performed around the winter solstice, celebrating the turn of the year. They often have comic and farcical sequences and characters such as Father Christmas and St George.

Did you know?

Aristotle was born in 384 BCE in Chalcidice at the northern end of the Aegean Sea, and after studying for 20 years in Plato's Academy he eventually became the tutor of Alexander the Great.

Aristotle on comedy

The word 'comedy' is obviously connected to the Greek word *komoida*. Aristotle, a Greek philosopher, thought a lot about drama, and in particular tragedy and comedy. He wrote more extensively on tragedy, but he also understood comedy. In his main work on drama, *The Poetics*, he writes that comedy:

- is 'an imitation of inferior people' – by inferior people, Aristotle seems to mean 'normal' people (that is, not kings, gods or leaders, who often feature in tragedy)
- 'the laughable is a species of what is disgraceful' – we laugh when we witness the disgraceful behaviour of others – maybe behaviour that we ourselves would not do, but might like to do
- 'does not involve pain or destruction, for example a comic mask is ugly and distorted, but does not involve pain' – watching comedy does not involve 'pain', whereas it would seem that watching tragedy is much more mentally anguishing.

These simple rules of Aristotle continue to have an effect on how comedies are structured and how they affect audiences.

Figure 9.2 *A bust of Aristotle*

Roman comedy

The Romans enjoyed watching comedies, and the writers of this period developed the genre of dramatic comedy in several ways. Roman writers such as Plautus (254–184 BCE) and Terence (190–159 BCE) acknowledged their debt to the structure of Greek comedies, but added a number of new elements.

Activity 3

1. Look at the following elements added to the development of comedy by Roman dramatists.
   - Stereotypical characters (e.g. young lovers, angry and/or grumpy old man)
   - A sub-plot
   - A unity of place (the action takes place in the same or a similar place)
   - Mistaken identity
   - Games with language and the misuse of words (**malapropism**)
   - A love of comic servants
   - Hidden characters
   - The importance of chance encounters and meetings
   - The use of everyday speech, asides to the audience and overhearing as dramatic techniques
   - Interlocking plots
   - The division of the comedy into acts and scenes
   - Long-lost siblings or rivals returning

   How many of them of do you see in modern comedies that you know? Once you have thought about this, compare them with your own list.
2. Do you think the above elements could be applied to any Shakespearean comedies you know?

Key terms

Malapropism: a comical confusion of words, for example saying 'expedition' instead of 'exhibition'.

Commentary on Activity 3

Again, you should find that many of these Roman elements seem curiously modern. That is because they are some of the core ingredients of how comedy operates dramatically. Despite the considerable time period between the Roman comedies and a 21st century film or television programme, the ingredients are very similar.

In Praise of Folly – Erasmus and Umberto Eco

The medieval period developed dramatic comedy in new ways. Although dramas were usually Christian-themed, and either explored episodes from the Bible or scenes from the lives of saints, they often had comic sequences within them. These were usually **bawdy** and contained down-to-earth humour. The language they were written in had lots **puns** and ***double entendres***, which the audience would find amusing. Often the dramas poked fun at local people and their environment. These sequences offered a break from the more theological themes of the dramas.

Some writers and observers felt that religious dramas should contain nothing comic or amusing within them, and that sacred texts should be treated as such. Other writers disagreed, and felt that humour could often be used very well to instruct. Comedy also appealed to the bulk

Key terms

Bawdy: generally applied to language that is coarse or lewd.

Pun: a play on words – often exploiting either similar-sounding words or words with a variety of meanings. They are often used to comic effect.

***Double entendre*:** an expression or figure of speech that has two meanings. The first meaning may be obvious, but a second meaning may be either ironic or intentionally rude.

Did you know?

You may like to look at some of the surviving mystery plays from this period. The best can be found from York, Coventry and Cornwall.

of the people who were watching the plays. It seems that by the end of the medieval period, attitudes had changed and comedy was now a legitimate and important genre of writing. One writer who praises the use of comedy and satire is Desiderius Erasmus, who was born about 1469. He was a **humanist** who wrote a volume called *Praise of Folly* during one week in 1509. Although a sharp criticism of the failures of the Church of the period, it is written as a piece of comic satire with many jibes and jokes.

Key terms

Humanist: a humanist focuses study and investigation on human values and concerns. Dramatic comedy often appeals to humanists.

The debate over the function of comedy is no better expressed than in the novel *In the Name of the Rose*, written by the Italian writer Umberto Eco, published in 1980 and made into a film in 1986. The story is a murder mystery set in an Italian monastery in the year 1327. William of Baskerville discovers that a series of deaths have occurred because of a forbidden book in the library. The book is controlled by the Venerable Jorge, the most ancient monk there, who has poisoned the pages to stop the transfer of dangerous ideas: that is the use of comedy to teach the message of the Bible. Jorge believes that laughter is an instrument of the devil, so with the poison kills those who have dared to read the book. It is William who sees merit in the use of comedy for instruction.

As we shall see, comedy and dramatic comedy can be quite controversial forms of literature. Echoes of the debate over festival and comedy and their interaction with Christianity and piety are found in some of Shakespeare's dramas, for example *Twelfth Night*. Comedies explore the themes of both religious and social control.

Comedy in literature

While the examples we have looked at previously incorporate comic elements, we have perhaps still used the term 'comedy' very loosely. Dramatic comedy is a specific genre of literature, which operates within a set of **conventions**. As you will have gathered by now, comedy is one of the oldest literary traditions that exist in the world. Over time the conventions from successive historical periods have helped define what needs to happen on stage, and why writers construct comedies in certain ways. One of the things the audience should feel when watching a comedy is that somehow the world is absurd and that all of us do foolish things. As we continue through this unit, keep in mind popular and everyday ideas of comedy, but try to compare them with the literary genre of comedy. You will need to examine these conventions within your coursework, and comment on their use in the dramas you study.

Key terms

Conventions: the accepted rules, structures and customs we expect to see in a specific genre of writing.

Ideas for coursework tasks

In each of Chapters 9–15 we offer you and your teacher some suggestions for coursework tasks, related to what you have studied in the chapter. These are broad suggestions and the exact wording of your task will need to be negotiated with your teacher.

Essay (conventional response)

To what extent does the Shakespearean comedy you have studied offer an interpretation of human folly and greed?

Re-creative response

Write a version for a popular magazine, such as *Hello* or *OK!* of events at the end of the comedy you are studying. Make sure that your writing gives a clear indication of how readers of your story are meant to respond to events. You may wish to focus on the observations of characters on the sidelines of the main story.

In your commentary say why you chose this reading of the play's final scene and other readings that could have been possible.

Summary

In this chapter you have been introduced to dramatic comedy as a literary genre, to some of the range of forms it can take and to some of the conventions it involves. You have considered examples of comedy in other fields, such as television, films and computer games, and explored some of the historical development of comedy. Your understanding of the conventions of literary comedies and how they compare with popular and everyday ideas of comedy, will underpin your coursework on the dramas you study.

Further reading

- *The Elizabethan World Picture* by E.M.W. Tillyard (1943). This book explains how Elizabethan people imagined the world to be ordered. Shakespeare's comedies involve an interaction with that order.
- *A National Joke: Popular Comedies and English Cultural Identities* by Andy Medhurst (2007). This book explains the tradition of popular comedy in England, from theatre, television and film, and how it has shaped identity.

10 Shakespearean comedies: green worlds

This chapter:

- Describes some of the characteristics of Shakespearean comedies.
- Explores the dramatic structure in which Shakespearean comedies operate, by particular study of *A Midsummer Night's Dream*.
- Considers a range of interpretations of these comedies as texts and in performance, in order to inform your own response.
- Considers some new theories of comedy and applies them to the texts you are studying.

AQA Examiner's tip

Your teacher will guide you as to which comedies you will be reading for your coursework, but because dramatic comedy is probably a new genre for you to study, you may find it helpful to look at *A Midsummer Night's Dream* and then *Twelfth Night* because they are useful examples of how Shakespearean comedies work.

Key terms

Pastoral: a style of living and working concerned with the countryside. It is a recognised genre of literature. The pastoral is often conceived as a reaction to the urban.

Anachronistic: something that is out of harmony with the period in which it is placed.

In this chapter we examine a well-known Shakespearean comedy, *A Midsummer Night's Dream*. The reason this text has been chosen is because it has some very useful characteristics that can be applied to other comedies by William Shakespeare.

Shakespeare and comedy

The main kind of comedies Shakespeare wrote are often labelled romantic comedies. These plays are quite light-hearted, but do have some darker and more disturbing elements to them. Most of these were written in the early to middle years of his career. Some of his comedies, however, have very dark themes to them – and almost become tragedies, seemingly stepping back from the brink before the end. He also wrote a number of plays that are often called the 'Romances'. These are plays such as *A Winter's Tale* and *The Tempest*. Although they do not always follow the usual structure of Shakespearean comedies, they do have comic elements to them. These plays were written towards the end of his career.

Like the model set in previous centuries, Shakespeare realised that the best kind of comedy is generated by a series of mix-ups where disorder is rife and life is turned upside down. All of his comedies look at the foolishness of human beings. It is worth bearing in mind that watching or performing a play of this kind will give you much more insight into how the comedy is generated. As we proceed through this chapter we will give you a set of further theories and different readings of comedy to help you in your studies.

Lovers, fairies and fools: *A Midsummer Night's Dream*

A Midsummer Night's Dream was written around 1595. Although notionally it is set in Athens, the play could almost be set in a **pastoral** British environment. In fact, many of Shakespeare's comedies are set abroad or in fictional realms. Some people believed this was helpful because it prevented Shakespeare from upsetting anyone in Britain and negated any censorship. Even though the plays are set in other locations – real (like Greece) or fictional (like Illyria) – these still contain many images, words and ideas from British society of the time. This can make some concepts **anachronistic**.

As you might expect from the comic theory you have already learned, the play begins with a fundamental problem: Hermia is ordered by her father Egeus to marry Demetrius. She refuses because she actually loves Lysander, while Demetrius has already professed his love for Hermia's friend Helena and Helena does love Demetrius. Under the law of Athens, Duke Theseus gives Hermia four days to obey her father or else she must suffer death or enter a nunnery (this is one of the darker components of Shakespearean comedy). Hermia and Lysander decide to leave Athens secretly in order to be married where the Athenian law cannot pursue them.

In this sense, one might argue that this comedy is actually initiated by the characters resisting an arranged marriage. The moment Hermia and Lysander leave the **urban** environment of Athens, the typical comic structure is allowed to happen. In the forest, the otherwise realistic events are complicated by the machinations of the fairy characters: Oberon, the King, and Titania, the Queen of the Fairies. It is the mischievous sprite Puck who assists further in the mix-up of identity and partners in the wood. These two plots interlock with a third plot in the drama – that of a set of Athenian tradesmen, also in the wood, who are secretly rehearsing a play to be performed at the Duke's wedding. These **rustic** characters, or 'Mechanicals' as they are often known, are essentially foolish, working-class characters.

The three interlinked plots

Already you can see that the plot of *A Midsummer Night's Dream* is quite complicated. There are three plot threads, but they are interconnected. The working-class characters and the lovers bump into the fairies within the wood. The wood, as we shall see, is a significant space for these events to be occurring in. You may like to think of the wood in the light of the English folk hero, Robin Hood of Sherwood Forest – a space that is outside the law, and where people can hide. Each group of characters has a problem that needs to be resolved: the Athenian lovers want to marry the right partners, the tradesmen want to successfully put on the play for Duke Theseus's wedding, while Oberon and Titania are in disagreement over a changeling boy.

Activity 1

To understand a Shakespearean comedy it is often useful to consider the overarching structure of the play. Even if you do not know *A Midsummer Night's Dream*, consider the following stage directions at the start of each scene below. With a partner, consider what this tells you about comic structure:

Act 1 Scene 1	Enter Theseus, Hippolyta, Philostrate, with Attendants.
Scene 2	Enter Quince the Carpenter; and Snug the Joiner; and Bottom, the Weaver; and Flute, the Bellows-mender; and Snout, the Tinker; and Starveling, the Tailor.
Act 2 Scene 1	Enter a Fairy at one door, and Puck at another.
Scene 2	Enter Titania, Queen of the Fairies, with her Train.
Act 3 Scene 1	[Titania still lying asleep] Enter Quince, Bottom, Snug, Flute, Snout and Starveling.
Scene 2	Enter Oberon, King of the Fairies.
Act 4 Scene 1	Lysander, Demetrius, Helena, and Hermia, still lying asleep. Enter Titania, Queen of the Fairies, and Bottom; Peaseblossom, Cobweb, Moth, Mustardseed, and other Fairies; Oberon, the King, behind, unseen.
Act 5 Scene 1	Enter Theseus, Hippolyta; Lords and Attendants, among them Philostrate.

Commentary on Activity 1

Although by no means giving us a full picture of all the comings and going of various characters, the above does offer some useful ideas on the patterns and structure of comedy. At the beginning we see the Athenian world, where the central problem will be established. Philostrate is found at the beginning and end of the play. Although you may not know who he is, you may not be surprised to learn that he is the Master of Revels – the coordinator of the wedding entertainment. The high-order world of

Key terms

Urban: concerned with the town or city.

Rustic: concerned with country life.

Did you know?

William Shakespeare lived between 1564 and 1616. His birthday is believed to be 23 April, which was also the date of his death. Most of his comedies were written before 1600. The first folio, the first collected edition of his plays, was printed in 1623.

Did you know?

A changeling is a child or thing believed to have been substituted secretly for another. Changelings are often associated with fairies, and the fairy child usually ends up in the human world, with the human child in the fairy world. Many folk-tales around the world are also about changelings, and folk-tales often form the inspiration for dramatic comedies.

Figure 10.1 A Midsummer Night's Dream *at Stratford-upon-Avon in 1981, with Juliet Stevenson as Titania and Mike Gwilym as Oberon*

Athenian gentry soon swaps to the working-class world of the men who wish to rehearse their play. You will have noticed that their professions help to define their characters.

The move to the wood suggests that disorder in imminent and this is reinforced with the entry of Puck in the next scene. Note that opposition is set up – Puck enters from another door to the other fairy, suggesting his independence and function. Titania is then introduced and linked in the next scene with the Mechanicals, suggesting how the human and fairy worlds are colliding. In Act 4 this is enhanced further, showing how the lovers are also embroiled in this world. Acts 3 and 4 are precisely where we should expect most comic confusion. By Act 5 we are back to the order of Athens and seemingly events of the play have been resolved. Philostrate's presence here would indicate some kind of celebration.

This type of analysis can be applied to any Shakespearean comedy.

Interpretations by other readers

As you proceed through your studies of English Literature you will come to understand that different readers offer different interpretations of texts. The ways in which they have been interpreted are often influenced by the time period the criticism was written in, as well as other trends in literary criticism. You should aim to read and recognise a number of different points of view that will help you to understand the text. It is often good to include or indicate these different readings in your coursework. Use their views to reflect on your own. You may also find new criticism and emerging interpretations. It is always worth keeping an open mind on what different observers are saying.

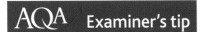

AQA Examiner's tip

Always keep a reference of your reading and add to your coursework in the Notes and References or Bibliography.

Different readings: Northrop Frye

The Canadian scholar Northrop Frye (1906–91) has had a considerable influence over the way modern literary studies interpret Shakespearean comedy. In 1957, Frye wrote *The Anatomy of Criticism*. One of the main ideas argued in his book is that Shakespearean comedy is written in harmony with the four seasons of the year: spring, summer, autumn and winter.

You may now be thinking of the titles of the two plays we are considering in Chapters 10 and 11 – relating to midsummer and twelfth night. Frye also saw patterns in Shakespearean comedies and comments that they:

> are usually divided up into four main phases, the four seasons of the year being the type for four periods of the day (morning, noon, evening, night), four aspects of the water cycle (rain, fountains, rivers, sea or snow), four periods of life (youth, maturity, age, death).

Northrop Frye, The Anatomy of Criticism, *1990 [1957], p160*

These patterns were not necessarily chronologically ordered across the play, but were part of the overall narrative of the drama.

Activity 2

See if you can apply some of Frye's ideas to *A Midsummer Night's Dream*. You may want to think of spring occurring at the end of the play as a kind of new beginning. Where do you find the four periods of life in a comedy like *A Midsummer Night's Dream*? Think about these ideas and design a table that illustrates your findings.

Commentary on Activity 2

Frye's theory is potentially useful since it relies on age-old concerns of human beings, and may be related back to original functions of comedy in pagan, pastoral Ancient Greece. Maybe the idea of winter applies when the characters suffer the mix-ups and confusion and have to push through this to reach the 'spring' in their lives. Comedies also often have a unity of time (a concept Aristotle introduced) – working through 24 hours – and darkness and night usually represent confusion. Dawn represents, like spring, a new era. In this way the play is filled with **symbols**.

Frye's 'green world'

Frye argued that Shakespearean comedy 'is the drama of the green-world, its plot being assimilated to the ritual themes of the triumph of life and love over the waste land' (Northrop Frye, *The Anatomy of Criticism*, 1990 [1957], p182). By this, and his other arguments, he seems to mean the following:

- The rural world means that urban and business concerns can be forgotten.
- Time is also forgotten. There are no clocks.
- The older, restrictive generation can be dispensed with.
- There is often gender confusion.
- The mythical and real merge.
- It is a temporary holiday atmosphere.
- There is no social hierarchy.

Frye notes that this can be seen again and again in Shakespearean comedy – notably in the play under consideration here, *A Midsummer Night's Dream*, but also in the forest of Arden in *As You Like It*, the location of Belmont in *The Merchant of Venice* and, as we shall see in the next chapter, the coast of Illyria in *Twelfth Night*. Since Frye's work, a consensus about Shakespearean comedy has emerged. This is outlined next.

Old world, green world, new world

One useful model to use to help you understand Shakespearean comedy draws on the theories of Frye. The central idea is that in any comedy by Shakespeare there are three worlds operating.

The 'old world'

The first is a world belonging to older people or parental figures. It is usually repressive and often urban. There is generally a lack of freedom due to the laws and established ways of doing things. Most often it is a world that is resisted by the young people, who find it unfair and unsympathetic to their needs. The 'old world' may only be seen for a very short while in the play, and we can probably project backwards in time to understand its operation further. This 'old world' structure is very clear in the Athenian society of *A Midsummer Night's Dream*.

The 'green world'

The second world is called the 'green world' because it often takes place in a forest, a wood or another non-urban environment. It is a world of freedom, but it is also a world of confusion. In Britain and Europe during the time in which Shakespeare was writing, huge, dense swathes of forest were untouched and unpopulated. They were therefore sometimes viewed as being magical and dangerous places (think of all the dark forests in fairy stories). Obviously, this is an environment most suited to fairies, mix-ups, disguise and misinformation. The 'green world' represents disorder. As comedies become more sophisticated over time, there are new ways in which this 'green world' operates. We need to remember that despite an overlay of Christianity, people in this period were still very superstitious, believing in the work of fairies and little people.

Key terms

Symbol: something that stands for something else in literary texts. The connection is usually not directly stated and the reader is expected to recognise the symbol for what it represents. Symbols are often used in comedies.

Extension tasks

1. Analyse the metaphorical language of *A Midsummer Night's Dream*, and see where this language connects with Frye's theory.
2. Connect the theories outlined in Chapter 9 with those here. How might the theories here be considered an extension of those outlined previously?

AQA Examiner's tip

You may find it useful to apply these three terms of 'old world', 'green world' and 'new world' to other comedies because they help to explain the structure and development of such comedies. They can even work for modern and contemporary comedies, although obviously it may not literally be a forest. Try it out with television programmes and films too.

The 'new world'

This is the world created out of the resolution in the play. It is a world that has learned from its past mistakes and has resolved any previous problems. Usually, characters return from the 'green world', often back into the urban world, but this time, a new order is established. This is symbolised by several elements – notably a marriage, or very often multiple marriages. Multiple marriages are important because they usually cut across all classes of people, suggesting social harmony. Other important elements that represent this 'new world' are dancing (a celebratory act), feasting and an opportunity for those doling out the 'law' to reform and rethink. Sometimes a character will offer an **epilogue**, explaining what their hopes are for the future. Obviously, marriage not only signifies a union, but also the opportunities for children, and therefore progress in the future. Because love is a kind of uncontrolled and irrational force, marriage demonstrates that it is also a way of controlling and managing it in the 'new world'.

Key terms

Epilogue: the short concluding section of a play or poem, sometimes summarising the content or theme.

In Oberon's speech below, there is much that can be related to the overall function of comedies. Oberon refers to solutions and new beginnings. There is an emphasis on the importance of children. There is a notion that we would all wish fairies to bless our homes in this way. The structural importance of the new dawn is also noted. It works as an epilogue. This was a common convention in this period. You will gain a good understanding of how comedies operate by looking at concluding speeches.

Activity 3

Look at Oberon's speech at the very end of *A Midsummer Night's Dream*. It is significant because it seems to summarise so much about the function of Shakespearean comedy. As you comment on the language, consider how this speech ties together the various strands of the comedy as outlined so far in this chapter. Note that like most 'high status' characters in Shakespearean comedy, Oberon uses verse.

Analysis of Act 5 Scene 2

Oberon Now, until the break of day,
Through this house each fairy stray,
To the best bride-bed will we,
Which by use shall blessed be;
And the issue there create
Ever shall be fortunate.
So shall all the couples three
Ever true in loving be;
And the blots of Nature's hand
Shall not in their issue stand:
Never mole, hair-lip, nor scar,
Nor mark prodigious, such as are
Despised in nativity,
Shall upon their children be,

Oberon is speaking in rhyming couplets. These suggest that a certain harmony has been reached at the end of the play.

Multiple marriage is an important signifier at the end of a Shakespearean comedy.

This refers to Theseus and Hippolyta, Hermia and Lysander, and Helena and Demetrius.

Because of the fairy's blessing, the children of the three couples will not have any disfigurement and will be born healthy.

With this field-dew consecrate,
Every fairy take his gait,
And each several chambers bless
Through this palace with sweet peace;
And the owner of it blest,
Ever shall in safety rest,
Trip away; make no stay;
Meet me all by break of day.

A Midsummer Night's Dream, Act 5 Scene 2

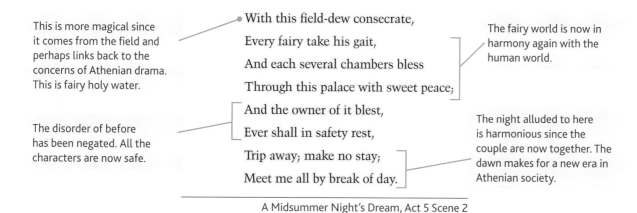

This is more magical since it comes from the field and perhaps links back to the concerns of Athenian drama. This is fairy holy water.

The fairy world is now in harmony again with the human world.

The disorder of before has been negated. All the characters are now safe.

The night alluded to here is harmonious since the couple are now together. The dawn makes for a new era in Athenian society.

Commentary on Activity 3

In this short speech, there is much that can be related to the overall function of comedies. Oberon refers to solutions and new beginnings. There is an emphasis on the importance of children. There is a notion that we would all wish fairies to bless our homes in this way. The structural importance of the new dawn is also noted.

Puck as trickster and Bottom as clown

Obviously the study of particular characters and their impact on a dramatic comedy is a significant area to investigate in your coursework. You should focus on how the author (in this case, Shakespeare) has constructed them and what their purpose is at different points through the drama. In most comedies, although the characteristics of a character stay basically the same, the character still goes through a developmental process. Two of the key characters in *A Midsummer Night's Dream* are Puck and Bottom.

To an extent, both Puck and Bottom represent 'types' in European thought and culture. Puck might be described as a **trickster** figure. He is unpredictable, somewhat manic, and delights in the chaos and disorder he manages. He loves making mischief in the mortals' world. Puck has multiple functions within the comedy. On one level he is a manifestation of the evil malevolence of Oberon (representing another dark strand of the comedy) and he can sometimes make audiences feel uncomfortable. On another level he is playful – exhibiting the kind of bad behaviour we sometimes admire in others! The relationship between Oberon and Puck has some similarities to the relationships between other Shakespearean-created kings and their fools (as in *King Lear*), but Puck is no ordinary fool. Whereas other fools debate and test their masters, Puck does what he is asked.

Bottom is more the classic kind of fool we might find in comedy, although he may more rightly be called a **clown**. Usually played in a clumsy, **slapstick** style, Bottom is enthusiastic (to the extent he wishes to play everyone's part) and good-hearted. When he is transformed into an ass, his language alters and becomes polite, pretentious and affected. He also becomes extremely courteous. Like Puck he has a number of structural functions within the drama. His characteristics may be observed in the following encounters with the fairies in Act 3 Scene 1:

Extension tasks

1. How does the ending of *A Midsummer Night's Dream* compare with the ending of the dramatic comedy you are studying?
2. How do you think modern audiences respond to the ending of *A Midsummer Night's Dream*? Do you think they would believe in the capacity of fairies to bless a house? Are superstition and folklore important?

Key terms

Trickster: the trickster has a wide number of interpretations across the world. In European culture he is often a thief or liar, a practical-joker and sometimes clever at disguise.

Clown: often a person who does comical tricks, but is better defined by the word 'buffoon'. The character is usually clumsy and unsophisticated.

Slapstick: a kind of physical comedy invented in the 20th century but applied on the past. It involves falling over, blows and mishaps.

Key terms

Verse: rhymed or (most usually) unrhymed poetry that is found in Shakespearean and other dramas of the period, and is usually spoken by higher-class or noble characters. The unrhymed form is written in iambic pentameters (ten-syllable lines with five stresses) and when performed closely imitates the rhythm of speech in English. It is sometimes called blank verse. Some characters speak in rhyming couplets.

Bathos: a key concept in comedy, this means taking an elevated form (such as tragedy) and descending it into the ridiculous.

Travesty: when something important or crucial is made ridiculous.

Transgression: to break a law or rule, and to go beyond the normal limits of tolerance.

Bottom:	I cry your worship's mercy, heartily, I beseech your worship's name?
Cobweb:	Cobweb.
Bottom:	I shall desire you of more acquaintance, good Master Cobweb: if I cut my finger, I shall make bold with you. Your name, honest gentleman?
Peaseblossom:	Peaseblossom.
Bottom:	I pray you, commend me to Mistress Squash, your mother, and to Master Peascod, your father. Good Master Peaseblossom, I shall desire you of more acquaintance too.

A Midsummer Night's Dream, Act 2 Scene I

Both characters are types that we will see repeatedly in dramatic comedy.

The play within a play: tragedy as comedy

Although not always found in other comedies, one particularly interesting comic sequence in *A Midsummer Night's Dream* is when the Mechanicals are given the opportunity to perform their tragedy, 'Pyramus and Thisbe', which has been in rehearsal throughout the play. Theseus, Hippolyta and the Athenian court have to watch the performance in which the play is performed so badly that it comes across as a comedy.

This is a very common technique in dramatic comedy, where something that is meant to be serious and pretentious is brought down to earth and made funny by inept acting. The workmen have spoken in prose through most of the play, but when performing they speak in **verse**. The comedy is heightened by the other noble characters commenting on the action. The play is delivered chaotically – perhaps mirroring the earlier chaos, although the actors are well-intentioned. At points Bottom comes out of character to directly inform the audience what is happening. The play is filled with **bathos** and is a **travesty** of what a tragedy should be.

Activity 4

Read the sequence from the performance of 'Pyramus and Thisbe', Act 5 Scene 1, which begins with Thisbe saying '*This is old Ninny's tomb*...', and think about the following:

1. How is comedy achieved in the sequence?
2. What is the effect of the over-dramatic verse delivered by Bottom?
3. Where do you see the bathos and travesty of the original tragedy?
4. Can you think of other film, television or stages comedies where some of the characters are engaged in a larger project to stage a play, a concert or an event?

Commentary on Activity 4

1. The comedy is achieved by timing ('timing is everything in comedy'), by the ornate and grand language and by the observational humour of those watching.
2. The effect of the over-dramatic verse is to render Bottom's portrayal ludicrous. Over-the-top acting is always funny because it departs too much from realism.
3. We can see both bathos and travesty in the death sequences. These are meant to be emotionally draining, tear-jerking and powerful. Instead, they are amusing.
4. Many of the films and television programmes mentioned in Chapter 9 have characters who have bigger projects on their minds. Usually, their ambitions for glory end up broken and shattered – warning us not to be too ambitious. A particularly good example is in *Only Fools and Horses* when Del and Rodney try to clean a chandelier. Or in *Twelfth Night*, when the character of Malvolio has ambitions to impress Olivia by wearing cross-gartered yellow stockings. His travesty and **transgression** of the normal order are again cut down to size.

Character as 'construction' – not as 'real'

One of the main errors many students make in their coursework is to present studies of characters in dramatic comedies as if they are somehow 'real', explaining their characteristics, personality and traits as if they actually exist, and somehow forgetting that they are a fictional construct. You should think about the way the dramatist constructs the character – using form, structure and language. It may also be useful to consider their dramatic function in the play. Keep checking your coursework to make sure you have not viewed them as 'real'.

Ideas for coursework tasks

Essay (conventional response)

What are the limitations of Frye's 'green world' model as applied to the Shakespearean comedy you are studying?

Re-creative response

In modern English prose, write Quince's reflections on the successes and failures of today's performance of 'Pyramus and Thisbe'. Aim to comment on the actors, the audience reaction and your own direction.

In your commentary say how you developed this reading of Quince and the workmen and other readings that could have been possible.

Summary

In this chapter you have considered some initial ways to approach a Shakespearean comedy, with particular reference to *A Midsummer Night's Dream*. These have provided you with a critical approach to the text and offered some development of the comic theories offered in Chapter 9. There have been a number of pointers about ways forward with your coursework, particularly regarding ways to deal with comedic characters and their construction.

Further reading

- *The Cambridge Companion to Shakespearean Comedy* edited by Alexander Leggatt (2001). This is an informed and wide-ranging introduction to Shakespeare's major comedies.
- *Shakespeare: The Biography* by Peter Ackroyd (2005). This is useful guide not only to the writer himself, but also to many of the conditions in which he was operating and where his plays were performed.

Extension (this reading may be challenging)

- *English Stage Comedy 1490–1990* by Alexander Leggatt (1998). This is a comprehensive guide to comic theatre, with a useful section on Shakespeare.
- *The Rise and Fall of Merry England: The Ritual Year 1400–1700* by Ronald Hutton (1994). This volume explains how comedy in England connects to the ritual year and demonstrates the seasonal impact of folkloric traditions on drama. It looks at whether disorder can be found in celebration.

Did you know?

In 1970 the famous director Peter Brook staged a production of *A Midsummer Night's Dream* for the Royal Shakespeare Company that was set in a blank, white box. All of the fairies were male, except for Titania, and they were suspended on trapeze wires. All the characters wore white clothes. Another recent production cast the fairies as Hell's Angels.

Extension tasks

1. Compare another play-within-a-play sequence from *Hamlet* known as 'The Mousetrap' (Act 3 Scene 2). Hamlet is a tragedy, but it may be useful to compare how Shakespeare uses this form within two genres.
2. With people in your class, see if you can mount a comic performance of 'Pyramus and Thisbe'. Other students can add in the commentary. You should aim to make the acting over-the-top.

AQA Examiner's tip

It is important that you remember that comedy is drama, intended to be performed on stage. Whenever possible you should contribute to the practical performance of the text you are studying and working on. Standing up and delivering the lines – or even recording them – will give you a better sense of how the drama operates, and what issues face playwrights, directors, actors and designers. You will also have more empathy with what the playwright is seeking to do – thus better understanding language, form and structure.

11 Other Shakespearean comedies: festival, carnival and misrule

This chapter:

- Enables you to analyse another Shakespearean comedy – *Twelfth Night*.
- Explores other ways of examining Shakespearean comedy.
- Considers the impact of festival, carnival and the concept of misrule in relation to comedy.
- Explores some of the other Shakespearean comedies.

To build on your knowledge of how Shakespearean comedy operates, in this chapter we have chosen *Twelfth Night* as a useful text to focus on. Like *A Midsummer Night's Dream*, it is a helpful model of comedy, which as well as incorporating many of the elements discussed so far, has a number of additional components that are useful to consider. Again, you will be able to take these elements and apply them to the text you are studying for your coursework.

Jesters, twins and cross-dressing: *Twelfth Night*

The comedy of *Twelfth Night* was written around 1601. It was certainly performed at the Middle Temple in London in February 1603 – denoting that it was, in some ways, a comedy celebrating the season of winter. The Middle Temple was a large indoor hall, unlike the traditional style of the **Globe Theatre** most associated with Shakespeare, although it is probable that it was performed at that sort of theatre as well.

The main plot in the play involves the separation of Viola and Sebastian. They are twin brother and sister who look alike, and after a shipwreck off the coast of the imagined country of Illyria, cannot find each other. Viola disguises herself as a page and takes service with Duke Orsino there. She **cross-dresses** to become a man. Orsino is in love with the Lady Olivia, but she rejects his **suit** for marriage. Orsino makes Viola (now disguised as Cesario) complete his wooing for him, but inadvertently Olivia starts to fall in love with Cesario. Things are only resolved when Sebastian arrives – with the mix-up over his identity eventually resolved – and Cesario admitting she is a woman.

There are several sub-plots in the comedy – one involving members of Olivia's household. Here, a number of characters – Sir Toby Belch (Olivia's uncle), Sir Andrew Aguecheek (another suitor for Olivia), Maria (Olivia's waiting gentlewoman) and Feste (Olivia's jester) – devise a plot to fool the pompous steward of the house, Malvolio. Malvolio is a Puritan and is against traditional celebration involving dancing, alcohol and singing. You may be able to see that structurally this makes for a conflict between those comic figures and Malvolio as an anti-comic and controlling figure. This is a pattern seen elsewhere in dramatic comedy.

Key terms

Globe Theatre: the most famous of the theatres found on the South Bank in London during Shakespeare's day. It is characterised by its circular shape, thrust stage and three tiers of seating. A modern re-creation of the theatre was built in 1997 and Shakespeare's dramas are performed there in original performance conditions.

Cross-dress: any form of disguise that turns one gender into another.

Suit: a request or wish for something.

Activity 1

The starting point for the analysis of any comedy you encounter is always the list of characters at the start of the play – sometimes called the *dramatis personæ* ('people of the drama'). Have a look at the list of characters in *Twelfth Night*. You may already know the plot, or at least have heard of some of the characters – but even if you do not know the story, try to think about the relationships in the play.

- Consider issues of power and control and who might be the confidant of other characters.
- Can you identify three interlocking plots in the text?
- Which characters do you conceive of as the most comic, and which might be the most serious?

Did you know?

Puritans were an important Protestant Christian group that developed in the 16th and 17th centuries. They wanted a simpler kind of church ceremony and changes in behaviour. Broadly, they were anti-theatre, anti-festival, anti-sports and anti-drinking.

***Twelfth Night*: The cast**

Orsino, Duke of Illyria

Valentine Curio	gentlemen attending on the duke
1st Officer 2nd Officer	in the service of the duke

Viola, a lady, later disguised as Cesario

Sebastian, Viola's twin brother

A Captain, of Viola's wrecked ship, who befriends her

Antonio, another sea captain, friend of Sebastian

Olivia, a countess

Maria, Olivia's waiting woman

Sir Toby Belch, Olivia's kinsman

Sir Andrew Aguecheek, companion to Sir Toby

Malvolio, Olivia's steward

Fabian, a member of Olivia's household

Feste, the clown, Olivia's jester

Servant to Olivia

Musicians, lords, sailors, attendants

Commentary on Activity 1

This is a good activity to do with any comedy. The presence of twins is likely to be of dramatic importance (you may note this in films, such as the *Star Wars IV*, *V* and *VI* trilogy, and *Twins*). There is a parallel set-up between Olivia and her waiting woman and Orsino and his gentlemen. The servant characters are likely to know very well the life and loves of their superiors. Feste will obviously be a humorous character, but we also note the surname of Sir Toby. We might already imagine him as being rather rotund and a drinker. Sir Andrew sounds comic simply because of his name. Fabian and Antonio are more difficult to know about, but they must be of importance to the plot since they are both named. You may have noted the presence of musicians. In Shakespearean comedy, music and song have an important place. The songs often comment on the other stage events.

Extension tasks

1. Work your way through the character list and randomly pick some short pieces of dialogue from each character from throughout the play (roughly about 10 lines). What do these pieces of dialogue say about the characters?
2. Research the names given to the characters. These can often indicate personality types or characteristics – a technique used to great effect in Restoration comedy, but also in modern pantomime.

Conventions and performance conditions

Shakespeare often took advantage of some of the restrictions about performance conditions during the era he was writing. The authorities in the city of London frequently disapproved of dramas that cut 'too close to the bone' in their criticism of contemporary Britain. As a result, Shakespeare set *Twelfth Night* in the imagined country of Illyria.

One of the major plot elements in *Twelfth Night* is the disguise of the female Viola as the boy Cesario. You may know that women were not permitted to act on the stage during this time, so teenage boys (young actors in training) generally took the role of women – using voice, costuming and wigs to create the effect. Thus the conversion of a woman back into a boy again would be relatively easy. A number of other plays also take advantage of this condition, such as *As You Like It* (where the central character Rosalind takes the identity of a countryman named Ganymede).

Figure 11.1 *Nigel Hawthorne as Malvolio in the 1996 film adaptation of* Twelfth Night, *directed by Trevor Nunn*

Did you know?

Ritual terms

A ritual is a repeated series of actions used for ceremonial or festive purposes.

Epiphany falls on 6 January and is the festival that commemorates the showing of Christ to the Three Kings.

Solstices are either 21 June (approximately) or 22 December (approximately), when the sun is furthest from the equator.

AQA Examiner's tip

Dealing with the complexity of a Shakespearean comedy is not easy. When you study one, there are four main steps to dealing with it:

1. Try to see the main pattern of the plot.
2. Look at some key scenes in the opening, middle and end sections of the play. These scenes will inform the rest of your reading.
3. Keep in mind how form, structure and language are used in each of the scenes.
4. See if you can apply some critical views, but also try to formulate your own response to the text.

Applying comic theory

Even knowing only a little bit about the play *Twelfth Night*, you will be able to apply some of the comic theory learned so far. There is obviously a connection to the theories of Northrop Frye, and although the 'old world, green world, new world' model may be slightly harder to spot in *Twelfth Night*, it still exists. The 'old world' is defined by events before the shipwreck. The 'green world' reigns because the twins are separated and Viola is in disguise. It is worth re-emphasising that here the catastrophic event of the shipwreck is the ignition point of what follows.

The 'green world' itself does not necessarily need to be always in a forest or wood. It can just be the space created for the confusion, though most often the play is given a rural/pastoral setting. The 'new world' begins when the imprisoned Malvolio is released and when the multiple marriages take place between Viola and Orsino, and Olivia and Sebastian. There is some suggestion that Sir Toby and Maria are also married.

Love is very much a motivating force in the play, and we understand that when people are in love they do foolish things. Caricature is used a lot in the play (in the form of Sir Toby Belch and Sir Andrew Aguecheek). To some extent, the custom of Olivia's seven years of mourning for the death of her brother is also made to look foolish. The absurd fight that Viola is placed in with Sir Andrew is something she finds hard to escape from.

Part of the ritual year

Twelfth night is a point in the ritual year of Britain. Traditionally, twelfth night was the moment of celebration of the festival of Christmas and it is sometimes known as epiphany. Epiphany means a 'showing forth'. Over time, twelfth night has become less significant as a festive point in the year – but it is still known today as the date before which we are meant to take down our Christmas decorations.

Within the year in Britain and in most other European countries are a set of key dates and festivals that were cause for celebration. Some of these festive points are now hidden by the demands of the modern world, but you will know Christmas, Easter, May Day, Harvest Festival, Hallowe'en, and perhaps the winter and summer solstices. The play *A Midsummer Night's Dream* takes place, of course, on midsummer night – the shortest night of the year – so it, too, relates to the ritual year. The reasons for these dates becoming associated with the calendar is not always obvious, but they are probably related to pre-Christian pagan markers of the year. It is clear, however, why the winter and summer solstices are marked: the winter solstice marks a turn in the year when the days become longer again, and its proximity to Christmas (as a major festival) may be the reason such celebration takes place then.

It seems that at least Shakespeare and some other dramatists of the period in which he was writing were aware of the significance of these points in the ritual year, and often developed comedies that were either inspired by or celebrated these key points.

Festival in Britain

In some parts of Britain, during festivals, local people get to become Mock Mayors and are paraded around the town they live in. Mock Mayors are comic figures who tend to make popular and absurd declarations ('Free beer for everyone!' or 'Cabbages must be worn!'). The behaviour is called **inversion theory** – some people believed that allowed the working classes to be 'King for a Day', which lessened their need to revolt or overthrow their masters.

This tolerated foolery and riotous behaviour was generally allowed at key moments in the ritual year, for example on May Day or at the winter solstice. It was, for example, the custom in some parts of the country for morris dancers to lead the festivities, or for other performers known as guisers (related to the key concept of disguise in comedy) to put on May Plays or Mummers' Plays.

Activity 2

Read and perform Act 3 Scene 4 from the play. Here, the normally Puritan Malvolio has been inspired by the wording of a false letter to dress and behave in a very different way from normal. How might this be an example of inversion? Why is the sequence so comic?

You may also want to see how it is conceived in the *Cartoon Shakespeare* illustrated by John H. Howard, which you can find by searching the internet.

Commentary on Activity 2

This is good example of comic inversion theory in operation, because, as a Puritan, Malvolio is doing everything he should not be doing. He has been transformed into an unstoppable 'love machine', which of course, offends Olivia, making her think of him as mad. Love, or lust, as we know, makes people do crazy things. Note that Olivia labels it 'midsummer madness' – another time of the year when people do 'odd' things outside normal patterns of behaviour.

It is an ironic parallel to the more traditional ritual year inversions made by Feste, Sir Toby and Sir Andrew. It is at this point that the characters gain **revenge** on Malvolio. You may want to think about the value of revenge in comedies.

Different readings: C.L. Barber

Frye's reading of Shakespearean comedy was revised by the author C.L. Barber. Barber thought that the comedies were constructed in direct relation to the range of holidays and festivities available in Elizabethan society. He outlined these principles in his book *Shakespeare's Festive Comedies: A Study of Dramatic Form and its Relation to Social Custom* (1959). We might summarise Barber's arguments in the following statements:

- Shakespearean comedies should be read in the light of village marriages, wassails (an ancient custom intended to ward off evil spirits from cider apple trees) or wakes.
- Holidays such as Candlemas, Shrove Tuesday, Hocktide, May Day, Whitsuntide, Midsummer Eve, Harvest Home, Hallowe'en and Christmas are all starting points for comedy.
- Comedy is all about pleasure and merrymaking.

Key terms

Inversion theory: when the everyday or normal experience is altered for the purposes of ritual or celebration.

Revenge: a kind of mental or physical injury inflicted on someone who has caused you suffering. Revenge is not just a theme of dramatic tragedy, it can be found in comedy too.

Did you know?

Guisers lead folk drama performers through towns and villages. They sometimes disguise themselves with extravagant costumes or blackened faces.

May Plays are simple plays performed on or around May Day. They were sometimes led by Kings and Queens of Summer, and often told Robin Hood stories.

- Comedy offers a form of release.
- Comedy reacts against social conformity.

According to Barber, comedy also has a function to mock killjoy and authority figures who try to prevent merrymaking from happening. You can see this in the figure of Malvolio in *Twelfth Night*, but elements of it also exist in the characters of Shylock in *The Merchant of Venice* and Don John in *Much Ado About Nothing*.

AQA Examiner's tip

Build your own glossary of terminology and concepts used to discuss comedy and the play you are studying. This will be very useful when it comes to writing your coursework.

Did you know?

Twelfth Night has a subtitle, 'Or What You Will', which suggests that if you, as a member of the audience, do not particularly like the title, you can call it what you like.

Did you know?

A recent Royal Shakespeare Company performance updated the look of Malvolio by dressing him in an ergonomic set of yellow-and-black motorcycle leathers. The sequence is also often staged with him being cross-dressed and wearing a yellow-and-black suspender belt and stockings under a long coat.

Activity 3

Examine the sequence from Act 2 Scene 3 of *Twelfth Night*, where Malvolio interrupts the activities of Sir Toby Belch, Feste, Maria and Sir Andrew Aguecheek.

What elements of Barber's theory can be applied? Does this make for a relevant reading of a Shakespearean comedy?

Commentary on Activity 3

Here, we read this sequence in the light of the fact that it is a period of celebrations in the ritual year. Christmas is a starting point for the comedy. While Feste, Sir Toby and Andrew seek pleasure and merrymaking in part-songs (catches), this being a form of release from their day-to-day concerns (how Toby gains money and how Andrew might woo Olivia), we also note that they go against social conformity and invert the normal order of things ('rouse the night-owl'). Maria is the first to note that they are 'caterwauling' and disrupting the household.

The dramatic build-up to Malvolio's entry is made all the more powerful with the witty puns exchanged and the focus on the word 'peace'. The other thing they will not do is 'Hold their peace'. Feste talks of Sir Toby's 'admirable fooling'. Malvolio's insistence that they are 'mad' shows his Puritan ideology, but also, to the audience, it shows that he needs to be mocked for he is operating as a killjoy. He will need to be belittled, which is how part of the complication stage of the comedy is developed. You may have noticed that Malvolio describes Sir Toby as having 'disorders' – a reference to his like of drinking, but also offering an insight into what is happening.

Extension tasks

1. Look at another sequence in the play where social conformity is mocked. You may like to consider Act 2 Scene 1 (Malvolio with Viola) or Act 2 Scene 5 (the placing of the letter near the box tree).
2. Practise the delivery of Malvolio's speeches here. What are the different ways in which they could be said? How pompous can you make them?
3. Try writing down Malvolio's thoughts about what he has encountered. This might form the basis for some re-creative writing.

Another reading: Mikhail Bakhtin

A useful response to Shakespearean comedy is offered by the Russian critic Mikhail Bakhtin (1895–1975). In the 1930s, Bakhtin formulated some of his ideas on the work of a French novelist, François Rabelais (1494–1553), which was eventually published in English as *Rabelais and his World* in 1968. In the book he makes observations on the contrast between the official culture of the state and religious organisations, and the culture of the market-place and people.

Within this he notices that carnival is a significant celebration because it allowed freedom for the people away from the official culture. Carnival allowed both indulgence in food and sexual activity, as well as any kind of misrule. Misrule permitted a temporary suspension of the normal rules. In Catholic countries this happened during Mardi Gras before the restrictions of Lent.

In this way, some bad and comic behaviour was tolerated. When, in *Twelfth Night*, Olivia says 'There is no slander / in an allowed fool' (Act 1 Scene 5), she is commenting on this phenomenon of misrule. Like carnival and festival, dramatic comedy may be a way of the official society and church tolerating dissent and discontentment. Some people might say that in order to prevent riotous or revolutionary behaviour, the ruling authorities have allowed working-class people the opportunity for a kind of controlled misrule.

It has been argued that events such as the present-day Glastonbury Festival of Performing Arts, or the Reading/Leeds music festivals, offer young people a contemporary opportunity for 'controlled misrule'. Britain is also a country that now seems to use festival events at every opportunity to celebrate the diversity and identity of local communities. Comedy therefore has an extremely important social function. Bakhtin's theories tell us much about the issues of control and freedom within the genre of dramatic comedy.

Figure 11.2 *Is the Glastonbury Festival of Performing Arts a kind of modern-day example of controlled misrule?*

Jesters

One of the things we learn about the figure of the jester in *Twelfth Night* is that Olivia tolerates his insight. In comedies, jesters usually operate as a kind of corrective to the irrational thoughts of other characters. Jesters have insight because they see the world through comic and ironic eyes. Feste is allowed to call Olivia 'madonna' and she asks him for advice about relationships and life. Even though she is irritated by him ('Take the Fool away') she also realises he is perceptive enough to be her counsellor. In this sense, he is a licensed or permitted fool.

Jesters are also constructed as being more observant than other characters. It is Feste who first notices the attraction between Duke

Orsino and Cesario. While the attraction is 'unnatural' because homosexuality was conceived of in this way, he is also insightful, noticing Cesario's lack of a beard, to which 'she' replies, 'By my troth, I am almost sick for one'. This is a recognisable aspect of humanity – that sometimes people offer comic insight into events and situations.

Activity 4

Jesters are often presented in art and literature in a certain way. Discuss with a partner the characteristics of jesters.

To what extent does Feste fulfil these? How do you imagine jesters to be dressed? Maybe you could sketch what they look like. You may also want to think about ways in which jesters have been re-thought and re-imagined in plays or films.

Commentary on Activity 4

Jesters are primarily seen as being honest, witty and clever (with word puns). Feste seems to fulfil these characteristics. Jesters are traditionally imagined in brightly coloured clothes (often red and yellow) in a motley pattern. They wear hats made of three points, each with a bell on the end of them – supposedly a re-creation of the ears and tail of a donkey. Jesters are also seen as carrying a mock sceptre.

In the 1996 film version of *Twelfth Night*, Ben Kingsley's interpretation of Feste imagines him as more of an itinerant storyteller or musician, effectively singing for his supper as he wanders through Illyria. Very often contemporary productions of *Twelfth Night* seek to find alternative ways of presenting Feste from the stereotypical view outlined above.

Did you know?

Following the Civil War, the Lord Protector, Oliver Cromwell, stopped the tradition of jesters. He was – like Malvolio – a Puritan. After the Restoration, Charles II did not bring back the tradition, but he did support the theatre – and dramatic comedy in particular.

Disguise and cross-dressing

Disguise and mistaken identity form crucial plot devices in *Twelfth Night* and in other Shakespearean comedies. What is significant is how the disguise delays the process of resolution. In *Twelfth Night*, Sebastian and Viola first come to recognise each other with Sebastian's colleague Antonio noting 'How have you made division of yourself? An apple, cleft in two, is not more twin / Than these creatures'. Here the disguise is still fooling Antonio.

Disguise is associated with considerable festive activity in Elizabethan England. It is still a highly visible strand of comedy, allowing characters to move unnoticed in certain situations. Very often, if the disguise is not very good, the comedy is actually enhanced because, despite the audience knowing who it is, we suspend our disbelief enough to go along with it. Disguise is also echoed in *Twelfth Night* in Feste's imitation of Sir Topaz at Malvolio's cell. This is a scene you may wish to consider further. In your studies, look to where the sub-plots echo themes and developments of the main plots.

AQA Examiner's tip

Although you do not have to read every single Shakespearean comedy, gaining an awareness of the genre will help in your overall understanding for your coursework. Many Shakespearean comedies have been made into films and these will be useful to watch. One good example is *Much Ado About Nothing* (1993), which starred Keanu Reeves and Kenneth Branagh. Look at your local theatre to see which comedies are being performed.

Other Shakespearean comedies to consider

Most of the concepts and theories presented so far could be applied to other Shakespearean comedies. Other plays you might like to read and consider include:

- *The Merry Wives of Windsor* (1597)
- *Much Ado About Nothing* (1598)
- *As You Like It* (1599).

Ideas for coursework tasks

Essay (conventional response)

Explore and debate the function of the jester or fool figure in the Shakespearean comedy you are studying. To what extent do they offer honest insight to both other characters and the audience?

Re-creative response

One of the minor characters in *Twelfth Night* is Fabian. Using his confession at the end of Act 5 Scene 1 as a starting point, write some diary entries about the fate of characters (such as Malvolio, Sir Andrew Aguecheek and others you may choose) after the play has finished.

In your commentary say why you chose these developments, relating them to your reading of the play. Refer to critical interpretations if possible.

Summary

In this chapter you have gained an understanding of another Shakespearean comedy and explored some helpful ways of understanding it, relating to the ritual year, festival and misrule. The chapter has also offered you opportunities as to how to go about the process of exploring a Shakespeare text and managing the material.

You have also considered two further critics and their theories about comedy, and through textual analysis you have explored some key sequences and issues within the play.

Further reading

- Twelfth Night: *A Guide to the Text and its Theatrical Life* by Paul Edmondson (2005). This is useful history of the play's performance history.
- *Fools and Jesters at the English Court* by John Southworth (1998). This easy-to-read volume examines the function and place of jesters in relation to the Kings and Queens of England.

Extension (this reading may be challenging)

- *Renaissance Self-Fashioning: From More to Shakespeare* by Stephen Greenblatt (1982). This book offers enquiry into core ideological concepts that underpin many of Shakespeare's comedies.
- *The Place of the Stage: Licence, Play and Power in Renaissance England* by Stephen Mullaney (1988). Mullaney examines the legality of performances of dramatic comedy in the Renaissance.

12 Problem comedies, dark comedies and tragi-comedies

This chapter:

- Considers more complex comedies, which integrate aspects of other genres.
- Appreciates and understands how comedies deal with problematic issues.
- Explores and investigates the characteristics of 'dark' comedies and 'tragi-comedies'.
- Considers that there can be comic sequences in other kinds of drama.

Key terms

Revenger: the main character who seeks revenge. Although often found in tragedies, they can also be found in comedies.

Tragi-comedies: comedies that have more serious subject matter.

When Malvolio shouts, 'I'll be revenged on the whole pack of you', at the end of *Twelfth Night*, we can see a different direction for Shakespearean comedy. Most comedies offer a solution to the mix-ups and complications that have occurred during the play, but here Malvolio indicates a darker intent, that of revenge. He wants to return to the fray and, ultimately, defeat the happiness of the rest of the characters. Revenger's tragedies are dramas where the **revenger** never really has a happy outcome. *Hamlet* is, in essence, a revenge tragedy, since it involves him getting his own back on Claudius, the man who killed his father.

Revenge and comedy

Revenge is sometimes constructed in literature as a non-Christian concept. Christians are supposed to practise forgiveness, a central tenet of many comedies, so that the characters who have been outwitted or are fooled will somehow forgive the perpetrators of their unhappiness. Many comedies feature moments of revenge or push the limits of what comedy can do. Watching such comedies often feels like watching a tragedy where a small twist of the plot could result in the death of one or more of the major characters. Such comedies do not offer perfect solutions to the complications of the play and in this way they may well be more realistic portrayals of what life is really like.

When Malvolio is imprisoned and lampooned, he is treated very harshly. Audiences in Shakespeare's time appear to have enjoyed such characters getting their come-uppance, and a number of dramatists in the Renaissance and afterwards use this interest to good effect. Such plays often look at other issues of identity, ethnicity and sexuality that are explored through the dramatic medium. Some 'History' plays and 'Romances' of Shakespeare also include comic sequences that complicate the action. In these, dramatic comedy is used as a structural break in what is otherwise intensive drama, in the same way that comedy is also used in tragedy, both to alleviate tension and to see events from a new perspective.

Tragi-comedy

One way of understanding **tragi-comedy** is to think of the 'old world, green world, new world' model established in Chapter 10. In tragedy, the 'old world' and the 'green world' exist in just the same way, only the 'green world' of confusion does not end. Tragedies can only move to a 'new world' once some of the characters die. In tragi-comedy, the development of the 'new world' is much more in peril. It can feel as if the 'green world' is spinning out of control, instead of it being resolved. There is often a dark thread running through the world of confusion – and if the characters are not careful, they could die or be harmed in some way.

Usually tragi-comedies pit young lovers against authority figures in a much harsher way. The plays examine how society tries to control individuals, and there is more of an interest in crime, punishment, legality and imprisonment. Sometimes the lovers (who in regular romantic comedies would marry comparatively easily) are threatened with being parted or killed for their crimes. A particular focus is on the twin themes of justice and mercy. You may see here a connection between the concepts of revenge and forgiveness. Tragi-comedies grapple with a much more realistic vision of life.

In such plays by Shakespeare and other dramatists of this period (and immediately after), some of the controlling characters are likely to be more disturbing and unattractive. These will be contrasted, though, with those characters with whom we have **empathy**.

Key terms

Empathy: our ability as an audience to step into the shoes of an on-stage character.

Fornication: premarital and extramarital sexual activity.

Moral double: two characters' morality at opposite ends of the spectrum, who are the protagonist and antagonist of the play.

Bawd: a woman who is humorously indecent.

Sexuality, oppression and power: *Measure for Measure*

One of the characteristics of Shakespeare's 'problem' comedies is that they have very complicated multi-layered plots, and this is certainly the case with *Measure for Measure*. This tragi-comedy, first performed in 1604, has a plot that centres on the illegal marriage of Claudio and Juliet. **Fornication** outside of marriage in the city of Vienna is punishable by death, and this sentence is put in place by the unbending judge Angelo. Angelo is in charge of the city because the Duke of Vienna is to leave the city on a diplomatic mission.

Claudio's sister Isabella is a novice nun and she is asked to intercede on his behalf and plead for leniency after he is sentenced to death. Angelo abuses his position and power, since he says that he will only release Claudio if Isabella will sleep with him. However, the Duke has not left the city, but remains there disguised as a friar. It is he who helps Isabella to thwart Angelo's evil intentions. His disguise draws on more typical elements of dramatic comedy. The real possibility of Claudio's execution is why the play comes close to being a tragedy.

As you can see, this is a very different kind of Shakespearean comedy from those we looked at in Chapters 10 and 11. The usual structure is inverted since the comedy begins with a problem marriage. Happiness seems in peril because of the oppression of the state. A male figure in the play (Angelo) plans to use Isabella's sexuality for his own objectives. The construction of women in *Measure for Measure* is interesting because both Isabella and Juliet are in peril. As you will see, a third female character, Mariana, is also 'used' by the men.

Often in these kinds of tragi-comedy there is a trial scene, and this is the case here, with the Friar (the disguised Duke) being blamed for some false accusations against Angelo. The play has a problematic ending, too. Two of the women are forced to marry men: first, Mariana to Angelo, and then the Duke himself proposes marriage to Isabella. She seems to accept the offer, but does not speak. Many critics have commented on these 'silences' in the play, which seem not to offer the joyful nuptials of other comedies.

One way of understanding this play is to think of Isabella as the **moral double** (opposite) of Angelo. Angelo is the kind of inflexible authority figure we have witnessed before in the form of Malvolio. He is incapacitated by his lust. Comedies of this kind often use this moral doubling technique.

A number of other minor characters contribute to the sub-plots of the drama. These include Elbow (a simple constable), Froth (a foolish gentleman) and Mistress Overdone (a **bawd**). Again, their names indicate their characteristics.

Figure 12.1 *Lucky Strike Film productions promotional poster for* Measure for Measure, *2007*

The two tricks

In these kinds of comedy, quite unpleasant tricks are sometimes used to complicate the drama. For modern audiences these tricks may seem distasteful, but they were clearly appealing to earlier audiences. You may like to debate their impact in the drama.

The first is a 'bed' trick. In this, Isabella submits to Angelo, but substitutes his former fiancée Mariana in her place. Mariana has sex with Angelo and he believes that she is Isabella. Because Mariana and Angelo have now consummated their marriage, this leads to their eventual union. This trick is a new take on the idea of disguise, with Mariana acting as a 'body double' for Isabella.

The second is a 'head' trick. When Angelo says he wishes to see the executed head of Claudio, the Duke instigates the substitution of another head. At first this is to be another prisoner (a drunken villain named Barnadine), but eventually they use the head of a pirate named Ragozine who recently died of fever. Fortunately, Ragozine resembles Claudio. In this, you can see the lengths that characters go to in order to provide solutions to the comedy – even if it involves abusing other characters. This darker edge is very typical of tragi-comedy.

AQA Examiner's tip

Remember that creating some kind of debate in your coursework is central to producing a good answer. Without debate, your response will not hit the required assessment objectives.

Activity 1

Look at Act 3 Scene 4 from *Measure for Measure*. This is the moment when Isabella comes to plead for her brother's life, and when Angelo asks her to sleep with him. With a friend, read through or perform the dialogue.

- Comment on the structure and language of Shakespeare's writing.
- Does this have the feel of other comedies you have already encountered?
- To what extent is it more like a tragedy?

AQA Examiner's tip

The terms 'How far ...' and 'To what extent ...' often make good starting points for the creation of a good coursework title. Discuss these with your teacher and focus in on an area that interests you.

Commentary on Activity 1

This is Angelo's 'indecent proposal' to Isabella. In tone, this sequence has a much harsher feel than most other comedies we have encountered. You may already see the moral double issue at work in how they respond to each other. Angelo's language is very legal and logical, whereas Isabella's is much more impassioned. You may also note the Christian imagery at work.

In Isabella's final speech we note her helplessness, and that she is dominated by a patriarchal society. In some senses, this does not seem to set up the usual comic confusion. It is much more a life-and-death situation and the language here reflects that. Isabella is also confronting the power of the government – quite a task for a young woman. Her final **soliloquy** expresses her fears.

Key terms

Soliloquy: a speech spoken by a character who is usually alone on the stage, in which they tell or confess their thoughts to the audience.

Measure for Measure in performance

Measure for Measure was adapted for performance in the Restoration period (see Chapter 13). Audiences then seemed to continue to like its plot and tricks. One title for the play then was *Beauty, the Best Advocate*. In Victorian times, though, the play's subject matter surrounding sexual commerce was controversial and it was often edited. Modern productions have tended to focus in on the psychological and surveillance aspects of the play. Another characteristic of *Measure for Measure* is the unclear location of the scenes, which contemporary directors have used to their advantage to make the play fast-paced.

Extension tasks

1. Complete more research on performances of *Measure for Measure*, looking at how different directors have dealt with the difficulties of the Isabella and Mariana plots.
2. With most Shakespearean comedies, it is possible to update the look and feel of the production. What considerations would need to be explored in order to do this with *Measure for Measure*?

Sexual politics

A useful investigation for your coursework might be the sexual politics of *Measure for Measure* and plays like it. By sexual politics, we mean the power games that are played by both men and women in such dramas, which reflect the changes in society at the time when Shakespeare was writing. The old medieval order was changing and women were slowly beginning to be more assertive.

You might read into the play that Mariana is complicit with the old order, wishing to do what men want of her. Isabella, though, is more feisty and reactive, almost a new kind of modern woman. However, the sexual politics of the age still force her to marry and be reliant on men. You may like to discuss some of the roles for female characters in comedies. Look at the images of nuns, virgins, wives and prostitutes that are presented. Do you think that women had limited choices within the comic format?

Did you know?

The character of Mariana inspired Tennyson to write his 1830 poem *Mariana*.

Activity 2

Bearing in mind the issues of the sexual politics of *Measure for Measure*, look at Act 5 Scene 1 in the play. Examine the way the Duke questions Mariana about who she is, and the subsequent reaction of Angelo.

Commentary on Activity 2

It seems that women during this period had no other function beyond being a maid (a virgin), a wife or a widow. In many senses this scene is a classic revelatory moment, when the disguise of the 'bed trick' is revealed. An earlier revelation has already occurred with the Friar revealing himself to be the Duke. The position of Mariana is, for some readers, quite problematic. She is seemingly a pawn in a male world. You may like to reflect on whether comedies treat women poorly. Meanwhile, Angelo is repositioned here as having 'the vanity of wretched fools'. It seems that rather than marriages organically bringing the play to a conclusion, instead they are fixed or manipulated into place.

Different readings

Jonathan Dollimore and Alan Sinfield

In 1980, the Marxist literary critic Raymond Williams wrote an influential book called *Problems in Materialism and Culture*. In this book he explained that culture and literature need to be read as a material product. In 1985, Jonathan Dollimore and Alan Sinfield started to apply this idea to the writings of Shakespeare, examining in more detail how his texts could be related to the context of production. This theory has come to be known as 'cultural materialism'. It has proved to be useful in terms of understanding some of the problem comedies. Their ideas about literary criticism offer the following core concepts:

- We always need to think about the historical context of a play.
- Plays are not transcendent (this means they are not merely 'great for great's sake' – a view commonly applied to Shakespeare).
- Cultural materialism is interested in marginal groups in plays – like the women in *Measure for Measure*.
- It is interested in how texts are re-processed over time and how different time periods read and engage with the text. For example,

Measure for Measure would be read very differently after the development of feminist criticism from the 1960s onwards.

- It understands that culture sometimes exploits people in terms of their race (as we shall see with *The Merchant of Venice*), class, gender and sexuality.

Try applying some of these debates to the comedy you are exploring for your coursework. In an essay in Dollimore and Sinfield's *Political Shakespeare: New Essays in Cultural Materialism*, Dollimore looks at 'Transgression and Surveillance in *Measure for Measure*' and shows that issues of transgression (stepping outside of the normal code of sexual behaviours) are vital to understanding the play.

Jacqueline Rose

In an essay on sexuality in *Measure for Measure*, published in 1985, the critic Jacqueline Rose examines the sexual politics of the play in its context of production. She says of Isabella that

> ... 'uniting in her person are those extremes of attraction and recoil' and that the 'woman who refuses to meet that desire is as unsettling as the one who does so with excessive haste', arguing for her to be a 'hussy' and 'revered as the divine'. She posits that the 'two positions are, however, related and that the second can tip over into the first, with Angelo making the connection when he says, "What is't I dream on? O cunning enemy, that, to catch a saint, With saints dost bait thy hook?"'

Jacqueline Rose, 'Sexuality in the reading of Shakespeare: Hamlet *and* Measure for Measure', *in John Drakakis (ed.),* Alternative Shakespeares, *1985, p104*

You may wish to consider Isabella in the light of this comment: is she a mixture of saintly qualities and cunning? To an extent, unmarried women were supposed to have saintly qualities, but in Renaissance Britain maybe women needed more skills to survive. Isabella therefore assumes a more male role of cunningness to outwit the controlling male characters. Such roles blur the boundaries between the genders.

Link

Look at Chapter 16 of this textbook to see the different ways in which the observations of Rose (or other critics) could be integrated into your coursework.

AQA Examiner's tip

Often students think only about character and theme in their coursework. These areas are quite limited. Think about other readings you may be able to make: political, religious, cultural or gender-based.

Ethnicity, identity and usury in *The Merchant of Venice*

Another tragi-comedy worthy of our consideration is *The Merchant of Venice*, which was written sometime between 1596 and 1598. It is one of Shakespeare's most controversial plays. Set in the rich city of Venice, it concerns events surrounding the merchant Antonio, who works as the guarantor for a cash loan of 3,000 ducats. The cash is needed by Bassanio, who wishes to marry the beautiful heiress Portia. Antonio is wary and insulting towards the Jewish **ethnicity** of the moneylender Shylock, but nevertheless goes to him for a loan. Shylock practises usury normally, but offers his loan to Antonio with an unusual condition: that if Antonio is unable to pay him back, Shylock will take a pound of Antonio's flesh. Shylock remains proud of his **identity**, in the face of other characters' racism towards him.

Portia, meanwhile, has many suitors. They undergo a trial by choosing the correct casket. The first two suitors choose incorrectly the gold and silver caskets, but Bassanio rightly chooses the lead one. Meanwhile, we learn that Antonio's ship has been lost at sea. The climax of events comes at a trial before the Duke of Venice. Antonio cannot pay back the money he owes Shylock, so is under arrest. A young 'doctor of the law'

Key terms

Ethnicity: a person's ethnic origins.

Identity: a person's sense of themselves and their cultural heritage.

Did you know?

A guarantor is someone who guarantees repayment of a loan.

Usury is a process of lending money at excessively high interest rates.

named Balthazar is brought before the court, who is actually Portia in disguise. A flaw in the contract is eventually exposed and then Shylock is exposed as an 'alien'. He must submit his property to both the state of Venice and to Antonio and convert to Christianity. A sub-plot of the play involves Shylock's daughter Jessica, who has eloped with Lorenzo, and plans on converting to Christianity. Jessica steals from Shylock, and when we examine the story, this may be a greater tragedy than events in the main plot.

Activity 3

Read Act 4 Scene 1 from *The Merchant of Venice*. This scene is a famous examination of the issue of mercy. Portia is asking Shylock to show mercy towards Antonio. Examine the way that structure and language create an effect on the court and the audience.

Commentary on Activity 3

Disguise is a key component of this sequence. We know by now that this kind of deceit helps to unravel the complications. Portia is employing a great deal of Christian terminology to evoke the issue of mercy – all of which are alien to Shylock's belief system.

There is talk of justice, which Shylock is relying on to back up his claim. In his final lines from this extract he seems to evoke the reliability of the legal system. Ironically it is this system that is eventually going to bring his business and his lifestyle to an end. Portia's eloquence contrasts with both Shylock and the monosyllabic answers of Antonio.

The legal nature of this scene is seemingly far-removed from the regular romantic comedies in Shakespeare's work. There are the germs of a debate here as well: is the society of the period asking those who exhibit difference to conform or to continue to resist? The emphasis on legal proceedings also precedes the complex modern criminal justice system.

Key terms

Anti-Semitic: hostile towards Jewish people.

Avaricious: greedy for financial gain.

Different readings

The anti-Semitic

One of the core debates about *The Merchant of Venice* is whether or not the play is **anti-Semitic**. We know that Renaissance society was broadly unsympathetic to Jews (they had been expelled from England in the Middle Ages), and on stage they were usually presented as caricatures, with hooked noses and red wigs. This anti-Semitism had built up over time, since apparently Jewish people had killed Christ (all this seemingly ignoring the fact that Christ himself was Jewish).

At the time, Jewish people were generally seen as being deceitful and **avaricious**. In Shakespeare's play, Shylock might be seen as being presented unsympathetically, and the ending suggests that his forced conversion to Christianity makes for some kind of happy ending, since he will now be able to enter Heaven and have his soul saved. It also appears that Shakespeare contrasts the vengefulness of Shylock with the mercy and forgiveness of the Christian characters. He was probably once played as a bloodthirsty and evil character.

Figure 12.2 *Dustin Hoffman as Shylock in Peter Hall's 1989 London production of* The Merchant of Venice

The sympathetic

Other readers have a different interpretation of this tragi-comedy. They suggest that Shylock is a sympathetic character and that the play is about

Did you know?

A sham trial is a trial that is based on a ludicrous premise or wrongful evidence. They are quite common in dramatic comedy.

Key terms

Presentism: a theory of literary criticism, which proposes that in any text there is a never-ending dialogue between the past and the present, and that aspects of present culture always and inevitably inform our readings of a text.

tolerance. Their main evidence for this is the trial itself. They consider it to be a sham trial and that the Christian characters use tricks to mock Shylock and to win. Shylock is also presented as very eloquent (and therefore more likeable) in his 'Has not a Jew eyes?' speech. Generally, the trend in performance has been to present more sympathetic conceptualisations of Shylock, with those around him as 'bloodthirsty'. This has come through more sympathetic understandings of different ethnicities.

Presentism

A very new kind of literary criticism has been developed recently by critics such as Hugh Grady and Terence Hawkes. This approach is labelled **Presentism**. It suggests that with any text there is actually a never-ending dialogue between the past and the present, and that aspects of present culture always and inevitably inform our readings of a text.

It would be hard for us to read *The Merchant of Venice* without knowledge of, for example, the Jewish holocaust of the 20th century or contemporary hostilities between Arabic countries and Israel. One Presentist critic, John Drakakis, observes that *The Merchant of Venice* shows signs of the 'radical instability' of the Elizabethan era, when it comes to looking at other ethnicities and economic developments.

Activity 4

1. Have a look at Shylock's famous speech in Act 3 Scene 1. See if you can adapt it to another ethnic group that represents a minority within a majority culture. Examine issues of prejudice and stereotypes. Feel free to update the language, but aim to keep the feel of the original.
2. You may like to look at the way other ethnicities are presented by Shakespeare and his contemporaries. Look at Shakespeare's construction of *Othello* and Christopher Marlowe's *The Jew of Malta*. With a slight change to the dialogue, could other ethnicities be cast in the role of Shylock?

Commentary on Activity 4

You may have chosen one of a wide range of contemporary ethnicities, which might be specific groups or 'stateless nations' across the European Union. There are other ethnicities across the globe that find themselves operating in cultures that are not sympathetic to them. Consider, for example, Maori culture in New Zealand, Native Americans in the USA or Aboriginal people in Australia.

There are probably people from many ethnic groups who could step into the role of a figure such as Shylock, perhaps showing the universality of his position – as someone on the edge of a more mainstream society.

Extension tasks

1. Examine the construction of Shylock and discuss with your class whether you find Shakespeare's presentation of him to be sympathetic or anti-Semitic. This might lead into re-creative writing or into a conventional essay.
2. How far do you find a 'Presentist' reading of comedy to be useful? You can apply this idea to *The Merchant of Venice*, *Measure for Measure* or any other comedy you are examining. Discuss your thoughts with a partner.

Did you know?

The playwright Arnold Wesker (b.1932) wrote a play entitled *The Merchant*, which tells the story from Shylock's point of view. This might make an interesting starting point for re-creative work.

Other 'problem' and 'dark' comedies to consider

Shakespeare was not the only writer in the Renaissance to tackle more difficult issues in his comedies. A number of other playwrights wrote plays that pushed the boundary between comedy and tragedy, including:

- *Bartholomew Fair* by Ben Jonson (1614)
- *A Fair Quarrel* by Thomas Middleton and William Rowley (1617)
- *The Birth of Merlin* by William Rowley (1620).

Romance and history

Shakespeare's final comic plays (*Pericles*, *Cymbeline*, *The Winter's Tale* and *The Tempest*) are often called the 'Romances'. These are quite stylised plays, often about how an evil force disrupts and displaces a noble family. To some extent this matches the confusion stage of the more established Shakespearean comedies, and many of the plays enter a 'green world'. The plays, which have the feel of fairy-tales, do not have the social realism of some of the tragi-comedies. Instead, they are set in a mythical or fantasy world. *The Winter's Tale* has an unusual structure: the first half of it appears to be a tragedy, while the second half is a comedy. The debate about their categorisation could be an interesting area for you to investigate.

The so-called 'History' plays of Shakespeare also have a number of comic sequences within them. Although they obviously do not follow the usual comic dramatic structure, the range of characters, humour and situations can be explored productively. Among the plays you might wish to read are *Henry IV: Part I* and *Part 2* (which feature Falstaff – later seen in *The Merry Wives of Windsor*) and *Henry V*. You may be able to consider how the comedy informs our appreciation of the history.

Ideas for coursework tasks

The problem, dark or tragi-comedies offer lots of interesting areas of investigation for your coursework, because they push the genre of comedies and what they can do.

Essay (conventional response)

Do you consider Shakespeare's *Measure for Measure* to be closer to a tragedy or a comedy?

Re-creative response

Write some scenes in contemporary English set before *Measure for Measure* begins, involving discussions between Angelo and Mariana, and why their relationship did not lead to marriage the first time round. In your commentary, say why you chose these moments relating to your reading of the play. Refer to critical interpretations if possible.

AQA Examiner's tip

Avoid saying obvious things about a comedy. Do not, for example, complete a coursework task that asks why a particular comedy is funny or why a main character is a comic hero. This is because both strands are obvious enough already. Exploring the less obvious aspects of a play, or the difficulties of a text, make much more rewarding areas of investigation.

Did you know?

Shakespeare is supposed to have written a number of apocryphal plays, beyond the usual canon ascribed to him. These include *Edward III*, *Love's Labour's Won* and *Mucedorus*.

AQA Examiner's tip

Remember that although understanding the historical period and its features is important, this will only get you so far up the grading of the assessment objectives. It is your exploration, analysis and ability to consider different interpretations that will get you the best marks.

Summary

In this chapter you have learned about the kind of issues raised in 'problem' comedies that do not always fit the usual model of comic drama. By examining two Shakespeare plays – *Measure for Measure* and *The Merchant of Venice* – you have examined how these plays extol the genre of tragi-comedy and what kinds of characters and situations you might expect to find in them. Some alternative views of the plays by other readers have been offered, and you have an idea of the other kinds of 'dark' comedy being written in the period. Sexual politics, the treatment of women and different ethnicities or identities may also be productive areas of investigation for your coursework. Finally, you have looked at how the genres of romance and history might intersect with dramatic comedy.

Further reading

- *Shakespeare Criticism 1935–1960* edited by Anne Ridler (1963). In this book, Ridler assembles many useful essays on 'problem' comedies.
- *Political Shakespeare: New Essays in Cultural Materialism* edited by Jonathan Dollimore and Alan Sinfield (1985). This is a well-considered application of cultural materialism to Shakespeare, with many interesting insights into the plays.

Extension (this reading may be challenging)

- *Problems in Materialism and Culture* by Raymond Williams (1980). This is the classic account of the theory of cultural materialism and gives you lots of ideas on how to apply it to literary texts.
- *Shakespeare's Problem Plays* by Simon Barker (2005). This looks at *Measure for Measure* and *All's Well That Ends Well*, but also offers some general pointers on how to deal with problem comedies.

13 Restoration comedy and the comedy of manners

This chapter:

- Allows you to reflect further on the core debates within comedy.
- Explores further genres and historical periods of comedy.
- Explores feminist readings of genre and considers the investigation of women within comedy and as writers of comedy as a productive area of debate.
- Considers how past comedy can be recovered and reinterpreted for modern audiences.

Key terms

Status quo: the current or established state of affairs.

Subversive: seeking to overthrow the establishment.

Stock: the usual or stereotypical characters.

Beaus: relaxed, attractive and self-confident men.

Rakes: men who live an irresponsible and immoral life.

Fops: men who are dandy-like and a little effeminate. They often pay a lot of attention to their appearance and clothes.

Valets: personal servants who took care of a gentleman's clothes and lifestyle.

Squires: gentlemen from the countryside. They are usually satirised in Restoration comedy as not having the manners or fashions of the city. They often come from the north or the west.

By now, you should understand some of the basic functions of comedy as a genre. Often, the lack of self-knowledge by the characters causes the disorder and misrule. You might want to ask if the comedy you are studying subverts or supports the **status quo** of the time period in which the text was first produced. The representation of women in comedies is also clearly a productive area of investigation for your coursework.

In your thinking about comedy, a number of debates should have emerged as well: can comedies still be criticised for their lack of seriousness and does the genre only offer one-dimensional characters? You may also be considering whether characters really develop in comedy or do they just stay the same? A crucial discussion you may have in your class is whether comedy does 'laugh us into understanding' or whether it remains trivial. You may also have started to consider the idea that comedy can be highly **subversive**. Those in authority or in control are sometimes worried about the effect on audiences.

Restoration comedy

Puritanism (imagined on stage in an earlier period by the character of Malvolio in *Twelfth Night*) and the Civil War had put a stop to much comedy on the stage in Britain in the middle of the 17th century. However, during the final decades of that century and in the aftermath of the coronation of King Charles II, dramatic comedy flourished again. There was a counter-reaction to past restrictions and after the restoration of the King, comic dramatists became preoccupied with dramas that looked at sexual relationships within polite society. This new type of comedy has now come to be known as Restoration comedy.

These kinds of comedy used many elements from previous centuries, but they were usually light and sometimes farcical in their themes, with confusion generated by a web of intrigue and deceit. Their plots often involved amorous and illicit relationships. The plays rarely took on serious themes, but heroism and sentiment were important ideas. One crucial change from the previous age, however, was that women were allowed on stage for the first time. This meant that the characters played were much more realistic, but their place in the theatre attracted a lot of criticism.

Key components of Restoration comedy

Although not the case for every comedy produced in this period, if we look at the range of comedies produced by writers such as William Congreve, John Dryden, William Wycherley, George Farquhar, George Vanbrugh, George Etherege and Aphra Behn, we discover the importance of the following components:

- Marriage is a central theme.
- Key **stock** characters include **beaus**, **rakes**, **fops**, bawds, scheming **valets**, young and older women, and country **squires**.
- They are mainly written in prose, though with some verse sections.
- There is a focus on repartee and wit.

Key terms

Affectation: a form of pretence in behaviour.

Blasphemous: to talk irreverently about something sacred.

Figure 13.1 *Sheila Hancock as Lady Wishfort in* The Way of the World *at the Lyric Theatre, London, 1992*

Did you know?

Jeremy's Collier's 1698 attack on Restoration comedy was called *A Short View of the Immorality and Profaneness of the English Stage*. It is, in fact, quite a long book.

AQA Examiner's tip

Do not imagine that your text always has one audience. Most plays have different audiences over time.

- The tone is bawdy, cynical and amoral.
- There are often double or triple plot-lines.
- Money, sexual commerce and social standing are key issues.

There are components of older comedies here. However, it is worth bearing in mind that the plays often dealt with the issue of human beings' belief in their own self-importance, and the absurdity of a world with elaborate rules and codes of behaviour or manners. What comes across is an artificial world of pretence and hiding from the truth. The plays suggest that under apparent civilisation is a kind of rampant disorder. The plays are about satirising pretence and artificiality. The core source of comedy is to be found in the character's **affectation**.

Criticism of Restoration comedy

Just as some modern comedies come in for criticism, so did the comedies of this era. People who considered themselves to be respectable and the 'guardians of morality' avoided the theatres that promoted comedies. They felt such comedies were **blasphemous** and were the reason for corruption and immorality in the society of the period. The playwrights were often attacked for their themes being frivolous and rude. One of the leading critics of these kinds of comedy was the Reverend Jeremy Collier (1650–1726), who was instrumental in leading public opinion against the immoral nature of such plays.

The playwrights, meanwhile, defended themselves, saying that in fact their works were pieces of social criticism and that they merely mirrored the age they were writing in. For example, William Wycherley's play *The Country Wife* (1675) satirised the sexual desires of people in a corrupt society.

Affectation, wit and repartee: *The Way of the World*

The Way of the World by William Congreve (1670–1729) is a useful starting point for exploring Restoration comedy because it has many of the components mentioned previously. It also has many similarities to Shakespearean comedies that you will recognise. The comedy is set in motion by the characters of Mirabell and Millamant. The former is in love with the latter, a niece of Lady Wishfort, and he has pretended to have made love with the aunt to conceal his suit of the niece. The deceit has been revealed to Lady Wishfort by Mrs Marwood, who enacts revenge on Mirabell because he rejected her advances.

Much of the comedy in the play is offered through the servant Waitwell, who impersonates an uncle of his called Sir Rowland. Sir Rowland aims to make love to Lady Wishfort and then pretend to marry her. Disguise, therefore, remains an important fuel of the plot in the play. Another amusing character is Lady Wishfort's country nephew Sir Wilfull Witwoud, who is, in effect, a clumsy fool from the rural world, struggling to cope in the city. The play proves that love can endure in a very mercenary society, but that in order to achieve this, one has to use wit and repartee to survive. Affectation is to be cut down at every opportunity.

The importance of names

Following an older tradition in comic drama, Congreve gives his characters names that suit their personalities:

Fainall: insincere and deceitful

Mirabell: honourable and chivalrous

Witwoud: tries to be witty but is unsuccessful

Petulant: disagreeable person

Millamant: someone with a thousand admirers

Mrs Marwood: spiteful tendencies and would do you harm

Lady Wishfort: a woman who wishes for love/sex

Mincing: someone who walks in this way and is affected

Waitwell: a servant.

In this way, an audience does not require lots of character background. They instantly recognise the type. See if you can apply this on the comedies you encounter. It is still a technique used by playwrights today.

Activity 1

In the 1700 edition of *The Way of the World* are found two **epigrams** that contain two Latin quotations from Horace's *Satires*. Translated, they read as follows:

It is worthwhile, for those of you who wish adulterers no success, to hear how much misfortune they suffer, and how often their pleasure is marred by pain and, though rarely achieved, even then fraught with danger.

I have no fear in her company that a husband may rush back from the country, the door burst open, the dog bark, the house shake with the din, the woman, deathly pale, leap from her bed, her complicit maid shriek, she fearing for her limbs, her guilty mistress for her dowry and I for myself.

Now read the following excerpt from the Prologue of *The Way of the World*:

Of those few fools, who wit ill stars are curst,
Sure scribbling fools, called poets, fare the worst:
For they're a sort of fools which Fortune makes,
And after she has made 'em fools, forsakes.
With Nature's oafs 'tis quite a diff'rent case,
For Fortune favours all her Idiot -race:
In her own nest the Cuckow-eggs we find,
O'er which she broods to hatch the Changeling-kind.
No portion for her own she has to spare,
So much she doats on her adoption care.

What do these epigrams and the Prologue tell you about the purpose and place of comedy during this period? If you look at *The Way of the World*, and have started to read the text, see if you can apply it there. If you are looking at another comedy, what insights do these give you?

Key terms

Epigram: a short and witty saying at the beginning of a text.

Commentary on Activity 1

Both these epigrams focus on the inherent danger in adulterous (and thus comic) behaviour. They indicate that, just like the 'problem' plays that were looked at in Chapter 12, the comedy here looks at something more sinister. These plays contain much behaviour that, these days, we would term risky. There is therefore learning and advice to be taken from them. The folly of others will help us learn how to conduct our own lives. The excerpt from the Prologue offers a more complex idea about Fortune. Here, the character of Fortune (derived from the medieval concept of Fortune's Wheel) suggests that the dramatists (or poets) themselves are fools for even daring to dramatise comedy. Fortune also seems to nurture fools – perhaps because they are in search of fortune (financial gain). Note, too, the metaphor of the cuckoo. Being 'cuckolded' is an idea found, for example, in some of Geoffrey Chaucer's *The Canterbury Tales* – the idea that someone can be fooled or tricked is an obvious theme in these kinds of play. The notion of the changeling is also present: that disguise and the swapping of people can cause confusion.

Link

To complete Activity 2 you will need to use *The Way of the World*, which is printed in the Extracts section at the back of this book, Extract 2 (p132).

Activity 2

In Act 1 Scene 5 of the play, Mirabell and Fainall discuss the imminent arrival of Sir Wilfull Witwoud. Read their discussion and try to work out how the lines would be spoken.

- What is the effect of talking about this character before the audience meets him?
- Discuss the use of witty repartee in their dialogue.

Extension tasks

1. Although most Restoration comedies are read as a conflict between the witty and the foolish, examine the play you are studying with an eye on the battle between good and evil.
2. Investigate the performance conditions of Restoration comedy.
   - What do you learn about the theatres and audiences of the period?
   - Consider whether Restoration comedy is easy or difficult to present to contemporary audiences.

Commentary on Activity 2

In essence, this section shows how two sophisticated urban characters regard country characters, showing the difference in value systems and ideology. Generally, it is funny when very rural characters enter the urban environment and vice versa. There is also a funny sequence about exporting fools and how the English ought not to do this. Extended puns (for example, the 'crab', 'apple' and 'rotten' imagery) give the audience an idea of how Sir Wilfull does not understand the manners and conventions of the age. They also compare him with Caliban, from Shakespeare's *The Tempest*. A long-established technique in comedy is for two characters to talk about another character before that character arrives. The audience then tests their own theories about the character. Sir Wilfull's incompetence is extended by comparison with his brother. The text also comments on the importance of originality in wit (not using other people's humour).

Different readings

Robert D. Hume

There are many different approaches to Restoration comedy. Robert D. Hume has written extensively on the genre. He commented in 1976 that 'Restoration comedies are about people, not ideas or ethical abstractions... they present the complexities and ambiguities of human experience rather than a simple white-or-black picture of what man should or should not be.' He also observes that the substance of the genre is composed of

> stock characters and situations... The same plots are used over and over again: the young man wins his girl and usually reforms in the process; fortune is won; adulterous copulation is achieved; without discovery – or the consequences are evaded. The same perils of discovery are run in comedy after comedy. The wanton wives, young libertines, jealous husbands, and witty young ladies produce highly repetitive patterns of events and situations.

Robert D. Hume, The Development of English Drama in the Late Seventeenth Century, *1990, pp71–2*

Jocelyn Powell

In an earlier essay on George Etherege's plays, Jocelyn Powell (1965) notes a tension in Restoration comedy between a 'comedy of criticism' and a 'comedy of experience'. Powell observes that

> the essential difference between the comedy of criticism and the comedy of experience is that in the former, though a good character may be given faults and a bad character virtues, there is never any serious doubt as to the category to which the character belongs; whereas in the latter there are no categories. Criticism sees characters from one angle, but experience is constantly modifying the angle from which a character is seen, so that, like a shot silk, his colour changes with the light.

Jocelyn Powell, 'George Etheredge and the Form of a Comedy' in John Russell Brown and Bernard Harris (ed.), Restoration Theatre, *1965, p60*

L.C. Knights

L.C. Knights (1907–97) was a famous literary critic who had a quite a dismissive view of Restoration comedies. In 1937 he wrote the following:

> The trouble is not that Restoration comic writers deal with a limited number of themes, but that they bring to bear a miserably limited set of attitudes... The criticism that defenders of Restoration comedy need to answer is not that the comedies are 'immoral', but that they are trivial, gross and dull.

L.C. Knights, 'Restoration Comedy: The Reality and the Myth', in Scrutiny, *1937*

Activity 3

1. With these three readers' thoughts on Restoration comedy in mind, apply their ideas to either *The Way of the World* (Act 5 Scene 14) or the Restoration comedy you are studying. Decide which reading you are more sympathetic towards.
2. Develop a paragraph of criticism about this section that integrates these three views – but which culminates in you coming to your own conclusion. Integrate other critics if you wish.

Commentary on Activity 3 and Activity 4

There is no commentary on these activities, but discuss your written responses with your class and your teacher.

Other Restoration-style comedies to consider

There is a wide range of other Restoration-style comedies that are worth exploring. The same basic principles that are found in *The Way of the World* are also to be found in these plays:

- *The Provok'd Wife* by George Vanbrugh (1679)
- *The Recruiting Officer* by George Farquhar (1706)
- *Wild Oats* by John O'Keeffe (1791).

A woman's voice: Aphra Behn

You will have already noticed that much Restoration comedy seems to embody a very male and **patriarchal** perspective on the world. Aphra Behn (1640–89) is broadly regarded as Britain's first female playwright, and she was developing her drama in the Restoration period. Up until

Did you know?

Although *The Way of the World* is now considered the best-crafted of all the Restoration comedies, when it was first produced at the Lincoln's Inn Fields Theatre in 1700 it was not successful at all.

AQA Examiner's tip

Always suggest a range of possible interpretations in re-creative commentaries and then explain why you chose a particular one.

Link

To complete Activity 3 you may wish to use *The Way of the World*, which is printed in the Extracts section at the back of this book, Extract 3 (p133).

Activity 4

Restoration comedies offer lots of opportunities for re-creative work. If you are looking at a Restoration comedy, choose one of the servant characters and develop some writing around their feelings about their masters. Servants and masters always make for good comedy. Aim to imitate the style and language choices of the base text.

Did you know?

The Recruiting Officer is used in an **intertextual** way in the 1988 drama *Our Country's Good* by Timberlake Wertenbaker, which is about an Australian penal colony attempting to put on the play there.

Key terms

Intertextual: when one text makes reference to another.

Patriarchal: pertaining to men and male views.

Figure 13.2 *Aphra Behn: A portrait*

Key terms

Interregnum: the period of time in which no king or queen is on the throne. In Britain, this lasted from 1649 to 1660.

Royalists: supporters of the king and the monarchy.

Courtesan: a female member of a court, but one who is independent and has free morals.

Disenfranchisement: when a particular group of people feel they are deprived of their rights.

Complicit: being involved with a wrongdoing.

Did you know?

Aphra Behn worked as a spy for Charles II against the Dutch.

fairly recently, literary critics have not celebrated Behn's work, but in the wake of the development of feminist literary criticism in the 1960s and 1970s, her work has been re-evaluated and she is now seen as an important writer.

Wine, women and song: The Rover

The Rover premiered in 1677 and it has a subtitle, *The Banished Cavaliers*. Like other Restoration comedies of this time, three plot-lines dominate and merge. The play is set during the **interregnum** when **royalists** sought exile abroad, and the drama tells the story of three Englishmen in Naples during the carnival there. The carnival allows disguise and duplicity, as well as alcohol, singing and the pursuit of the opposite sex.

The 'rover' of the title is Willmore, a rakish naval captain, who travels to Naples with Colonel Belvile and a fool called Blunt. Willmore falls in love with Hellena, who is trying to experience what love is like before her controlling brother sends her to a convent. The complication stage of the comedy occurs when a **courtesan** – Angelica Bianca – falls in love with Willmore. When she learns of his betrayal, she seeks revenge on him. A second story involves Hellena's sister Florinda wishing to marry Belvile, with Blunt being deceived by Lucetta – a prostitute and thief.

In some respects *The Rover* is close to becoming a tragedy, and it has a seriousness that we find in other plays such as *Measure for Measure*. There are disturbing moments of rape and near-rape in the play, and the revenge of Angelica also sets a darker tone than that of most other Restoration comedies.

The Rover and feminist literary criticism

The Rover is of great interest to feminist literary scholars, not least because it stands as one of the first plays written by a female dramatist, but also because of the instances of rape in the play, and the issue of Angelica being rejected by Willmore. The play is often read as a text highlighting the powerlessness and **disenfranchisement** felt by women during Behn's time. In this sense, the drama steps over a line and becomes something of a 'problem' comedy.

There is a lot of debate about the rape sequences in the play and about the behaviour of men within it. Some critics argue that by showing these scenes on stage, Behn exposes the stupidity and folly of men. This seems to match the 'reform' of the main rake of the play – Willmore, who eventually marries Hellena. Other observers have viewed Behn as being **complicit** with the lascivious and sexist behaviour of men during this period. It is likely that she had to write a play that at least followed the conventions of the day, or as a play written by a woman it would never have been produced.

Different readings

John Doran

A 19th-century male critic called John Doran was decidedly unimpressed with the work of Aphra Behn. In his history of the English stage, published in 1864, he described her as the 'most shameless woman who ever took pen in hand, to corrupt the public... she was a mere harlot who danced through uncleanness, and dared them to follow.'

W.R. Owens

The critic W.R. Owens, writing in 1996, has re-examined *The Rover*. He sees the comedy as less of a 'romp' and more a 'powerful social satire' and comments that:

> Behn is offering a serious criticism of contemporary social and sexual conventions. In particular, she is opening up the whole question of the sexual 'double standard' by which 'rakish' behaviour in men seems to be tolerated, and is certainly no bar to their marrying well, whereas women who engage in sex outside marriage are to wreck irretrievably any chance of respectable marriage.

W.R. Owens, 'Remaking the canon: Aphra Behn's The Rover*' in W.R. Owens and Lizbeth Goodman (eds.),* Shakespeare, Aphra Behn and the Canon, *1996, p132 and p162*

Activity 5

Think about both John Doran's and W.R. Owens' views of *The Rover*. Certainly, double standards seem to be at work, and perhaps comedy is a good way of exploring these. In this sense, the message of *The Rover* is very contemporary, since double standards over the behaviour of men and women still exist now.

Discuss the following points with a partner and share the results with your class.

- Why do you think Doran took this view of a female comic playwright?
- What kind of performance conditions could be used for a modern take on this play?

Link

To complete Activity 5 you may want to use the extract from Act 1 Scene 1 of *The Rover*, which is printed in the Extracts section at the back of this book, Extract 4 (p133).

Commentary on Activity 5

Doran is clearly an uninformed observer who failed to see the vitality of Behn's play. He confuses the writer's identity with the **discourse** of the drama. This is why it is sometimes good to be cynical about criticism that only looks at the writer's life in relation to the text. Owens is much more open-minded and comments favourably on what the play achieves. In the sequence from Act 1 Scene 1, you should have noticed that women seem to be subject to the will of men, and that resisting that is difficult. The extract supports Owen's view. Clearly, within the limitations of the genre, Behn was quite a radical voice – very different to the kind of comedy that would emerge later on. A play like *The Rover* is very open to modern interpretations.

Key terms

Discourse: the language and texture of the play.

The comedy of manners

For many people, the roots of the so-called genre of 'the comedy of manners' can be traced back to elements of Restoration comedy. Comedy of manners is usually a type of play that satirises the affectations of a particular social class. Such plays are usually characterised by scandal, witty dialogue and the presence of stock characters. Among the best-known writers of comedies of manners were the French dramatist Molière (for example, in his *Tartuffe*, 1664, and *The Misanthrope*, 1666) and the Irish-born playwright Oscar Wilde (1854–1900). His play *The Importance of Being Earnest* is a classic example of the genre. In the latter play, the financial and familial objections to two marriages are overcome.

AQA Examiner's tip

Always think about the sub-genre of the comedy you are looking at. Try to clarify the characteristics of the sub-genre. Sometimes new types of comedy are formed by the merging of two sub-genres.

Ideas for coursework tasks

Essay (conventional response)

To what extent do wit or incompetence fuel the development of the comedy in William Congreve's *The Way of the World*?

Re-creative response

One of the characters in Aphra Behn's *The Rover* is Moretta. Write a set of letters to Governess Callis, criticising the behaviour of the female characters (such as Hellena, Florinda, Angelica Bianca and others you may choose) after the play has finished.

In your commentary say why you chose these criticisms relating to your reading of the play. Refer to critical interpretations if possible.

Summary

In this chapter you have explored a new genre – Restoration comedy. Restoration comedy builds on the historical development of comedy, but also offers a new take on dramatic comedy, based on satirising affectation. You have also considered a range of other comedies, culminating in discussion of a female comic playwright, Aphra Behn. Her work proves useful in applying a more feminist reading of this kind of comedy. You have understood the impact of Restoration comedy in helping to shape sentimental comedies and the comedy of manners.

Further reading

- *The Cambridge Introduction to English Theatre, 1660–1900* by Peter Thomson (2006). There is lots of good discussion of dramatic comedy throughout the period – relating to the theatre, actors and texts.
- *The First English Actresses: Women and Drama, 1660–1700* by E. Howe (1992). The book looks at the problems and difficulties of being a female comic performer in this period.

Extension (this reading may be challenging)

- *The Cambridge Companion to English Restoration Theatre* edited by Deborah Payne Fisk (2000). This volume will give you lots of insight into the variety of dramatic comedy performed after the Restoration.
- *Rereading Aphra Behn: History, Theory and Criticism* by H. Humer (1993). This takes a new look at the work of Aphra Behn.

14 Modern comedies, absurdist comedy and farce

This chapter:

- Considers how a range of comedies from the late 19th and 20th centuries develop the genre.
- Understands absurdist comedies and how they reflect postmodern life and society.
- Explores and investigates the characteristics of modern farce as a dramatic genre.
- Understands that modern forms of dramatic comedy can be more complex than earlier ones, and integrates many other aspects.

Key terms

Postmodern: this literally means 'after the modern' but it has come to mean texts whose construction shows the alienation and disruption of the modern world.

Alienation: the process through which a person feels exiled from and forgotten about by their own community.

Naturalistic: a style of drama that aims to be more natural in terms of performance than previous dramas.

Farce: a comic play featuring improbable situations.

Did you know?

Constantin Stanislavski (1863–1948) was a Russian actor and theatre director who developed an innovative style of acting based on organisation and naturalistic techniques known as 'the system'. It is still employed by many actors and directors today.

Many of the plays that were written in the late 19th and early 20th centuries do not always appear to fully fit the dramatic comedy genre. The 19th century did produce dramatic comedies, but their form has perhaps been eclipsed by the rise of the comic novel (by writers like Charles Dickens and Anthony Trollope). Some dramatists of this period used aspects of comedy within plays that critiqued the conventional social order. By the 20th century, there was a sense that the old value system was being eroded. Modern comedies of this period dealt with how society was decaying and disintegrating.

The 20th century also witnessed two world wars, which changed people's perception of the established order, and caused them to have less faith in Christianity and traditional values. In some respects, the comic dramas prior to World War One anticipate this collapse of normality, while those coming in the aftermath of the World War Two reflected a **postmodern** sense of **alienation**, frustration and helplessness.

Although these 20th-century plays took on 'big' issues – for example the conflict in Ireland or the liberation of women – they relied on the historical mechanisms of comedy to make their point. The defining elements of previous comedies, such as marriage and disguise, dropped away, but other elements, such as their focus on festival, ritual and the transition from 'old world', through 'green worlds' to 'new worlds' continued.

Seriously funny: Anton Pavlovich Chekhov and George Bernard Shaw

The Russian-born dramatist Anton Pavlovich Chekhov (1860–1904) wrote a set of dramas that in some respects defy categorisation. In the early part of his career he wrote a number of short comic plays, but in the later part of his career he used more **naturalistic** techniques, to show that the world seemingly has no concern for the individual. This comedy technique comes out in plays such as *The Cherry Orchard* (1903). Chekhov intended the play to be a comedy about the return of a family to their country estate. It even contains elements of **farce**, but, interestingly, it was directed by Constantin Stanislavski as more of a tragedy, which perhaps shows the new seriousness in these kinds of play. You may find this play an interesting example of a comedy that defies the usual rules and is open to several interpretations.

George Bernard Shaw (1856–1950) wrote many comedies in his lifetime. Like Chekhov, he seems to combine several genres at once, though his writings are full of much comic invention. His plays were a progression from the kind of sentimental comedies of the Victorian period, since they looked at the darker forces that might restrict an individual. Shaw was interested in comic conflicts of thought and belief – a kind of intellectual comedy.

A typical example is *Arms and the Man* (1894), which is set during the 1885 Serbo-Bulgarian War. Unlike lots of other comic writers, Shaw chooses to make dialogue and discourse the main comic moments of such plays, but they still follow the established comic format – with

Arms and the Man, and others by Shaw culminating in multiple marriages. In *Arms and the Man*, the 'green' world is the war itself – a place of confusion and disguise.

Other modern comedies to consider

There is a wide range of other modern comedies that are worth exploring. The same basic principles that are found in the plays of Chekhov and Shaw are also to be found in these plays:

- *The Magistrate* by Arthur Wing Pinero (1885)
- *Lady Windermere's Fan* by Oscar Wilde (1892)
- *The Playboy of the Western World* by J.M. Synge (1907).

Absurdist and black comedy

In the immediate aftermath of World War Two, across many territories, there seemed to be a development of a new genre of comedy that we now define as **absurdist comedy** or sometimes **black comedy**. In such plays, laughter from the audience is generated by them watching characters operating in a world they cannot understand. The main aim of many of these dramas was to show that the established social order around us is, in fact, a complete illusion and that life is full of absurd and odd moments. It is also a comedy that reflects a move away from an essentially Christian view of the universe to a more humanist or **secular** position.

Absurdist or black comedy draws on some of the conventions established by kitchen-sink dramas. These were comedies or plays that were not set in the middle-class environments of plays from the early 20th century, but instead were in working-class bed-sits, flats or kitchens. The characters were often drawn from the working-class or under-class. Homelessness, personality disorders and mental illness formed some of the themes. Sometimes, the settings were more **abstract** and unclear, however, showing that the same issues and problems face all people.

You might even begin to see a link between the bizarre situations that some characters are placed in by these dramatists and the more absurdist television comedy of the 1950s, 1960s and 1970s, such as Spike Milligan's *Q* series, *The Goon Show* and *Monty Python's Flying Circus*.

A tree, some tramps and secularism: *Waiting for Godot*

Waiting for Godot (1953), written by Samuel Beckett, is an important black comedy and an early piece of 'theatre of the absurd'. Beckett (1906–89) was born in Dublin, but spent much of his life in France, initially writing *Waiting for Godot* in French. In English, the play is subtitled 'A tragicomedy in two acts'.

The play's initial stage direction is 'A country road. A tree. Evening' and the audience meet two men – Estragon and Vladimir – who appear to be tramps. They are waiting for someone called Godot (pronounced God-oh), who never actually arrives. Many observers comment that Godot is a symbol for God, and the fact that he does not arrive shows how secular the world had become in the post-World War Two period. It also makes a wider comment on human beings seeking something more spiritual in their lives but never really finding it.

It is not a traditional piece of dramatic comedy, but it is written in such a way as to be highly comic. This is because Beckett develops the characters into types that the audience recognises, and has them do things that are absurd and puzzling. Other characters contribute to the

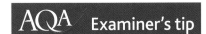

AQA Examiner's tip

You are permitted to study one text in translation in your coursework.

Key terms

Absurdist comedy: drama that examines life outside common sense and the usual conventions.

Black comedy: comedy that looks at dark or depressing themes in a comic way.

Secular: the system of thought concerned with worldly matters – and not those of religion or spirituality.

Abstract: not always representing things pictorially or realistically.

Figure 14.1 *Sir Patrick Stewart (as Vladimir) and Sir Ian McKellan (as Estragon) in* Waiting for Godot, *at the Theatre Royal Haymarket, London*

comedy: Pozzo is a dominating character who possesses a slave, ironically called Lucky. The dialogue of the play is very disjointed, circular (in that things are repeated), and bleak in language and theme. The soliloquies use a **stream-of-consciousness** style of writing. The play has several themes: **existentialism**, secularism and the pointlessness of life. Estragon summarises much of the play's theme with his repetition of the line 'Nothing to be done'.

Beckett's comedies can also be seen as a response to the **realist tradition** in comedy. In his writing he disregards the unities of time and place, and focuses more on the issues that face all of us. The normal plot of comedy is also rejected. There is no happy resolution in the form of marriage, and the 'green world' of the countryside the characters find themselves in does not enter a new phase. In fact, Beckett seems to suggest that in the absurdity of life, the comic 'green world' of confusion never actually ends and that we are perpetually trapped within it.

Activity 1

Consider the extract of Samuel Beckett's *Waiting for Godot* that begins with Vladimir saying 'One is what one is ...' and ends with him saying 'Not at all!'.

Please note that this extract is not printed in the Extracts section. You will need to use a class copy of the play to complete this activity or find the extract on the internet.

- Examine the sequence and try to work out what is comic about it.
- How is black humour developed, and what aspects of the comedy are absurd?
- Can you imagine the effect of this piece of dramatic comedy when it was first performed in 1953?

In order to help you make your conclusions, you may wish to try to perform the section.

Commentary on Activity 1

You will first notice that this section of Beckett's play is very different from the kind of comedies you have encountered so far. Estragon's opening comment seems to suggest that nothing will alter or change. The detailed stage directions mean that comic timing is very well organised, and the length of the rope makes the audience wonder what is coming behind Lucky. Clearly, one human being using another human being in this way is a very 'black' piece of humour. It is making fun of the issue of slavery. Even in this absurd and non-realist world we do not expect human beings to treat others in this way. Therefore Beckett disrupts our normal sense of reality and the effect is comic.

There are absurd items: the carrot, the folding stool, the picnic basket and the whip. Lucky cannot possibly do anything to harm Estragon or Vladimir, so Pozzo's line, 'Be careful! He's wicked', is highly comic. There is confusion at the end of the sequence over the name Pozzo being similar to the name Godot. The piece would have undoubtedly shocked audiences in 1953 because such sequences were unexpected in other plays of this era.

Different readings

A play like *Waiting for Godot* is a useful postmodern play to explore within your coursework because there are so many different ways of reading it. The absurdity and lack of realism of the play have enhanced

Key terms

Stream-of-consciousness: a writing system that involves writing down ideas as soon as they are thought of and not ordering them, to imitate more accurately the reality of experience. It was practised by the novelist James Joyce, who greatly influenced Beckett.

Existentialism: a system of thought that emphasises that people are free to choose their own actions.

Realist tradition: where literature seeks to hold a mirror up to life and seeks to reproduce it as accurately as possible.

AQA Examiner's tip

Avoid excessive concentration on *only* analysing language in your essays. Make sure that you look at form and structure as well. Structure is usually harder to write about as it requires a higher level of analysis, but it will gain you a better mark.

Remember

Postmodern has come to mean texts whose construction shows the alienation and disruption of the modern world.

the range of interpretations taken from it. Debating and discussing this range of meanings is important and you will gain greater understanding of the play by doing so. Remember, too, that your interpretation is just as important as other people's.

Key terms

Cold War: the period of tension between the USA and Soviet Russia in the 1950s and 1960s.

Futility: a process that produces no result or change.

Link

For more information on Presentism, look back to Chapter 12.

Political comedy

Political readings of this dramatic comedy have been made. Some readers have commented that it is an allegory of the **Cold War**, while others have argued that it is symbolic of the relationship between Britain and Ireland. Others, noting Beckett's time in France, say that it is a play about the French resistance movement during World War Two. Presentist readings often adapt the play according to relevant contemporary political issues. In South Africa, Estragon and Vladimir were recently played by two black actors, while Pozzo and Lucky were played by white performers. This has ramifications in a country with a history of racial tension.

Christian

Despite the secular theme of the play, some critics see a Christian undertone to it and observe that the plot is based on a section of the Bible (Luke 23:39–43) about two thieves and their debate over repentance. This view also says that the play is a debate over religion and that the 'road' is a metaphor for the journey to heaven.

Psychological

Psychological readings of the play have also been made. The two tramps represent different parts of our personalities: Estragon is the irrational and dreamy aspect of us all, while Vladimir is the rational and sensible one. This has implications in dramatic comedy as we see different sides of our personalities explored. It also shows that a number of different readings can be derived from modern comedies.

Menace, dialect and procrastination: *The Caretaker*

Another play that offers the audience a number of different interpretations is Harold Pinter's 1960 play, *The Caretaker*. The play is a tightly written three-hander, and is set in a small flat in London. It concerns two brothers, Mick and Aston, and a tramp named Davies. Aston, who has been mentally unwell, brings back Davies to a flat that is being done up, with a view to him becoming the caretaker of the property. We are later introduced to the bullying but visionary Mick, who has plans for the future of the place. In the end, Davies is rejected by both brothers and sent on his way. The play seems to offer a message that blood is thicker than water and that family ties are stronger than one might think.

Much of the comedy of the play relies on the menace of Mick. He sees that Davies is a victim, and using slapstick and dialogue Pinter creates Mick as a character who intimidates and bullies the tramp. This is intercut with irrelevant and seemingly inconsequential dialogue, and odd changes in rhythm and subject matter that reflect the absurd reality of our lives.

Comedy is also centred on the tramp Davies, who always has plans for improvement and a better life, but never quite achieves them. In this way, he procrastinates over everything – and in so doing, reflects all our sense of needing to do important things, but putting them off if we can. On the face of it, *The Caretaker* may not seem like a dramatic comedy, but there are some highly comic moments in the play, which, as in *Waiting for Godot*, seem to show the **futility** of modern life.

The language of *The Caretaker* is filled with cockney-style dialect of London. In Davies's recollection of places he has been, and Mick's properties and associates, we have a litany of language, which, when put together, sounds amusing. This is because of the precision of detail and the relative common-ness of the locations talked about. Dialect is often used for comic purposes in comedy because it is non-standard and features exotic or different phrasing or language. When compared with standard English it dislocates and sounds amusing.

Dialect and comedy

You may wish to consider the use of dialect in the comedy you are studying. There is a debate here, however. Is the dialect used by certain characters either stereotypical or derogatory towards the ethnic or regional group being satirised? For example, in Britain a lot of comedy is set in the south, and satirises northern characters (clearly based on the **North–South divide**). Characters from the periphery of Britain (Wales, Cornwall, Scotland and Ireland) have been included in plays for comic purposes (they seemingly talk 'funny' for mainstream English audiences) since the time of the Renaissance, and were a considerable part of Restoration comedy too. Other regional or distinctive parts of Britain – for example, the North East, Essex or Liverpool – may also provide comic dialects.

Comic drama represents these groups in certain ways, often using eye-dialect as a comic mechanism. Most often eye-dialect is **pejorative** and is sometimes unintelligible. Dialect and its use may be a fruitful area of investigation for your coursework. Think of your own regional dialect as a source of comedy. The way in which television comedians use dialect may also be useful to consider.

Commentary on Activity 2

The dialogue here is both surreal and realistic. Whoever Mick is talking about has had a mysterious and intriguing life. The piece is full of absurd comments and observations, but they are often the kinds of observation that make us laugh in real life. They frequently seem to make little sense, but at the same time give an impression of life and experience. For example, his skill as a long-jump specialist is disrupted by his penchant for nuts. The analysis below gives you further detail on how the comedy is achieved in this monologue.

Analysis

You remind me of my uncle's brother. He was always on the move,

that man. Never without his passport. Had an eye for the girls. Very

much your build. Bit of an athlete. Long-jump specialist. He had a

habit of demonstrating different run-ups in the drawing-room round

about Christmas time. Had a penchant for nuts. That's what it was.

Nothing else but a penchant. Couldn't eat enough of them. Peanuts,

This is suggesting an unsettled lifestyle, similar to that of Davies. (move)

This is an absurd description. Does he actually mean his father? (brother)

Has he really travelled abroad? (passport)

The obscurity of this makes it amusing. (specialist)

This is comic because Davies is not really athletic at all. (athlete)

This is a strange thing to do. (Christmas)

His practice is undercut by his interest in this more traditional Christmas food. (nuts)

'Penchant' is an amusing and anachronistic piece of vocabulary. (penchant)

Key terms

North–South divide: a stereotypical view of the economic and cultural divide in Britain between the North and the South in the 21st century.

Pejorative: negative or derogatory.

Activity 2

Read aloud or perform Mick's monologue from early in Act 2 of *The Caretaker*.

- Work out how the comedy is achieved in the sequence.
- Write a short piece of literary critical analysis, commenting on its form, language and structure.

Link

To complete Activity 2 you will need to use *The Caretaker*, which is printed in the Extracts section at the back of this book, Extract 5 (p134).

walnuts, brazil nuts, monkey nuts, wouldn't touch a piece of fruit cake.

A bizarre thing to remember.

An amusing list.

Had a marvellous stop-watch. Picked it up in Hong Kong. The day

after they chucked him out of the Salvation Army. Used to go in

We wonder what he could have done that was so bad that he was thrown out of this charity group?

An amusing anecdote about cricket.

number four for Beckenham Reserves. That was before he got his Gold

Medal. Had a funny habit of carrying his fiddle on his back. Like a

papoose. I think there was a bit of the Red Indian in him. To be honest,

This dislocates us totally from what we have heard before.

How could this possibly be if he is from London?

I've never made out how he came to be my uncle's brother. I've often

thought that maybe it was the other way round. I mean that my uncle

was his brother and he was my uncle. But I never called him uncle. As

Again, we are unclear about the relationship Mick has with this man.

a matter of fact I called him Sid. My mother called him Sid too. It was

This indicates a possible affair or an illegitimate child.

a funny business. Your spitting image he was. Married a Chinaman

In this context, this is again, absurd.

and went to Jamaica.

The Caretaker, Act 2

Activity 3

Read the 'bag throwing' sequence from Act 2 of Harold Pinter's *The Caretaker*. Examine how both menace and slapstick are used in the sequence to create comedy. You may find it helpful to try performing the 'bag throwing' before you comment on it.

Link

To complete Activity 3 you will need to use *The Caretaker*, which is printed in the Extracts section at the back of this book, Extract 6 (p134).

Commentary on Activity 3

This is a very famous sequence from the play. It relies on a combination of Mick's menace working against Davies's naivety – with Aston as the peacemaker. In essence, the physicality described in Pinter's stage directions allow for a comic piece of 'piggy in the middle'. However, further comedy is developed by the fact that at one point the menace is reversed, with Aston grabbing the bag and Mick giving it to Davies. This comic reversal undercuts our expectations and makes us laugh. The drip of the bucket is amusing because it operates as a repetitive motif in the play and unites the three characters.

Different readings

Comedy of menace

Many critics have described Harold Pinter's plays as being 'a comedy of menace', which may well be an accurate description of how they operate. Pinter was once asked what his plays were about and he said they were about the 'weasel under the cocktail cabinet'. Although he has since retracted that observation, it still seems profoundly relevant when it comes to his style of comedy of menace. It suggest that under the 'glitzy cocktail party of life', there is something more dark and menacing. Comedy can therefore expose and explore this.

This is a profoundly relevant comment to all the comedies we consider within Aspects of Comedy.

Pinteresque

'Pinteresque' is a word that has entered the English language. *The Online Oxford English Dictionary* defines this as 'Resembling or characteristic of his plays... Pinter's plays are typically characterised by implications of threat and strong feeling produced through colloquial language, apparent triviality and long pauses'. You may like to apply Pinteresque to other dramatic comedies you read.

Pauses and silences

The pauses and silences in Pinter's comedies have given many critics a view of his plays that they are based on 'what is not said, rather than what is said'. See if you can identify these in the Pinter play you have considered, or in other dramatic comedies.

'Quick! Hide in the wardrobe! My husband's home!': how farce operates

Although writers like Samuel Beckett and Harold Pinter have helped to define a certain kind of comedy from the 20th century, other writers have taken a different approach. One of the most popular forms of dramatic comedy in the 20th and 21st centuries is the genre of farce.

If you ask many people how they would define modern farcical plays, they may well respond with something like the expression in the sub-heading, and they would expect to see several comic characters opening and shutting doors, trying to hide from other characters. Modern farces are usually set in domestic or familiar situations and, like earlier comedies, involve ludicrous and improbable situations, disguise and mistaken identity. Core elements you might expect to see in a farce include:

- word play and witty banter
- a fast-paced plot that increases to a frantic speed as the play continues
- physical humour or slapstick
- the characters are often vain, neurotic or silly
- the plays often have a twist.

Modern farce has a long comic pedigree, and elements of it may be traced back to plays such as William Shakespeare's *The Comedy of Errors* (1592), Molière's *Tartuffe* (1664) and Aphra Behn's *The Rover* (1677). The genre is widely used in television situation comedies, and in the theatre there are several different sub-genres. Bedroom farces usually involve people having secret affairs or liaisons like the one indicated in the heading to this section.

Farce, 'Englishness' and the village green: *Gosforth's Fete*

The best-known modern writer of farce is Alan Ayckbourn (b.1939). He quickly established himself as a comic writer who likes to satirise the lifestyle of the suburban middle class in Britain. Often the kind of middle-class characters featured in his dramatic comedies are aspirational – wanting to be upper-class, but failing to be so. They are engaged with gaining material wealth and money, but also often try to do the right thing for their immediate community. Marriage also forms a key theme within his work, and although his plays may seem conservative, they often have inventive structural elements to them; for example, *Intimate*

Extension tasks

1. There are many other Pinter plays that have very similar comic ingredients to *The Caretaker*. *A Night Out*, *The Birthday Party* and *The Dumb Waiter* are a few of the more famous of his works. Read some of these plays and identify further ways in which Pinter creates dramatic comedy.
2. Try a piece of creative writing in the style of Pinter. Aim to blend menace, circular-style dialogue, procrastination and a regional dialect.

AQA Examiner's tip

When analysing a comedy it may be useful for you to consider the macro-structure and micro-structure of the text. The macro-structure is the larger structural elements of the play, like the acts and scenes. The micro-structure refers to individual smaller sequences and how they are constructed.

Exchanges (1982), has 16 different endings to it. Some of his most successful plays include *Absurd Person Singular* (1975), *The Norman Conquest Trilogy* (1973) and *Bedroom Farce* (1975).

One useful play to consider in the light of our discussion of dramatic comedy is his 1974 play, *Gosforth's Fete*. The play is quite short, and is set in a quintessential English village in which a church fete is occurring. The characters include a vicar, Gosforth himself (a controlling organiser type), a Boy Scout leader (Stewart) and a local councillor (Mrs Pearce). During the course of the play it is revealed that the Boy Scout leader's girlfriend Milly is pregnant from a one-night stand with Gosforth. Chaos and confusion follow as Mrs Pearce is electrocuted during her speech to open the fete.

Such characters and events (a broken tea urn, misbehaving Boy Scouts, loudhailers for making announcements) define a certain kind of middle-class Englishness, which many audience members would recognise. Many comedies, in fact, have a vision of 'Englishness' that may well be fading fast. You might like to consider them as cultural resistance to wider social change, hence their popularity with amateur dramatic groups in particular. Pretentious or aspirational characters are bound to have fun poked at them, however. A number of other comedies feature these ingredients and it is possible to read them in a variety of ways.

Although written four hundred years after the period of Shakespeare's comedies, perhaps you can see a connection. The village green (a green world) is still the place of confusion (the play is part of a longer group of plays called *Confusions*). Gosforth is pretentious (like Malvolio) and his undoing is his lust (getting Milly pregnant). It seems that fundamentally the strands of comedy do not alter very much. It is merely the updated setting and circumstances that change.

Activity 4

With a partner, read this section from the middle of *Gosforth's Fete* in which Milly reveals that she is pregnant. Perform the text, testing out different tones of voice, speed and accent. Are any funnier than others? If so, then you will have a greater insight into how dramatic comedy works.

Link

To complete Activity 4 you will need to use *Gosforth's Fete*, which is printed in the Extracts section at the back of this book, Extract 7 (p134).

Commentary on Activity 4

This piece contains typical Ayckbourn-style dialogue, which is a sharp satire of middle-class behaviour. The core narrative point is that their conversation is heard by everyone at the fete because the microphone is switched on. You might recognise the character types here as well as a portrayal of an imagined Englishness, and vocabulary such as 'darling girl' and 'frightfully'. Interestingly, the confusion about the pregnancy causes the forthcoming marriage between Stewart and Milly to be thrown into disarray. The play ends without the audience knowing if their marriage takes place. The technique of overhearing 'hidden' information is something that is used in Shakespeare's plays and throughout the development of comic drama.

Did you know?

After Shakespeare, Alan Ayckbourn is the second most popularly performed playwright in the world. He has written more than 70 plays.

AQA Examiner's tip

In the re-creative option, ensure that you show understanding of form, structure and language of the base text. The base text is the one you are basing your re-creative work on.

Extension tasks

1. Now that you are familiar with the conventions of farce, try writing your own sequence of dialogue. It might be for an imagined stage play or perhaps even a radio play. By doing this, you will come to better understand the conventions used.
2. Find other examples of farces. To what extent do they follow the model suggested above? How much do they differ from the established format?

Ideas for coursework tasks

Modern comedies, absurdist comedies and farcical comedies offer lots of interesting areas of investigation for your coursework, because, like tragi-comedies, they push the genre of comedy and what it can do.

Essay (conventional response)

To what extent can dramatic comedy offer serious criticism of contemporary social and sexual conventions? Discuss with reference to the comedy you have studied.

Re-creative response

Write some additional scenes to follow the ending of *The Caretaker*, between Aston and Mick, comically revealing more about their childhood and background.

Alternatively, write a comic monologue by Davies, explaining how bitter he feels about his treatment by the two brothers.

In your commentary say why you chose this material, relating it to your reading of the play. Refer to critical interpretations if possible and explain how you constructed the dramatic comedy.

Summary

In this chapter you have examined a wide range of modern comedy operating from the end of the 19th century through the 20th century. Initially, modern comedy looked at satirising the manners and lifestyle of the middle classes, but in the post-war period it turned to more absurd themes and black humour for its inspiration. The postmodern plays of Beckett and Pinter ask big questions about humanity and its purpose in a world where existence itself is comic and absurd. The 'green world' seems inescapable. A different trend may also be identified in the form of farce. Though borrowing from earlier comic traditions, farce is a very popular genre. The dramatic comedy offered here provides many ways of developing coursework responses.

Further reading

- *The Complete Critical Guide to Samuel Beckett* by David Pattie (2000). Pattie explores many of the main critical approaches to the comedies of Samuel Beckett.
- *Harold Pinter: Faber Critical Guide* edited by Bill Naismith (2004). This is a helpful examination of why Harold Pinter is an important comic playwright.

Extension (this reading may be challenging)

- *Literature, Politics and Culture in Post-War Britain* by Alan Sinfield (1989). This is a really useful volume that locates dramatic comedy and other literature in the context of the post-war period.
- *Writing Englishness 1900–1950* edited by Judy Giles and Tim Middleton (1995). This is an anthology of how different comic writers have imagined classic ideas about English identity.

15 Contemporary dramatic comedy

This chapter:

- Understands the diversity and cross-genre borrowings of contemporary dramatic comedy.
- Examines some examples of contemporary dramatic comedy.
- Shows the political dimension of contemporary comedy.
- Explores comedy as a reforming force in culture.

Key terms

'In your face' theatre: a form of theatre that is quite aggressive and tough, reflecting a very realistic look at contemporary life.

Politically incorrect: language and culture that maximise offence to certain groups.

AQA Examiner's tip

Within English Literature B, our ideas about comedy are not fixed. You do not need to follow a particular model or offer a historical survey in your coursework. The historical material in this book is to help you better understand the major developments in dramatic comedy.

Contemporary comedy is more difficult to define than the dramatic comedy of the past. This is because contemporary plays, such as those discussed in this chapter, incorporate lots of elements of other styles of drama. Contemporary comedy still uses many of the generic elements of the past, but re-works them in new and alternative ways. Very often, the traditional settings for dramatic comedy are revised, with playwrights seeking new ways of how comedy can be used to expose and discuss the human condition. Sometimes tragedy and comedy are combined in new ways, beyond the established format of the tragi-comedy.

Contemporary dramatic comedy: what to expect

Contemporary comedies often incorporate dark and surreal elements, and can be of the genre known as **'in your face' theatre**. The moves in dramatic comedy match the moves in television stand-up comedy and situation comedies. For example, mainstream stand-up comedy has now moved away from telling jokes about mothers-in-law or offering stereotypical or racist depictions of other groups. Modern comedy is much more observational, concerned with the ironies and dislocations of living in the 21st century. Situation comedies have also changed: they no longer just offer depictions of middle-class suburban Britain. Instead, more alternative situations and locations are used. You may find it useful to think about contemporary dramatic comedy in a similar way.

Modern dramatic comedy draws on trends and developments in contemporary Britain – so we might expect new work to consider mobile phones, iPads, the internet and iconic television programmes such as *Big Brother* or *The X Factor*. As ever, the comedy will also reflect the political, social, economic and religious concerns of the era. At the time of writing, these could be issues such as the world economic crisis, the response to terrorism, or devolution in Great Britain. Usually, playwrights try to find new ways of exploring the same themes. Black comedy is quite popular, perhaps because it matches the cynicism of the contemporary era. In terms of both structure and theme, contemporary dramatic comedy is still innovative.

Bad comedy and good comedy: *Comedians*

One notable example of a political dramatic comedy is a 1975 play by the Manchester-based writer Trevor Griffiths (b.1935). The drama, titled *Comedians*, is interesting because it is a comedy about comedians and the comic process. The play was written during a period when ideas of what was funny were being challenged and questioned, perhaps shaping the comedy we are more used to seeing on television today.

The play debates what we laugh at, and whether there is *good* comedy (which questions the status quo) and *bad* comedy (which reinforces stereotypes, and is inevitably sexist, racist and demeaning to minority groups).

During the 1970s and into the 1980s, many people felt that old-fashioned comedy no longer held a purpose and that it was, in effect, **politically incorrect**. Emergent comedians (such as Ben Elton in the

1980s and Lee Evans in the 1990s) were telling different kinds of jokes that were based more on observations. Griffiths's play examines this moment of transition.

The play is set in a schoolroom, and focuses on an evening class for budding working-class comedians. It is the night of an audition for them in front of an agent's man from London. Their tutor Eddie Waters is giving the aspiring comics a final briefing. The premise is that comedy will offer them a way out of the drudgery of their normal lives, and each of the potential comedians has developed a routine – some of which are examined in the course of the play.

Conservative or alternative?

Many of the comedians are somewhat stereotypical, with Sammy Samuels ('forty-one, fat, Manchester Jewish, cigar, heavy finely cut black overcoat, homburg, white silk scarf') telling Jewish-themed jokes, and Mick Connor telling inventive but broadly still Irish-style gags. The other comedians present (Ged Murray and George McBrain) tread a conservative path of typical humour of the period. Only one character, Gethin Price, offers more challenging and alternative comedy. His alternative routine is absurd and challenging. It is what comedy *should* do, but there is no place for him on the books of the agency: he is too outlandish for his own good.

In the second half of the play, the audience in the theatre becomes each comedian's audience, and therefore the various kinds of humour test out the audience's attitudes. Griffiths politicises the action by making the audience laugh at jokes they really should not laugh at, forcing them to think about notions of comedy. In this way the play is structurally innovative, as the audience is both observer and participant in the dramatic comedy.

Commentary on Activity 1

This is an important speech in the play, and you might be able to see that it really applies to the kind of alternative and innovative humour that Gethin Price is trying to develop. There is also awareness that comedy's purpose is to tell the truth and to be inherently honest. This might make you think of the function of the Fool character in some of Shakespeare's comedies –

AQA Examiner's tip

It is worth spending considerable time with your teacher shaping the direction and title of your coursework. Remember, you do not have to cover the whole text. You can focus on an aspect of it or on a specific key moment.

Activity 1

In Act 1 of the play, Eddie Waters, their teacher, gives the would-be comedians some advice. Read what he says in his monologue. You may like to consider his observations in the light of your studies of the function and purpose of dramatic comedy.

Link

To complete Activity 1 you will need to use *Comedians* 1, which is printed in the Extracts section at the back of this book, Extract 8 (p135).

Figure 15.1 Comedians *at the Lyric Theatre, Hammersmith, London, 2009*

Activity 2

Read the stage directions and speech of two of the comedians, Samuels and Price (Price *emerges, carrying the tiny violin and bow*...), which they perform before the agent's man and the 'real' audience. Examine the different kinds of comedy used in each act. Try to relate each style of performance to contemporary comedians you know.

Link

To complete Activity 2 you will need to use *Comedians* 2, which is printed in the Extracts section at the back of this book, Extract 9 (p135).

again, to tell the truth. The liberation alluded to suggests the political nature of comedy: that laughing at difficulties or problems in a culture can prompt change. Staying in favour as a comedian seems the safe option, which most of Waters's comedians take. Only Gethin challenges this.

Commentary on Activity 2

Samuels has the typical patter of comedians at this time. He is sexist towards women in the audience and pokes fun at his own community. The deer gag is an old-fashioned style of joke, which works towards a verbal and physical punchline. We can deduce that his routine will be filled with a set of linked narratives. Griffiths purposely structures the drama to show the difference between that kind of comedy and the kind suggested by Price. Price's physical image is striking to begin with. For a working-class club audience it would be utterly bizarre. The opening lines of his routine suggest a violence and absurdity that are unexpected. He does not tell gags in the normal sense of the word.

Extension tasks

1. Investigate further examples of political comedy. Examine reactions to particular plays and their critical reception. Two good starting points are *Product* by Mark Ravenhill (2005) and *Enron* by Lucy Prebble (2009).
2. The writer Horace Walpole (1717–97) suggested that 'The world is a comedy to those that think, a tragedy to those that feel'. Is this statement still relevant to contemporary comedies such as *Comedians*?

Different readings

R.A. Banks

Comedians is a good example of how critical receptions of comedies change over time. R.A. Banks, writing in 1985 (10 years after it was first performed), observed that it was concerned with 'those laughing in society, those giving in to society and those outside the division who think they could change it'. He further observed that 'as with most comics, below the jests there lies smouldering frustration and the deep sadness of disappointment'. This gives a flavour of what initial readings of the play were made.

Brian Logan

The theatre critic Brian Logan saw a revival of the play in 2009 and commented that

> There is certainly still dishonesty in comedy, even if it's perhaps better able to disguise itself than in earlier eras. When the going gets tough, Griffiths's amateur standups resort to lazy stereotypes about the Irish, the Africans and the wife. Today's get-laughs-quick equivalents might be less blatant, but they're scarcely more 'truthful': the knob gag; the provocative misogynist or *outré* remark; the national (but safely non-racist) stereotype.

Brian Logan, Thursday 22 October 2009, www.guardian.co.uk

Logan suggests that time has been less kind to the play, and that whereas once the divisions between comedians and comic styles were easier to note, they are now more difficult. He also observes that modern comedians have modified humour to make it less offensive, but that it still draws on stereotype for effect.

Reception of the dramatic comedy you are studying is important to consider.

Magical realism, feminine structure and working women: *Top Girls*

Another interesting political and comic play emerged in 1982. This was *Top Girls* by Caryl Churchill (b.1938). Set in the era of radical change brought on by the then Conservative government (led by Margaret Thatcher), the play examines how values from that age engage with the concerns of feminism. The main character in the play is Marlene, a career-oriented woman, who has a 'simple' daughter named Angie, whom she has left to be brought up by her sister Joyce. The play asks difficult questions about women trying to combine a successful career with family life.

This theme is examined in Act 1 when Marlene hosts a celebratory meal. Churchill constructs her as having no real friends, so she invites female guests from history, art, folklore and literature; for example, Patient Griselda from 'The Clerk's Tale' in Geoffrey Chaucer's *The Canterbury Tales*, Pope Joan (a woman disguised as a male pope) and Dull Gret (a warrior woman found in a painting by Peter Breughel).

Matching moves in fiction during this phase, this act has a **magical realist** feel, where the real combines with fantasy. The women have several things in common, but fundamentally they are all coping with either giving up or losing children. Retaining earlier comic elements, there is an emphasis on disguise, gender confusion, dialect and language, and (in many productions) **doubling** actors and roles. *Top Girls* is a serious play in many ways, but in its blending of magical realism, absurdism, black humour and observation, it has a number of notable comic sequences.

Figure 15.2 *Peter Breughel the Elder,* Dull Gret c. 1562. Museum mayer van den bergh, Antwerp

Key terms

Magical realist: a term often applied to some postmodern fiction, but essentially it indicates a combination of magical and realistic elements in literature.

Doubling: when the same actor plays two roles. It is usually to save money, but can have interesting effects on how an audience perceives characters.

Activity 3

Read and perform a section from one of the office scenes in *Top Girls*, Act 2 Scene 3. At this point, Churchill's focus turns on the women who work at the employment agency, and this piece is set on a Monday morning. Examine the humour and comic writing contained in the sequence. You may also like to think about how women use wit and observational comedy.

Link

To complete Activity 3 you will need to use *Top Girls*, which is printed in the Extracts section at the back of this book, Extract 10 (p135).

The structure of *Top Girls* makes it an interesting play. Act 1 is, in fact, the ending of real time in the play, whereas Act 3 takes place a year earlier than the main body of the play. Some critics have commented that this format of structuring a play matches much more directly the busy lives of women, and that it does not have the normal 'exposition, development, solution' structure of 'male'-written plays. Churchill is also a great pioneer of attempting to show more realistically how speech operates and uses the / (backslash) symbol to indicate where characters interrupt and talk over others. Very often this is done for comic effect.

A number of other plays by Churchill might be classified as political or even feminist comedy. You may find them a fruitful area of investigation for your coursework.

Commentary on Activity 3

This sequence is found in the middle of Act 2 of the play, and we encounter two of the office girls – Win and Nell – talking about their weekend. Both are world-weary and, in typical Churchill dialogue, made up of short and witty lines, they discuss relationships and marriage. We learn that Nell has been on two dates. This is then undercut by her observation that Sunday was her favourite night of the weekend. Both are strong women who are 'tough birds'. At the end, we learn that it is a man (Derek) who is at the receiving end of their wit: he appears to be a hapless character who does not know when he is beaten. The dialogue here has much of the comic wit and quick-fire humour that you might expect to see in a Restoration comedy.

Different readings

Juli Thompson Burk

The female critic and director Juli Thompson Burk read the dramatic comedy of *Top Girls* as a play that asks important questions about women's roles in both the theatre and society. There are relatively few dramatic comedies that have an all-female cast. Writing in 1996, she argued that

> Reading *Top Girls* as a feminist text helped me to find ways to dramatise the price women pay for success in a patriarchal society. For me, and, I hope, for the spectators who attended this production, Marlene and the other women of the play embodied the dangerous and complex situation faced by many women in today's world, a world in which the consequences of success are almost as frightening as those of failure.

Juli Thompson Burk, 'Women's Roles in theatre and society: creative writing' in Lizbeth Goodman (ed.), Literature and Gender, *1996, pp246–7*

You can see that in Thompson Burk's words, the comedy of *Top Girls* has a serious function: to expose the difficulties women face in a patriarchal world. You may like to compare this observation with the concerns of an earlier female comic writer, Aphra Behn.

Michael Coveney

Male critics have also responded to the play. Michael Coveney reviewed a 2011 production of *Top Girls* and observed the following:

> I've always loved and admired the play, but I had forgotten how ingeniously it makes its effects and arguments. And of course we

> see it now in even sharper relief in the march of history. 'I think the 1980s are going to be stupendous!' says Marlene, and she was right, by her lights. But now look what happened. *Top Girls* is not so much historical pastoral as ironical satirical.

Michael Coveney, search for the review on www.whatsonstage.com (17 Aug 11)

Coveney demonstrates that the passage of time has allowed the play's comedy to be further foregrounded. This can sometimes happen with more contemporary comedy, as people are able to look back over more recent history. Comedy can therefore help us to reflect on changing attitudes over time. The position of women at work and in the home is very different now compared with the situation in 1982, when this play first emerged.

Anarchy, Albion and Rooster Byron: *Jerusalem*

One of the most successful dramatic comedies of recent years is Jez Butterworth's 2009 play *Jerusalem*. The play's title is derived from a poem by the English poet, William Blake (1757–1827), in which he imagines Britain being visited by Jesus Christ (accompanying the merchant Joseph of Arimathea), thus connecting Britain to a glorious and mythic past. The play's central theme is to contrast this incredible past with the hard-hitting reality of modern Britain. Britain was once named Albion and the drama often references this idea.

The play is set in contemporary Britain near Flintock, a town in Wiltshire. As a location, Wiltshire is significant, since it contains mythic structures such as Stonehenge and the Avebury stone circles. The play is set on St George's Day and the community is hosting its local fair. In the middle of this part of the ritual year, a local waster, traveller and drug dealer, Johnny 'Rooster' Byron, holds his own gatherings, which involve loud rave music, drug misuse, alcohol and underage drinking. The council wishes to evict him, but he is resisting this. The play follows Byron's connections with the local community and how they represent modern life in England. The comedy blends popular culture with imagery and **icons** of traditional England. It is no surprise, then, that the central character is partly named after the hell-raising poet, George Gordon – or Lord Byron.

One way of understanding *Jersualem* is as a kind of anarchic *A Midsummer Night's Dream*. The play's vision of contemporary Britain reflects the topsy-turvy inverted world of confusion that we recognise in past comedies, as well as an image of a 'green world' of anarchy and disorder. Johnny 'Rooster' Byron may be a modern manifestation of the trickster figure found in Shakespeare's comedies. He also has some attributes of the jester – outwardly showing signs of foolery, but inwardly having insight about other characters as well as the 'state of the nation'.

Key terms

Icons: key images or events that become symbolic of a particular time period.

Figure 15.3 *Mark Rylance as Johnny 'Rooster' Byron at the Royal Court Theatre, London*

Activity 4

Read Blake's poem *Jerusalem* on the following page before you read Butterworth's play.

- Why do you think the glory of England's past, juxtaposed with its present, might make for an interesting contemporary comedy?
- Identify lines from the play that echo this poem.

Did you know?

Jerusalem is the anthem of the Women's Institute in Britain and the England cricket team.

Activity 5

Examine the sequence from *Jerusalem* beginning with Johnny's words, 'Last night, you say'. Here, Ginger is remonstrating with Johnny over his behaviour in the local public houses. Examine the dialogue. How realistic do you consider the dramatic comedy presented here is?

Link

To complete Activity 5 you will need to use *Jerusalem*, which is printed in the Extracts section at the back of this book, Extract 11 (p136).

Extension tasks

1. Butterworth's play contains numerous motifs and themes relating to the festival and folk tradition in Britain. Research these and find out how they connect to dramatic comedy.
2. Consider the relationship between *Jerusalem* and other traditional English comedies you may have read or encountered. What continuities are there?

AQA Examiner's tip

When considering characters for your coursework task it is useful to think about whether they are positive or destructive forces in the text you are studying. Sometimes they may be constructed by the dramatist as both positive and negative.

Jerusalem

And did those feet in ancient time
Walk upon England's mountains green?
And was the holy lamb of God
On England's pleasant pastures seen?

And did the Countenance Divine
Shine forth upon our clouded hills?
And was Jerusalem builded here
Among those dark Satanic Mills?

Bring me my Bow of burning gold!
Bring me my Arrows of desire!
Bring me my Spear! O clouds, unfold!
Bring me my Chariot of fire!

I will not cease from Mental Fight,
Nor shall my Sword sleep in my hand,
Till we have built Jerusalem
In England's green and pleasant land.

William Blake, 1804

Commentary on Activity 4

The central metaphor of this poem gives hope that one day, a glorious future (as glorious as the city of Jerusalem itself) might be constructed in England. However, the dramatic comedy of Butterworth's play undercuts this, and satirises what England has become. In part, the play is a response to the social changes that occurred under the New Labour governments between 1997 and 2009 (the latter date being when the play was first performed).

The notion of Jerusalem is replaced with an illegal caravan in the middle of the countryside, arguments over planning, illegal raves and drug and alcohol abuse. There is a sense that the comedy is able to look at the way 'dark Satanic Mills' continue to over-run and destroy 'England's green and pleasant land'. The comedy asks the audience questions about the future direction of England in a changing contemporary world. Many of the lines in the play echo the concerns of this poem.

Commentary on Activity 5

This is an excellent example of black comedy. The humour is generated by Ginger's catalogue of Johnny's misdemeanours and Johnny's protestations of why events happened. It draws on popular culture and some illegal activity. The example of the killing of the pig on the Kiddies' Fun Day is made funny by Johnny declaring it to be a rural display. This notion also fits the idea of this dramatic comedy being a celebration of 'England's green and pleasant land'.

Other contemporary comedies to consider

In this chapter we have suggested four comedies that you might wish to look at within your coursework. None of them precisely defines the genre, however, as (say) a Restoration or Shakespearean comedy does. Here are four contemporary comedies that are also worth exploring:

- *Abigail's Party* by Mike Leigh (1977)
- *Bouncers* by John Godber (1983)

- *Henna Night* by Amy Rosenthal (1999)
- *Artefacts* by Mike Bartlett (2008).

Ideas for coursework tasks

Contemporary comedies offer lots of interesting areas of investigation for your coursework, because they ask difficult questions about modern life and experience.

Essay (conventional response)

'Women's roles are often tokenistic in dramatic comedy.'

To what extent do you believe this to be the case in relation to the play you are studying?

Re-creative response

Having read Jez Butterworth's *Jerusalem*, develop extra scenes of off-stage action that reveal to the audience more about the characters and the state of contemporary Britain.

In your commentary say why you developed this material, relating this to your reading of the play. Refer to critical interpretations if possible and explain how you constructed the dramatic comedy.

AQA Examiner's tip

When writing your commentary in the re-creative option, ensure that you show awareness of the detail of the represented speech. You may like to use textual evidence from the base text to help support this.

Summary

In this chapter you have explored the diversity of contemporary comedy. You have also understood that, increasingly, dramatic comedy has become a highly political form, where writers have used comedy to try to expose problems or ignite change in our society. Although sometimes dissimilar in subject matter, contemporary comedies do have some structural similarities. They often play games with the genre of comedy, and have inter-textual connections with other genres. They often integrate popular culture to useful effect, making contemporary comedy much more accessible to a wide audience.

In comedies such as *Comedians* and *Jerusalem*, you have seen many similarities to comedies written four hundred years ago. In other work, by writers such as Churchill, the lives of women are explored in a challenging but resoundingly comic way. Contemporary comedies still have the ability to expose the stupidity and pretentiousness of human beings.

Further reading

- *State of the Nation: British Theatre Since 1945* by Michael Billington (2009). This is a very readable book on theatre in this period, considering many dramatic comedies.
- *Caryl Churchill* by Elaine Aston (2010). This book is a detailed study of the plays of Caryl Churchill.

Extension (this reading may be challenging)

- *Rewriting the Nation: British Theatre Today* by Aleks Sierz (2011). This is a great overview of the kinds of dramatic comedy (and other plays) being performed in contemporary Britain.
- Albion: The *Origins of the English Imagination* by Peter Ackroyd (2005). A useful guide to Britain's mythic and ritual past.

16 Preparing for the coursework submission

This chapter:

- Explains what you need to do to submit your best possible coursework.
- Gives you advice on how to cover all the assessment objectives.
- Provides you with details of how to prepare bibliographies and/or endnotes.

Link

See the introduction to this book for an outline of the full AS requirements, or go to www.aqa.org.uk.

AQA Examiner's tip

Always make sure that your preparation and writing of coursework is well-focused. Although your coursework will take time to research, plan, shape and eventually write, each stage should lead quickly to the next. Endless tinkering, and endless planning, without actually getting on with the job in hand, can lead to a stale final product.

This final chapter gives you some hints on writing your AS Level English Literature coursework. These hints are based on the assumption that you have studied the texts and know them well.

One obvious way of preparing for coursework is to use this book. Take each of the chapters in Unit 2 in turn and apply its focus to the actual plays you have been studying. Consider which aspect of comedy you would like to focus on in each text. A different, but equally important part of preparation involves making the best use of time given to you in class.

What is coursework?

Coursework is different from examinations. For examinations, you have to prepare for all possibilities. In coursework, you can decide, with your teacher, which particular aspects of the texts you want to focus on. You can only know this, though, when you have read each text in full. Once you have negotiated a task with your teacher, always make sure that you understand fully what is required. After the task has been negotiated and finalised, make sure that you keep to the task – relevance is as important in coursework as in an examination.

Here are some other points to consider, bearing in mind that you will be required to produce a portfolio of two pieces of coursework, each 1,200–1,500 words in length.

- You must write separately about two texts, both of them comedies.
- You will probably complete each piece of coursework at a different time in your AS course.
- The word limits are important. They are designed for you to write substantially but with sharp focus.
- One of the assignments can be re-creative. This will be explained later in this chapter.
- How much time do you expect to spend on each assignment? How many drafts will you need and how will you amend the first draft? This will also be looked at in more detail later in this chapter.
- The marking criteria for coursework are available and can help you understand what you have to do. Ask your teacher for a copy, look at the introduction to this book or follow the link to the AQA website.

Types of written coursework

Broadly speaking, there are two types of task you can work on for this unit. One or both of your responses can be in the more traditional form of the essay, answering a question that has been negotiated with your teacher. There is, though, an alternative option for one of the pieces: this can be a response that is re-creative, so is unlikely to take the form of an essay. If you go for this option, you must also write a commentary to go with it. The combined word limit for a re-creative response and commentary is still 1,200–1,500 words.

The essay

As mentioned previously, the essay question you work on will have been negotiated with your teacher, who may also discuss your task with an AQA adviser. It could focus on one of the aspects of comedy considered in this unit, or it could ask you to consider the play as a whole and the extent to which is shows aspects of the comic genre. Whatever the focus, though, ideally it will ask you to debate a proposition rather than just *describe* a feature.

A straightforward task on a Shakespeare play might be something like:

> To what extent does Shakespeare's *Measure for Measure* conform to the models of comedy you have studied?

Preparing your task 1

After the task has been set and you have discussed it with your teacher, get started, whatever the deadline might be. Putting off the process because there is plenty of time can be fatal. By the time you get round to it, you will have lost momentum and will have started to forget the text and the task.

Preparing your task 2

Before you start writing, you will need to organise your thoughts and sort out the references, textual and critical, that will support your ideas. Make sure that the ideas come first, though – otherwise you will tend to take the play chronologically, rather than in the sequences that best suit your argument.

So, for example, as you first think about the task:

> To what extent does Shakespeare's *Measure for Measure* conform to the models of comedy you have studied?

you might come up with the following ideas, bearing in mind the word limit you are working to:

- What possible models of comedy might be relevant to the text?
- Does *Measure for Measure* have some aspects of comedy, but aspects of other genres too? How far is it a tragedy?
- To what extent are those other genres present and what impact do they have?
- How does Shakespeare construct the play following the 'usual' model, but to what extent is that disrupted?
- How does the author construct characters to both confirm and disrupt expectations?
- Consider the historical context, performance conditions and how the play has been received by audiences over time.
- What critical positions or evaluations might be relevant to my response?

In English Literature the best essays confront the task head-on. There is no need to write a lengthy introduction that says what you intend to do in your essay – just get on and do it. Punchy and dynamic starts make for effective reading because they will grip your reader from the outset. If you look at the list of points above, clearly any one of them might be a suitable starting point for your argument, depending on the overall line of argument you intend to take.

It is often said, rather loosely, that there is no right answer in English Literature. And, when studying a play, this can be even more the case, because in addition to the text of the play itself you can consider the possible performances that can come from the text. None the less, there are certainly answers that are 'right' in that they argue logically, using suitable evidence to reinforce the points being made.

So how do you decide the best sequence for your ideas? The best way is to try out different sequences in note form and to draft different openings. When you find an opening paragraph that clearly leads on to the next ones, you are in business. Then complete your first draft quickly, giving the task your full attention.

Structurally, within coursework, you are at liberty to move paragraphs around and re-insert them, especially when the essay is being drafted. This is perfectly valid as your ideas become more organised and shaped. This is where coursework is different from the examination. It is obviously harder to change the structure of an examination essay.

AQA Examiner's tip

Do not follow the play sequentially. The best answers are those that move around the play, referring to whatever part suits the argument as it progresses. This 'ranging' around the text is an important skill to develop at this stage.

Although it may seem strange, from the outset have an eye on what you might want to say in the conclusion. Many students rush their conclusions, or just write a paragraph that more or less repeats the start of the essay. Better conclusions outline what other issues a text might raise, or further ways of interpreting an aspect of comedy. You may even wish to write a draft of your conclusion first of all – that way your essay will be less of a mystery trip and have a destination to it. You can always revise the conclusion in the light of what you write about in the main body of your essay.

How many drafts?

You may want to show your teacher a draft of your work in progress. If so, there are several points to be clear about:

- You are only allowed to show your teacher one draft of your coursework.
- Your teacher can only make general comments, especially if it is a full draft.
- Those comments will be about things like structure and reference, both textual and critical.
- Technical accuracy (e.g. spelling, punctuation, grammar and quotation) is your responsibility.
- Your teacher will make helpful suggestions: it is up to you what you do with these.

Above all, remember that coursework exists to give you the opportunity for independent study. It is your teacher's job to supervise, not to do all the hard work for you.

Covering the assessment objectives

In order to obtain a good mark in your coursework, you need to keep an eye on all four Assessment Objectives and make sure that you are covering them in your response. Here is some advice about how to respond to each AO within your coursework.

AO1

- Aim for a clear, fluent and well-structured argument, but also one that is not too mechanical. Your individual voice is valued.

- Use some critical vocabulary and concepts of comic theory, but make sure you understand and apply them.
- Use quotation in a focused and supportive way. Do not just quote for the sake of it.

AO2

- It is relatively easy sometimes to comment on language, but ensure that you also comment on the form and the structure of the text.
- Avoid seeing literary characters as 'real'. Keep an eye on how they are constructed by dramatists.
- Make sure your task is not too broad, and make sure you do not just tell the reader the plot.

AO3

- You do not need to make lots of references to other forms of comedy. By studying two comedies you are doing that anyway.
- Explore a range of different interpretations of definitions of comedy and how they might be applied.
- Remember: it is always a good thing to show that the same text can be interpreted differently by different readers.

AO4

- Make sure you are accurate about issues of context.
- Avoid a biographical approach.
- Integrate historical context into your coursework as part of the conceptual argument. Do not just bolt it on.

Good coursework responses tend to have the following key characteristics. Use this as a checklist for your response:

- A close focus on a section of the play
- A close focus on an aspect of both drama and comedy within the text
- A genuine debate around different readings of the text
- An independent response
- A close focus on the playwright's methods.

Quotation and reference: text of the play

Earlier in the book, you learned how to quote and refer in the Unit 1 examination. The difference with coursework is that you have more time to research the quotations and references you need. This does not mean, however, that large chunks of the play should now be copied out. Exactly the same rules apply for coursework as for examinations:

- You should support your arguments with frequent and relevant textual evidence.
- Quotations should be brief.
- Quotations should be accurate.
- The best quotations are embedded in your own sentences.
- Quotations in brackets can be a useful way of integrating them.
- Reference to the text can also help to give evidence: close references can often work better than quotation.
- Quotations and references should never stand alone: they should be used in support of specific points you are making.

Quotation and reference: critical sources

Your coursework essay should present a debate and an argument. To help with this debate you can read the work of critics and then refer to it and/or quote from it as appropriate. Again, there are some rules to observe:

- Critical comments can help in the shaping of your argument.
- Such comments may support your argument or provide a counter-argument.
- These comments should be tested against the text of the play.
- You should reference the critics by providing the source in your **bibliography** or in **endnotes**, as described below.
- Quotations count as part of the overall word limit.

Key terms

Bibliography: list of texts you have referenced or quoted from **in** your work.

Endnotes: list of texts you have referenced within the essay and stated at the end of your work.

As part of your initial preparation for writing coursework, it is worth practising the use of critical sources and comments. Earlier in this unit there was a quotation from the critic Jacqueline Rose, in which she discussed aspects of Isabella's identity in Shakespeare's *Measure for Measure*.

Here are two examples of the ways you can use a piece of criticism and the original text in your writing.

One is to quote directly:

> Jacqueline Rose says of Isabella that 'uniting in her person are those extremes of attraction and recoil' and that the 'woman who refuses to meet that desire is as unsettling as the one who does so with excessive haste', arguing for her to be a 'hussy' and 'revered as the divine'. She posits that the 'two positions are, however, related and that the second can tip over into the first, with Angelo making the connection when he says, "What is't I dream on? O cunning enemy, that, to catch a saint, With saints dost bait thy hook?"' (Act 2 Scene 2, lines 180–1)

Another is to refer to a critic and the original text:

> Jacqueline Rose notes that Isabella unites the two extremes of attraction and recoil and that any woman who resists desire is as dislocating as one who comes to it readily. Rose further argues that these two aspects are in fact combined in Isabella, with Angelo in Act 2 Scene 2 (lines 180–1) understanding both her cunning nature and her saintly qualities.

Either is valid. Remember: it is important to correctly attribute what other readers have said about texts. You must ensure that you do not inappropriately make what they have said sound like your own ideas.

Bibliographies and endnotes

Bibliographies and endnotes are useful for examiners to see because they demonstrate the range of reading you have completed during the course, as well as the references made to critics in your essays.

Bibliographies are usually listed alphabetically according to the author's surname. Order your entries in the following way: author's surname, author's first name or initial(s), title in italics, place of publication and publisher, date of publication. For example:

> Billington, Michael, *State of the Nation: British Theatre Since 1945*, London: Faber and Faber, 2007.
>
> Hampton-Reeves, Stuart, *Measure for Measure: A Guide to the Text and its Theatrical Life*, Basingstoke: Palgrave Macmillan, 2007.

Sometimes you might also want to refer to a chapter within a longer edited book of essays. You can do this in the following way:

> Dollimore, Jonathan, 'Transgression and surveillance in *Measure for Measure*' in Dollimore, Jonathan and Sinfield, Alan (eds), *Political Shakespeare: New Essays in Cultural Materialism*, Manchester: Manchester University Press, 1985.

Alternatively, you may like to use endnotes, where you include a number in the text of your essay, and reference the book at the end of your essay. Here are the same books as above, referenced 1, 2 and 3 in the text of the essay, and now including the relevant page numbers:

> 1 Michael Billington, *State of the Nation: British Theatre Since 1945*, London: Faber and Faber, 2007, pp.288–9.
>
> 2 Stuart Hampton-Reeves, *Measure for Measure: A Guide to the Text and its Theatrical Life*, Basingstoke: Palgrave Macmillan, 2007, pp.38–45.
>
> 3 Jonathan Dollimore, 'Transgression and surveillance in *Measure for Measure*' in Jonathan Dollimore and Alan Sinfield (eds), *Political Shakespeare: New Essays in Cultural Materialism*, Manchester: Manchester University Press, 1985, pp.72–87.

Your teacher will explain how to use the terms ibid. and op. cit. so that you do not have to keep repeating the book titles when you refer to them again.

Internet sources

Many students now reference websites from the internet. These can sometimes be difficult because articles can be anonymous, and websites may disappear overnight or be unavailable. If you can find the name of the author of an article alongside the title, add it and state the site where you found it. The convention is generally to add the date when the site was accessed. For example:

> Charles Isherwood, 'Hold onto your morals: life is tough' – review of *Measure for Measure*, http://theater.nytimes.com. Accessed 1 September 2011.

If you cannot find the name of the author, make sure you reference the website, adding when you accessed it:

> www.william-shakespeare.info. Accessed 2 September 2011.

The internet can be useful because it can refer to more contemporary material than in some published sources.

AQA Examiner's tip

Although website references are easy to find and locate, we would recommend that you use a combination of books, articles and websites. This shows that you are reading widely, above and beyond the internet alone. This will also be good practice for the A2 component of the syllabus. Always ensure that material is properly attributed.

A re-creative response

In addition to writing an essay, you have the opportunity, if you wish, to write a re-creative response, with commentary.

The word 're-creative' is used because what you are being asked to do in this option is to explore the original text by coming at it from a different angle. A re-creative response is not easier than an essay: it is different, and in the process offers you the chance, if you wish, to have fun by writing in other formats. It is vital, though, that you consult with your teacher if you wish to take this approach.

There are many different tasks that could be devised, depending very much on the plays you are studying. One common aspect of all plays that you study, though, is that they have an ending, and given that they are comedies, they usually end up with marriages and solutions to earlier anarchy and mix-ups. Shakespeare often gives the last word to the happy couple – or the mother and father figures – and a re-creative response might allow reflection on events and why the mix-up happened, and how it is to be avoided in the future.

It is clear, however, that the best kind of re-creative tasks often involve minor characters or silent characters on the sidelines, who may well be able to offer additional insights into events. Choosing major characters can sometimes be a problem because we know everything there is to know about them. A minor character offers opportunities for greater development and a more creative interpretation. Most plays also have ambiguities within them and these are often good starting points for re-creative activities.

It is important to consider the form/genre in which you write this re-creative response. Imitation of the original language is often not successful, but your own response will depend on your interests and the time period in which you consider the play to be set. Often, however, an innovative use of genre can be both productive and rewarding. Despite a play coming from the 17th century, a more contemporary mode of writing may work very well indeed. Sometimes good re-creative work comes out of experimentation within your classroom – using re-creative tasks to help you better understand the base text.

Diaries or journals are often used by students for the purposes of the re-creative response, but really there is a far wider range of genres to be used. Among those you may wish to consider are:

- Script: think of extra scenes before the play begins, during the play or after the play.
- Reports: formal reports such as those made by psychologists or journalists can be productive.
- Blog: pretend you are writing a series of blogs for a website about events in the drama.
- Dramatic monologues: this is a good way to explore the reflections of minor characters.

Other inventive genres include sermons, imagined debates, phone calls, email exchanges and responses imitating contemporary and new literary forms.

AQA Examiner's tip

In preparing a re-creative response, ask yourself what critical issues you are hoping to raise in the process. Make sure that you do more than simply retell the story or copy the style. Indeed, there is little point, for example, in trying to copy Shakespeare's verse/language. Use modern English to make your point, even if you do sometimes echo the language of the original.

Activity

Look at the endings of any comedies you can access. What is said at the very end of the play?

Now turn to the play you have been studying. In what ways can you reflect on the nature of its ending, either by changing it, adding to it or giving it a fresh context? For example:

- Write a series of final words spoken by other characters whom we do not hear from at the end.
- Instead of replacing the final speech, add to it with further responses from characters to the final words, perhaps challenging the final sentiments in new ways.
- Write two 500-word newspaper reports on events in the comedy, perhaps from the perspective of two different kinds of newspaper, showing potentially different responses to how the characters/events can be perceived.

There is no commentary on this activity.

The re-creative commentary

The commentary that accompanies a re-creative piece has two purposes. One is to allow you to discuss what you have been trying to do in terms of re-creating the comedy. The other, and the more important one, is to allow you to reflect on how the re-creative process has thrown light on potential meanings and ambiguities in the play.

How much you write will depend on how much you wrote in the initial re-creative piece. The longer the initial piece, the fewer words you will both need and have available. When planning a re-creative piece, though, do take into account the word limit of the full package. In the third option suggested in the Activity on the previous page, you would have 500 words for your commentary. Most students find that devoting around 50 per cent of the word limit to the task itself and 50 per cent to the commentary is a good balance.

Here are some of the things you can address in a commentary, although this is not a complete list:

- Why the original play lends itself to the approach you have taken
- The debates and ambiguities in the play that you have attempted to highlight
- Further insights you gained into the play through writing this piece
- Further ways of approaching the play and/or further ideas you could have explored given more time and words.

There is no need, though, to dwell on how well you think you have done this exercise. That will be reflected in your mark.

Key factors for success in the re-creative response

Here are some important tips based on successful re-creative responses seen by examiners:

- Ensure your response recognises that you are dealing with a dramatic comedy.
- Silent or marginal voices often make for successful work.
- Use the re-creative response to illustrate a particular reading of the base text.
- The commentary should complement and reinforce your reading.
- Do not spend time saying how you could have improved the work further.
- In the commentary, talk about the choices you made about language to highlight issues in the base text.
- Give your work a clear title so that the examiner knows what you are doing.

AQA Examiner's tip

When you are assembling your portfolio of coursework, make sure each piece of work has an accurate word count written at the end, with a full bibliography, and that the responses are bound together using a single treasury tag in the top left-hand corner. The portfolio should be organised so that the Shakespeare piece is first. Also ensure that the task is clearly written at the top of each piece of work.

Conclusion

Coursework is included in the assessment of AS Level English Literature so that you can reflect on texts and create individual responses to them. If you work sensibly, it offers the perfect balance to the demands of working under examination conditions.

Extracts

1 *The Patriot*

An Old Story

I

It was roses, roses, all the way,
With myrtle mixed in my path like mad;
The house-roofs seemed to heave and sway,
The church-spires flamed, such flags they had,
A year ago on this very day.

II

The air broke into a mist with bells,
The old walls rocked with the crowd and cries.
Had I said, 'Good folk, mere noise repels--
But give me your sun from yonder skies!'
They had answered 'And afterward, what else?'

III

Alack, it was I who leaped at the sun
To give it my loving friends to keep!
Naught man could do, have I left undone:
And you see my harvest, what I reap
This very day, now a year is run.

IV

There's nobody on the house-tops now--
Just a palsied few at the windows set;
For the best of the sight is, all allow,
At the Shambles' Gate--or, better yet,
By the very scaffold's foot, I trow.

V

I go in the rain, and, more than needs,
A rope cuts both my wrists behind;
And I think, by the feel, my forehead bleeds
For they fling, whoever has a mind,
Stones at me for my year's misdeeds.

VI

Thus I entered, and thus I go!
In triumphs, people have dropped down dead.
'Paid by the world, what dost thou owe
Me? '--God might question; now instead,
'Tis God shall repay: I am safer so.

2 *The Way of the World* Act 1 Scene 5

Mirabell What, is the chief of that noble family in town, Sir Wilful Witwoud?

Fainall He is expected to-day. Do you know him?

Mirabell I have seen him, he promises to be an extraordinary person: I think you have the honour to be related to him.

Fainall Yes, he is half-brother to this Witwoud by a former wife, who was sister to my Lady Wishfort, my wife's mother. If you marry Millamant, you must call cousins too.

Mirabell I had rather be his relation than his acquaintance.

Fainall He comes to town in order to equip himself for travel.

Mirabell For travel! Why the man that I mean is above forty.

Fainall No matter for that; 'tis for the honour of England that all Europe should know we have blockheads of all ages.

Mirabell I wonder there is not an act of parliament to save the credit of the nation, and prohibit the exportation of fools.

Fainall By no means, 'tis better as 'tis; 'tis better to trade with a little loss, than to be quite eaten up, with being over-stocked.

Mirabell Pray, are the follies of this knight-errant, and those of the squire his brother, anything related?

Fainall Not at all; Witwoud grows by the knight, like a medlar [*a kind of apple*] grafted on a crab. One will melt in your mouth, and t'other set your teeth on edge; one is all pulp, and the other all core.

Mirabell So one will be rotten before he be ripe, and the other will be rotten without ever being ripe at all.

Fainall Sir Wilful is an odd mixture of bashfulness and obstinacy – But when he's drunk, he's as loving as the monster in the "Tempest"; and much after the same manner. To give t'other his due, he has something of good nature, and does not always want wit.

Mirabell Not always; but as often as his memory fails him, and his commonplace of comparisons. He is fool with a good memory, and some few scraps of other folks' wit. He is one whose conversation can never be approved, yet it is now and then to be endured. He has indeed one good quality, he is not exceptious; for he so passionately affects the reputation of understanding raillery, that he will construe an affront into a jest, and call downright rudeness and ill language, satire and fire.

3 *The Way of the World* Act 5 Scene 14

Lady Wishfort, Millimant, Mirabell, Mrs Fainall, Sir Wilfull, Petulant, Witwood, Foible, Mincing, Waitwell.

Lady Wishfort O daughter, daughter, 'tis plain thou hast inherited thy mother's prudence.

Mrs Fainall Thank Mr Mirabell, a cautious friend, to whose advice all is owing.

Lady Wishfort Well, Mr Mirabell, you have kept your promise—and I must perform mine. First, I pardon for your sake Sir Rowland there and Foible—the next thing is to break the matter to my nephew—and how to do that—

Mirabell For that, madam, give yourself no trouble—let me have your consent—Sir Wilful is my friend: he has had compassion upon lovers, and generously engaged a volunteer in this action, for our service: and now designs to prosecute his travels.

Sir Wilfull 'Sheart, aunt, I have no mind to marry. My cousin's a fine lady, and the gentleman loves her, and she loves him, and they deserve one another; my resolution is to see foreign parts—I have set on't—and when I'm set on't, I must do't. And if these two gentlemen would travel too, I think they may be spared.

Petulant For my part, I say little—I think things are best off or on.

Witwood I gad, I understand nothing of the matter, —I'm in a maze yet, like a dog in a dancing school.

Lady Wishfort Well sir, take her, and with her all the joy I can give you.

Millamant Why does not the man take me? Would you have me give myself to you over again?

Mirabell Ay, and over and over again [*kisses her hand*]. I would have you as often as possibly I can. Well, Heaven grant I love you not too well, that's all my fear.

Sir Wilfull 'Sheart, you'll have time enough to toy after you're married; or if you will toy now, let us have a dance in the meantime; that we who are not lovers may have some other employment, besides looking on.

Mirabell With all my heart, dear Sir Wilfull. What shall we do for music?

Foible O sir, some that were provided for Sir Rowland's entertainment are yet within call.

Lady Wishfort As I am a person I can hold out no longer; —I have wasted my spirits so today already, that I am ready to sink under the fatigue; and I cannot but have some fears upon yet, that my son Fainall will pursue some desperate course.

Mirabell Madam, disquiet not yourself on that account; to my knowledge his circumstances are such, he must of force comply. For my part, I will contribute all that in me lies to a reunion; in the meantime, madam [to Mrs Fainall], let me before these witnesses restore you to this deed of trust; it may be a means, well managed, to make you live easily together.

From hence, let those be warned, who mean to wed;
Let mutual falsehood stun the bridal bed:
For each deceiver to his cost may find,
That marriage frauds too oft are paid in kind.

4 *The Rover* Act 1 Scene 1

Florinda With indignation, and how near soever my father thinks I am to marrying that hated object, I shall let him see I understand better what's due to my beauty, birth and fortune, and more to my soul, than to obey those unjust commands.

Hellena Now hang me, if I don't love thee for that clear disobedience. I love mischief strangely, as most of our sex do, who are come to love nothing else. But tell me dear Florinda, don't you love that fine *Anglese* [Englishman]? For I vow, next to loving him myself, 'twill please me most that you do so, for he is so gay and so handsome.

Florinda Hellena, a maid designed for a nun ought not to be so curious in a discourse of love.

Hellena And dost thou think that ever I'll be a nun? Or at least till I'm so old I'm fit for nothing else? Faith no, sister, and that which makes me long to know whether you love Belvile, is because I hope he has some mad companion or other that will spoil my devotion. Nay, I'm resolved to provide myself this Carnival, if there be e'er a handsome proper fellow of my humour above ground, though I ask first!

Florinda Prithee be not so wild!

Hellena Now you have provided yourself of a man, you take no care for poor me. Prithee tell me, what does thou see about me that is unfit for love? Have I not a world youth? A humour gay? A beauty passable? A vigour desirable? Well shaped? Clean limbed? Sweet breathed? And sense enough to know how all these ought to be employed to my best advantage? Yes, I do and will: therefore lay aside your hopes of my fortune by my being. a devote, and tell me now how you came acquainted with this Belvile, for I perceive you knew him before he came to Naples.

Florinda Yes, I knew him at the siege of Pamplona: he was then a colonel of French horse, who, when the town was ransacked, nobly trusted my brother and myself, preserving us from all insolences. And I must own, besides great obligations, I have I know not what that pleads kindly for him about my heart, and will suffer no other to enter.—But see, my brother.

Enter Don Pedro, Stephano *with a masquing habit, and* Callis.

Pedro Good morrow, sister. Pray when saw you your love Don Vincentio?

Florinda I know not, sir—Callis, when was he here?—for I consider it so little, I knew not when it was.

Pedro I have a command from my father here to tell you you ought not to despise him, a man of so vast a fortune, and such a passion for you.

5 *The Caretaker, 2*

Mick You remind me of my uncle's brother. He was always on the move, that man. Never without his passport. Had an eye for the girls. Very much your build. Bit of an athlete. Long-jump specialist. He had a habit of demonstrating different run-ups in the drawing-room round about Christmas time. Had a penchant for nuts. That's what it was. Nothing else but a penchant. Couldn't eat enough of them. Peanuts, walnuts, brazil nuts, monkey nuts, wouldn't touch a piece of fruit cake. Had a marvellous stop-watch. Picked it up in Hong Kong. The day after they chucked him out of the Salvation Army. Used to go in number four for Beckenham Reserves. That was before he got his Gold Medal. Had a funny habit of carrying his fiddle on his back. Like a papoose. I think there was a bit of the Red Indian in him. To be honest, I've never made out how he came to be my uncle's brother. I've often thought that maybe it was the other way round. I mean that my uncle was his brother and he was my uncle. But I never called him uncle. As a matter of fact I called him Sid. My mother called him Sid too. It was a funny business. Your spitting image he was. Married a Chinaman and went to Jamaica.

6 *The Caretaker, 2*

Mick What's this?
Davies Give us it, that's my bag!
Mick (*warding him off*). I've seen this bag before.
Davies That's my bag!
Mick (*eluding him*). This bag's very familiar.
Davies What do you mean?
Mick Where'd you get it?
Aston (*rising, to them*). Scrub it.
Davies That's mine.
Mick Whose?
Davies It's mine! Tell him it's mine!
Mick This your bag?
Davies Give me it!
Aston Give it to him.
Mick What? Give him what?
Davies That bloody bag!
Mick (*slipping it behind the gas stove*). What bag? (*To* Davies.) What bag?
Davies (*moving*). Look here!
Mick (*facing him*). Where you going?
Davies I'm going to get... my old...
Mick Watch your step, sonny! You're knocking at the door when no one's at home. Don't push it too hard. You come busting into a private home, laying your hands on anything your can lay your hands on. Don't overstep the mark, son.
Aston *picks up the bag.*
Davies You thieving bastard... you thieving skate... let me get my—
Aston Here you are. (Aston *offers the bag to* Davies.)
Mick *grabs it.* Aston *takes it.*
Mick *grabs it.* Davies *reaches for it.*
Aston *takes it.* Mich *reaches for it.*
Aston *gives it to* Davies. Mick *grabs it.*
Pause.
Aston *takes it.* Davies *takes it.* Mick *takes it.* Davies *reaches for it.* Aston *takes it.*
Pause.
Aston *gives it to* Mick. Mick *gives it to* Davies.
Davies *gives it to him.*
Pause.
Mick *looks at* Aston. Davies *moves away with the bag.* He drops it.
Pause.
They watch him. He picks it up. Goes to his bed, and sits.
Aston *goes to his bed, sits, and begins to roll a cigarette.*
Mick *stands still.*
Pause.
A drip sounds in the bucket. They all look up.
Pause.
How did you get to Wembley?
Davies Well, I didn't get down there.

7 *Gosforth's Fete*

Milly Have you got a minute? Please.
Gosforth (*sitting on a chair, still fiddling with the mike*) Darling girl, does it look like I've got a minute?

Milly It's frightfully urgent, Gordon.
Gosforth All right, old girl, go ahead. I'll just keep fiddling.
Milly Well... (*She pauses.*)
Gosforth Uh-hun...
Milly It's really rather awful. It does seem terribly as if perhaps I might be pregnant.
Gosforth Oh yes.
Milly Yes.
Gosforth *drops the mike, as he realizes what she has said. The jolt causes the mike to become live. We hear, distantly, their voices echoing away on a series of loudspeakers. They alone, in their concern, remain unaware of this.*
Gosforth Did you say pregnant!
Milly I'm frightfully sorry.
Gosforth Me?
Milly There's no-one else it could have been, Gordon.
Gosforth Oh my God. (*He rises, with the mike.*)
Milly I'm really awfully sorry. What are we going to do?
Gosforth Well...

Milly What am I going to say to Stewart?
Gosforth Oh…
Milly He'll be dreadfully upset.
Gosforth Yes, I can see that he might, yes.
Milly He might refuse to marry me.
Gosforth Yes, I can see that he might, yes.
Milly (*her lip trembling*.) I don't know what to do.
Gosforth Now, easy, easy, Milly. (*He puts his arm round her*.) Now you're absolutely sure.
Milly Yes.
Gosforth Yes. Well. This needs thinking about.
Milly What's Stewart going to say when he finds out? What's it going to do to him? Everyone knows we're engaged. How's he going to face his Cubs?
Gosforth Well, he's a good bloke. He's a Scout, isn't he, after all. He's pretty decent. Now listen, Milly, we must just get through today first. Then we'll talk about it. You see?
Milly Yes.
Gosforth Don't worry.
Milly No.
Gosforth You're not to worry, we'll sort it out. But first things first. You get your tea organised and I'll see if I can get this wretched thing to – one, two, three – ah, success, it's working – don't know what it was I did but I – ah…
They look at each other appalled.
Milly How long's it been on for?
Gosforth Very good point.
Stewart Stokes *enters in full Scout kit. Normally a pink young man – he is now red with fury.*
Milly Stewart…!
Stewart You bastard, Gosforth…
Gosforth Hello, old boy.
Stewart You complete and utter bastard, Gosforth.
Gosforth Now keep calm, Stokes.

8 *Comedians* 1

Waters It's not the jokes. It's not the jokes. It's what lies behind 'em. It's the attitude. A real comedian—that's a daring man. He *dares* to see what his listeners shy away from, fear to express. And what he sees is a sort of truth, about people, about their situation, about what hurts or terrifies them, about what's hard, above all, about what they want. A joke releases tension, says the unsayable, any joke pretty well. But a true joke, a comedian's joke, has to do more than release tension, it has to liberate the will and the desire, it has to change the situation. (*Pause*.) There's very little won't take a joke. But when a joke bases itself upon a distortion—(*At* Price, *deliberately*)—a 'stereotype' perhaps—and gives the lie to the truth so as to win a laugh and stay in favour, we've moved away from a comic art and into the world of 'entertainment' and slick success (*Pause*.) You're better than that, damn you. And even if you're not, you should bloody well want to be.

9 *Comedians* 2

Samuels A message for any nymphomaniacs in the audience… Hello. Sit down, lady, we'll have no rushing towards the stage. 1929 I was born. Year of the Great Crash. The sound of my father's jaw dropping. He took one look at me and said, I'm not that Jewish. Nobody's that Jewish… Here, there was this poacher, see. Poacher? And he catches this deer. And he slings it over his shoulder and he's humping it through the forest and a gamekeeper catches him and he says, Hey you, you're poaching. And the guy says, How do you mean? And the gamekeeper says, You've got a deer on your back. And the guy goes… (*Looks over his shoulder and screams*.)
(Price *emerges, carrying the tiny violin and bow. He wears baggy half-mast trousers, large sullen boots, a red-hard wool jersey, studded and battered denim jacket, sleeves rolled to elbow, a red and white scarf tied to an arm. His face has been whitened to deaden and mask the face. He is half-clown, half this year's version of a bovver boy. The effect is calculatedly eerie, funny and chill…*)
Price (*to himself, not admitting the audience's existence*): Wish I had a train. I feel like smashing a train up. On me own. I feel really strong. Wish I had a train. I could do with some exercise.

10 *Top Girls* Act 2 Scene 3

Win Good weekend you?
Nell You could say.
Win Which one?
Nell One Friday, one Saturday.
Win Aye aye.
Nell Sunday night I watched telly.
Win Which of them do you like best really?
Nell Sunday was best. I liked the Ovaltine.
Win Holden, Barker, Gardner, Duke.
Nell I've a lady here thinks she can sell.
Win Taking her on?
Nell She's had some jobs.
Win Services?
Nell No, quite heavy stuff, electric.
Win Tough bird, like us.
Nell We could do with a few more here.
Win There's nothing going on here.
Nell No but I always want the tough ones when I see them. Hang onto them.
Win I think we're plenty.
Nell Derek asked me to marry him again.
Win He doesn't know when he's beaten.
Nell I told him I'm not going to play house, not even in Ascot.
Win Mind you, you could play house.
Nell If I chose to play house I would play house ace.
Win You could marry him and go on working.
Nell I could go on working and not marry him.

11 *Jerusalem* 1

Johnny Last night, you say. *(Beat.)* It's coming back. No, it is. And I can categorically say that that is bollocks. For a start, I was drinking brandy and Cokes. And I was not starkers. If you examine the CCTV footage, it clearly shows I had my socks on.

Ginger (*makes the umpire signal*). I think we'll refer that one upstairs.

Mate It's taken years but you've finally done it. You're barred from every pub in Flintock. Phoenix Arms, you broke the bog. They let you back, you locked Jim's lad in the freezer cabinet.

Johnny And he deserved it. Lippy bastard.

Ginger Moonrakers, you broke the security cameras then a week after they let you back, you pick a fight with a squaddie.

Johnny I never started that. Bloody Rambo…

Ginger First night back you set fire to the Christmas tree. Royal Oak, you were doing whizz off the bar during the meat raffle. Then on Kiddies' Fun Day you slaughtered a live pig in the car park.

Johnny It was a rural display.

Glossary

A

abstract: not always representing things pictorially or realistically.

absurdist comedy: drama that examines life outside common sense and the usual conventions.

affectation: a form of pretence in behaviour.

alienation: the process through which a person feels exiled from and forgotten about by their own community.

ambiguity: part of the drama which might have two or more possible meanings or interpretations.

anachronistic: something that is out of harmony with the period in which it is placed.

antagonist: this refers to the second character, who usually disagrees in some way with the protagonist. Some comic dramas also have a third actor – the tritagonist.

anti-Semitic: hostile towards Jewish people.

archaic: belonging to a much earlier period; archaic vocabulary is 'old' words deliberately used to suggest an earlier time.

attributed: describes direct speech that is identified (i.e. the reader is told who is speaking).

avaricious: greedy for financial gain.

B

bathos: a key concept in comedy, this means taking an elevated form (such as tragedy) and descending it into the ridiculous.

bawd: a woman who is humorously indecent.

bawdy: generally applied to language that is coarse or lewd.

beaus: relaxed, attractive and self-confident men.

bibliography: list of texts you have referenced or quoted from in your work.

black comedy: comedy that looks at dark or depressing themes in a comic way.

blasphemous: to talk irreverently about something sacred.

C

caricature: an exaggerated portrayal of a person or type of person for comic effect.

characterisation: the way in which an author creates and uses characters, and why.

charade: an absurd pretence.

chorus: in Greek dramas, this was usually a number of performers who comment with a collective voice on the play's action. In later dramas, the chorus could be a solitary performer, who assists the audience with narration and understanding.

chronological order: the sequence of events as they happen, in a timeline that goes from A, the start of events, to, say, E, the end.

clown: often a person who does comical tricks, but is better defined by the word 'buffoon'. The character is usually clumsy and unsophisticated.

Cold War: the period of tension between the USA and Soviet Russia in the 1950s and 1960s.

complicit: being involved with a wrongdoing.

context: the circumstances surrounding a text (e.g. where it first appeared, social attitudes today) which affect the way it is understood. The word is formed from *con* (= with) + *text*, so literally it means 'what goes with the text'.

contexts of production: circumstances that might affect a text at the time of its writing.

contexts of reception: circumstances that might affect a text at the time of its being read.

conventions: the accepted rules, structures and customs we expect to see in a specific genre of writing.

courtesan: a female member of a court, but one who is independent and has free morals.

cross-dress: any form of disguise that turns one gender into another.

cultural stereotype: some authors present characters with features that we are conditioned to recognise as having a certain meaning. Bright eyes, for example, will often suggest wisdom and creativity.

D

dialect: regional and sometimes social variations in language.

direct speech: the actual words spoken by characters in a narrative.

discourse: the language and texture of the play.

disenfranchisement: when a particular group of people feel they are deprived of their rights.

disorder: inversion (turning upside down) of the normal order in a society.

***double entendre*:** an expression or figure of speech that has two meanings. The first meaning may be obvious, but a second meaning may be either ironic or intentionally rude.

doubling: when the same actor plays two roles. It is usually to save money, but can have interesting effects on how an audience perceives characters.

E

empathy: our ability as an audience to step into the shoes of an on-stage character.

endnotes: list of texts you have referenced within the essay and stated at the end of your work.

end-stopped: a line of poetry where a grammatical unit of sense, usually a sentence, is completed at the end of a line.

epigram: a short and witty saying at the beginning of a text.

epilogue: the short concluding section of a play or poem, sometimes summarising the content or theme.

establishment: refers to how texts begin, the work the author does for the reader at the beginning of the text. Establishment can involve introducing people, places, time, and so on.

ethnicity: a person's ethnic origins.

existentialism: a system of thought which emphasises that people are free to choose their own actions.

eye-dialect: the representation of the vocabulary, grammar and sound of dialect in ordinary letters, in contrast to the phonetic representation (with special symbols) that a linguist would use; the use of non-standard spelling to draw attention to how words should be pronounced.

F

farce: a comic play featuring improbable situations.

farcical: a method of entertaining an audience that uses improbable situations and useless pretence.

first-person narrative: a story told through the voice of one of the characters, using 'I'.

folly: a foolish act.

fops: men who are dandy-like and a little effeminate. They often pay a lot of attention to their appearance and clothes.

form: the aspects of a text in its totality that enable it to be identified as a novel, a poem, an epistolary novel (i.e. a story told in the form of letters), a sonnet (a poem of 14 lines), and so on.

fornication: premarital sexual activity.

free: in a technical sense, describes thought or speech that is not attributed (i.e. the reader is not told specifically who is speaking or thinking).

futility: a process that produces no result or change.

G

genre: a type of text (e.g. a crime novel, a narrative poem).

Globe Theatre: the most famous of the theatres found on the South Bank in London during Shakespeare's day. It is characterised by its circular shape, thrust stage and three tiers of seating. A modern recreation of the theatre was built in 1997 and Shakespeare's dramas are performed there in original performance conditions.

H

homodiegetic narrator: the narrator who is part of the story they describe.

humanist: a humanist focuses study and investigation on human values and concerns.

I

iconic: when some aspect of culture is established as important and definitive.

icons: key images or events that become symbolic of a particular time period.

identity: a person's sense of themselves and their cultural heritage.

ideology: the attitudes, values and assumptions that a text contains or which a character or group of characters share.

indirect speech: speech that is reported by the narrator, giving a version of the words spoken rather than the words themselves.

interregnum: the period of time in which no king or queen is on the throne. In Britain, this lasted from 1649 to 1660.

inter-textual: when one text makes reference to another.

intradiegetic narrator: the narrator who is not omniscient and does not know everything, usually because they are part of the story rather than in control of it.

inversion theory: when the everyday or normal experience is altered for the purposes of ritual or celebration.

'in your face' theatre: a form of theatre that is quite aggressive and tough, reflecting a very realistic look at contemporary life.

L

language: in this context, generally refers to specific words or phrases in the text.

M

magical realist: a term often applied to some postmodern fiction, but essentially it indicates a combination of magical and realistic elements in literature.

malapropism: a comical confusion of words, for example saying 'expedition' instead of 'exhibition'.

metaphor: involves the transfer of meaning, with one thing described as another. When one thing is described as being like another it is known as a simile.

moral double: the morality of two characters, at opposite ends of the spectrum, who are the protagonist and antagonist of the play.

motif: a recurring element in a story that has symbolic significance.

N

narrative: involves how the events and causes are shown, and the various methods used to do this.

narrative persona: a useful term used to describe the unnamed 'I' who sometimes narrates a story. Be aware that the 'I' is rarely the author, so the term persona is a helpful point of reference.

naturalistic: a style of drama that aims to be more natural in terms of performance than previous dramas.

North–South divide: a stereotypical view of the economic and cultural divide in Britain between the North and the South in the 21st century.

P

pantomime: in modern culture, a play generally based on a fairy-tale or folk-tale, often performed around Christmas. In theatre, pantomime has a long tradition of a variety of styles.

parody: a comic or grotesque imitation of another text.

pastoral: a style of living and working concerned with the countryside. It is a recognised genre of literature. The pastoral is often conceived as a reaction to the urban.

patriarchal: pertaining to men and male views.

pejorative: negative or derogatory.

plot: the chain of causes and circumstances that connect the various events and place them into some sort of relationship with each other.

politically incorrect: this is language and culture that maximises offence to certain groups.

postmodern: this literally means 'after the modern', but it has come to mean texts whose construction shows the alienation and disruption of the modern world.

Presentism: a theory of literary criticism that proposes that in any text there is a never-ending dialogue between the past and the present, and that aspects of present culture always and inevitably inform our readings of a text.

prologue: an introduction to a play.

prose: 'normal' speech in paragraphs, not poetry. It is usually spoken by lower-class characters.

protagonist: in dramatic terms, this refers to the first major character who offers a particular view.

pun: a play on words – often exploiting either similar-sounding words or words with a variety of meanings. They are often used to comic effect.

R

rakes: men who live an irresponsible and immoral life.

realist tradition: where literature seeks to hold a mirror up to life and seeks to reproduce it as accurately as possible.

re-creative response: a piece of writing that throws light on the original text in a creative rather than an analytical way.

repartee: the ability to make witty replies and remarks. It is often a key component of both Shakespearean and Restoration comedy.

revel: to take delight in an event, and to complete this with lively festivities.

revenge: a kind of mental or physical injury inflicted on someone who has caused you suffering. Revenge is not just a theme of dramatic tragedy, it can be found in comedy too.

revenger: the main character who seeks revenge. Although often found in tragedies, they can also be found in comedies.

royalists: supporters of the king and the monarchy.

rustic: concerned with country life.

S

secular: the system of thought concerned with worldly matters – and not those of religion or spirituality.

semiotics: relates to the meanings of signs.

significance: in a literary sense significance is to do with signification, the making of meanings, so when asked to find significance you are being asked to think about potential meanings.

slapstick: a kind of physical comedy invented in the 20th century but applied on the past. It involves falling over, blows and mishaps.

soliloquy: a speech spoken by a character, who is usually alone on the stage, in which they tell or confess their thoughts to the audience.

speaker: the person whose voice is heard in a poem, as opposed to the author.

speech marks: inverted commas used to indicate the start and end of direct speech.

squires: gentlemen from the countryside. They are usually satirised in Restoration comedy as not having the manners or fashions of the city. They often come from the north or the west.

status quo: the current or established state of affairs.

stock: the usual or stereotypical characters.

story: all the various events that are going to be shown.

stream-of-consciousness: a writing system that involves writing down ideas as soon as they are thought of and not ordering them to imitate more accurately the reality of experience. It was practised by the novelist James Joyce, who greatly influenced Beckett.

structure: how the significant parts of a text work together to form a whole (e.g. the connection between chapters in a novel).

subversive: seeking to overthrow the establishment.

suit: a request or wish for something.

symbol: something that stands for something else in literary texts. The connection is usually not directly stated and the reader is expected to recognise the symbol for what it represents. Symbols are often used in comedies.

T

third-person narrative: a story told through the voice of a narrator who is not one of the characters in the story.

tragi-comedies: comedies that have more serious subject matter.

transgression: to break a law or rule, and to go beyond the normal limits of tolerance.

travesty: when something important or crucial is made ridiculous.

trickster: the trickster has a wide number of interpretations across the world. In European culture he is often a thief or liar, a practical-joker and sometimes clever at disguise.

U

urban: concerned with the town or city.

V

valets: personal servants who took care of a gentleman's clothes and lifestyle.

verse: rhymed or (most usually) unrhymed poetry that is found in Shakespearean and other dramas of the period and is usually spoken by higher-class or noble characters. The unrhymed form is written in iambic pentameters (10-syllable lines with five stresses) and when performed closely imitates the rhythm of speech in English. It is sometimes called blank verse. Some characters speak in rhyming couplets.

Index

N

O

P

R

S

Acknowledgements

The authors wish to acknowledge the help and advice they have received from Janice Ashman, Peter Bunten, Chris Hawkes, Katherine Clements, Chris Davies and Rob Gardner in the preparation of this volume.

The authors and the publisher would also like to thank the following for permission to reproduce material:

Text

p7 Caters News Agency for extracts from Charlotte Dalton, 'He Died a Hero', *Woman's Own*, 30.10.06; p11 'Stopping by Woods on a Snowy Evening' from *The Poetry of Robert Frost*, edited by Edward Connery Latham, published by Jonathan Cape. Reprinted by permission of the Random House Group Ltd; p12 'The Road Not Taken' from *The Poetry of Robert Frost*, edited by Edward Connery Latham, published by Jonathan Cape. Reprinted by permission of the Random House Group Ltd; p14 from *Fingersmith* by Sarah Waters, published by Virago Press, 2003. Reproduced with the permission of Little Brown Book Group; p16 Roger, Coleridge & White on behalf of the author for extracts from Richard Ford, *A Multitude of Sins*, Vintage Books (1996); p21 and p42 Copyright © 1934 by W.H. Auden. Reprinted by permission of Curtis Brown, Ltd; p23 Faber and Faber Ltd for Sebastian Barry, *The Secret Scripture* (2009); p25 and p40 from *Enduring Love* by Ian McEwan, published by Vintage Books 1997. Reprinted by permission of The Random House Group Ltd; p32 from *The Kite Runner* by Khaled Hosseini, published by Bloomsbury 2004. Reprinted with the permission of Bloomsbury; p36, p37, p38, p48 from *Small Island* by Andrea Levy, published by Headline Review 2004. Reprinted with permission; p47 from *Birdsong* by Sebastian Faulks, published by Vintage Books 1993. Reprinted by permission of the Random House Group Limited; p76 from *The Anatomy of Criticism* by Northrop Frye, published by Princeton University Press. Reprinted by permission of Princeton University Press 1990; p94 from 'Sexuality in the reading of Shakespeare: *Hamlet* and *Measure for Measure*', in John Drakakis (ed.), *Alternative Shakespeares* (London: Methuen, 1985). Reproduced with permission from Taylor & Francis Group; p102 *The Development of English Drama in the Late Seventeenth Century* by Robert D. Hume (1976). By permission of Oxford University Press; p103 from 'George Etherege and the Form of Comedy' by Jocelyn Powell taken from *Restoration Theatre* edited by John Rissell Brown and Bernard Harris (1965); p103 from 'Restoration Comedy: The Reality and Myth' by L.C, Knights, taken from *Scrutiny, 6* (1936). Reprinted with the permission of the author's estate; p105 from 'Remaking the canon: Aphra Behn's *The Rover*' by W.R. Owens and Lizbeth Goodman, taken from *Shakespeare, Aphra Behn and the Canon*, London: Routledge, 1996; p111 and p134 Faber and Faber Ltd for Harold Pinter, *The Caretaker* (1960); p118 extract from 'Griffith's Comedians still has the last laugh' by Brian Logan. Copyright Guardian News & Media Ltd 2009; p120 From 'Women's Roles in Theatre and Society: Creative Writing' by Juli Thompson Burk in Lizbeth Goodman (ed.), *Literature & Gender* (London: Routledge, 1996). Reproduced with permission from Taylor & Francis Group; p121 extract from 'Review: Top Girls' by Michael Coveney. Copyright Independent News and Media Ltd 2011; p134 Alan Acykbourn, *Confusions* © Methuen Drama, an imprint of Bloomsbury Publishing Plc; p135 Faber and Faber Ltd for Trevor Griffiths, *Comedians* (1976); p135 Caryl Churchill, *Top Girls* © Methuen Drama, an imprint of Bloomsbury Publishing Plc; p136 excerpt from *Jerusalem* copyright © 2009 Jez Butterworth reprinted with permission from the publishers, Nick Hern Books: www.nickhernbooks.co.uk

Photos

p15 © Craig Lovell/Corbis; p30 The Stapleton Collection; p59 © Swim Ink 2, LLC/ Corbis; p66 © Elnur; p70 © The Art Gallery Collection/Alamy; p75 Joe Cocks Studio Collection © Shakespeare Birthplace Trust; p84 © Moviestore collection Ltd/Alamy; p87 © Roger Cracknell 01/classic/Alamy; p91 www.debbieattwell.com; p95 © Shaun Higson colour/Alamy; p100 © Robbie Jack/Corbis; p104 Getty Images; p108 © Geraint Lewis/Alamy; p117 © Geraint Lewis/Alamy; p119 Giraudon; p121 © Geraint Lewis/Alamy.

Every effort has been made to contact copyright holders and we apologise if any have been overlooked. Should copyright have been unwittingly infringed in this publication the owners should contact the publishers, who will make the correction at reprint.

The right formula for success

Teamwork

This book has been planned and written alongside the AQA English Literature B AS specification by two senior examiners.

Their objective has been to produce a book that provides clear guidance for learning and plenty of assessment materials for practice.

Confidence

This book matches the specification precisely and you can have confidence that it will cover everything you need to study for your AS Level exams.

Adrian Beard has taught in Newcastle upon Tyne and York. He is a chair of examiners in English Literature and is the series editor for the Literature B Student Books and electronic resources. He is also a co-author for the AQA Literature B A2 Student Books. He has written widely on topics in both English Language and English Literature.

Alan Kent Ph.D. M.Ed., M.Phil. has taught GCE English Literature and Drama, and Theatre Studies for twenty-five years and is a Associate Lecturer in Literature with the Open University. He is a senior examiner for both *Aspects of Narrative* and *Dramatic Genres: Aspects of Comedy* in the AQA GCE English Literature B specification.